Anglo-Saxon
Food and Drink

Ann Hagen

First Published 2006 by

Anglo-Saxon Books
Hereward, Black Bank Business Centre
Little Downham, Ely, Cambs. CB6 2UA

reprinted 2010 in paperback

Printed and bound by Lightning Source
Australia, England, USA

PL

British Library Cataloguing-in-Publication Data. A catalogue record for this
book is available from the British Library.

ISBN 9781898281559

To Ant, Tom and Lizzie

For their patience and good company

Acknowledgements

First of all I would like to record my thanks to Sir David Wilson who taught me Anglo-Saxon Archaeology, and supervised the earliest stages of this project. A grant from University College London enabled me to visit York, where Peter Addyman was kind enough to conduct me round the excavations. Professor John McNeill Dodgson helped with documentary sources at an initial stage, and it is with great regret that I learned of his death. My late parents, Peggy and Arthur Smallridge, provided support, moral and financial, whereby I could get work under way. Working from home, I relied on the staff of the Information Desk at Bedford Central Library whom I would like to thank for treating my requests as interesting challenges, in particular Robert Napthine, who rarely failed to get his book.

A multidisciplinary work of this kind has to be to some extent a co-operative venture, in that many people have provided me with information. To the specialists listed separately, my colleagues at Clarendon School, and friends who produced books and items of interest, my thanks. I also wish to thank my farming relations in Devon and Bedfordshire, in particular the late Harry Newman and his widow, Iola, who generously lent me books as well as answering agricultural questions, and my brother, David Smallridge, at Chasestead Engineering, Letchworth, where the answer to various questions metallurgical and technical was only a phone-call away.

Debby Banham and Paul Callow helped me more than they know by discussing this subject with me. I owe an enormous debt of gratitude to Professor James Graham-Campbell at the Institute of Archaeology, London, who provided me with information, encouragement and made corrections. From him I received counsels of perfection: that the work has shortcomings is due to my own failings.

Pearl and Tony Linsell made a number of suggestions and improvements at the publication stage, and I am very grateful for their expertise. It was with great sadness that I heard of Pearl's illness and death. Thanks also to Steve Pollington for his help with the Old English and the Index.

Special thanks to Michael Miller at Cambridge.

Ann Hagen

July 2005

Contents

The Author

Ann Smallridge Hagen was born at Kempston, Bedford. After leaving Bedford High School, she had a number of jobs, from toffee apple wrapping to metallurgical analysis. She read English with Honours at University College London, 1965–8, taking Anglo-Saxon Archaeology as a special subject. On leaving university she worked as a Museum Educational Officer, before becoming an English teacher. She was also a partner in a firm of antique restorers for ten years, additionally bringing up a family during this time. She enrolled as a postgraduate student at University College London, and was awarded her M.Phil. and the Isobel Thornley prize of the University of London in 1992. She lives in Haynes, Bedfordshire, and now works at Bedford Museum.

Introduction

The intention of this synthesizing study is to bring together for the first time information from various primary and secondary sources in order to build up a composite picture of the production, processing, distribution, and consumption of food during the Anglo-Saxon period. The period covered is the seven centuries from the beginning of the fifth century to c.1100, and an attempt is made to trace changes and development in food production and the access to a food supply over this time.

The area covered is limited to Anglo-Saxon England and the Celtic west of Britain – the latter is included so that use could be made of the detailed *Ancient Laws and Institutes of Wales*, although these were not recorded until the end of the period. In the matter of privileges in those laws for which earlier texts exist, those attributed to Hywel Dda (died 949 or 950), are not widely different from those recorded in the sixth and seventh centuries, and it is reasonable to assume other material is similarly conservative.[1] Occasionally, reference is made to continental sites for archaeological evidence to verify points in the literary sources when, by the accidents of (non) recovery, such evidence is unknown in the archaeological record in England.

Primary Sources

The primary source material is of two kinds: documentary and archaeological. Material in Anglo-Saxon manuscripts in the vernacular has been supplemented on occasion by that in Latin manuscripts. Bosworth & Toller's *Anglo-Saxon Dictionary* and *Supplements* were used as the basis for references to foodstuffs, processing or consumption, although the *Toronto Microfiche Concordance of Old English* and ensuing *Dictionary of Old English* (in progress) is superseding this. Manuscripts of all types were used: there was no attempt to select manuscripts on particular subjects which might have been thought more relevant. This was just as well, as references to food turn up in all types of Anglo-Saxon literature and records, either as the basis of land units, or because wages, taxes and dues were often paid directly in food, and it was a medium of trade and charity. There are more specialised references in medical recipes and charms. Religious writings contain direct references to diet, to the precariousness of the food supply and therefore the need to balance the numbers of those in establishments with their food resources. As feasting, which always involved the consumption of liquor, amounted to a lay ceremony, there are many references to it in Laws and Guild Statutes. Purely literary works also contain valuable references, particularly to feasting as an element of the noble life. However, most of these writings were not primarily about food, and the references are incidental to the main subject, or they have a special emphasis which has to be taken into account.

Surviving manuscripts have been preserved by chance. Leofric, the first bishop of Exeter, gave his new cathedral about sixty books in the mid-eleventh century: most of these were dispersed, but the Exeter Book which remains is a most important source. Writing in 1549, after the Dissolution, John Bale recorded, 'Those who bought the monasteries kept the books to scour their candlesticks, some to rub their boots, some

---

[1] Owen 1841, *Preface* ix.

they sold to the grocers and soap-sellers, some they sent over the sea to the book-binders...at times whole ships full'. Collections made by antiquarians were not always safe from disaster: 114 volumes were lost in the Cotton Library fire of 1731.[1] Given this state of affairs it is reasonable to assume that there are bound to be lacunae in the documentary record, notwithstanding the fact that the occasional important source may yet be discovered – the very informative tenth-century O.E. will of Æthelgifu came to light in an outbuilding in 1939.[2]

The documentary record is heavily weighted towards the end of the Anglo-Saxon period, with the majority of Anglo-Saxon manuscripts dating from about 1000 and the eleventh century, about twenty from the tenth century, and very few before this date (although original texts, like the writings of Bede, of which only copies are extant, are known to have been written from the period of the conversion onwards).[3] Documents relating to agriculture refer to large holdings in the hands of wealthy owners. But even when the size of an estate can be established, and we have some knowledge of its produce, the number of individuals to be supported from the holding at any one time is not recorded. Since circumstances changed over the seven centuries, it is unwise to use these sources to generalise about earlier conditions, particularly conditions in the fifth and sixth centuries (from which there are no O.E. written sources).

As for deficiencies in my method of using these sources, I have used printed versions of the manuscripts and accepted the readings of their editors and their judgement as to authenticity. In the case of *Ancient Laws and Institutes of Wales*[4] I have accepted this editor's translation too, although The Law of Hywel Dda has been newly translated by D. Jenkins (1986). I have tried to exercise the necessary caution where manuscripts are translations from Mediterranean writers, and therefore do not refer to conditions in Britain, and with certain cartularies or laws which may be later than their purported dates. I have not listed every reference to a foodstuff, but selected representative material and indicated how common references are. Where there is an important unique reference not based on emendation, then this is noted.

Illustrations are valuable for showing animals, equipment and agricultural processes which are not otherwise described, and these occur not only in manuscripts, but on textiles, notably the Bayeux Tapestry. However, these illustrations are all found in late Anglo-Saxon manuscripts, and the Bayeux Tapestry is, of course, post-Conquest, so this material, like the literary evidence, is of limited value for the early and mid-Anglo-Saxon periods. Lack of artistic perspective means we have to make judgements on the size of what is depicted. For example, the large bird-sized bees in Bodleian MS, Ashmole 1511, folio 75v, would not fit into their hive. Moreover, manuscript illustrations could be (and were) copied by Anglo-Saxon artists from continental sources.

Although many place-names are often not recorded for the first time until after the Conquest, if they are made up of O.E. elements it is reasonable to assume they were in use during the Anglo-Saxon period.[5] It is difficult to assess whether O.E. place/field

---

[1] Earle 1884, 28.
[2] Rennell in Whitelock 1968, 2,3.
[3] Ker 1957, xv-xviii.
[4] Owen 1841.
[5] Cameron 1985, 183, 96, 204.

names indicate the cultivation or merely the presence of certain plants, e.g. clover at Claverley.[1] Some field names must indicate the presence of undesirable weeds: Cockle Close – corncockle, Dockey Field – dock, Twitch Piece – couch grass. However, when there is confirmatory evidence from other sources, then place/field names can be related to crops and animal husbandry: Royden – rye, Bean Croft, Ewster Ham – land with a sheepfold, Loose Hay – land with a pigsty. The name 'Arras' – summer sheilings for stock, indicates a system of transhumance.[2] In dealing with evidence of this kind, I have accepted the linguistic derivations of the various authors.

Archaeological evidence is very valuable to supplement the evidence from the literature in the late period. But, unlike the literature, it provides evidence for the whole of the Anglo-Saxon period, and is the main source of data for the early period. However, again, as with the manuscripts, the recovery of evidence is a matter of chance. Soils preserve remains differentially, acid soils being the most destructive. The bone preserved on a site may well represent less than 1% of what was originally deposited. Animal bones from early excavations were not usually retained. Recovery techniques themselves will bias a sample.[3] Unsieved samples are biased towards larger mammals; sieved samples increase the proportion of pig, sheep and goat remains, and water-sieved samples the proportion of fish, bird and small mammal bones.[4] The most commonly represented bone fragments are those that are formed of dense, compact bone, and where the epiphysis fuses early in the animal's life. The least well-represented bones are small bones and more fragile last fusing bones. The effect of this is to bias the age of a population towards 'youth'.[5] Of the animal bones recovered, a proportion will, in all likelihood be unidentifiable, some may be wrongly identified, and bones diagnostic as to breed, (skulls in particular or the scapula/neck of sheep), may be missing. It is generally impossible to tell sheep and goats apart in the animal bone record.

Different methods of quantifying the numbers of animals involved and the relative proportions of species produce different results. It would be much easier to make valid comparisons between sites if the presentation of statistical material in bone reports was done in a uniform manner.

The inadequacies of my own method in dealing with this material are that I have used only the major bone assemblages. I have accepted the report writers' assessments of species, numbers, age of specimens, etc., without reworking the figures. I have also taken the end of December 1986 as the cut-off point for a close study of archaeological reports. While a bulk of material has seen the light of day more recently, it has not necessarily seen the pages of archaeological reports. Later excavations have added to the amount of evidence without changing the basic conclusions to be drawn from it. I have tried to exercise extreme caution in interpreting animal bone remains. For example, the absence of particular bones may not be an indicator of food preferences. It may, in the case of the recovery of only a small number of fish bones, indicate, not that few fish were eaten, but that many fish

[1] Smith 1956, 96.
[2] Field 1972.
[3] O'Connor 1982.
[4] Maltby 1979.
[5] Grant 1974.

were eaten, bones and all.[1] Absence of particular bones may not be an indicator of butchering techniques or preferences but of an industrial process. The absence of cow ribs from one part of the *Hamwih* excavations may indicate the presence elsewhere of a leather industry, as they were often used instead of scudding knives to remove hair from more tender hides. Animal bones in graves may not represent food for the next life, but may have other, possibly totemic, significance.[2]

Before the last decade or so, plant remains were rarely recorded unless they were in the form of wood or nuts/stones or charred/carbonised grain. Modern techniques now permit the recovery of more fragile remains, particularly from waterlogged layers. The range of plant material recovered on a site is directly linked to the type of preservation, and the methods of sampling may lead to bias.[3] Some of the problems of interpreting pollen from urban sites are dealt with by Grieg.[4] I have accepted the identifications given by the writers of reports, which is not to say these are free of problems related to taxonomy and interpretation.

Chemical analysis of organic remains in archaeological contexts can give clues to the food consumed.[5] Gas chromatography techniques developed by Dr Richard Evershed and his team provide useful confirmation of cooked plant foods. The thermal history of a cereal, i.e. how it was cooked, can be reconstructed by the technique of electron spin resonance.[6]

Plant remains need to be treated with caution: unless they come from faecal layers or the area of the stomach cavity they cannot be proved to have been consumed, though reasonable assumptions can be made. Some plants remain problematic – weeds of habitation sites and cultivated ground may have been eaten in times of famine.

Plant remains reflect agricultural practices and help to build up a chronological picture of how diet developed, but it has to be borne in mind that certain crops may result from local conditions, and not indicate general custom or preference. Working independently on what was generally the same body of material, Debby Banham and I came to the same overall conclusions, but her forthcoming work on Anglo-Saxon Food Plants, (meanwhile her unpublished Cambridge Ph.D. thesis) explores this area, particularly the taxonomy, in much more detail than is appropriate here.

Animal bones, plant remains and chemical analyses help to answer the question, 'What did the Anglo-Saxon eat?', but only in quite exceptional circumstances 'How much of it did they eat?'

Human skeletal material can provide useful information about diet which is not available from other sources. Here again, I have accepted the writers' diagnoses and interpretations as to pathology and the physical damage caused by dietary factors, although the etiology of caries, for example, is complex, and may not point to plentiful cereal food.[7]

---

[1] Jones, undated paper.
[2] Meaney 1981.
[3] Green in Hall & Kenward 1982, 40ff., 154; Monk 1977, 29, 148, 334; Jones & Dimbleby 1981, 130; Jessen & Helbaek 1944, 23; West 1982, 319.
[4] Grieg in Hall & Kenwood 1982, 47.
[5] Arrhenius 1985, 339.
[6] Robins 1988, 49.
[7] Wells 1964; Miles 1972, 309.

Some excavated structures like fish weirs relate specifically to obtaining food, and the presence of mills, kilns and ovens for processing cereals gives additional evidence for their production. Kitchens and hall structures also exist in the archaeological record.

Secondary Sources

'Anglo-Saxon Food and Drink: Production, Processing, Distribution and Consumption' has not been treated as the main subject of any similar multidisciplinary research before, and so I cannot deal with the history of research into the subject as such, but there is a vast range of secondary material – ancient, medieval and modern.

1.Classical and later medieval documents.

(i) Treatises by Roman writers such as Varro and Columella may throw light on certain aspects of Anglo-Saxon practice, even if the documents were not specifically known to the Anglo-Saxons. *On the Observance of Foods* by Anthimus written in early sixth century Gaul gives details of foods, though there is no evidence for the more exotic of these in Anglo-Saxon contexts. Similarly, as well as the basic methods of cooking, he refers to more elaborate dishes resembling chicken soufflé or quenelles of pike, but we have no reference to Frankish chefs at Anglo-Saxon courts.

(ii) Medieval, Tudor and later traditions may also reflect Anglo-Saxon conditions as in some ways these are unlikely to have changed rapidly in the interim. The great improvement in stock was an eighteenth- and nineteenth-century phenomenon, and the hybridisation of cereal breeds is more recent still. However, it is important to realise the changes and not to extrapolate from existing practices or livestock breeds without qualification. Later medieval works on the Monastic Rule can provide detailed information on diet, food supply, etc., relevant to the lives of a certain proportion of the Anglo-Saxon population, to supplement such primary source material as the Old English *Rule of Chrodegang*.

2. Modern secondary writings:

(i) **Histories of the Anglo-Saxon period.** Antiquarians like Archbishop Parker and Sir Robert Cotton gathered libraries of Anglo-Saxon manuscripts after the Dissolution. Various, particularly religious, institutions had retained Anglo-Saxon documents. As such important sources as laws, wills, charters, the *Anglo-Saxon Chronicle*, Bede's *Ecclesiastical History*, Ælfric's *Glossary*, *Gerefa* and *Rectitudines Singularum Personarum* were published by editors like Dugdale, Birch and Liebermann, they were used as a basis by historians like Turner and Kemble in the nineteenth century, Stenton and Whitelock in the twentieth. A further development has been the publication of translations, for example, *English Historical Documents*, *Volumes I & II*, and *Early Charters* published in the 'Studies in Early English History' series by Leicester University Press. More recent historical surveys have incorporated archaeological evidence.

(ii) **Surveys of food in antiquity.** These can be very wide in scope, as with the very useful *Food in Antiquity* by D. and P. Brothwell (1969). When limited geographically, as with Drummond & Wilbraham's *The Englishman's Food* (1939), the Anglo-Saxon period tends to be dealt with briefly.

(iii) **Publications on specific foodstuffs, and animal husbandry.** Later medieval and modern publications are invaluable for background information to prevent the drawing of false inferences. Ethnographical parallels have been referred to when this has seemed helpful.

Presentation of Material

The text is divided into five main sections.

Section I Production (Chapters 1–15)

Chapters 2–4 deal with the production of vegetable foods; Chapters 5–8 with domestic food animals, poultry and eggs. Chapter 9 deals with wild animals and birds as a food resource; Chapter 10 with Honey, 11 with Fish and Molluscs. Relatively small amounts of food and drink were brought into the country, but these were prestige items with an importance out of all proportion to their bulk, and are covered in Chapter 12. Chapter 13 deals with prohibited foods. The provision of a water supply and the production of fermented drinks are the subjects of Chapters 14 and 15 respectively.

Section II Processing (Chapters 16-20)

Chapter 16 deals with the processing of cereal crops, primarily for breadmaking; Chapter 17 with dairying. The next two chapters cover butchery, preservation and storage, and Chapter 20 cookery methods.

Section III Distribution (Chapters 21-27)

Ensuring Access To A Food Supply

This section attempts to show the importance of food in the system of finance and administration. Chapter 21 shows the importance of land as the basis for food production. Chapter 22 deals with measures and weights and Chapter 23 with the theft of food. Provision for the monastic food supply is treated in Chapter 24. Chapters 25, 26 and 27 deal with the food supply for those who could not draw directly upon the land for their sustenance, either because they lived in towns, were away from home or were destitute.

Section IV Consumption (Chapters 28-33)

Chapter 28 covers meals and mealtimes; Chapter 29 & 30 fasting and feasting respectively. Special regimes for infants, invalids & monastics are dealt with in Chapter 31. Chapters 32 & 33 cover food shortages and deficiency diseases, and the damage caused by dietary elements, including adulteration.

Section V Conclusion

This attempts to bring together the main findings on the production and distribution of food and drink in Anglo-Saxon England. There is also an account of the main changes over the period, where these can be traced. The chapter ends by looking at Anglo-Saxon attitudes to food, and the comparisons and contrasts between Anglo-Saxon and modern English diet and nutrition.

I Food Production

1. Cereal Crops

The Land and Cultivation

Bede begins his *Ecclesiastical History of the English People* with a description of the fertility of the island of Britain. 'The island is rich in crops and trees of various kinds' (*Hit is welig þis ealond on wæstmum 7 on treowum misenlicra cynna*).[1] After the Angles and Saxons Vortigern had called in to fight the Picts had won the victory, 'then they sent home messengers and told them to report the fertility of the land and the cowardice of the Britons' (*þa sendan hi ham ærenddracan 7 heton secgan þysses landes wæstmbærnysse 7 Brytta yrgþo*).[2]

The importance of cultivation is suggested by the amount of imagery it gives rise to. Daniel, bishop of Winchester, writes to Boniface c.723–5, 'who, trusting in the might of the faith has boldly attacked the stony and hitherto barren hearts of the heathen, and working them tirelessly with the plough of gospel preaching dost strive to change them daily'.[3] Presumably Ælfric's listeners would have been familiar with the farmer who brought waste into cultivation since he writes, 'so the husbandman loves the field which, after thorns and brambles, yields abundant crops, more than he loves that which was not thorny nor is fruitful' (*Ealswa se yrðling lufað ðone æcer, ðe æfter ðornum and bremelum genihtsume wæstmas agifð, swiðor þonne he lufige ðone ðe ðornig næs, ne wæstmbære ne bið*).[4] Not surprisingly harvest gives rise to many images, from the brief, 'who multiplies the harvest from a few grains of corn' (*Hwa gemenigfylt ðæt gerip of feawum cornum*); to the poetic description from *The Phoenix* in the Exeter Book:

> . . . *sumes onlice*
> *swa mon to andleofne eorðan wæs(t)mas*
> *on hærfeste ham ge læded*
> *wiste wynsume ær wintres cyme*
> *on rypes timan þy læs hi renes scur*
> *awyrde under wolcnum þær hi wraðe metað*
> *fodor-þege gefean þonne forst and snaw*
> *mid ofer-mægne eorþan peccað*
> *winter-gewædum of þam wæstmum sceal*
> *eorla ead-wela eft alædan*
> *þurh cornes gecynd þa ær clæna bið*
> *sæd onsawen*

. . . much as men bring home for their sustenance the fruits of the earth at harvest, pleasant food at reaping time before winter comes, lest the rain shower destroy

---

[1] Miller 1890, I 1 26.
[2] op. cit., 51.
[3] Kylie 1911, 51.
[4] Thorpe 1843, 89/343/377.

them under the clouds; there they find benefit, the delights of food, when frost and snow, with overpowering might, cover the earth with winter weeds. From those fruits the riches of men shall again come forth, through the nature of grain, which is sown at first as a mere seed.[1]

The Value of Land

Land suitable for growing cereals would have been far scarcer in Anglo-Saxon times than today, when vast areas are suitable for cultivation only because they have effective drainage systems and no forest cover.[2] The importance of land is suggested by the care taken over records of ownership. A lease of land by Abbot Ælfweard and the community at Evesham to Æthelmær for three lifetimes, had fifteen witnesses including one archbishop, two bishops, four abbots and two earls.[3] Such a witness list is not exceptional among the records that have come down to us.[4] The Welsh Laws deal with a number of claims over land, in particular in the first Chapter of Anomalous Laws.[5] To buy a large acreage of land outright required considerable resources: Osgar, abbot of Abingdon, paid 100 mancuses of gold for an estate of twenty hides at Abingdon.[6]

Land units probably reflected the area that would support a family group.[7] Kemble observes that ten acres would support a man and his family 'very well' in his day.[8] The *kotsetle* of *Rectitudines Singularum Personarum* was to have at least five acres 'and it is too little if it ever be less', so perhaps with the other common rights to which he was entitled, he could support himself on this area.[9]

Land was used for *mædue* (pasture) as well as for crops, but it was often made a condition of leases that the land was to be returned with a proportion already sown, or with corn in hand: 'and with twenty acres sown with corn' (*7 mid xx æcerum gesawenes cornes*) 'and with fifty fothers of corn' (*7 half hundred foðra cornes*).[10]

The Fertility of Land

Obviously the fertility of the land was of prime importance, and various prognostications, charms and prayers dealing with this are recorded.[11] In the first category are 'By the Moon's Age', 'From Days', 'From the Sun'[12] and 'From Dreams'.[13] The most often cited – and complicated – charm seems to retain pagan elements. 'Here is the remedy by which you may improve your land if it will not yield well or if any sorcery or witchcraft is suspected' (*Her ys seo bot hu þu mæht þine æceras betan gif hi nellaþ wel wexan oþþe þær hwilc ungedefe þing onegedon bið on*

---

[1] Bosworth & Toller 1898, I 432.
[2] J. Graham, pers. comm.
[3] Robertson 1939, 156.
[4] Whitelock 1955, 467, 468, 471, 477.
[5] Owen 1841, II.
[6] Robertson 1939, 107.
[7] Kemble 1879, 109 ff.
[8] op. cit., 119.
[9] Douglas & Greenaway 1953, 814, 816.
[10] Robertson 1939, 156, 154–5.
[11] Bonser 1963, 431–3.
[12] M.S. Junius 23 folio 148.
[13] M.S. Cott. Tiberius A iii folio 36a/38a; Cockayne 1851, III.

dry oððe on lyblace). Oil, honey, barm and milk of every animal on the land, part of every tree and plant known by name *butan glappan* (except ?buckbean) and holy water was to be dripped on four places from which turves had been cut. The turves were to be taken to church where masses were said over them. Then they were to be returned to their original positions and a cross of quickbeam erected. After that the protagonist was to turn round three times and say more Latin prayers. The next part of the charm may have been efficacious, as 'strange seed from an almsman' (*uncuþ sæd æt almesmannum*) was to be taken. A different strain of seed could well have proved more fertile. Then styrax, fennel, hallowed soap and salt were to be put in a hole in the plough, and a chant beginning *Erce, Erce, Erce* (the name of an earth goddess – 'Mother Earth', perhaps), was to be said over it. The chant goes on to list 'bright crops, broad barley, white wheat, shining millet'. Then a broad loaf was to be baked and placed under the first furrow, after which another prayer to God was to be said.[1] Another charm involved taking four pieces of a loaf which had been marked with the cross and baked at *hlafmæsse* (Lammas – 1st August, originally a Celtic festival). These four pieces were to be crumbled on the four corners of the barn.[2]

Prayers for good harvests were incorporated into the rites of the church: for example, corn was one of the blessings asked for at the coronation of Æthelred II.[3] On April 25 'all God's folk humbly visiting relics shall pray to God to bring a peaceful year and fair weather and sufficient harvests to maintain their bodily strength' (*eall godes folc mid eadmodlice relicgonge sceal god biddan þæt ne him forgefe þone gear siblice tid ond symtelico gewidra and genihtsume wæstmas on heora lichoman trymnysse*).[4] The mention of relics is interesting, since in Wales anyone possessing the bones of St. Cadog – or one of his disciples – would be able to ensure abundance and fertility.[5] Bishop Oswald assured an *ealdorman* at Edgar's court that among the other benefits brought about by the prayers of monks 'corn springs up more abundantly, famine and pestilence withdraw'. Duly impressed, the nobleman founded Ramsey Abbey.[6]

More obviously practical measures were taken to maximise agricultural production. The Welsh Laws stated, 'There are three domestic arts, being primary branches: husbandry, or cultivation of the land; pastoral cares and weaving: and the chiefs of kindreds are to enforce instruction in them; and to answer in that respect in court, and in village, and in every assembly for worship'.[7] 'There are three common protections: of court, place of worship and a plough and team at work'.[8] The Laws of Ine at the end of the seventh century laid down procedure for communal farming – in particular responsibilities for fencing out cattle so they could not damage crops.[9]

---

1 M.S. Cott. Calig. A vii folio 171a in Cockayne 1851, III.
2 M.S.Cott. Vitell. E xviii, folio 16a in Cockayne 1851, III.
3 Turner 1828, III 156–495.
4 Herzfeld 1900, April 25.
5 Davies 1982, 180.
6 Turner 1828, III 495.
7 Owen 1841, II 515.
8 op. cit., 543.
9 Whitelock 1955, 368–9.

Harvesting

Danish raids resulted in the ravaging of various areas of the country, but although a Danish force first overwintered c.855, it was not until 893 that we hear Alfred had organised his army 'so that always half its men were at home, half on service, apart from the men that guarded the boroughs'.[1] In 895 we learn that the king camped in the vicinity of the borough so that the Danes 'could not deny them the harvest'.[2]

Harvest brought a crisis of a different kind at the monastery in Inishboffin: 'at harvest time when men gather in the crops, (the Scots) left the monastery and wandered about the district which they knew and then in the winter they would return and expect to share the stores which the English had worked to get in' (*on hærfest tide þonne mon wæstmas insomnode þon forleton heo þæt mynster 7 þurh cuðe stowe swicedon 7 foron 7 þonne on wintra eft ham hwurfon 7 wilnedon þara goda gemænelice brucan þe Ongle gewunnon 7 gegear wodon*).[3] Presumably the Scots either did not have highly evolved arable agriculture and so were not used to the work, or, because they knew the district, could obtain hospitality without working for their food. Colman solved t4.2he problem by founding another monastery for the English.

Agricultural Methods

Cereals cannot properly be considered without some consideration of what is known of arable farming in the Anglo-Saxon period. Work on open field agriculture suggests that the very early Saxon sites were the homes, sometimes temporary, of small groups of settlers.[4] They usually worked light soils using primitive techniques.[5] Tilling the ground with handtools was a possibility from the earliest times. A sixth-century Preface on Penance refers to Welsh monks who dug by hand.[6] Digging sticks, if not spades, would have been available to the early settlers.[7] The skeletons of early Saxons in East Anglia show a low, bony ridge on the front of the femur, produced by the action of the muscles as the body swung to and fro in the heave and drag of hoeing and mattocking heavy clay soils.[8] Probably most people in the sixth and seventh centuries were involved in subsistence agriculture, expending a considerable physical effort for their returns. On some sites, such as Red Castle, arthritis is more or less universal among adults over the age of thirty. At North Elmham arthritis was also common, though the men suffered more severely than the women. This pattern was repeated at Monkwearmouth and Jarrow, though there the overall incidence of arthritis was much lower, affecting only about a quarter of the population.[9] At Burgh Castle Wells found a case of 'poker' spine, caused, at least in part, by continual straining of the back in lifting and carrying heavy loads, and of Anglo-Saxon populations from early and mid period sites generally he recorded the impression of

---

[1] op. cit., 185.
[2] op. cit., 188.
[3] Miller 1890, IV iv.
[4] Rowley 1981, 85–6.
[5] op. cit. 34ff.
[6] Davies 1982, 38.
[7] Evans 1969, 19.
[8] Wells 1964, 134.
[9] Wells 1967.

1. Cereal Crops

continuous and heavy labour.[1] The ploughman of Ælfric's *Colloquy* (c.1000) exclaims, 'Oh! Oh! it is very hard work . . . Sir, it is very heavy labour, because I am not free' (*Hig! Hig! micel gedeorf ys hit . . . Geleof, micel gedeorf hit ys, forþam ic neom freoh*).[2] This suggests that the work was still heavy, but was exacerbated by the ploughman's servile status which precluded a proper return for his work.

One argument is that, by the end of the eighth century, population pressure was leading to the establishment of nucleated villages and the laying out of some sort of open field system farmed communally, as Ine's Laws seem to imply.[3] However, it may have been periods of heightened mortality and consequently perhaps of demographic decline and reduced labour resources that were the cause of rationalisation and the establishment of a system that was more economical of labour.[4]

As well as dealing with the responsibility for fencing out cattle from common meadow or other land divided in shares, Ine's Laws also deal with the methods of payment for hiring another's yoke of oxen.[5] This suggests that the scratch plough or ard, which may have been available to some groups from migration times, was probably drawn by oxen from at least the seventh century. The tenth-century Cædmon manuscript shows a plough drawn by two oxen.

One of the graves at Sutton Hoo appears to have contained a wooden ard and a ploughman placed as if running with it,[6] but a robust form of one-way plough which could have turned the furrow to either side if the ploughman leaned on it, may have still been in use at the end of the Anglo-Saxon period.[7] A share from a plough of this type was deposited at Nazeing, Essex, probably at the beginning of the eleventh century;[8] an eleventh-century manuscript illustrates a plough of this type,[9] but the layout of this part of the manuscript is for the most part identical with the ninth-century Utrecht Psalter.[10] There is some evidence for mould board ploughing in a seventh century context at Whithorn Priory, Galloway, and complex micro-stratigraphy suggests this was the method used in the mid ninth century.[11] There is more evidence for the technically developed plough, with coulter, share and mouldboard in the late Saxon period. Ploughshares from such ploughs have been found at St. Neots, Hunts., and Westley Waterless, Cambs., and date to the late tenth/early eleventh centuries.[12] The latter example also had a coulter. It is likely that a wheeled plough incorporating these technological advances increased cereal production significantly although other authorities think that the major effect would have been to improve the regulation depth of furrow which may have been beneficial and, therefore, that no great change in production resulted.[13] Incidentally, the

[1] op. cit.
[2] Garmonsway 1978, 21.
[3] Rowley 1981, 19, 36.
[4] op. cit., 123ff.
[5] Whitelock 1955, 371.
[6] Welch 1992, 42.
[7] Monk 1977, 241.
[8] Morris 1983, 32.
[9] BL Harley 603 folio 51v, illustrated in Temple 1976, 205.
[10] op. cit., 82.
[11] Gaimster *et al.* 1990, 241.
[12] Addyman 1973, 52, 94.
[13] Langdon 1986, 268.

increasing use of horses for ploughing in the tenth century in some areas probably did little to improve crop yields either directly or indirectly.[1]

The strip field of ridge and furrow form produced by use of a plough which could turn a furrow was widely established in the Anglo-Saxon period. Such fields have been discovered in secure pre-Conquest contexts: under blown sand at Gwithian, Cornwall, beneath the banks of castle baileys at Hen Domen, Montgomery, and Sandal, Yorks.[2] Subdivided fields ensured a more equitable division of sunny and shadowy shares, and they may have been seen as an insurance against crop failure or destruction, though this may not have been the reason for their establishment.[3]

At the end of the period at least animal power was also used for drawing harrows. In the Bayeux Tapestry a mule-like animal is illustrated pulling a harrow with a square frame and what are presumably metal spikes. It is certainly not just brushwood as earlier harrows may have been.[4] The accounts of property at Thorney Abbey presumably refer to similar pieces of equipment: 'three harrows worth three ores' (*iii ege [ðan þr]eora orena wyrþe*).[5] The horse began to be used for harrowing from the tenth or eleventh century onward and would have increased efficiency, since the horse can pull a load at least fifty per cent faster than an ox.[6]

Gerefa lists handtools necessary for various jobs on an estate. These include seedlips, mattocks, hoes, spades, shovels, beetles, rakes, flails and sieves. Tools illustrated in Anglo-Saxon manuscripts differ little from those in use up to recent times. An early eleventh-century calendar illustrates recognisable scythes, pitchfork, bucket and whetstone.[7] The overall strategies would have remained the same too, so that a farmer speaking early this century would reflect Anglo-Saxon preoccupations. 'A good farmer sowed his seed so that he could take his crop of corn before the weeds came on. You had to be a good farmer to do that, a good practical farmer'.[8] August, the harvest month, was called *weod monað* (weed month), and contamination by weed seeds maturing at the same time and height as the grain could present serious problems (see below). A recognition of the value of a skilful manager is recorded by Werfrith, bishop of Worcester; 'I give Wulfsige my reeve for his loyal efficiency and humble obedience one hide at Easton as Herred held it for three lives' (*sylle Wulfsige minum gerefan wið his holdum mægene eadmodre hernesse anes hides lond on Easttune swa swa Herred hit hæfde on ðreora monna dæg*).[9]

Probably by the end of the period a slightly smaller percentage of the population was engaged in agriculture than had been the case in earlier centuries, and was therefore suffering the associated occupational diseases, in particular arthritis. However, the amount of cereal food produced was probably generally greater, despite Danish raids or poor harvests. Agriculture appears to have been highly organised. On expiry of leases, land was to be left with stock, men and oxen to work it, and stores of sown

[1] op. cit., 264–268.
[2] Clarke, forthcoming.
[3] Rowley 1981, 136.
[4] Trow-Smith 1951, 44.
[5] Robertson 1939, 255.
[6] Langdon 1986, 21.
[7] Temple 1976, 274.
[8] Evans 1960, 144.
[9] Robertson 1939, 35.

corn. In other words a farm was to be passed on as a going concern.[1] The amounts of corn referred to e.g. fifty fothers, suggest large-scale farming, as do documents like *Gerefa* and *Rectitudines Singularum Personarum*, both written by people familiar with the management of a large estate and which assume a demand for such information on the parts of others, with estates in different parts of the country, since the latter refers to local differences.

Treatises

There is evidence that Roman writers on agriculture, certainly Pliny and Columella, were much copied and studied.[2] That, for example, the value of manure was recognised, is demonstrated by the recording of the rights of folding animals on the land, as well as by *Gerefa*. Archaeological evidence for manure/compost heaps comes from Southampton, and stalled cattle may have been valued not just as a luxury food, but as a source of manure.[3] It appears that the Anglo-Saxons followed a system of crop rotation while still living on the continent,[4] and as two ploughings are mentioned in *Gerefa*, it may indicate that a three-field system was in operation, at least by the end of the period. The restricted area of land at Portchester Castle was presumably regenerated, implying a knowledge of the value of manuring, and possibly of crop rotation.[5] The presence at West Stow of a seed of stinking mayweed *Anthemis cotula* characteristic of the heavy boulder clay of Norfolk and Suffolk may indicate the importation of seed corn.[6] (See the *Erce* charm above).

Later Developments

Towards the end of the period owners of large estates seem to have had the interest and resources to improve their estates. *The Assignments of Property to Thorney Abbey* refer to the financing of such improvements. 'And apart from this, the abbot gave the monk Ælfsige ... mancuses of gold for improvement of property belonging to Thorney'. Iron for three mills is mentioned, and perhaps stock and slaves as well as equipment would be bought. 'The bishop in the first instance gave three pounds for improvements at Yaxley, and then three pounds-worth of gold was given ... the second for digging at Farcet (?) and the third for improvements at Yaxley'.[7] By the mid-tenth century the Saxon abbots of Glastonbury had begun the reclamation of their vast marshland endowment in mid-Somerset to produce rich grazing land, and a century later the reclamation of low-lying land in the Exe valley was in hand.[8] Thurston, the first Norman abbot, brought in a drainage engineer, Girard Fossarius. The great coastal manor of Brent Marsh more than trebled in value a few years before 1086, which could only be the result of the construction of a sea bank along the coast of the Bristol Channel, or the substantial repair of an earlier work. Several inland manors in the Levels more than doubled in value in the same years, and must have

---

[1] op. cit., 154 156.
[2] Talbot Rice 1965, 293; Gneuss 1981.
[3] Monk 1977, 446.
[4] Grube 1934, 140.
[5] Cunliffe 1976, 286.
[6] Murphy 1982, 323.
[7] Robertson 1939, 254–5.
[8] Allen et al. in Haslam 1984, 404.

been the scene of much embanking and ditching.[1] This also happened in the fenland estates of Peterborough, Ely and Ramsey. As well as more efficient feeding of communities, the sale of surpluses could enable the acquisition of prestige goods, including food, equipment, tableware.[2]

Problems of the Evidence

It is important to realise that the documents which survive tend to refer to large holdings in the hands of wealthy owners: there is an absence of information relating to the holdings of peasant farmers. Moreover, even when the size of a large estate can be established, and we have some knowledge of its produce, the number to be supported from the holding at any one time is not recorded. In particular it seems virtually impossible to quantify the yield of crops in Anglo-Saxon England. The first variable is climate. There is evidence for colder summers and wetter conditions generally in the late sixth century, while in the eighth century conditions were more continental: summers were drier and warmer, winters colder. Similar conditions prevailed in the tenth century, but a warmer period began around 980.[3] Rye can cope with drier summers than wheat, oats with damper conditions, so yields of these crops would vary with climatic conditions.[4] Soils too will influence yield: rye and oats will yield better than wheat on acid soils. Te Brake considers that early medieval fields produced only a small proportion of the total diet, since early medieval crop yields could be appallingly low, and this is why food provisioning in *De Villis* is so broadly based.[5] Figures for wheat are given as eight bushels per acre, though much higher yields are possible with primitive strains.[6] Trow Smith estimates that ten bushels an acre were possible, but that the average was much less.[7] Seebohm estimates ten bushels an acre in the thirteenth century, dropping to six in the fourteenth.[8] Eleven bushels of wheat a year were needed to support a Roman soldier, and that has been calculated as slightly more than the product of an acre in Roman Britain. In early modern Britain a three-fold yield was not uncommon, and a fifteen-fold yield would have been regarded as particularly good.[9] The yield from Carolingian royal estates in Northern France was approximately 1:3, not very different to the yield recorded in thirteenth-century Winchester documents.[10] Certainly there can be no comparison with modern conditions, where the yield is now three tons of wheat per acre, a one hundred and twenty-fold return. Another variable is the amount of land newly taken into cultivation. In Scania rye planted after clearing and burning gave a 16–24-fold return, compared with a two-five-fold return on the normally tilled village fields.[11] 'Run rig' methods may have been more common in Anglo-Saxon England, and yields correspondingly higher.

---

[1] Poole 1958.
[2] Hodges 1982, 104.
[3] Jones & Dimbleby 1981, 60.
[4] op. cit., 109.
[5] Biddick 1984, 172.
[6] Jones & Dimbleby 1981, 114.
[7] Trow Smith 1951, 48.
[8] Trow Smith 1952, 162.
[9] Davies 1982, 38.
[10] Monk 1977, 352–3.
[11] Evans 1969, 20.

1. Cereal Crops

It seems to have been the case in late Anglo-Saxon England that cereal crops were a staple food. In Ælfric's *Colloquy* agriculture is the most important craft 'because the ploughman feeds us all' (*forþam se yrþling us ealle fett*). The smith protests that without his skill the ploughman would have neither share nor coulter, but the teacher replies, 'but all of us would rather dwell with the ploughman than with you, because the ploughman gives us bread and drink' (*ac eallum us leofre ys wikian mid þe yrþlincge, þonne mid þe, forþam se yrþling sylð us hlaf and drenc*). While stating his own case the baker says, 'and without bread every food is turned to loathing' (*7 buton hlafe ælc mete to wlættan byþ gewyrfed*), which adds support to the ploughman's case. The conclusion is, 'and to agree always with the ploughman who provides us with food and fodder for our horses' (*7 geðwærian symble mid þan yrþlinge, þær we bigleofan us 7 foddor horsum urum habbaþ*).[1]

Archaeological evidence, while tangible, presents its own problems of interpretation. Green deals with the problem of interpreting plant remains, particularly when criteria for sampling vary from site to site.[2] Monk considers the three different methods of analysing material: presence, total presence and dominance.[3] Impressions in briquetage are not random: specific wastes were used for particular technological and domestic purposes.[4] Helbaek's findings of cereal impressions in hand-made pots of the Anglo-Saxon period (80 hulled, 3 naked barley, 14 oat, 1 wild oat, 2 flax) may present a biased view.[5] Hand-made pots may or may not have been made close to a domestic hearth, and have picked up grains lost on the floor during food preparation. The impressions could reflect diet, or merely those crops where the grains were used whole in soups or stews.[6] Impressions in the cremation urns found at Spong Hill were identified as being caused by barley (31), bread wheat (5), oats (4) and rye (2), which presents a rather different picture.[7] Although barley is still the dominant species, this may not indicate it was the staple, or even the preferred cereal crop, simply that wheat and rye were more likely to have been ground and consumed as bread.

Corn

From the earliest references to the end of the period, documents refer to corn, the generic term for grain. In the Laws of Ine and Cnut's Ordinance of 1027, the type of grain for church scot is not specified.[8] Church dues often refer to corn, as at Lambourne: 'at Martinmas two sesters of corn . . . one acre as tithes or a hundred sheaves at harvest and every *geneat* a sester of corn for church scot' (*on Martines mæssan twegen sester cornes . . . oenne æker to teoþunge oððe an hundred sceafa on hærueste and ælc geneat ænne sester cornes to syricsceatte*).[9] Two hundred and three acres of seed from its twenty-four manors were rendered to Peterborough Abbey. Other places also contributed *æcer*

[1] Garmonsway 1978, 39, 40, 36, 41.
[2] Green in Hall and Kenward 1982, 154.
[3] Monk 1977, 29, 148, 334.
[4] Jones & Dimbleby 1981, 130.
[5] Jessen and Halbaek 1944, 23.
[6] West 1982, 319.
[7] op. cit., 318.
[8] Whitelock 1955, 371, 418.
[9] Robertson 1939, 241.

sed tiþunge (acres of seed as tithes, but the kind of grain is unspecified).[1] The reference to part of the *feorme* retained by Offa from an estate at Westbury, Glos., is to thirty ambers of unground corn.[2] Corn is also referred to in other types of transactions. An inventory refers to 'fifty fothers of corn' (*[he]alf hund foþre cornes*) and 'three ores to Leofric of Strethamfor his corn' (*iii oran Leofrice at Strætham æt his corne*).[3] Under the will of Ealdorman Alfred (871–8), Eadred was to have land at Farley and to pay thirty ambers of corn from that land annually to Rochester.[4] According to *Rectitudines Singularum Personarum*, a slave was to have twelve pounds of good corn for food annually, a female slave was to receive eight pounds.[5] This was the 'large pound' – see Chapter 22. The sower was to have a seedlip of every kind of seed 'when he has properly sown every seed throughout the space of a year'. The granary keeper was to have the corn split at the barn door at harvest time 'if his overseer grant it to him and if he deserves it'. This proviso would probably stop the chicanery of obviously unnecessary spillage.

The Ancient Laws and Institutes of Wales deal with compensation to be made for damage to corn and state that one was free to stone animals in the corn. A cartload of the best corn on the land of the man was part of a woman's pay for nursing a child for a year.[6] If a couple parted, the husband was to keep the corn, though a woman could have as much meal as she could carry between her arms and knees into the house from the storeroom.[7]

The Abbotsbury Guild Statutes lay down a fine of a guild sester of corn if a guild brother had not supplied the amount of wood specified.[8] Domesday corn rents refer to *annona* or *frumentum*.

Wheat

In the above cases the receiver presumably could not insist on a particular type of grain, but documents do sometimes refer to specific crops. The Abbotsbury Guild may have considered the non-supply of wood a more trivial affair than other offences for which wheat was to be paid. Three sesters of wheat was to be paid by anyone who undertook a brewing, but did not do it satisfactorily. It was also the fine to be paid by a guild brother who insulted another 'deliberately, inside the guild', or who brought in more men than he should without the permission of the steward and purveyors. The annual subscription (to be paid five weeks before St. Peter's Mass, the first of August) was a guild sester of pure wheat, and if it was not paid within two days the fine was the amount of the entrance fee, namely three sesters of wheat.[9]

Wheat presumably commanded a higher price than other cereals, as the Anglo-Saxon chronicler recorded the high price of wheat. In 1040 'the sester went to 55 pence and even higher' (*Eode se sester hwætes to lv penega and eac furðor*). This followed a

---

[1] op. cit., 74–5.
[2] Whitelock 1955, 467.
[3] Robertson 1939, 249, 257.
[4] Gelling 1979, 155.
[5] Whitelock 1955, 877.
[6] Owen 1841, 741, 783, 679.
[7] op. cit., 83.
[8] Whitelock 1955, 560.
[9] op. cit., 560.

year in which a great gale had occurred. An eighth/ninth century Irish poet wrote of the wind, 'It has broken us, it has crushed us', reminding us of the damage wind can do to the standing crop.[1] In 1043–4 during a severe famine the sester of wheat went above 60 pence, the highest price men could remember, and Henry of Huntingdon added that a sextarius of wheat used to be the burthen of one horse.[2]

In Wales wheat is specified more frequently than any other sort of grain, suggesting it was preferred by those who had the right to demand renders.[3] The king's *gwesta* was a horseload of wheat flour; the three summer *dawnbwyds* sixty loaves of wheaten bread.[4] Wheat was to be provided as food for a very young child.[5] When St. Cuthbert took up residence on Farne Island he planted wheat, and only when this did not grow, did he ask for *beresæd* (barley seed), and miraculously, although 'well beyond the time for sowing' (*ofer ealle tide to sawenne*), it sprang up and produced an abundant crop.[6] It is interesting that the saint's first choice had been wheat: a diet of barley bread is mentioned in association with other saints in such as way as to emphasise their asceticism.

In the year of Christ's birth 'ears of wheat were seen to grow on trees' (*man geseah hwætes eare weaxan on treowum*), and, less exceptionally but still considered worthy of mention, 'good wheat grew this year' (*god hwæte geweaxeð togeare*). It was wheat flour (boiled in milk) that an angel advised as a poultice for a swollen knee.[7] References to wheat, twice in the form of *smedman* (fine meal), are made in *Leechdoms*, fewer references than to barley.[8]

Wheat was specified for church scot as at Elmstone Hardwicke, Glos., where three measures were to be paid annually.[9] The peasants at Hurstbourne Priors, Hants., in about 1050 had to render 'first from every hide . . . 3 sesters of wheat for bread' (*ærest æt hilcan hiwisce . . . iii sesðlar hlafhwetes*).[10] In 977 reference was made to a certain piece of land which the archbishop had attached to his manor at Kempsey, Worcs., 'as wheat-growing land' (*to hwætlande*).[11]

Food rents to be paid to monasteries often include wheat as the specified grain. The surveys from Bury St. Edmunds (1087–98) include 'half a measure of wheat from Barton' (*halmet hwæte . . . on Byrtune*) and 'half a bushel of wheat' (*hælf sceppe hwæte*) from Newton, plus similar dues from over a dozen other places.[12] Evidence for the high status of wheat is the statement that 'At Abbot Ufi's anniversary we shall have half a pound for fish and 40 pence for mead and two measures of wheat' because 'the brethren should enjoy better food on the anniversaries of those whose names they do not hesitate to repeat in their prayers frequently'.[13]

---

[1] Jackson 1971, 127.
[2] Bosworth & Toller 1898, I 349, 222.
[3] Davies 1982, 38.
[4] Owen 1841, 769, 533.
[5] op. cit., 519.
[6] Miller 1890, IV 28.
[7] op. cit., 230.
[8] Cockayne 1851, I viii, lxi 2, III xxxix, lxv, *Lac.* XXXIX.
[9] Finberg 1972, 51.
[10] Robertson 1939, 207.
[11] op. cit., 115.
[12] op. cit., 199, 193.
[13] op. cit., 197.

One important reason for the preference of wheat is that the gluten it contains forms a tough, rubbery material in contact with water. When yeast is added the bubbles of carbon dioxide gas it produces are trapped, producing a light, puffy loaf, whereas barley gluten in contrast tends to dissolve into a watery suspension.[1]

The archaeological record provides evidence of wheats of different kinds. Emmer (*triticum dicoccum*) is found in the early Saxon period, for example as chaff in pottery in early Saxon Canterbury, as seed impressions in pottery and bricks at Buckden Down, Hunts..[2] But it may also have been present in middle Saxon *Hamwih* and as pollen from the 850–950 ground surface in the north bailey of Durham castle.[3] Emmer is gastronomically highly regarded and has good survival characteristics but is not as high yielding as other forms of wheat.[4]

Another variety of wheat, *triticum turgidum*, made up 48% of the sample of grain from two corn-drying kilns at Victoria Street, Hereford, but does not seem to have been identified elsewhere.[5]

Spelt, (*triticum spelta*) was also a hulled wheat, like emmer, but was more frost-hardy, and although it was thought that spelt had gone out of cultivation in the post-Roman period, in favour of free-threshing wheats, it is present throughout the early and mid Saxon periods: in early Saxon Canterbury and at Buckden Down, Hunts., (in association with emmer), probably at *Hamwih*, associated with a bread oven at middle Saxon Fladbury, Worcs., and in an eighth-century waterlogged deposit at Gloucester.[6] It is present in tenth-century Winchester, but more surprisingly, spelt, a major component of cereal assemblages from post-Roman Gloucester, was the most dominant cereal there in the ninth century, and was present also in the tenth, eleventh and twelfth centuries. Perhaps the particular soils and climatic conditions, or even simple rural conservatism favoured the retention of spelt in this area.[7] In the east of the country spelt seems to have died out. Present at West Stow until the mid-fifth century, suggesting a degree of continuity with the Roman period, there was no trace in later seventh-century samples, or in middle Saxon samples from Brandon or Ipswich.[8]

The Gloucester evidence is an exception to the rule that by the late Saxon period, bread wheat (*triticum æstivum*) and club wheat (*triticum compactum*) were the main types of wheat grown. These naked wheats thresh clean from their glumes, so do not need to be parched before threshing as the hulled species do. These wheats were grown as crops, or as a mixed crop, from the Roman period onward, and occur on early Saxon sites like West Stow, as impressions on cremation urns at Spong Hill and at Hawkshill, Leatherhead.[9] They were present at the early/mid Saxon site of Walton, Bucks., and in association with an eighth-century bread oven at Fladbury, Worcs.[10] The middle Saxon site of *Hamwih* produced evidence of *T. æstivum* and *T.*

[1] J. Graham, pers. comm.
[2] Jones & Dimbleby 1981, 136; Monk 1977, 291.
[3] Monk 1977, 308, 312, 294.
[4] Jones & Dimbleby 1981, 106–7.
[5] Monk 1977, 290.
[6] op. cit., 291, 302, 308, 294.
[7] Green 1975, 186.
[8] West 1982, 490, 325.
[9] op. cit., 314, 318; Monk 1977, 291.
[10] op. cit., 302.

compactum, as did Chalton Manor Farm.[1] The middle/late site of Fuller's Hill, Great Yarmouth, provided 6% of *T. æstivum*, slightly more barley and a much higher percentage of oats. The Anglo-Danish Lloyds Bank site, York, provided evidence of *T. æstivum*, also with barley and oats, and a similar assemblage was present in tenth- and eleventh-century Winchester.[2]

It is common to find both dense and lax eared forms of wheat together in a way that indicates that the selection of specific strains had not taken place until at least the late Saxon period in Wessex, although lax eared wheat would be easier to thresh.[3] *T. æstivum* and *T. compactum* may have been grown together and some grain forms showed characteristics of both species. Perhaps the purity of the different strains was not important to Anglo-Saxon farmers as long as bread could be produced from the grain.[4] Since leechdoms mention *hwætene wyrte* (*wyrte* being the wort of beer), wheat may have been used for brewing.[5] British beer brewed today may contain up to 30% wheat, although the admixture usually contains maize, but some German breakfast beers are brewed entirely from wheat.[6]

It seems likely that wheat was the dominant cereal species at least by the tenth century, in place of barley.[7] It is possible that bread wheat was favoured only when it was possible and desirable to invest the greater amount of fertilizer, and man hours in the form of cultivation and weeding, necessary to obtain the high yield potential of bread wheat.[8] This accords well with the documentary evidence that suggests it was the preferred crop.

Barley

Barley is one of the three cereal crops of the *Erce* charm, the others are wheat and millet. It is specified for dues in a similar manner to wheat. The Laws of Ine state that as barley rent six weys must always be given for each labourer. At Hurstbourne Priors c. 1050, the peasants were to give 'three pounds of barley as rent' (*ðreo pund gauol bæres*) as compared with three sesters of wheat for bread from every hide.[9] *Rectitudines Singularum Personarum* refers to the *gebur's* right as 23 sesters of barley at Martinmas after the harvest.[10]

The compound *hlafbere* does not exist in Old English. As the barley gluten lacks the qualities of wheat gluten, it makes a much heavier, as well as more strongly flavoured, bread. Barley is mentioned by eleventh- and twelfth-century Welsh writers as barley bread, but wheat bread seems to have been more in evidence.[11] Barley bread is still sold in Wales, and when fresh is quite palatable. In *The Ancient Laws and Institutes of Wales* a sheaf of barley at one half-penny was double the

---

[1] Holdsworth 1981, 130; Monk 1977, 321.
[2] op. cit., 294, 292, 325, 327.
[3] Jones & Dimbleby 1981, 139; J. Graham, pers. comm.
[4] Monk 1977, 332.
[5] Cockayne 1851, II, 268.
[6] D. Maule, pers. comm.
[7] Jones & Dimbleby 1981, 139; Monk 1977, 338; Green in Hall & Kenward 1982, 44.
[8] Jones & Dimbleby 1981, 107.
[9] Robertson 1939, 207.
[10] Douglas & Greenaway 1953, 814.
[11] Davies 1982, 38.

price of oats.[1] The barley corn was established as a unit of measure – there were three barley corn lengths to the inch.[2]

Barley was probably the main raw material for malt as it is today, and malt is often mentioned in dues. For example, the royal manor of Tidenham was to provide eight sesters of malt at Lammas, and Newton was to pay a bushel of malt to Bury St. Edmunds.[3] There is some archaeological evidence that barley was used for brewing rather than bread making, since hulled barley *hordeum vulgare*, is found throughout the period. At the early Saxon site of West Stow barley was present.[4] At Victoria Street, Hereford, *H. vulgare* made up 28% of the grain sample.[5] At Canterbury, on another early site, *H. vulgare* was present, as at the early/mid Saxon site of Walton, Bucks.[6] At *Hamwih* a large sample of *hordeum vulgare* was found in association with a dryer or kiln (Feature SAR XV). However, the other large deposit of carbonised grain in Feature SAR V, consisted almost entirely of wheat, and Monk's observation is that, assuming chances of accidental carbonisation and recovery were equal for each species, wheat was produced in equal quantities with barley.[7] *Hamwih* also produced evidence of two-row barley, *Hordeum distichum*, which is otherwise assumed not to have been introduced until well into the medieval period.[8] At Chalton Manor Farm barley was the most important cereal found at the lowest level, probably in association with a corn-drying kiln, and was also present in the later levels.[9] The mid/late site of Fuller's Hill, Great Yarmouth, produced 7% of *H. vulgare*, and the tenth- and eleventh-century site of Sussex Street, Winchester, produced 58%, but also naked barley *H. nudum*.[10] At the York Lloyds Bank site *H. vulgare* was again in evidence: two-thirds of the cereal pollen came from this variety of barley, the remainder from oats.[11]

Helbaek's evidence from the early period revealed 80 impressions of hulled barley but only three of naked barley.[12] Not only does hulled barley remain the commonest form, but in the late Saxon period naked barley almost entirely disappears.[13] If barley was being threshed and used for bread, then one would expect the naked forms which are easier to thresh to have been preferred, as happened with wheat. But as the grains are allowed to germinate in the first stage of making malt, the presence of husks is of no account. *H. vulgare* is the form used for brewing today. In the Saxon period the varieties of six-row barley were genetically highly mixed, but within individual grain deposits from late Saxon sites there was much less diversity. The differences between such deposits can be closely compared with modern lax-and dense-eared crops, and so may indicate selection for particular varieties of hulled barley.[14] When barley was found specifically associated with what is believed to have been a bread oven at

---

[1] Owen 1841, 281.
[2] op. cit., 185.
[3] Douglas & Greenaway 1953, 818.
[4] West 1982.
[5] Monk 1977, 290.
[6] op. cit., 292, 300.
[7] op. cit., 308, 316.
[8] Holdsworth 1980, 130; Monk 1977, 340.
[9] Monk 1977, 321, 325.
[10] op. cit., 294, 327.
[11] op. cit., 293.
[12] Jessen & Helbaek 1944, 23.
[13] Jones & Dimbleby 1981, 37.
[14] op. cit., 140.

Fladbury, Worcs., the dominant species of barley was *H. testrastichum*, a lax-eared species much easier to thresh than *H. vulgare*.[1]

While barley was generally considered to have been the major cultivated species of the post-Roman period in southern England, and some sites show equal dominance of barley and wheat over other cereal crops where evidence is from carbonised material associated with domestic activities, Green points out that most evidence comes from areas of chalk downland well-suited to barley growing. In Gloucestershire, where the soil is not of this type, then spelt was the dominant species.[2]

The percentage of late Saxon sites at which both bread wheat and barley were found was more than double that of early sites. The percentage of late Saxon sites at which bread wheat alone was found, had declined by half, but there were no sites of either period on which barley was found alone.[3] This suggests that barley and wheat had different uses, that wheat was perhaps the more important, but that both were wanted. Almost certainly the wheat was wanted for bread, the barley for brewing, perhaps also for use in soups and stews, as it still is, and possibly also for feeding stock. Ruminant animals can be fed barley during the winter.[4]

One conclusion is that archaeological evidence does not support the view that barley was the staple crop in Anglo-Saxon England: the balance suggests larger quantities of wheat.[5] However, Monk records hulled six-row barley in the highest percentages throughout the Saxon period, although it diminishes very markedly in the middle period, showing only a gradual recovery by the late Saxon period.

Oats

There is evidence that oats were quite widely grown in Anglo-Saxon England. *on athylle* (on oat hill) is recorded in 779, and although Oteley Grove and The Nakers are not recorded until after the Saxon period, they are based on O.E. forms: *ate leah* and *atten æcer*.[6] The bishop of Worcester's oat land is mentioned in a boundary charter of 984.[7] However, oats do not feature in dues and rents as wheat and barley do. In leechdoms oats are mentioned only three times, less often than wheat, barley or rye.[8]

Oats may have been used for human consumption: while Pliny was not complimentary about oats he noted they were made into porridge in Germany.[9] Giraldus was perhaps sensationalising matters when he commented that the whole population of Wales lived almost entirely on oats.[10] In times of dearth they may have been utilized quite generally, but they could have been a staple crop in areas with damp, acid soils.

---

[1] Monk 1977, 342.
[2] Green 1975, 189.
[3] Jones and Dimbleby 1981, 137–8.
[4] J. Graham, pers. comm.
[5] Jones & Dimbleby 1981, 139.
[6] Smith 1964, I 218, III 255, 53.
[7] Finberg 1972, 123.
[8] Cockayne 1851, I lxxxv, xlvii and *Lac.* 8.
[9] Monk 1977, 349.
[10] Thorpe 1978, 233.

In *The Ancient Laws and Institutes of Wales* oats as part of the king's *gwesta* are 'for provender'. The apparitor (an official of the court) was to get a sieve of oats if he was insulted when cases were being heard.[1] These laws also stated that oatmeal was to be provided as compensation for a dry cow from the calends of winter to the feast of St. Curig.[2] This may have been for human consumption as porridge, or in stews and pottage, since oats would presumably not have been ground into meal if they were intended for animal food. Oats may have been used for brewing. *atena gratan* (to be taken with cream) are referred to in an addition in a twelfth-century hand to leechdoms in MS Cotton Faustina A x, folio 115b. Cockayne translates *gratan* as 'groats . . . the residuary materials of malt liquor', and in the Orkneys oats were added on special occasions to make the beer more intoxicating.[3] However, an alternative translation for *gratan* is grain with the hull removed.[4]

In the archaeological record cultivated oats (*avena sativa*) can only be distinguished from the wild species (*A. fatua*) when the floret base of the chaff is present.[5] At West Stow small numbers of oat grains were found, of which only one large grain may have come from cultivated oats. It is considered that oats were probably not cultivated as a separate crop and may represent contamination.[6] Jessen and Helbaek reported 14 impressions of cultivated oats (as compared to 83 of barley and five of wheat, and Murphy found four impressions of oats on the Spong Hill cremation urns, compared with 31 of barley and five of wheat.[7] Two corn-drying kilns at Victoria Street, Hereford, produced 24% of oats, which were not thought to be the result of mixed cropping.[8] Chaff in sixth-century pottery at Portsdown, Portsmouth, came from *A. sativa* and *A. strigosa*, and another early site at Hawkshill, Leatherhead, yielded *A. sativa*.[9] Carbonised grain discovered in pits at the early/mid Saxon site of Walton, Bucks., gave two grains of *A. sativa* and two of *A. fatua*.[10] At *Hamwih* (Feature SAR XV) one tenth of the grains in a large deposit were identified as *avena sp.* and the only other large grain deposit, (Feature SAR V) contained only two grains of oats.[11] The oats could have been a contaminant, or a crop in their own right.[12] At the lowest level at Chalton Manor Farm almost all the grain was from barley and oats, and the latter were present also in the later levels.[13] At the mid/late site of Fuller's Hill, Great Yarmouth, 55% of *avena* was found, the density being highest in an oven rake-out.[14] In Anglo-Danish York, at the Lloyds Bank site, carbonised *A. sativa* was found, and the cultivated oat also provided one third of the cereal pollen found.[15] In tenth-century bell-mould fragments found at Winchester, the majority of grains were *avena sp.* and

---

[1] Owen 1841, 199, 67.
[2] op. cit., 273.
[3] Renfrew 1985, 17.
[4] Grube 1934, 148.
[5] Jones & Dimbleby 1981.
[6] West 1982, 315, 321, 425.
[7] op. cit., 318.
[8] Monk 1977, 290.
[9] op. cit., 291.
[10] op. cit., 300.
[11] op. cit., 308, 316.
[12] Holdsworth 1980, 130.
[13] Monk 1977, 321, 325.
[14] op. cit., 294.
[15] op. cit., 293.

A. sativa, and a possible source was animal feed or dung.[1] On the tenth/eleventh century Sussex Street, Winchester, site, *avena sp.* was thought to be a contaminant.[2] Without modern methods of weed control, the proportion of 'weed' oats could have been quite high in Anglo-Saxon England.[3]

Small rural and semi-urban sites produce greater evidence of oats (and legumes) than large urban centres like Winchester.[4] This suggests the primary use of oats was as provender, and they were not the preferred cereal of those who purchased their food. The frequency cultivation of *A. sativa* may have increased very slightly through the Anglo-Saxon period.[5]

Rye

Rye (*secale cereale*) was grown in Anglo-Saxon England. *Ryton* (rye-farmstead) is recorded in 892, *rige cumb* (rye valley) in 955–9, and *Rwirdin* recorded in 1086 may be *ryge worðign* (rye enclosure).[6] A lease of land by Oswald, archbishop of York and bishop of Worcester, refers to *hryancrofte* (to the rye-growing croft).[7]

It is mentioned in leechdoms as *riges seofoþa* (siftings of rye), *siglan dust* (rye powder), *rigen mela* (rye meal), and *surre rigenre grut* (sour rye groats).[8] Wihtred, who was ruling in Kent in 695, issued his laws in that year on the sixth day of *Rugern*, which probably means 'rye harvest'.[9] For rye to have given its name to a month would suppose it was of considerable importance, although this may have reflected continental i.e. pre-Migration, conditions. A charter of Offa refers to thirty ambers of rye corn.

In the archaeological record also rye is present throughout the period. Rye chaff was found in the sixth-century pottery from Portsdown, Portsmouth, and in early pottery from Canterbury.[10] It is common at Old Buckenham Mere, Norfolk, from the fifth century on until the thirteenth, peaking at around 600–700. Rye would have been the ideal crop to exploit the dry, sandy soil conditions of this area.[11] The large rye at West Stow are the earliest known from Anglo-Saxon contexts in this area at present. It was a minor contaminant of the spelt crop in the Roman samples, although it was cultivated elsewhere in Roman Britain.[12] One seventh-century deposit almost entirely of rye grains: a fully-processed crop ready for consumption or sowing. The other sample was largely of rye grains, but included a significant number of poisonous corncockle seeds (*agrostemma githago*) and small grass caryopses. Since the seeds of corncockle are almost as big as rye they would have been almost

[1] op. cit., 325.
[2] op. cit., 327.
[3] J. Graham, pers. comm.
[4] Jones & Dimbleby 1981, 146.
[5] Monk 1977, 339.
[6] Smith 1964, III 169, 116, 240.
[7] Robertson 1939, 117.
[8] Cockayne 1851, I iv 6, liii, lxxiii, II lix.
[9] Whitelock 1955, 361.
[10] Monk 1977, 291.
[11] op. cit., 292.
[12] West 1982, 320.

impossible to remove by winnowing or sieving, and this contaminated batch may have been deliberately burnt.[1]

Rye was present in ninth-century Gloucester and is now increasingly found on other sites of the period, although only in exceptional circumstances, as in the wholesale destruction of granaries at Lydford, Devon, is it found in large quantities.[2] The small quantities in which it is usually encountered may indicate it was a weed of cultivation, rather than a major cereal crop.[3] The Chalton Manor Farm site produced only one possible example of rye, and the mid/late Saxon site of Fuller's Hill, Great Yarmouth, produced only 0.6% of rye.[4] However, there is a significant late deposit from what was probably a corn-drying kiln at Wallingford, Berks.[5] An important mill in Shropshire paid a rent of eight sesters of rye at the time of Domesday.[6]

Rye was the staple crop on the continent because it was able to thrive under adverse conditions of soil and climate, but better conditions in Britain meant that the settlers could indulge their preference for other crops.[7] Ergot would have flourished in the damper conditions prevailing in England, and this may have been the major factor in relinquishing rye as an important cereal crop. Marling must have taken place in the eleventh century when there was 'capitalistic estate management' (the expense of marling is heavy) in order to introduce or extend wheat cultivation in lieu of rye.[8]

There is some evidence that wheat and rye were already being grown together as a mixed crop (maslin). *The Ancient Laws and Institutes of Wales* give the price of a thrave of maslin as eight pence, double that of oats. Archaeologically it is possibly indicated by the occurrence together of fragments of the bran of rye and wheat in faecal layers of Anglo-Danish York.[9] There is evidence that the Welsh also grew rye as a separate and relatively common crop, in the details of the compensation to be paid for a dry cow. This was to be a pancheon-shaped measure of oatmeal until the feast of St. Curig, of barley meal until the feast of St. Michael, of rye meal until the calends of winter. However, another code substitutes wheat meal for the rye meal.[10]

Millet

Although millet occurs frequently in the continental record, its absence from Anglo-Saxon England may be explained in terms of a lack of demand for a new cereal that was not tolerant of unfavourable situations in the same way as the other oncoming species.[11] The *Erce* charm for fertility apparently refers to 'bright millet' (*scira herse*) together with wheat and barley. This requires an emendation of *henre*, the word in the manuscript, although Cockayne keeps this reading and translates the phrase as 'rural crops'. Schlutter however, thinks the charm is evidence that the Anglo-Saxons did grow

---

[1] op. cit., 317.
[2] Green 1975, 186.
[3] op. cit.
[4] Monk 1977, 321, 325, 294.
[5] Med. Archaeol. XI, 284.
[6] Ashley 1928, 132.
[7] Monk 1977, 343.
[8] Ashley 1928, 139.
[9] Jones, undated paper.
[10] Owen 1841, 273, 563.
[11] Jones & Dimbleby 1981, 110.

millet, but there is at present no other evidence for it, and the word *herse* (modern German *hirse*) may not have been known to the copyist, hence his mistake.[1] Parts of the *Erce* charm may be very ancient, and have related to continental conditions.

Weeds

In addition to the conventional cereal species, use may also have been made of wild grasses. In Denmark to the present century, the seeds of chess (*bromus sp.*) were collected and ground to flour as a famine food in the years the rye crop failed. Chess, a natural weed contaminant of cereal crops would have dominated these failed fields.[2] The archaeological evidence for *bromus* in Anglo-Saxon contexts invariably comes from bulk cereal deposits, in particular barley crops that seem not to have been thoroughly cleaned of such impurities.[3] But it may be that the Anglo-Saxons did not regard *bromus* as an impurity, but an addition, and that, if the barley was to be used for brewing (or as animal feed) the seeds would not have been considered to contaminate the sample.

Excavations in Winetavern Street, Dublin, indicate that the townsfolk ate the seeds of goosefoot (*chenopodium album*), and three species of polygonum: knot grass (*P. persicaria*), black bindweed (*P. convolvulus*) and pale persicaria (*P. lapathifolium*).[4] All three polygonum species were likely to be collected by the reaper.[5] The early/mid Saxon site of Walton, Bucks., yielded one seed of *C. album* and this species was present at the mid Saxon site of Fladbury, Worcs., (in association with a bread oven), with seeds of *bromus*, *rumex* and *vincia sp.* (vetch), although as very few weed seeds were present, the crop had presumably undergone cleaning.[6] At *Hamwih*, feature SAR XV which yielded a large sample of seed, contained *gramineæ* and *bromus sp.*, but no other weed seeds, and is regarded as having been 'thoroughly cleaned', in which case perhaps the seeds of these two species were tolerated.[7] The middle/late Saxon site of Fuller's Hill, Great Yarmouth, yielded 30% *gramineæ* from layers associated with two ovens, pits and floor, and also *P. persicaria*, *rumex crispus* and *chenopodium album*.[8] *Bromus secallinus/mollis* were found at the tenth/eleventh-century site at Sussex Street, Winchester, and the late Saxon sites of Hungate, York, and Little Paxton, Hunts.[9]

Anglo-Saxon crops were probably heavily infested with weeds. The manure used as fertilizer almost certainly contained a number of viable weed seeds, and weeding by hand, or with handtools would be the only way of reducing their numbers. Cutting the stalks a little way below the ears would free the gathered corn from the lower-growing weeds, but some species of bindweed, for example, would remain attached to the ears, and only seeds that were smaller or larger than the corn could be separated

---

[1] Schlutter 1907, 125–7.
[2] Jones & Dimbleby 1981, 108–9.
[3] op. cit., 145.
[4] Med. Archaeol. XV, 77.
[5] Jones & Dimbleby 1981, 32.
[6] Monk 1977, 300, 302.
[7] op. cit., 303.
[8] op. cit., 294.
[9] op. cit., 298, 297, 295.

by sieving. Even modern grain cleaning techniques cannot remove all weed seeds.[1] The presence of the seeds listed above probably did not matter: they might contribute their own taste to the final cereal product, but might in some seasons be welcomed as bulking out the crop.

However, this would not have been the case with corncockle (*agrostemma githago*). A weed of cereal crops, its seeds mature at the same time and at the same height as the ears of corn. It taints flour and contains haemolytic toxins known as saponins.[2] The O.E. for 'tares' was *coccel*, so presumably it was corncockle that was referred to in metaphors like the following: ' . . . in order that, if any tares had spoilt those crops, sown with the best seed, which the blessed Pope Gregory had planted through the mouth of St. Augustine, we might be zealous with our highest endeavour to uproot completely anything harmful and to secure most wholesome fruit'.[3]

It is found on a number of middle and late sites: Fuller's Hill, Great Yarmouth; Sussex Street, Winchester; Little Paxton, Hunts., and Anglo-Danish sites in York, particularly Lloyds Bank and Hungate.[4] On the latter site corncockle seeds were frequent in samples from late Saxon layers, and may have increased the susceptibility to leprosy of those who consumed them. The seeds, together with cereal bran and parasite ova, form a characteristic suite of fossil remains, often fused together in concreted lumps. One eleventh-century pit fill from 16–22 Coppergate, York, yielded as much as 4% by volume of corncockle seed, though it is difficult to tell what proportion this formed of the bread – or porridge – from which it undoubtedly came. It is also possible that slow cooking removes the poison, and that contaminated samples would therefore be used for porridge or in stews; it is also possible that the anti-helminthic properties of corncockle were known, and the population were trying to rid themselves of worm infestations.[5]

Ergot is a fungal infection of cereal crops to which rye is more susceptible than wheat.[6] It is a serious contaminant causing poisoning of humans and stock. Gangrene is the most common symptom, but it can cause abortions, hallucinations, and other unpleasant effects.[7] Ploughing and crop rotation can be effective against infestation, but crops can become reinfected from certain wild and cultivated grasses on which ergot is very common. The technology existed in Anglo-Saxon times to get rid of ergots, by soaking grain in a salt solution, then floating off the ergots and drying the grain, but it is not known if this was practised or not.[8] The murrain of cattle recorded in the chronicles might be related to cool, wet conditions during the flowering period of grasses and cereals, as this would be ideal for the spread of ergot infection. Ergotism may have been partly responsible for the decrease of rye through the Anglo-Saxon period.

---

[1] J. Graham, pers. comm.
[2] Forsyth 1968, 47.
[3] Smith 1964, I, 23; Legates' Report to Pope Hadrian in 786, in Whitelock 1955, 770.
[4] Monk 1977, 294, 327, 295, 293, 297.
[5] Hall 1981, 5ff.
[6] Dickens 1974, 1, 3.
[7] Masefield et al. 1986, 4.
[8] Dickens 1974.

Conclusion

As far as the cereal diet of the Anglo-Saxons was concerned, this must have varied from area to area, according to soil type and climatic conditions; from year to year, as well as changing gradually through the period; but probably social status was the most important single determinant. Wheat seems to have been the preferred cereal, no doubt because its properties made it particularly suitable for bread-making, and it became more common. Naked types which were easier to thresh became more popular, the hulled types tending to die out in most areas. This was not paralleled by barley, the other important cereal crop, where naked types were not selected for, and this suggests barley was not threshed and used for bread, but was probably very important for brewing. The ploughman *sylð us . . . drenc* (gives us drink) as well as *hlaf* (bread) according to Ælfric's *Colloquy*.[1] Other crops were oats and rye, and all four cereals may have been used for brewing.

The development of a plough capable of turning a furrow made more effective cultivation possible, and the use of oxen for motive power also increased productivity. This may have produced the supply of cereal food per head, since the population seems not to have increased dramatically. Pollen evidence shows considerable tracts of land falling waste, and forest re-establishing itself. Only at the end of the period did the pressure on land reach that of the Iron Age.[2] The evidence of Ælfric's *Colloquy* is that cereals, as raw material for bread and ale, were the single most important source of food by the end of the period. It has been argued that the increasing incidence of caries in the Anglo-Saxon population is evidence that cereal food became steadily more important, but scurvy and other damage can cause bad periodontal health.[3] This is not to say that most individuals could always be assured of cereal food: bad harvests could reduce a *ceorl* to a slave, rich harvests might mean he could aspire to the status of a *thegn*.[4]

The traditions of farming in the classical period probably influenced farming across Europe until changes in the eighteenth century.[5] Communal activity to pool resources probably started in the middle Saxon period, most evidence coming from the south Midlands, the type area for open field farming in the thirteenth century.[6] The evidence of *Gerefa* is that ploughing was carried out in the autumn and spring, and at least a two-field system of rotation was being practised. Spelt and most wheats are winter-sown. However, three-course rotation: wheat or rye, followed by oats/barley/peas/beans, third year fallow, may have been introduced from the ecclesiastical estates of northern France.[7]

While it is obvious that the yield of crops today – about one hundred and twenty-fold for wheat – cannot be compared with the much lower yields of Anglo-Saxon times, it may be less apparent that the chemical make-up of grain may have changed. The Laws of Edward I stated that a penny was to be round without clipping, and to weigh

---

[1] Garmonsway 1978, 40.
[2] Jones & Dimbleby 1981, 71–2.
[3] Wells 1964; Miles 1972, 309.
[4] Trow-Smith 1951, 501.
[5] Monk 1977, 351.
[6] op. cit., 247.
[7] Trow-Smith 1951, 47.

32 grains of wheat from the middle of the ear. A simple experiment with modern wheat shows that only 24 grains are now needed to equal the weight of such a penny. However, even though the grains of 'unimproved' varieties of wheat were smaller than modern varieties, they may have contained as much protein. Harlan found that wild grain was almost twice as rich in protein as domestic wheat.[1] However, the protein content of any sample of modern grain depends almost entirely on the fertility of the soil in which it is grown.[2] It is therefore difficult to state that Anglo-Saxon varieties may have been more nutritionally valuable, weight for weight, than modern varieties, since samples from exhausted soil would contain less protein. Harlan's evidence perhaps gives clues as to why what are thought of as 'wild' grasses may have been consumed. However, Anglo-Saxon cereals may also have been different from modern samples in that they might have been contaminated, potentially fatally, with the vegetable poisons of corncockle and ergot. Erysipelas, or ergotism, was one of the common complaints dealt with in Anglo-Saxon medical writings.[3]

[1] Ucko & Dimbleby 1971, 80.
[2] J. Graham, pers. comm.
[3] Deegan 1986, 20.

2. Vegetables, Herbs and Fungi

Gardens

Alcuin, writing to Charlemagne in 796–7, says he hopes that not only in York but in Tours there may be a 'garden enclosed', but he points out that this imagery has come from the *Song of Songs*.[1] However, Anglo-Saxon Glosses do translate the Latin terms for garden by *wyrttun* or *leactun*.[2] A timber hall at Chalk Lane, Northampton, dated by a St. Edmund memorial penny unlikely to have been deposited after 917, was associated with a small cultivated plot.[3] Before the Conquest, the garden of Lefstan Bittecat in Winchester yielded 12 pence.[4] Gardens are mentioned in Domesday Book, particularly in towns, where the pressure on space may have made their presence more noteworthy: eight *cotarii* and their gardens in *Fuleham*, Middlesex, and a house and garden at Hertford, for example.[5] Other examples from the *Inquisitio Eliensis* are quoted in Seebohm 1952, 122. The conclusion has been drawn that 'Most men had a small croft for growing vegetables and the herbs required for seasoning and medicinal purposes'.[6]

Earlier evidence is forthcoming from the continent and probably parallels the situation here. A possible vegetable garden was excavated at Wijster.[7] Charlemagne's *Capitulare De Villis* c. 800, detailed the plants to be grown on crown lands, and in England too vegetables and herbs, and perhaps flowers and trees, were probably grown on the kings' estates.[8] Between 816 and 836, a plan for an ideal monastery, which included lists of plants for the herb and vegetable gardens, was sent to the abbot of St. Gall, where it has been preserved.[9] The monastery of St. Gall had been founded in the eighth century by Irish missionaries and maintained strong links with Anglo-Saxon England.[10] In his life of St. Æthelwold, Wulfstan writes of the saint 'cultivating the garden and getting the fruit and different kinds of vegetables ready for the monks' meal'.[11]

Links with continental houses were well established, and it would not have been necessary to wait for the visits of English bishops to St. Gall (like those of Cenwald, bishop of Worcester, in 929, or of Oda, bishop of Ramsbury in 936), before such information was passed on.[12] Walafrid Strabo writes in about 840 of his garden at Reichnau, that it contained sage, rue, southern wood, poppy, pennyroyal, parsley, mint and radishes, and 'for love's sake only' gladioli, lilies and roses.[13]

---

1   Whitelock 1955, 786.
2   Bosworth & Toller 1898, I 1291, 624.
3   Williams 1984, 113.
4   Barlow 1976, 49.
5   Turner 1828, II 548.
6   Whitelock 1952, 104.
7   Wolters 1967, 405.
8   Harvey 1981, 29.
9   op. cit., 32.
10 Deegan 1986, 16.
11 Lapidge 1991, 17.
12 Hart 1975, 311.
13 Waddell 1932, 80.

Gardens were established in the Celtic west some time before the Welsh Laws were codified in the first half of the tenth century. The Venedotian Code mentioned 'cabbage . . . leeks, and everything that pertains to a garden', and that the land of a *corddlan* was to be shared as gardens.[1] No-one was to retain gardens in his possession more than a year, and the gardens were to be manured each year.[2] One of the three thieves subject to a *camlwrw* was a stealer of garden herbs.[3]

Leechdoms advise that *missenlice wyrts* (various plants – herbs and vegetables), are to be avoided in some cases: 'particularly in summer when they are commonly eaten' (*swiþost on sumera þonne þa mon þigð*).[4] While some of these plants may have been gathered from the wild, the likelihood is that a number of them were cultivated.

Allium Species

Very early on, *laukaz* (leek) was a magic word, inscribed in runic form on a number of objects, and therefore likely to have been of some importance in the culture.[5] *Leac* (leek) occurs as a place- or field-name element as at Leckhampton, Gloucs., and *lectun*, a *litil mede* (leek-enclosure, a little meadow) is recorded in 1180.[6] Given that *leactun* is a term for garden, and *leac(tun)weard* for gardener, the many mentions of leeks and other plants of the onion family are not surprising. We have seen that, with cabbages, leeks were one of the crops pertaining to a garden.[7] The list of vegetables in the St. Gall monastery plan opens with *cepas* (onions), *alias* (garlic), *porros* (leeks) and *ascolonias* (shallots). The same four plants had appeared in *De Villis* with the addition there of *britlas* (chives) and *uniones* (the Welsh onion, *allium fistulosum*).[8] Ælfric Bata wrote that *algium* (garlic) was one of the plants that was cooked and eaten daily.[9] Garlick Close is recorded as a field name.[10]

Leechdoms refer to *por* (leek), although here it is said to be hard to digest and bad for the eyes.[11] There are a further six references to *por* or *porr*. *Cropleac* (*A. sativum*) is mentioned in I ii 14, and in another 17 recipes when it is particularly recommended for cases of madness. *Garleac* (garlic, *A. oleraceum*) is mentioned first in I ii 16 and then in another twelve recipes, one of which calls for *clufe garleac* (cloves of garlic). There are three references to the onion (*cipe, ciepan, cipan*); and three to *secgleac* (*A. schoenoprasum*). There is one mention each of *brade leaces* and *holleac*. Glosses do not throw any light on these two references, but the *Durham Glossary* and the *Epinal Gloss* add *ramsons* (*A. ursinum*), as a translation for *vamuscium* and *accitula* respectively, to the list of oniony plants.[12] Salads in late medieval England tended to

---

[1] Owen 1841, 325.
[2] op. cit., 181.
[3] op. cit., 553.
[4] Cockayne 1851, II xxxvi.
[5] Elliott 1963, 68.
[6] Smith 1964, II 109, 197.
[7] Owen 1841, 325.
[8] Harvey 1981, 32.
[9] Stevenson 1929.
[10] Field 1972, 85.
[11] Cockayne 1851, I ii 1.
[12] Pheifer 1974, 6.

be heavy on the onion family: one recipe includes garlic, scallions, onions, leek, young leeks plus herbs.[1] This would seem to reflect a long-term preference.

St. Eastorwine at Wearmouth *leac sette* (planted leeks).[2] According to Bede's latin life of St. Cuthbert, the saint remained five days in one spot whereupon he was asked, 'Surely you have not stayed so long in one place without taking food?' He drew back the coverlet . . . and showed five onions . . . 'This was my food these five days; for as often as my mouth was parched and burned through excess of dryness and thirst I sought to refresh and cool myself by tasting these.' His questioner commented, 'And indeed somewhat less than half of one of the onions seemed to have been nibbled away'.[3]

Rather different from these saintly connections, is Riddle 25 from the Exeter Book, a *tour de force* of sexual innuendo for which its inventor could have disclaimed all responsibility as it refers accurately to an onion.[4] The answer to Riddle 65 is likewise an onion. Riddle 85 is somewhat contentious, as the answer unfairly requires the garlic seller to be one-eyed.[5]

Archaeological evidence for vegetables is sparse, but two bulbs, which on the balance of probabilities were onions, were found in a hanging bowl in a barrow burial at Ford, Hampshire. The burial was dated to the late seventh century by the shield boss, seax and buckle.[6] Also in the bowl were four crab apples, which suggests some ceremonial provision of food, if not a meal, as Elizabeth Fowler suggests.[7] Remains of the outer layer of an allium species, some at least of leek, (*A. porrum*) have been found in many cesspit samples from Anglo-Danish York.[8]

Root Vegetables

Carrots are listed in the *Capitulare De Villis*, and in the list of vegetables in the St. Gall plan as *mangones*, though on the plan itself they are *carritas*.[9] There is a reference in leechdoms to *broþ moran* which Cockayne translates as 'carrot broth'.[10] He translates other references to *feldmore* as 'carrot' in I xi, but 'parsnip' in I xlviii 2. Bonser agrees with the latter attribution.[11] However, seeds of wild or cultivated carrot (*daucus carota*) have been recovered from a number of late Saxon sites in Wessex, particularly Winchester and from ninth-century and later contexts in Gloucester.[12] Early varieties would have been red, purple or black with anthocyanin pigment, the orange variety was not produced until the seventeenth century in Holland.[13]

[1] McGee 1986, 103–1.
[2] Herzfeld, 1900 March 7.
[3] Colgrave 1940, 277.
[4] Mackie 1934.
[5] op. cit.
[6] Musty 1969, 109.
[7] in Cole & Simpson 1968.
[8] Hall 1987, 5.
[9] Harvey 1981, 29, 32, 34.
[10] Cockayne 1851, I xviii.
[11] Bonser 1963, 358.
[12] Jones & Dimbleby 1981, 143; Green 1975, 186.
[13] McGee 1986, 191.

Parsnips (*pastinaca*) are listed as a separate vegetable in *De Villis* and the St. Gall plan. The former also includes *silum*, which may have stood for *sium* – skirret, a very similar but sweeter root.[1] Ælfric Bata writes that parsnip was cooked and eaten daily.[2] The *Durham Glossary* translates *pastinaca* as *mora*. If we accept that carrots and parsnips were known and eaten, this leaves the problem of how *englisce moran* (English root) is to be identified.[3]

Radish is listed for Charlemagne's gardens, for the ideal monastery and Walafrid Strabo's garden.[4] It is also mentioned by Ælfric Bata.[5] There are over twenty references in leechdoms, where radish is recommended for various problems, such as warding off a woman's chatter and 'for depression' (*wið innoðes hefignesse*).[6] There are two references to *superne rædic* (southern radish) which may be the large white radish eaten on the continent today.[7]

There is only one reference to turnip in leechdoms: *smale napes*, although *Lacnunga* xxx mentions *ængliscne næp* (English turnip).[8] However, glossaries regularly translate *napi* (turnip) by *næp* (*Epinal*) or *nep*, (*Erfurt* and *Durham*) and *nep* remains a dialect and Scottish term for turnip.[9] Ælfric Bata too lists it, and later the turnip and parsnip were important staple foods before the introduction of the potato.[10]

Wild roots were almost certainly eaten, particularly in times of dearth. The pignut (*conopodium majus*), a member of the carrot family common in parts of Britain is still eaten, mainly though as a famine food. The small sweet-chestnut-like tubers can be roasted or eaten raw.[11] A tenth-century Irish hermit praising his hut and its surroundings includes pignuts 'with good-tasting savour' as one of the advantages of the site.[12] Pennant reported that the dried roots of the cormeille (*orobus tuberrosus*) were used by Highlanders on long journeys. Trunkfuls of silverweed root were stored for winter use in Scotland in recent historic times.[13] Unfortunately, those who had recourse to such food, were those who were least likely to record the fact.

Pulses

The situation with regard to pulses is very different: there are so many references, particularly to beans, that they must have been an important item of diet. The kidney bean (*faba domestica*) is listed in *De Villis* and the St. Gall plan; the broad bean (*faba maiores*) in the *De Villis*.[14] The account of the royal palace at Annapes c.820 lists one muid of beans, twelve muids of peas, immediately after the amounts of barley, spelt,

---

[1] Harvey 1981, 29–32.
[2] Stevenson 1929.
[3] Cockayne 1851, I ii 23.
[4] Harvey 1981, 29; Waddell 1932, 80.
[5] Stevenson 1929.
[6] Cockayne 1851, III lvii, *Lac.* 73.
[7] op. cit., I xvii 2, *Lac.* 115.
[8] op. cit., III *Peri Did.* 61.
[9] Pheifer 1974, 37.
[10] McGee 1986 , 191.
[11] Howes 1948, 226; Foley 1974, 47.
[12] Jackson 1971, 69.
[13] McNeill 1963.
[14] Harvey 1981, 33.

wheat and oats.[1] A number of place- and field-names recorded in the Anglo-Saxon period have 'bean' as an element.[2] Green writes that it is not possible to envisage that legumes were widely grown as specific field crops.[3] However, this is not the impression given by the sums of money for bean seed in the *Assignments of Property to Thorney Abbey*: to '40 pence for bean seed . . . 15 pence for bean seed at Yaxley' (*beansæde xl pene(ga) . . . xv penegas wyþ bean (sæ)de to Geaceslea)*; nor by the 1016 charter of Leofsige, bishop of Worcester, to whose thane, Godric, every third acre of beanland at Bishopton was assigned.[4] 'To sow beans' (*beana sawan*) is one of the spring tasks in *Gerefa* after 'to plough and to graft' (*eregian 7 impian*), and this would seem to suggest large-scale production.[5] The reeve of a large estate would have to ensure that he had sufficient beans in store to provide female slaves with 'one sester of beans for food in Lent' (*I syster beana to lægtensufle*), one of the food allowances laid down in *Rectitudines Singularum Personarum*.[6] The novice, who was likewise an inhabitant of a large – monastic – estate, lists beans as one of the seven items of diet specifically mentioned.[7] Monk classes beans as a field crop, and this is certainly the inference I would draw from the documentary evidence.[8] It is supported by archaeological evidence. The tenth- to eleventh-century site of Sussex Street, Winchester produced evidence of *vicia*, possibly *vicia faba* (bean).[9] The pollen and pods of *vicia faba* present at tenth-century Anglo-Danish sites in York sites no doubt represent locally-grown field beans.[10] These were the same size and shape as modern-day field beans.

Involuntary bodily functions, including flatulence, tended to be seen as signs of man's fall from grace. St. Jerome considered that beans were particularly offensive in this connection, and forbade them to nuns in his charge because 'they tickle the genitals' (*in partibus genitalibus titillationes*).[11] Leechdoms also observe that peas and beans cause flatulence.[12] This is more likely to happen with the vegetables in their dried state, and certainly this would have been the obvious way to preserve large quantities of beans, for Lent, for example, when they were needed as a fasting food. The references to *adrige beana* (dried beans) and *bean mela* also suggest beans were preserved by drying.[13] *Lacnunga* gives the instruction 'dry beans and then grind (*drige mon beana 7 grinde hy siðþan*).[14] *Swearte beanen* (black beans) are specified one case.[15]

Green writes that it is unlikely that many remains of legumes will be recovered since they leave fewer archaeological traces than cereals, for example.[16] However, bean

1 Hodges 1982, 132.
2 Ekwall 1960, 37; Field 1972, 11, 14, 16.
3 in Jones & Dimbleby 1981, 141.
4 Robertson 1939, 253; Hart 1975, 85.
5 Liebermann 1898, 454.
6 op. cit., 450.
7 Garmonsway 1978, 46.
8 Monk 1977, 3.
9 op. cit., 327.
10 Hall et al. 1983, 207; 1987, 2.
11 McGee 1986, 257.
12 Cockayne 1851, II xxxix – contents, xxiv.
13 op. cit., I xxxv, III *Peri Did.* 26.
14 op. cit., *Lac.* 116.
15 op. cit., *Peri Did.* 4.
16 in Jones & Dimbleby 1981, 141.

pods were identified at Coppergate, York, indicating that the crop was probably grown locally.[1] Although the fossil beans are of the same species as modern broad beans, the seeds would probably have been similar in size and shape to field beans grown today for human and animal consumption.[2] Unfortunately the single pea-sized leguminous seed found in SFB 63 at West Stow could not be identified, though it was possibly a pea.[3] Pod fragments of pea which may have been cultivated were found in a ninth-century context in Gloucester and it is being increasingly found on sites of the period, for example, at the middle Saxon site of Fladbury, Worcs., and small numbers of peas were also found on tenth- to eleventh-century sites in York and Winchester.[4]

A Gloucester boundary charter of about 1055 includes the phrase *ofer peos hylle* (over pease hill).[5] Field-names based on the Old English form *pisen* (of peas) are recorded.[6] Peas and chick peas are mentioned in *De Villis* but not in the St. Gall plan.[7] Ælfric's novice does not include peas in the list of foods he eats, although they may be comprised in the term *wyrta* (vegetables).[8] However, leechdoms contain more references to peas than beans. They were presumably eaten as part of a normal diet, since one is cautioned that 'a windy swollen state of the milt' is caused by eating *pysena*.[9] However, peas stewed in wine, water or vinegar were recommended for a painful stomach.[10] References to *geseawe peas* (juicy peas) are presumably to fresh peas, which suggests that peas, like beans, were very often dried.

In leechdoms *pisena cyn* (sorts of pea) are part of a recommended diet; three recipes earlier is the mention of 'a sort of pea called lentils' (*sum pyse cyn hatte lenticulas*), with the recommendation to 'eat a hundred and twenty of them raw' (*ete þara hund teontig hreawa*).[11] In Ælfric's *Lives of the Saints*, Zozimus took to Mary in the desert – inter alia – 'lentils soaked in water' (*lenticula mid wætere ofgotene*) and later they are mentioned as 'those lentils that are peas' (*þære lenticula þæt syndon pysan*).[12] Perhaps 'dried peas' was the nearest approximation to lentils for Ælfric, although lentils have been recovered from late Saxon sites, where they occurred either as an imported crop, or a species accidentally imported as a crop weed, although casual cultivation may have taken place.[13]

Leaf Vegetables

Lettuce was certainly known on the continent in the Anglo-Saxon period. It is included with the salad plants in the *De Villis*, and in the St. Gall monastery plan.[14] 'Wild lettuce' is used by Ælfric to translate the bitter herbs Israelites ate at passover.[15] The evidence

[1] Hall 1987, 2.
[2] op. cit.
[3] West 1982, 321.
[4] Green 1975, 186–9; Monk 1977, 307, 327; Hall et al. 1983, 179.
[5] Finberg 1972, 72.
[6] Field 1972, 162.
[7] Harvey 1981, 31.
[8] Garmonsway 1978, 46.
[9] Cockayne 1851, II xxxix.
[10] op. cit., I ii 2.
[11] op. cit., II xvi.
[12] Skeat 1881, l.663, 715.
[13] Green in Jones & Dimbleby 1981, 141.
[14] Harvey 1981, 32.
[15] Swanton 1975, 95.

from Glosses may indicate a process of introduction to and cultivation in this country. The Erfurt Gloss written in the eighth century but based on one written in the second half of the seventh, gives *þuðistel* (sow thistle) for *lactuca*.[1] An eleventh-century Gloss gives both *þiðistel* and *leahtrice*, while a second eleventh-century Gloss gives only *leahtric*.[2] Although the place-name *Lettrintone* is not recorded until 1205, the elements are O.E. *leahtric*, and *tun*.[3] However, the Anglo-Saxon form *leahtrice* does occur earlier, in Werferth's translation of Gregory's *Dialogues*, where there is the cautionary tale of a nun who thoughtlessly ate a lettuce leaf without first making the sign of the cross over it. The devil complained, 'I was sitting on a lettuce when she came and bit me' ('*Ic sæt me on anum leahtrice, þa com heo and bat me*').[4]

Cress was listed in *De Villis*, and *cærsan* translates *cresco* in a list of garden plants in Ælfric Bata's *Colloquy*.[5] A reference to *tuncersan sio þe self weaxað* (self-set garden cress) suggests that it was normally sown, and elsewhere it is recommended as part of a diet.[6] Cress is known from the Norwegian Oseberg grave.[7] It seems to have been particularly popular in Ireland. In a ninth-century reference Cuchulain welcoming Fergus says he shall have a handful of water-cress, and a handful of brooklime.[8] A tenth-century Irish hermit praising his hut and its surroundings mentions 'cresses of the stream – green purity', and there are several twelfth-century references to cress.[9] Often the mention of cress is coupled with brooklime: 'spring of Traigh Dha Bhon, lovely is your pure-topped cress; since your crop has been neglected, your brooklime is not allowed to grow'.[10] This suggests a regular cutting of the cress. *Cærs* (cress) occurs very frequently in O.E. place-names.[11] The term in *cærsihtan wyll* (to the stream where watercress grows) occurs in a boundary charter of lands at Madeley in 975, and *eacersan* (watercress) is referred to in leechdoms,[12] and probably *stime* is also watercress.[13]

In the early *Epinal* and *Erfurt* Glosses, *cressa* translates *sinapio* (mustard), and in the second Erfurt Glossary mustard is confused with watercress.[14] *Nasturcium* is as *tuuncressa* in the *Epinal* Gloss and *leccressæ* in the *Erfurt* Gloss.[15] *Læccersan* also occurs twice in *Leechdoms* III xv and xix and this is translated as *eysimum alliaria* by Cockayne.[16] There are three mentions of *holan cersan* (hollow cress) which cannot be identified with any certainty: all one can say is that there were apparently a few varieties of cress-like plants that were eaten.[17]

---

[1] Pheifer 1974, 32.
[2] Wright & Wulcker 1968, 432, 7; 297, 18.
[3] Smith 1964, 25.
[4] Earle 1884, 197.
[5] Stevenson 1929.
[6] Cockayne 1851, I i 14; II iv.
[7] Roesdahl 1982, 119.
[8] Jackson 1971, 35.
[9] op. cit., 69, 73, 254, 255.
[10] op. cit., 125, 74.
[11] Smith 1964, III 157, 175, 207, 235.
[12] Hart 1975, 96; Cockayne 1851, I xxxviii.
[13] op. cit., *Lac.* 45.
[14] Pheifer 1974, 48.
[15] op. cit., 36.
[16] Cockayne 1851.
[17] op. cit., I ii 17, xxxii 4, lxiii.

Cabbage (*brassica oleraceo*) is known in Britain from the Roman period.[1] Several seeds of the *brassica* family (cabbage, mustard and rape – *B. napus*) were found at *Hamwih*.[2] At Hungate cabbage and rape have been tentatively identified, and there is a possibility of cabbages at Portchester since *cruciferæ* pollen was discovered in Well (Pit) 135.[3] Kale is listed in *De Villis* and coleworts (caulas) in the St. Gall plan.[4] According to the Welsh Laws, cabbage was one of the plants that characterised a garden, the other was leeks.[5] Ælfric Bata wrote that *caula* (coleworts) were cooked and eaten every day.[6] *Cawel/caul* is mentioned several times in leechdoms, and the comment that it was hard to digest indicates it was part of a normal diet.[7] Cockayne thinks the single reference to *se brada cawel* is to cabbage (*brassica oleracea*).[8] The term *brassica* is used once in a recipe which calls for it to be cooked with beet, mallow and pork.[9] The field-name *cawker thorn* may indicate an area where cabbage was grown.[10]

A new approach to determining the leafy vegetable constituents of early diets, using chromatography and GC/mass spectrometry, can identify epicuticular leaf wax compounds absorbed in potsherds. These can serve as chemotaxononic indicators of the vegetables cooked in the vessels. Sherds from the late Saxon/Medieval site at W. Cotton, Northants., have produced evidence of *Brassica sp.*, cabbage leaves or possibly juvenile turnip leaves.[11]

It is likely that only the leaves of beet were eaten.[12] The beet recorded in a late Saxon context in Winchester may have been leaf beet, chard or beetroot.[13] One leechdom instructs that the root of beet is to be dug up, the earth shaken off, and then stewed to a pulp.[14] Another specifies 'beet with its roots' (*betan mid hire wyrtruman*).[15] But in both these cases a medicament is being prepared, and the second example may suggest that beet was normally eaten without its roots. That it was a cultivated plant is shown by its inclusion in the *De Villis* and the St. Gall plan.[16] Fossil remains of beet, originally a coastal plant, have been found inland as far as York, but Hall thinks that if it was consumed, it would have been poor eating.[17]

Other leaf vegetables are referred to, in particular mallow, orache, spinach and goosefoot/fat hen (*Chenopodium sp.*). Mallow is included in the pot herbs section of *De Villis* and was cooked and eaten daily according to Ælfric Bata.[18] In leechdoms it coupled with lettuce as part of a recommended diet, used to make broth when boiled

[1] Jones & Dimbleby 1981, 37.
[2] Holdsworth 1980.
[3] Monk 1977, 297; Cunliffe 1976, 299.
[4] Harvey 1981, 29, 32.
[5] Owen 1841, 325.
[6] Stevenson 1929.
[7] Cockayne 1851, I ii 1.
[8] op. cit., I xxxiii.
[9] op. cit., I xxx 1.
[10] Cameron 1985, 204.
[11] Evershed et al. 1991, 541–3.
[12] Brothwell 1969, 117.
[13] Jones & Dimbleby 1981, 143.
[14] Cockayne 1851, II xxx.
[15] op. cit., II lix 14.
[16] Harvey 1981, 29.
[17] Hall 1987, 4.
[18] Harvey 1981, 32; Stevenson 1929.

with a hen, and boiled with cabbage, beet and pork.[1] Orache is referred to in *Lacnunga 77* as *meldon þa wyrt* (orache, the plant). It was present at *Hamwih*.[2] It was evidently cultivated under the name *tun melde* (garden orache) here, as well as on the continent where it was listed in *De Villis*.[3] Blite, a form of spinach, is also included in *De Villis* and spinach (*atriplex hortensis*) was discovered in York.[4] Chenopodium was found at York and at *Hamwih*.[5] It was evidently used as food at Winetavern Street, Dublin.[6] Other evidence for its consumption comes from bog-found corpses to whose diet it made a substantial contribution, and in recent historical times it was eaten after the widespread evictions in Scotland.[7] It may at times have constituted a crop plant, and it may equally well have been resorted to in times of dearth.[8]

Celery (*apium graveolens*) was known in Britain from the Roman period, and there is evidence for celery from late Saxon sites in Winchester.[9] It was cooked and eaten every day according to Ælfric Bata.[10] It occurs in a Latin charm and in Cotton Vesp. DXX folio 93, where an early eleventh-century cure recommends that it be taken in wine for toothache.[11] Like celery, fennel (*foeniculum vulgare*) is known from the Roman period and occurs on late Saxon sites in Winchester.[12] It is included in the garden on the St. Gall monastery plan and as *finol* occurs in the list of garden plants in Ælfric's *Colloquy*.[13] There is no evidence for cucumber in Anglo-Saxon archaeological contexts although it is known from Roman sites and *De Villis*.[14] However, the Latin name *cucumeris* is translated by an Anglo-Saxon word which is not based on this form: *hwerhwette*. It is called for by *Leechdom* I xxiii and a further four 'cures'.[15] It is just possible that a form of artichoke was known, since *De Villis* lists *cardones* which can arguably be translated as 'cardoons'.[16] The same plant may be meant by the term *mete þistel* which translates *camerion* in the *Durham Glossary*.

It is difficult to know how important herbs were to the Anglo-Saxon diet. Ælfric Bata's *Colloquy* lists some sixty herbs as being grown in the garden of a monastery and adds *et cetera multa* (and many others).[17] Of the three hundred or so herbs mentioned in leechdoms, some are virtually impossible to identify and others must be purely medicinal, but generally those most frequently cited are also those referred to in other sources. Dill, chervil, mints, parsley, rocket, horseradish, rosemary, rue, sage, savoury, tansy, bay, cumin, lovage, houseleek, pennyroyal, fenugreek, coriander, poppy, black cumin, agrimony, betony, wormwood, mugwort and white horehound

1 Cockayne 1981, II xvi, III xliii, II xxx 1.
2 Holdsworth 1980.
3 Wilson 1973, 330; Harvey 1981, 29.
4 op. cit, 29; Monk 1977, 297.
5 *Med. Archaeol.* XV, 46; Holdsworth 1980, 128.
6 *Med. Archaeol.* XV, 77.
7 Brothwell & Higgs 1963, 178; McNeill 1963.
8 Jones & Dimbleby 1981, 143.
9 op. cit., 37, 43.
10 Stevenson 1929.
11 Storms 1948, 290.
12 Jones & Dimbleby 1981, 37, 43.
13 Harvey 1981, 32.
14 Jones & Dimbleby 1981, 37; Harvey 1981, 29.
15 Cockayne 1851, II lxv 2; *Lac.* 21, 52, *Peri Did.* 31.
16 Harvey 1981, 29.
17 Stevenson 1929.

are also listed in *De Villis* and/or the St. Gall plan.[1] Of these, the first four: dill, chervil, mint and parsley were eaten every day according to Ælfric's *Colloquy*.[2] Dill may have grown, or been grown at, for example, Dilcar in Cumberland and Dilwick in Bedfordshire.[3] A reference to *wudu cearfillan* (wild chervil) suggests the presence of a cultivated variety, like the reference to *wildne rue* (wild rue). A tenth-century Irish hermit mentions wild marjoram when he praises the surroundings of his hut.[4] Leechdoms mention three kinds of mint: 'mint, water-mint, and a third kind which has white flowers' (*mintan, fenmintan 7 þæt ðridde cyn mintan þæt bloweð hwite*).[5] Of the other herbs mentioned, poppy has been found in Anglo-Saxon contexts, and black cumin (*nigella sativa*) which translates *gitto* in the St. Gall plan, is almost certainly what is meant by *gitte* 'the southern wort that is good to eat on bread'.[6] However, in addition, basil, sweet gale, mustard seed, thyme, saffron, comfrey, nettle, sorrel and tarragon are all mentioned in leechdoms, and may have been used for food, flavouring or medicinal drinks, as they still are today. In an eleventh-century Irish account of St. Columba, the saint meets an old woman cutting nettles for broth. This was unusual enough for the saint to question her, when he learns she is waiting for her cow to calf (when she would have various dairy products – 'white meats'). The saint decides to eat the same, practising what is seen as self-denial.[7] This suggests nettles were not eaten from choice, but as a 'famine food'.

Seaweeds

Seaweeds were probably exploited much more as a food resource, at least in coastal districts, than they are today. Irish and Scottish cooking make a great deal of use of the various varieties.[8] St. Columba was said to have gathered *duileasg* (dulse) from the rocks.[9] In a ninth-century Irish source Cuchulain welcomes Father Fergus with a promise of a handful of dulse, as well as goose and salmon, and the following century Donnan, one of Senan's disciples, went to gather dulse along the shore with two small boys.[10] Nowadays laver, which may be the *laber* of the Old English *Herbarium*, can bought in Wales as laver bread and in North Devon, but the iodine taste is too strong for most palates.[11]

Fungi

The term *swam* seems to indicate fungi generally.[12] *Meteswam vel tuber* Cockayne thinks refers to the edible truffle, which can be found in some areas of Britain. Truffles may have been searched for by pigs, when they were regularly driven into the woods.[13] Other species like the beefsteak fungus, (*fistulina hepatica*), and various

[1] Harvey 1981, 29–32.
[2] Stevenson 1929.
[3] Smith 1964, 133.
[4] Jackson 1971, 69.
[5] Cockayne 1851, *Lac*.XXXIV.
[6] Jones & Dimbleby 1981, 143; Cockayne 1851, II xxxix; Holden 1843.
[7] Jackson 1977, 296.
[8] Hartley 1954, 287; McNeill 1963.
[9] Jackson 1971, 279.
[10] op. cit., 34, 285.
[11] De Vriend 1984, 176.
[12] Cockayne 1851, *Lac*. 66.
[13] Zeuner 1963, 267.

mushrooms may have been eaten too. Mushrooms contain more protein by weight than vegetables and a significant amount of vitamin D, and would have been valuable in dietary terms.[1]

Conclusion

It would be a mistake to assume that the Anglo-Saxons' attitude to what was edible was the same as ours. Almost certainly they did not draw a line between what was cultivated and culinary and what was wild and weedy. Today our choice of vegetables and herbs is generally limited to what can be cultivated on a large scale and what travels or freezes well. However, a process of bringing species into cultivation was clearly under way during the period as the names *tun cerse*, *tun mint* and *tun melde* imply.[2] Perhaps there was already a preference for the bland, rather than the highly-flavoured, and a dislike of what was tough and stringy.

Our knowledge of what can be eaten tends to be limited to what we can buy as food, or as seeds to grow ourselves. The information that a whole range of shoots and roots are edible is available, but only rarely in cookery books, the notable exception being Dorothy Hartley's *Food in England*.[3] We cannot assume that the species commonly eaten today were the only food plants in Anglo-Saxon times. One might think, for example, that the 15 seeds of *Juncus sp.* recorded from *Hamwih*, the highest number recorded of any of the species, indicated only that the plants were growing wild in the vicinity, if it had not been recorded that the poor in England used the great bullrush in bread and broths as recently as the eighteenth century.[4]

Most wild vegetable foods are very rich in vitamins.[5] The custom of eating hawthorn buds under the name 'bread and cheese' is a reminder of what was formerly a widespread practice: gathering the first green shoots of spring to counteract the pre-ascobutic state of a number of the population after a winter's diet of dried pulse and salt meat.[6] In the Calder Valley *polygonum bistorta* is used to make 'dock pudding'. Other ingredients include onions, nettles and oatmeal, and the dish is fried in bacon fat. It is regarded as a spring medicine for cleaning the blood.[7] *Horta* are wild plants gathered from the edges of fields and vineyards in Greece , including such species as dandelion, dock, bladder campion, chickory, sow thistle, mustard, fennel, wild lettuce, rocket and young red poppy leaves. These are collected and given to friends, or sold in the market by the very poor who have nothing else to trade. They are an important source of winter vegetables.[8] Perhaps *Elmari Picteurte* (Elmer Pickwort) of Winchester owed his name to this practice.[9] Dandelion (*taraxacum officinale*) is still used as a salad plant in Europe.[10] In addition to the species mentioned above, the Anglo-Saxons may also have eaten bittercress, yellow rocket, ivy-leaved toadflax,

---

[1] Renfrew 1985, 20.
[2] Wilson 1973, 330.
[3] Brothwell 1969; Harris 1961; Hartley 1954.
[4] Holdsworth 1980, 128; Harris 1961, 95.
[5] Hill 1939, 5.
[6] Bonser 1963, 9.
[7] Sir Bernard Ingham, pers. comm.
[8] Kuper 1977, 31–3.
[9] Barlow 1976, 51.
[10] Kundegraber in Fenton & Owen 1981, 171.

lambs' lettuce, wood sorrel, red clover, and salad burnet.[1] The Anglo-Saxons probably exploited some species for flavourings. For example, tansy (*chrysanthemum vulgare*) tastes of ginger; sweet cecily (*myrrhis oderata*) of aniseed and sorrel (*rumex acetosa*) of vinegar.[2]

The daily consumption of dill and celery recorded by Ælfric Bata,[3] is probably related related to their qualities in aiding the digestion of such vegetables as beans, turnip and cabbage, wholemeal rye and other coarse breads.[4] Interestingly the tenth-century Anglo-Scandinavian sites of York have yielded dill and wild celery.[5] Given the availability of herbs and vegetables, the Anglo-Saxons probably evolved a diet in which the vegetable, herbal and other elements were complementary .

---

[1] Renfrew 1985, 18–9.
[2] op. cit.
[3] Stevenson 1929.
[4] Harris 1961, 101.
[5] Hall et al. 1983, 206–7.

3. Fruit and Nuts

Fruit Trees

By the end of the Anglo-Saxon period some fruit trees were being cultivated in orchards. The Anglo-Saxon term *orceard* was derived from *weortyeard*, which meant a garden – a 'plant yard'.[1] It appears that the word *orceard* was beginning to take on its modern meaning towards the end of the period: 'may their orchards be filled with apples/fruit' (*beoþ hyra orcerdas mid æpplum afyllede*).[2] But the quotation, 'orchards are suitable for apples/fruit' (*synt orceadas gedafenlice æpplum*) suggests the term *orceard* was not automatically associated with apples/fruit. Other terms, *æppuldretun*, *appeltun*, signified apple orchard.[3] Perhaps to start with some fruit trees were planted in gardens, as Alcuin's letter of 796/7 to Charlemagne seems to imply. He wants books from York so that not in York alone is there a 'garden enclosed' but there will also be in Tours 'plants of Paradise with the fruit of the orchard'.[4] The royal palace of Annapes c.820 had 'a little courtyard, surrounded with a hedge, and planted with trees of different kinds', and these are unlikely to have been large forest trees.[5] The *Capitulare de Villis* lists apples, pears, plums, peaches, quinces, figs, cherries, medlars, and service tree berries as being grown on royal estates.[6] Egbert had been at the court of Charlemagne from 787–802, and by 827 he was back in England, ruling over most of the country which enjoyed relative peace in his reign.[7] It seems likely, therefore, that he would have had the opportunity to establish fruit trees on his own estates.[8] The Welsh Laws also write of trees planted within a garden.[9] Different varieties of apples and pears were already recorded on the continent at this time.[10]

Towards the end of the period orchards are appurtenances of estates, as in a charter of Wulfstan, archbishop of York, to his brother Ælfwig in 1017, but there is no evidence that the orchards referred to were for apples or other fruit trees.[11] Similarly the Welsh Laws refer to an orchard as one of the three 'ornaments of a kindred' and state that the produce is to be shared only between those that have a right to it, without specifying what form the produce took.[12] An extensive apple orchard is recorded in the Domesday Book. At Nottingham 'the king leases William Peverel ten acres of land to make an apple orchard' (*Wittmo Peurel cessit rex x acras terrae, ad faciendu pomerium*).[13] This suggests a large scale production of apples, presumably as a cash crop, or for cider making.

---

[1] Commissioners 1819, 411.
[2] Cockayne 1851, III 252, 22.
[3] Bosworth & Toller 1898, I 17, 47.
[4] Whitelock 1955, 786.
[5] Hodges 1982, 191–2.
[6] Roach 1985, 16–17.
[7] op. cit..
[8] op. cit.
[9] Owen 1841, 142.
[10] Roach 1985, 118–9.
[11] Finberg 1972, 126.
[12] Owen 1841, 179.
[13] Commissioners 1819, 411.

According to *Gerefa*, men worked on orchards in winter. Grafting was carried out in spring, and pruning appears to be the activity depicted for February in the illustration to an Anglo-Saxon calendar.[1] Information on grafting and pruning was available in classical treatises like those of Palladius and Columella. An Anglo-Saxon herbal indicates that at Glastonbury plums were cultivated by grafting onto sloe rootstocks.[2] The Welsh Laws value a graft at four pence, more as it takes successfully and gives fruit.[3] With these techniques the Anglo-Saxon could select for the preferred types of apple, and increase the productivity of his trees. More importantly, he could propagate domesticated varieties of pears and plums whose seedlings are degenerate. A pruning hook was found with mid/late Saxon pottery at Portchester, and other examples have been found in the St. Neots area.[4] That they were common items by the end of the period is suggested by Alexander Neckham's twelfth-century treatise, *De Utensilibus*. He wrote that a peasant living in the country should have a large knife for cutting grafts.[5]

Fruit probably constituted an important part of the monastic diet when available, since fresh vegetables and fruit provided the third dish at the chief meal, and probably also the second meal, of the day.[6] Religious communities had the incentive to improve their stocks of fruit trees, and would have had access to the classical treatises dealing with grafting and pruning. They also had contacts with continental religious houses and may have exchanged cuttings of different varieties. Ely became famous for its vineyards, refounded in 872 by Æthelwold, and subsequently Britnoth was responsible for establishing orchards and a nursery of various fruits there.[7] Some estates may have developed their own fruit trees, though there is no documentary evidence of this during Anglo-Saxon times. The earliest reference seems to date from the twelfth century when a variety of pear, 'wardouns', was developed at Warden Abbey in Bedfordshire.[8]

In an earlier period in England and in the time of Hywel Dda in Wales, pear and apple trees in personal ownership were not necessarily cultivated, but seem to have grown wild in forests and hedgerows as laws and charters indicate. A grant by Æthelheard, king of Wessex in 739, lists four trees and one grove belonging to different owners on the boundary of an area of land.[9] Apple trees are often mentioned as landmarks in boundary charters and so are pear trees.[10] A wood is referred to as *Pyriæ* 'Perry Wood'.[11] Compensation was payable to the owners of trees. An apple tree was rated at 60 pence and a crab apple at 30 pence in the Gwentian Code.[12] The Venedotian Code valued fruiting trees (unspecified) at 24 pence, but apples, presumably, higher, since they are bracketed with the oak, although no figure is given.[13] The Dimetian

[1] Liebermann 1898, 454; MS Cott. Tiberius B5 folio.
[2] Roach 1985, 146.
[3] Owen 1841, 291.
[4] Cunliffe 1976, 197; Lethbridge & Tebbutt 1933, 133–51; Addyman 1973, 44–99.
[5] Holmes 1952, 201.
[6] Knowles 1940, 462.
[7] Roach 1985, 18.
[8] Hartley 1954, 447.
[9] Whitelock 1955, 456–7.
[10] Cameron 1975, 22–3; Finberg 1972, 80.
[11] op. cit., 126.
[12] Owen 1841, 725.
[13] op. cit., 291.

3. Fruit and Nuts

Code stated that 'the woods are interdictable in respect of fruits from the fifth day before the feast of St. Michael until the fifteenth day after Epiphany and of the swine found in them let one tenth of the animals be killed, then let every one be killed...even to the last'.[1] This suggests that woodland provided an important food resource in autumn, and that people would gather what they could before pigs were allowed back into the woods.

Obviously this resource could not be exploited to the same extent by people in areas where woodland was relatively scarce. Charter evidence suggests far fewer hedges in the downland of south-west Wiltshire, and north Berkshire, than in the London or north-west Dorset areas.[2] Presumably fruit trees were scarcer in such areas where there were fewer naturally occurring trees. It is likely that other areas of the country had a greater density of fruit trees. William of Malmesbury wrote that the vale of Gloucester was so fertile that 'one may see public paths clad with fruit-bearing trees, not grafted by the hand of man, but thanks to the quality of the soil itself'.[3] Place-names in Gloucestershire like *Periton* (1086), *Hardepiry* (1167) *Apeldresham* (c.1130) and *Pirton* (*Pyritune* in 972) in Worcestershire suggest that fruit was grown in and around the Vale of Evesham in pre-Conquest days.[4] After his extensive travels in Europe Moryson recorded, 'England hath such abundance of Apples, Peares, Cherries, and Plummes, such variety of them, and so good in all respects, as no countrie yeelds more or better'.[5] Perhaps this was also the case some centuries earlier.

Apples

Apples were asked for as a blessing in the coronation service of Æthelred II, together with grapes.[6] According to leechdoms, apples are variously to be avoided, or taken as cooling and strengthening.[7] Sour apples, crab apples, sweet (*milisc*) apples, wood apples and green apples are specifically mentioned. In his list of plant names Cockayne thinks that 'sour apple' is *mala acidiora*, that crab apples and wood apples are *M. agrestia* or *M. acerba*, and that sweet apple is *M. hortulana*.[8] He also notes the term *cod æppel* – a codling, *M. maiusculum*, *M. coquinarium*, but points out that in Gloss. Cleop. folio 44a the same term interprets *malum cydonium sive malum cotonium*. Perhaps all that can be said is that there were different kinds of apple known in Anglo-Saxon England. 'Many kinds of apples, pears and medlars' (*manigfeald appelcyn, peran, æpeningas*) are recommended for a delicate stomach.[9] References to apple trees in Irish sources from the eighth century on, leave no doubt as to their popularity: 'a tree of apples of great bounty', 'sweet apples', 'little apple tree, violently everyone shakes you'.[10]

It is possible that the round items in a bowl which feature in a drawing of Lot feasting the angels are apples.[11]

---

[1] op. cit., 555.
[2] Biddick 1984, 74.
[3] *De Gestis Pontificum Anglorum* iv, 153, Rolls Series.
[4] Smith 1964, III 259, 155, 137; Mawer & Stenton 1969, 223.
[5] Moryson 1617, IV 165.
[6] Turner 1828, III 156.
[7] Cockayne 1851, II xxiii etc., II i 1.
[8] op. cit.
[9] Cockayne 1851, II ii 2.
[10] Jackson 1971, 69, 73, 153, 181.
[11] MS Cott. Claud. B4 folio.

There is some archaeological evidence for the consumption of apples. Four small crab apples were found in a bowl together with onions in a late seventh-century barrow burial at Ford, Wilts.[1] Pips of apples and crab apples were present at Gloucester and *Hamwih*, and were frequently found in the faecal layers of Anglo-Danish York.[2]

Pears and Peaches

Pears and peaches are translated into Old English by the translator of the Leechbook as *peran 7 persuccas*, but he omits from his translation pomegranates, nectarines, and grapes of a cold and dry flavour.[3] Presumably the translated items were available, or at least known to him, whereas the others were not. There is evidence for pear from tenth- and eleventh-century Winchester.[4] Elsewhere in leechdoms the words for peach are *persoce*[5] and *persogge*.[6] In the latter section 'the stone that is inside the peach' (*þane cyrnel þe byð innan þan persogge*) is referred to.

Soft Fruit

Also mentioned in leechdoms are elder (numerous times), plums and mulberries (*byrig bergena*).[7] The latter are also mentioned in *The Maccabees*, but here they are called *mor-berium* and they have the non-culinary and extremely specialised function of emboldening elephants.[8] The fruit of the mulberry is very soft, and cannot be conveyed any distance, so the hundred or so Roman excavated instances indicate the fruit was grown here.[9] The mulberry is very long-lived, specimens six hundred years old have been recorded, and moreover it comes true from seed, so Roman plantings could have lasted into Anglo-Saxon times.[10] An Anglo-Saxon herbal dating from the early tenth century, and held at Glastonbury indicates plums were cultivated in the gardens grafted on to sloe as the rootstock.[11]

Blackberries (*bremel æppel, bremelberian*) and strawberries (*streawbergan*) are mentioned a few times each in leechdoms, and blackberries also by Ælfric Bata as *blaceberian*.[12] He translates *fragaria* as *streabariye* 'stray-berry', presumably because of its runners.[13] References to raspberries (*hind bergean*, translating *acinum* in an eighth-century Kentish glossary), cherry trees (*ciristreow, cyrstreow*), bilberries (*hæpergean*), the myrtle (*wir treow*) and the sloe (*slah*) occur very rarely in leechdoms.[14] A Gloucestershire place-name '*Hortham*' derives from the O.E. *horte*, and means 'whortleberry enclosure'.[15] A tenth-century Irish source refers to the sloe, food of whorts, red bog berries, whortleberries, haws, yew berries and bird cherries as

---

[1] Musty 1969, 109–10.
[2] Green 1975 186; Holdsworth 1980, 129; Jones, undated paper.
[3] Cockayne 1851, II i 1.
[4] Monk 1977, 393.
[5] *Lac.*
[6] *Peri Did.*, 31.
[7] Cockayne 1851, II xxx.
[8] Skeat 1881, 1.575.
[9] Roach 1985, 215.
[10] op. cit.
[11] op. cit., 146.
[12] op. cit., 325.
[13] op. cit.
[14] Wright & Wulcker 1884, XCLIV.
[15] Smith 1964, III 107.

well as blackberries, and also to 'delicious' strawberries and rowan berries in such a way as to suggest they were all eaten.[1]

Unfortunately the archaeological evidence for soft fruit is always likely to be scarce, but what finds there have been confirm the documentary evidence.[2] Plum and sloe stones have been recovered from York and Gloucester.[3] In London eleventh-century rubbish and cess pits have yielded large quantities of plum, sloe and cherry stones, and grape pips as well as cereal bran. At Walton, Bucks., and Winchester the stones were of bullace, a cross of sloe and domesticated plum, as well as sloe itself.[4] At *Hamwih* the plums were cultivated varieties probably similar to a damson.[5] Damsons were probably also present at York.[6] *Prunus* timber was recovered from the shaft of Well II at North Elmham.[7] Blackberry and wild raspberry were recovered from *Hamwih*, as were wild cherry, bullace and elder.[8] There is evidence that strawberries were cultivated in Wessex, probably in hedgerows.[9] Remains of strawberries were found, with blackberries at Gloucester in ninth-century and later contexts.[10] There is no evidence for the consumption of rowan berries on Anglo-Saxon sites, although both rowan berries and strawberries were consumed in early medieval Dublin and Hedeby.[11] Hips may have been consumed in Anglo-Saxon England as they were in Hedeby. This assumption is given more weight by the Welsh Laws: compensation for thorns is put at eight and a half pence, and this is followed by the statement 'every tree that does not bear fruit is four pence'.[12] Of course, the primary use of such fruit may have been as animal feed, but hips would have been valuable nutritionally, and not just in times of dearth.

Grapes were mentioned together with apples as blessings at the coronation service of Æthelred II.[13] This suggests that grapes grew here and did not have to be imported. Vineyards were established at least by the end of the Anglo-Saxon period, and would have flourished during those periods when continental climatic conditions prevailed. This was the case when Moryson was writing, and some vineyards have been established recently.[14] At Winchester c.1100 the abbess had a gardener (*ortolanus*) who lived outside the south gate and may have tended the abbey's vineyard there.[15] Grape pips were found at *Hamwih*, but they may have been present in the residue from wine.[16] Most grapes would have been used to make wine, but some individuals may have had the opportunity to eat the fresh fruit (see Chapter 15).

---

[1] Jackson 1971, 69–73.
[2] Green 1979, 39.
[3] Radley 1971, 46; Green 1975, 186.
[4] Monk 1977, 302, 365.
[5] Holdsworth 1980, 129.
[6] Roach 1985, 146.
[7] Jones 1980, 112.
[8] Holdsworth 1980, 129.
[9] Jones & Dimbleby 1981, 144.
[10] Green 1979, 39.
[11] Radley 1971, 77; Foote & Wilson 1970, 149, 212.
[12] Owen 1841.
[13] Turner 1828, III 156.
[14] Moryson 1617, IV 165.
[15] Barlow 1976, 135, 323.
[16] Holdsworth 1980, 129.

Dates and Figs

Possibly dates were known. Old English did have a special term for 'palm tree fruit'. Zozimus takes to St. Mary in the wilderness 'a little basket filled with figs and with palm tree fruit that we call finger apples' (*ænne lytelne tænel mid caricum gefylledne and mid palm treowa wæstmum þe we hatað finger æppla*).[1] However, 'finger apples' is a straight translation from the Latin *dactylus* – a finger; dates were called 'finger fruit' by the Romans. In this passage a Latin term (*caricum*) for figs is used, but apparently the Old English word *fic* found elsewhere derives directly from the Latin *ficus*. References to figs as well as dates tend to be biblical in inspiration. In *The Book of Dreams by the Prophet Daniel*, interpretations are given as to what seeing a *fic treow* betokened.[2] However, date stones were found in a seventh-century context in Paris and fig seeds were found in eleventh-century levels at Castle Yard, Winchester.[3] As fig trees here do not now produce seed, the fruit may have been imported, or may signify warmer conditions. Fig seeds were also found in thirteenth-century levels in Dublin, and Moryson recorded that fig trees grew in some parts of England and the fruit ripened well.[4] Figs could have been grown here, but both dates and figs could have been traded into England as they will last a matter of months when dried.

Dried Fruit

No trace would remain from currants or seedless raisins, and dried fruits including raisins and prunes are known to have been imported from Portugal and the Levant as early as the thirteenth century.[5] These items could have been traded in Anglo-Saxon times, or given as gifts: Bede bequeathed dried prunes and raisins (as well as exotic spices) to his brethren on his death in 735.[6]

Flowers

There is evidence that flowers (hawthorn and elder blossom, rose petals) as well as fruit, were used in composite dishes, but again, there is unlikely to be any trace of the practice in the archaeological record.

Nuts

Hazel Nuts

References to nut trees occur in charters, like that of 969: 'to the slope where nuts grow' (*on hnut clyf*).[7] Presumably the native hazel, (*corylus avellana*), was the nut most commonly found. Field-names with this element are plentiful: e.g. *hasfield, hesedene, haseden*, all recorded in 1086.[8] *Hæselnutu* glosses *abelana* in an eighth-century Kentish glossary.[9] The hazel was valued at fifteen pence in the Dimetian Code, but only four

[1] Skeat 1881, St Mary of Egypt l. 661.
[2] Cockayne 1851, III.
[3] Eydoux 1966, 86; Monk 1977.
[4] Radley 1971; Moryson 1617, IV 165.
[5] Drummond 1958.
[6] McKendry 1973, 10.
[7] Cameron 1975, 18, 20.
[8] Smith 1964, III 148, I 106, 174.
[9] Wright & Wulcker 1884, CCCXCLIV.

pence in the Venedotian, though a hazel grove was valued at 24 pence.[1] Davies points out that according to the late eleventh-century life of St. David, the people of St. David's were accustomed to gather nuts, and that the food value of nuts should not be underestimated as 1.6 square miles of hazel could supply four families with 25% of their diet for four of the winter months.[2] Young hazel trees yield about a pound of nuts at six years old, an amount which steadily increases.[3] Irish sources refer frequently to the hazel in contexts which indicate it was valued for its nuts, e.g. a 'seemly crop' of nuts, a coffer of hazel nuts.[4]

The remains of hazel nuts have been found in archaeological contexts as at *Hamwih*, Yeavering and York, whereas at Faversham, Kent, they were discovered as grave goods in a bowl in an inhumation burial.[5] At Broadstairs, Kent, fruit and hazel nuts in a bronze bowl were found in a warrior's grave.[6] Continental parallels have been found and the suggestion has been put forward that these nuts were used in pagan times as a symbol of fertility and perhaps rebirth.[7]

Walnuts and Sweet Chestnuts

By the end of the period walnuts may have been known.[8] They have been recorded at tenth-century Anglo-Danish sites in York.[9] They were known too in Viking Denmark, but were probably often imported.[10] An eleventh-century gloss for 'nut tree or *nux* gives *hnutbeam oððe walhhnutu*.[11] It is possible that it was known earlier, since among the timbers from a ninth-century well at North Elmham, wood from walnut and sweet chestnut was provisionally identified.[12] It is not unlikely that a monastic house would have obtained specimens of trees from continental houses, and would have had the knowledge that such trees need to be reproduced by grafting to yield well. It is possible that such trees would have yielded better than they do today, during the spells of continental weather towards the end of the period. However, walnuts or their oil may have been imported from France. An invalid diet for asthma gives the instruction to stew chicken in wine and then add 'oil that comes from French nuts' (*ele to þe beo of frencissen hnutu*).[13]

Seebohm states that chestnuts were known in Anglo-Saxon England, as does Howes, but the latter adds that sweet chestnuts in Britain are at the limit of their range and are unlikely to have been as common or to have fruited as well as in Mediterranean countries where chestnut flour was the staple food of some communities.[14] As early the eighth century a gloss gives *cistenbeam* for *casteneo*, chestnut timber is recorded from tenth-century Anglo-Danish York and by the twelfth century sweet chestnut

---

1 Owen 1841, 585, 291.
2 Davies 1982, 33.
3 Howes 1948.
4 Jackson 1971, 69, 73, 66, 71.
5 Holdsworth 1980, 129; Hope-Taylor 1977, 333; Radley 1977, 46; *Med. Archaeol.* II 1967, 16.
6 Webster 1975, 223.
7 Ellis Davidson 1964, 165–6.
8 Foote & Wilson 1970, 149.
9 Hall et al. 1983, 179.
10 Roesdahl 1982, 119.
11 Wright & Wulcker 1884, CCCLII.
12 *East Anglian Archaeol. Report* 9, 112.
13 Cockayne 1851, Peri Did.
14 Seebohm 1952, 112; Howes 1948, 130.

trees (*castanea vesca*) in the Forest of Dean had gained a considerable size, and a tithe of the chestnuts was granted to the abbey of Flaxley.[1]

Pine Nuts, Almonds and *Swegels Appel*

Pinhnyte, the nuts of the stone pine (*pinus pinea*), are listed in a recipe in *Leechdoms*, and are mentioned in a description in *Starcraft*: 'like a pine nut' (*an gelicnysse ancre pinnhnyte*).[2] The translator does not expand on this, so perhaps he thought pine nuts would be known by his readers. Pine nuts were imported into Britain in Roman times and may have been traded into Anglo-Saxon England.[3] *Amigdales* (almonds) are mentioned together with other nuts as suitable for sensitive stomachs.[4] However, Anglo-Saxon medical opinion seemed divided on nuts: elsewhere we find the caution that they cause 'a windy swollen state of the milt'.[5]

The evocatively named *swegles appel* (fruit of Paradise) Cockayne translates as 'betel nut', which could have been traded here from India.[6] However, later, cardamom seeds were known as *graynes of Paradyse*, and any unusual exotic fruit, nut or spice may be meant. In any case the reference is only to external use, and it is not included as the constituent of any diets.

Acorns and Beech-Mast

Welsh Laws lay down that the woods were to be kept free of pigs from the fifth day before Michaelmas until the fifteenth day after Epiphany, perhaps so that nuts, including beech-mast and acorns, as well as fruit, could be gathered.[7] It is possible that acorns were eaten raw like nuts, given the warning against a pregnant woman eating 'nuts or acorns or any fresh fruit'.[8] 'If a woman is four or five months pregnant and she often eats nuts or acorns or any fresh fruits then it sometimes happens that the child is stupid' (*Gif wif biþ bearn eacen feower monoð oþþe fife 7 heo þonne gelome eteð hnyte oþþe æceran oþþe ænige niwe bleda þonne gelimpeð hit hwilum þurh þ þæt þ cild biþ it disig*).[9] A woman on this sort of diet was presumably foraging, living off the land, and if the child was born damaged in some way it was probably because her diet generally was insufficient, not because she ate nuts, acorns or fresh fruit. The acorns referred to, since the manuscript has a continental source, were probably those of the holm oak (*quercus ilex*) which are not dissimilar to sweet chestnuts in taste and food value.[10] 'Sweet acorns' are referred to, together with hazel nuts, in a tenth-century Irish source.[11] Acorns have been found in archaeological contexts as at Broadwater Crescent, Stevenage, where a small hoard of charred acorns split down the middle were found on the floor of a Saxon hut.[12] However, it may be that acorns were not normally regarded as food in Anglo-Saxon England. Alfred

---

[1] Hall et al. 1983, 190; Cox 1905, 71.
[2] Cockayne 1851, II ii 2, III 259.
[3] Howe 1948, 165.
[4] Cockayne 1851, III 63.
[5] op. cit., xxxix.
[6] op. cit., I xxiii.
[7] Owen 1841, 55.
[8] Cockayne 1851, III.
[9] op. cit.
[10] Howes 1948, 171.
[11] Jackson 1971, 66.
[12] B. Adams, pers. comm..

omits from his translation of Boethius' description of the Gold Age that, 'it was accustomed to end its late fasts with the ready acorn'.[1] In the Mediterranean region, the use of acorns for food is referred to by many Greek and Latin writers, among them Theophrastus, Pliny, Virgil and Ovid.[2] Perhaps in Britain acorns from a different oak, *quercus robor*, were used only in times of famine to eke out supplies. One cannot assume that because leechdoms call for *ac mela* (acorn meal) or *ac melwes* dust (acorn flour) that native British acorns were habitually ground for use as flour, though this is a possibility; some form of treatment would have been needed because of the high tannin content.

Beech-mast has been used in recent times to make meal for bread, and is known to have been a useful standby in time of famine, as it is rich in protein and oil.[3] Beechnuts were found in a grave at Hitchin.[4] However, the importance of beech-mast mast and the acorn as a food resource in Anglo-Saxon times was to fatten pigs, though other livestock – cattle and poultry – would have eaten the mast. Nuts may have been used for oil in Anglo-Saxon times, as they were later, when Walter of Henley records that a quarter of nuts produces four gallons of oil.[5] Beech-mast is still used to manufacture cooking oil on the continent.[6]

---

[1] Turner 1828, II 36.
[2] Howes 1948, 171.
[3] op. cit., 204.
[4] Whittock 1986, 152.
[5] Lamond 1890.
[6] Howes 1948, 204.

4. Cattle

Breeds

The Anglo-Saxons probably found two breeds of cattle in England: *bos longifrons*, a very small-boned, probably black, breed of cattle imported in Neolithic times, and white cattle, some polled. These white cattle were probably ancestors of the present-day White Park cattle.[1] Although samples of hair from Chillingham cattle are much coarser than the normal cattle range, whereas primitive breeds apparently have finer hair, it is generally accepted that White Park cattle are ancient, and were probably present in the Celtic fringes of Britain and pre-Christian Ireland two millennia ago.[2] White Park cattle are white with black points (Chartley & Dynevor herds) or red points (Chillingham cattle), and in the Welsh Laws white cattle with red ears are of special value. The *saraad* (lordly goods payable in livestock) due to the King of Aberfraw on account of his wife included a hundred cows from each *cantrev* with a white bull with red ears to each hundred cows. If the cattle were black, then a black bull was payable with each hundred cows.[3] Small black cattle suggest the Kerry and Dexter breeds, and also the Galloway, whose fine hair would mark it out as a primitive breed.[4] The Laws of Kenneth MacAlpine (844-60) at Scone refer to black cattle, and cattle in the Western Isles of Scotland as late as the seventeenth century were black, and almost always very small.[5]

The cattle in a late tenth-century illustration to Prudentius' *Psychomachia* are the size of the pigs they are following, when in fact even small Anglo-Saxon cattle were larger than Anglo-Saxon pigs.[6] If, however, the horns were to be considered an accurate representation, then we might suppose a Kerry or Ayrshire was being depicted.[7] They are certainly similar in form to those of the beast about to be killed for a feast in honour of William after his arrival at Hastings, depicted on the Bayeux Tapestry.

White Park cattle have a good growth rate, although they are small, no more than 110 cm. at the shoulder when full-grown, and are noted for their longevity and vigour. Like the carcasses of other 'unimproved' and primitive breeds, those of White Park cattle contain less saturated fat than those of modern breeds.[8] They can live out all year, do not suffer from brucellosis or tuberculosis and carry negligible worm burdens.[9] Today's Shetland cattle may be taken to characterise the breed of small black cattle, and these are also very hardy, free from disease, and have the ability to convert poor-quality fodder into excellent beef.[10]

---

[1] Zeuner 1963, 210; CA Wilson 1973, 76.
[2] Ryder in Ucko & Dimbleby 1971, 517; *Ark* May 1986 & April 1988.
[3] Owen 1841, 509, 235.
[4] Ryder in Ucko & Dimbleby 1971, 517.
[5] Trow Smith 1951, 224–5.
[6] Temple 1976, 70.
[7] J. Fensom, pers. comm.
[8] *Ark* May 1986.
[9] Hall 1989, 15, 46, 48.
[10] Bowie 1988, 442.

The Anglo-Saxons probably brought with them the red cattle surviving as Lincolns, Suffolks and Norfolks, Sussex, Devons and Herefords, which were largely ousted from central and southern England by longhorns and shorthorns in the eighteenth century.[1] Trow Smith thinks a Roman or pre-Roman origin for the red cattle is equally likely, and the matter is likely to be determined only as a result of further genetic studies.[2] However, the authorities seem to agree that, whatever their origins, the Anglo-Saxons had three breeds of cattle, the very small-boned dark cattle, and the larger white and red varieties. The Norse, thinks Seebohm, brought in their own cattle, the large type customary on the continent and akin to those brought in by the Anglo-Saxons.[3]

Unfortunately the animal bone record cannot provide direct information as to breeds. At Portchester, for example, there were no complete, or even fairly complete skulls, which might have provided diagnostic features.[4] At the mid-Saxon site of Ramsbury, Wiltshire, there was one hornless animal, while the rest were medium or long-horned, but no further evidence as to breed was available.[5] From the middle-Saxon site of Medmerry Farm, Selsey, came evidence for short-horned cattle.[6] Horn cores, skulls and complete leg bones of oxen from Anglo-Scandinavian York apparently belonged to a small breed similar to prehistoric shorthorns.[7]

Size

The animal bone record does provide evidence for the size of cattle. The fifth to seventh-century site of West Stow provided the remains of cattle of a moderate size comparable to cattle recovered from later sites. The shoulder height range of 104.6–121.4 cm fell within the *Hamwih* range of 101.7–137.7 cm.[8] The lateral lengths of West Stow astragali ranged from 53.6 to 70.3 mm with means of 61.1 for period 1, 60.1 for period 2, and 60.7 for period 3. Measured astragali from *Hamwih* provided a mean of 60.9 mm. As astragali from Iron Age sites were consistently smaller, it has been suggested that Romans introduced larger cattle into Britain, and that Saxon cattle were maintaining the general improvement.[9] However, the rate of size increase was not maintained throughout the period, or perhaps was not general to all areas, since the average lateral length for cattle at the later site of Cheddar was about 60.0 mm.[10] At another early site, Old Down Farm, Andover, the size of the cattle fell below their *Hamwih* counterparts.[11] This again indicates that the size of cattle varied according to region, rather than date.

The two different size groups of cattle present at Yeavering indicate either sexual dimorphism in the breed of cattle present in the area at the time, or two different breeds. The physiography of the site suggests highland and lowland forms of agriculture would have been practical, so the size of cattle may have depended on the

---

[1] Wilson 1909, 38ff.
[2] *Ark* April 1988.
[3] Seebohm, 1952, 118.
[4] Cunliffe 1976, 283.
[5] Coy in Haslam 1980, 47.
[6] Welch 1983.
[7] *Med. Archaeol.* XV, 47.
[8] Crabtree 1984, 229.
[9] op. cit., 230.
[10] Rahtz 1979, 360.
[11] Davies 1980, 177.

area from which they came.[1] On the whole Yeavering cattle were smaller than those from Sedgeford, Northold, and Kirkstall.[2] A pagan period grave at Nassington, Northants., yielded a piece of bone, 'possibly the pisiform of one of the Bovidiae, of the size of the Chillingham ox'.[3] At the seventh-century site of Puddlehill, Beds., the cattle were small, probably slightly smaller than the small cattle of the Neolithic. At 59mm the astragalus can be compared with that from a modern shorthorn at 70mm.[4]

Perhaps small (and peaceable) cattle were an advantage in terms of handling, although they would not have provided as much meat as modern varieties.[5] The average height at the withers of cattle from the comparable urban sites of Dorestad and *Hamwih* was the same, but much higher than cattle from Hedeby. If entire, or particularly if castrated, males predominate in a sample, the sample will be taller, but taking such factors into account, the conclusion is still that cattle from Hedeby were smaller. Husbandry at *Hamwih* and Dorestad may have been better, or they may have been wealthier sites, able to command the best of the animals.[6] The mid-Saxon site of Ramsbury, Wilts., produced cattle within the size range for Melbourne Street, Southampton, but the Ramsbury cattle were ready for eating slightly earlier, reflecting the higher grade of land.[7] At the later site of Exeter, cattle were no bigger than they had been in the Roman period, with a withers height of 104–8 cm compared with 115–7 cm for *Hamwih*.[8] The closest modern parallel to the cattle on the late urban site of Flaxengate, Lincoln, is the Kerry. On this site there was a possible size decrease in the later eleventh-century.[9] The size of cattle at Cheddar, another late Saxon site, overlaps with that of present-day Chillingham cattle, with the Saxon cattle slightly smaller.[10] Thetford yielded a similar result, and the general conclusion is that many of the Anglo-Saxon cattle must have been as small as present-day Kerrys.[11]

Husbandry

It has been suggested there were probably advantages to small cattle, and certainly large cattle do not seem to have commanded a premium.[12] The small size of animals is not therefore necessarily an indication of poor standards of husbandry. Cattle from Portchester, occupied throughout the Anglo-Saxon period, showed only a low incidence of disease, implying healthy stock, although it could have meant diseased specimens were quickly killed and eaten.[13] At Exeter fewer than 20% of the cattle were immature, so the mortality rate of young animals was low.[14] At *Hamwih* most animals reached maturity healthy and of a good size. What troubles there were, and these were rare, stemmed from

[1] Hope-Taylor 1976, 332.
[2] op. cit.
[3] Meaney 1981, 145.
[4] Hawkes 1985, 109.
[5] Zeuner 1963, 214.
[6] Prummel 1983, 174–5.
[7] Coy in Haslam 1980, 47.
[8] Maltby 1979.
[9] O'Connor 1982.
[10] Higgs & Greenwood in Rahtz 1979, 357.
[11] Clutton Brock in Wilson 1976, 380.
[12] Zeuner 1963, 214.
[13] Cunliffe 1976, 283.
[14] Maltby 1979.

use and age.[1] At Anglo-Saxon sites in Bedford there was little evidence of periodontal disease on the jaws of cattle (or sheep).[2] The disease that did manifest itself was osteoarthritis, on the first phalanges of cattle.[3] This situation was repeated at Flaxengate, and suggests that the animals concerned were used for draught, not primarily as food.[4] At Exeter the splaying of the distal portion of the metacarpi is possibly also a direct result of ploughing, although it can also be an indication of a mature male animal.[5]

Continuity of practice is observable in the sex ratios of stock. One bull to every hundred cows, as specified in the Welsh Laws, suggests a modern dairy herd, where the bull is penned separately for most of the time.[6] There were very few bulls recorded at Portchester or at Flaxengate, Lincoln, which might suggest a similar ratio.[7] If a bull is run with the herd, then a ratio of 1:20 is the average. Unfortunately the animal bone record is likely to be incomplete, both in terms of material recovered, and in the accurate assigning of bones to sex. The figures from Hedeby (13% bulls, 32% castrates 55% cows) give a larger number of bulls than might be expected.[8] This may indicate that individual herds consisted of fewer than twenty cows. The main difference is that now the numbers of castrates indicate food animals; in Anglo-Saxon times the high percentage (two-thirds at Portchester, for example) almost certainly indicated plough oxen.[9]

Diseases are recorded in the literature, notably in the chronicles where severe outbreaks are recorded, for example in 800, and 1041.[10] It is virtually impossible to identify the various cattle murrains, but anthrax may have recurred. Contact with diseased meat can transmit the infection, and some cattle plagues did spread to humans. One might expect tuberculosis to be widespread, since this was common in herds until recently, and exacerbated by keeping cattle in dark or badly-ventilated byres, but primitive breeds in general have a lower incidence of disease.[11] According to the Welsh Laws, a seller of cattle was to answer that it would be free of the staggers for three days, the glanders for three months and the farcy for a year.[12] More comprehensively, the Laws of Ine stated that cattle developing any unsoundness could be handed back to the seller unless the latter swore that he knew of no fraud, but there was a time limit of 30 days.[13] Cattle may have suffered from ergotism.

Byres

Bede wrote of Ireland 'no-one there mows hay or builds stalls for his cattle as a provision against the cold of winter' (*þær nænig mann for wintres cyle on sumera heg ne maweþ, ne scypene his neatum ne timbreþ*).[14] This suggests that both activities were carried on in

[1] Holdsworth 1980, 105.
[2] *Beds. Archaeol. J.* 1974, 106.
[3] op.cit., 105.
[4] O'Connor 1982.
[5] Maltby 1979.
[6] Owen 1841, 7; J. Fensom, pers. comm.
[7] Cunliffe 1976, 283; O'Connor 1982.
[8] Zeuner 1963, 214.
[9] Cunliffe 1976, 283.
[10] Whitelock 1955, 250, 235.
[11] Barton 1913, 144; *Ark* April 1988.
[12] Owen 1841, 715.
[13] Whitelock 1955, 370.
[14] Miller 1890, I 1 28–9.

England. Wooden *scypene* may not be easily recognised in the archaeological record, but where they were built in stone as during the Viking Age at Kvívík in the Faroes, then there is evidence for the stabling of 8–12 animals in halls 1.6m deep, with stone slabs marking stall divisions.[1] There is early continental evidence for the practice, for example at Wijster, where the byre took up a considerable proportion of all long houses, providing accommodation for 8–44 animals.[2] At Chalton one building probably contained cattle stalls, and at tenth-century Mawgan Porth the most completely excavated house was divided into a byre, complete with drain, and living quarters.[3]

That cattle were stalled, is not necessarily evidence that they were being fattened for slaughter. In any case there seem to be only two references to stalled bullocks: *fal'd'reþere* (a stalled bullock) in the inventory of stock at Yaxley, part of the gift of bishop Æthelwold to Peterborough, and *xxxvi faldhriþera* (36 stalled bullocks) in an eleventh-century inventory from Bury St. Edmunds.[4] These may only be variant spellings of the term *feldhryper*, a bullock kept in a fold, i.e. out at pasture. The term *reþere* or *hriþer* does however suggest a beef animal (see below).

Fodder

Hay would almost certainly have been the most important source of fodder for stalled animals. The element *heg* (hay) is present in a number of field-names, Haycroft, for example, indicating land on which grass was grown to be cut for hay.[5] According to the Laws of Ine ten hides were to furnish 'twenty pounds of fodder' (*xx pundwæga fodres*). Liebermann translates 'pound' by *wispel*, a German measure of about twenty-four bushels.[6] These laws also specify that payment for hire of a yoke of oxen was to be made in full in fodder, and even if the hirer was short of fodder, half the cost of hire was still to be paid in fodder, half in other goods.[7] According to early West Midlands charters, one estate was paying six trusses of fodder yearly to *Bloccanlea*, while another was released from a provender rent for three years.[8] In *Rectitudines Singularum Personarum*, as part of the gebur's duties, 'he shall be ready on occasion for many jobs as his lord orders, besides mowing his meadows' (*he sceal hwiltidum geara beon on manegum worcum to hlafordes willan to eacon maðmæwecte*).[9] The *folcgerihtu* (folk-rights) included *mæðmed* (mowing reward) and *hreacmete* (food given to the labourers on completion of a rick).[10] The rick could be of corn, but in the services and dues rendered at Hurstbourne Priors, Hants.: 'the *ceorl* (is to mow) half an acre of gavel-meadow in his own time, and to bring it (i.e. the hay) to the rick' (*ceorlas healfne æcer gauolmæde on hiora agienre hwile and ðæt on hreace gebringen*).[11] Hay was probably cut, raked and turned pretty much as it still is in places, since 'a rake' is the answer to one of the Exeter Book riddles, and it is described as 'a creature ... that feeds the

---

1 *Med. Archaeol.* XIV, 69.
2 Wolters 1967, 380ff.
3 Welch 1983; Todd 1987, 305.
4 Robertson 1939, 74, 248.
5 Field 1972, 100.
6 Whitelock 1955, 371.
7 op. cit., 371.
8 Finberg 1972, 61, 96.
9 Liebermann 1898, 448.
10 op. cit., 452.
11 Robertson 1939, 207.

cattle...wanders about walls, seeks for plants' (*wiht . . . seo þæt feoh fedeð . . . weapeð geond weallas wyrte seceð*). Wooden hay rakes are unlikely to survive, and neither is there likely to be clear archaeological evidence of ricks, but haymaking must be regarded as an established Anglo-Saxon activity.[1] Hay could also be bought. High Mangergate was the street to find *heymangari* (hay-sellers) in York.[2]

Winter shelter and fodder were indirectly but importantly concerned with food production since thereby provision was made for cows in calf, and for plough oxen. Part of the duties of the ploughman of the *Colloquy* was 'to fill the mangers of the oxen with hay, to water them, and muck them out' (*fyllan binnan oxan mid hig, 7 wæterian hig,7 scearn beran ut*).[3] According to Walter of Henley, plough oxen were fed three and a half sheaves of oats a week from 18 October to 3 May, and Anglo-Saxon oxen may also have been fed grain.[4] Winter fodder could have included beans, dried bines, chaff, straw, and vetches. The ninth-century Welsh poet of *Canu Llywarch Hen* says that in winter the cattle got thin but the implication is that they managed to overwinter, and the archaeological record at Dinas Powys shows some overwintering took place.[5] Saxon cattle were almost certainly more hardy than modern breeds: the primitive Chillingham cattle, for example, are fed hay only in extreme weather conditions.[6] Evidence from Flaxengate suggests that cattle were carefully tended on good grass for most of the year, with little foddering.[7]

Browse

The leaves and young wood of trees were also used for fodder. Pollarded and coppiced trees would provide browse wood for animals in hard winters, and as woodland and wood pasture covered 15% of the country, this would have been a useful resource.[8] The young twigs of elm, lime, ash and hazel, were all palatable, as well as the leaves, and foliage was cut for cattle during summer droughts into this century.[9] Field-names like Holney acre recall the importance of holly as browse, although sheep can cope with holly better than cattle.[10] There is evidence that other evergreens, among them ivy and mistletoe, were used as stock feed.[11] The supposition that cattle would be fed on the leaves of trees is confirmed by the account of the death of the worthy Hadwald, occasioned by his fall from an oak. One text explains his otherwise puzzling presence up a tree – he was feeding cattle on the foliage.[12]

Pasture

Pasture was seen by Bede as one of the assets of the country: 'it is suitable for grazing sheep and cattle' (*7 hit is gescræþe on læswe sceapa 7 neata*); one of the reasons

---

[1] *Med. Archaeol.* XIV, 163.
[2] Interim 2, 1 48–9.
[3] Garmonsway 1978, 21.
[4] Oschinsky 1971, 319.
[5] Davies 1982, 41.
[6] Oschinsky 1971, 102.
[7] O'Connor 1982.
[8] Rackham in Biddick 1984, 87, 75.
[9] op. cit., 89; I. Newman, pers. comm.
[10] Field 1972, 106.
[11] Dimbleby 1971, 534, 538.
[12] Pope 1968, II 150.

4. Cattle

why, after defeating the Britons, the Anglo-Saxons sent back messengers reporting on 'the fertility of this land' (*þysses landes wæstmbærnysse*).[1] Land was conveyed 'with all pastures', with 'food and pasture for swine and cattle'.[2] When lands were leased by Werfrith, bishop of Worcester, in 904, these included 'the meadowland to the west of the Severn . . . also very generously 12 acres in addition of excellent meadowland' (*þ medwe land bewestan Sæferne . . . ec swyþe rumedlice xii æceras þærto fulgodes mædlandes*).[3] A lease made by Oswald to Goding also included meadowland, this time 'seven acres in the pasture belonging to Tibberton' (*vii aceras in þæm homme þe gebyrað into Tidbrihtingctune*).[4] Land leased to Wulfic by Stigand, bishop of Winchester, included 'the meadow belonging to the reeveland and pasture for two teams and ten cows along with the lord's' (*þa mæde þa gebyrað to ðam gereflande 7 twegra getymæna læse 7 tyn cuna forð mid þas hlafordes*).[5] Rights to pasture were carefully recorded; the dues rendered to the church at Lambourne entitled the priest to pasture for 10 oxen and 2 cows along with the king's, and pasture for his bullocks.[6]

The oxherd stayed out in the pasture with his animals at night: 'I lead them to pasture and stand over them all night' (*ic lædde hig to læse 7 ealle niht ic stand ofer hig*).[7] At least one lease refers to *oxna leage* (the oxen's pasture), so obviously certain areas were so designated.[8] The field-name 'Nightleys' (from *niht-læs*, pastures used at night) may refer to this practice, although Anglo-Danish farming practice involved the collecting of cattle into a central township fold at night, from where they were taken to feeding grounds in the morning.[9] Other field- and place-names like Garston (*gærs-tun*, grass enclosure, paddock), and Angerton (*anger*, pasture land) also indicate grazing land.[10]

Seasonal transhumance, not only to upland areas, but also to lowland riverside grazing in Somerset and Oxfordshire, may have been a feature of pastoral The field-name *Arras* indicates upland pastures used in summer, and names like Summercroft clearly also indicate seasonal use.[12] The use of low-lying water meadows, flooded in winter, but used for fattening cattle in summer, is still an element in modern farming practice.

As now, cattle were almost certainly fattened for slaughter on grass. Oxen retired from the plough could be fattened on ten pence worth of grass, according to Walter of Henley.[13] They may also have been turned on to the stubble after gleaning. Probably the animals eaten by the nobility were larger and carried more flesh than those eaten by the common folk, as was demonstrably the case in Tudor England.[14]

[1] Miller 1890, I 1 26, 50.
[2] Whitelock 1955, 475.
[3] Robertson 1939, 36.
[4] op. cit., 125.
[5] op. cit., 203.
[6] op. cit., 241.
[7] Garmonsway 1978, 22.
[8] Robertson 1939, 126–7.
[9] Field 1972, 149; Seebohm 1952, 118.
[10] Field 1972, 87; Smith 1970, 11.
[11] Davies 1982, 40.
[12] Field 1972, 7, 222.
[13] Oschinsky 1971, 319.
[14] Armitage in Kenward and Hall 1982, 97–8.

Culling & Killing

There seems no particular reason for conducting an autumn killing, neither is there evidence for this among prehistoric groups.[1] There is no definite evidence for an autumn killing in Anglo-Saxon England either. Theoretically it is possible to tell by the outer layer of tooth enamel at which season an animal was killed.[2] However, this technique does not seem to feature to any extent in animal bone reports. Bede recounted that the pagan Saxon name for November was *blotmonaþ* (sacrifice month), but this has become confused with *blodmonaþ* (blood month) and used as evidence for autumn slaughter.[3] There is clearly a difference between the sacrifice of 'the cattle that they wished to offer' (*ða neat ða ðe ... woldon syllan*), and wholesale slaughter. To kill a number of cattle at once would be a wasteful way of using a food resource, to say nothing of the work involved in processing a number of carcasses at the same time. The reality was probably closer to Tusser's picture, although this relates to the first half of the sixteenth century:

> At Hallontide, slaughter time entereth in,
>   and then doth the husbandmans feasting begin:
> From thence unto Shroftide kill now and then some,
>   their offal for household the better wil come.[4]

If animals were to be culled, autumn and winter would be a good time, since it would save on fodder, and also meat would hang and keep better in the colder months. The place of the dairy products – 'whitemeats', and fresh vegetables of summer was supplied to some extent by the fresh meat of winter.

The situation described in the post-Conquest *Seneshaucy* probably described older practice; there was some culling in winter of old, barren and young animals that were not thriving.[5] This is no more than good farm practice and does not suggest that fodder was not available. But the situation that Martin described in eighteenth-century Scotland may sometimes have occurred during bad winters in Anglo-Saxon England: namely that some cattle died from lack of fodder and others became mere skeletons, unable to rise from the ground without help, having to be carried out to pasture in the spring.[6]

Cattle & Mixed Farming

The lists of livestock in the documentary evidence, and the analyses of animal bone deposits, give a picture of mixed farming recognisable in today's terms. A late ninth-early tenth-century lease of Beddington, Surrey, by bishop Denewulf of Winchester to King Edward the Elder included an inventory of the stock 'surviving this severe winter': 9 full-grown oxen, 114 full-grown pigs and 50 wethers, besides the sheep and the pigs which the herdsmen have a right to have, 20 of which are full-grown, and there

[1] Higgs & White 1963, 282–9.
[2] Chaplin 1971, 84.
[3] Boswoth & Toller, I 112, 113; Seebohm 1952, 113.
[4] Grigson 1984, 49.
[5] Oschinsky 1971, 284.
[6] Trow Smith 1957, 228.

are 110 full-grown sheep.[1] Behind every recorded plough-team, traditionally of eight oxen, would be two cows whose first purpose was to breed new oxen, the *animalia* of Domesday. *Animalia otiosa* on the demesne were the breeding herds for plough-team replenishment. There must have been several young cattle at various stages of growth up to the age of four, when they could become draught oxen, which were not included in the Domesday stock figures. Extensive ratio sampling more often than not produces an equation in line with the ratio of team strength and breeding strength. Where it does not, the animals in excess of the team breeding herd must constitute a vaccary, with production of veal; plough oxen for sale, or beef animals for a rich table.[2] The late tenth-century will of Æthelgifu refers to 80 oxen, 65 cows plus two more if available, 6 bullocks, 600 sheep, 6–7 herds of swine plus 30–40 other pigs.[3] The inventory of stock at Yaxley, given by bishop Æthelwold to Peterborough, included 'thirteen able-bodied men and five women and eight young men and 16 oxen and a stalled ox and 305 sheep and 30 pigs' (*þryttene wepmen weorce wyrþe 7 v wimmen 7 æhta geonge men 7 xvi oxan fal'd'reþere 7 iii scepa 7 v scep 7 xxx swina*).[4] Property on another estate consisted of 100 sheep, 55 swine, 2 men and 5 yoked oxen.[5]

Animal Bone Evidence – Cattle as a Major Food Resource

Unlike the documentary record, animal bone evidence is available from the earliest period, and for continental sites too. For example, cattle bones predominate on the early continental site of Wijster and were the most important of the livestock on contemporary *terp* sites too.[6] One might expect the settlers to go on practising the same form of husbandry as they had always done. At the mid fifth- to sixth-century site of Bishopstone, Sussex, cattle made up 25% of the bones, sheep 39%, and pig 17%.[7] Cattle at the West Stow site (fifth-seventh century) made up 35% of the faunal sample.[8] This compared with 40% at the sixth-century site of Old Down Farm, Andover.[9] A family group of minor aristocrats settled at Puddlehill in Bedfordshire in the early seventh century, and this site produced evidence of 21 mature and 6 immature oxen, and that cattle would have provided the largest amount of meat.[10] At Yeavering the percentage of cattle bones was probably above 97.2%.[11] At another royal site, Cheddar, but towards the end of the period, it was just above 40%.[12] Late eighth- early ninth-century Ramsbury, Wilts., produced a percentage of 35%, which was appreciably lower than the figure of 49.2–54.3% from mid-Saxon *Hamwih*.[13] The late ninth-century Whitehall, London, site gave minimum numbers of 57 cattle, 54 sheep and 26 pigs, with the weight of meat from cattle at least 12 times greater than

[1] Whitelock 1955, 501.
[2] Trow Smith 1957.
[3] Whitelock 1968, 76–81.
[4] Robertson 1939, 74–5.
[5] Turner 1828, III 89.
[6] Wolters 1967, 404.
[7] Bell 1978, 267 ff.
[8] Crabtree in West 1982, 269.
[9] Arnold 1984, 71.
[10] Hawkes et al. 1985, 106.
[11] Hope Taylor 1977.
[12] Higgs and Greenwood in Rahtz 1979, 356.
[13] Coy in Haslam 1980, 47.

that from sheep.[1] At the later London sites of Billingsgate Buildings and St. Magnus the percentages of cattle bones were over 50 and over 75 respectively.[2] Sixty-five percent of the bones from the Lloyds and Barclays Bank sites in Anglo-Scandinavian York were chiefly leg and rib bones from cattle.[3] The proportion of cattle bones at Flaxengate declines from about 70% (870–80) to 50% (c.1100), so cattle provided 86%–74% of the meat in a period which saw sheep increase from 20% to 40%.[4] Cattle would also have provided most of the meat on the late urban sites of St. Mary's Vicarage and Midland Road, Bedford, and in tenth-century Skeldergate.[5] Other urban sites also produce high percentages of cattle bone, and so may have reflected the preferences of consumers, since they could buy the meat they chose, unlike farmers who would, for example, have had to eat up old sheep after using them for wool production. However, salt pork was not likely to leave traces in the archaeological record, and so may have been popular too (see Chapter 7). In general, the West Saxon sites produced a higher proportion of cattle than other parts of the country, which reflects a present-day concentration of pastoral husbandry in the west.[6]

Age at Death

As well as providing comparison with modern-day husbandry, the age of cattle at death provides useful information about the exploitation of cattle as a food resource. However, this subject presents one major difficulty in that the information given in much of the recent literature is based on the ages at which the teeth of modern cattle erupt, and since there may have been changes over time, information based on extrapolation from modern material has been shown to be untrustworthy.[7] A similar observation was made by Maltby, who considered that the age of peak slaughter for the Exeter cattle given as four and a half to five years old underestimated the age of the animals possibly by several years. He considered that eighteenth-century figures probably reflected Anglo-Saxon practice more closely. In 1794 oxen were turned off for fat at 5–6 years, though others might still be worked to the full age of 10-12 years. At Exeter the absence of extremely old cattle indicated that their owners sold beasts off at an age when they could get a better return for their investment.[8] Although absolute ages at death may be inaccurate, relative ages can still be assessed, and comparison between the sites made.

At the early site of West Stow a significant number of very young calves died early in their first year, and a sizeable number were killed at about two years. About half survived to maturity, and of these a significant number were well over five years old. Of these most were females, so milk production may have been important, but so may have been the production of the surplus males killed off for beef at about 2 years.[9] At Portchester 30% of cattle were killed in their third or fourth year, but almost 60% of

---

[1] Chaplin 1971, 124, 134.
[2] Kenward & Hall 1982, 96.
[3] *Med. Archaeol.* XV, 47.
[4] O'Connor 1982.
[5] *Beds. Archaeol. J.* 70ff, 94ff; O'Connor 1984, 16.
[6] West 1982, 273.
[7] Beasley, Brown and Legge 1987, 22–4.
[8] Maltby in Jones & Dimbleby 1981, 183.
[9] Crabtree 1984.

the bones came from fully mature animals. There were few animals less than two years old (although survival factors adversely affect the proportion of bones from young animals).[1] In the mid and late periods, from the eighth to eleventh centuries, a slightly larger proportion was killed at between two and four years old; fewer were kept beyond four years.[2]

This pattern is similar elsewhere, at *Hamwih* and St. Peter's Street, Northampton, for example, and at Whitehall, London, where about a quarter of the cattle were killed between 18 and 30 months, and the rest were killed when they were over four years old.[3] At *Hamwih* a quarter of the cattle were killed in late adolescence, a time that gives the best returns in terms of meat provided in relationship to foodstuff consumed, but after that many beasts reached full maturity and wore their teeth heavily, probably over many years.[4] A very small proportion of cattle shows evidence of very long hard work, so perhaps contributed more to the food supply in terms of cereal crops than beef.[5] The cattle killed in late adolescence were the males not required for breeding or working.[6] On the rural site of North Elmham most of the cattle were old, eaten only after a long and useful life.[7] But in another rural and only slightly later site, Ramsbury, Wilts., there were peaks at 6–18 months and a second when the third molar came into wear.[8] At Flaxengate cattle were killed off when they were mature, usually over four years, though there were some elderly milch cows.[9] On the Saxo-Norman site of St. John's, Bedford, most cattle were killed in their third or fourth year, although some bones came from older animals and a few from animals in their first year. This age structure suggests that they were raised primarily for food, although osteo-arthritic conditions on the first phalanges of cattle indicates some were used as plough oxen.[10]

It is interesting that at Yeavering most cattle were killed around two to three-and-a-half years, but there were also peaks at 6–12 months and 18–35 months.[11] The young animals may have been killed because of a shortage of winter fodder, and there may have been ritual significance in the autumn killing, but obviously the older animals had been overwintered.[12] It appears that at this high status site cattle were kept primarily for the production of tender meat. This was also the case at royal Cheddar, where the indications are that animals were slaughtered at a prime age for eating.[13]

The Value of Cattle

Not all cattle were necessarily slaughtered. The Welsh codes deal with the disposal of an animal found dead. 'If a person find the flesh of an animal not his own, whether killed by dogs or hidden and taken away without permission, *dirwy* is payable'.[1] The

---

[1] Cunliffe 1976, 275.
[2] op. cit.
[3] Maltby in Jones & Dimbleby 1981, 183; Chaplin 1971, 132.
[4] Holdsworth 1980, 105, 89.
[5] op. cit., 82.
[6] Bourdillon and Coy 1980, 105–8.
[7] Clarke, forthcoming.
[8] Coy in Haslam 1980, 47.
[9] O'Connor 1982.
[10] *Beds. Archaeol. J.* 13 103ff.
[11] Hope-Taylor 1977, 329, 331.
[12] op. cit.
[13] Higgs & Greenwood in Rahtz 1979, 357.
[1] Owen 1841, 247.

obvious course of action was to tell the owner of the land, and then – if the flesh was eatable, the finder was to be rewarded with a hindquarter.[1] On the other hand, if the animal had been skinned, it could not be sworn to by its owner, however sure he was that it was his animal.[2]

From later medieval evidence it would seem that cattle provided 300lb of meat, sheep 22lb. On this basis cattle gave about fourteen times more meat than sheep.[3] As might be expected, in view of the much greater amount of meat they provided, cattle had a higher monetary value than sheep or pigs, but they also had – and conferred – a higher status. By definition, a man of rank in Wales owned a house, a cornyard and a cattlefold.[4] It was in terms of cattle that values were sometimes assessed and payments and/or compensation had to be made.[5] According to the Welsh Laws, a fine of three cattle was imposed for disturbing the silence of a court.[6] In England even after the Conquest an ox was the fine if a man refused to attend a court to which he had been summoned.[7] One of the Privileges of Arven was for the man, on separation from his wife, to have two oxen from the herd before the woman had a choice.[8] Cattle were to be paid as tribute by the sons of a Welsh woman who had married a foreign chieftain.[9] The Welsh Laws also lay down how many cattle the king and court officials were to get from border raids. For example, the judge could choose an ox after the king had taken his share, and the apparitor was entitled to a bull and a milch cow.[10]

Cattle were always to be accounted for. If an ox was killed by another, the testimony of the oxherd was to be decisive when it came to arranging compensation.[11] If cattle were held without surety and the lord of the estate attached them, then the cattle were to be given up, and 20 ores paid as a fine.[12] Although a case of pig rustling was recorded (see Chapter 7), it was cattle thieving that the laws were concerned to stamp out. As early as the seventh century a number of regulations was codified to this end. For example, a man charged with stealing or receiving stolen cattle had to deny the theft by an oath of 60, or 120 hides if he were Welsh.[13] If found guilty, a man had to forfeit his possessions, although his wife could retain a third if she could declare on oath that she had not tasted the stolen meat.[14] (Clearly cattle thieves prudently easily recognisable individual animals to less readily identifiable carcasses.) Presumably because the purchase of cattle represented a substantial capital investment, the buyer of an unsound beast was given redress against the seller, providing that this was sought within thirty days, although the seller could swear that he knew of no fraud when the animal was sold.[1]

---

[1] op. cit., 97.
[2] op. cit., II 341.
[3] Rahtz 1979, 362.
[4] Owen 1841, II 493.
[5] op. cit., 675; Davies 1982, 39.
[6] Owen 1841, 145.
[7] Robertson 1925, 240.
[8] Owen 1841, 107.
[9] op. cit., 99.
[10] op. cit., 7, 19, 23, 67.
[11] op. cit., 111.
[12] Whitelock 1955, 404.
[13] op. cit., 369.
[14] op. cit., 370.
[1] op. cit., 370.

4. Cattle

A number of subsequent codes contained refinements and further details on this subject. Edgar's Code at *Wihtbordesstan* stated that buyers and sellers were to have two or three of the official witnesses present at their transactions in either borough or wapentake.[1] The Laws of Cnut increased the numbers of witnesses required for a transaction over 4 pence in value to four, and the procedure for swearing title to livestock was further elaborated in the Code of William I.[2] According to Edgar's Code, anyone going to make a purchase of livestock was to tell his neighbours beforehand, but if he bought animals unexpectedly, he was to bring them onto the common pasture within five days with the witness of his village, or to forfeit his cattle.[3] Should he declare that he bought the livestock with official witness and this was false, then he was to be executed and forfeit all he owned. A further section suggests that resistance was common, and that informants were sometimes killed.[4] Many copies were to be made of this Code, and were to be sent to Ealdormen Ælfhere and Æthelwine, for distribution 'in all directions', indicating that establishing legal title to cattle was of widespread concern.[5] The Welsh Codes also gave formulas for reclaiming lost or stolen animals and for swearing a new animal had been born and reared in one's ownership.[6]

The Viking army, in search of self-transporting, easily-prepared food, was no doubt responsible for some cattle rustling at various times, and Alfred's code refers to a situation whereby a man has entrusted cattle to a friend who then says the army has taken it.[7] (If he had no witness to this, the trustee was to bring an oath that this had indeed been the case.) More importantly, raiding by the Scandinavian army may have contributed to the general lawlessness which seems to have been a feature of the later period. In the tenth century the concern was that thieves, and above all, cattle thieves, might 'prevail more than they had previously done'.[8]

A letter to King Edward the Elder concerns the history of an estate at Fonthill, Wiltshire, and is interesting for the information that Helmstan stole the untended oxen at Fonthill, by which he was completely ruined, and drove them to Cricklade where he was discovered by a man who tracked and recovered the stolen cattle.[9] It is even more interesting that the cattle were unattended, since they were usually guarded. In the words of the oxherd of the *Colloquy* 'When the ploughman unyokes the oxen, I lead them to pasture and I watch over them all night because of thieves' (*Þænne se yrþlingc unscenþ þa oxan, ic læde hig to læse, 7 ealle niht ic stande ofer hig waciende for þeofan*).[10] The danger of leaving cattle unattended is intimated in the Welsh Laws make provision for the cattle of someone who had taken sanctuary: they were to the kept with the cattle of the community and the abbot.[1] Fields may sometimes have been

---

[1] op. cit., 399, 422.
[2] op. cit., 422; Robertson 1925, 264–5.
[3] Whitelock 1955, 399–400.
[4] op. cit., 400.
[5] op. cit., 401.
[6] Owen 1841, 249, 251, 441, 789.
[7] Whitelock 1955, 373.
[8] op. cit., 390.
[9] op. cit., 503.
[10] Garmonsway 1978, 22.
[1] Owen 1841, 141.

locked, since the field-name *Aspage* (although not recorded until 1181) derives from the Old English *hæpse, hecg* and means a hedged enclosure secured with a lock.[1]

Detailed instructions as to who was responsible for tracking stolen cattle are given in Æthelstan's Code at Exeter. Not only the owner of the cattle, but also the owner of land over which the trail of the stolen cattle was traced had to join in the pursuit, though fortunately expenses could be claimed.[2] According to the slightly later *Ordinance of the Bishops and Reeves of London*, those who failed to follow the trail were to forfeit thirty pence or one ox, but expenses were available for those who helped with the search.[3] According to this code, cattle owners seem to have formed a syndicate to insure against theft. Members of the peace guild 'noble or commoner' (*ge eorlisce ge ceorlisce*), seem to have had to pay an annual premium of a shilling, from which pool of money compensation could be paid out to whoever had stock stolen.[4] However, the system was subject to abuse: 'many men bring forth impudent claims'.[5]

The Laws of William I provided for guards on roads who were to look out for stolen livestock taken along or across their section. If they did not raise the alarm or could not prove that force had been applied to them, they were to pay compensation for the stock.[6] There was provision for an individual who took temporary charge of strayed stock, 'which is called *forfang* in English' (*que est forfang apele en Engleis*), to be paid for his trouble, but as there was a maximum charge (of eight pence) it was in his interests to locate the owner and return the stock as soon as possible.[7] The use of the Old English t erm suggests this custom was established in Anglo-Saxon times. Later it became the job of the pindar to collect stray animals (and birds and swarms of bees).[8]

The value of cattle was such that remedies for cattle disease, as for pig and sheep disease, are included in the leechdoms. Reciting Psalms li, lxviii and the Athanasian Creed was reputedly particularly efficacious.[9] Charms for finding cattle that had been stolen or hidden, one by putting a qualified curse on the thief, are likewise recorded.[10] Cattle were important enough to warrant inclusion in the sections *On Auguries* and *Of the Moon's Age*. Wind on the eleventh of the twelve days of Christmas meant that 'all cattle shall perish' (*æale nytenu forweorðað*), but when the moon was new on a Sunday then 'it betokened a want of cattle' (*hit tacnað nytena wædla*)[11]

The Ordinance of the Bishops and Reeves of London issued in Æthelstan's reign, gave the value of an ox as a mancus, a cow at twenty pence, a pig at ten pence and a sheep at a shilling.[12] (The horse was even more valuable, at up to one hundred and twenty pence.) But in Æthelred's code of 991 stealing cattle and murder are equated, and if the charge was brought by 'one viking and one man of this country there is to be no

[1] Field 1972, 8.
[2] Whitelock 1955, 387.
[3] op. cit., 388–90.
[4] op. cit., 388.
[5] op. cit., 390.
[6] Robertson 1925, 266–7.
[7] op. cit., 256–7.
[8] Seebohm 1952, 142.
[9] Cockayne rep. 1965, I 389.
[10] op. cit., 385, 390–1.
[11] op. cit.
[12] Whitelock 1955, 388.

denial'.[1] After the Conquest, the heriot of a villein was to include 'the best animal he has: a horse, an ox or a cow' (*le meillur aveir qu'il averad, u cheval u bof, u vache*).[2] The same order of value, but with a monetary equivalent, is given in details for the payment of wergild: 'he can pay a stallion at twenty shillings, a bull at ten shillings and a boar at five shillings' (*purra il rendre chevil ki ad coille pur xx sol, e tor pur x sol et ver pur v sol*).[3] Prosperous farmers would presumably not have been unduly concerned about having to pay Peter's Pence, but it would be interesting to know if any farmers on a small scale were deterred from keeping cattle because this would bring them within this tax bracket: 'he who possesses livestock to the value of thirty pence shall pay Peter's Pence' (*cil ki ad aveir champestre xxx den. vaillant deit duner le den. Sein Piere*).[4]

The value of cattle increased with age until, presumably, maximum size was reached. The Welsh Laws allow for the payment of oxen worth twenty, thirty and sixty pence to a woman after the breakdown of a marriage.[5] In one case a steer whose horn and ear were of equal length was to be paid.[6] In present-day terms this would be a yearling bullock, but with slower maturing stock the animal referred to may have been slightly older than a year.

That the value of cattle – unlike that of the horse – lay as much in its use for food as for draught is indicated by the concern with the meat. According to the Laws of Ine, if the owner of land which he wished to protect from damage by cattle which had invaded it, killed the animals concerned, then he was still to return the hide and meat to the owner of the cattle.[7] The Welsh Laws apportioned different joints to the various officials: the watchman had the aitchbone and the apparitor the shanks of every ox.

Food Rents

Before proceeding to a survey of food rents, it is necessary to look first at the various terms for cattle. *Cu* (cow) and *cealf* (calf) are straightforward enough, and *fearre* clearly meant a bull, since a pregnant woman was warned against eating 'bull's flesh or ram's or buck's or boar's or cock's or gander's or any from animals that are able to procreate' (*fearres flæsc oððe rammes oþþe buccan oþþe bæres oþþe hanan oþþe ganran oþþe æniges þara neata þe strynan mæg*).[8] A *bulluc* seems to have been a young male, as was a *steor*, and a *hreþer* would seem to have indicated a castrated male older than a bullock but younger than an *oxan*, presumably the term used when an animal was ready for work at four years old. The terms *hryþer* and *oxan* were not interchangeable: a leechdom calls for 'bullock's, or best of all ox's gall' (*hyþeres oþþe swiþost mid oxan geallan*).[9] This is the only reference to ox in the leechdoms; there is no mention of ox's flesh in the various diets, and this cure is for external use. *Lacnunga* includes a

[1] op. cit., 402.
[2] Robertson 1925, 262–3.
[3] op. cit., 256–7.
[4] op. cit., 260–1.
[5] Owen 1841, 89.
[6] op. cit.
[7] Whitelock 1955, 369.
[8] Cockayne 1851, III 146.
[9] op. cit., II 45.

reference to 'old ox's marrow' (*ealdes oxsan mearh*), but again, this is for external use.[1] The term *heofor* is modern English heifer, a cow that has not yet calved. Heifers are considered to provide inferior meat, but are now included in the term 'bullock' if they are being raised for meat. *Hreþer/hryþer* is the term which seems to have indicated an animal reared for food, so 'bullock' seems an appropriate translation, and there is no way of knowing if *hreþer* included heifers. Now, because the beasts are usually slaughtered at 18 months anyway, the term 'bullock' is general, although some older farmers still use the term 'steer', and butchers use the term in reference to an animal 2–3 years old. The term 'ox' is still seen as referring to a draught animal, except in the term 'ox roast', where it is recognised as deliberately archaic, and for which a mature bullock or steer of 2-3 years old is used.[2]

Leechdoms indicate that the *hryþer* was a comparatively young animal. *Hryþeren flæsc* (bullock's meat) stewed in vinegar and oil with herbs, leeks, etc., was recommended for a 'labouring maw'.[3] And while *hryþeres flæsc* was slowly digested, *fearra* (bull), took still longer, like 'those four-footed animals that are very old' (*þa þe swiðe eald beoð on feowerfotum nietum*). *Geong hryþer* (young bullock) however digested well.[4] The three references to *fearres geallan* (bull's gall) and one to *fearres gelyndo* (bull's suet) seem to indicate that bulls' carcasses were available.[5]

When it comes to references to cattle in legal documents it is clear that sometimes these are not intended for food. For example, Ealdgyth was granted an estate on the terms that when she left it she was to pay eight oxen and ten cows and four men.[6] This looks very much as though she was to leave the estate as a going concern with its workforce. An early eleventh-century lease of Luddington, Warws., specifically states the estate is 'with full equipment' and itemises two teams of oxen (as well as slaves and two sheep), so the cattle were presumably not for consumption, at least, not immediately.[7] When the abbot of Evesham leased an estate at Norton for three lives, it was returnable with 6 oxen.[8] Under the terms of a marriage agreement made before King Cnut between Godwine and Brihtric when he wooed his daughter, the lady was to receive two estates plus 30 oxen, 20 cows, 10 horses and 10 slaves, i.e. two well-stocked farms, rather than food.[9]

Sometimes the words used make it obvious that the cattle were for food. By the terms of the lease of Sempringham by Ceolred, abbot of Peterborough, to Wulfred, in 825, he was to render to *Medeshamstede* (Peterborough) every year 'two cattle for slaughter' (*tua slegne'a't*).[10] Æthelgifu bequeathed oxen in multiples of two, presumably for plough teams, but to St. Alban's with other food a *hryþer* and a *slegeryþer*.[11] Presumably the *slegeryþer* was ready to be killed. Charitable gifts to Bury St. Edmunds

---

[1] op. cit., *Lac.* xxxv.
[2] W. Smallridge and A.E. Cook, pers. comms.
[3] Cockayne 1851, II vii.
[4] op. cit., II xvi 2.
[5] op. cit., I ii 16, iii 6, iii 9, iv 6.
[6] Robertson 1939, 230–1.
[7] Trow Smith 1957.
[8] op. cit.
[9] Robertson 1939, 151.
[10] op. cit., 13.
[11] Whitelock 1968, 11.

included *an slægryðer* (a bullock for slaughter), and the monastery's food rents included *an ryðer* from Barton, and from Tivetshall 'a quarter of beef' (*7 forðendæl an ryðer*).[1] For a first funeral feast two ores were provided for *an repær* (a bullock).[2] Under the terms of Æthelwyrd's will one day's food rent was to be paid at Michaelmas to the community at Christchurch, and this included 'a hindquarter of beef' (*an hriðres læuw*).[3] Denewulf, bishop of Winchester had to pay annually as rent 'two bullocks – beef carcasses, one salted the other fresh' (*tu hrieðeru oþer sealt oþer fersce*).[4] The Laws of Ine included 'two old, i.e. full-grown, bullocks' (*tu eald hriðeru*) in the food rent payable from ten hides. When Bishop Æthelwold gave Peterborough an estate at Yaxley, this was stocked, *inter alia*, with sixteen oxen (presumably two plough teams) and a *fal'd' repere* (stalled? [see above] bullock).[5] This was clearly not a 'retired, intractable or surplus beast' as has been thought, but a prime meat animal.[6] A fragment of another inventory at Bury refers to *xviii oxana* (18 oxen) and the very high number of *xxxvi faldhriþera* (36 stalled? grazing? bullocks).[7] The cattle market at Canterbury was referred to as *Hryþera Ceap* in 923, and *Ryþerceap* in 1002, which suggests it was primarily a meat market.[8]

However, not everyone had the chance to eat prime beef. According to *Rectitudines Singularum Personarum* a male slave was provided with a *metecu* (cow for food) every year.[9] Perhaps the cow provided a calf and milk before it was eaten, but more probably it was a cow retired from the lord's vaccary since he had a *kuhyrde*.[10] According to the Welsh Laws the king's *gwesta* and *dawnbwyd* included the carcasses of oxen, and a fat cow 'without skin or entrails'.[11] Of course it may have been his retainers, rather than the king himself, who had to eat up old oxen and cows. Certain of the officials of the Welsh court were entitled to particular parts of the cattle. The smith was to receive the heads and feet of the cattle slaughtered in the palace, with the exception of the tongues, which were to go to the judge, since he was concerned in a metaphorical sense with 'tongues'. The tongue was presumably a delicacy, since its absence had to be compensated for with prime meat: the king's share of the thigh.[12] Perhaps one should not speculate on the metaphorical connection in the case of the porter, who received the rectum and milt from each of the slaughtered cattle, but perhaps he merely fed his dogs on them; the falconer received the hearts to feed his hawks, although the cook received the rest of the entrails.[13] The lord might not be able to choose particular animals for his rents. Sometimes no doubt it was a case of taking what there was. The *gebur* for instance might have to pay his rent in meat (the alternatives were honey or ale), but he might not have had the resources to raise stock just for food.[1]

---

[1] Robertson 1939, 193, 199, 201.
[2] op. cit., 253.
[3] op. cit., 59.
[4] op. cit., 39.
[5] op. cit., 74.
[6] Trow Smith 1952.
[7] Robertson 1939, 249.
[8] Tatton Brown in Haslam 1984, 8.
[9] Liebermann 1909, 449.
[10] op. cit., 450.
[11] Owen 1841, 533, 535, 769, 199.
[12] op. cit., 649, 681.
[13] op. cit., 667.
[1] Liebermann 1909, 448.

Cattle Bones as Non-Food Waste

Cattle remains turn up in contexts other than food waste. Mid sixth-century cemeteries in Kent produced several ox teeth, and a large ox tooth was found in the grave of a seventh-century woman at Garton, Yorks. This may have represented some sort of ceremonial or ritual practice. In another grave at Garton, ox bones over the body were probably the remains of food deposits.[1] At the Suffolk site of Butley, pits full of ox heads were discovered, and one head was placed on a spearhead. At Soham and Girton too ox heads were buried in pagan cemeteries.[2] Harrow Hill, Angmering, Sussex, yielded large numbers of ox skulls. The name points to the presence of a pagan Saxon shrine, and it may be that the heads of cattle were offerings. In 601 Pope Gregory wrote to Mellitus about the English habit of sacrificing many oxen to devils, and Bede recounts it in his explanation of *blot-monaþ* as the old name for November, and there are other traces of an ox-cult among Germanic peoples.[3] At Yeavering the large deposits of cattle bones with an overwhelmingly high proportion of skulls may represent periodic feasts or possibly pagan ritual.[4] The two may of course have been combined, and presumably, even if the heads were left as a sacrifice, the rest of the carcass was eaten. At the cremation cemetery of Illingworth, Norfolk, ox bones (together with sheep bones) were deposited with male and female remains. These were not, says Wells, food for the underworld, but represent some form of totemism.[5]

Changes in the Importance of Cattle as a Food Resource over the Period

Changes over the period are not particularly marked, although at Portchester, the only site known to have been occupied throughout the period, the percentage of cattle bones fell from 57% during the fifth to eighth centuries to 31% at the end of the period, a fall comparable to those found elsewhere, although cattle remained the most important animal in terms of meat yield.[6] There may have been several reasons for this: one may have been that the status of sites changed. With the extension of the cultivated area one would expect oxen to become more common, as indeed they did at Portchester, both because they were needed for ploughing and because there would have been more cereal crops available for fodder.[7] Agricultural efficiency and prosperity may well have improved, but a loss of grassland would have lessened the numbers of cattle that could be raised for beef. There would have been local, and sometimes general, dearths of cattle as a result of murrain, as in 987, 986, 1046, 1049, and 1086.[8] The Viking campaigns and the English countermeasures also took their toll of cattle populations. In 793 the pagans slaughtered cattle, and in 909 King Edward's army ravaged Danish territory severely, killing all kinds of animals.[9]

---

[1] Meaney 1981, 144.
[2] Whittock 1986, 148, 152.
[3] Meaney 1981, 144.
[4] Hope-Taylor 1977, 158.
[5] Wells 1960.
[6] Cunliffe 1976, 263, 267.
[7] op. cit., 286.
[8] Creighton 1891, 26–7, 29.
[9] Whitelock 1955, 247, 192.

4. Cattle

Cattle from the early site of West Stow were of a good size compared with the mid-Saxon cattle of *Hamwih* and North Elmham, and were comparable in size to cattle recovered from later Anglo-Saxon sites.[1] They were killed at consistently younger ages than domestic stocks from later Anglo-Saxon sites.[2] The number of neo-natal deaths is not high on any site, so the winter keep must have been adequate, and the standard of husbandry high, as it was in post-Conquest times.[3] Presumably though, the Anglo-Saxons had no strategy for dealing with murrain. The explanation 'that some of your cattle are suddenly killed when the devil is vexed by your steadfastness' hardly points to any scientific understanding of the disease.

What differences there are in cattle production seem to be regional rather than temporal. In her comparison of animal bones from eight medieval sites in Britain, Barbara Noddle points out that 'the proportion of cattle bones seems to be more dependent on region than anything else; it is nearly twice as high in western Hereford as eastern North Elmham, both in the Saxon and medieval periods'.[4] This may have been due to the availability of cattle from Welsh upland areas. According to William of Malmesbury, Æthelstan sought an annual tribute of 25,000 oxen from the rulers of the north Welsh in the third decade of the tenth century, and, even allowing for some exaggeration, this still suggests that Wales had a cattle population in excess of draught requirements.[5] An analysis of the Domesday Book, and associated contemporary documents shows a situation comparable with that of today, in that there was more pastoral farming in the hilly and wet west. The important manors in North Devon had concentrations of cattle greatly in excess of their draught needs, which means that they were probably producing cattle for milk and meat.[6]

Cattle could presumably be bought in towns in the mid-Saxon period, and in 1002 a grant by King Æthelred of a small property in or outside Canterbury, records the boundary of the sixth acre as being on the south side of the cattle market.[7] The fact that two ores were left in a will for *an repær* (a bullock) for a first funeral feast indicates that it would be possible to buy one.[8] It would have been convenient to have an established market where the buying and selling could be done in front of the official witnesses for the district to comply with the law. However, the formula *toll and team* is a very common one in writs, and indicates the right to take toll on animals sold within an estate and to 'vouch to warranty'.[9] This proves the existence of a trade in cattle and goods outside borough markets, and there are definite references to purchases made *upp on lande*. Perhaps cattle were sold on to other farmers, for fattening for example, before they were sold in towns for meat.

Probably joints from plough oxen were lean and sinewy, as their absence from invalid regimens in leechdoms seems to suggest. Although William of Henley thinks they could be successfully fattened on grass, they seem never to have been regarded as highly as

---

[1] Crabtree in West 1982, 276, 277.
[2] Crabtree 1984.
[3] Trow Smith 1957, 117.
[4] Noddle in Clason 1975, 248.
[5] Whitelock 1955, 281.
[6] Trow Smith 1957.
[7] Whitelock 1955, 540.
[8] Robertson 1939, 253.
[9] Harmer 1952, 76–7.

those from younger animals. A situation like that described in the late eighteenth century in the Western Isles of Scotland must have been paralleled on occasion in Anglo-Saxon England. Cattle kept on near starvation rations in winter and allowed to flesh rapidly in spring produced a marbled beef 'the fat and lean is not so much separated as in other cows, but as it were larded, which renders it very agreeable to the taste'. Martin went to say that a cow might be twelve years old but its beef not above 4–6 months old.[1] The much-travelled Fynnes Moryson, making implicit comparison with cattle from other European counties, wrote, 'England...particularly hath very great oxen, the flesh whereof is so tender as no meat is more desired'.[2]

Very few documents survive from earlier times, but no doubt some cattle were raised for meat as soon as settled husbandry was established. The term *hryþer* for a beef animal is used as early as the Laws of Ine. In the later period from which most documents survive it is clear that large establishments ensured a good supply of beef cattle, and archaeological evidence from the royal sites of Yeavering and Cheddar indicate a plentiful supply of prime beef.

There are many references in leechdoms to the fatty sorts of meat: marrow (the bones to be broken with the back of an axe), grease, suet and lard, and injunctions to invalids to eat 'fat meat' (*fæt flæsc*) or 'fresh meat where it is fattest' (*fersc flæsc þær þær hit fætost sie*).[3] Nutritionally this was probably perfectly sensible. Lean meat needs to be supplemented by calorie-rich substances in order to prevent the meat's amino acids from being converted into energy, rather than body-building proteins. Although calorie for calorie carbohydrates are more efficient than fats in sparing proteins, fats provide 100% more calories than starch or sugars per gram. This means far fewer grams of fat than carbohydrates are needed to achieve a given protein-sparing effect.[4] Eating fatty meat then does away with a need for carbohydrates. By eating copious amounts of meat and bone marrow, the Eskimo maintained themselves in excellent health on an all-meat diet without the slightest trace of scurvy or other Vitamin C deficiency diseases, and moreover had lower than expected rates of cardio-vascular disease.[5] Carcasses of the unimproved breeds of cattle eaten by the Anglo-Saxons would have contained low amounts of saturated fats (see above); the Anglo-Saxon lifestyle was outdoor and active, rather than sedentary, and so it is almost certain that the incidence of heart disease in Anglo-Saxon times was much lower than it is today. Until the twentieth century fibre was the easiest and cheapest food element to acquire. Everyone had more fibre than they needed from imperfectly milled cereals, and so its absence from animal foods was a positive aspect.[6] Animal foods are concentrated sources of the essential minerals; iron occurs in greater abundance and in a more usable form than in spinach and other leafy foods. Meat is a very good source of zinc, essential for male fertility, as well as copper, iodine, and almost every other element needed in trace amounts.[7] It is not, therefore, surprising, that those who had most power organised a supply of this food in its most palatable form.

---

[1] Trow Smith 1957, 224–5; Seebohm 1952, 127.
[2] Moryson 1617, IV 356.
[3] Cockayne 1851, e.g. *Peri Did.* 38, Leechbook III lxv.
[4] Harris 1986, 41.
[5] op. cit., 36, 39.
[6] op. cit., 37.
[7] op. cit., 36.

5. Sheep

Summary of the Evidence

Contemporary documentary evidence, which includes illustrations, is augmented by information from some major animal bone assemblages, in particular those from Portchester, West Stow, *Hamwih* and King's Lynn. Tooth eruption and bone fusion data can establish the age of sheep at death, although estimates are derived from modern improved breeds whose development is much faster than the primitive breeds, though by how much is at present unclear.[1] Primitive short-tailed types of sheep have a short scapula neck, improved breeds a long scapula neck.[2] However, not all sites have provided the diagnostic evidence necessary for making these assessments. Some information on modern strains of primitive breeds is now available, thanks in the main to the Rare Breeds Survival Trust, and this can provide reasonable comparisons with Anglo-Saxon sheep types.

Habitat

Suitable areas were soon exploited for sheep-farming. The sheep is tolerant of most habitats except fresh-water marsh, but it prefers pasture to scrub or woodland, conditions the goat is better suited to exploit. Place-names with the element *sceap* are among the first to be recorded. Early in the eighth century the abbess of Gloucester acquired Pinswell in the Cotswolds for a sheep walk.[3] In the ninth century boundary charters referred to, for example, 'the sheep lea' and Sheepswick.[4] Ewehurst in the Weald is referred to in a charter of 822, and although swine, cattle and goats are listed as the animals for which there is pasture, sheep-rearing had presumably been carried on there.[5]

By the time of Domesday flocks must have been plentiful. In general the numbers were highest in the east, though there were concentrations round Cheddar for example, and desmesne lands round Exeter carried 9,689 sheep and 1,613 goats.[6] Other areas of intensive sheep husbandry included Devon with an average of 50 sheep per thousand domainal acres. The salt marshes of East Anglia supported large numbers of sheep. In 1086 Norfolk had approximately 92,000 sheep and the number on the Essex marshes alone was put at over 18,000. Mutton grazed on salt marshes is a particular delicacy today as *de pré-salé*.[7] Anglo-Saxon populations may have similarly appreciated it.

Pre-Saxon Sheep in England

Anglo-Saxon sheep had three possible ancestors: the brown Soay, the Iron Age vari-coloured and the third a Roman white sheep with a long tail. The Danes may have introduced a black-faced horned sheep, with a hairy fleece, which is thought to persist in the Scottish blackface. The area occupied by the Danes corresponds very roughly with the

---

[1] Maltby in Jones & Dimbleby 1981, 171.
[2] Ryder in Crossley 1981, 23.
[3] Trow Smith 1957.
[4] Turner 1828, II 570.
[5] Whitelock 1955, 475.
[6] Noddle in Clason 1975.
[7] David 1960, 32.

area in which this type later emerged, and some Danish textiles excavated in York contained true hairy wool. There is evidence too that a similar sheep existed in Denmark which gives support to this theory, although the black-faced horned type may have evolved independently in Britain.[1] The white sheep introduced by the Romans could have evolved into a primitive longwool, of which the white-faced polled Romney breed is an example. Crossed with the Soay it may have produced the Cheviot and Welsh Mountain breeds.[2] Potentially therefore an Anglo-Saxon sheep could have been a direct descendant of the three breeds here at the time of the Migration, or, late in the period, of the Danish type; a cross between any two of these types, or an admixture of them.

Breeds – Manuscript Evidence

There are a number of Anglo-Saxon illustrations of sheep. Of two eleventh-century calendar illustrations for the month of May, Trow Smith observes that the rams are horned like Exmoor Horn, while the ewes are apparently hornless.[3] The Caedmon manuscript also has an indication of horned rams and polled ewes.[4] However, problems of perspective and therefore size suggest the 'ewes' might be lambs. At Exeter naturally polled sheep appear for the first time in twelfth-century deposits.[5] However Ryder thinks that medieval sheep (which showed no evidence of a change from Anglo-Saxon sheep), could come from a horned breed or breeds (i.e. both sexes horned), or from a polled breed (neither sex horned) or from a breed in which only the rams were horned, or all could have come from a general variability within the same type of sheep.[6] The illustrations bear out the archaeological evidence in that the sheep appear long-legged and rangy compared to modern breeds. Seebohm thinks the sheep on the M.S. Cott. Julius A vi calendar show a remarkable resemblance in the length of leg, general build and curve of horns to modern St. Kilda sheep.[7] A ram shown in M.S. Cott. Vitellius C iii is the same long-legged animal, but with curiously foliate horns. Assuming the same artistic licence does not extend to the body, it does have a mane of long hair which is a feature of the adult Soay, though it is more pronounced in the ram.[8] However, all three manuscripts show long-tailed sheep – the Soay is a primitive short-tailed breed. This suggests a Soay-Roman longwool cross, which may have resulted in the Norfolk Horn, hardy and thrifty enough to flourish on the poor grass and heather of the Breckland.[9] The Norfolk Horn was kept for wool and cheese, and only slaughtered at the end of its productive life, a typically Anglo-Saxon pattern. Ryder thinks the white-faced polled sheep of medieval illustrations show something like today's Ryeland breed.[10] By 900 there could well have been a large and growing element of improved woolly and more nearly white sheep from the Mediterranean countries, and of derived crosses between them and the resident small, hairy sheep.[11]

---

[1] Ryder in Jones & Dimbleby 1981, 226.
[2] Ryder in Ucko & Dimbleby 1971, 510.
[3] Temple 1976, Nos. 198, 73; Trow Smith 1951, 44.
[4] Ryder in Jones & Dimbleby 1981, 226.
[5] Noddle in Clason 1975.
[6] Ryder in Crossley 1981, 23.
[7] Seebohm 1952, 98-9.
[8] R.B.S.T. n.d., 2; Zeuner 1963, 189.
[9] Henson 1982, 17; Cassidy 1989, 143.
[10] Ryder in Ucko & Dimbleby 1971, 510.
[11] Carter in Whitelock 1968, 76-7.

Archaeological Evidence

Presumably it was as a symbolic source of meat that the hind leg of a sheep (or goat) was deposited in a seventh-century grave at Shudy Camps, Cambridgeshire, although this was in a Christian cemetery.[1] Less surprising were the joints of lamb deposited in several graves in a sixth-century cemetery at Cotgrave, Northamptonshire, or the lamb chops in a grave at Burwell, Cambs.[2]

Archaeological evidence establishes only a general type: a small, generally lightly built, long-legged breed, although the sheep at the early seventh-century site of Puddlehill, Beds., are comparable with, though slightly smaller than, Welsh mountain sheep.[3] Whether sheep were polled or horned can be established from animal-bone evidence, but externals such as colour can only be established from textiles, where there is no linking to skeletal material.

Sheep from the sixth-century site at Old Down Farm, Hants., were small compared with sheep from middle Saxon *Hamwih*.[4] However, sheep from the fifth- to seventh-century site at West Stow were very similar in size to sheep from middle-Saxon North Elmham and Thetford sites, and at the top of the Anglo-Saxon size range. The differences between the West Stow and *Hamwih* sites were not significant, and there is no evidence for a size change through time.[5] All crania at *Hamwih* were horned, and as at the other sites, the sheep were small in height and lightly built, but larger – at 0.612m at the withers – than Wessex Iron Age material, so some 'improving' had taken place, but this had not necessarily been the work of the Anglo-Saxons.[6]

Sheep from King's Lynn in the period 1050–1250 were little larger than a Soay, but the bones were rather more robust. The scapulae, which are diagnostic of primitive semi-improved modern breeds, here approximate to the Orkney primitive short-tail. There were two smooth curved horn cores, one round core (as in the present-day Orkney), one oval core (as in the present-day Soay), and two have carrying scurs, which occur in both Orkney and Soay breeds.[7]

Four types of sheep were identified at Portchester on the basis of horn cores. One had a small horn core, one had a very much larger core, four individuals had an average size core, and one type was hornless.[8] One skull from a late Saxon site at Bedford was clearly from a hornless animal.[9] At *Hamwih* the horn cores of ewes were not less numerous than those of rams, although the rams' horns were relatively heavy.[10]

The sheep at North Elmham were larger than average. Some had horns with a longitudinal groove on their outer surface. This is seen in the modern Norfolk Horn, a semi-improved breed.[1] The Norfolk Horn was supposed to be of Saxon origin, though

[1] Lethbridge 1936, Grave 12.
[2] Wilkinson 1986, 16; Lethbridge cited in Alcock 1987, 293.
[3] Hawkes et al. 1985, 109.
[4] Davies 1980, 178.
[5] West 1982, 276.
[6] Holdsworth 1980, 109.
[7] Clarke & Carter 1977, 94.
[8] Cunliffe 1976, 283.
[9] *Beds. Archaeol. J.* 13, 70.
[10] Prummel 1983, 193-4.
[1] Noddle in Clason 1975.

a modern representative of the breed weighs about 110 lb., the average Saxon sheep about 90 lb.[1] Several scapulae of the North Elmham sheep indicated a breed approaching the mutton sheep type, although the majority of these bones are intermediate between this, and a primitive Soay type.[2] The sheep at Flaxengate were higher at the withers than a Soay ram, and were perhaps also stock from which the Norfolk Horn descended.[3] The sheep at Exeter at the end of the period were smaller than the stock represented in other parts of England, and similar in several respects to modern breeds of Soay sheep.[4] The size of the sheep on the early medieval site of St. Magnus, London, also compares to that of the modern Soay.[5]

Evidence from Present-Day Primitive Breeds

The growth rate of Soay and St. Kilda sheep is not as high as that of modern improved breeds but they require the minimum of food and management and do well on areas of low fertility. Soays have an unusual pelvic structure which makes for easy lambing.[6] The Manx Loghtan, another comparable primitive breed, is very hardy: lambing is usually trouble-free. They are unlikely to succumb to foot-rot or mastitis. Because they do not put on weight rapidly, slaughter is not recommended before 18 months, and they do not put on much fat before they are 2 years old.[7] The flavour – like that of other primitive breeds, the Soay, the North Ronaldsay – is particularly fine.[8]

Husbandry

Numbers

Sheep seem to have been kept in much greater numbers than goats. On a number of estates both animals were kept and, looking at figures for Somerset in the Domesday survey, ratios of sheep to goats range from 2:1 to 16:1, with an average of 6:1. The flocks of sheep range up to 800 on the royal manor of Chewton, but flocks of over a hundred are common.[9] Ratios from animal-bone assemblages at *Hamwih* are 8:1, and 20:1.[10] As compared with animals other than goat, sheep are preponderant in terms of numbers.

Composition of Flock

At least 22.5% of the sheep bones at *Hamwih* were from castrates, 7.5% certainly from rams, and the assumption is that the animals were basically kept for wool, and were only secondarily a food resource.[11] However, animal-bone assemblages, particularly in towns, may not be indicative of the flocks from which they came. An official Welsh flock consisted of 30 sheep and a ram, but makes no mention of

[1] Clutton Brock in Wilson 1976, 382.
[2] Noddle in Clason 1975.
[3] Crabtree in Biddick 1984, 183.
[4] op. cit.
[5] Armitage in Hall & Kenward 1982, 101.
[6] Morris 1990, 402.
[7] Wade-Martins 1986, 168-9.
[8] Petch 1987.
[9] C & F Thorn 1980, 87b, 86 a-d, 87 a-d.
[10] Holdsworth 1980, 109.
[11] op. cit., 109.

wethers, which are often mentioned in Anglo-Saxon documents.[1] No doubt a dairy flock would differ in composition from a wool flock, but the picture is complicated by the fact the sheep was a multiple-purpose animal, providing milk, wool, fertilizer, skins and meat. The thrifty Anglo-Saxon farmer would want it to supply as much as possible of the first three items before it finally supplied the last two, unless the meat was likely to command a premium, compensating him for the loss of the other products. Æthelgifu's will of c.990 provides information on the composition of the flocks on her estates, and this suggests wethers were kept for both wool and meat.[2]

The Shepherd

The care of shepherds for their flocks should have been exemplary, but the metaphor Boniface uses in a letter to Cuthbert of Canterbury suggests this was not always the case: 'Let us not be ... hirelings who flee from the wolf, but zealous shepherds'.[3] Wolves were a danger in some areas; the terms *wulfseaðe* and *wulf pytte* (wolf pit) occur in boundary charters, as does the term *wulfhaga* (an enclosure to protect flocks from wolves).[4] Unlike the hirelings Boniface wrote of, the shepherd of the *Colloquy* declares: 'I am true to my master. In the early morning I drive my flock to their pasture and stand over them in the heat and in the cold with my dogs, in case wolves should devour them, and I lead them back to their fold' (*ic eom getrywe hlaforde minon. On forewerdne morgen ic drife sceap mine to heora lease 7 stande ofer hig on hæte 7 on cyle mid hundum, þe læs wulfas forswelgen hig 7 ic agenlade hig on heora loca*).[5] Even after the end of the Anglo-Saxon period Alexander Neckham wrote that 'the treachery of wolves' necessitated a shepherd spending all his time guarding his sheep.[6] He also advised the shepherd be accompanied by a faithful dog. Some idea of the importance of a sheepdog is suggested when its value in the Welsh Laws is the same as that of an ox.[7]

Nutrition

At *Hamwih* the sheep were slender, and possibly undernourished.[8] Indentations on horn cores may be related to severe winter conditions and malnutrition. Nearly a quarter of the horn cores from Saxon Southampton show this feature, but further studies are needed to establish the cause.[9] A very large number of sheep from Wicken Bonhunt had periodontal disease, which is related to some extent to dietary health. However, the Saxon sheep at *Hamwih* were remarkably free of this oral pathology, a fact which is in conflict with the horn core evidence.[10] Gum inflammation may have deterred feeding and malnutrition may have resulted from, rather than caused, the disease.[11] There was an absence of periodontal disease also at the late Saxon sites of St. John's, Bedford, and Flaxengate, Lincoln, where the stock were healthy and well-fed, living on good grass

[1] Owen 1841, 743.
[2] Carter in Whitelock 1968, 78.
[3] Kylie 1911, 188.
[4] Bosworth & Toller 1898, I 1281, II 751.
[5] Garmonsway 1978, 22.
[6] Homes 1952, 201.
[7] Owen 1841, 731.
[8] Holdsworth 1980, 109.
[9] Ryder in Jones & Dimbleby 1981, 239.
[10] op. cit.
[11] op. cit.

with little foddering.[1] Saxon wools were relatively fine, which may have been due to poor nutrition, but probably was the result of interbreeding with the finer-fleeced Roman sheep.[2] Sheep may have been kept under cover from Martinmas to Easter and fed with hay, a little straw and pea-haulms, as later medieval sheep were.[3] However, as they were hardy or only semi-improved, it is likely they needed shelter and supplementary food only in very hard winters.

General Management

The sheeps' tails, according to contemporary illustrations, were not docked. This probably did not result in maggot infestation as would be likely to be the case with improved breeds today, as primitive breed are rarely troubled by this.[4] Disastrous epidemics among domestic animals were recorded in the Anglo-Saxon Chronicle, but the diseases concerned are difficult to identify. The Welsh Laws made the seller of sheep answerable for sheep with rot, scab, and red water, and stated sheep were not to have had contact with a house where there was mange up to seven years previously.[5] This indicates some of the diseases that might strike sheep. There is a recipe in leechdoms for a sick sheep – it was to be given new ale.[6] Penning elbow, a traumatic joint condition of sheep, is linked with the use of pens for management purposes, and might be expected to occur in Anglo-Saxon sheep. It is rarely mentioned in bone reports, so either Anglo-Saxon shepherds were very careful with their sheep, or it goes unrecognised. At the late ninth-century Whitehall Farm site the figure for young sheep dying in their first year is very near to normal losses encountered in modern sheep production, which suggests adequate management.[7]

The sheep was probably kept in rural contexts and brought into towns on the hoof for slaughter – a suggestion made about the *Hamwih* sheep.[8] However, there was evidence that some of these sheep were kept tethered by their front legs, and these may have been kept by households in the town, much as pigs were.[9] The sheep in late eighth- early ninth-century Ramsbury, Wiltshire, were probably older than two years at death, so more young stock was slaughtered in urban *Hamwih*, presumably to satisfy a demand for food.[10]

Inventories give some idea of the organisation and the size of flocks. A fragment from Bury St. Edmunds refers to 96 sheep.[11] According to An Assignment of Property to Thorney Abbey: 'sixty pence was allotted to Brandon for sheep . . . and ten pence to the shepherd . . . and when Ælfnoth was entrusted with his office at Hatfield there were 250 sheep there' (man seald to sceap[um?] to Bromdune lx þ . . . 7 x þ þæm sceaph[yrd]e . . . þa man betæhte Ælfnoðe þone folgað æt

[1] *Beds. Archaeol. J.* 13, 106; Crabtree in Biddick 1984, 183.
[2] Ryder in Ucko & Dimbleby 1971, 510.
[3] Seebohm 1952, 128.
[4] Wade-Martins 1986, 168.
[5] Owen 1841, 717.
[6] Cockayne 1851, E xviii fol 13b.
[7] Wells 1971, 137.
[8] Holdsworth 1980, 109.
[9] op. cit., 96.
[10] Coy in Haslam 1980, 47-9.
[11] Robertson 1939, 249.

5. Sheep

Hæðfel[da] þa wæs þær . . . þrydde healf hund sceapa).[1] When Beddington, Surrey, was leased to King Edward the Elder (899–908) by Bishop Denewulf, an inventory of the stock which survived the severe winter included fifty wethers, besides the sheep which the herdsman has the right to have...110 full-grown sheep.[2] In about 963 there were 305 sheep on an estate at Yaxley which Bishop Æthelwold gave to Peterborough, compared with thirty pigs, four oxen and two cows.[3] Æthelgifu bequeathed 350 sheep from her estate at Langford to various churches, leaving 200 to Ælfnoth who was to inherit the property. She left sixteen wethers to St. Alban's from her Offley estate, and it is presumed these were for slaughter.[4]

Age at Slaughter

At *Hamwih* about a fifth of the animals were killed young, at just under a year. This is a good option in modern terms – yearling lambs are sometimes sold in March and April when lamb meat is in short supply and they command a good price.[5] A concentration were killed at three-four years, which may have been a culling of breeding ewes or entire males. Until comparatively recently mutton was usually four years old, as ewes were killed off after breeding, and the meat was lean and well flavoured.[6] But more than a third of the *Hamwih* sheep had molars all fully in wear. A comparatively large proportion of mature animals almost certainly does mean an economic concern with breeding, dairying, and dunging, but it does not mean that sheep were valued for these factors rather than meat. By this time the wethers at least would have put on some amount of fat, and fat meat was specially valued in Anglo-Saxon times. It is more tasty, tender, and would provide extra calories. The fifteenth-century drinking song presumably picks out a common fault of mutton:

> Bryng us in good ale
> Bryng us in no mutton,
> for that is often lene.[7]

It is known that after the Conquest old and feeble sheep were fattened for sale on or about St. John's Day (June 24th), and that this was considered superior mutton.[8] The use of the sheep as a meat animal did not therefore run counter to its other functions as is sometimes suggested. This is not to say that all old sheep were for human consumption: the Welsh king's falconer was to have an old crone as food for his hawks.[9] However, the king's hawks, like his hounds, were well fed, since they provided him with a variety of more prestigious food, and it is quite possible that someone at the bottom of the hierarchy would have been grateful for the meat, however elderly.

At West Stow nearly half the sheep were dead before the end of their first year, and nearly two-thirds by the end of their second year. Assuming that the sheep were intentionally killed, rather than meeting with death from natural causes, these figures suggest a meat

---

[1] op. cit., 257.
[2] Whitelock 1955, 501.
[3] Robertson 1939, 135.
[4] Carter in Whitelock 1968, 77.
[5] Wade-Martins 1986, 169.
[6] Hartley 1954, 136.
[7] Furnivall 1868, 285.
[8] Seebohm 1952, 128.
[9] Owen 1841, 369.

and milk scheme, rather than wool production.[1] Perhaps there was some pressure on meat supplies for so many animals to be killed comparatively young. At early seventh-century Puddlehill, Beds., twenty percent of sheep were eaten when immature, but, as might be expected from this well-to-do settlement, none of the animals were old when slaughtered – all were of a prime age for eating.[2]

According to the evidence from Portchester, peaks occur at certain stages in the tooth wear which might suggest some seasonal or annual killing.[3] In the early period from the fifth to eighth centuries, and in the middle period from the eighth to the tenth centuries a large proportion of sheep were killed between 18 months and 3½ years. By the late period the majority were killed in their second year.[4] This suggests a standardisation of procedure, and also perhaps a pressure on the food supply. Similarly at Exeter in the late period a large proportion of sheep were slaughtered at between 15 and 36 months with a peak at 18–30 months. Most were younger than 25 months old; presumably they had been culled and sent to town for meat.[5] At North Elmham nearly all the sheep were wethers at least six years old. The presumption is that they were kept for wool.[6] However, their ultimate end would almost certainly have been to be eaten.

Sheep in Legal Documents

According to the Laws of Ine (688–94), ten hides were to furnish two full-grown cows or ten wethers, as well as other provisions.[7] Offa retained six wethers as part of a food rent from Westbury, Gloucs.[8] In an exchange of land at 'Wassingwell' and Mersham between Æthelbert, king of Kent, and his thegn Wulflaf in 858, twenty lambs had been part of the royal dues previously paid by Wassingwell.[9] Welsh kings too provided themselves with sheep in their food rents. The bond *mænol* was to provide a three-year-old wether in summer, and the king's summer *dawnbywds* included a fat wether.[10] In Herefordshire and Gloucestershire the old Welsh dues of sheep, honey, etc., remained undisturbed until Domesday.[11]

Other landowners exacted sheep as part of their rents. When Oswald, Archbishop of York, leased land at Henbury, Worcs., to Æthelmær in the late tenth century, the annual rent included thirty ewes and their lambs.[12] An estate was leased to Denewulf, Bishop of Winchester in return for, *inter alia*, six wethers.[13]

The church received sheep as a result of charitable giving. In two mid-ninth-century food rents a wether sheep was paid to the church of Llandaff by Rhys ap Ithael, the king of the district.[1] A noblewoman's estate was to give annually an old ram and four wethers.[2]

[1] West 1982, 290.
[2] Hawkes et al. 1985, 109.
[3] Cunliffe 1976, 279.
[4] op. cit., 277.
[5] Noddle in Clason 1975.
[6] Clutton-Brock in Wilson 1975, 382.
[7] Whitelock 1955, 371.
[8] Loyn 1970, 304.
[9] op. cit., 489.
[10] Owen 1841, 199, 533.
[11] Seebohm 1883, 211.
[12] Trow Smith 1957.
[13] Robertson 1939, 39.
[1] Seebohm 1883, 209.
[2] Turner 1828, II 547.

5. Sheep

Under the terms of the will of Athelwyrd, one day's food rent, which included a *weðær* (wether), was to be paid to the community at Christchurch.[1] Another gift, this time to Bury St. Edmunds, was of 'five sheep' (*v scep*).[2] According to the Bedwyn Guild Statutes, at the Rogation Days two members of the guild were to contribute to the priest a young sheep or two pence.[3] Possibly this was for services rendered to the guild, rather than a charitable gift. The church was officially entitled to some dues: among those paid at Lambourne were 'the tenth lamb' (*þat teoþe lamb*), and at Hurstbourne Priors 'and at Easter two ewes and two lambs, and we [reckon] two young sheep to a full-grown sheep' (*7 to easran two ewe mid twam lamban 7 we two geong sceap to eala sceapan*).[4] This suggests some negotiation was possible: perhaps those who had to pay would rather part with two lambs than an ewe, or perhaps they were more prepared to get rid of an old ewe than two healthy lambs. It also points to a lambing date roughly the same as that today.

A *gebur* was to pay to his lord according to *Rectitudines Singularum Personarum*: 'at Easter one young sheep or two pence' (*on Eastran an geong sceap oððe II p*).[5] Some humbler members of society received sheep in return for services rendered. A male slave was to receive 'two sheep carcasses' (*II scipæteras*) a year, a female slave 'one sheep or three pence for winter provisions' (*I sceap oððe III p. to wintersufle*).[6] After the Conquest, on the lands of Glastonbury and Canterbury a she-lamb and a ram respectively were among the foods to be paid for mowing service.[7]

Sheep in Leechdoms

Ram's grease (or buck's grease) is to be employed in one remedy for external application.[8] Another two similar remedies call for *sceapes smeru* (sheep's grease – presumably mutton fat rather than lanolin), and *sceapes mearh* (sheep's marrow) is similarly for external application.[9] Ram's flesh was considered hard to digest, but it was recommended as part of a a diet.[10] One leechdom calls for sheep's flesh to be avoided; a second says sheep's flesh and none other is to be taken.[11] 'Stewed ram's bladder' (*rammes blædre gesodene*) is to be taken internally, and one leechdom gives the instruction: 'make an incision in a sheep and quickly drink the sheep's blood while it is still hot' (*sniðe sceap raðe drince hat þe sceapes blood*).[12] The first presumably worked by sympathetic magic – if it worked at all – since it was to provoke urine, and the second perhaps took the patient's mind off the fact he had swallowed *wyrm* ('a creeping thing' – Cockayne) in water, and for which it was prescribed.

---

[1] Robertson 1939, 59.
[2] op. cit., 193.
[3] Whitelock 1955, 559.
[4] Robertson 1939, 241, 207.
[5] Leibermann 1898, 446.
[6] op. cit., 449-50.
[7] Seebohm 1952, 157.
[8] Cockayne 1851, III xxxi.
[9] op. cit., I viii 2, xxiii, I ii 23, xxxviii 8.
[10] op. cit., II xvi.
[11] op. cit., II xliii, lxxii.
[12] op. cit., I xxxvii, xlv 6.

The Value of Sheep

Sheep were important enough to be included in Prognostications. By a simplistic and surely non-scientific rule, if the mass day of mid-winter fell on a Sunday 'sheep shall thrive' (*sceap beoð weaxende*); if on a Tuesday, they were 'imperilled' (*frecnode*); but if the mass day fell on a Saturday 'sheep will perish' (*scep cwellað*). The same unfortunate outcome was to be expected if the wind blew on the ninth of the twelve days of Christmas.[1]

Sheep had a definite financial value. The Laws of Ine in the section 'Concerning the value of ewes' (*Be eowe wyrðe*) stated: 'a ewe with her lamb is worth a shilling until a fortnight after Easter' (*Ewo bið mid hire giunge sceap scill. weorð oþþæt XIIII niht ofer Eastran*).[2] The alternative of two full-grown cows to ten wethers in Ine's food rent from ten hides suggests the average sheep was more valuable in relation to the average cow in the Saxon period than now. The present-day ratio in dead carcass weights is 1:20. The likelihood is that the Anglo-Saxon cattle were proportionately smaller than the sheep. The guild compensation figures of 12 pence for a sheep and 20 pence for a cow, narrow the differential even more.[3] The law code *VI Æthelstan* established compensation for a sheep at a shilling.[4] However, 'compensation' may have involved a punitive element: according to *Rectitudines Singularum Personarum* a sheep was equated with three pence, and the Bedwyn Guild Statutes refer to a lamb or two pence.[5] Edgar's Andover code (959–63) fixes the price of a wey of wool at ten shillings, which suggests, though far from proves, that the value of the sheep as a wool producer was very low in relation to its value as an animal which had other useful functions, namely the production of meat, milk and fertilizer.[6]

In the Welsh Laws sheep seem to have been equated with the pig, in that to deny a swine or a sheep took the oaths of five men.[7] Elsewhere the impression is that they were less valuable: if a husband and his wife parted, the husband was to have the swine, the wife the sheep.[8] However, it is possible this was an equitable settlement based on the fact that the sheep was a dairy animal, and dairying was a woman's province, but the *net* of the king, *gwrda* and *tæog* consisted of horses, cattle and swine (sheep were not included), which perhaps indicates they were less valued.[9] The monetary value of a sheep which should give milk was four pence; a ram was worth double.[10]

Changes During the Period

It is impossible to build up a comprehensive picture on the evidence of a very few animal bone assemblages, particularly when only one published site, Portchester, gives continuous evidence. Here the percentage of sheep bones was highest in the

[1] Cockayne 1851.
[2] Attenborough 1922, 54.
[3] Trow Smith 1957.
[4] Whitelock 1955, 388.
[5] Liebermann 1898 449-50; Whitelock 1955, 559.
[6] Trow Smith 1957.
[7] Owen 1841, 243.
[8] op. cit., 87.
[9] op. cit., 7.
[10] op. cit., 277.

middle (eighth- to tenth-century) and late (tenth- and eleventh-century) groups.[1] There was a steady increase in the relative importance of sheep, and more sheep than cattle were kept from the eighth century on.[2] Another change over the period was that in the early and middle periods only 17% of the sheep were older than three years at death; in the late period 36% were fully mature animals. In the early to middle, and to a lesser extent the middle to late periods, a large proportion of sheep were killed when aged between 18 months and three-and-a-half years. In the late period the majority were killed in their second year.[3] This may not reflect a general change, but that the status of this site changed.

At West Stow there was an increase in the population of sheep/goat, with a corresponding decrease of pigs, from the fifth to the seventh centuries.[4] At Flaxengate, Lincoln, there was an increase in sheep bones from 20% c. 870–80, to about 40% by 1100.[5] Here the animals were mainly one- to two-year-old wethers so were meat animals).[6] On the rural sites of North Elmham, Sedgeford, Sandtun, Mawgan Porth, Old Down Farm, Hants., and Bishopstone, Sussex, sheep were the most numerous animal.[7]

At the royal site of Yeavering sheep were relatively rare, and at Cheddar, also a high status site, sheep were third in number to cattle and pig in the tenth and early eleventh centuries, though in the later eleventh century they became more common than pig.[8] At mid-Saxon Hamwih, tenth-century Skeldergate, York, and two late London sites (Billingsgate Buildings and St. Magnus) sheep were second in importance to cattle.[9] At the late Anglo-Saxon site of St. John's, Bedford, sheep provided the largest percentage of bones, but butchery marks on cat and dog bones on the site suggests they too were eaten.[10] Perhaps where sheep bones were in a majority on an urban site, then the site may have been comparatively poor.

The archaeological evidence provided by Portchester is corroborated by the figures in the Domesday survey. According to these records, sheep were absent only on a few manors, and then mainly on run-down and understocked holdings. The numbers of sheep recorded exceeded those of all other farm animals put together.[11] Comparisons between Domesday sheep populations and those recorded earlier this century show they were not dissimilar. In 1086 Norfolk had approximately 92,000 sheep, in 1936 the figure was 112, 000. Essex also had 92,000 sheep at the time of Domesday; but 78, 000 in 1937.[12] The large flocks of sheep run on the coastal marshes of Essex were mostly the property of lay landlords, like Suen who had grazing for over 4,000 sheep, but Ely Abbey had 13,400 sheep on its estates in 1086.[13] By the end of the period

[1] Cunliffe 1976, 263.
[2] op. cit., 284.
[3] op. cit., 277.
[4] West 1982, 269.
[5] Crabtree in Biddick 1984, 183.
[6] op. cit.
[7] Clutton Brock in Wilson 1976, 377; Arnold 1984, 71.
[8] Hope-Taylor 1977 326; Rahtz 1979, 354.
[9] Crabtree in Biddick 1984, 231; Hall & Kenward 1982, 96; O'Connor 1984, 16.
[10] Beds. Archaeol. J. 13, 103.
[11] Trow Smith 1957.
[12] op. cit.
[13] Poole 1958, 21; Loyn 1970, 367.

important landowners were initiating a policy of running breeding flocks of ewes on the hills, and fattening wethers on the better lowland pastures.[1] In these circumstances the wethers will fatten up well. The wether, a meat animal at least from the time of Ine's food rents, seems at the end of the period to have been singled out as a meat resource in the same way as the bullock. Maltby however, sees the development of wool production as the most important component of sheep farming by the end of the period, a conclusion he is led to by the high percentage of adult sheep on most late Saxon sites.[2] It is also true that the wool of castrates grows more luxuriantly than that of other sheep.[3]

There are indications of an increase in the average size of sheep during the Anglo-Saxon period, though regional variation was marked, and sheep in the south-west continued to be small.[4] Better husbandry, and/or the introduction of other stock, could account for this. The fact that the sheep at Portchester were already large in the early period suggests Roman sheep had already been crossed with native Iron Age breeds.

Nutritional Value of Mutton

Intensively produced animals, because of their scientific feeding and lack of exercise provide protein containing large amounts of saturated fat. The meat of naturally-reared animals, and this would include the Anglo-Saxon sheep, contains only unsaturated fat. Moreover these animals produce three times as much protein as fat – intensively produced animals vice versa.[5] The fat so much desired in meat by Anglo-Saxon populations would have been beneficial unsaturated fat.[6]

Status of Mutton as Food

Simply because the sheep was so common, its flesh was probably not considered a delicacy. We have seen from *Rectitudines Singularum Personarum* that the only meat mentioned as being provided for slaves was mutton. Perhaps a number of people owned at least one sheep: in later medieval times even Chaucer's *povre wydwe* had one, though how she or the Wife of Bath felt on consuming *Malle* or '*Wilkyn oure sheep*' is not recorded.[7] The household of Edward III's mother had boiled beef and mutton for dinner and roast beef or mutton for supper three times a week.[8] Perhaps more humble individuals had to eat beef and mutton even more frequently: a fifteenth century scholar writes, 'I have no delyte in beffe and motyn and such daily metes. I wolde onys have a partridge...or sum such'.[9] Although *VI score carcas of shepe fressh* were listed for a royal feast in 1387, neither sheep, mutton nor lamb is named in the seventy-two dishes. It may have been included in '*Grete Flesh*', or used to make

---

[1] Trow Smith 1957.
[2] Maltby in Jones & Dimbleby 1981.
[3] Clarke unpub.
[4] Maltby in Jones & Dimbleby 1981, 189.
[5] Pullar 1970, 227.
[6] Walker & Cannon 1985, 56.
[7] Robinson 1957, 80, 199.
[8] Mead 1931, 114.
[9] Pullar 1970, 94.

soups and other composite dishes like brawn or jelly, for which the *VI score hedes of shepe fressh* may have come in handy.[1]

Mutton has suffered from a bad press: hell for Sydney Smith was 'a thousand years of tough mutton', and it was inflicted daily on the unfortunate Victorian child since it was considered appropriate nursery fare.[2] However, to a gourmet at a Lord Mayor's dinner in the same era, Southdown mutton 'three or four years old if it's a day' was 'fit for a prince'. Edwardian mutton depended for its succulence and flavour on its maturity and proper hanging.[3] Nowadays saltmarsh reared mutton, and joints from the primitive breeds naturally reared, command premium prices.[4]

---

[1] Austin 1888, 67; Hartley 1954, 135.
[2] Pullar 1970, 183, 186.
[3] op. cit., 210.
[4] Petch 1987.

6. Goats

Evidence

Evidence for the goat as a meat animal comes mainly from documentary sources. This is due in part to the difficulty of telling goat and sheep bones apart. Osteologically skulls and horns are diagnostic, but long bones, for instance, present great difficulties.[1] Consequently in a number of important animal-bone reports reference is made to ovicaprine samples, and the assumption is that the majority of the animals represented are sheep.[2] However, where documentary and archaeological information is compared for an area, correspondence is very close.[3]

Habitat

Goats exploit a different ecological niche to sheep. Thriving on scrub and rougher land,[4] the goat could live on woodland like the pig, as a grant by Ceolwulf I, king of Mercia, to Archbishop Wulfred in 822, confirms: 'Again in Andred [the forest of the Weald] food and pasture for swine and cattle or goats'.[5] Felling of timber and assarting during the Anglo-Saxon period would have reduced the area the goat was best suited to occupy and may have accelerated a decline in numbers.[6] Allowing some goats to run with a flock of sheep may have had a beneficial effect in that the weeds were removed by the goats, allowing better grazing for the sheep.[7]

The elements *ticcen* (a kid), *hæfer* (a he-goat), and *gat* (goat) all occur in place-names[8]. References in boundary charters to 'the kids' field' and 'Kidburn' also evince the presence of goats.[9]

Breed

Evidence from the ovicaprine samples at *Hamwih*, shows the animals were small in stature and slightly built, with a withers height of 0.612m. This is larger than the Wessex Iron Age material and might argue a breed in process of improvement[10]. However the animals in the ovicaprine sample at the fifth- to seventh-century site of West Stow are very similar in size to those from the later sites of North Elmham and Thetford, and so there does not seem to be evidence for a change in the size of goats or sheep over the period[11]. What is apparently a goat with beard and horns (although rams of the Soay breed have both features), is depicted in the Bayeux Tapestry in the illustration to the fable 'Hunting with the Lion', and a second goat appears further on, but little can be judged of size or

---

[1] Zeuner 1961, 129.
[2] Maltby in Jones and Dimbleby 1981, 161.
[3] Noddle in Clason 1975.
[4] Zeuner 1961, 151.
[5] Whitelock 1955, 475.
[6] Trow Smith 1957.
[7] Ryder 1987, 335.
[8] Smith 1970, II 178, 214, 195–6.
[9] Turner 1828, II 570.
[10] Holdsworth 1980, 109.
[11] West 1982, 276.

breed[1]. The horns are not unlike those of the feral goat.[2] Some bones from Anglo-Danish sites in York are very similar to those of the feral goat.[3]

Husbandry

Such terms as *gat-hus* (goat house) and *gata loc* (an enclosure for goats) do not necessarily indicate that goats were farmed since they are glosses to Latin words.[4] However, there is definite evidence from *Rectitudines Singularum Personarum*, in that a *gat-hyrde* was one of the workers on a great estate. Apart from receiving the milk from his herd after Martinmas, and his share of the whey before that, 'the goatherd is entitled to a kid born that year if he tends his herd well' (*gat-hyrde gebyreþ . . . an ticcen of geares geogoþe gif he his heorde wel begymeþ*).[5] Moreover an actual goatherd (*mediator capraru*), was recorded in the Domesday survey for the hundred of Neatham in Hampshire.[6]

According to the *Assignments of Property at Thorney Abbey*, 'When Ælfnoth was entrusted with his office at Hatfield there were . . . 47 goats there' (*Þa man betæhte Ælfnoðe þone folgað æt Hæðfel[da] þa wæs þær . . . xlvii gata*), compared with 250 sheep, 40 oxen and 15 calves, and 190 pigs.[7] These figures are paralleled more or less closely by the ratios recorded in Domesday. For example, in Somerset at Congresbury there were 200 sheep and 40 goats; at Old Cleve 300 wethers and 50 goats; the manor of the bishop of Coutances had 317 sheep and 43 goats.[8] In general, the larger the numbers of sheep, the smaller the percentage of goats. The royal manor of Chewton with 800 sheep had only 50 goats.[9] It was unusual to have goats without sheep, although at Pitminster there were 36 goats but no sheep.[10] Chilcompton, Rodney Stoke, Shepton Mallet and Croscombe Blagdon all had flocks of she-goats ranging in size from 45 to 90, and, while their primary function would have been dairying, they perhaps provided kids for meat.[11] The demesne lands around Exeter carried 1,613 goats, and 9, 689 sheep, a ratio of approximately one to six, which is the same as that produced by the comparison of goat to sheep bones - identified by various criteria - at Exeter.[12] The animal bone evidence from the mid-Saxon site of *Hamwih* yields a ratio of goats to sheep of 1:8 based on the width of the distal metacarpus, and a ratio of approximately 1:20 from a minimum number count based on the radius. About one fifth of the animals were killed young - at just under a year in modern terms, but the concentration was killed at 3-4 years.[13] On the basis of horn-core sexing females made up only 12% of the sample. Perhaps the horns of males/castrates were brought into *Hamwih* because they were better for horn working.[14] However, a preponderance of castrate horns would be expected if the goats were being raised for meat.

---

[1] Wilson 1985, Plates 6, 60.
[2] Ryder 1987, 335.
[3] *Med. Archaeol.* XV, 47.
[4] Bosworth & Toller 1898, 363.
[5] Liebermann 1898, 451.
[6] Munby 1982, 47b 33 1.
[7] Robertson 1939, 257.
[8] C.& F. Thorn 1980, 87a, 86d.
[9] op. cit., 87b.
[10] op. cit., 37c.
[11] Trow Smith 1957.
[12] Noddle in Clason 1975.
[13] Holdsworth 1980, 109.
[14] op. cit., 111.

Goats as a Source of Meat

Goats were used for meat as well as milk in Roman times, so one might expect this function to continue.[1] Goats' meat is said to be tougher than that of sheep.[2] However, we should not allow our contemporary preferences for tender meat from young animals to be a guide to how the Anglo-Saxons regarded goat-meat. In his *Tours in Wales* (1772), Pennant records that goats' meat was salted and dried, and that 'the meat of a splayed goat of 6 or 7 years old (which is called *hyfr*)[3] is reckoned the best; being generally very sweet and fat . . . little inferior to venison'.

There were a large number of mature animals in the ovicaprine sample at *Hamwih*: more than one third had all molars fully in wear. This presumably does reflect concern with the other functions of the animals: dunging, breeding, dairying, the provision of wool/hair/skins, although these would not have been at odds with meat production if the meat of older animals was preferred.[4] There were an appreciable number of males kept in late eleventh- to twelfth-century Skeldergate, York, presumably for meat.[5] Castrates (where dairying, perhaps the most important function of the goat, was clearly not an issue) were kept until several years old in later medieval King's Lynn.[6]

The liking for kid meat, which makes excellent eating, is more understandable to us, and in the post-Conquest period the Berkeley estates of Edward III provided 300 kids every year for their lord's table.[7]

The skull of a goat was found in grave AX at Yeavering.[8] *Gefrin* meant 'hill of the goats', and the goat may have had a totemic significance. Totemic significance and importance as a meat animal are not mutually exclusive, however, although use of a skull suggests a symbolic function, an obviously meaty joint would suggest food.

Goats in *Leechdoms*

'Goat's grease/fat' (*Hæferes smera*) is prescribed for external use in *Leechdoms*, though it is to be taken internally for dysentery.[9] 'Kid's gall' (*ticcenes geallan*) is prescribed for external use, 'goat's gall' (*gate geallan*) is to be taken internally.[10] In one prescription 'goat's meat burned to ashes' (*gate flæsc gebærned to ahsan*) is required, in another a 'goat's bladder' (*gate blædre*) is to be fried and eaten.[11] In a section on diet, goat's flesh is recommended as being slow to digest and in addition for making good blood, kid's flesh is recommended as being easy to digest.[12]

---

[1] Seebohm 1952, 79.
[2] Zeuner 1963, 151.
[3] cf. O.E. *haefere*.
[4] Pennant 1772; Holdsworth 1980, 109.
[5] O'Connor 1984, 16.
[6] Clarke & Carter 1977.
[7] Seebohm 1952, 131.
[8] Hope-Taylor 1977, 69.
[9] Cockayne 1851, I xxxi, xxxvii, II vi 4.
[10] op. cit., I ii 5, ii 16, iii 5.
[11] op. cit., I xxxi 3, xxxvii.
[12] op. cit., II xvi 2, xxxvii.

Value

Goats would seem to be less valued than sheep - 2 pence as against a shilling in the time of Æthelred.[1] The same comparative values seem to have held for Wales, in that, if a couple parted and the only animals they possessed were sheep and goats, the husband was to have the former, while the wife was left with the goats.[2] The Welsh Laws gave a value of 4 pence for a goat, though one penny of this was for milk and a halfpenny for the kid, so at two and a half pence the Welsh goat's value was only marginally more than that of its English counterpart.[3] According to the Dimetian Code, its value was the same as a roebuck.[4] This probably indicates that both animals would yield about the same amount of meat, and also that some goats were feral, especially when we are given the information that the king has 'of the spoil (of a hunt) . . . the goats . . . without sharing with anyone'.[5]

The usefulness of the goat may have declined generally when cattle were domesticated.[6] Certainly the goat seems to have declined in importance with the development of dairying based on cows, and as wool became more important after the Conquest.[7] Although the goat provided more milk per animal than sheep and it was considered efficacious against many diseases, two points noticed by Neckham, it became less popular after the Anglo-Saxon period.[8]

---

[1] Seebohm 1952, 99.
[2] Owen 1841, 81.
[3] op. cit., 279.
[4] op. cit., 575.
[5] op. cit., 793.
[6] Zeuner 1963, 152.
[7] Trow Smith 1957.
[8] Seebohm 1952, 131.

7. Pigs

The Anglo-Saxon pig was small, a domestic version of *sus scrofa* and a smaller, apparently more populous type, *s. scrofa pallustris* (the early domestic – tubary – pig), which was probably descended from the small wild pig of S.E. Europe.[1] Celtic literature may preserve a folk memory of the first domestication of the pig in Wales. Taliesin tells of a woman who first 'brought swine from the south', and in *The Mabinogion*, Gwydion introduces 'hogs or swine' (*hoben* or *moch*) as newcomers to Gwynedd, whose flesh 'is better than the flesh of oxen'.[2]

Appearance

Pigs were certainly bristly. The most impressive evidence comes from the Welsh Laws. The Porter of the Welsh court was to have 'of the swine taken in pillage that pass through the gate, the sow which he shall be able, with one hand, to lift by her bristles until her feet are as high as his knees'.[3] While the main effect of this regulation would be to limit the weight of the sow the porter could claim, it indicates that the pig's bristles were long enough to grasp. Pigs apparently remained bristly for some centuries: in 1508 John Patriche, a scalding-house keeper thought it worthwhile to retain, under the terms of an agreement with the butchers of Eastcheap, the bristles of the slaughtered pigs.[4] Bristly pigs are shown in Anglo-Saxon illustrations, for example in B.L. Cott. Claudius C. VIII, where the pigs are tusked, with curly tails.[5] They may have been dark in colour: Riddle 40 refers to 'a dark/black boar' (*bearg won*), and Wiseman thinks they were dark brown.[6] However, when one Wærlaf, Wærstan's father was a serf at *Hæðfeld*, he held 'the grey pigs' (*þa grægan swin*).[7]

Size

Pigs at the fifth- to seventh-century site of West Stow were considerably larger, ranging from about 50–70 cm. at the withers, than pigs from British Iron Age sites at 50–60 cms. All were quite large, and comparable in size to those found at later Anglo-Saxon sites.[8] Comparison of proximal radial breadths showed no difference between pigs from West Stow, and the middle-Saxon sites of *Hamwih*, Ramsbury and North Elmham.[9] The average withers heights of *Hamwih* pigs calculated from the astragalus and calcaneus were 68.7 and 70.1 cms. respectively, which makes them comparable in height to the pigs of Dorestad, Hedeby and Rijnsburg.[10] But when the height was calculated on the basis of the humerus, radius, femur and tibia, *Hamwih* pigs were slightly taller than pigs from the continental sites, and were also, to judge from the distal tibial width, the heaviest too.[11] Although Ramsbury pigs were smaller

---

[1] Wiseman 1986, viii.
[2] Trow-Smith 1957; Jones 1973, 56.
[3] Owen 1841, 69.
[4] Jones 1976, 88.
[5] illus. in Wright 1871, 88.
[6] Mackie 1934; Wiseman 1986, viii.
[7] Kemble 1876, I 226.
[8] Crabtree in Biddick 1984, 277.
[9] op. cit., 230–1.
[10] Prummel 1983, 215.
[11] op. cit.

than wild boar, they were not very much so, but by modern standards they were very small.[1] After all, the porter at the Welsh court would hardly have been able to lift a sow (as opposed to a piglet) one-handed, if it was as heavy as a modern-day breed. Unfortunately, contemporary illustrations can not be relied upon to indicate size. A tenth-century illustration to Prudentius' *Psychomachia* shows pigs just as big as cattle, at a quarter the size of horse.[2]

Conformation

The Anglo-Saxon pig was shorter in the leg than wild boar, but was still long-legged compared with modern breeds, as illustrations, for example in B.L. Cott. Tiberius B. V, show.[3] They had shorter jaws and smaller teeth than wild pigs and there is no evidence for cross-breeding with wild boar.[4] That they were nevertheless comparatively long-snouted is shown by illustrations, and this is a feature elsewhere remarked on.[5] The Dorestad pigs are thought to have retained the straight snout of their wild forebears.[6] Such long-legged and long-snouted pigs survive in country districts in Europe. The herd pig of Spain may be regarded as representative of the external appearance of most early European pigs.[7] Wiseman describes Anglo-Saxon pigs as long-legged, razor-backed and prick-eared, and considers that it is unlikely that any attempts were made to improve the breed in Anglo-Saxon times.[8] The Tamworth is the most primitive surviving breed of British pig, and has not, it is thought, been interbred with Chinese pigs, which was the usual way of 'improving' breeds during the eighteenth century. The Tamworth and the Gloucester Old Spot, another primitive breed, are hardy pigs, producing only small litters (7–8 piglets), but capable of rearing their young outside, without the controlled environment needed by modern commercial pig strains.[9] They are particularly able to thrive on low-quality feed inputs – low quality, that is, in modern terms.[10] Their natural diet would be a varied one, probably consisting in the main of nuts and acorns, slugs, insects, worms, fungi, vegetation, roots, carcasses, eggs and reptiles.[11]

The Anglo-Saxon pig seems to have grown slowly, reaching maturity in its third year. Pre-Conquest inventories differentiate between young pigs, hogs, and full-grown swine (see below). The modern bacon pig matures at around eight months. The boar in B.L. Cott. Vitellius C. iii is the usual long-legged, long-snouted beast, but is noticeably bulky.[12] There is no doubt pigs could and did put on weight, and that the Anglo-Saxons favoured fat pigs. They would have recognised fat as a concentrated source of dietary energy, essential for the hard physical existence of labourers. Not until the end of the eighteenth century is there any suggestion that leaner meat was favoured, and then it was by the gentry who left the larger animals for their servants.[13]

---

[1] Coy in Haslam 1980, 47.
[2] Temple 1976, 70.
[3] Clarke Appendix to Alecto edition of Domesday.
[4] Coy in Haslam 1980, 47.
[5] Temple 1976, 70; Zeuner 1963, 267–8.
[6] Prummel 1983, 217.
[7] Zeuner 1963, 267–8.
[8] Wiseman 1986, viii.
[9] Henson 1982.
[10] Wiseman 1986, 105.
[11] Zeuner 1963, 263.
[12] Meaney 1981, 133.
[13] Wiseman 1986, 28.

Husbandry

Conditions in early Anglo-Saxon England may have been more favourable for the pig, perhaps because the countryside was more wooded than on the continent, since at Wijster pig bones were extremely rare.[1] Pigs have large and frequent litters, and consequently were valuable in providing a safety margin in primitive husbandry, whereas the enlargement of breeding herds of cattle and sheep takes several years.[2] However, like the other domestic animals they were subject to disease and *Lacnunga* contains a remedy 'for sudden death of pigs' (*wið swina fær steorfan*).[3] According to the Welsh Laws the seller of pigs was answerable for them not being infected with the quinsy and strangles, and for not devouring their young.[4]

The Welsh Laws also laid down the composition of a legal herd of swine as twelve sows and a boar. Males not wanted for breeding would have been castrated, and Prognostications recommend the third moon as being the best time 'to castrate boars' (*baras fyran*).[5] Unfortunately, the animal bone record does not add very much to the picture as the bones are rarely diagnosed as to sex. At *Hamwih* the numbers of female to male pigs were 76.5: 23.5, but presumably not all the males were boars.[6]

Seebohm's assumption that Anglo-Saxon pigs may have been only partially domesticated, seems to rest on his belief that, after they were bred on farms, they were 'turned out' into the public forests.[7] If this had been the case, they would probably have interbred with wild pigs but the animal bone record does not seem to show this. Even at the early site of West Stow measurements from the largest pig were not incompatible with those for a large domesticated boar, and this situation is paralleled by that at North Elmham.[8] There is no evidence of a wild strain at *Hamwih* where the size of the third molar, taken as diagnostic, is within the domestic size range; nor at Ramsbury.[9]

Swineherds

It was the job of the *inswan* to take the pigs to the wood in the autumn, and 'each *gebur* is to give six loaves to the *inswan* when he drives the pigs to the wood' (*ælc gebur sylle VI hlafas ðam inswa[ne] ðonne he his heorde to mæstene drife*).[10] *Inswan* is glossed as 'the lord's swineherd' (*porcario curie*), but it seems possible that the term could have referred to the pig-keeper associated with the home-farm, hence his fee for driving the pigs to mast – an extra responsibility, perhaps. It seems likely to me that swineherds would have stayed with the pigs once they were in the forest, not least to guard them from predators, including pig rustlers. The Welsh Laws stated that the woods were to be guarded 'from the feast of St. John (29 September) when the

---

[1] Wolters 1967, 404.
[2] Copley 1958, 138.
[3] Cockayne 1851, *Lac.* 82.
[4] Owen 1841, 717.
[5] Cockayne 1851, III, *Prog.*
[6] Holdsworth 1980, 112.
[7] Seebohm 1952, 97.
[8] West 1982, 277.
[9] Holdsworth 1980, 112; Coy in Haslam 1980, 47.
[10] Liebermann 1907, 447.

swine go into the woods, until the 15th day after the Kalends of January'.[1] One manuscript illustrates swineherds, armed with spears, and their dog, driving the pigs into the forest.[2] They also carry horns, perhaps to keep in touch with each other or their dogs, or perhaps to comply with the regulation that anyone leaving the public highway should advertise his presence by blowing a horn, otherwise he might be taken for an outlaw. In one lawsuit over pannage, a number of swineherds seems to have been responsible for pigs in a forest.[3] Pigs of one proprietor were only entitled to forage in two-thirds of the forest, and since there are no references to physical boundaries, the swineherds must have kept the pigs within their assigned areas[4] (see below). It seems likely that pigs may have become used to being herded, and so this was not the difficult job that it might seem. Moryson observed that German pigs 'come home of their own accord without any beating or driving' although they were attended by a swineherd.[5] Wild pigs probably avoided the domestic herds, with their accompanying swineherds and dogs. We know from what the hunter of the *Colloquy* says that there were still wild pigs in the forests, and the Welsh Laws lay down who was to get the meat if one came across a dead wild sow. (It belonged to the owner of the land, but the finder was to have the fore-quarter).[6]

There is evidence that pigs were kept in settlements, perhaps sometimes foraging on the loose, since the Welsh Laws deal with the situation when swine had got into a house and scattered the fire about.[7] There is animal-bone evidence from *Hamwih* that some pigs were tethered by the back leg.[8] The presence of pig is not necessarily an indication of a rural or frontier economy.[9] In York layers of pig manure were found on the Coppergate and Clifford Street sites.[10] At Flaxengate there is a dearth of evidence for pig-breeding, but it seems likely that pigs were brought into the town and fattened on scraps.[11] Certainly in the later medieval period pigs were kept on a 'one per household' basis and fed predominantly on kitchen waste.[12] In about 1422 feeding offal to pigs in the street became punishable, and as late as 1576 it was thought that the Wardens of the Butchers company were keeping pigs near their offal house in London from where they were conveniently slipping them the offal.[13]

There is evidence for sty-husbandry from place-names, e.g. Loscombe, Dorset; Loseley, Surrey; and Loose, Kent, (deriving from O.E. *hlose* – a pig sty); and from *Rectitudines Singularum Personarum*, where 'the swineherd who belongs to the property is entitled to a pig for the sty' (*æhteswane, ðe inhe[or]de healt, gebyreð stifearh*).[14] The sty may have been part of a building complex, or simply an

[1] Owen 1841, II 41.
[2] Cott. Claudius C. VIII; Wright 1871, 82–3.
[3] Robertson 1939, 8–9.
[4] op. cit.
[5] Moryson 1617, IV 29.
[6] Owen 1841, 497.
[7] op. cit., 261.
[8] Holdsworth 1980, 96.
[9] op. cit., 112.
[10] *Med. Archaeol.* XV, 47.
[11] O'Connor 1982.
[12] Wiseman 1986, 9.
[13] Jones 1976, 77–8, 88–90; Sabine 1933, 335–53.
[14] Smith 1970, I 253; Liebermann 1907, 449.

enclosure.[1] In the sty the pig may have been fed on grain to fatten it. In 1306–7, the abbey of Bec at Combe fed the porkers with *beremancorn*, *brotcorn*, peas and vetch. A nursing sow was fed on dregecorn.[2] William of Henley said that pigs needed extra fodder from February to April. The spent grain from the brewhouse – *drasch* – was often used for this.[3] In more recent times pigs were fed on skimmed milk and whey from the dairy, but it seems that this would have been an extravagant proceeding in Anglo-Saxon times. Pommace from cider-making may have been available as in more recent times when it was fed to the Gloucester Old Spot, a primitive breed.[4]

The most important food for the pig was what could be foraged in the woods in autumn. In Anglo-Saxon times the foraging season was from August 29th to the New Year, though after the Conquest the period was shortened to October and November, perhaps because of the decrease of woodland.[5] During this period payment had to be made – in pigs – to the owner of the wood, at other times perhaps pigs could be kept in the woods without payment. Acorns and beech-mast were the most important foods. Acorns of the common English oak, *quercus robur*, or *q. pedunculata* have long been recognised as food for livestock. There are large quantities of digestible carbohydrate in acorns, which are comparable to a mixture of oats and maize, and acorns have about half the nutritional value of barley meal.[6] An excess of acorns can lead to *trousse galante*, a sweating sickness.[7] However, there do not seem to be any specific references to this in the Anglo-Saxon context, and perhaps primitive pigs were not susceptible to it. The rhizomes of bracken are also fairly rich in starch. With a thin top-cover of trees a thick bracken stand will develop a root system of 45 tons an acre within the reach of the rootling pig. The rhizomes of couch grass and other roots also have some nutritional value.[8] This diet certainly seems to have fattened pigs: some Shropshire entries in the Domesday Book have the following formula, *silva* (number) *porcis incrassandis* (woodland for fattening [number] pigs).[9] An evocative image of the fat mast-filled pig occurs in Riddle 40 of the Exeter Book:

> Mara ic eom ond fættra þonne amæsted swin
> bearg bellende *[þe]* on bocwuda
> won wrotende wynnum lifde

I am greater and fatter than the mast-fed pig, the grunting black boar which, rooting around, leads a joyful life in the beechwood.[10]

A single well-grown oak tree would serve to produce well over 100 lbs of pork per year. Pigs fattened on acorns in Portugal can double or triple their weight in three months. The flesh is said to be soft and the fat oily, but the flavour is good.[11] This conflicts with another view, that pork was thought too firm when the pig had fed on

---

[1] Bosworth & Toller 1898, I 919.
[2] Trow-Smith 1957, 117.
[3] Seebohm 1952, 129.
[4] Jones 1988, 431.
[5] Seebohm 1952, 129.
[6] Howes 1948, 175; Trow Smith 1957.
[7] Howes 1948, 175.
[8] Trow Smith 1957.
[9] op. cit.
[10] Gollancz reprint 1972.
[11] Howes 1948, 174, 173.

peas, beans or acorns, because of the high tannin content of these feeds.[1] In any case, considerable attention was paid to acorns and beech-mast: both are specifically mentioned in charters.[2]

Landowners appear to have recognised the importance of preserving the woodlands so they would provide food for pigs and thus be a source of income, 'pannage' (*æfesan*).[3] From as early as the time of Ine, comes the regulation 'If, however, anyone cuts down a tree that can shelter 30 pigs, and it becomes known, he shall pay 60 shillings' (*Gif mon þonne aceorfe an treow þæt mæg xxx swina undergestandan, 7 wryð undierne, geselle LX scill.*).[4] In 866 Burgred, king of the Mercians, granted land with pasturage for seventy swine in the common wood of Wolverley to one Wulferd.[5] Presumably if Wulferd did not choose to run a herd of seventy pigs himself, he could transfer his right and collect payment in pigs. The Council of *Clofesho* in 825 considered a lawsuit about the 'wood pasture' (*wuduleswe*) at Sinton: 'The reeves in charge of the swineherds wanted to extend the pasture, and take in more of the wood than the ancient rights permitted' (*Waldon þa swangerefan þa leswe forðor gedrifan 7 þone wudu geþiogan þonne hit ald geryhta weron*). The bishop and the community of Worcester said they would only allow mast for 300 swine, since they should retain two-thirds of the wood and the mast, and later declared on oath that this is what had been agreed in Æthelbald's day. Hama, the reeve in charge of the swineherds observed, but did not challenge, the oath.[6] The community evidently continued to be concerned about the provision of wood pasture for pigs, since when Oswald was bishop of Worcester in 967 he made an exchange of lands with his brother Osulf in order to provide mast yearly for one hundred swine belonging to the clergy.[7]

At one time the Weald seems to have been used as unenclosed swine-pasture by the Kentish people, but before long portions were assigned to individual manors. In 785 Offa granted some land, with permission to feed swine in the wood of Andred.[8] Ceolwulf I, king of Mercia, granted land at *Mylentun* in Kent in 822, with 'in Andred, food and pasture for swine and cattle or goats in Ewehurst [?], *Sciofingden* and *Snadhyrst*'.[9] In 858 an exchange of land between King Æthelbert of Kent and his thegn, Wulflaf, refers to the swine pastures 'which we call in our language *denbera*, namely *Lamburnan-den, Orricesden, Tilden, Stanehtan-den*, and the wood called Sandhurst'.[10] In a grant by Godwine of swine pasture at *Surrenden* (presumably also in Kent, since the witnesses include ecclesiastics and citizens of Canterbury) in exchange for two pounds and forty pence and eight ambers of corn from Leofwine the Red, the term used is *dænnes*.[11] In 996 King Æthelred granted to his mother Ælfthryth, Brabourne and other estates in Kent. This grant included 'six swine pastures in the Weald which belong to Brabourne: one is Crudenhole, the second Hemsted, the third *Beginge* [Bayden?]; the

---

[1] Wiseman 1986, 80.
[2] Finberg 1972, 87–8, 101, 105, 113.
[3] Cox 1905, 305.
[4] Attenborough 1922, 50–1.
[5] Finberg 1972, 105.
[6] Robertson 1939, 8–9.
[7] Finberg 1972, 113.
[8] Turner 1828, II 54.
[9] Whitelock 1955, 475.
[10] op. cit., 489.
[11] Robertson 1939, 148.

fourth *Hereburne*, the fifth *Strætden*, the sixth *Biddendene*'. The boundaries refer to 'one swine pasture which is called Bingdene' and the grant gives the information that 'this swine pasture belongs to Nackington: *Wigreding* acres'.[1] G.B. Grundy deduces from the frequent occurrence of the suffix -*denn* (swine pasture), as a place-name element in the Kentish part of Andredsweald that this was an important pig-breeding district in Anglo-Saxon England.[2] This seems very likely, but counties to the north and west of Kent also provide evidence of pig-keeping. In 962 Edgar granted his relative Ælfheah ten *cassati* at Sunbury, which had mast for fifty swine annually.[3] In 967 he granted lands to Chertsey monastery, including 30 *mansæ* in Sutton with its swine pastures in Thunderfield Castle; but the 20 *mansæ* he granted in Cheam had swine pastures in the Weald.[4]

At the time of the Domesday survey, some villages had woodland sufficient for 2,000 pigs.[5] A recurrent phrase, or variant of this, in the survey is 'there is wood for ... swine'. Attempts are made to equate woodland area with its swine potential. In Essex ratios range from 15 to 75 pigs per 100 acres, so evidently there were good feeding woods and bad feeding woods. At Lubbesthorpe, Leics., there was 'infertile woodland' (*silva infructosa*). In Rutland at Hambleton and Ketton woods were 'fruitful only in places' (*fertilis per loca*), or of 'little value' (*silva villis*). The numbers of pigs that could be carried at Buxton in Norfolk declined from 1000 in 1066 to 200 twenty years later. At Homersfield, Suffolk, the numbers went down from 600 to 200, and in Essex, at Little Easton, the numbers fell by half, from 800 to 400. The decline in the amount of productive woodland was probably brought about by the clear felling which accompanied charcoal burning and the other industrial uses of timber, and also the expansion of the area of arable land.[6]

Pigs did not have to roam the woods. The dues to the church at Lambourne included free pasture for 40 pigs in wood and open country.[7] And *gærs-swyn* (*id est porcum herbagii* – a pig fed on grass) had to be paid by the *geneat*, according to *Rectitudines Singularum Personarum*.[8] The payment made in return for feeding pigs on grassland seems to have varied from one pig in seven in Sussex, to one pig in ten in parts of Cornwall.[9] Repayment for pig food seems to have been directly related to its quality, the emphasis always being on the fatness of the pig.

Pannage

It seems likely that woods were soon claimed as personal property, and their owners exacted pannage from those who fed their pigs in the woods. The Welsh Laws establish that three things were in common to a country and kindred, hunting, an iron mine, and the mast of woods.[1] Although this meant a pig owner was entitled to take

[1] Whitelock 1955, 531–4.
[2] Bonser 1963, 349.
[3] Gelling 1979, 110.
[4] op. cit., 159.
[5] Bonser 1963, 350.
[6] Trow Smith 1957.
[7] Robertson 1939, 241.
[8] Liebermann 1907, 445.
[9] Seebohm 1952, 97.
[1] Owen 1841, I 533.

his pigs into the woods, he had to make payment to the landowner. Mast was 'free', but this declaration is followed immediately by an interesting legal definition of this term. 'The meaning of that is, if a lord find swine in his wood, from the fifth day before the feast of St. Michael to the fifteenth day after New Year's Day, he is entitled to the tenth animal; and so from one to one to the last. And a proprietor is not to preserve his wood, but from three days before the feast of St. Michael (24 September) to the tenth day after New Year's day; and of the swine he may find in the wood, within that time, let him kill the tenth sow, and he has not the right of killing the swine from one to one, as the lord is entitled to do'.[1] A 'proprietor' presumably did not have the status of a lord, and so his rights were curtailed. As always, the superior in the hierarchy used his position to ensure his food supply. According to other of the Welsh Laws, pannage could be exacted even if the owner of the wood found only three pigs belonging to someone else, so the relatively poor pig farmer would find himself paying a greater proportion of his stock in pannage.[2]

The Laws of Ine deal with the rights of the owner of woodland.

Gif mon on his mæstenne unaliefed swin gemete, genime þonne VI scill. weorþ wed.

l.Gif he þonne þær næren oftor þonne æne, geselle scill. se agenfrigea 7 gecyðe, þæt hie þær oftor ne comen, be þæs ceapes weorðe.

2.Gif hi þær tuwa wæren, geselle twegen scill.

3.Gif mon nime æfesne on swynum æt þryfingrum[spic] þæt ðridde, æt twyfingrum þæt feorðe, æt þrymelum þæt fifte

If anyone finds swine intruding in his mast pasture, he may take security to the value of six shillings.

l.If, however, they have not been there more than once, the owner [of the swine] shall pay a shilling and declare [by an oath equivalent to the value of] the pigs, that they have not been there before.

2.If they have been there twice, he shall pay 2 shillings.

3.If pannage is paid in pigs, every third pig shall be taken when the bacon (?where the fat) is three fingers thick, every fourth when the bacon is two fingers thick, and every fifth when it is a thumb thick.

Towards the end of the Anglo-Saxon period, between 1044–6, King Edward granting land at Chalkhill to Westminster does so 'with mast and pannage' (*mid mæste 7 mid æuesan*). 'And also with this land I likewise grant with full freedom the third tree and the third pig of the pannage of the nearest wood, which belongs to Kingsbury, which is held in common as it was constituted in olden times' (*7 æac swycle to þeosum lande mid fullan freodome ic ann þ þridde treow 7 þ þridde swiin. of æuesan þæs nextan wudes þe lið to Kyngesbyrig. se is gemæne swa he onn ældum timum gelegd wæs*).[3] According to the survey of Tidenham, Gloucs., it was the rule that he who had seven pigs should give three as pannage, and thereafter always the tenth, and, in spite of this, should pay for the right of having mast when

---

[1] op. cit., II 269.
[2] op. cit., II 41.
[3] Harmer 1952, 344–5.

there was mast. According to Domesday, on Sussex manors one pig in seven or in ten was paid to the lord as pannage. Archbishop Lanfranc's manor of Malling yielded 300 pigs from the pannage.[1]

Early documentation indicates the king had the right to call on other landowners to provide food for the royal pigs. A grant by Æthelweard, king of the Hwicce, to Bishop Ecgwine in 706, of an estate at Ombersley, frees it of all secular dues 'except that if the island belonging to the estate shall bring forth an unusually large crop of acorns, beech-mast (sic) sufficient for one herd of swine shall be contributed to the royal provender-rent'.[2] This implied that the acorns/beech-mast were gathered and transported to the pigs. This situation seems to have applied in Wales too. One of the three *motes* of mutual protection was mast gathering: 'herein the hand of everyone is to assist according to his ability'.[3] In 855 Burgred, king of the Mercians, exempted Alhuun, bishop of Worcester's three hides in Bentley 'which is called fern pasture' from the pasturing of the king's swine.[4] Fern roots are one of the foods specifically mentioned as being eaten by pigs when they are free to forage.[5]

Place-Name Evidence

Bær in West Saxon, *ber* in Kentish, meant 'pasture, especially in woodland; a woodland feeding ground for swine'. The element occurs only in Old English charters, although the compounds *den-bær*, *weald-bær* and *wudu-bær* are common, and equate with *pascua* and *pascua porcorum* (swine pasture). It is particularly common in the southern counties from Kent to Devon, although it is usually impossible to distinguish it from *beoru* (a wood, grove). Beer in Dorset and Somerset, Bere in Hants. and Stockbury, Kent, are place-names derived from this element.[6] The name Tenterden, means 'swine pasture of the men of Thanet', and makes it clear that this Wealden settlement was an offshoot from villages in a region that was among the first occupied by the Anglo-Saxons.[7] Hognaston, Derbyshire, may contain the element *æfsn* (swine pasturage, pannage).[8] A grant by Æthelheard, king of Wessex, to Forthhere, bishop of Sherborne, of land at Crediton in 739, refers to *Swincumb*.[9] In 846 a grant by Æthelwulf, king of Wessex, of land to himself, refers to the old swine enclosure. This was on land at South Hams, Devon.[10] The will of King Alfred (873–88) refers to an assembly at *Swinbeorg*, a place which has not been positively identified.[11] Swineshead, Beds., Gloucs., Lancs., Wilts., etc., may have been a totem name. The element *bar*, meaning a boar, wild or domestic, is fairly common, though it is not found combined with *tun*; Barley, Lancs., and Barlow, Derbyshire, are examples of such place-names.[1] Among the Germanic tribes oaths were sworn with

[1] op. cit., 498.
[2] Finberg 1972, 87–8.
[3] Owen 1841, 477.
[4] Finberg 1972, 104.
[5] Zeuner 1963, 267.
[6] Smith 1970, I 16, 22.
[7] Copley 1958, 170.
[8] Smith 1970, I 3.
[9] Whitelock 1955, 457.
[10] op. cit., 483.
[11] op. cit., 493.
[1] op. cit., 19.

the oath takers' hands on the back of boars, and boar-crested helmets seem to have had a special significance (see below).[1]

Swineherds

The swineherd, together with the bee-keeper, had pride of place among the specialists on the Anglo-Saxon estate, according to *Rectitudines Singularum Personarum*. Like the bee-keeper, the self-employed swineherd was also to keep a horse for his lord's use. His duties are given in some detail:

> *Gafolswane gebyreð, þæt he sylle his slyht, be ðam ðe on landum stent. On manegum landum stent, þæt he sylle ælce geare XV swyn to sticunge, X ealde 7 V gynge – hæbbe sylf, þæt he ofer þæt arære –; on mangum landum gebyreð deopre swanriht.*

> The swineherd who pays tribute has to provide pigs ready for slaughter according to the rule on the particular estate. In many places he has to provide annually 15 pigs for slaughter, ten old and 5 young, from those he has bred himself; but in many other places the demands on him are heavier.[2]

The swineherd whose job it was to look after the lord's herd of pigs received some perquisites, since he had no pigs of his own, like the *gafolswane*:

> *Æhteswane, ðe inhe[or]de healt, gebyreð stifearh 7 his gewirce, ðonne he s[p]ic behworfen hæfð, 7 elles ða gerihtu, ðe ðeowan men to gebyriað.*

> The swineherd who looks after the lord's herd of the pigs on his estate is entitled to a pig from the sty, and the entrails [?], when he has seen to the bacon/lard, and otherwise he has the same rights as other slaves.[3]

This is very similar to the swineherd's payment on the Glastonbury estates in the twelfth century. He received one sucking pig every year, and the entrails of the best pig, but also the tails of all pigs slaughtered, presumably to make pig-tail soup, which was regarded as something of a delicacy.[4] It is possible that the swineherds put the entrails to use in making sausages, since filling intestines with chopped meat is first mentioned as a Graeco-Roman practice.[5] *The Assignments of Property to Thorney Abbey* put a value on a swineherd:

> *þonne dyde man æf[te]r ðæm hundeahtatig swyna 7 þone swan from Middeltune . . . þa geeahtade man þa [swi]ne to oðran healfan punde 7 þone swan to healfan pund*

> after that 80 swine and the swineherd were transferred from Milton . . . the pigs were valued at one and a half pounds and the swineherd at half a pound.[6]

A swineherd then was equated with 26 or 27 pigs.

---

[1] Whittock 1986, 148; Meaney 1981, 133.
[2] Liebermann 1907, 449.
[3] op.cit.
[4] Wiseman 1986, 4.
[5] Zeuner 1963, 263.
[6] Robertson 1939, 252–5.

Swineherds are listed in the Domesday survey: 296 for Devon, 87 for Wiltshire, 57 for Somerset, 23 for Surrey, 14 for Herefordshire, and 7 in Cambridgeshire.[1] This presumably reflects the concentration of pigs in the southern counties. In the counties where the population of pigs can be calculated, there are generally far fewer than sheep, but the survey does not take into account the pigs of free and servile sub-tenants.[2] In the wooded valleys of the Exe and Creedy there were probably herds of some thousands of pigs. The bishop of Exeter's great manor of Crediton contained 30 swineherds who paid a rent of 150 swine a year. At Bampton, for example, there were 15 swineherds paying 105½ swine, and at Bishop's Tawton 22 swineherds paying 100 swine. At Forthampton, Gloucs., 4 swineherds rendered 35 pigs from those they pastured in the royal wood, which was 9 square leagues in extent. At Hanley Castle, Worcs., 6 swineherds rendered 60 swine.[3]

Values

In the Laws of Æthelstan the domestic animals are given monetary values.

> *7 oxan to mancuse 7 cu to xx 7 swyn to x 7 sceap to scll.*

> An ox shall be valued at a mancus, and a cow at 20 pence, a pig at 10 pence and a sheep at a shilling.[4]

The amendments to the laws of Edward the Elder and Æthelstan at *Dunsættan* reduced the value of the pig. The new values were an ox at 30 pence, a cow at 24 pence, a pig at 8 pence, while the sheep remained at a shilling.[5] *The Assignments of Property to Thorney Abbey* seems to indicate a value of six pence for pigs:

> *man sealde fram Hæþfelda xxx ealdra swyna ælce [t]o vi pænegum ofer*

> 30 full-grown swine were given from Hatfield, each over . . . worth six pence.[6]

Leis Willelme gave the values of the male breeding animals:

> *En la were purra il rendre cheval ki ad la coille pur xx sol., e tor pur x sol., e ver pur v sol*

> In payment for wergild he can give a stallion as 20 shillings, and a bull at ten shillings and a boar at 5 shillings.[7]

The Welsh Laws seem to have equated the values of pigs and sheep since to deny a horseload took the oaths of six men, but to deny a swine or sheep (or backburden) took the oaths of five men.[8] The Welsh Laws differentiated between pigs at various stages in their growth, so that a pig in a litter was worth one penny. From the time it went out until it was weaned it was worth 2 pence, then it was worth 4 pence until the feast of St. John when it was worth 10 pence until the calends of January. Ultimately it was worth 30 pence, although a boar was worth three times this amount.[1] A *tæog* was not to sell swine without his lord's permission, and horses, pigs and honey all had to be

---

[1] Turner 1828, III 255.
[2] Trow Smith 1957.
[3] op. cit.
[4] Attenborough 1922, 11.
[5] op. cit., 214.
[6] Robertson 1939, 252–5.
[7] Loyn 1970, 293.
[8] Owen 1841, 243.
[1] op. cit., 717, 277.

offered to the lord in preference to another.[1] If a couple parted, the husband was to have the pigs and the wife the sheep, and one of the privileges of Arvon was that the man was to have the pigs before the woman had a choice.[2]

Pigs were certainly valuable enough to be rustled. Sometime before 995 Æthelsige forfeited 2½ hides of land in Dumbleton, Gloucs., to the king, because he stole the swine of Æthelwine, the son of Ealdorman Æthelmær, whose men rode to Æthelsige's house and brought out the bacon, while Æthelsige escaped to the wood.[3]

Pigs in Food Rents

In some places in Anglo-Saxon England the 'free tenant' (*geneat*) had to render 'a grass-fed pig annually' (*gærsswyn on gære*) to his lord.[4] At Tidenham, Gloucs., the manor survey states

> *On ðam sylfum lande stent se ðe vii swyn hæbbe þ he sylle iii 7 swa forð a þ teoþe 7 ðæs napulæs mæstenrædene þonne mæsten beo*

> On that same estate it is the rule that he who has seven pigs shall pay three and thereafter always the tenth, and in spite of this shall pay for the right of having mast when there is mast.[5]

The dues rendered to the church at Lambourne included 'the tenth young pig' (*þæt teoþe fearh*) and at Martinmas 'a pig' (*an swyn*).[6] Pigs are mentioned in food rents like that to be paid by King Edward the Elder for a lease of land at Beddington, Surrey, namely one hundred and fourteen pigs (plus nine full-grown oxen and fifty wethers) and twenty flitches of bacon.[7] A food rent due to Bury St. Edmunds included 'ten flitches ... to be ready by September 4th' (*x fliccen ... þ sceal beon gære on pridie NONAS Septembrio*). Abbot Leofstan added 'six flitches and another six to complete it, to the old food rent' (*vi fliccen 7 oþer vi to fyllinge into þan ealdan fyrme*).[8] Abbot Baldwin granted to his brethren 'two fat pigs for lard, or three ores' (*II fætte swyn ... to smolte oððe III oran*). Later this was amended to 'two fat pigs or four shillings for lard' (*II porcos pingues aut IIII sol. ad saginam*).[9] The food rent to Bury St. Edmunds from Barton included two pigs, and 'half a pig' (*an half swin*) was due from Tivetshall.[10] In return for a lease of land, Denewulf, bishop of Winchester had to pay, *inter alia*, 'four pigs and four flitches' (*feower swin 7 feor fliccu*).[11]

Royal food rents recorded in the Welsh Laws refer to pigs a number of times. Part of the *gwesta* from a free *mænol* in winter was a three-year old swine, and a salted flitch of three-finger breadths in thickness; a bond *mænol* had to pay just the three-year old pig.[1] The king's summer *dawnbywrds* included a sow of three winters with fat three

[1] op. cit., 79, II 345, 265.
[2] op. cit., 81, 107.
[3] Whitelock 1955, 530.
[4] Liebermann 1907, 445.
[5] Robertson 1939, 241.
[6] op. cit., 241.
[7] Whitelock 1955, 501.
[8] Robertson 1939, 193.
[9] op. cit., 197, 199.
[10] op. cit., 199.
[11] op. cit., 39.
[1] Owen 1841, I 199.

fingers thick; the *dawnbywrds* from the villeins included a sow three fingers thick in her hams, ribs and gammons, and a flitch of salted bacon.[1] The winter *dawnbywrd* was a sow of three fingers thick in her shoulder, and in the long ribs or in the ham, and a salted flitch.[2]

Assignments of Property

*The Assignments of Property to Thorney and St. Edmunds Abbey*s give some idea of the importance of the pig. The first extract uses the terms 'mature pigs' (*ealdra swin*), 'hogs – pigs in their second year' (*hogga*) and 'young pigs – pigs in their first year' (*geongra swin*).

> *Æt byryg xlvii ealdra swin 7 cc geongra bu[tun] ðrim; æt Strætham xx sugen[a] æt . . . xx sugena 7 l hogga; æt Horningesige xviii [eal]de swyn 7 xl hogga; æt . . . 7 xliiij hogga; æt Hafucestune xxx ealdra swyna 7 c hogga butun i; æ[t] [M]eldeburnan xxiij suge[na]; Of þære heorde þe Alfwold heold æt Hæðfelda xiii sige 7 lxxxiij [ge]ongra swina; 7 Ælfnod [of] þære oþre heorde xiiij sige 7 lx hogga . . . Þa man betæhte Ælfnoðe þone folgað æt Hæðfel[da] þa wæs þær xl oxana . . . þrydde healf hund sceapa xlvii gata 7 xv cealfra cc [swin]a(?) butun x; xliii flicca*

At St. Etheldreda's burh 47 full-grown swine and 200 young ones all but 3, at Stretham 20 sows, at . . . 20 sows and 50 hogs; at Horningsea 18 full-grown swine and 40 hogs; at . . . and 44 hogs; at Hauxton 30 full-grown swine and 100 hogs all but one; at Melbourne 23 sows; from the herd of which Ælfwold had charge at Hatfield 13 sows (?) and 83 young swine, and Ælfnoth from the other herd 14 sows and 60 hogs . . . When Ælfnoth was entrusted with his office at Hatfield there were 40 oxen there . . . 250 sheep, 47 goats and 15 calves, 200 swine all but 10 and 43 flitches of bacon.[3]

An inventory of the stock at Yaxley included 'thirty pigs and 100 flitches and all the delicacies that go with them . . . and one fat pig' (*xxx swina 7 hundteongig fliccena 7 eal þa smean ðe þerto gebyriað . . . 7 i fedelswin*).[4] [Unfortunately there is no clue as to what the 'delicacies' included: lard, perhaps, or meat puddings or sausages.] 'A hundred pigs and seven hundred flitches' (*hundteontig swina . . . sifon hund flicca*) are recorded elsewhere.[5] In comparison stock at Egmere after Cole left it seems to have been more than a little depleted, with only 'one flitch and one pig' (*i flicce 7 i swin*).[6] A lease by bishop Denewulf of Winchester to Edmund the Elder (899–908) included an inventory of the stock 'which has survived this severe winter . . . 9 full-grown oxen, and 114 full-grown pigs and 50 wethers besides the sheep and the pigs which the herdsmen have a right to have, 20 of which are full-grown; and there are 110 full-grown sheep and 7 bondsmen and 20 flitches'.[1]

---

[1] op. cit., 533.
[2] op. cit., 771.
[3] Robertson 1939, 254–7.
[4] op. cit., 74.
[5] op. cit., 249.
[6] op. cit., 197.
[1] Whitelock 1955, 501.

Wills

The largest number of pigs mentioned in a document seems to be the 2000 pigs, bequeathed to his wife and daughter, along with land, in the will, dated between 871 and 888, of Ealdorman Alfred, who held lands in Kent and Surrey, counties which have previously been mentioned in connection with extensive pig husbandry.[1] His son Æthelwold was to receive three hides and 100 pigs; his kinsman Brihtsige one hide and 100 pigs. His wife was to give 100 swine to Christchurch, and another hundred to Chertsey, 'the surplus to be divided among the monasteries of God's churches in Surrey and Kent'.[2] Pigs are the only animals specifically referred to in this will. Æthelgifu's mid-tenth-century will bequeaths numbers of sheep and cattle as well as six herds of pigs, most with a swineherd, which seem to have been run in the wooded areas of Ashridge and Gaddesden in Herts., and the Ivel valley between Clifton and Henlow in Beds.[3] Leofsige, a major beneficiary, received a herd of pigs, a swineherd and the land at Tewin as swine pasture, and six pigs were included in the annual food rent he was to pay to St. Alban's.[4] Ælfgifu and Leofwine each received a herd of swine with a swineherd.[5] In one case the swineherd who had served Æthelgifu was to be freed, and his son was to go with the herd. According to the will of Æthelwyrd, one day's food rent was to be paid at Michaelmas to the community at Christchurch, and this included a flitch of bacon.[6] Another similar grant included eight gammons.[7] A fragment of a will from Bury St. Edmunds refers to:

> 7 hoþær hæræ at an flychca 7 seuentene peniges at an swin

and another ore for a flitch of bacon and seventeen pence for a pig.

This was part of the provisioning for a funeral feast.[8]

The Animal Bone Record

The animal bone record presents a number of problems. The higher rate of decay of pigs bones has been commented on.[9] One contributory factor is that pigs were generally killed younger than other animals, before the epiphysis fused, and the porous bone is more liable to decay, and less likely to be recovered.[10] Pig meat was very often eaten salted and salt pork produces no bones at the point of consumption. Salt pork was known to have been the principle source of meat for Fort Lingonier, USA, from 1758–66, but this left no trace in the faunal remains.[1] The observation has been made that the lack of large numbers of pig bones from Anglo-Saxon sites is perhaps because the meat was customarily eaten boned and salted.[2]

---

[1] op. cit., 496.
[2] op. cit.
[3] Whitelock 1968, 6–10.
[4] op. cit., 8–11.
[5] op. cit.
[6] Robertson 1939, 59.
[7] Turner 1828, II 547.
[8] Robertson 1939, 253.
[9] Arnold 1984, 71.
[10] Grant unpublished Animal Bone Report on Bedford Excavations, Bedford Museum.
[1] Prummel 1983, 66.
[2] Clutton Brock in DM Wilson 1976, 378.

When remains of pig have been recovered, there may be doubt about how to interpret their presence. The hams buried in the Vendel graves of Uppland in Sweden presumably reflected the use of the pig as a food animal.[1] However, the significance of pig teeth, even when these have not been perforated, in Anglo-Saxon graves, may be amuletic, rather than representative of a food deposit.[2] Pigs buried in a cremation cemetery at Illingworth, Norfolk, may have been totemic, signifying that the adolescents with whom they were buried had been swineherds.[3] At Frilford the head of a pig was buried in a pagan cemetery, and perhaps indicated a boar cult.[4]

It is difficult to avoid inferences based on present-day tastes and eating habits. For example, in Viking Age York, bones representing the 'poorer parts' of pigs, in particular heads and feet (together with the heads and feet of cattle and most parts of sheep) were recovered from the floor of a Viking-age building. The fact that metapodial bones – from pigs' trotters – were sometimes present in great numbers adds weight to a story of 'scrupulous making do'.[5] This may have been the case, but trotters may equally have been something of a delicacy. They were certainly well-regarded in the medical literature. 'Pigs' feet' (*swines fet*) being slow to digest were good for a sensitive stomach.[6] Elsewhere the *Leechbook* states 'the extremities of the limbs of swine are easy to digest' (*þa ytmestan leomo swina beð eaðmelte*).[7] The boar's head is still considered something of a speciality, and even if the heads were boiled, rather than roasted as the centre-piece of a feast, the brawn made from them was a delicacy. MS Cott. Claud B4 shows an illustration of a boar's head at a feast. Trotters may have been present at Coppergate because they were not salted, and the meat of other joints was stripped from the bone at the place of slaughter. Salt pork may have been eaten, and so may boneless joints of beef.

An important problem when it comes to comparing the importance of pork in the diet on different sites is that the data is recorded in different ways: percentage of bone fragments, of the weight of bone, minimum numbers, and percentage of meat provided, are the most usual forms, but comparison of like with like is not always, or indeed often, possible.

Age of Pigs at Slaughter

On the early (fifth- to seventh-century) site of West Stow, most pigs were killed when their second and third molars were in early wear, representing pigs in approximately their second and third years of life. The highest mortality was in the early third year – about the stage at which the pig reached bodily maturity. Continuing to feed the animal beyond this stage would not substantially increase its body weight or meat yield, so killing pigs at this stage maximised the meat yield to fodder input ratio. The second peak of mortality corresponded to mid-adolescence.[1] Newborn and young piglets were also killed as the farmer selected runts, weak and sickly pigs for early

[1] Zeuner 1963, 263.
[2] Meaney 1981, 132–3.
[3] Wells 1960.
[4] Whittock 1986, 148; Meaney 1981, 133.
[5] O'Connor 1984, 26.
[6] Cockayne 1851, II i 1.
[7] op. cit., II xvi 2.
[1] Crabtree in Biddick 1984, 227–8.

slaughter.[1] It is possible that sucking pig was a delicacy: on the continent roasted sucking pig was sometimes buried in rich Germanic graves.[2] As with the sheep and cattle, numbers of West Stow pigs were younger at death than those from other large Saxon sites. At a rural site like West Stow, one would expect to see a wide range of age classes, including a larger number of young pigs not needed to maintain the breeding stock. The West Stow area was not ideal pig country: the nearest wooded area was several miles from the site. Substantial amounts of food would have been needed to supplement the pannage available, and the practice of sty husbandry would have provided a strong economic motive to eliminate excess animals. The figures for the pigs' ages at death contrasts strongly with those from North Elmham. During the middle Saxon period 50–85% of the N. Elmham pigs were mature, more than four years old at the time of death, and many were elderly, with heavy wear on all teeth. The explanation given is that, during the Saxon period the pigs were almost wild and difficult to catch when young. However, the presence of such a large number of mature pigs is atypical for a Saxon site. At North Elmham in the post-medieval period the proportion of mature pigs dropped to 20%, when they were probably kept in sties. At West Stow the high proportion of young animals killed and the availability of fodder may well indicate the practice of sty husbandry at an early date.[3] The age distribution in the pig kill patterns is most similar to those at a number of Roman sites, which suggests a continuity in exploitation practice.[4]

At seventh-century Puddlehill, Beds., the settlement site of a family group of minor aristocracy or middle-class West Saxons, 40% of the pigs were eaten when immature, at a prime age for eating, and none of the animals were old.[5] The West Stow peak killing period is also paralleled by evidence from mid-Saxon Ramsbury, Wilts., where probably only a few pigs survived to be more than 2–3 years old and this is not dissimilar to the situation at the mid-Saxon site of Melbourne Street, Southampton.[6] At *Hamwih* the pigs were likewise killed young, although 26.6% of the pig mandibles had all the cheek teeth in wear.[7] This situation was paralleled by that at the contemporary and similar continental urban settlement of Dorestad.[8] At Dorestad, however, only 9% of the pigs were slaughtered when older than 3–3½ years, and this is seen as evidence that the townspeople were producing some of their pork themselves.[1] Presumably, since there is a greater proportion of mature pigs at *Hamwih*, so were the townsfolk there.

On the later site of Flaxengate, Lincoln, the modal age of slaughter fell from 2–3 years before the mid-eleventh-century to 1–2 years after this date (at the same time as there was a decline in the slaughter age of sheep), and the lower slaughter age of pigs was maintained through subsequent centuries. This might suggest that some improvement in the breed may have been made, but the pigs in the later sample were – if anything – smaller, which suggests the change in the slaughter pattern was

---

[1] op. cit., 228.
[2] Zeuner 1963, 263.
[3] Crabtree in Biddick 1984, 228.
[4] op. cit., 229.
[5] Hawkes et al. 1985, 103.
[6] Coy in Haslam 1980, 46–7.
[7] Bourdillon 1980, 112, 184.
[8] Prummel 1983, 210.
[1] op. cit., 211.

due to economic pressures alone.[1] At Exeter too most of the pigs – 79% – were killed in their second and third years, only 8% surviving longer than three years. The peak age for slaughter was 16–26 months, with most of these pigs killed in the earlier part of the range.[2] On the late Saxon sites in Bedford pigs seem usually to have been killed at 1 to 2½ years old, with only a few bones coming from animals 2½ to 3½ years old.[3]

The evidence from Portchester typifies the changes on other sites over the period. From the fifth to eighth centuries 25% of pigs were killed between 1 and 1½ years old, 50% between 2 and 3½ years old. In the middle and late periods these figures were reversed, so that 50% were killed between a year and eighteen months old, and only 25% between 2 and 3½ years old. Relatively few pigs were kept longer than 3½ years.[4] Perhaps the earlier age of slaughter in the late Saxon period was caused by pressure on the food resources, or probably in a more prosperous economy preferences for younger carcasses could be indulged. It would seem that there would be nothing to be gained by keeping pigs beyond the age of thirty months or so, unless they were kept to have the benefit of an autumn season when a diet of mast and acorns would cause them to put on fat.

Fat carcasses were easier to preserve than lean ones, and were preferred. The household pig may have had its slaughter delayed until Christmas or some other festival, but it is more likely that a group of neighbours would kill their pigs in rotation, sharing the perishable offal after each slaughter.

Pig Bones as a Proportion of Animal Bone Assemblages

The early Dark Age site of Dinas Powys in Wales yielded 61% of pig bones from a midden, and only 20% of cattle and 13% of sheep bones.[5] These proportions are exceptional, and seemed to indicate that Celtic husbandry was different to Anglo-Saxon farming. However, when the complete assemblage was assessed identified fragments were: cattle 50.67%, sheep 24.43% and pig 24.76%.[6] At the early site of Yeavering in Northumbria pig bones were much less important than those of cattle.[7] At Old Down Farm, Hants., only 8% of the bones were of pig, which may indicate that little woodland was available for pannage.[1] In any case the faunal assemblage is unusual in that the proportion of sheep bones is very high.[2] The site could have been based on a shepherd's hut, although the animal bone assemblage is not so different to the early settlement at Bishopstone, where pig made up 19%. Although the proportion of pig bone is still small, it represents an increase from the Roman period.[3] The Old

[1] O'Connor 1982.
[2] Maltby 1979.
[3] *Beds. Archaeol. J.* 13; 72, 94, 105.
[4] Cunliffe 1976, 280.
[5] Davies 1982, 39.
[6] Alcock 1987, 34, 81–2.
[7] Hope-Taylor 1977, 326.
[1] Arnold 1984, 171.
[2] Davies 1980, 177.
[3] Arnold 1984, 72.

Down Farm percentage is paralleled by the figures for Sedgeford, Sandtun and Mawgan Porth (7.6%, 8.7% and 3.2% respectively). In all cases pigs are third to sheep and ox.[1]

This order of importance is different at the late seventh- to ninth-century site of *Hamwih* where the ratios by fragment count are cattle:sheep:pigs – 53:32:15, by bone weight 72:15:12. The high ratio of cattle to pigs is the strongest indication of the substantial provisioning of the town. At Hedeby the ratio was 1.25:1 by fragment count, changing to 1.5:1. Early Stettin and Wollin started with a strong predominance of pigs over cattle, but as these towns developed, the balance was sharply reversed, but even *Hamwih*'s early pits give 2.5:1, and the later pits, 5:1. At Dorestad the overall ratio for the settlement was as high as the *Hamwih* peak.[2]

The pits at *Hamwih* yielded 15.3% of pig bone (by minimum numbers count the percentage of pigs reaches 28.5%). On the surface the percentage of bone was 21.9%. What was left on the occupation surface was presumably fairly late, and possibly pig was relatively more important in the late days of *Hamwih*, or perhaps more remains were then left lying around than were buried.[3] It is possible that pigs were run in the New Forest and transported to *Hamwih* and other towns as flitches, leaving no trace in the archaeological record. Bones could be fed to surviving pigs.

At the urban site of Melbourne Street, Southampton, the proportion of pig bone was less than at the more rural site of Ramsbury which dated from approximately the same period.[4] This suggests that location was the most important factor in determining the proportion of pork in the diet.

The more usual West Saxon cattle, sheep, pig order is not found at the East Anglian settlements of West Stow or North Elmham. At West Stow pig are still third in the order, but numerically sheep predominate.[5] There was an increase in the proportion of sheep/goat and a corresponding decrease of pig in the sixth century, but this was followed by a reversal of these trends in the seventh century. This may represent responses to altered circumstances, such as access to and availability of forest pasture. The West Stow assemblage compares well with that from North Elmham.[6] Here pig is again second to sheep at 28%.[7]

Approximately ten percent of pig bones were found at Flaxengate as compared to the bones of cattle and sheep together. This proportion remains fairly constant from c.870 to 1100. As the proportions of cattle and sheep alter considerably during this period, whatever influenced their availability did not apply to the pig. It is suggested that pigs were kept at the household level and not farmed on a larger scale. Cats and dogs, reared and kept by the households, were likewise consistently present.[1] Ten percent (or less) is the figure for pig bones on the Lloyds, Barclays Bank and Hart's Store sites in urban York also.[2] In tenth-century Skeldergate, York, pig was third in importance to ox and

[1] Clutton Brock in DM Wilson 1976, 377.
[2] Bourdillon 1980, 183–4.
[3] Holdsworth 1980, 104, 112.
[4] Coy in Haslam 1980, 46.
[5] Crabtree in Biddick 1984, 223.
[6] West 1982, 269, 273.
[7] Clutton Brock in DM Wilson 1976, 377.
[1] O'Connor 1982.
[2] *Med. Archaeol.* XV, 47.

sheep.[1] This was the situation also at sites in Bedford where the ratio of beef:mutton:pork on the ninth- to thirteenth-century site of St. John's has been calculated as 6:3:1.[2] At Exeter from 1000–1150 (calculated according to minimum numbers) pigs made up 25–19%, from 1000–1200, 18.82%, providing between 8 and 12 percent of the meat. This compares with a percentage of 6.61% for pigs on demesne lands in Devon according to the Domesday Survey. However, the survey clearly does not record all the pigs, since there are instances of manors where swineherds are mentioned, but there would appear to be no pigs.[3] At Portchester the percentage of pig bones remains a fairly constant 13%–16% from the fifth to the eleventh centuries.[4] Pork provided about 20% of the meat, and pigs were more numerous than cattle and almost as numerous as sheep with the possible exception of the earliest period.[5] At Cheddar before 930 pig provided 29% of the meat, and was second in importance to ox. This proportion is only very slightly increased (to 30.1%) in the period from 930 to the eleventh century. In the later eleventh century to the early thirteenth century pig was third to ox and sheep.[6] At Beckery Chapel pig provided a 'good part of the meat diet'.[7] It would appear that the more rural the settlement, the more likely it would be to be close to substantial woodlands, as at Cheddar, and the higher the proportion of pigs would be. The impression is of a slight increase in the percentage of pigs through the period, although the one continuously occupied (and published) site of Portchester does not bear this out.[8]

Pigs in Leechdoms

As might perhaps be expected pigs' grease is prescribed for external use in a number of salves: Cockayne 1851, I iv 5, xii, xx, xxi, xii, for example, and Schaumann & Cameron *Anglia* XCV 292. Two of these leechdoms specify 'old grease' (*ealdne rysele*). 'Fresh pig meat' (*geonge swines flæsce*) together with vegetables in a broth is recommended, and 'half-grown pigs' (*healfeald swin*) were considered good for the blood.[9] In one case 'fresh pork' (*fe[r]sc swin*) is to be avoided, although salt pork was acceptable.[10] In another case pork was to be avoided altogether, and a pregnant was not to eat *swines flæsc*.[1] This is the only food to be specifically prohibited, though she was enjoined against consuming salt, sweet or fatty foods or drinking *beor*. In the literature the pig was seen as a masculine symbol: heroes' helmets were 'boar-adorned', and one such helmet was discovered at Benty Grange, Derbyshire, which might explain such a prohibition.[2] Other leechdoms call for a 'boar's or pig's hoof' (*eofores clawa* or *swines clawa*) to be burned to ashes and taken in liquid.[3] The bladder of a 'a sow that has not yet had a litter, that is, a gilt' (*swines untydrendes þ is*

[1] O'Connor 1984, 16.
[2] *Beds. Archaeol. J.* 13; 70, 94, 125.
[3] Maltby 1979, 15ff.
[4] Cunliffe 1976, 263.
[5] op. cit., 284.
[6] Rahtz 1979, 356.
[7] Noddle in Rahtz and Hirst 1974, 39.
[8] Cunliffe 1976, 263.
[9] Cockayne 1851, II xxx, xxxvii.
[10] op. cit., I xxxvi.
[1] op. cit., II xliii, III xxxvii.
[2] Wilson 1960, 120–1, etc., pl. 28 & 29.
[3] Cockayne 1851, I xxxvii, II xxxii.

gylte) is to be utilised in the same way.[1] To avoid against intoxication Pliny's (surely ineffectual) instructions are repeated: 'take a pig's lung, roast it, and at night fasting take five slices always' (*genim swines lungenne gebræd 7 on neaht nestig genim fif snæda simle*).[2]

Conclusion

The pig is generally associated with the poorer classes, and most households may have kept at least one pig although the pig does not have the very poor/rural connotation of sheep.[3] However, they were run in herds on the estates of the aristocracy, and in such numbers that some must have been sold for meat. The will referring to the funeral feast implies pork and bacon could be bought easily and that they were feast food.[4] In post-Conquest times Ipswich was doing a thriving trade in the export of bacon.[5] Perhaps the basis for this trade had been set up in the Anglo-Saxon period. Traders were allowed to buy three live pigs, and lard, at the port of London to provision their ships according to a law code of about 1000.[6]

Pigs would have been important to the Anglo-Saxons as a source of essential fat.[7] How much of the carcass of a Dark Age pig was fat can only be guessed at, though this may have been about 10–15%.[8] For this reason fat pigs were particularly valued, as food rents indicate, and this continued to be the case into the seventeenth century when an immensely fat sow was sold for the proportionately large price of fifty guldens.[9] The fat in the meat would have provided calories, which would have otherwise have had to be derived from lean meat, nutritionally more valuable as a source of protein. Presumably for this reason early recipes generally contained a high proportion of fat.[10] The fat from pigs was used to lard other roast and boiled meats fish.[11]

Because of its high proportion of fat, pig meat was comparatively easy to preserve and was important because it could be preserved. This is no doubt why flitches are mentioned in inventories, while the carcasses of sheep or cattle are not, and why the emphasis seems to have been on bacon and lard production.

Pigs were also valuable because they did not compete with man for food, being fattened primarily on woodland or grass, rather than grain.[1] They would be in better condition than other stock in late winter since they could find natural forage, and may have been useful for fresh meat at a time of year unfavourable for the slaughter of ruminants. Corsican pigs live very much as Anglo-Saxon pigs are likely to have done, and the pig meat is used mainly for the production of specialist preserved products,

---

[1] op. cit., I xxxvii.
[2] op. cit., I lxxx.
[3] Bonser 1963, 249–50; Wiseman 1986, viii.
[4] Robertson 1939, 253.
[5] Poole 1958, 227.
[6] Whitelock 1955, 119.
[7] Wiseman 1986, 5.
[8] Prummel 1983, 261.
[9] Moryson 1617, IV 29.
[10] Ayrton 1975, 18.
[11] Moryson 1617, IV 29; Robertson 1939, 199.
[1] Wiseman 1986, 5.

some of which may resemble the 'delicacies' referred to in the Anglo-Saxon sources.[1] There seems to be some evidence that numbers of pigs were slaughtered in November, but the numbers killed at other times of the year in combination was as high or higher than the November figure, at least in *Hamwih* and Dorestad.[2] Other sites, for example seventh-century Puddlehill, Beds., gave no evidence of autumn killing.[3]

---

[1] op. cit., 176.
[2] Prummel 1983, 212.
[3] Hawkes et al. 1985, 103.

124

8. Poultry and Eggs

Rich early continental Germanic graves contained fowl and piglets: the latter was definitely considered a luxury food, and so poultry is likely to have been a prestige food too.[1] This impression of a luxury food is reinforced by the fact that poultry was exacted by those who could call on food rents. Poultry is mentioned from the earliest references. Legal documents refer to hens and geese. In the Laws of Ine 688–694, the food rent from ten hides includes ten geese and twenty hens.[2] The food rent from Barton to Bury St. Edmunds Abbey included *iiii ges and xx hennen*, that from Tivetshall, *an gos 7 v hennan*.[3] Incidentally this 1:5 ratio is very close to that found at Exeter, where 72.08% of the bird fragments were of domestic fowl, and 14.86% were of geese.[4] The will of Æthelwyrd left one day's food rent to the community at Christchurch to be paid at Michaelmas, and this included *iiii hæn fugulas*.[5] The *gebur* in *Rectitudines Singularum Personarum* had to pay 'two hens at Martinmas' (*on Martinus mæssedæg . . . II henfugelas*), as well as other dues.[6] The fact that numbers are so small and the amount of food provided so tiny, suggests poultry was the delicacy that it remained until recently.[7]

Some idea of how common poultry keeping became, is suggested by the Gwentian Code which gives the 'three signs of the inhabitancy of a country' as 'little children, dogs and cocks'.[8] By the time of Æthelred, hens were being brought into London for sale, and one hen was paid as toll from a hamper.[9] By the end of the period at least, on large estates roosts were constructed for the hens, according to *Gerefa*: 'in winter . . . many things have to be done in the farmstead – yes, a hen roost too' (*on wintra . . . fela ðinga sceal to tune – ge eac henna hrost*).[10] Poultry may also have been kept in towns. Wynkyn de Worde (1513) states that '*the skynne of capon, henne or chekyn ben not so clene, for the[y] ete foule thynges in the strete*'.[11] Despite the fact that poultry keeping was general, chicken and capons remained a prestige food. Thirteen chickens were ordered for the coronation feast of Henry III in 1220.[12] Although a later medieval drinking song is facetious, it may reflect reality:

> *Bryng us in good ale*
> *Bryng us in no capouns flesch*
> *For that is ofte der;*
> *Nor bryng us in no dokes flesche,*
> *For thei slober in the mer.*[13]

---

[1]   Zeuner 1963, 263.
[2]   Whitelock 1955, 371.
[3]   Robertson 1939, 199, 201.
[4]   Maltby, 1979.
[5]   Robertson 1939, 59.
[6]   Liebermann 1898, 446.
[7]   Harris 1987, xii.
[8]   Owen 1841.
[9]   Robertson 1925, 72.
[10] Liebermann 1898, 454.
[11] quoted in Furnivall 1868, 165.
[12] Harris 1987, xiii.
[13] Furnivall 1968, 285.

Judging from leechdoms, poultry was an invalid food: hens were often used to make broth, with the addition of worts and butter.[1] They could also be 'cooked in wine with the addition of oil' (*cicene mete seoþ on wine do þanne ele to* . . .).[2] The extremities of geese were recommended, as was 'hen's flesh not very boiled' (*hænne flæsc næs swiþe gesoden*).[3] Geese wings were 'the better the fatter and fresher'.[4] Goose giblets were good for a sensitive stomach.[5] Fresh goose was to be avoided for some complaints.[6] Bede mentions a goose which hung on the wall in the guesthouse for a week before Cuthbert prevailed on some visiting brothers to boil it;[7] the reluctance was presumably because it was a delicacy. Goose was also salted.[8] It was considered highly dangerous to eat goose on 'Egyptian Days'. These were the Monday at the end of April, the first Monday in August, and the first Monday after the end of December. Statements of how long it would be before death ensued varied from the three days of *Meddygon Myddfai*, the fifteen days of Bede's *De Minutione Sanguinis*[9] to the forty days of *Lacnunga*: 'and whoever on those three days eats goose flesh will die within the space of forty days' (*7 se þe on þys ylcum þrim dagum gose flæsces onbyrigeð binnan feowortiges daga fyrste he his lif geændeð*).[10] A pregnant woman was not to eat cocks or ganders (in common with bulls, rams, boars and bucks), in case the child was born *hoforode 7 healede*, which Cockagne translates as 'hump-backed and bursted'.[11]

Bird bones are fragile, and are less likely to have survived on sites than more robust animal bone. They are likely to be more fragmented, and therefore it is likely that a large proportion of the evidence was lost before more sophisticated recovery techniques were developed and put into practice. However, bird bones have been found on sites dating from early in this period. There was a small percentage of domestic fowl at Old Down Farm, Hants., dated to the sixth century.[12] Domestic goose and fowl bones were found at Bishopstone, Sussex, on a site dated from the mid fifth century onwards by metalwork in the adjacent cemetery.[13] A goose wing was found in a mid seventh-century grave of a male of some rank at Farthing Down, Surrey.[14] Domestic goose, fowl and duck bones were found on the fifth- to seventh-century site of West Stow. These species were also found on the mid period sites of Ipswich and Medmerry Farm, Selsey, Sussex.[15]

The late eighth- to early ninth-century site at Ramsbury, Wilts., gave evidence of geese, cocks, hens, capons and small fowl the size of modern bantams.[16] There was a high proportion of immature fowl bones, perhaps because the population preferred younger, tender poultry, although this is not the only interpretation possible. It is

---

[1] Cockayne 1851, II lvi 1, III xii 1, xliii.
[2] op. cit., *Peri Did.* 51, 52.
[3] op. cit., II xvi 2.
[4] op. cit.
[5] op. cit., II i 1.
[6]   op. cit., I xxxvi.
[7] Colgrave 1940, 269.
[8] Cockagne 1851, I xxxvi.
[9] Bonser 1963, 298–9.
[10] Cockayne 1851, *Lac.* 118.
[11] op. cit., III MS Cott. Tib. A III fol. 40b.
[12] Davies 1980.
[13] Bell 1977, 283.
[14] Hope-Taylor 1950, 170.
[15] West 1963, 243; 1982, 268; Welch 1983.
[16] Haslam 1980, 49.

similar to the situation at Exeter, where 20% of the domestic fowl were killed at under six months of age.[1] The geese were large, indistinguishable from the wild greylag *anser anser*. Again, this parallels the situation at Exeter where geese were allowed to attain their full size. There were a few bones of duck which could belong to the wild mallard *anas platyrhynchos* or an unspecialised domestic form.[2]

The report on the animal bones from Flaxengate, Lincoln, gives a comprehensive picture of the presence of poultry and wild birds.[3] Overall the fowl were small, compared with those from medieval Exeter and King's Lynn, though not small enough to justify descriptions as bantams.[4] Three large unspurred bones could possibly be those of capons. At *Hamwih* the smallest fowl are comparable with bantams, the largest with modern laying fowl, and again, these may be capons.[5] A good number of bones could have come from cockerels killed for food while young and tender. At Flaxengate there is a decrease in the number of fowl and an increase in the number of geese from c.870 until about the mid eleventh century, followed by a small increase in fowl. From the twelfth century the fowl are again more numerous than geese. At about 1000 the numbers of hens and geese are the same.[6] A very few bones of domestic fowl were found in the tenth-century layers at Skeldergate, York.[7] This suggests that fowl were indeed brought into towns for food, but that they were scarce, and probably expensive.

Geese were scarce in late ninth-century Lincoln, when they were perhaps kept around the city, but became gradually more common. This increase in geese at the beginning of the medieval period was also noticed by Maltby at Exeter and perhaps indicates that geese were being brought into the city from grazing outside. The late eleventh-century examples seem to be rather smaller, and taken with other contemporary changes in husbandry observed on site, this suggests an increased demand for meat – smaller, not previously saleable geese were coming to market. The Flaxengate geese are larger than those recorded at King's Lynn. (The two much smaller specimens were probably wild greylag geese.)

Geese were probably grazed on grass, like the *gandran dune* (gander down/hill) mentioned in the boundaries of Tichborne.[8] They were not allowed to imperil the main source of food, and, in Wales, geese in corn could be killed by the owner of the crops, and if found in the corn yard they could be strangled, presumably by whoever discovered them.[9]

Ducks were never very abundant at Flaxengate.[10] There are no trends as regards numbers at particular periods. There is a small proportion of mallard. As a recent domesticate, there would have been a majority of ducks with intermediate skeletal

---

[1] Maltby 1979.
[2] Haslam 1980, 49.
[3] O'Connor 1982.
[4] Clarke & Carter 1977.
[5] Holdsworth 1980.
[6] O'Connor 1982.
[7] O'Connor 1984, 16.
[8] Robertson 1939, 40.
[9] Seebohm 1952, 93; Owen 1841, 561.
[10] O'Connor 1982.

characteristics and hybridization with wild duck may have been common. Place-names suggest the keeping of ducks, e.g. *æt Ductune* (duck farmstead) (775–8).[1]

Apart from bird bone evidence, what was possibly a fowl keeper's house, fowl run and store was found at Cheddar (though the suggestion this was a horse mill has been put forward). This identification is based primarily on the St. Gall monastery plan, but such a construction was probably a feature of most large estates by the end of the period according to *Gerefa*.[2] Charlemagne's *De Villis* stated that a minimum of one hundred chickens and thirty geese were to be kept on large royal farms, fifty chickens and twelve geese on smaller ones.[3] The numbers actually found on the royal estate at Annapes c.820 were thirty geese, twenty-four chickens and twenty-two peacocks.[4] In the twelfth century Alexander Neckham wrote of straw and coarse grains being fed to hens, ducks and geese and birds of the kitchen yard.[5] There is documentary and archaeological evidence that swans and peacocks were regarded as domestic birds, and kept on large estates.[6]

There seems to be no parallel to the hen (together with the dove and the fish) that was found in Grave 31 in Bonn Cathedral in Anglo-Saxon graves.[7]

Eggs

However, 43 eggs were discovered in a grave at Barfriston, and other graves in the Cambridge area at Holywell Row.[8] Barbara Noddle points out (in Clason 1975) that poultry at this period shows a regional variation with the greatest number of domestic fowl in East Anglia. This is what one would expect, as fowl prefer drier conditions. They also lay better in dry and warm conditions, so almost certainly more eggs would have been available in the eastern part of the country. Eggs were being brought into London for sale by the eleventh century, as the Laws of Æthelred specify that five eggs were to be rendered as toll from a hamper on coming to market (*de uno dossero cum ovis v ova telonei, si veniant ad mercatum*).[9]

It is difficult to quantify the number of eggs that would be produced by a hen in a year as this is not mentioned in Anglo-Saxon treatises. Walter of Henley's *Husbandry* in Grosseteste's translation of 1240–1 suggests that a hen produces 180 eggs a year. While the modern figures for egg production are much higher, they are not relevant, as battery conditions bear very little relation to free-range conditions. Certainly the figures given by this treatise for pigs (3 farrowings a year producing 13 piglets on each occasion) are unrealistically high in terms of modern stock and husbandry. The figures for 1985 are weaners per sow reared average 9.05, high 9.55, with 2.15 and 2.35 farrowings a year respectively.[10] The figure of 180 eggs also seems very high,

---

[1] Smith 1964, I 111.
[2] Rahtz 1979, 54, 130–132; 1990, 269.
[3] op. cit., 376.
[4] Hodges 1982, 132.
[5] Holmes 1952, 200.
[6] Cockayne 1851, II xvi 2; Holmes 1952, 195; Clutton Brock in Wilson 1976, 248.
[7] *Med. Archaeol.* XI 33, F.note 56, 137.
[8] Whittock 1986, 152.
[9] Robertson 1925, 72.
[10] Nix 1985.

though it is by no means impossible with good management.[1] It is likely that Anglo-Saxon hens may have had resemblances to the modern Dorking, and these begin laying early in the year.[2] An *Anonymous Husbandrie* of the same century gives much more realistic figures for pigs (2 farrowings a year with 7 piglets produced) and 122 as the annual figure for egg production (or 115 eggs and 7 chickens) seems a reasonable assessment.[3]

'One hen's egg' (*an henne æg*) was eaten in the evening by Bishop Cedd during the Lenten fast.[4] Eggs (*æigra*) were one of the foods eaten by the novice in the *Colloquy*, and an important addition to monastic diet generally.[5] They would have supplied iron, which otherwise may have been in short supply. In leechdoms hens' eggs were regarded as light, and recommended as part of an invalid diet.[6] As part of a cure they could be taken raw, beaten up with curds, or in hot water or ale.[7] If the lung disease for which many beaten hen's eggs were to be taken raw with curds was in fact tuberculosis, this would have been a very helpful dietary supplement.[8] Soft (*hreren bræden*) and hard boiled eggs are mentioned, and on one occasion the egg is to be eaten with bread.[9] One recipe approximates to an omelette: 'beat in butter and cook in oil over the fire' (*gesleah þonne in buteran lege in ele ado þonne hwon ofer fyr . . .*).[10] Another recipe is similar but it calls for the addition of sage and pepper and specifies that the mixture should be cooked in a clean pan.[11]

The fact that hen's eggs are called for in the leechdoms suggests that the eggs of other birds were eaten, as now. Such delicacies as gulls' and plovers' eggs were probably more available for the Anglo-Saxons at a time when a much smaller population did not require such intensive land use.

Two of the Welsh law codes say that a hen's egg is to be paid as a fine for a hen trespassing in a flax garden or barn, or for each lamb or kid damaging corn.[12]

---

[1] J. Graham, pers. comm.
[2] Thompson 1989, 25.
[3] Lamond 1890.
[4] Miller 1890, I 2 232.
[5] Garmonsway 1978, 46.
[6] Cockayne 1851, II xxv, xxvi.
[7] op. cit., III xxxv, II xlix.
[8] op. cit., II li.
[9] op. cit., *Peri Did.* 62, 63, *Lac.* 37, II lii 3, xvi 1, I xxxix 3, xxxii 2, etc.
[10] op. cit., *Lac.* XXXVIII.
[11] op. cit., *Peri Did.* 63.
[12] Owen 1841, 561.

9. Wild Animals and Birds

Wild Animals

It is necessary in this chapter to consider what animals were both available and normally regarded as food. There are references in leechdoms to the flesh of boars, hares, harts and bucks; bears, badgers, foxes and wolves.[1] Of these animals there is evidence that the first four were eaten as part of a normal diet.[2] Bears are also mentioned in the *Gnomic Verses*,[3] 'to attack boars or bears' (*onginan eofor or beran*) but both this manuscript and *Leechdoms* show continental influence and the only account of bear hunting comes from the eleventh-century *Chronicle of Nantes*.[4] Here it is recorded that Alan killed boars and bears with a wooden staff, but this suggests a heroic sport, rather than efficient hunting for food. While bear was consumed in a Norse/Icelandic saga,[5] it may have been in short supply in Anglo-Saxon England: I have come across only one record of bone on sites. Badger presents a problem in that while various parts of the animal were to be taken for different disorders, the flesh was recommended as being good for you: 'eat and consume [badger's] meat – it is good for you and your household' (*hys flæsc* [i.e. that of the *broc*] *gesoden etest & þigest, hyt biþ god þe 7 þinum weorudum*).[6] A fifteenth-century Irish elegy praises Scotland and says, 'Fish and venison and badger's fat, that was my food in Glenn Laigh', so it was presumably not a hardship to consume this.[7]

The *Gwentian Code* was unable to fix the value of a badger or hare (because the latter at least was thought to change sex every month).[8] Various other animals including the fox and wolf are referred to as doing only mischief and are hence valueless, which suggests some value was put on the badger and hare even if this could not be quantified, and it seems likely that it was as food they were valued, since the pelts of fox and wolf would have had some use. Two bones of badger were found at Flaxengate, and while this does not amount to proof that badger was eaten there, it is a possibility. The picture is complicated by the presence of badger together with fox and beaver at Ramsbury.[9] At West Stow hare, bear, badger and beaver remains were found, and badger and hare were found in middle and later contexts at Portchester and hare at Anglo-Scandinavian York.[10] Hare bones were found at Flaxengate in all levels.[11] The eleventh- to twelfth-century Billingsgate Buildings site in London produced a very small percentage of hare, as did Exeter.[12] Hare was allowed as food according to the Penitential of Theodore.[1] References to

---

1 Cockagne 1851; de Vriend 1984.
2 op. cit., II iv, xvi.
3 Gollanz 1934, 1.175.
4 Whitelock 1955, 317.
5 Jones 1980, 266.
6 De Vriend 1984, 234–6.
7 Jackson 1971, 256.
8 Owen 1841, 733, 735.
9 Coy in Haslam 1980, 49.
10 Crabtree in West 1982, 268; Cunliffe 1976, 265; Hall 1983, 186.
11 O'Connor, 1982.
12 Hall & Kenward 1982, 96; Maltby 1979.
1 CA Wilson 1973, 365.

the fox and wolf in leechdoms are purely medicinal, and wolf bones do not seem to have turned up on sites.

Ælfric's *Colloquy* provides useful evidence. Hunting with nets or hounds, the hunter says, 'I catch harts and boars and roe deer – male and female – and sometimes hares' (*Ic gefeo heortas 7 baras 7 rann 7 rægan 7 hwilon haran*). Boar hunting is illustrated in Cotton Tiberius B5. Wild boar remains were found at Thetford.[1] Because of the similarity of wild and domestic pigs, which may have interbred, it may be difficult to isolate the bones of wild pig in deposits: size seems to be the determining factor. In the Domesday Survey there is one instance of a *warenna Leporum* on the lands of Earl Alan at Hache, Lincs.[2] According to a life of the saint, St. Martin saved a hare that was being hunted.[3] The Bayeux Tapestry apparently depicts hare coursing and, in another section, a hare.[4] Anglo-Scandinavian Coppergate and Pavement sites, York, produced hare bones.[5]

The evidence for the consumption of deer is relatively plentiful. Deer fragments are found at a number of sites, though it is necessary to remember that shed antlers were often collected as raw material, and so a fragment count is likely to be distorted by the inclusion of antler. At the beginning of the period the breakdown in ordered life consequent on the Roman withdrawal led to a greater dependence on game animals. The fifth-century inhabitants of Latimer villa in the Chilterns consumed deer in far greater numbers than their predecessors had done, and Gildas lamented that because of troubles in the fifth century, the only source of food had been that which huntsmen could find.[6] At the mid-fifth- to sixth-century site of Bishopstone there was a little evidence for the hunting of red and roe deer.[7] At the fifth- to seventh-century site of West Stow post-cranial bones as well as antler from both red and roe deer were present in low numbers.[8] At the mid-Saxon site of Ramsbury, Wilts., the fragments of roe deer (*capreolus capreolus*) peak at 1–2 years old, and it is pointed out that this may either indicate that younger, inexperienced deer were more likely to be caught, or that they had been selected because they would be more tender.[9] There were also remains of red deer (*cervus elephus*). At Chalton the excavators remarked on the frequency of the bones of sheep, deer and pig, and stated that the economy of the village depended more on hunting and sheep farming than cattle raising.[10]

As far as urban sites are concerned, Thetford also yielded remains of red and roe deer as did Hamwih which gave a minimum of 11 red deer of which at least 2 were stags, and eight fragments of roe deer which gave a minimum of 7 animals with at least one buck and one doe.[11] Red deer alone were present at the Lloyds and Barclays Bank sites in York, and Flaxengate, Lincoln, where a few post-cranial bones suggested a very

---

[1] *Med. Archaeol.* XV, 75.
[2] Commissioners 1819, 410, 347.
[3] Skeat 1881, *St Martin* l. 1056.
[4] Wilson 1985, plates 2, 3, 5.
[5] Hall et al. 1983, 186.
[6] CA Wilson 1973, 76.
[7] Bell 1977, 283, Fig. 111, Table XX.
[8] West 1982, 273.
[9] Coy in Haslam 1980, 49.
[10] *Med. Archaeol.* XVI, 31.
[11] *Med. Archaeol.* XV, 75; Holdsworth 1980.

limited use of venison.[1] The large size of the animals indicates a wild herd. The presence of deer can indicate either a high-status site, or a site where the inhabitants needed to supplement their diet at the risk of severe punishment. The abnormally large amount of remains of red deer bones, all from food remains with no antler, in the late Saxon ditch at Southampton, coupled with the presence of horse bones, suggests a time of dearth.[2] In a short stretch of ditch, the weight of deer bones exceeded the total weight of red deer bone in the whole of *Hamwih*'s Melbourne Street site, suggesting that *Hamwih*'s inhabitants were well-nourished.[3]

What are presumably red deer are illustrated in two eleventh-century manuscripts; one is present in a scene of the garden of Eden, the other is being disembowelled by a hunter.[4]

One deer species not available to the Anglo-Saxon was the fallow. Writing on the naturalised animals of the British Isles, Lever states it is generally agreed that the fallow deer (*dama dama*) were well established in Roman times.[5] He goes on to say that Ælfric refers to fallow as 'bucks' in his *Colloquy*. However, in Saxon glosses *buc*, *buk*, *bucca*, or *bucce* never translate either *dama* or *cervus palmatus*. The late eighth-century – early ninth-century transcript of a late seventh century text in the Erfurt Gloss translated *damina* as *elch* 'elk'.[6] The only reference to fallow deer in these glosses seems to occur in an eleventh-century vocabulary where *da* translates *damma vel dammula*. Moreover, while the Domesday survey does record thirty-one parks in Southern England, it does not specify that these are for fallow deer. References are very often to 'parks for wild animals' like that at (Bishops) Waltham: *Ibi e parc bestiaru* and the terms *parcus bestium siluaticarum* and *parcus ferarum siluaticarum* are common.[7] With the exception of one fragment of fallow deer bone identified in pre-930 levels at Cheddar (to be compared with 51 fragments of red, and 44 of roe, deer) fallow deer remains are not known before eleventh- to twelfth-century levels; for example in the 1000–1150 and 1000–1200 deposits at Exeter where they are in company with rabbit bones.[8] Although not completely naturalistic, the deer with branching antlers illustrated in the Bayeux Tapestry are not spotty.[9]

Place-names like *Deorhyrste* (a wooded hillock frequented by deer), and *Rawelle* (roebuck well or stream) indicate areas where deer were to be found.[10] The establishment of deer parks seems to go back before the Conquest. The place-name Dyrham (*Deorham* in 950) indicates a deer enclosure.[11] Welsh Laws deal with punishments for stealing animals from enclosed parkland.[12] Deer parks are not therefore directly connected with the Norman introduction of fallow deer. A boundary charter of 780 has the phrase, 'to the roe deer hedge' (to þan rahhege).[13]

---

1 op. cit.; O'Connor 1982.
2 Bourdillon 1980, 189.
3 op. cit.
4 Temple 1976, figs. 190, 275.
5 Lever 1977, 248, 426.
6 Pheifer 1974, 19.
7 Munby 1982, 40b; Commissioners 1819, 409ff.
8 Rahtz 1979, 355; Maltby 1979.
9 Wilson 1985, plates 5, 44.
10 Smith 1964, II 78, 21.
11 op. cit., III 49.
12 Owen 1841, 533.
13 Smith 1964, II 92.

A lease of land to Wulfgeat by Oswald, the Archbishop of York and Bishop of Worcester gives a boundary as 'along the dyke to the deer park' (ondlong þære dic to deorleage).[1] The elements hliep, geat, (leap gate for deer) occur very frequently in place and field-names and there are pre-Conquest examples.[2] It might well have been sensible to contain deer in some sort of enclosure to avoid damage to crops. However, the reference to the deer hedge the geneat is to cut and maintain may refer to a method of hunting deer whereby they were driven into enclosures.[3] Haiæ occur in the Domesday survey chiefly in Worcestershire, Herefordshire, Shropshire and Cheshire and were actually in the woods. The entry for Ruiscop, Herefs., reads, 'here there is a enclosure in a great wood' (ibi e una haia in una magna silua). They were for the capture of animals: 'enclosures in which they used to capture wild animals' (haia in qua capiebant feræ) (Chintune, Worcs.), and specifically for deer 'they capture roe deer' (capreolis capient) (Cortune, Salop.).[4] According to Domesday, the duty of stabilitio, driving deer to a point where they made their stand, was expressly laid on some of the citizens of Hereford, Shrewsbury and Berkshire.[5] This custom seems to have predated Rectitudines Singularum Personarum (c.1000), as in 964 Oswald, Bishop of Worcester wrote down the conditions on which he granted leases. The lessees were to erect a hedge for the bishop's hunt (and lend their own hunting spears if required).[6]

No doubt other animals were eaten in time of dearth and by deprived members of the community. Centuries later Shakespeare makes Poor Tom complain

> But rats and mice and such small deer
> Have been Tom's food for seven long year

> King Lear Act III scene iv.

His audience would no doubt have found mice as disgusting as Lughaidh and his companions in ninth, or tenth-century Ireland. Forced to eat mice under pain of death the author comments, 'never had a more distressing vexation been put upon them', and one unfortunate gagged on the tail.[7]

A brief summary of the ways wild animals could be caught will give an idea of those who would have been able to exploit them for food. All members of the community would have had access to a stone to cast at an animal, as mentioned in the Welsh Laws, though not all could have thrown with the force and accuracy required. 'Casting with an arrow' would have been much more effective, but limited to those who could make, or buy, and draw a bow.[8] Most people would have had access to the materials to make traps and snares to take at least the smaller animals. That snaring was practised is indicated by the Welsh Laws, which lay down the procedure to be followed when a domestic animal had been taken in a snare.[9] Again, skill would have

---

[1] Robertson 1939, 116.
[2] Smith 1964, II 158; Mawer & Stenton 1969, 243.
[3] Liebermann 1898, 445.
[4] Commissioners 1819, 408–10.
[5] Loyn 1970, 366.
[6] Finberg 1972, 113.
[7] Jackson 1971, 205.
[8] Owen 1841, I 737, II 7, 9.
[9] op. cit., 103–5.

been at a premium, both in terms of constructing snares and knowing where to set them. Pits could have been dug by most people who had access to a suitable location, and the Welsh Laws lay down compensation in the case of people or domestic animals falling into them.[1]

Hunting spears would have been necessary for dealing with the larger animals, particularly boars, and, judging by the number of spearheads found in early Anglo-Saxon graves, a large proportion of men probably possessed them. Nets could have been made by a number of people and used for small and large game. The hunter of Ælfric's Colloquy used max (mesh) and nettan (nets), and their use is implied in Ælfric's *Lives of the Saints* where St. Eustace is confronted by the hart he is hunting and told 'and for him that you hunt and take with the nets of my mercy' (*and for hine þe ge huntian and gefon mid þam nettum minre mildheortnysse*).[2]

A number of animals could be hunted down by dogs, and in very many cases the bones of dogs on Anglo-Saxon sites could have come from hunting dogs. At Ramsbury, Wilts., remains of a large, well-exercised dog, long-legged and with long jaws was found.[3] The dog found at St. Mary's Vicarage site, Bedford, in a tenth- to twelfth-century context, was a slender, but very large animal of wolf size.[4] The Thetford dogs were large animals, some large enough to fall into the category of buck hounds.[5] Most of the dogs found at Flaxengate 'were of medium to large size, suitable for hunting purposes' and most were long-snouted.[6] That there were very few immature bones presumably reflects the care with which they were being kept. A number of households, if not short of food themselves, could have kept one dog on scraps and bones, though to have kept a pack necessary to bring down larger animals would have needed more resources.

Nobles and the king were able to own numbers of superior dogs. Something of the king's overall privilege is suggested by the fact that horses and dogs are left to him in his nobles' wills. Æthelgifu left 'to her lord the king two steeds that he is entitled to and my hounds' (*hyre hlaforde þam cynge . . . twegen stedan þe him to beodonne bioð 7 mine header hundas*).[7] Æthelstan made Wales supply as tribute dogs that were especially good at following a scent.[8] According to Domesday, Oxfordshire and Warwickshire paid 23 pounds to the king for dogs.[9] The Welsh Laws gave the price of the king's covert hound when trained at one pound, and his greyhound at 120d. (compared with the price of 4d. for a cur).[10] English dogs were prized on the continent: at least, Alfred sent two to the archbishop of Rheims in return for help with his educational reforms.[11] Two fine greyhounds were to make part of the three-yearly toll to Customs in Lombardy in the early eleventh century.[12]

---

[1] op. cit.
[2] Garmonsway 1978, 23; Skeat 1881, *St Eustace* l.49.
[3] Haslam 1980, 49.
[4] *Beds. Archaeol. J.*, 13.
[5] Clutton–Brock in Wilson 1976, 387.
[6] O'Connor 1982.
[7] Whitelock 1968, 7.
[8] Whitelock 1955, 281.
[9] Whitelock 1952, 66.
[10] Owen 1841, 281, 499.
[11] Whitelock 1952, 92.
[12] Poole 1958, 221.

Most people would have had access to wasteland in the form of hedgerows and thickets, fallow, or steep slopes unsuitable for agriculture, where they could have set snares or nets for the smaller animals. However, Rackham points out that medieval England was not a very wooded land and many settlements were a day's journey from substantial woodland, and so the inhabitants of such settlements may have been precluded from hunting larger animals.[1] However, the hunting rights of the citizens of London in the Chilterns (the second largest concentration of woodland in Domesday) were confirmed by Henry I in terms which suggest their antiquity.[2] Perhaps other members of important urban settlements had rights in distant woodland. Biddick suggests that the ancient commons had been apportioned out to specific manors by the ninth century and this may have reduced hunting rights.[3] Depopulation may have increased the land available for hunting. In the time of Edward the Confessor three Saxon thegns were recorded as hunting over 52 and a half hides of waste arable.[4]

Hunting was seen as a vocation. In *The Endowments of Men* in the Exeter Book, God distributes faculties to the world's inhabitants so that 'one goes hunting, a pursuer of ferocious wild beasts' (*sum bið on huntoþe hred – eadigra deora dræfend*).[5] When the professional hunter of the *Colloquy* explains how he *ofstikode* the boar which his hounds drove to him, and his listener comments, 'you were very brave then' (*swyþe þryste þu wære þa*), his response is 'a hunter must not be fearful, because various wild animals live in the woods' (*Ne sceal hunta forhtfull wesan, forþam mislice wildeor wuniað on wudum*).[6] That the dogs were sometimes seriously injured is indicated by the fact that the Welsh Laws accorded special importance to the needle of the chief huntsman, used for 'sewing the torn dogs'.[7] The hunter of the *Colloquy* was clothed and fed and sometimes rewarded by the king for whom he worked. In one manuscript,[8] he adds, 'I hold the first place in his hall'. Under the Welsh Codes he would have rated only tenth.[9]

There is evidence that the king's huntsmen and foresters were rewarded with estates. Wulfric, the king's huntsman in 957, had received small estates at Zeal and Donhead on Cranbourne Chase, Wilts., and a five-hide property at Ebbesborne.[10] In 987 Æthelred gave three hides, three perches to his huntsman, Leofwine.[11] In 1015 Ætheling Æthelstan, the eldest son of King Æthelred, left the stud at Coldridge to his stag huntsmen. Nobles also kept huntsmen among their retainers.[12] Æthelgifu left two oxen and two cows to Wulfric, her huntsman, and his wife and children were to be freed.[13] A number of *venatores* are named in Domesday.[14]

Rather than accompanying the king at all times, the royal huntsmen seem to have progressed separately. Feeding the huntsmen, horses and hounds was a burden from

---

[1] Biddick 1984.
[2] Robertson 1925, 292.
[3] Biddick 1984.
[4] *Med. Archaeol.* XV, 60.
[5] Mackie 1934.
[6] Garmonsway 1978, 25.
[7] Owen 1841, I 783.
[8] Whitelock 1952, 105.
[9] Owen 1841, 22–3.
[10] Hart 1975, 372.
[11] Whitelock 1952, 105.
[12] Whitelock 1955, 550.
[13] Whitelock 1968, 9.
[14] Commissioners 1819, 408.

which landowners sought relief. A grant by Brihtwulf in 843–4 to his ealdorman Æthelwulf at Pangbourne expressly freed the estate from 'the entertainment of ealdormen and from . . . *fæstingmen*, neither are to be sent there men who bear hawks and falcons, or lead dogs or horses'.[1] Burgred's charter of 855 to Alhwine gives exemption from feeding all huntsmen of the king, and in 875 the diocese of the Hwicce was freed from the charge of feeding the king's horses by Ceolwulf II of Mercia.[2] The Dimetian Code says that the king's huntsmen were to have a progress among the king's villeins in the spring when they hunted hinds, and in October when they hunted stags.[3] A grant of one hide at (East) Hendred was made to Godric the sheriff's wife, because she was supporting the king's hounds.[4] Just before the Conquest Cirencester was rendering 3,000 loaves yearly for dogs.[5]

Perhaps the huntsmen built up supplies of game in preparation for the king's visits, or perhaps they sent the animals to the court, where ever that happened to be. Post-Conquest documents tell us that deer and boars caught by the royal huntsmen were salted and transported to the court in barrels; boars' heads were pickled in wine.[6] This may account for the very low percentage of deer bones (0.4%) in pits at *Hamwih* where one would expect more because of the proximity of the New Forest. Boneless joints were salted, and the bones, etc., fed to dogs on the spot.[7] However, the inhabitants of *Hamwih* may not have had hunting rights in the forest, or perhaps they had a satisfactory diet without supplementing it with game. The fact that the majority of deer bones from the ninth-century on, turned up at the Bedford Castle site, rather than the St. Mary's Vicarage or St. John's sites, would seem to indicate social differentiation.[8]

The Gwentian Code gives details of the procedure to be followed if a hart was killed and the king's huntsman did not turn up. If this happened in the morning, the hart had to be flayed after noon and the skin, liver and hind quarter had to be kept (plus the hounds who had presumably made the kill). If the huntsman had not turned up by the following day, all the flesh could be used, and only the skin and hounds kept for the huntsman to collect. If the hart was caught in the afternoon it was to be kept whole overnight.[9] Delight at the sudden augmentation of the food supply might have been qualified if the hounds had to be fed for any length of time.

According to the same code, the king's hounds always took precedence over other dogs. Normally, if a man's hounds started an animal he was entitled to it, even if stray dogs came up and killed it. However, if the dogs belonged to the king, the king was to have the animal.[10]

Hunting for the larger animals with hounds, if not a horse, was probably beyond most people's means. The food resources consumed by horses and hounds may well have outweighed quite literally the game caught over a year since there were closed

---

[1] Whitelock 1955, 481.
[2] Finberg 1972, 48–9.
[3] Owen 1841, 381.
[4] Gelling 1972, 69.
[5] Seebohm 1883, 211.
[6] Cox 1905.
[7] Copley 1958, 180.
[8] *Beds. Archaeol. J.* 13, 125.
[9] Owen 1841, 493–5, 737.
[10] op. cit., II 7–9.

seasons for hunting. Asser says hunting was one of the pursuits fitting for a nobleman.[1] Alfred wrote in his *Preface to St. Augustine's Soliloquies* that 'every man likes to stay on the land his lord has leased him, and to go hunting and fishing and fowling'.[2] The Laws of Wales list the three noble pursuits as arms, horsemanship, and hunting, and state they were only free to an innate *Cymro*.[3] Certainly the nobility were the one class of people able to command the necessary resources for hunting. *Rectitudines Singularum Personarum* specify that 'every two *geburs* have to maintain one hunting dog' (*geburs twegen 7 twegen fedan ænne headorhund*) for their lord.[4]

It seems that everyone was entitled to hunt on his own property. *II Cnut 80* runs: 'Concerning hunting. I decree that every man can hunt in the woods and fields on his own property' (*Be huntnaðe. And ic wylle þæt ælc man sy his huntnoðes wyrðe on wudu 7 on felda on his agenan*). But it warns: 'and no-one is to hunt where the hunting is reserved for myself alone, under pain of the full penalty' (*7 forga ælc man minne huntoð lochwar ic hit gefriðod wille habban* [*on mine agenan*] *be fullan wite*).[5] No-one was to go hunting on a Sunday. In Wales there was a special concession for travellers. A traveller wounding a wild animal in the king's forest by casting a stone or arrow from the road was entitled to pursue it and catch it as long as he could see it. If it escaped his sight, he had to give up the chase.[6]

King Alfred was praised for his love of, and skill in hunting by Asser; Edward the Confessor was reputed to have hunted every morning.[7] Harold I went hunting with his dogs when others were attending divine service.[8] On the Bayeux Tapestry Harold and other nobles are depicted with hounds running before them.[9] Harold had apparently taken his hounds with him as they are shown being carried on board ship.[10] In 1087 the *Anglo-Saxon Chronicle* states that King William 'loved the high harts as if he was their father'.[11] Nowhere are such comments linked with the provision of food, rather these kings were seen as displaying their nobility through hunting.

The king's parks are enumerated in Domesday, together with those of earls and bishops. The king could call on men to fulfil the duty of *stabilitio venationis*. In Berkshire before the Conquest twelve men on horses and 36 men on foot could be requited to act as beaters. In the Gwentian Code the *tæogs* were required to make nine buildings for the king: the last two were the stable and the dog kennel.[12] By exacting such rights, the king must on occasion have made those whose food supply was not completely assured, contribute high status food to his own plentiful larder. The king relied on food from hunting only in very extreme circumstances: for example, when

---

[1] Whitelock 1955, 267.
[2] op. cit., 844.
[3] Owen 1841, II 515.
[4] Liebermann 1898, 447.
[5] Robertson 1925.
[6] Owen 1841, II 7, 9.
[7] Turner 1828, III 63; Poole 1958, 616.
[8] op. cit., 66.
[9] Wilson 1985, plates 2, 3, 12.
[10] op. cit., plate 4.
[11] Douglas & Greenaway 1953, 164.
[12] Owen 1841, 773.

Alfred was on Athelney.[1] However, the venison obtained was important: the Welsh Laws state that a hind-quarter of the animal was to be given to the owner of the land, but the hunters retained the bulk of the carcass. This contrasts with the situation today, where the huntsmen and followers gain only small portions of the liver.[2]

Clearly hunting carried a social cachet, and would be indulged in by those who had the means. It is presumably for this reason that bishops have to be warned against it. Wulfstan's *Canons of Edgar* are quite precise on the matter:

> *And riht is þæt preost ne beo hunta ne hafecre ne tæflere ac plegge on his bocum swa his hade gebiraö ... Se canon segö gyf hwylc gehadod man on huntaþ fare, gyf hit biö clerec forga xii monaö flæsc, diacon twa gear mæssepreost þreo, bisceop vii*

> It is not fitting for a priest to be a hunter or a falconer or gambler, rather he should busy himself with his books as suits his vocation. The law says that if a man in orders goes hunting he must forgo meat for a year if he is a cleric, two years if he is a deacon, three if he is a priest and seven if a bishop.[3]

Perhaps for this reason a bishop would licence others to hunt on his land, so hunting rights could be vested in someone other than the owner of the land. The Christchurch Writ[4] suggests that poaching was going on:

> *Mando 7 precipio uobis ne siluis uel terris Eadsini archiepiscopi ceruos uel ceruas nec capreolos nec lepores capiatis, nec omnino aliquam uenationem faciatis, preter eos quibus ipse Eadsinus archiepiscopus preceperit uel licenciam dederit.*

> I order and command you that neither in the woods or lands of Edsinus the Archbishop are stags or hinds or roe deer or hares to be taken, nor is any hunting whatever to be practised on account of those to whom Edsinus the Archbishop has himself authorised or given his licence to.

By the end of the period and probably from comparatively early times, the larger game animals tended to be prestige foods for the nobility – like the larger game birds taken by hawking. Or they might provide food on special occasions. A fragment from a will from Bury St. Edmunds allows for a funeral feast 'another ore for a flitch of bacon and for a buck'.[5] The feast on the first anniversary is to be celebrated with *þræ buces* for which one ore is allotted. This might suggest buck were not particularly common – the funeral feast would be held without much notice, and a flitch of bacon might be easier to come by than two more bucks. The anniversary feast, however, could be planned for in advance, giving time to acquire more game. Noddle[6] summarises that deer bones of the period are primarily *cervus elaphus* (red deer) bones from the richer sites. At the Cheddar palace site however, deer bone was relatively scarce, which is surprising in view of the importance of hunting as the principal recreation of the king and his court and that *Cedderclyff* was a known hunting area.[7] Edmund, the grandson of Alfred, was

---

[1] Turner 1828, I 545.
[2] A. Milton, pers. comm.
[3] Fowler 1972, 15.
[4] Harmer 1952, 185–6.
[5] Robertson 1939, 253.
[6] in Clason 1975.
[7] Rahtz 1979, 379, 11, 17.

hunting at *Ceoddri* when many stags were disturbed by the dogs. From these the king with his pack selected one for hunting.[1] That game was as plentiful in other suitable locations is confirmed by the evidence from late Saxon Southampton.[2] The Gwentian Code gives a stag as equal in value to an ox, a hind to a cow, a roe to a goat, a roebuck to a he-goat and a wild sow to a domestic sow.[3] Roesdahl observes that game must have been a luxury in Viking Denmark and this is likely to have been the situation in Anglo-Saxon England too.[4]

After the Conquest the Laws of William I decreed that anyone found guilty of hunting a wild boar should have his eyes put out: perhaps demonstrating a concern for restricting hunting to the king and nobility, rather than with conservation.[5] In the same period large dogs had to have their forefeet maimed so that they could not chase deer, and there is some evidence pigs were used as hunting or retrieving dogs instead.[6]

Wild Birds

Wild birds are often mentioned in leechdoms. 'Wild hens' (see below) and 'all the birds which live on the downs' were considered good to eat for certain illnesses, whereas birds that lived in the fens were not.[7] Web-footed birds (*flohtenfote fugelas*) that were to be avoided fresh could be eaten salted.[8] This is part of a diet, rather than special treatment, so presumably these items would normally have been eaten. No species are referred to, and the term 'web-footed' would include a large number of different birds. The flesh of *smælra fugla* (small birds) (again no species are mentioned) could be eaten boiled or roasted for a sore maw.[9] Wild culvers (doves/pigeons) are mentioned, and 'pigeons that are culvers' chicks'.[10] Starling and sand martin chicks are mentioned as a treatment, rather than as part of a diet, and might not therefore be consumed under normal circumstances, although a fifteenth-century *Boke of Kervynge* refers to certain birds by name, and then to 'all maner of small byrdes' which suggests the identification as to species was not important,[11] and the Northumberland household book lists small birds at 12 for a penny.[12] Meats considered slow to digest were *pawa, swan, æned* (peacock, swan, duck).[13] All three are referred to as normal items of diet but may be considered domesticated.

Cockayne translates 'wild hens' as '?pheasants'. It seems likely to me that these are partridges, present at Exeter and King's Lynn, if not Flaxengate.[14] The earliest reference to pheasant seems to be a mention of *unus phasianus* being served to members of the

[1] Turner 1828, III 63.
[2] Bourdillon 1980, 189.
[3] Owen 1841, 733.
[4] Roesdahl 1982, 120.
[5] Wiseman 1986, 5.
[6] Zeuner 1963, 266.
[7] Cockayne 1851, II xxxvii, xliii.
[8] op. cit., I xxxvi.
[9] op. cit., II ii 2.
[10] op. cit., II xxx 2, xxxvii.
[11] op. cit., III xix, I xxxv; Furnivall 1868, 151–2.
[12] Austin 1888, 182.
[13] Cockayne 1851, II xvi 2.
[14] op. cit., II xxxvii; Maltby 1979; Clarke & Carter 1977; O'Connor 1982.

canons' household at Waltham Abbey.[1] This occurs in a manuscript in the British Museum dated to about 1177 entitled *De inventione Sanctae Crucis nostrae in Monte Acuto, et de ductione ejusdem apud Waltham*. This gives details of the rations specified for the six or seven members of the canons' household at Waltham Abbey from Michaelmas 1058 to Ash Wednesday of the following year. They were to get either twelve blackbirds or two ?magpies (*agauseæ*) or two partridges or one pheasant (*unus phasianus*). The rest of the time they could have either geese or fowl. A charter of 1098 in *Monasticon Anglicanum*,[2] shows the bishop of Rochester assigning the monks sixteen pheasants, thirty geese and three hundred fowl from separate manors. Later references treat the pheasant as game: the *Beauchamp Cartulary* contains a writ issued between September 1114 and June 1115 forbidding the poaching of Walter of Beauchamp's *fesandos*.[3] It seems to have remained scarce: a feast for King Richard in 1387 had *four fesauntes* as against *xii dozen partrych*.[4]

Writing in 1933 P.R. Lowe found no positive evidence of pheasant in the Roman or Saxon material he examined, although it was previously assumed to be present.[5] A single pheasant bone occurs at Flaxengate in a mid-twelfth-century context, so a late date in the Anglo-Saxon period is suggested for the introduction of pheasant, which probably had to be keepered then as now.[6]

Lever writes that the remains of what were probably capercaillie have been discovered in deposits in Somerset, Yorkshire, and Co. Durham.[7] This bird was not extinct in England until c.1660, and so must have been available to the Anglo-Saxon population. However, it does not seem necessary to argue that *pavones* refers to capercaillie and not peacock. Peacocks were kept in Charlemagne's estates, and Neckham considered them as one of the birds of the court in the twelfth century.[8] The bones and feathers of a peacock were found beside the steering oar of the Gokstad Viking ship dated to the late ninth century.[9] Peacock remains have been found in the excavations of Anglo-Saxon Thetford.[10] Two peacocks are illustrated in the top margin of the Bayeux Tapestry above William's palace.[11]

A proportion of the bones of wild birds tend to be small and fragile, and was therefore probably not recovered, but the following species were all represented at Flaxengate: woodcock, rock dove, swan, small goose, mallard, teal, shelduck, pochard, tufted duck, crane, grey plover, golden plover, curlew, whimbrel, wood pigeon, jackdaw, crow, raven, bittern, gull species.[12] Most of these species were found at the fifth- to seventh-century site of West Stow, where, in addition, heron, moorhen, lapwing, greenshank, snipe and thrush were present.[13] This is basically the same pattern as at Exeter and King's Lynn, though partridge is absent at Flaxengate.[14] Some of these

---

[1] Lever 1977.
[2] Dugdale 1718.
[3] Mason 1980, 1.
[4] Austen 1888, 67.
[5] Lowe 1933, 332–43.
[6] O'Connor 1982.
[7] Lever 1977, 248, 426.
[8] Harvey 1981; Holmes 1952, 195.
[9] Brøndsted 1940.
[10] Clutton Brock in Wilson 1976, 388.
[11] Wilson 1985, plate 74.
[12] O'Connor 1982.
[13] Crabtree in West 1982, 268, 297.
[14] Maltby 1979; Clarke & Carter 1977.

species would have been present mainly or exclusively at winter time, in large flocks presenting an attractive target to the fowler. It is suggested that at a slack time agriculturally, the labourers may have turned to wildfowling to provide a welcome supplement to their food. A Breton source of 1519 provides the following, 'As in the season of ice there are caught in the snares birds seeking their food', which again suggests winter as a time for taking birds.[1]

According to later medieval accounts of wildfowling, very large numbers of birds were taken. Thomas of Ely wrote that he had seen at midwinter or when the birds moult their feathers, waterfowl caught by the hundred or even three hundreds.[2] While his account in the *Liber Eliensis* dates from the twelfth century, it is unlikely the situation had changed from Anglo-Saxon times. Moreover, his account that the birds were taken in nets and snares as well as with lime, accords well with what the fowler says in Ælfric's *Colloquy*: 'I catch birds in many ways: sometimes with nets, with snares, with lime, with whistling, with a hawk, with traps' (*On feala wisan ic beswice fugelas: hwilon mid neton, mid grinum, mid lime, mit hwistlunge, mid hafoce, mid treppan*).[3]

Hemp and flax were cultivated at Old Buckenham Mere, Norfolk, in the Anglo-Saxon period, and at Anglo-Scandinavian sites in York in the tenth century.[4] There is definite evidence of fowlers and fishermen using nets made of hemp in the sixteenth century, and the likelihood is that hemp nets were made much earlier.[5]

Trapping and netting birds must have been well-established practices: in 737 Boniface, writing to all the English clergy, asks that 'we may be delivered from the snares of Satan, the fowler'.[6] The elements *cocc, sciete* (glade where woodcocks were netted) are extremely common in field-names with the modern forms cockshut, cockshoot.[7]

The list of species found at *Hamwih* includes duck (domestic or wild mallard), three smaller species of duck (possibly widgeon), a teal, woodcock, herring and black-backed gulls, buzzard, carrion crow, jackdaw, Great Northern diver, starling, song thrush, redwing and ?wagtail.[8] Knife marks suggesting that a sharp knife was used to transfer meat directly to the mouth were found on all species except the gulls, buzzard and jackdaw. However, it would perhaps be dangerous to argue that any of the birds whose remains have been found on sites were never eaten. Gulls were eaten until recently in Scotland, and were part of the diet at the Viking settlement of Kvívík in the Faroe Islands.[9] Lest it might be thought that gulls were subsistence items only, it is interesting to note that the Northumberland Household Book of 1512, records the purchase of seagulls at one to one-and-a-half pence, the same price they were giving for plovers and woodcocks.[10] Rooks are still eaten, and so are young gannet and puffin.[11]

[1] Jackson 1971, 299.
[2] Darby 1940, 36.
[3] Garmonsway 1978, 31.
[4] Godwin *Antiquity* XLI Part 161, 45; Hall et al. 1983, 179.
[5] Furnivall 1868, 127.
[6] Kylie 1911, 194.
[7] Smith 1964, III 110, 113, 173, 182, etc.
[8] Holdsworth 1980.
[9] McNeill 1963; *Med. Archaeol.* XIV, 69.
[10] Austin 1888, 182.
[11] *Sunday Times* Sept. 28, 1975, 21; Kuper 1977, 48.

The case of Portchester is of particular interest as the site was occupied throughout the Anglo-Saxon period. The early to mid-Saxon period provided evidence of very few wild birds: bittern, mallard, curlew, partridge and wood pigeon, whereas in the late period another seventeen species are recorded, making up about a quarter of all the bird bones. This may well indicate the increase in the social status of the settlement.[1] Generally bones from wild species are a very small proportion when compared with those from domestic birds. At King's Lynn the percentages are 3–4 and 96–7 respectively, which is virtually the same as for *Hamwih*, although Site V Feature 16 yielded 8% of wild bird bone as against 92% of domestic bird bone. The situation at Exeter is not markedly different. Domestic geese and fowl made up 86.92% of the bird fragments, and of the remaining percentage of wild bird fragments, woodcock provided 5.65%.[2]

Barbara Noddle observes that the presence of wild bird bones on sites coincides almost exactly with the presence of hawk bones.[3] This certainly appears to be the case at – *inter alia* – Ramsbury: bones of the snipe and bones of the red kite; Flaxengate: a wide range of species plus goshawk in some quantity and peregrine falcon; *Hamwih*: various species plus buzzard.[4] It does not necessarily follow that the hawks were responsible for the presence of the other birds: methods of trapping might have captured the hawks as well, even if they were not intended for food.

Suggestions that the hawks might not have been eaten come from the Anomalous Welsh Laws. 'There are three animals whose foot and life are of the same worth: a horse, a greyhound and a hawk . . . they are unclean and worthless when they are lame.' The eagle's marrow mentioned in *Leechdom*s was to be applied externally, and the buzzard bones at *Hamwih* did not display any knife cuts. Lists of ingredients for medieval banquets do not include any varieties of hawk.

But the probability is that hawks found on sites had been used for hawking, otherwise they would have been discarded where they had been caught. Moreover hawking was established at least by the first half of the eighth century, and probably earlier, since 'no good hawk flies through the [deserted] hall' (*ne god hafoc geond sæl swingeð*) described in *Beowulf*.[5]

References in two of the riddles of the Exeter Book[6] connect hawking with members of the nobility, or at least those who were rich enough to afford horses. In *The Battle of Maldon* a noble 'let his loved hawk fly from his hand to the wood' (*let him þa of handon leofne fleogan/ hafoc wið þæs holtes*) before he advanced into battle.[7] In legal documents hawks are mentioned in connection with those of high status. One left two hawks as well as all his staghounds to his natural lord.[8] The situation was similar in Wales, where a lord, an edling, and a chief of household owed no *ebediws* but their steeds, their greyhounds and their hawks.[9] There are several references to kings and

[1] Eastham in Cunliffe 1976, 287ff.
[2] Bramwell in Clarke and Carter 1977, 399; Maltby 1979.
[3] Clason 1975.
[4] Haslam 1980, 49; O'Connor 1982; Holdsworth 1980.
[5] Zupita 1959, 106.
[6] Mackie 1934, Riddles 19, 64.
[7] Sweet 1954, 111.
[8] Turner 1828, III 65.
[9] Owen 1841, II 327.

hawking. Sometime between 748 and 752 King Æthelbert of Kent was writing to Boniface for two hawks.[1] Apparently Alfred wrote a treatise on hawking, recorded in the Christchurch Library catalogue in 1315 as *Liber Alured, regis, de custodiendis accipitribus*.[2] This seems reasonable in view of Asser's report that Alfred was accustomed to teach his falconers and hawkers and hound trainers.[3] William of Malmesbury noted that the Welsh were to pay trained hawks as tribute to Æthelstan.[4] When Adelard of Bath wrote a treatise on falconry, he tells that he derived information from King Harold's books, and certainly the latter, and other nobles, are shown with hawks on their wrists in the Bayeux Tapestry.[5] The illustration for October in the Anglo-Saxon calendar shows two hawkers, one mounted, beside a river. There are two goose-like birds and one crane.[6]

Land is conveyed 'with all . . . fowling grounds', which were evidently an asset.[7] Alfred wrote in his *Preface to St. Augustine's Soliloquies* that 'every man, when he has built a village on land leased to him by his lord . . . likes to stay in it sometimes and go hunting and fowling and fishing'.[8] This sounds very like the modern 'hunting, shooting and fishing', which his country estate provides for a rich enough gentleman today, and does not intimate a purposeful or methodical way of obtaining a food supply. The passage continues 'and to support himself in every way on that leased land', but almost certainly cereal crops and stock-rearing would have provided most of his food. Presumably it was the recreational aspects of hawking which were objected to by Boniface, writing to Cuthbert, archbishop of Canterbury in 747, 'The servants of God we forbid to hunt and wander in the woods with dogs and to keep hawks and falcons'.[9] However, well-to-do monks continued to follow these gentlemanly pursuits (as Chaucer's monk did centuries later), for this prohibition is repeated in Wulfstan's *Canons of Edgar*: *And riht is þæt preost ne beo . . . hafecere*.[10]

Hawking as practised by the nobility themselves was probably mainly recreational and secondarily a way of obtaining delicacies. Provision of food as such can hardly have been its function. As practised by the king's falconer, it became primarily a way of providing expensive, prestige foods. The Chief Falconer was the fourth officer of the Welsh Court – the Chief Huntsman ranked only tenth. He was to supply the other officials with hawks, presumably for recreational purposes or as status symbols, rather than as a means to a food supply. He was honoured with three presents on the day his hawk killed one of the three 'notable' birds: crane, heron and bittern (Dimetian Code), or crane, heron and curlew (Gwentian Code). William I had to be restrained from striking his steward when offered only half a roast crane at a banquet.[11] These four birds continue to feature on the menus of feasts well into the late medieval period. Two

---

[1] Kylie 1911, 157.
[2] Turner 1828, II 96.
[3] Whitelock 1955, 267.
[4] op. cit., 281.
[5] Wilson 1985, plates 2, 4, 9, 14.
[6] B.L. MS Cott. Claud. C. viii.
[7] Whitelock 1955, 474.
[8] op. cit., 844.
[9] Kylie 1911, 178.
[10] Fowler 1972, 15.
[11] Groundes-Peace 1971, 12.

cranelike birds are part of the decoration of a Canterbury manuscript of c.1020, and are referred to in Irish sources of the ninth and tenth centuries.[1]

The hawks that could tackle such difficult game were themselves difficult to procure. Some time between 748 and 754, Æthelbert II of Kent begged two falcons from Boniface in Germany, which should have 'skill and courage enough' to bring down cranes. 'We make of you this request to secure and send the birds because in our country, that is to say in Kent, very few falcons of this kind are found, which will produce such good brood, and can be trained and subdued to quickness and courage in the aforementioned art'.[2] Boniface also sent a hawk and two falcons to Æthelbald, king of the Mercians, between 732 and 751. That there was a scarcity of falcons in England is suggested by *The Fates of Men* which describes the taming of a hawk referred to as *se wælisca*, 'the foreign'. Since William of Malmesbury noted the Welsh paid trained hawks as tribute to Æthelstan, the hawk may have been Welsh.[3] The fact that the goshawk found in a tenth- or early eleventh-century context at Flaxengate is paralleled on a number of sites, but the peregrine falcon found there is much rarer, seems to reflect the situation Æthelbert was complaining of earlier.[4] At the time of Domesday foreign hawks appear to have been particularly valued: Worcester had to provide a Norwegian hawk, probably a gyr-falcon or an extra ten pounds in rent.[5] Nests of native hawks, though, were still referred to as assets.[6]

Hawking primarily as a means of procuring food would probably have been practised in the way the fowler in the *Colloquy* describes. He says that while his hawks feed themselves and him in winter, he lets them fly away to the woods in spring because he will not feed them in summer because they eat so ravenously. He catches and trains others in the autumn. Others, he acknowledges, keep their hawks through the summer in order to have them ready trained. And certainly those nobles who had managed to procure expensive foreign hawks would not have wanted to let them fly off after a season's hawking. Such owners would of course have been landowners who had access to enough food for their hawks. That provision for hawks was not negligible is suggested by charters, like that of Burgred, king of the Mercians, who in 855 freed Blockley minster from paying for the feeding of all hawks and falcons in Mercia, of all huntsmen of the king, of ealdormen except those in the province of the Hwicce, of the men called Walhfæreld and from lodging all mounted men, in return for 300 silver shillings.[7] The clause referring to feeding of hawks and falcons would hardly have been included had not this been a drain on the resources of the community. In the Domesday survey of Gloucestershire 54 vills rendered 28 shillings for the hawks, though this was perhaps for the provision, rather than provisions, of hawks.[8] According to the Dimetian Code, the falconer of the Welsh court was to have an old crone as food for the hawks.[9]

[1] Temple 1976, fig. 223; Jackson 1971, 67, 70.
[2] Kylie 1911, 157.
[3] Whitelock 1955, 281.
[4] O'Connor 1982.
[5] Hinde 1985.
[6] Loyn 1970, 355.
[7] Whitelock 1955, 486–7.
[8] Darby & Terrett 1954.
[9] Owen 1841, 369.

So hawking them seems to have had two roles: the provision of prestige foods for the aristocracy, where the food for the hawks outweighed the prey they brought down, and a subsistence function for the ordinary members of the community like Ælfric's fowler who had the skill to tame hawks. The provision of fresh meat obtained by hawking in winter would have been particularly important nutritionally for the latter group.

10. Honey

Honey was certainly the most important sweetening agent in Anglo-Saxon Britain. The sugary sap of some trees may have been tapped, as field-names like *pildash* (peeled ash) seem to imply.[1] This century birch trees were still occasionally tapped for their sweet sap, which was boiled down to make sweetmeats.[2] Malt would have been available as a sweetening agent, though in the documentary sources it is mentioned as a raw material for beer.[3] However, in leechdoms, wort drinks and vegetables are to be 'sweetened with honey' (*geswet mid hunige*).[4] Honey will also have been important as the major ingredient in mead, and as a means of increasing the alcohol content in other fermented drinks.

Beekeeping

Although the Romans had introduced beekeeping, it seems that at the beginning of the Anglo-Saxon period bees were not domesticated.[5] Anyone finding honey and wax was entitled to keep them.[6] The first stage in domestication was to cut into the tree trunks which contained bees' nests and to make a portion of the trunk into a door through which the honey was collected. This was done in living memory in the New Forest.[7] Presumably this method would have been used in the Anglo-Saxon period.

Primitive bark or log hives (*rusca*) were the next development, and one such hive, dated to 400–500, is recorded for Vehne Moor, N. Germany.[8] A tenth-century continental manuscript[9] illustrates one of these hives, and it is possible they were used in England too. The Domesday Book records *ruscæ* in Suffolk: two at Winburgh and three at Compsey, but Frazer thinks this term refers to wicker hives.[10] A wicker skep pre-dating our period survives from Feddersen Wierde, and such skeps were in use in Anglo-Saxon England.[11] They were probably *clomed* – covered with clay – and this successful design persisted into the last century. Small conical wicker skeps are shown on a capital which dates to 1120, in the Madeleine Chapel, Vezelay.[12] *Hyfa* (hives) could also be made of straw. Straw skeps were used by the Germanic tribes west of the Elbe, and if they were introduced into eastern districts of England, it might account for the different terms found in Domesday: *vascula* (small hives) in the south and west, and *vasa apium* for the eastern counties where the larger straw skeps had superseded the earlier form.[13] Hives are illustrated in B.L. MS. Royal 12 CXIX, Vit. C. iiii.

---

[1] Field 1972, 166.
[2] Edlin 1949, 44.
[3] *The Times*, Letters, 14th May, 1986.
[4] Cockayne 1851, I xlvii, xxxix, xix.
[5] Seebohm 1952, 18.
[6] op. cit., 99.
[7] Crane 1983, 77.
[8] op. cit., 91.
[9] reproduced in Marchenay 1979, 71.
[10] Frazer 1955, 183.
[11] Crane 1983, 91.
[12] op. cit., 91.
[13] Frazer 1955, 177.

Harvesting the honey causes the bees to go on producing honey as long as the weather is favourable and, while honey could be systematically collected from the nests of bees in forests and woods, there were advantages to having the bees in hives, of whatever form. The four gardens of the royal palace at Annapes before about 820, yielded three *muids* of honey: presumably the bees which produced this honey were kept in hives in the gardens.[1] Hives kept near the homestead were less likely to be stolen – and the beekeeper could perhaps stop the honey being eaten by other bees, a contingency the Welsh Laws deal with.[2] The small size of hives encouraged swarming, and an owner on hand would stand more chance of tracking a swarm. He could also feed his bees on honey syrup in bad seasons. Keeping bees in hives would have helped ensure a regular and plentiful supply of honey, even if the yield from Anglo-Saxon bees would be accounted very low by a present-day beekeeper. An anonymous thirteenth-century Husbandry gives two gallons as the average annual yield from a hive.[3] A good hive today would yield about four times that amount.

Processing

Processing the honey is relatively simple. After cutting the comb from the inside of the hive, the wax cappings could be cut off, and the liquid honey allowed to drip into a container. This 'run' honey is considered the best today, and probably was in Anglo-Saxon times too, under the term *huniges teares*.[4] Sometimes it is better to strain the honey, through a strainer, or better, a cloth, to remove brood, etc., and the term 'strained honey' (*aseowones hunige*) also occurs in leechdoms.[5] More honey could be forced through the strainer or cloth, but this is not considered so good, and the Anglo-Saxon may have made this distinction too, since the term 'pure honey' (*huniges seaw*) is found.[6]

Heating to 68 degrees Celsius will destroy honey-fermenting yeasts, but we do not know if this was practised.[7] Occasionally 'new honey' (*nifes huniges*) or 'new honeycomb' (*nywe bleoblæd*) is specified.[8] For external use 'spoilt honey' (*gemered hunig*) is listed.[9] Honey gathered in a bad season, or kept above 55 degrees Fahrenheit will tend to produce an acidic scum and become less palatable, but could probably still have been used to make mead, so 'spoilt honey' may have been honey into which a mouse, hen or other creature had fallen. Regulations were laid down for the permitted use of such honey, and are dealt with under Tabooed Food (see Chapter 13).

Honey Gathering

However, there would still have been wild bees nesting in woods and forests and this food resource would have been exploited in the Anglo-Saxon period as it was later, when forest courts in the thirteenth and fourteenth centuries imposed fines on anyone

[1] Hodges 1982, 132.
[2] Owen 1841, II 111.
[3] Lamond 1890.
[4] Cockayne 1851, I ii 1 & 2.
[5] op. cit., II xviii.
[6] op. cit., I ii 9.
[7] McGee 1986, 373.
[8] Cockayne 1851, III *Peri. Did.* 55, 66.
[9] De Vriend 1984, 150.

taking honey, wax or bees from 'old tree trunks'.[1] The Welsh courts recognised this resource and allocated honey to the *mær* and *canghellor* who kept the king's waste.[2] The nine *mellitari* of Westbury, Wilts., and the five of Lustleigh in Devon may have been gatherers of honey, rather than beekeepers.[3]

Leechdoms make reference to *dorena hunige*, the honey from a bumble bee *bombus terrestris*.[4] In *Lacnunga dorena hunig* is a translation for Attic honey.[5] This was presumably not procurable, so the translator gave what he considered a viable alternative. 'Honey from the hills' (*dunhunige*) is given as an alternative, and this also suggests honey from wild bees, as does 'field-bee honey' (*feldbeon hunig*).[6]

Wild swarms seem to have been needed to supplement domestic stocks. This may have been because to harvest the honey the stock of bees was killed.[7] The Welsh Laws contain detailed reference. The finder of a wild swarm was to have one penny or the wax, while the landowner kept the swarm, according to the Venedotian Code, but the Dimetian Code awarded him four pence and his dinner, or all the wax.[8] The value of a swarm is suggested by the arduous procedure to be followed if a wild swarm was found on a boundary. 'It is right for the owner to hew the tree on each side, and he on whose land the tree may fall, is to have the swarm.[9]

Archaeological Evidence

Archaeological evidence for honey, bees and beekeeping is, not surprisingly, sparse. As honey is water soluble, it is unlikely that it would survive as a residue in a container, and I have not heard of any positive identifications from Anglo-Saxon contexts. However, a swarm of honey bees was discovered in a twelfth-century context in York, together with what may be the remains of a straw skep.[10] The latter is a rare survival, given the perishable nature of such hives. The remains of wicker hives would not necessarily be readily recognisable as such, nor would the benches, single stones or 'bee stones' on which the hives might have stood. There are few Anglo-Saxon walls left standing in which bee boles might be discovered: the earliest in England seems to be in a twelfth-century wall in an enclosed garden in the Buckfast Abbey ruins. Metal hackle rings to secure straw bundles over the skep could survive, but like snecks (wooden or metal plates with several small entrances to fit over the gap in the base of skeps), might not be easily identified.[11]

---

[1] Cox 1905, 39–40.
[2] Owen 1841, 491.
[3] Frazer 1955, 183.
[4] Cockayne 1851, I ii, 1, 4, 7, 10, 16.
[5] op. cit., *Lac.* XIIIa.
[6] op. cit., III vi.
[7] Crane 1983, 91.
[8] Owen 1841, 289, 503.
[9] op. cit., II 97.
[10] Hall 1978, 25; Crane 1983, 91.
[11] op. cit., 104.

Place-Name Evidence

Place-names may give further information. 'Bee-clearing' (*beoleah*) recorded in 972, may have meant a place where bees often swarmed, or it may have been an area in which hives were kept, like the much later New Forest bee gardens.[1] Place-names and field-names may indicate the former presence of beehives. Rahtz & Hirst,[2] accept Finsberg's derivation of Beckery (*Beocere Eo* – Beekeeper's Island) from the form of the 971 charter. Honey names for fields may be complimentary, referring to fertile land, or derogatory, alluding to sticky soil, but where the name indicates a small piece of land, then it may refer to the location of beehives, e.g. Honey Spots, Honey Butts, Honey Piece.[3]

Documentary Evidence

Fortunately there are a great many documentary references to honey. Because of its sweetness, honey is a favourite vehicle for metaphor. Altfrid wrote of St. Liudger before 849 that he desired 'to saturate himself in the sweetness of the honeycomb of which he had had a foretaste' (i.e. spiritual doctrines).[4] Monks from St. Benedict's, Fleury and Ghent were sent for so that their praiseworthy customs could be incorporated into the *Regularis Concordia*: 'even as honey is gathered by bees from all manner of wild flowers and collected into one hive' (*ut apes fanum nectaris diversis pratorum floridus in uno alueario*).[5] Such references are literary commonplaces. More direct is Aldhelm's assertion that honey 'excels all the dishes of delicacies and peppered broths'.[6]

Honey is also referred to when the fertility of areas is described. The writer of the Life of St. Illtud in the early twelfth century praised the fertility of Llantwit by stressing not only the good harvests of the area, but also the abundance of flowers and honey.[7] A number of references to land 'flowing with milk and honey' or 'oil and honey' should be treated with caution as they are clearly based on biblical phrases.

Less poetically and more practically, honey is mentioned in specific amounts in various legal documents. According to Ine's Laws, ten hides were to furnish ten vessels of honey. These may have been larger than the sester, which was later the standard measure for honey, since the Welsh Laws gave the height of the honey tub for the king's *gwestra* as nine handbreadths measured diagonally.[8]

Between 801 and 805 Ealhmund, bishop of Winchester, allowed land to Byrhthelm, reserving from 24 hides two nights' entertainment in Farnham and ten jars of honey annually.[9] In the late tenth-century will of Æthelgifu, Leofsige is to pay to St. Alban's, *inter alia,* 'one sester of honey' (*anne sester huniges*).[10] In the period

---

[1] Mawer & Stanton 1969, 186.
[2] Rahtz & Hirst 1974, 10–11.
[3] Field 1972, 107–8.
[4] Whitelock 1955, 725.
[5] Symons 1953, *Proemium* Section 5.
[6] Turner 1828, III 27.
[7] Davies 1982, 34.
[8] Owen 1841, I 533.
[9] Gelling 1979, 153.
[10] Whitelock 1968, 10.

immediately following the Conquest, Queen Edith writes to the Hundred of Wedmore that she has given land at Mark to Bishop Giso. She goes on to say, 'I ask you to pronounce for me a just judgement concerning Woodman, to whom I entrusted my horse[s], and who has withheld my rent for six years – both honey and money.' (*And ic bidde eow þat ge deme me richtne dom of Wudemann þe ic min horse bitachte 7 mi gauel haueð ofhealden six gear eiðer ge hunig 7 eac feoch*).[1] References to honey and money are relatively common as rents continued to be paid in sesters of honey after the other dues were commuted to a money payment. Honey was not bulky in proportion to its value, and, if it is kept cool and airtight, will last for ten years or thereabouts, so presented no great problems of transport and storage.

Rectitudines Singularum Personarum groups the swineherd and *beo ceorl* next to each other in the lowest rank of free men. The *beo ceorl* held his land by virtue of his office, and his bees reverted to the lord on his death. If his land was good, he was required to keep a horse for his lord. 'It behoves the beekeeper, if he hold a taxable hive, that he shall pay what is ordered in the district. With us it is ordered that he shall pay five sesters of honey as a tax' (*Beoceorle gebyreþ gif he gafol heorde heallt, ðæt he sylle ðonne lande geræd beo. Mid us is geræd ðæt he sylle v. sustras huniges to gafole*). This suggests the beekeeper was usually found on a large estate. Frazer suggests he may have looked after the bees of the village as the local expert, and not just those of the lord.[2] The reeve was to find out if the *gebur* paid his tribute in honey, or meat or ale.

Domesday Book contains numerous references to hives and honey. The most noticeable point is that important towns were paying tax in the form of money and honey. Oxford paid the king twenty pounds, and six sesters of honey for toll, *gafol* and all customs.[3] Norwich paid six sesters of honey to the king in 1066.[4]

The *mellitarii* (honey gatherers?) have already been mentioned. The Domesday entry for Stocks, Salop., states there was a *custos apium*, with no further details. At Suckley, Heref., the *custos apium* was called the king's beekeeper and he had twelve 'small hives' (*vascula*). The Bolden Book entry for Wolsingham, Co. Durham, gives Ralph as the *custos apium*, and he holds six acres of land for 'guarding' the bees there.[5]

The Domesday records for East Anglia refer to relatively small numbers of hives – most places had only two or three. However Saffron Walden had 30 'now', where it only had 4 'then'. Shortgrave had 23 'then', but only 11 'now'. Some places previously had no hives recorded where there were several 'now', others had none where they had hives T.R.E. (in the time of King Edward the Confessor) Frazer considers that, as there seems to have been no difficulty in stating the numbers of hives, the hives probably stood on a bench under a penthouse roof, and they belonged to the lord whose bailiff kept accounts. The villeins did not pay taxes direct to the king, and so their hives were not registered.[6]

---

[1] Harmer 1952, 286.
[2] Frazer 1955.
[3] Turner 1828, III 107.
[4] Loyn 1970, 381.
[5] Frazer 1955, 183.
[6] op. cit., 182.

Generally speaking the western counties rendered more honey: Cirencester was taxed at six and a half sesters. Welsh men in these districts also rendered honey. One in *Westwode* provided one sester, at *Clive* eight Welshmen rendered ten and a half sesters and six shillings and fivepence.[1] In the Domesday Annexe to Gloucestershire, 54 *villæ* rendered 46 sesters of honey (40 pigs, 41 cows and 28 shillings for hawks); 7 *villæ* rendered six sesters of honey (6 pigs and ten shillings). At Ardenfield the king had 96 men who gave 41 sesters of honey. This had been kept as a payment in kind, although they were paying twenty shillings instead of the sheep they used to give. Other rents feature only honey and money. For example, in *Penedecdoc*, one under-tenant having four teams rendered six sesters of honey and ten shillings. In the recently Welsh districts, honey is the most prominent item.[2]

Honey is often mentioned in connection with woods, suggesting the continuation of honey gathering. At '*Beodum* in Worcestershire . . . the bishop holds woods two miles long and one and a half miles wide from which he has ten shillings and all the produce of the chase, honey and other things. The same bishop holds *Fledburie* . . . there are . . . woods two miles long and half a mile wide from which the bishop has all the issues arising from hunting and honey'.[3] In Sussex a wood yields twenty pigs and two sesters of honey as rent. In the manor of Wallop the reeve used to have the honey 'but now the foresters enjoy this'.[4] The last entry seems to indicate a trend which was to become more noticeable in later medieval times when foresters claimed the honey.[5]

The worth of the swarms of bees was carefully documented in the Welsh Laws. The Gwentian Code includes a section on 'The Law of Bees'. An old stock was worth 24d (the price of an ox ready for the yoke or a millstone), the first swarm 16d, the second (or bull) swarm 12d, the third swarm 8d, the swarm from a first swarm 12d, etc.[6] This code goes on to give the value of a swarm after 4th August as 4d, 'and that is called a wing swarm. And so they continue until the calends of winter. From the calends of winter is 24d . . . only a wing swarm does not become an old stock until the calends of May and then is 24d in value.' The *alveary* (probably the small wicker hive) was also worth 24d. Post-August swarming suggests bees in Wales were taken to the heather then as now: skep colonies at the heather still swarm frequently.[7]

The value put on bees is suggested by the Laws of Alfred (9.2). This states that formerly the fine for the stealer of gold, the stealer of stud horses and the stealer of bees and many fines were greater than the others, now all are alike, except for the stealer of a man: 120 shillings.[8]

[1] Seebohm 1883, 217.
[2] op. cit., 184–5.
[3] Crane 1983, 77.
[4] op. cit.
[5] Cox 1905.
[6] Owen 1841, 360.
[7] Frazer 1955, 181.
[8] Whitelock 1955, 375.

Charms to prevent bees from swarming, to catch bees, against the loss and theft of bees and to keep bees safe in their garden likewise indicate their importance. A charm 'catching a swarm of bees' (*wið ymb*) runs in part: 'Sit ye, wise women, sink to earth . . . be ye as mindful of my good as every man is of meat and estate' (*Sitte ge sige wif sigað to earþan . . . beo ge swa gemindige mines godes swa bið manna gehwilc metes 7 eþeles*).[1] There is also a simple and amazingly optimistic charm against the loss of bees: 'put a sprig of madder on your hive then no one can lure your bees away or steal them so long as the plant remains on the hive' (*mædere cið on þinre hyfe þonne ne aspond nan man þine beon ne hi ma[n] ne mæg forstelan þa hwile þe se cið on þære hyfe bið*).[2] A charm to keep bees safe in their enclosure is much more complex: 'This is St. Columcille's circle. Inscribe this circle with the point of your knife on a maumstone and drive a stake into the middle of your bee garden. Put the stone on the stake so that everything is below the ground, except for the inscription.' (*Þis is Sancte Columcille Circul. Writ þysne circul mid þines cnifes orde on anum mealmstane and sleah ænne stacan on middan þan ymbhagan and lege þone stan on uppan þan stacan, þæt he beo eall under eorðan butan þam gewritenan.*) The circle is divided into four quadrants, and in the upper right-hand section the inscription reads: *con t̄ apes ut salvi sint et in corda eorum sāh* (for bees, in order that they may remain safe and in their ?). If *sāh* was emended to *san* for *sana*, then the literal translation might be 'healthy in their hearts/bodies'.[3] '*Sāh* remains a mystery'.[4] *Sa* is given for *libitorium* (tub, pail, vessel) in an eighth-century Kentish gloss, and so may refer to the hive: 'safe in the heart of their hive').[5]

The term 'swarm enclosure' (*ymbhagan*) recalls Roman beekeeping, when the bees were kept in an enclosure and attended by the *mellarius*.[6] The name 'Bee Garden' was given to a rectangular medieval earthwork in the New Forest, although the people who used this term had never heard tell that bee skeps were put there. No fences or enclosures were allowed in royal forests, and so banks may have been used instead to mark out the protected areas.[7]

Recovering stolen bees was a difficult matter as the Welsh Laws indicate, because, as one swarm looks very much like another, you could not swear to your property, no matter how convinced you were as to your ownership.[8]

Perhaps honey was not all that plentiful in Anglo-Saxon England. Wulfstan remarks on the great quantity of honey in Estonia – so much indeed that 'the poor and the slaves drink mead' (*þa unspedigan and þa þeowan drincað medo*). To preserve the distinction of rank, one imagines, the rich had to drink (fermented) mares' milk.[9] The situation was probably comparable to that in the last century when vast numbers of forest beekeepers in Eastern Europe harvested very large amounts of honey.

---

[1] Cockayne 1851, I 384.
[2] op. cit., 397.
[3] op. cit., 395.
[4] Storms 1948, 309.
[5] Wright & Wulker 1884 .
[6] Frazer 1955, 178.
[7] Crane 1983.
[8] Owen 1841, II 213.
[9] Sweet 1954, 21.

Those who could, made sure of their supply. The king received honey from his own estates, and also from towns. Like the king, other important landowners exacted honey as part of their rents. In Wales the lord of a *tæog* had the right of buying up all his honey, and in North Wales all the honey of the king's *aillts* or *tæogs* was reserved in the court.[1] As we have seen, honey was retained as an item of tax in the trevs of Gwent after their conquest by Harold.[2]

Guild regulations refer to honey as the medium of guild fines. For example, the regulations of the Thegns' Guild in Cambridge state, 'If any guild brother die, all the guildship is to bring him to where he desired, and he who does not come for that purpose is to pay a sester of honey. If any guild brother insult another, he is to pay a sester of honey, unless he can clear himself with two of his bench fellows . . . if a retainer sits within the *stig* (probably a railed-off dais) . . . if anyone has a *fotsetla* . . . if the guild brother does not attend his morning conference (he is) to pay his sester of honey'.[3] The Exeter Guild Statutes state each brother is to have two sesters of malt and each retainer one, and a sceat of honey.[4] Probably the honey was important in its capacity as the raw material for mead, as malt was for ale.

Although bees are not mentioned in the *Anglo-Saxon Chronicle* as they are in the *Annals of Ulster* where, for example, mortalities of bees are recorded for the years 950 and 992, they were important enough to be included in *Prognostications*.[5] 'If the mass day of mid-winter fall on a Sunday, then there shall be good vineyards, sheep shall thrive' and 'honey shall be sufficient' (*hunu beoð genihtsum*)'. However, if it fell on a Wednesday, so that a fierce winter and a bad spring would follow, even if there was a good summer 'honey will be short' (*hunig byð lesse*).[6] Honey was also one of the ingredients to be dug into the earth as part of a charm to ensure its fertility.[7]

Monasteries may have had a special incentive to keep their own bees because of the need of wax for candles. As the introduction to the Laws of Bees in the Gwentian Code puts it, 'The origin of bees is from paradise, and on account of the sin of man they came from thence, and God conferred his blessing upon them; and, therefore, the mass cannot be sung without the wax'.[8] If this was the case, then monasteries would also have harvested the honey. They had access to a number of classical treatises, including those by Columella, Varro, Virgil, Palladius, Celsus, the Elder Pliny and later, the *Geoponica*, a compilation written in Constantinople c.950.[9] The Anglo-Saxons might not have been able to carry out some of the suggestions, like that of Pliny the Elder for an observation hive with sides made of transparent stone; and other statements, that brick hives were not to be recommended because they were too heavy to move, for example, would appear to be self-evident, but other information would have been helpful. Additional evidence for medieval monastic beekeeping is

---

[1] Owen 1841, II 265.
[2] Seebohm 1883, 208.
[3] Whitelock 1955, 558.
[4] op. cit.
[5] Frazer 1955.
[6] Cockayne 1865, III *Prog.*
[7] op. cit., I 399.
[8] Owen 1841, 360.
[9] Crane 1983, 96; Frazer 1933, 102.

provided by the earliest bee bole recorded in England, in the inside wall of the enclosed garden in Buckfast Abbey ruins.[1]

Perhaps because of the notion that bees were blessed, honey seems to have been considered a suitable food for a religious. Additional support for this idea is perhaps indicated by an Old English Martyrology where it is stated that after his resurrection Christ and his disciples ate 'broiled fish and honeycomb' (*gebrædne fisc and huniges beobread*).[2] Boniface, in a letter to Daniel, bishop of Winchester in 742–4, criticises over-ascetic priests, who, 'feeding themselves on honey and milk alone, reject bread and other foods'.[3] While honey often contains B vitamins, vitamin C and some minerals, one would not imagine that a diet of milk and honey would be nutritionally sound.[4] In her will of 980–90, Æthelgifu directs that 'one sester of honey' (*anne sester huniges*) is to be given annually to St. Alban's Abbey.[5] A fragment of an inventory at Bury St. Edmunds lists seven sesters of honey.[6] Land was given to a monastery to provide . . . honey for the brothers.[7] While there may be 'every reason to think that . . . honey figured at the monastic table', it is likely that mead was as important in monastic establishments as it was in secular establishments.[8]

---

[1] Crane 1983, 104.
[2] Herzfeld 1900, March 27.
[3] Whitelock 1955, 749.
[4] McGee 1986, 373.
[5] Whitelock 1968, 11.
[6] Robertson 1939, 249.
[7] 3 Gale Script. 445 quoted in Turner.
[8] Knowles 1940, 462–3.

11. Fish and Molluscs

It is probable that fish and molluscs were more plentiful in coastal and inland waters in Anglo-Saxon times than they are today. There is unlikely to have been overfishing or much pollution, although this may have been a factor locally in rivers late in the period. In this case there may have been a local scarcity of clean-living fish.[1] Bede wrote in his *Ecclesiastical History*: 'this land produces . . . various . . . sea creatures and it abounds in springs and waters full of fish' (*swylce eac þeos eorþe is berende . . . missenlicra . . . sæwihta 7 fiscumwyllum wæterum 7 wyllgesprungum*).[2] From later evidence, for example from Leicestershire, quite small streams were rented as fisheries.[3] In particular Bede notes: 'here are often captured seals and whales and porpoises and here are often found different kinds of whelks and mussels' (*her beoþ oft fangene seolas 7 hronas and mereswyn 7 her beoþ oft numene missenlicra cynna weolcscylle 7 muscule*).[4] The Latin version of the *Ecclesiastical History* listed 'salmon' (*issicio*) and 'eels' (*anguilla*), and the abundance of eels in the fens round Ely gave the place its name, Bede thought.[5] In 1125 William of Malmesbury wrote of the Fens: 'Here is such a quantity of fish as to cause astonishment in strangers, while the natives laugh at their surprise'.[6] The *Liber Eliensis* indicates the variety of fish in the Fens: 'innumerable eels, large water wolves (*lupi aquatici* – pike?), even pickerels, perch, roach, burbots and lampreys which we call water snakes. It is indeed said by many men that sometimes salmon (*isicii*), together with the royal fish, the sturgeon, are taken'.[7]

In the medieval period England exported herrings in return for wine from Gascony, and in the sixteenth century herrings were still being 'taken in gret hepis togeder . . . with nettis'.[8] There seems no reason to suppose that herring stocks were any smaller in the Anglo-Saxon period.

Climatic factors may have played a part in influencing the availability of fish. The colder continental climate of the eighth and tenth centuries may have extended the southerly range for some species, but limited the growth of oyster stocks, for example.[9] Oysters would have benefited from the warming up which began c.980 and continued beyond the end of the Anglo-Saxon period.

Deep sea fish are referred to in documents and are present in the archaeological record. Some fish were imported: merchants from Rouen brought 'salt whale' (*craspois*) on which Æthelred laid down the tolls payable at London Bridge, which suggests it was a luxury item.[10] *Egil's Saga* records the importation of dried fish from Norway into England in the tenth century.[1] Spring shoals of cod caught along

[1] O'Connor 1982, 32.
[2] Miller 1890, I 1 26.
[3] Hartley in Aston 1988, 291.
[4] op. cit.
[5] Miller 1898, I 1 19.
[6] Hamilton 1870, 322.
[7] Darby 1940, 28.
[8] Poole 1958, 232; Furnivall 1868, 114.
[9] Lamb 1981, 60; Laver 1916, 8.
[10] CA Wilson 1973, 28.
[1] Seebohm 1952, 109.

the western seaboard of Norway could be dehydrated in the cold, sunny air to a point at which they would keep almost indefinitely.[1] Stockfish from Norway were certainly a delicacy in medieval France.[2]

Some fish were apparently not readily available. The translator of the Leechbooks omits crayfish, scallops and conch shellfish in his original text, from the list of fish which take a long time to digest.[3] Perhaps the non-availability of octopus is what leads Ælfric to translate *polipodes* by *lopystran* (lobster) in his *Colloquy*.

Fishing

Leaving aside those members of an early landed gentry for whom fishing seems to have been primarily a recreation along with hunting and hawking,[4] some individuals with access to inland or coastal water presumably fished, using a variety of methods. In the late sixth-century Welsh poem *The Gododdin*, the father in the interpolated cradle song, 'killed fish in his coracle . . . he would bring back . . . a fish from the falls of Derwennydd'.[5] Much later, the Gwentian Code stated that whoever set a net in a river was to have one-third of the fish, two-thirds were to go to the owner of the river.[6] This suggests, firstly, that fishing rights had been established, at least in Wales, towards the end of the Anglo-Saxon period, a fact commented on by Wendy Davies in *Wales in the Early Middle Ages*.[7] Secondly, that as long as the owner of the fishing rights was compensated generously, individual initiative was allowed.

Most people would have been able to procure a rod and line, and this method had the advantage, according to the Anomalous Welsh Laws, that 'if you were taking fish on hooks you were not obliged to give anyone else who came along a share'.[8] A manuscript of c.1000, probably from Canterbury, shows fishing with a rod and line.[9] A trident fish spear was found in a late Anglo-Saxon hoard at Nazeing, and has parallels in more recent folk collections.[10] Neckham, writing in the twelfth century, stated that a peasant should have a 'fishing fork shaped like a hook that he may get himself fish' but it is difficult to know if he meant simply a small bifurcated hook for use with a line, or some sort of fish spear.[11] A tenth-century legend refers to a fishing line of hemp being sold in Lincoln.[12] Hemp and flax were cultivated in the Anglo-Saxon period at Old Buckenham Mere, Norfolk, and were present on tenth-century Anglo-Scandinavian sites in York.[1] Hemp was the usual material for both fisher and fowler to make their nets of in the sixteenth century.[2]

---

[1] CA Wilson 1973, 30.
[2] Kuper 1977, 19.
[3] Cockayne 1851, I i 1.
[4] Alfred's *Preface to the Soliloquies of St Augustine*: Whitelock 1955, 844.
[5] Jackson 1969, 151.
[6] Owen 1841, I 553.
[7] Davies 1982, 125.
[8] Owen 1841, II 9.
[9] Temple 1976, fig. 176.
[10] Morris 1983, 34.
[11] Holmes 1952, 200.
[12] Godwin *Antiquity* XLI Part 161, 44.
[1] op. cit., 45; Hall et al. 1983, 179.
[2] Furnivall 1868, 127.

A *gebur* on the manor of Tidenham was expected to provide a ball of good net twine, which suggests it was not too exotic an item to come by, and although netting is a skilled craft, it was probably widely practised.[1] Pieces of ropes and net from Viking age Denmark have all proved to be made from bast, usually of oak but with a significant proportion from lime. The rope was presumably finished with grease.[2] The Gwentian Code details the values of various nets from a bow net at 4d to a salmon net at 24d.[3] The net for fishing, according to Anomalous Welsh Laws, was to be large enough at least to entangle an ox.[4] These Laws suggest that the fish were driven into the nets, since they state that whoever started the fish was to have them, even if they went into the nets of another.[5]

Fish-weirs

Taking fish in weirs, traps and stationary nets were probably the commonest methods, and perhaps the most efficient in terms of results for time expended, since all could be left unattended for most of the time. At Lincoln a succession of hurdles/stake-built structures dating from c.900–1200 was erected in shallow water on the river Witham. These may have been fish weirs put up to funnel fish into areas of still water near the shore. At the St. Benedict's Square site a series of wicker fences of c.975–1025 may indicate the presence of a fish-farm.[6] Brushwood weirs could be set up in rivers and also on the sea shore. The sea weir at Southwold referred to in Domesday indicates a fishing industry already well-developed by the eleventh century.[7] There were probably extensive fish-weirs on the mud flats of the Bristol Channel, and there were certainly fish-weirs at Dunster and Carhampton by the late eleventh century.[8] It is usual to find weirs, which were often in personal ownership, mentioned in grants of property, as for example in the formula 'in marsh and meadow, weir and water' (*on merisce 7 on mæduen on weren 7 on wætere*) used in King Edward's grant of land at Claygate.[9] The earliest reference to weirs in the Severn is in a reputed Saxon charter for Ombersley, Worcs.[10]

Kidells, *hedges* or *stops* were rough brushwood structures angled across the current in the shape of a shallow V or W with a net at the apex. A V-shaped Saxon fish-weir carbon-dated to the eighth to ninth centuries was discovered in the Trent at Colwick, Notts. This was formed of boulders, posts and a fish-tight fence, built very obliquely across the river.[11] It was probably for catching eels, since according to Domesday all the 22 *piscaria* in Notts. were for eels.[1] Domesday records that the renders from eight fisheries on the Severn were usually of eels.[2]

---

[1] Seebohm 1883, 155.
[2] Roesdahl 1982, 100.
[3] Owen 1841, I 203.
[4] op. cit., II 5.
[5] op. cit., 9.
[6] P. Chitwood *Lincoln's ancient docklands: the search continues* in Good *et al.* 1991 p. 172.
[7] Taylor in Aston 1988, 466.
[8] Bond & Chamber in op. cit., 394, 401.
[9] Harmer 1952, 359.
[10] Bond and Chambers in Aston 1988, 375.
[11] Losco-Bradley & Salisbury in Ashton 1988, 329–348.
[1] Day in op. cit., 346.
[2] Bond & Chambers in op. cit., 375.

Boundary charters refer to weirs, which seem very often to be in private ownership.[1] Place or field-names may give clues to the whereabouts of Anglo-Saxon fisheries even when the first record of a name is post-Conquest. *Bykeleswere* (1305) contains the O.E. personal name *Biccel* with O.E. *wer* (weir). *Noweria* is probably a Latinised form of New Weir.[2] *Hersepol* (*piscar*) (Hersa's pool) (1141) records another fishery.[3] *Dunywere* (1392) and *Ellesmoreswere* (1395) record the position of weirs in the Severn.[4]

The survey of the manor of Tidenham refers to a number of 'basket-weirs' (*cytweras*) and 'hackle-weirs' (*hæcweras*) on the Wye and Severn.[5] Such devices were presumably the 'fisheries' which had been constructed to the hindrance of the Thames, Trent, Severn and Yorkshire Ouse, and which Edward the Confessor ordered to be destroyed in 1066.[6] *Gerefa* lists making a fish-weir as one of the summer tasks (*fiscwer . . . macian*).[7] The reeve was also in charge of the eel container, according to Seebohm.[8] However, he is presumably translating *ælhyd* (eel skin). If emended to *ælhyð*, (eel landing-place) then the pits dug in front of the causeways at Dorestad which held baskets of wickerwork and possibly served as fish containers come to mind,[9] but eelskin has uses for which the reeve may have kept it: for providing the leather flexure between the two wooden members of a flail, as hinges for doors, and as a membrane through which liquids could be filtered. Were there eel traps they may have resembled the trap made from young willow shoots found in the thirteenth-century levels in Bryggen, Norway, or the two traps made of birch and willow found at Dorestad.[10] Eel traps, *bucks*, perhaps equivalent to the *putt* or *butt* of the Severn, were in position on the Thames well into the last century and a photographic record of them exists.[11] *Bucks* were often positioned in mill cuts, and renders in eels from mills were mentioned more often in Domesday than renders in corn. For example, at Alveston, Warwickshire, a mill rendered one thousand and twelve *stitches* of eels. A stitch was *xxv anguillis*.[12] At times it is expressly stated that the render must be of large eels.[13] 'Eel mill ditch' and 'eel dikes' often occur in boundary charters.[14] On the border of the Bayeux Tapestry below the river Couesnon are fishes and eels, and a man with a knife who is 'either drowning, or catching' eels.[15]

[1] Bosworth & Toller 1898, I 1206.
[2] Smith 1964, III 243, 208.
[3] op. cit., II 166.
[4] op. cit., 162.
[5] Robertson 1939, 205.
[6] Wilson DG 1977, 35.
[7] Liebermann 1898, 454.
[8] Seebohm 1952, 109.
[9] Van Es 1980, 24.
[10] Bruce-Mitford 1975, 71; Prummel 1983, 10–11.
[11] Wilson DG 1977, 35; Edlin 1949, fig. 67, 68.
[12] Commissioners 1819, 417.
[13] Loyn 1970, 359.
[14] Turner 1828.
[15] Wilson 1985, plates 19, 20, p. 179.

Fishponds

Those who had resources in terms of land and labour might dig out fishponds which are therefore generally associated with manorial property or monastic buildings.[1] Quite complex feats of water engineering were needed to prevent the build up of fish waste products.[2] Robert Malet had *xx piscinæ* at *Tuduuorde*, Yorkshire, which returned two thousand eels. The abbot of Bury St. Edmunds had eleven *vivaria* and *piscinæ ad victum monachorum*.[3] Even a small and poor monastic house founded before 1161 had extensive fishponds.[4] Two tenth-century Oxfordshire charter references to *stirigan pole* and *strygan pol* have been identified with a artificial rectangular pond 48.8m x 9.1m.[5] *Vivarium piscium* are recorded at various places in the Domesday survey, and the pond fishes they were likely to contain, according to a source of 1170, were bream, pike, roach and perch.[6] An acre pond would produce only 40 lb of bream a year and even the very large (130 acre) pond of St. Swithun's at Fleet would not have made the community self-sufficient in fish.[7] A number of fishponds have no doubt already been destroyed, and others are difficult to date.[8] These fish were likely to have been consumed mainly by the rich or those in monastic orders.[9] The *Second Penitential of Theodore* dealt with the finding and eating of dead fish found in fishponds, but may relate only to continental practices.[10]

Fishermen

Professional fishermen may have been provided with boats by their employers. In the Assignment of Property to Thorney Abbey two ores are spent on a boat and net, and a further five boats are bought for two ores apiece for the Fenland fisheries.[11] Freelance fishermen may have been able to finance the manufacture of vessels from their trading activities. Coracle-like craft would have continued to be made throughout the period in Wales and probably in the Anglo-Saxon region too. They would have been economical in terms of materials, not requiring the larger timbers used in clinker-built ships. Logboats have been shown by radiocarbon assay to have been made well into medieval times.[12]

Inland waters were fished by professional fishermen like Thorulf, the fisherman of Farcet, and Wulfgeit, the fisherman of Hepmangrove, who were both witnesses to a writ.[13] Or they fished estuaries and coastal waters like the fisherman of the *Colloquy*. Others presumably went out further fishing for whales. Ælfric's fisherman appears to have been self-employed, but others were the servants of landowners, whether the king, (like the twenty-four fishermen in *Gememutha* – Yarmouth – who belonged to the royal manor of *Gorlestune*, Suffolk), or an abbot. Thorney Abbey had several

---

[1] Hartley in Ashton 1988, 296.
[2] Currie in op. cit., 271, 273.
[3] Commissioners 1819, 417.
[4] Shackley et al. in Ashton 1988, 301.
[5] Bond & Chambers in op. cit., 356.
[6] op. cit., 365.
[7] op. cit., 275–6.
[8] Dennison & Iles in op. cit., 210, 208.
[9] op. cit., 67.
[10] Wilson CA 1973, 365.
[11] Robertson 1939, 253.
[12] McGrail & Switsur 1979, 229–31.
[13] Harmer 1952, 253.

fishermen working to supply the monks. Domesday lists a number of fishermen county by county. Bedfordshire and Staffordshire had one and two respectively, Nottinghamshire 32, and Oxfordshire 38. Counties with sea coasts had more: Norfolk–72, Kent–158, but 211 are recorded for Lincolnshire which had both a sea coast and extensive inland fisheries in the Fens.

The presence of fishermen may be related to fish available for purchase, since even if fishermen were working for the king or a monastery there may have been surpluses they could sell. A detailed investigation of fishermen who returned money renders, and the sums of money involved, would indicate more accurately where quantities of fish could be bought. That fish were sold is indicated by the eleventh-century Assignments of Property to Thorney Abbey:[1] 'First of all 2000 herrings were bought for 40d'. The fishermen in the *Colloquy* sold his catch in the town to the *ceasterwara* and declares, 'I cannot catch as many as I could sell' (*Ic ne mæg swa fela swa ic mæg gesyllan*).[2] This situation is perhaps suggested by the 'three pence for fish' (*þræ peniges at fysc*) left in a will for the first funeral feast, that is on the first anniversary of the funeral.[3] Fish are not specified for the funeral feast itself, perhaps because organising the supply – as with the venison also to be provided at the anniversary feast – took time. The reference to *Laxbothes* – salmon stalls – near High Bridge at Lincoln is late – 1254,[4] but the fact both elements of the name are Old English probably reflects long-term use.

Documentary Evidence

There are a very large number of references to fish and fisheries in documents. Such documents are often associated with monasteries where the monks would have to eat fish on fast days. Hlothhere, king of Kent, granted land in Thanet ' ... with everything belonging to it ... fens, fisheries ... ' to Abbot Brihtwold in 679.[5] The following century, in 736, Æthelbald, king of Mercia, granted Stour in Ismere, Worcestershire, 'with fisheries' to Ealdorman Cyneberht.[6] The will of Theodred, bishop of London from 942–951 gave estates to St. Paul's, including one at Sothery, Norfolk, 'with all the fishing that belongs to it', and King Cnut restored land at Drayton, Hampshire to New Minster, Winchester, in 1019 with 'the inconceivable abundance of fish in Neptune's watery element'.[7]

Sometimes the fisheries are not mentioned incidentally to estates, but are themselves the subjects of grants. In 688 King Ceadwalla granted 5 *manentes* at the confluence of the rivers Avon and Wylye for a fishery, King Æthelstan granted to St. Mary's 'a fishery at Austan which already belonged to the church', and the monks of Winchcombe and St. Peter's, Gloucester, received equal shares of the fishery at *Fremelade* from King Edward.[8]

[1] Robertson 1939, 253.
[2] Garmonsway 1978, 27.
[3] Robertson 1939, 53.
[4] Cameron 1985, 183.
[5] Whitelock 1955, 443.
[6] op. cit., 453.
[7] op. cit., 509, 553.
[8] Finberg, 1972, 32, 52, 70.

Sometimes the lessor of a fishery and/or land would reserve rent in the form of fish. The lessee of 40 *agri* and a fishery at *Huneshom* was to render yearly from 996 to the Archbishop of York 15 good salmon on the first day of Lent.[1] Sometime between 1061 and 1065, Ælfwig, abbot of Bath, leased 30 hides at Tidenham reserving an annual rent of one mark of gold, 6 porpoises and 30,000 herrings.[2]

The large numbers of fish involved in the later documents suggest the mass catering arrangements monasteries had to make, not only for the monks, but for layworkers, travellers, and those who received their charity. At the time of Domesday 60,000 herrings were paid annually to the monks of Bury. Queen Ælfgifu had granted 4000 eels 'to the saint' in Cnut's Charter.[3] The will of Wulfric Spott (1002–4) granted lands between the Ribble and the Mersey and in the Wirral to two lessees 'on condition that when it is the shad season each of them shall pay 3000 shad to the monastery at Burton'.[4] Thorney Abbey received 26,275 eels as rent from individuals and from various weirs and watercourses.[5] King Edgar added to an earlier gift 10,000 eels yearly for the monks at Ely.[6] St. Peter, Winchester, received 38,500 herrings from their manor at Lewes, Sussex, and Sandwich, Kent, given by Cnut to Christchurch, Canterbury, yielded 40,000 herrings a year.[7] On a more modest scale, Eadsige granted an estate on condition that each year *þreo gebind æles* (i.e. 75 eels) should be rendered to Christchurch.[8] Unfortunately the documentary record is incomplete: we cannot be sure that we have the total amount of fish received by any one monastery, nor do we have details of the numbers to be fed, so it is not possible to estimate how much fish each monk consumed. Clearly most of the fish in these large renders must have undergone some sort of preservation treatment; even the very largest establishments could not have consumed these amounts of fresh fish.

Archaeological evidence for large numbers of herrings includes the compacted layer of between one and two thousand herrings on the St. Mary Bishophill Junior site in York, which appears to be the remains of stored or discarded fish.[9]

We have seen that the lessee of the *Huneshom* fishery was to pay his rent of 15 good salmon on the first day of Lent. Ærunketel and his wife Wulfrun granted 8 salmon to Ramsey Abbey 'for the brothers during Lent'. These were probably transported 55 miles from the River Smite.[10] Æthelgifu left in her will six measures of fish to be paid every Lent to Braughing and Welwyn by Ælfwold in return for his land at Munden.[11] Ramsey Abbey received every year from 20 fishermen 60,000 eels 'for the use of the brethren' to be paid at the feast of St. Benedict – i.e. in Lent.[12] However, Ramsey Abbey itself had to give each Lent 4000 eels 'as a voluntary gift' to the abbot and monks at Peterborough.[13] A

[1] op. cit., 135.
[2] op. cit., 77.
[3] Harmer 1952, 434.
[4] Whitelock 1955, 542.
[5] Robertson 1939, 257.
[6] op. cit., 100.
[7] Loyn 1970, 361.
[8] Robertson 1939, 171.
[9] Moulden and Tweddle 1986, 24.
[10] Hart 1975, 113.
[11] Whitelock 1968, 8.
[12] Darby 1940, 29.
[13] Harmer 1952, 262.

lease of land of Denewulf, Bishop of Winchester, states that if the render should occur in Lent, then the value of the meat was to be taken in fish unless this was impracticable.[1]

Fish seems to have been considered suitable for feasts on the anniversaries of funerals. A fragment of a will from Bury St. Edmunds assigns *præ peniges* for fish, but Abbot Ufi left half a pound for fish at his anniversary. Abbot Baldwin granted the same amount for fish at the anniversary of 'Edward, the good king, on condition that they remember him the oftener in their prayers'.[2]

Perhaps because the fish was a Christian symbol and was associated with self-denial, they seem to have been a particularly suitable subject for the exercise of miraculous powers, or simply, in the following cases concerning St. Cuthbert and St. Martin, the powers of observation. One day St. Cuthbert asked a boy travelling on foot with him, 'Do you think that someone has prepared your evening meal today?' He answered he knew none of their kindred along that way and he did not hope for any sort of kindness from unknown strangers. Whereupon Cuthbert replied, 'My son, be of good cheer . . . This is the eagle which the Lord has instructed to provide us with food today.' The boy ran to the eagle and found a large fish. Commendably he gave half to the eagle, and they proceeded to the next village. Giving the fish to be broiled (*dato ad assandum, pisciculo*), 'they refreshed themselves and those whose home they had entered with a most acceptable repast' (*gratissimo refecere convivio*). On another occasion when Cuthbert and two companions were afflicted by hunger they found 'three portions of porpoise's flesh as if cut up with a knife' (*tres partes delfini carnis quasi humano manu cum cultella sectas*). These were 'sufficient for three men for three days and nights. They cooked them and enjoyed the wonderful sweetness of the flesh'.[3] St. Martin wanted fish to eat one Easter day but the steward said neither he nor the fisherman had caught so much as 'a single sprat' (*ænne sprott*). The holy man told him to cast out his net and when he drew it up '*þær wearð on-innan an ormæte leax*' – 'a huge salmon', which he carried to the minster where the saint prepared it.[4] It was at least safe in legal terms to find a fish. To miraculously find a domestic animal was to run the risk of being confronted by a posse of searchers and an owner demanding compensation.

The miracle associated with St. Wilfred presents more of a problem. He found the folk in Sussex starving after three years of famine – although the coastal waters abounded in fish, because 'they knew only how to catch eels'. He showed them how to use the *ælnet* in the sea, and by God's grace 'they soon took three hundred fish of various kinds' (*hie sona gefengon þreo hund fisca missenlicra cynna*).[5] This is in conflict with the archaeological record, since whiting bones as well as eel bones were recovered from the mid-fifth early sixth-century site of Bishopstone in Sussex.[6]

The overriding impression is that, certainly by the end of the period and probably much earlier, a number of individuals as well as religious houses had secured access to plentiful supplies of fish and kept careful records of their entitlements. The

---

[1] Robertson 1939, 39.
[2] op. cit., 197.
[3] Colgrave 1940, 82–7; 82–5.
[4] Skeat 1881, l.126–7.
[5] Miller 1890, I, 2 304.
[6] Bell 1977, 276ff.

individuals who secured these benefits were once again the king and his nobles. As early as 688–694 Ine's Laws stated that 10 hides were to furnish 5 salmon and 100 eels (as well as other items).[1] Domesday supplies much more evidence: Marcle paid 6 salmon to the King, at Totnes two fisheries each yielded 30 salmon as rent, but a fishery belonging to Earl Edwin at Eaton by Chester paid 1000 salmon.[2] Petersham paid 1000 lampreys and 1000 eels, and at Wisbech 17 fishermen paid a rent of 59,260 eels. Lewes, Sussex, rendered 38,500 herrings, and Dunwich, Suffolk, 60,000.[3] Occasionally the king would appropriate someone else's fish as Harold Harefoot did c.1050. He had Sandwich taken from Christchurch for his own use for *twegen hæringc timan*.[4] *Niworde*,[5] paid 16,000 herrings annually to the Lord of Warenne.[6]

The lord of the manor of Tidenham claimed every alternate fish taken at the fish-weirs and 'every rare fish which is of value: sturgeon or porpoise, herring or sea fish'. No one had the right to sell any fish for money when the lord was on the estate without telling him – so he would have first choice, presumably.[7] The sturgeon (Lat:*acipenser*) was esteemed from Roman times.[8]

The Anomalous Welsh Laws point out that it is free for everyone to fish in the sea, 'what the sea casts ashore however, whether dead or alive belongs to the king from the day they are cast up until the third day; from the third day forth, if not taken by the king, let them be a booty to such as find them'.[9] A small fish washed up in the heat of summer might not be much of a prize to anyone after the third day, and no doubt even a moderately hungry man who was unobserved might make away with a free meal. The three-day limit does not seem to have applied in England, although the earliest record of a king claiming a whale 'whereof a great part has been carried away by certain evil doers' does not seem to be until 1337.[10] A whale's feelings on being stranded are inscribed on the early eighth-century Northumbrian Franks Casket, which was made of whalebone:

> Fisc flodu ahof on fergenberig
> warþ gasric grorn, þær he on greut giswom.
> Hronæs ban.

> The swell lifted the fish up onto the cliff bank. The whale became sad where he swam on the shingle. Whale's bone.[11]

Anglo-Saxon kings seem also to have had rights to anything, including fish, washed up by the sea, since occasionally they appear to have conferred these rights on others. Cnut granted St. Edmunds all the fishery that Ulfketel had and the *gafol* fish which accrue to the king himself.[1] King Edward granted to Ramsey 'everything cast up by

---

[1] Whitelock 1955, 371.
[2] Commissioners 1819, 417.
[3] Whitelock 1952, 118.
[4] Robertson 1939, 175.
[5] ?Ilford, Sussex.
[6] Loyn 1970, 361.
[7] Douglas & Greenaway 1953, 817.
[8] Clair 1964, 42.
[9] Owen 1841, I 53.
[10] Bland & Tawney 1914, 40.
[11] Elliott 1963, 99ff.
[1] Harmer 1952, 434.

the sea at Brancaster and Ringstead as well and as freely as I myself have it by the sea coast anywhere in England' (*þa sæupwarp of eallan þingen æt Bramcæstre 7 æt Ringstyde swa wel 7 swa freolice swa ic hit me seolf betst habbe bi ða særime ahwær in Engelande*).[1] King Edward granted to Urk his *huskarl* the shore adjoining his land 'and everything that is driven to his shore' (*7 eall to hys strande gedryuen hys*).[2] Urk's possessions came into the ownership of Abbotsbury and in 1315 Edward II confirmed their right to a 'fat fish' (*crassus piscis*) which had been washed up. This might have been a sturgeon, porpoise or whale. One hopes for the sake of the monks that the legal procedure was not protracted.[3]

'Fat Fish' seems to have been considered a delicacy. According to *IV Æthelred*, merchants who came to London Bridge with (wine or) blubber fish (*craspisce*) paid a duty of 6 shillings for a large ship and 5% of the fish.[4] This supposes the cargo would realise a high price, since a large ship carrying only *piscis* would have to pay only 1d as toll. We have seen that 6 porpoises were reserved as rent when Ælfwih granted land to Archbishop Stigand, and Southease paid four pounds 'for porpoises' at the time of Domesday.[5] A porpoise bone occurs in the secular family treasure of St. Ninian's Isle dated to c.800. Otherwise the hoard consists only of silver objects. Perhaps it was included as a status indicator but 'the deeper meaning of this bone remains an enigma'.[6] That porpoise was not merely a subsistence item is suggested by its inclusion (with seals) at the feast for Archbishop Neville at York in 1467.[7] Much earlier, Adamnan (624–704) speaks in his life of St. Columba of 'the little island where our sea calves breed', and these were presumably seals, since porpoise were referred to as 'sea-swine'.[8] Twelfth-century Irish praise of the cliff of Alternan refers to the fat seals that used to sleep there. Alfred interpolated Ohthere's account of whale hunting off Norway in his translation of Orosius[9] and from what the fisherman of the *Colloquy* says, it is clear that whales were hunted by the English: 'many capture whales and escape danger and make a lot of money by doing so' (*manige gefoþ hwælas 7 ætberstaþ frecnysse, 7 micelne sceat þanon begytaþ*).[10] Whales could have been driven by the fishermen into inlets and killed, as is still done in the Faroe Islands.[11]

Dr. Stonehouse[12] suggests that whales and porpoises would have provided a significant food source because fats when cured would keep better than proteins or carbohydrates. It would be interesting to know if this preference for fatty fish reflected some physiological need. Most people's lives would have been spent in the open air, and in the absence of efficient heating, dwellings would have been cold in winter.

[1] op. cit., 259ff.
[2] op. cit., 120.
[3] op. cit., 426.
[4] Robertson 1925, 72.
[5] Whitelock 1952, 118.
[6] Small, Thomas and Wilson 1973, 124.
[7] Mead 1931, 33.
[8] McNeill 1963.
[9] Sweet 1954, 17.
[10] Garmonsway 1978, 30.
[11] Foote & Wilson 1970, 146–7.
[12] pers. comm. Dr. D.J. Drewry, Scott Polar Research Institute.

The existing legal documents refer only to a relatively limited range of fish: usually eels, shad, salmon, herrings, porpoise and lamprey. This presumably relates to the ease of supply: it would be easier to fulfil an order for 1000 of the same fish that could be caught in its annual migration than for 100 each of ten species needing to be caught from different habitats by different fishing methods. The legal evidence is in contrast to the evidence the fisherman gives in the *Colloquy*, and to the archaeological record discussed below. The fisherman records 'Eels and pike, minnows(?) and eelpout, trout or shote, lampreys, and whatever swims in the water. Sprats' (*Ælas 7 hacodas, mynas 7 ælputan, sceotan 7 lampredan 7 swa wylce swa on wætere swimmaþ. Sprote*). When he fishes in the sea he catches 'Herrings, salmon, porpoise, sturgeon, oysters and crab, mussels, periwinkles, cockles, flounders, plaice, lobsters and many such' (*Hæringas, leaxas, mereswyn, stirian, ostran 7 crabban, muslan, winewinklan, sæcoccas, fagc, floc, lopystran, 7 fela swycles*).[1] It is possible that it was the lampern, rather than the lamprey referred to in both sources, that was fished for, as it was 'more common, more edible and certainly not so repulsive-looking as the larger yellow-blotched sea lamprey'.[2]

Archaeological Evidence

The archaeological record has its own limitations. There is evidence from the bones that survive, that they were chewed and perhaps eaten, but few recognisable bones survive digestion.[3] Fish bones are usually smaller and more fragile than those from most other groups of edible animals. As a consequence their survival at any site is less likely, a bias which it is impossible to assess.[4] More serious is the bias due to failure to retrieve the bones excavated. One experiment where spoil heaps were sifted showed at least nine species of fish where no fish remains had been recovered.[5] A more representative sample can be obtained only by wet sieving.

However, despite the fact that evidence was no doubt lost in the past, a number of recent archaeological excavations provide evidence of the consumption of many species. The mid fifth- to early sixth-century site of Bishopstone yielded the bones of conger eel, from specimens at least 100 cm long, and whiting.[6] At the fifth- to seventh-century site of West Stow, there was evidence for perch and pike.[7] The tenth- to thirteenth-century deposits of York's Coppergate excavation have been the subject of a comprehensive survey. Marine species were most important. These included cod, haddock, herring, ling, mackerel, horse mackerel, conger eel and thornback ray. Of these, cod, haddock and herring were the most important. Estuarine and fresh water species were also present, most importantly eel, but including smelt, flounder, salmon, pike, perch, roach, chubb and dace.[8] Barbel and grayling bones were only present in late ninth-century levels – evidence that points to pollution of the river after

[1] Garmonsway 1978, 27–9.
[2] Wheeler 1979, 64.
[3] Jones, *The End Product*, undated paper.
[4] Wheeler & Jones 1974, 208.
[5] op. cit.
[6] Bell 1977.
[7] Crabtree in West 1982.
[8] Spencer 1979, 9ff.

this time.[1] At the Melbourne Street site, *Hamwih*, just under a quarter of the fish bone fragments were identified. Many of the remains in one pit (F16) came from flat fish: plaice and flounder were positively identified. The fish would have ranged in weight from less than 50 to more than 400 grams. After flatfish, the commonest species was eel – in all sizes, some very large. Also recorded are thornback and sting rays. The bucklers of thornback ray frequently found on Wessex urban sites are scanty evidence for what may have been fish of 20 to 30 kilograms.[2] Dogfish were probably taken, but skeletal remains would not often survive. Bass and grey mullet, horse mackerel, mackerel, cod (one more than a metre long), whiting, salmon (one specimen weighing slightly over 9 pounds), gilt-head sea bream and a possible pollack were found. Most of the fish could be caught from the modern shingle bank of the estuary.[3] There were five fragments of whalebone, and a whale vertebra was used as a block in the manufacture of animal bone artefacts.[4]

Although the site is late Anglo-Saxon, rather than mid-period like *Hamwih*, Exeter provides a similar picture, although the emphasis is different. Hake was the commonest fish, followed by conger eel. Also common were whiting, cod, pollack, ling, haddock, sea bream, and plaice. Present were gurnards, wrasses, salmon, bass, horse mackerel, eel, thornback ray, and, represented by one bone, turbot. The emphasis seems to have been on line fishing, with surface netting, and river/estuarine traps.[5]

At another late site, Flaxengate, Lincoln, cod was the most common fish, with some large specimens – 60–110 cms – present; a similar size range is recorded at Durham and Northampton. Possibly, local inshore fishing in winter produced small cod, but the large cod would have had to have been imported, preserved, from northern coasts; the same situation would have prevailed at King's Lynn and Yarmouth. Mid-Saxon Ipswich also produced many bones of codfish.[6] At Flaxengate medium to large haddock were eaten, as were salmon and sea trout. Flatfish – plaice, flounder and sole – were present, as they were in the late Anglo-Saxon levels at King's Lynn.[7] Ling – large specimens caught in fairly deep water – were probably traded south to Lincoln, like the large cod. Small species of shark, possibly dogfish and spurdog, and herring complete the list of marine species. The absence of eel at Flaxengate, found at virtually all other sites where fish bones have been recovered, needs to be mentioned. In fact fresh-water species were in short supply, limited to pike and small roach.[8]

The range of species at Great Yarmouth is similar to that found at other east coast sites: cod and herring, the most abundant, were followed by whiting, mackerel, horse mackerel, plaice, haddock, conger eel, eel, thornback ray, with ling, bass, Dover sole, turbot, flounder, garfish, spurdog and gurnard all present with other flatfish and cartilaginous fishes.[1] Most species could be caught off Great

---

[1] O'Connor 1985, 29ff.
[2] Coy in Hall & Kenward 1982, 113.
[3] Holdsworth 1980, 118.
[4] op. cit.
[5] Maltby 1979.
[6] West 1963, 243.
[7] Clarke & Carter 1977, 378ff.
[8] O'Connor 1982.
[1] Wheeler & Jones 1974, 211ff.

Yarmouth at the present time, but haddock is now rare, perhaps as the result of climatic change or over-fishing. Ling and halibut may have been imported from more northerly ports, or fishermen from Yarmouth may have fished more northerly waters. The conclusion is that fishing was carried on at all seasons of the year, with nets and hook and line.

Excavations in Ipswich demonstrate a great increase in the number of herring bones between the end of the middle Saxon period and the beginning of the Saxo-Norman phase of occupation. Figures for other major food fish do not show this dramatic leap, so either the distribution of herring in the North Sea changed, or there was some technological innovation, for example development of the drift net, at this point.[1]

Molluscs

'Oysters and crabs, mussels, periwinkles, cockles . . . lobsters' (*Ostran, 7 crabban, muslan, winewinclan, sæcoccas . . . lopystran*) are the molluscs the fisherman of the *Colloquy* sells to the townsfolk.[2] Some of these species are represented in the archaeological record and sometimes in large numbers. At the mid fifth- to sixth-century site of Bishopstone, mussels were the most plentiful mollusc, with significant numbers of periwinkles, limpets and oysters.[3] Oysters were placed in a pagan grave at Sarre, Kent.[4] At Portchester Castle shellfish were found in early, middle and late Saxon periods. The only mention of mussels is in an early to mid-Saxon context, but the ninth and tenth centuries are represented by 'many thousands of oysters and other shellfish'. The molluscs are not otherwise quantified, and are not treated as a separate section within the report, so that information has to be gathered from the description of the features. The impression is that oysters were the most common species, with winkles mentioned several times, and limpets mentioned only once, as occurring in a pit with late Saxon pottery.[5] At Poole, Dorset, a vast midden of oyster shells radio-carbon-dated to the late Saxon period represents between 28.56 and 57.12 tonnes of raw oyster meat. No other food remains are incorporated with the oyster shells and it seems possible the oysters were being harvested, opened and processed (perhaps by salting or pickling) for redistribution. This is also the interpretation of an eleventh- twelfth-century shell midden at Braunton Burrows, North Devon.[6] Mussels were eaten by the inhabitants of a tenth-century fishing village at Mawgan Porth, Cornwall, and there were great quantities of edible molluscs found at ninth- to tenth-century Gosport, Hants., and oysters were evidently consumed in mid-Saxon Ipswich.[7] The Cheddar palace site provided relatively few shells: oysters were most frequently found, followed by limpet, winkle and mussel.[1]

---

[1] Jones in Hall and Kenward 1982, 84.
[2] Garmonsway 1978, 29.
[3] Bell 1977.
[4] Whittock 1986, 152.
[5] Cunliffe 1976, 62ff.
[6] Horsey, I. P. & Winder, J. M. *Late Saxon and Conquest-period oyster middens at Poole, Dorset* in Good *et al.* 1991 pp. 102–4
[7] *Med. Archaeol.* XVI, 155; West 1963, 243.
[1] Rahtz 1979, 362.

More surprising is the presence of oysters, cockles, mussels and winkles at the Anglo-Danish town of Thetford, forty miles from the coast, and oysters in quantity, together with tiny numbers of mussels, cockles and winkles were found on late Saxon/early Norman sites in Bedford, eighty miles from the sea.[1] In fact oysters will live out of water for many weeks at low temperatures, and traditionally they were transported in barrels of seawater.[2] Perhaps the other shellfish were too, and arrived fresh and in good condition. The inhabitants of the two urban centres of York and *Hamwih* consumed shellfish in some quantity: oysters, cockles and mussels were the most common species at York, with modest numbers of whelks and limpets. Also present were various scallops, clams, horse mussels and winkles. There were also non-edible varieties, suggesting trawling was practised. This would have been an obvious method of harvesting the large quantities of shellfish involved.[3] Some thousands of oysters from three sites at *Hamwih* would have produced getting on for 100 kg. of meat. Winkles and cockles were the next in order of importance, with whelk and mussel. There were also sting winkle, dog whelk, netted dog whelk, saddle oyster, scallop, limpets and tellins, etc.[4] Most of the oysters were in the middle of the size range, i.e. about 3–4 years old, the size favoured for marketing in Britain today. The thinner shell of the smaller oysters would shatter on opening, and the meat of the larger oysters would not be tender enough to be eaten raw. They were probably collected from a natural population on the lower shore when tides were suitable. Again, as with 'fat fish', it would be interesting if the apparent preference for oysters reflected a physiological need. Oysters are highly nutritious, containing vitamins A, B1, B2, C, D, & PP. A is absent from meat and fish, except for fish liver.[5] Something of this seems to have been known to the writer of *Leechbook II* as in xxxvii he diverges from his Greek original to add that shellfish make good blood, an opinion repeated of oysters eight centuries later.[6] Elsewhere he recommends a diet including winkles and oysters. However, the presence of oysters in large numbers may have been no more than a reflection of their abundance. Stocks were not over-fished in Anglo-Saxon times, and the oyster's main enemies nowadays, like the slipper limpet, have been imported, and were not then present.[7]

A document of Richard I's reign attests to the famous oyster fishery in the Colne at Colchester, that it had been in existence during the two preceding reigns, i.e. to 1135, and 'from time immemorial beyond that'.[8] This could take it back into the Anglo-Saxon period. It may have been that oyster fishing in particular areas continued more or less uninterrupted from Roman times when Rutupian oysters were exported to Rome from Kent, as were oysters from the river Colne at Colchester.[9] The presence of oysters in the grave at Sarre indicates that oysters continued to be harvested in Kent after the Roman period.[1]

---

[1] Clarke 1960, 28; *Beds. Archaeol. J.* 13, 291.
[2] Yonge 1966, 91.
[3] O'Connor 1985, 29ff.
[4] Holdsworth 1980.
[5] op. cit., 121.
[6] Laver 1916, 91.
[7] op. cit., 8ff.
[8] op. cit., 56.
[9] Yonge 1966, 91.
[1] Whittock 1986, 152.

The remains of crab, lobster, shrimp and crayfish have not to my knowledge been recorded, but as their remains would be particularly delicate, this is perhaps not surprising.

Another mollusc that may have been eaten in Anglo-Saxon times is a land snail, *helix aspersa*. Three complete shells and two fragments were found at Beckery Chapel.[1] This species was apparently eaten in Romano-British times, and was still sold in Bristol markets at the beginning of this century under the name 'wall fish'. This particular instance highlights the difficulty of deciding whether remains are naturally occurring, or are food remains.

There was a considerable demand for fish, which were considered a delicacy. Fresh fish seem to have been most favoured, though a number, if not most, fish must have been consumed in a preserved state. Consumed in great numbers by monastic establishments, fish also graced the tables of the rich. The evidence from all sources for medieval fishing and fish-farming, and the numerous sites of fishponds indicate fish must have played an important part in the food intake at least of the upper classes of society.[2] Areas like the Fens and the Somerset Levels continued to provide abundant freshwater fish, even after drainage operations began in the late Saxon period.[3] Fish were given as prestige gifts, either for the table or for stocking fishponds.[4] Fish are often the only identifiable food item in contemporary illustrations of individuals at table. Such illustrations are usually of important individuals, if not royalty.

Perhaps oysters and other shellfish were a relatively cheap food for town dwellers, and had little status as a food, as was the case into Victorian times. That the Cheddar palace site provided comparatively few shells, might bear this out.[5]

---

[1] Rahtz & Hirst 1974, 83.
[2] Taylor in Ashton 1988, 465.
[3] Bond & Chambers in op. cit., 391.
[4] Bond & Chambers in op. cit., 367, Aston & Bond in op. cit., 438.
[5] Rahtz 1979, 362.

12. Imported Food

A brief survey of the archaeological and documentary evidence introduces this chapter to indicate the range of Anglo-Saxon trading contacts, and show what edible substances (which are unlikely to have survived in archaeological contexts) may also have been imported.

New types of trading settlements on navigable rivers or natural harbours were established both in England and on the continent from the end of the sixth century to the beginning of the eighth. These included Quentovic, Wijk-bij-Duurstede, Schleswig, Brunswick, Bardowick, London, Ipswich, York, Swanage, Norwich, Dunwich, Harwich and *Hamwih*.[1] By the 560's Kent was trading with the Frankish kingdom of Charibert; East Anglia with Scandinavia and the Baltic.[2] Cowries (from the Indian ocean) have been found in sixth- and seventh-century graves, mostly in Kent but several reached Cambridgeshire, Bedfordshire, Buckinghamshire and Oxfordshire.[3] Garnets from India and Ceylon have been discovered in sixth- and seventh-century contexts.[4] Procopius, writing in Byzantium in the second and third quarters of the sixth century, had heard of farmers of the North Sea littoral who were ferrymen.[5] There is evidence that trade with Byzantine areas was established as early as the beginning of the seventh century.[6] In the first half of the seventh century, Byzantine silver and Coptic bowls from the eastern Mediterranean were buried in Suffolk.[7] Perhaps such goods arrived via the annual fair of St. Denis, near Paris, held from 634 and visited by Saxon merchants.[8] Later in the seventh century St. Cuthbert was buried with an ivory comb and a pectoral cross containing white shell imported from tropical waters.[9] Seventh-century west Frankish E-ware was traded into Somerset, seventh- and eighth-century wheel-turned pottery from Frankish territory on the middle and lower Rhine, and fragments of Neidermendig lava were excavated in *Hamwih*, and trade with Carolingian Gaul continued into the ninth century.[10] Frankish and Rhenish vessels were found also in Anglian York.[11] Ecclesiastical manuscripts and objects from Rome are recorded – other items were less likely to have been mentioned.[12]

In the first third of the eighth century London is mentioned by Bede as being the emporium of many people coming by sea and land.[13] Writing of the years shortly before 720, he remarked that a great many of the English race were in the habit of going from Britain to Rome, nobles and men of common birth, women as well as

---

[1] Tatton-Brown in Haslam 1984, 16.
[2] Whittock 1986, 225.
[3] Hawkes et al. 1985, 100.
[4] Welch 1992, 116.
[5] Hodges 1982, 32–3.
[6] Dodwell 1982, 155.
[7] Sutton Hoo Report Vol. III.
[8] Levison 1946, 7.
[9] DM Wilson 1960, 64, 66.
[10] Copley 1958, 178.
[11] Holdsworth 1974, 37.
[12] Dodwell 1982, 96.
[13] Whitelock 1955, 609.

men, officers of government as well as ordinary people.[1] Such individuals may have brought back exotic food, particularly if this was preserved, and valuable in proportion to its bulk.

In the first half of the eighth century, a number of royal grants remitting the toll on one or more ships at various ports were made to religious foundations.[2] This kind of grant continued to be made. For example, Cnut granted the dues from every ship arriving at Sandwich to Christchurch, Canterbury.[3] Records would seem to indicate that trade was well-established by the eighth century. At *Hamwih* the pottery argues the presence of wines from north-west France. At York a number of eighth-century silver coins: 'porcupine series stycas', the medium of international commerce, indicate that it was visited by, or was the home of, traders.[4] This archaeological evidence confirms Altfrid's *Vita Liudgeri*, which suggests York was visited by Frisian merchants, or even had a Frisian colony in the eighth century.[5] Sarre, Harwich, and Fordwich may also have been trading stations at this period, and some of the ancient Romano-British towns, e.g. Chester and Lincoln, may have performed a similar function.[6] York evidently continued as a centre of trade: in 974 it was recorded that merchants coming from York were taken prisoner by the islanders of Thanet.[7]

An ecclesiastical council of 785 ordered the clergy not to wear the tinctured colours of India, nor precious – presumably silk – garments.[8] The inference must be that some at least of the clergy were given to ostentatious display, and if dyes and fabrics were imported from India and the Far East, then other items could be too. There is other documentary evidence for the presence of silks from the eighth century on, and archaeological evidence for silk in early tenth-century Saltergate, Lincoln, and Coppergate, York.[9]

In 796 Charlemagne wrote to Offa to say that English merchants would be afforded protection and support in his kingdom, according to the ancient custom of trading. Similarly he asked for justice for his own subjects in Offa's realm. In the same letter he refers to the accompanying gift of two silk palls, establishing beyond doubt trade with the Near East.[10] In the following century Frankish coins found their way to England, like the half a denier of Charles the Bald excavated at York.[11] Theoretically, and almost certainly practically, such trade made Mediterranean products available to the Anglo-Saxons.

Hodges demonstrates that from c.490–600, trade was mainly between the Rhine and East Anglia and Kent; from 600–640, between the Rhone and Rhine and East Anglia, the Seine and eastern and southern England; from 690 to 830 between the Rhine and Thames; between 700 and 830 between the Seine and central and southern England.[1]

---

[1] Hunter Blair 1970, 190.
[2] Whitelock 1955, 451.
[3] Robertson 1939, 159.
[4] Kemp 1986, 11.
[5] Wilson 1986, 232.
[6] op. cit., 233.
[7] Whitelock 1955, 257.
[8] Turner 1828, III 46.
[9] Dodwell 1982, 129, 130, 145, 150, 151, 156, 165; McGregor 1982, 132.
[10] Whitelock 1955, 781–2.
[11] *Interim X*, No. 2, 19.
[1] Hodges 1982, 32.

Asser remarked that King Alfred showed daily solicitude for the nations which dwelt from the Tyrrhenian Sea to the furthest end of Ireland. He also received gifts and letters from Elias, Patriarch of Jerusalem.[1] In 883 Sigelm and Æthelstan took alms to Rome and continued on to St. Thomas and St. Bartholomew in India.[2] There was evidently an annual expedition to Rome, so that when this does not take place, as in 889, the fact is recorded, but nevertheless, King Alfred sent two courtiers with letters that year.[3] He received at his court Ohthere and Wulfstan, who had travelled in the Baltic to Eastonia, and round to the north of Norway.[4]

Very large numbers of Arabic coins found their way into northern Europe and Scandinavia from the end of the ninth century as a result of Viking raiding and trading.[5] At the end of the tenth century, trade was important enough for Æthelred to state that every trading ship which entered an estuary was to have peace, even if it came from a region outside the truce.[6] Likewise Vikings were not to attack English traders in the ports of Germany, the Low Countries or France.[7] Cnut's letter of 1027 states that princes through whose lands the route to Rome lay, confirmed that his subjects – merchants and others – would be afforded protection, and would be free from unjust tolls.[8]

By the end of the tenth century men from Rouen and other parts of France were well-known in England, importing wine and *craspois* (salt whale), and so were traders from Flanders.[9] Irish merchants were often in Chester, and Danes in York.[10] The Frisians dominated trade in northern Europe for long periods of time, and had colonies in London and York.[11] But grants remitting tolls to religious establishments state that these may be on their own ships too, and by the end of the period, if not earlier, the Anglo-Saxons may have been trading on their own account. There is certainly no suggestion that the merchant of Ælfric's *Colloquy* comes from another country (see below). By the tenth century it is likely that exotic produce could be bought in major ports. In the time of Æthelstan Exeter was a wealthy city, where, 'because of the great concourse of strangers, nothing would be desired in vain'.[12] By the twelfth century 'goods from every nation under heaven' were brought to London, according to FitzStephen.[13] This suggests not the sudden establishment of a trading centre, but gradual growth from the time of Bede.

---

1 Whitelock 1955, 272.
2 op. cit., 181.
3 op. cit., 183.
4 Sweet 1892, 38–44.
5 Graham-Campbell & Kidd 1980, 48.
6 Whitelock 1955, 401.
7 Poole 1958, 168–9.
8 Robertson 1925, 149.
9 D.G. Wilson 1975, 646.
10 Poole 1958, 221.
11 Wilson 1960, 85–6.
12 Whitelock 1955, 281.
13 Poole 1958, 226.

Riddle number 32 in the Exeter Book – *The Ship* – suggests that the Anglo-Saxons were used to the idea of imported food.

> *fere foddurwelan folcscipe dreogeð*
> *wist in wigeð and werum gieldeð*
> *gaful geara gehwam þes þe guman brucað*

It does the carrying of provisions for the people, brings in food, and every year pays tribute to men, of which they make use.[1]

The evidence of the trader of Ælfric's *Colloquy* is particularly interesting. He says that he is useful to the king and the nobles and wealthy and all the folk; that he sells his goods overseas, and goes on:

> *ic bicge þincg dyrwyrðe þa on þisum lande ne beoþ acennede, 7 ic hit togelæde eow mid micclan plihte ofer sæ 7 hwylon forlidenesse ic þolie mid lyre ealra þinga minra uneaþe cwic ætberstende*

I buy valuable things that are not produced in this country, and I bring them here to you across the sea at great risk, and sometimes I endure shipwreck with the loss of all my goods, scarcely escaping with my life.

In answer to the question, 'What do you bring us?' he replies,

> *Pællas 7 sidan deorwyrþe gymmas 7 gold, selcuþe reaf 7 wyrtgemancg, win 7 ele ylpesban 7 mæstlingc, ær 7 tin swefel 7 glæs 7 þylces fela*

Purple garments, silk, precious stones and gold; rare clothing and mixtures of herbs, spices and perfume, wine and oil, ivory and alloy, brass and tin, sulphur and glass and many such things.

These he sells for a greater price than he paid, so that he can make a living for his wife and family.[2] The items give an idea of the range of trading contacts available to the late Saxon merchant: the Near and Far East, India or Africa as well as continental Europe.

It is important to realise that trade did not grow steadily; there were some periods when there was little trading.[3] Wide fluctuations over short intervals are to be expected in the geographical range of trade, in the extent of local participation in trading networks, and in the selection of trading partners.[4] During the unsettled periods of Viking raids imported goods would not always have been available.[5] By the end of the eleventh century, however, harbours where boats were docked, not beached, were in use to cater for boats larger than eight tons which had been developed from c.1000, thought it was not until c.1300 that boats larger than 20–30 tons were developed.[6]

---

[1] Gollancz 1895.
[2] Garmonsway 1978, 33–4.
[3] Hodges 1982, 45, 53; Brisbane 1988, 103 in Hobley & Hodges 1988.
[4] Adams, quoted in op. cit., 20.
[5] op.cit.
[6] op. cit., 98, 100; R. Ward, pers. comm.

Imported wine, fruit and nuts, fish (and hops) are dealt with in the appropriate chapters, which leaves oil and spices, two of the merchant's lines, as the subject of this chapter.

Since oil is imported by the merchant of the *Colloquy* it was presumably a typical import. It had perhaps been imported from Roman times.[1] Wheel-made Frankish bottles found on early Saxon sites in southern England may have contained oil (or wine).[2] It seems to have been lands with a Mediterranean climate that were seen as producing the best oil. Daniel, Bishop of Winchester from 722–32, wrote to Boniface that the Christians possessed fertile lands and provinces fruitful in wine and oil and abounding in other riches.[3] It was probably olive oil which was most commonly met with, although walnut oil, and oil from other plants could also have been imported. In c.1173 FitzStephen gave olive oil as one of the luxury goods which was obtainable in London. That this was not simply a post-Conquest development is suggested by the evidence that London was an international trading settlement from c.630, and, although there were setbacks to its growth, by 1018 it was rich enough to pay Danegeld of 10,500 pounds, and c.1067 was considered 'a great city ' by Guy of Amiens.[4]

Presumably the writer of *Leechdoms* thought his readers knew of olives since an amount is defined as 'as much as the size of an olive' (*ele berge*, lit. oil berry), and *elebeam* (oil tree) translated olive tree.[5] The oil called for by *Leechdoms* was probably olive oil. In *Peri Didachaeon* walnut oil is specified: 'the oil that comes from French nuts' (*þanne ele to þe beo of frencissen hnutu*). Certainly walnuts were used for oil in the time of Walter of Henley.[6] Walnut oil, as well as olive oil, may have been imported. Oil of fenugreek is also separately specified.[7]

Various recipes make quite clear that oil had culinary uses very like those of today: for frying an omelette, or for cooking an egg beaten up in butter.[8] It was also to be used for cooking or moistening vegetables, or for cooking meat, or – with vinegar and herbs – as a marinade for beef.[9] *Leechdoms* call for oil to be taken internally in over twenty recipes. Sometimes 'best oil' (*selestan ele*) is called for.[10] The importance of oil as part of the diet is suggested by its inclusion in the ancient *Erce* charm (together with honey, yeast and all kinds of milk), and by its symbolic use in Prognostications: 'when you move into your new house, take three vessels full of oil and milk with you' (*fær in niwe hus 7 nim eac mid þeo þrio fata ful æles 7 meolc*).[11]

One reference to oil clearly shows its nature as an import, and focuses on its ritual use. Writing to Colcu early in 790, Alcuin discusses the dissension between Charlemagne and Offa which has resulted in the breaking-off of trade relations, and

---

[1] Thomas 1971, 87–8.
[2] Whittock 1986, 226.
[3] Whitelock 1955, 733.
[4] B Hobley *Ludenwic & Ludenburh: two cities rediscovered* in Hodges & Hobley 1988.
[5] Cockayne 1851, II xxx.
[6] Seebohm 1952, 165.
[7] Cockayne 1851, II ii 1.
[8] Cockayne 1851, III *Peri Did.* 63, *Lac.* xxxviii.
[9] op.cit., II xxv, li, lix 9, li 3, vii.
[10] op. cit., II ix, xiv.
[11] Cockayne 1851, I 399; III *Prog.* 178.

says, 'I have sent . . . some oil which is now scarcely to be met with in Britain for you to dispense where the bishops require it for the utility and honour of God'.[1] A recipe for 'unsanctified oil' (*unhalgodes eles*) suggests it was often come across in its sanctified form.[2] Another recipe calls for 'oil for the sick' (*ele infirmorum*), and the Laws of Edgar required that priests were always to keep oil for anointing the sick.[3] Oil was possibly used for preserving the bodies of saints,[4] and, by extension, other things as well.

This seems an appropriate point at which to mention that there probably were locally available oils. The flax seed in some cases belonged to the Apparitor of the Welsh court. On the break up of a marriage it belonged to the wife, so that it had some value – presumably for the production of linseed oil, since there is evidence for this in Northern Europe.[5] Helbaek found two flax seeds in an Anglo-Saxon context, and flax seeds were found in the intestinal tract of an Anglo-Saxon skeleton.[6] Like linseed, gold of pleasure (*camelina sativa*) was cultivated as an oil crop in Iron Age Denmark and Germany.[7] Oil may also have been produced from species of brassica – from rape and cole seed.[8]

The spice route from the Far East to Europe had been established well before the Anglo-Saxon period. By the second century caravans regularly left the Chinese city of Lo-Yang with ginger, cassia, malabathrum (cassia leaf) and cinnamon.[9] Some idea of the quantities involved is given by the fact that the barbarians who materialised outside the gates of Rome in the fifth century demanded as part of their tribute 3000lbs of pepper.[10] However, Tannahill goes on to point out that spices became much more expensive and were presumably scarcer after the fall of Rome. The final stage of the journey to Europe was probably from Alexandria or other Egyptian or East Mediterranean ports to Marseilles. There were frequent embassies between the Carolingian emperors and the Abissid caliphs, which no doubt strengthened trading links.[11] The visit of Haroun al Raschid to Charlemagne around 800 may have created a renewed interest and indulgence in spices: continental sauces of the time match or outdo those of Apicius in piquancy.[12] Trade in S.Europe, Asia and Africa was controlled by Arabs and Jews, and Ibn Khordadbeh describes the journey of a polyglot Jewish merchant from western Europe to Egypt, then by way of Arabia to India and China. He returned to Constantinople with musk, aloes, camphor, cinnamon and other products of the East.[13] As the products were dried, or otherwise preserved, the journey time – which may have run into years – was fortunately not critical.

---

[1] Whitelock 1955, 755.
[2] Cockayne 1851, I 375.
[3] op. cit., III lxii; Turner 1828, III 502.
[4] Bonser 1963, 191.
[5] Owen 1841, 677, 83; Tannahill 1973, 77.
[6] Jessen & Helbaek 1944, 23; J. McN. Dodgson, pers. comm.
[7] Brothwell 1969, 154.
[8] Seebohm 1952, 253, 255; Moryson 1619, I 98.
[9] Tannahill 1973, 55.
[10] op. cit.
[11] Poole 1958, 267.
[12] McGee 1986, 130.
[13] Wilson 1960, 86.

Exotic spices were known to the Anglo-Saxons and very highly valued: no doubt they were very highly priced and difficult to find. In about 754 Cyneheard, Bishop of Winchester, complained that he could not get hold of the foreign ingredients prescribed in his medical books.[1] In terms of location (Winchester was already an important market), and finance, one would have expected him to be well-placed to purchase such items, so perhaps this indicates there was not a steady supply of the more unusual imported commodities in the middle Saxon period.

Pepper is the spice most frequently mentioned. Just before he died in 735, Bede bequeathed his spices to the other brethren, and these included pepper.[2] Frisians were known to be handling spices in Mainz at the time of Bede.[3] A deacon at Rome once sent Boniface 2lb of pepper, besides smaller amounts of other spices.[4] Aldhelm regarded peppered broths as delicacies.[5] About sixty leechdoms call for pepper, sometimes as peppercorns in various quantities – often for as many as twenty or so, sometimes as finely ground pepper.[6] By the end of the period, the court, and probably other large households, seem to have secured supplies of pepper. 10lb of pepper was to be paid at Christmas and Easter by the subjects of Æthelred as part of a toll.[7] Those unable to obtain pepper so conveniently by edict were probably able to buy from pepperers who were already organised in the eleventh century.[8] The reeve had to see to the 'pepper horn' (*piperhorn*), which indicates there was pepper to be stored, but in small quantities.[9] The steward of the Welsh court was to supply the royal cook with all necessary seasonings, which specifically included pepper.[10] The impression given is that pepper was already second to salt as a seasoning. The verb 'to pepper' (*piporian*) was already in use.[11] According to leechdoms, pepper seems to have been used very much as we would do today: to season an omelette, or wort drinks, (which were like soup) for example, but it was also used in a dish with apple, wine and honey where we would now employ cloves, cinnamon or nutmeg.[12]

Other spices are recorded, and although the amounts concerned are tiny, they were clearly highly regarded. The impression is that spices were circulated among the religious fraternity, but in fact churchmen were much more likely to have made a record of such gifts in their accompanying letters, and their letters were more likely to have been preserved. However, the large religious communities of the English coast of the North Sea, with their vast resources are likely to have indulged in trade, or at least attracted it.[13] Royal households and those of the rich were also likely to have had supplies of spices.

[1] Deegan 1986, 17.
[2] McKendry 1973, 10.
[3] Hodges 1982, 127.
[4] Turner 1828, III 56.
[5] op. cit., 27.
[6] Cockayne 1851, II xxiv, xxx, lix.
[7] Loyn 1970, 94.
[8] Drummond 1958.
[9] Liebermann 1898, 455.
[10] Owen 1841, I 49.
[11] Bosworth & Toller 1898, 774.
[12] Cockayne 1851, III *Lac.* 63; II iii, iv.
[13] Wilson 1986, 236.

The spices Bede left to his brethren are said to have included lavender, aniseed, buckwheat, cinnamon. cloves, cubebs, cumin, coriander, cardamom ('grains of paradise' so called because they were believed to float down the Nile from the earthly paradise),[1] cypress roots (galingale), ginger (raw and preserved), gromic, liquorice, and sugar (as well as pepper).[2] Although this is a very early reference to sugar – it is not until the Pipe Rolls of Henry II that it is recorded again (as a condiment for the court) – there is written evidence for sugar making circa 500, centred on the coast to the west of the Indus delta, and in the Tigris-Euphrates delta. By the eighth century it was being exported to Venice, and the Arab expansion led to the expansion of sugar-making in the Mediterranean basin, so sugar could have reached Bede. Used as a spice it altered the flavour of food without clearly sweetening it.[3] Sucrose is a more effective preservative than honey, and Bede's preserved ginger could have come from Persia, although the documentary record does not refer to the export of fruit syrups, candied capers and other preserves until the century after Bede's death.[4] The Patriarch Elias' recommendation of *tyriaca* for 'inward tenderness' does not necessarily refer to treacle – the Latin *triaca* meant an antidote for a venomous bite, and then 'a sovereign remedy'. Sugar was popularised as a medicine, in the early medieval period, and this second sense was transferred to it. However, it is just possible that *tyriaca* which was to be mixed with water then strained through a cloth was the unrefined liquid residue from sugar-making.[5]

As well as 2lb of pepper, Boniface had received 4 ounces of cinnamon, 2 ounces of costus and 1 1b of cozombri from the deacon in Rome. An archdeacon sent him cinnamon and costus, as well as pepper. Boniface seems to have passed on some of what he received to others: an abbess was sent some frankincense, and cinnamon, as well as pepper, and another correspondent received storax and cinnamon.[6] About 745–6 Lul, Bishop of Mainz, sent Eadburga, Abbess of Thanet, some pieces of storax and cinnamon, and the accompanying silver stylus suggests the prestigious nature of the gift.[7]

The *Leechdoms* refer to a number of eastern spices, though there is a possibility that the names of what were originally exotic plants were given to native species. Cumin (originally *cuminum cyminum*) may have been used of the indigenous *nigella sativa* (known now as black cumin). 'Cumin' (*cumeð/cymen*) is referred to seventeen times, 'mastic, the gum of *pistachia lentiscus' (hwit cudu*), and 'aloes' (*alwan*) seven times each, and 'ginger' (*gingifen/gingifran*), five times. There are four references to 'balm' [probably Balm of Gillead] (*balsami*), which was evidently highly thought of. In one instance it was for an 'noble cure' (*æþele cræft*). It was recommended by the Patriarch Elias to Alfred for its therapeutic qualities. Another reference adds 'if you have any' (*gif þu hæbbe*).[8] In 1109 'Ralph . . . particularly asked a monk named Baldwin if he had some drops of balm' (although this was not for consumption, but

---

[1] Kuper 1977, 23.
[2] McKendry 1973, 10.
[3] Mintz 1985, 83, 23, 242, 79.
[4] op. cit., 123.
[5] Cockayne 1851, II lxiv.
[6] Turner 1828, III 56.
[7] Kylie 1911, 108.
[8] Cockayne 1851, I ii 2, 3; II lxiv; III *Peri Did.* 15.

for embalming St. Anselm's head).[1] Balm then, was hard to come by, but it was not out of the question that a monk should have some. 'Incense' (*recels*) is mentioned four times, and both incense and nard are mentioned in Riddle 40 in the Exeter Book.[2] Alfred gave Asser 'a strong man's load' of incense, and while in this case it was presumably for liturgical use rather than consumption or dispensing, it is a useful indication of the kind of quantities in which exotic spices were available.[3]

'Zedoary' (*sideware*) is referred to three times in *Leechdoms*. An aromatic, ginger-like substance made from the rootstock of East Indian plants, it was included in a list of herbs and spices that the monks of Cambrai planned to buy for their monastery in the ninth century.[4] Cinnamon is mentioned twice, as 'foreign bark' (*oferseawisc rind*) and 'Roman bark' (*romanisce rind*).[5] 'Crocus, saffron in French' (*Croh safran gallice*) is mentioned twice, so are castor oil seeds (*lybcorn*) and myrrh (*myrran*).

Some of the mineral substances recommended by the Patriarch to be taken internally, are mentioned only once in any source: 'mineral oil, white stone, red earth' (*petraoleum, hwita stan and rædan eorþan*). The same section of the *Leechdoms* also contains unique references to substances to be taken for various internal disorders: scamony, ammoniac drops, gum dragon and galbanum. However, writing immediately after the Anglo-Saxon period, Alexander Neckham knew of the latter, and also listed ginger, cloves, cinnamon, liquorice, zedoary, incense, myrrh, aloes, rosin, storax, balm, cypress (galingale), nard, gutta, and cassia fistula, not as exotic or rare substances, but as useful herbs which unfortunately did not grow in European gardens.[6] However, it has to be said that Neckham lived in Paris for some time, and, given that Anglo-Norman recipes are far more specific and discriminating in their suggested spicing of different dishes than their contemporary French counterparts, spices may have been scarcer and more expensive in England.[7] Probably they were not even used by the majority of the population, but were yet another way in which the rich were able to extend the range of dishes available to them. The prestigious nature of exotic objects and substances is indicated by the fact that, particularly in the early and middle periods, merchants were taken to the local royal vill.[8] Paradoxically, the very poor may have been more likely than the middle classes to have tasted spices, since they may have received the leavings of the rich, or been dosed by monks.

---

[1] Bonser 1963, 210.
[2] Gollancz 1895.
[3] Whitelock 1955, 271.
[4] op. cit., 45–6.
[5] Cockayne 1851, I vi 6, 376.
[6] Holmes 1952, 105.
[7] Hieatt & Jones 1986, 860.
[8] Hodges 1982, 55.

13. Tabooed Food

Marvin Harris argues that foods which are 'bad to think' in Claude Levi-Strauss's dictum, are tabooed because they are 'bad to eat' in the sense that the costs (in the widest sense) of eating them, outweigh the practical benefits. Thus apparently baffling prejudices and avoidances often turn out to be rational.[1]

In Anglo-Saxon times the obvious taboo, although unwritten, was against human meat, although this contains the highest quality protein one can eat.[2] The *Andreas* poet refers to cannibalism as a specifically heathen practice:

> *Leton him þa betweonum taan wisian*
> *hywclcne hira ærest oðrum sceolde*
> *to foddurþege feores ongyldan*

> Casting lots they let them decree which should die first as food for the others. 1.1099 ff.[3]

This taboo was eminently practical: if observed by everyone, no-one was going to be killed in order to be converted into food. However, once Christianized, with a belief in the resurrection of the body, the Anglo-Saxons would have been anxious to ensure that their corpses remained uneaten.[4] Burial ceremonies and interment in consecrated ground and the presence of usually adequate alternative sources of protein ensured that this was generally the case. However, this taboo, like others, was disregarded in emergencies, as it has been since.[5] Between 695 and 700 England and Ireland suffered from a three-year dearth during which 'men ate each other'. 936 saw the beginning of a four-year famine in Scotland when 'people began to devour each other'. After William's campaigns there was in 1069 a great dearth 'whereby many were forced to eat horses, dogs, cats, rats and other vermin; yea, some abstained not from the flesh of men'.[6] The phrasing suggests the horror with which cannibalism was regarded. *The Great Hunger*, about a famine among Eskimos in the last century, portrays the psychological distress, as well as the physical suffering, of people in these circumstances.[7]

As well as people, tabooed foods in Anglo-Saxon England included 'horses, dogs, cats, rats, and other loathsome and vile vermin'.[8] Evidence for the 'uncleanliness' of the horse, dog and cat comes also from the Ancient Laws and Institutes of Wales. These refer to a case where one-third of the worth of a cat was to be paid. 'The *teithi* of every clean animal is half its worth. The *teithi* of every unclean animal is one-third its worth'.[9] This implies the cat was unclean, as was its milk and those of a bitch and

---

[1] Harris 1986, 15.
[2] op. cit., 33.
[3] Elliott 1959, 65.
[4] Tannahill 1975, 31.
[5] op. cit., 174.
[6] op. cit., 47.
[7] Victor 1955.
[8] Harleian Miscellany III, 151.
[9] Owen 1841, I 111.

mare.[1] These laws also stated that a horse and greyhound were worthless when lame because they were unclean, i.e. they could not be utilised for food.[2] Dogs and cats would be inefficient converters of food to protein for human consumption and were evidently more useful for the services they could provide, than as routine items of diet. However, butchery marks were found on cat and dog bones, mixed with more usual food debris at the late site at St. John's, Bedford.[3] Rats and other vermin are not mentioned in the laws because they had no value as food to members of an agricultural community which could normally produce enough food for itself. People outside such a community might forage for vermin and small animals as Shakespeare's Poor Tom did centuries later.

The horse is only two-thirds as efficient in digesting grass as cattle or sheep and also has a higher metabolic rate, so is an inefficient source of meat or milk;[4] it was also useful as a form of transport. These two reasons would have been enough to justify a taboo, but the Romans had used the horse extensively for food,[5] and Egbert's Penitential did not prohibit the eating of horseflesh 'though many families will not buy it'.[6] However, in 723 Gregory III was writing to Boniface to ask him to stamp out the 'detestable practice' of eating wild and domesticated horses among the Germans. This was the year of the Battle of Tours which demonstrated that the horse was needed by the Christians to counter the advance of the (mounted) Muslims. 'With their survival threatened, the Church fathers could only take a dim view of the appetite for horseflesh'.[7] That the horse had a strategic importance is suggested by the references to the disposal of horses in the English and Welsh Laws. Horses for sale generally had to be offered first to the lord, but even if he did not want them, they were not to be sold abroad.[8]

However, Pope Hadrian's injunction to the English in 786 suggests that the church was trying to sever a connection with pagan practices by tabooing horseflesh: 'many among you eat horses, which no Christian does in the East. Give this up also'.[9] This follows a denunciation of the evil custom of mutilating horses in various ways because this was *reliquae paganorum rituum*. The horse was sacred to Woden.[10] How quickly or completely such a ruling took effect is difficult to assess. There is evidence that at the Anglo-Saxon site of Ramsbury, Wilts., horses of various ages were butchered in the late eighth and early ninth centuries. This might mean only that the horses were fed to dogs, except that the fragments were found alongside food remains and they did not show evidence of more chewing.[11] However, just over a century after the ruling, the Danes are condemned in 893 for eating horses although they were oppressed by famine.[12] Page points out that the word used is not the neutral *etan* (to eat), but *fretan*, a much stronger word with connotations of devouring greedily, and

---

[1] op. cit., 441.
[2] op. cit., II 335.
[3] *Beds. Archaeol. J.* 13, 106.
[4] Harris 1986, 92.
[5] Seebohm 1952, 78.
[6] Turner 1828, III 25.
[7] Harris 1986, 96.
[8] Whitelock 1955, 384; Owen 1841, I 79, II 345, 523–5.
[9] Whitelock 1955, 772.
[10] Bonser 1963, 128.
[11] Coy in Haslam 1980, 46.
[12] Whitelock 1955, 187.

tearing apart.[1] The author seems to be expressing his disgust at their reversion to a pagan custom, and the passage could be translated 'they had eaten a good part of their horses as you might expect from a set of heathens like that'.[2]

On the sixth-century site of Old Down Farm, Andover, Hants., horse bones had been chopped or broken into quite small fragments: the animals had probably been butchered.[3] At the middle Saxon sites of Sedgeford, Norfolk, and *Hamwih*, butchered horse bones were discovered, although the fact that adult animals predominated suggests that the horse was more valued for transport than food, though at Maxey, Northants., the horses may have been ridden until they were about five years old, and then eaten.[4] The horse bones in the tenth-century layers at Skeldergate, York, included limb bones which had been butchered in a manner similar to the cattle bones, which suggests horsemeat was being eaten. York at this time was an Anglo-Danish town and perhaps Danish preferences were at work.[5] It is less easy to explain the plentiful remains of horse (together with cattle and red deer) in the late Saxon ditch at Southampton: they perhaps indicate a time of dearth.[6] At the late site of St. John's, Bedford, several carpals and tarsals, and a scapula and femur of horse had knife marks on them, and a tibia had heavy chop marks on the side of its shaft.[7] Perhaps these bones indicate an eleventh-century dearth after William's army passed through the area. At the late site of Flaxengate, Lincoln, horse bones are uncommon and show no signs of butchery, which is similar to the situation at Exeter, though there the long bones had been fragmented for marrow extraction.[8] This evidence accords quite well with the idea of a taboo becoming established. Leechdoms do refer to products from horses for externally applied medicaments (which may suggest a use for the marrow extracted from the Exeter horses), but not to the flesh in diets.[9]

The horse, although it was only of pony size, since specimens rarely exceeded 14.2 hands, was probably scarce in Anglo-Saxon times, since it was very expensive. At 120 pence its value was four times that of an ox,[10] and, until the laws of Alfred standardised fines, the stealer of horses (like the stealer of gold or bees) was subject to particularly heavy penalties.[11] Despite deforestation, there were still numbers of horses roaming wild at the end of the period. The Old English will of the bishop of Crediton refers to wild horses on the land at Ashburton and Wulfric Spott left one hundred wild horses to the monastery at Burton.[12] There are references in Domesday to 'wild' (*silvaticae*) or 'unbroken' (*indomitae*) mares. These feral mares were frequently met with in East Anglia and the South West. The high percentage of fragments (7% and 14% in the late eighth-early ninth, and early ninth centuries respectively) at Ramsbury, Wilts., may be because the settlement was close to the Savernake forest. No doubt poor people ate horsemeat, albeit clandestinely, when it

[1] Page 1985, 13.
[2] op. cit., 18.
[3] Davies 1980, 177.
[4] Clutton-Brock in Wilson 1976, 383.
[5] O'Connor 1984, 17.
[6] Bourdillon 1980, 189.
[7] *Beds. Archaeol. J.* 125, 103.
[8] O'Connor 1982; Maltby 1979.
[9] Cockayne 1851, I xxxii 4, liv, II lxv.
[10] Whitelock 1955, 388.
[11] op. cit., 375.
[12] op. cit., 536, 543.

was available – if a horse died naturally, or on a battlefield, or if they could catch a wild one. However, it was in the interest of those who owned horses to enforce the view that 'civilized' people did not eat horsemeat.

In fact it was very unusual for the church to establish a food taboo. From the time of St. Paul the church was opposed to food taboos that placed obstacles in the path of potential converts. Neither did St. Paul attempt to forbid the practising of food taboos since this would lead to 'doubtful disputation'.[1] But while St. Paul wrote 'I know and am persuaded by the Lord Jesus, that there is nothing unclean of itself',[2] James suggested that Gentiles should abstain from food offered to idols and from things strangled, and from blood.[3] These two views recur during the Anglo-Saxon period. Gregory's answer to Augustine on the subject of unclean food concentrated on the gospel where the Lord says, 'Not that which enters the mouth of man defiles, but that which goeth out of the mouth . . . ' and paraphrases St. Paul, 'To the clean all is clean'. But Fulk, Archbishop of Rheims, writing to King Alfred about 890, repeats the injunction against food offered to idols, things strangled and blood.[4] Wulfstan's *Canons of Edgar* state, 'And we instruct that no Christian man consume blood.' (*And we læराð þæt nan cristen man blod ne þigce*).[5]

Fulk's first injunction may have been behind the banning of horsemeat since the horse was sacred to Woden, and it may have caused the decline in the status of shellfish as a delicacy during the first few centuries after the end of Roman rule, since they were sacred to Venus, a pagan goddess particularly disliked by the Early Church. They were only rarely eaten, for example, at the prosperous early Dark Age settlement of Dinas Powys, although whelks, cockles, mussels, limpets, and especially oysters had formerly been a considerable feature of the diet at the Roman villa of Llantwit Major, which was only slightly nearer the sea.[6] However, memories of pagan practices must have faded, and Bede stated that in Britain 'various kinds of shellfish and mussels are often taken' (*beoþ oft numene missenlicra cynna weolcscylle 7 muscule*).[7] Although he goes on to mention 'shellfish' (*weolocas*) from which "shellfish-red' dye' (*weolcreada tælgh*) is made, the first mention of molluscs follows seals, whales and porpoises, which were definitely food items.[8]

The second injunction was complied with since butchery techniques involved killing by pole-axing and/or cutting the throat of the creature concerned. If an animal was strangled, the supposition is that blood would remain in the tissues, and, as this is a perfect medium for microbes, decay would set in quickly.[9] However, blood is an extremely valuable source of nutrients, and the danger of infection would be destroyed by cooking. The taboo may have led to cooking blood in sausages and puddings, where it was not recognisable as a forbidden substance.

---

[1] *Romans* 14:1.
[2] *Romans* 14:14.
[3] *Acts* 15:20.
[4] Whitelock 1955, 815.
[5] Fowler 1972, 12.
[6] Alcock 1987, 37.
[7] Miller 1890, I 1 26.
[8] op. cit.
[9] Harris 1986, 69.

13 Tabooed Food

The Old Testament taboos do not seem to have been observed. The hawk is included in a list of tabooed birds,[1] and according to Welsh Laws it was worthless if lame, because it was unclean, but other birds on the list were eaten, and the taboo on hawks may have been because they were of more use when they were used to catch other birds for food.[2] The fisherman of Ælfric's *Colloquy* says he throws out *unclænan* fish, but the reference can hardly be to Deuteronomy 14:10: 'And whatsoever hath not fins and scales ye may not eat; it is unclean unto you' as he does a thriving trade in shellfish.[3] The commentary on the Old Testament prohibitions in *The Maccabees* shows that they were seen symbolically, for example: 'And those are unclean who do not chew the cud because they represent those who do not desire rightly' (*And ða synd unclæne þe heora cudu ne ceowaðe forðan þe hi getacniað þa ðe tela nellað*); and 'To the pure all things are pure' (*Ealle ðincg syndon clæne þam clænum mannum*) is repeated.[4]

Anglo-Saxon Penitentials sought to identify and taboo contaminated food which posed a health risk. Penances were imposed on those who broke these early hygiene regulations, though for those who broke them unwittingly the penance was not so great. An important subject was animals, birds and fish that were found dead, rather than killed for consumption. Section VII of Bede's Penitential *De carne immunda* runs as follows: 'He who eats impure flesh, or that of an animal which has died, or one which has been torn to pieces by wild beasts, shall do penance for forty days. The penalty shall be lighter if this has been rendered necessary through hunger'. Theodore gives similar instructions: 'Animals which have been mangled by wolves or dogs must not be eaten, nor deer, nor goat, if they have been found dead . . . Birds and other creatures if they are strangled in nets are not for human consumption . . . but fish may be eaten since they are of another nature'. This injunction concerning fish is modified in the Second Penitential in an eleventh-century manuscript which says, 'If anyone finds a dead fish in a fishpond and eats it, he shall fast for four weeks . . . but if the dead fish be found in a river, it may be eaten'.[5] Welsh Laws appear to reflect a more pragmatic approach. If someone discovered a dead animal 'if its flesh be eatable' then its flesh was to be shared between the owner of the land and the discoverer. If it proved uneatable, the owner of the land was to give one penny to the discoverer.[6] However, the Welsh Laws also contain an apparently irrational taboo against eating meat, or presumably killing animals for food between the first of January and St. John's Day: 'If any person break the leg or thigh of an animal belonging to another . . . that the animal pine away in consequence and the animal be clean, so that its flesh may be eaten . . . If the injured animal dies . . . from the feast of St. John until 1st January, two parts are to be paid for the flesh and the skin the third for the life, for then is the prime season, again, from 1st January to the feast of St. John two parts for the life and the third for the flesh and skin, because every animal is carrion during that period'.[7]

---

[1] *Deuteronomy* 14:15.
[2] Owen 1841, II 335.
[3] Garmonsway 1978, 27, 29.
[4] Skeat 1881, *The Maccabees* l. 37–8.
[5] CA Wilson 1973, 365.
[6] Owen 1841, 497.
[7] op. cit., I 111.

Penitentials were also concerned with the contamination of other types of food. Bede discusses this in *De carne immunda*: 'If a mouse shall have fallen into liquor, let it be lifted out and let the liquor be sprinkled with holy water. If the mouse be dead, all the liquor should be thrown away and not consumed. But if it were a large amount of liquor into which the mouse – or a weasel – fell and died, let it be purified, and let it be sprinkled with holy water, and let it be consumed if it should be expedient.' The Penitential of Egbert specifies: 'If a mouse or weasel be found dead in flour or any food or drink, or in curdled milk, let all that part which is adjacent to it be thrown away; what remains may be eaten.'[1]

Mice and weasels seem to have been particularly troublesome. An ecclesiastical council mentioned them: 'For giving another any liquor in which a mouse or a weasel shall be found dead, a layman shall do penance for four days; a monk shall sing 300 psalms'.[2] For eating or drinking what a cat or dog had spoiled the penance was a hundred psalms or a day's fast. Theodore's Penitential deals with the contamination of oil and honey: 'If a mouse or hen or similar creature has fallen into oil or honey, and there be found dead, let the oil be used for a lamp, and the honey for medicinal purposes or in any other useful ways.' The honey from bees that had killed a man could not be used for culinary purposes but could be used the same way; the bees were to be killed.[3]

The Church's taboo against half-cooked food (the penance for eating this unwittingly was three days' fasting; knowingly, four days' fasting) may have been to establish a distinction between pagan and Christian habits.[4] However, it was eminently practical since thorough cooking destroys bacterial infections, and trichinella and tape worms, in undercooked pork and beef respectively.[5] Similarly the view that food that had fallen to the ground was the devil's and should certainly not be eaten was sensible, given the condition of Anglo-Saxon floors.[6]

Certain foods, most commonly meat, were taboo to everyone on fast days and during Lent. Religious communities tended to extend such taboos.

Medical taboos probably started to have some influence towards the end of the period. The *Regimen Sanitatis Salerni* of the mid-eleventh century stated that peaches, apples, pears, cheese, venison, salt meat, goats' flesh and hare should be avoided, as should the entrails of swine and the crust of bread 'lest some dark flux should smite'.[7] In one or two cases reasons of hygiene may be behind the prohibitions and the recommended diet was probably richer in nutrients. A pregnant woman was to avoid the flesh of bulls, rams, bucks, boars, etc., since this might cause a deformity in the foetus.[8] She was also cautioned that 'she does not eat anything salt or sweet, or drink *beor* or swines' flesh or anything fat, or drink until she is drunk' (*hio aht sealtes ete oððe swetes oþþe beor drince ne swines flæsc ete ne naht fætes ne druncen*

---

[1] CA Wilson 1973, 365.
[2] Turner 1828, III 35.
[3] Bonser 1963, 429.
[4] Turner 1828, III 35.
[5] Harris 1986, 120, 70.
[6] Page 1985, 15.
[7] Mead 1931, 217.
[8] Cockayne 1851, II xlii.

gedrince).[1] Other foods were also considered dangerous: 'If a woman is four or five months pregnant and she often eats nuts or acorns, or other fresh fruit then it sometimes happens that the child is stupid' (*Gif wif bearn eacen feower monað oþþe fife 7 heo þonne gelome eteð hnyte oþþe æceran oþþe ænige niwe bleda þonne gelimpeð hit hwilum þurh þ þæt þ cild biþ disig*).[2] It would be interesting to know how widely known and followed this belief was; unduly limiting her intake of fresh fruit could have caused harm to a pregnant woman and her unborn child. However the likelihood was that if a woman had recourse to these foods (which she might get by foraging), then she was not getting enough high-quality nutrients to produce a healthy child, and tabooing nuts, acorns and fresh fruit would not improve the situation. Apart from these instances, vegetable food was not tabooed in the same way as flesh from animals, fish or birds, presumably because it was not perceived as inciting lust as flesh foods were thought to do.

Goose would presumably have been considered taboo on the three 'Egyptian' days of the year, since eating it then was thought fatal, though death might be delayed up to forty days (see above). However, such recherché medical 'knowledge' was in limited circulation. Those rich enough to have recourse to physicians who might give them this advice, or to manuscripts where they could read it for themselves, were presumably those who would be able to afford alternative foods.

---

[1] op. cit., III xxxvii.
[2] op. cit.

14. Provision of a Water Supply

It is a commonplace of settlement geography that a community needs access to a water supply. While it is possible that Anglo-Saxons could have survived on milk-based drinks and/or fresh or fermented fruit juices, and while it seems true that few people regularly drank water from choice, it also seems likely that some of the Anglo-Saxons' most important drinks needed a high volume of water for their production. Water would also have been needed for cooking processes and for cleaning utensils. According to the Welsh Laws, a spring was one of the three things without which no country was a good one, and an early attempt at town planning says every habitation should have a path to its watering place.[1]

The form of the water supply no doubt varied according to the natural constraints of rainfall, geomorphology, geology, and human factors such as political conditions and the density of settlement. It would seem evident that natural supplies of surface water – watercourses, ponds and lakes, and springs – would have been made use of, but the archaeological evidence shows that wells were constructed from the early period on, and this was the case even when the settlement was close to a river. Unfortunately the documentary evidence is not particularly helpful: the term *wel/well/will/wyll* can be translated as 'pool', 'well', 'spring' or 'fountain', and occasionally as 'rivulet' or 'brook'.[2] Sometimes the context makes the meaning clear, otherwise it is a matter of guesswork. Where translations are given, I have followed them, though only by locating and investigating these features when they are mentioned in charters, for instance, could one be quite clear as to the form they took.

Certainly the *wel* represented fresh water, and was often a named feature of the landscape, particularly in areas where the surface water supply is not plentiful.[3] Typical examples are 'to hawk spring . . . to the spring in the hollow' (*to hafoc wylle . . . oþ holan wylle*) in a document of 931, into maere wylle (to the boundary spring) mentioned in 1055.[4] Apparently these examples had not been allocated to individuals even towards the end of the period, but these features were often in personal ownership: 'first from Æscwulf's well' (*ærest of æsculfer willan*); 'along the green way opposite Cynewynn's well'; thence to Ælmarch's spring . . . to Behrat's spring.[5] Later place-names also give evidence of Anglo-Saxon owners: *Bernewell*, recorded in 1264, derives from 'Beorna's spring'.[6] *Wylls* were considered one of the assets of an estate. The grant of Ceadwalla, king of Wessex, between the years 685–7 of lands of Farnham, Surrey, for a monastery mentions everything belonging to them: 'fisheries, rivers and springs'.[7] In about 975 Wulfgeat left to Donnington 'the spring at the wic' (?Droitwich).[8]

---

1   Owen 1841, 491, 329.
2   Bosworth & Toller 1898, I 1225; Jember 1975, 173; Cockayne 1851, III *Lac*.No. 114.
3   Smith 1965, IV 8, 197.
4   Smith 1964, III 64, I 228.
5   Gelling 1979, 183; Whitelock 1955, 526, 551–2.
6   Mawer & Stenton 1969, 269.
7   Whitelock 1955, 445.
8   Finberg 1982, 149.

That springs were evidently well-regarded, is evinced by the number of times that a spring suddenly welled-up on the sites where martyrs were slain.[1] King Alfred added to his translation of Boethius on the Golden Age, 'they drank the water of the clear springs'.[2] Although a *fule welan* (dirty ?spring) is recorded, it seems likely that the water in such features was probably cleaner, and perhaps easier of access, than water in streams and rivers. Water in streams and rivers in full spate could be very turbid, and watercourses could be fouled by animals and humans upstream. It seems likely that springs would be the purest source of water, which is perhaps why eyes were to be washed *on clænum wylle*.[3]

The ideal was perhaps to have a dwelling with its own clean running water.[4] Naturally this could be arranged by a saint with miraculous powers. When St. Cuthbert withdrew to Farne and built a dwelling, he asked the brethren to dig a pit in the floor of the house. 'Now the earth was so hard and stony, that no trace of a spring could be seen' (*Wæs seo eorðe to ðæs heard 7 to ðæs stanihte, þæt ðær nænig wiht wyllsprynges beon mihte on gesewen*). However, the brothers dug, and 'next day it was found full of water' (*ða oðre dæge was he wætres ful gemeted*).[5] The Latin version is more dramatic: the spring broke out of the rocky ground immediately (*statim*).[6] The waters of the spring were very sweet, but in any case water blessed by St. Cuthbert had all the sweetness of wine.[7] St. Cuthbert's powers of observation have been shown before, when he spotted the eagle which had just caught a salmon, and perhaps he had done no more than study the lie of the land. There seems no mention of water-divining using a hazel rod here, or elsewhere in the literature, although this skill may have been known. Nor is there any evidence for the arguably less technologically advanced Scandinavian method: heating up a snake, tying a thread to its tail, following it until it dives into the earth and digging there for water.[8]

There is archaeological evidence for the provision of water inside buildings. One of the monastic buildings at North Elmham was divided into three rooms, and the largest, with internal dimensions of 43 feet by 21 feet, had a small waterhole four-and-a-half feet deep at its east end.[9]

The knowledge that wells could tap underground water was known to the Romans and almost certainly the Anglo-Saxons from the beginning of the period. The element *funta*, possibly through Primitive Welsh *funton*, but deriving from the Latin *fontana*, is found in southern counties from Essex to Warwickshire and especially in Hampshire and Wiltshire. In these areas English and Latin speakers may have lived side by side in the early fifth century, and reference is to artificial water sources. At a number of places the element *funta* was combined with O.E. *byden* (tub, butt). This may indicate a Roman water trough or irrigation channel still functioning when the

---

[1] Miller 1890, I 2 418.
[2] Turner 1828, II 36.
[3] Cockayne 1851, I ii 14.
[4] Hartley 1978, 21.
[5] Miller 1890, I 2 367.
[6] Colgrave 1940, 98.
[7] op. cit., 267.
[8] Palsson 1971, 107.
[9] *Med. Archaeol.* XVI, 150.

word passed on to English lips.[1] It may, however, refer to a spring encircled by a barrel, or a well lined with a barrel, since this method was often used.

Wells were dug even where the site was near a river. There are examples of wells from the early Anglo-Saxon period at Odell and Harrold, Beds., on settlement sites within easy reach of the Great Ouse, and similar later evidence comes from the southern Scandinavian settlements of Lindholm Høje, Saedding, Trelleborg, and Hedeby.[2] Presumably the effect of well-digging was considered worthwhile in terms of having water, which was probably cleaner than that from rivers, very close at hand. Fetching water was one of the daily tasks of Ælfstan, later to be a bishop, when he cooked for the builders of the monastery at Abingdon.[3] A convenient well would have had much to recommend it. Cuthbert's guesthouse on Farne had a well for the guests' use not far away.[4]

It is possible that the warm period beginning in the ninth century may have lowered the water table, and some streams may have dried up or become seasonal 'winter bournes'. This may have led to the construction of wells, perhaps deeper than they would have needed to be in previous years, or after the thirteenth century.

There is plentiful archaeological evidence for wells, perhaps because they are such easily discovered and identified features. As they are often lined with wood they can be closely dated. Lining techniques were presumably known to the continental Anglo-Saxons, since wooden linings are found in wells which date from 300–425 at Wijster.[5] The wells at Harrold and Odell in Bedfordshire have been ascribed to dates in the sixth to eighth centuries.[6] These had woven frameworks of hazel, dogwood and willow, or were lined with split oak timbers, and in one case a basket seems to have been incorporated to act as a filter.[7] On the Cattle Market site, Kent Street, York, a circular well, formerly wood-lined, contained the tumbled and burnt remains of a wattle-and-daub structure in its upper levels – perhaps evidence that it had been inside, or at least near, a building. It also contained a cross of eighth-century type, and coins of Eadberht (737–58).[8] A ninth- early tenth-century well, also at York, was associated with a cistern, which, it has been suggested, was so that the dirty water could have a chance to clear.[9] Well 1 at North Elmham was dug nearly 12 metres deep through boulder clay into the underlying sand where there was a good supply of clean water. The pit was dug first, then shored up. Then three different methods of lining were used: a square timber lining built up in position by using large internal corner posts and side planks held rigid by bracing boards; beneath this a prefabricated cylinder of closely woven wattles, and, at the bottom, a prefabricated, straight-sided barrel. The excavator observes that the design and construction of this well required considerable skill and initiative: in particular that the problem of overcoming waterlogged running sand in the bottom was a remarkable achievement. On the balance of probabilities, this well was constructed between 824

---

[1] Whittock 1986, 81.
[2] Dix, draft, 62; Roesdahl 1982, 120.
[3] Whitelock 1955, 834.
[4] Colgrave 1940, 217.
[5] Van Es 1967, 100–8, 374.
[6] Dix, draft 62.
[7] *Beds. Mag.* Vol. 18, No. 138.
[8] *Work in York* 1973, 4.
[9] Brinklow 1979, 28.

and 840.[1] *Hamwih* produced evidence of pits lined with wickerwork dating from the eighth to tenth centuries. These were interpreted as wells, with a back-filling of clay round the wattle-lined shafts. These are paralleled by a pit at Bishopshill, York, 1.5 metres in diameter and nearly 2 metres deep, with a stone lining at its base, although this may have been associated with tanning.[2] At Portchester Castle a possible sequence of development was *grubenhäuser* with a water hole dating to the second part of the fifth century, a refitting of this well in the sixth century, and two new wells in the seventh to late eighth centuries.[3] The latter had timber well-linings constructed of vertical planks, elaborately cross-strutted with frames carefully pegged together.[4]

Access to a well might be by means of steps, as was the case at Aldwinkle, Northants. Here the well was set into a larger pit, one side of which was filled with stones, alternating with horizontal planks. It seems that this arrangement supported steps which gave access to the water.[5] At Harrold, Beds., access would have been by means of a ladder to a narrow ledge from which the water could be reached.[6] There is documentary evidence for a shaduf-like device for raising water – the 'Riding Well' of Riddle 58 in the Exeter Book.[7] There are two manuscript illustrations, one from the first half of the twelfth century, one from the fourteenth, showing such a device – a lever with a weight at one end of a beam sufficient to raise the other end and draw up the bucket.[8] However, this has not been corroborated by the archaeological evidence, although this is perhaps unlikely to have survived, and in any case would be difficult to interpret. Neither is there evidence for the use of windlasses. Well poles with a hook for holding the handle of a bucket, rather than the spring-clip device used into the present century, must have been a possible way of raising water, but again, there is no evidence for their use.

While wells in chalk areas in particular might provide clear water, in other districts the percolating water might transport particles of earth into the well. We have seen that attempts were made to overcome this problem by providing a cistern in which the mud could settle out, or a basket-work sieve, but probably some well-water was as cloudy as river water. The leechdom for 'swallowing in water some creeping thing' suggests drinking water could be very murky indeed. Insisting on the antidote for this could have caused some consternation at the dinner table: the hot blood of a sheep was to be drunk immediately.[9] Leechdoms do specify clean water and in this case rain or spring water was more likely to be useful: 'take rain water or spring water that bubbles up and is clean' (*nim renwæter oððer wulle wæter þa upwærð wyllð 7 clæne byð*).[10] Another leechdom would need rather more research since one had to find 'a spring that runs away due east and ladle up a cupful' (*wylle þæt rihte east yrne 7 gehlade an cuppan fulle*).[11]

---

[1] *E. Anglian Archaeol.*, Report No. 9, 1980, 74–5, 100–1.
[2] Bishop n.d., 15–16.
[3] Cunliffe 1976, 122, 68, 96.
[4] *Med. Archaeol.* XV, 126.
[5] *Med. Archaeol.* XVI, 158.
[6] *Beds. Mag.* Vol. 18, No. 138.
[7] Mackie 1934.
[8] Wright 1971, 98, 99.
[9] Cockayne 1851, I xlv 6.
[10] op. cit., III *Peri Did.*14.
[11] op. cit., *Lac.*114.

The Anglo-Saxons may have constructed dewponds, particularly in chalk uplands, though none have been identified to my knowledge. Rain water was almost certainly collected in containers, and there was at Jarrow evidence of a system for collecting rain from roofs in an eaves-drip drain and channelling this into a 7 foot x 2 foot cistern, though the water may have been intended for washing, rather than drinking.[1]

Some evidence of the political constraints on water supply comes from the seventh-century settlement of Puddlehill, near Dunstable. The occupants seem to have been prosperous farmers, even aristocrats, but they settled some four hundred feet up on the north-facing slope of the chalk downs, probably to avoid conflict with an enclave of Britons on the much more desirable valley site.[2] There was evidence of a seasonal watercourse which passed within 150 yards of the settlement, but in very dry weather they would have had to travel a quarter of a mile to the permanent spring line. There was no evidence of the construction of dewponds, but excavation was carried out in the face of encroaching quarrying, and only features that were clearly artificial were dug.[3]

By the end of the period it is possible that some rivers with large settlements on their banks were polluted to some extent. This seems to have been the case at York, since barbel and grayling, clean-living fish whose bones were found in late ninth-century levels, were apparently not present after this period.[4]

In some areas which were relatively densely settled, wells may also have been polluted, if sewage pits and wells were in close proximity. Typhoid, cholera and other water-borne diseases may consequently have been more common, but we have to be cautious in assuming certain diseases were present: some, like typhus, are of comparatively recent introduction to Europe.[5] Those living in trading centres where there was contact with strangers may have been at greater risk. At three years old children are immune to every common pathogen in their environment, but would be at risk from infections brought in by outsiders.[6]

There is some evidence that water was transported in skins on horseback.[7] In towns there may have been water-sellers: a *wetmaungre* is recorded in Winchester.[8] There may have been a number of reasons for buying water from a good source. Some tenements may not have had space for the construction of a well, but if there were a number of wells in a small area, then a cone of depletion would result. Wells may have become contaminated from industrial processes like tanning, as well as cesspits.

Water does not seem to have been drunk as a matter of preference by many Anglo-Saxons, any more than it is by people today. No doubt it was drunk by anyone who was thirsty and had no alternative beverage; travellers in particular seem to have depended on it. Bede writes of King Edwin of Northumbria that 'that king established a benefit for his people in that in many places where clear springs/streams ran by

---

[1] *Med. Archaeol.* XV, 126.
[2] Meaney & Hawkes 1985, 63.
[3] R.K. Hagen, pers. comm.
[4] O'Connor 1985, 29ff.
[5] Burnet & White 1972, 146; Wheeler 1979, 28.
[6] Burnet & White 1972, 82, 152.
[7] Seebohm 1952, 167.
[8] Barlow et al. 1976, 429.

well-used roads, where they were most frequented he ordered posts with bronze cups hung on them to be set up for the refreshment of travellers. And yet no-one, out of awe and love for him, dared or would touch them, except for his necessary use' (*se ilca cyning to nytnisse fond his leodum, þæt in monegum stowum, þær hluttre wællan urnon, bi fulcuðum strætum, þær monna færnis mæst wæs, þæt he þær gehet for wegferendra gecelnisse stapolas asetton 7 þær ærene ceacas onahon: ond þa hwæðre nænig fore his ege 7 his lufan hrinan dorste ne ne wolde buton his nedþearflicre þenunge*).[1] Similar provision seems to have been made in ninth- or tenth-century Ireland: 'Cenn Escrach of the orchards, a dwelling for the meadow bees, there is a shining thicket in its midst, with a drinking cup of wooden laths'.[2] The Welsh Laws declared that no-one, native or a stranger, should be deterred from taking water from a spring, a brook or a river, although the term 'water not in a vessel' which could be taken by anyone without consent, seems to suggest free access to wells too.[3]

Water that was considered in some way magical was sought after for administering to the sick. Wells which were considered in heathen times to possess special healing properties naturally continued to possess them after the advent of Christianity, but often the church would not allow them to be officially used until they had been blessed by the bishop and placed under the auspices of a saint.[4] That the old tradition died hard, is suggested by the *Canons of Edgar*, which enjoined every priest to forbid well-worshipping and necromancies.[5] About a dozen leechdoms call for holy water, and in three cases it is clear that this was 'blessed in a font' (*on font . . . gehalgodum*).[6] Bonser considers that the fee paid to the prototype of the parish priest for supplying holy water for prescriptions was a part of his meagre income.[7] Water could also be sanctified by contact with a saint: water containing earth from the spot where King Oswald was killed cured many.[8] Water containing chips of wood from the tree on which Oswald's head was placed after his death, or moss from this tree, was equally effective.[9] Chips from a buttress on which Aidan had leaned at the time of his death were similarly used to sanctify water, as were bread which St. Cuthbert had blessed, and earth from the spot where the water which had been used to wash his dead body had been poured out.[10] The efficacy of such holy water must have depended entirely on the faith of those who were taking the cure.

Invalid regimes might call for water, and sometimes the type of water is specified: 'rainwater, seawater' (*ren wætere, sæwater*).[11] On occasion a sufferer might be advised to take water instead of a second helping of wine.[12] Much more commonly water was used to produce an infusion of herbs, vegetables or berries. The *Regimen Sanitatis Salerni* however, does not recommend drinking water at mealtimes because it chills the stomach, and states that wine is preferable. It does advise

---

[1] Miller 1890, I 1 144.
[2] Jackson 1971, 125.
[3] Owen 1841, 523, 329.
[4] Elliott 1963, 138.
[5] Bonser 1963, 137.
[6] Cockayne 1851, III lxii.
[7] Bonser 1963, 226.
[8] Miller 1890, I 1 180.
[9] Bonser 1963, 182.
[10] Miller 1890, I 1 205; Colgrave 1940, 256, 290.
[11] Cockayne 1851, I ii 1, 3.
[12] op. cit., II lix 9.

drinking from a cool spring if you were very thirsty, but then, somewhat confusingly, says rainwater is best.[1]

To be restricted to drinking only water was seen as a deprivation. Water only was to be drunk by all the nation on the Monday, Tuesday and Wednesday before Michaelmas in the year when the 'Great Army' came to England, probably 1009.[2] According to Æthelstan's laws, anyone who had to undergo the ordeal was allowed only water for the three preceding days.[3] The Old English version of *The Rule of Chrodegang* states that for persistently transgressing against the Rule a guilty party was to be forbidden 'all food except for bread and water until he has fully expiated his wrong-doing' (*ælce bilyfne butan hlafe 7 wætere, oð he hit fullice gebete*). If a culprit talked in church then he was to do penance for this by taking only bread and water for the rest of the day. Talking in church seems to have posed a particular temptation: the authorities had been obliged to establish 'three days on bread and water' (*þry dagas an hlafe & an wætere*) for talking a second time, and 'a week on bread and water' (syfon niht an hlafe 7 an wætere) for a third offence.[4] Water then, was the liquid for those on a punitive or penitential diet.

Ascetics of course declared a preference for water. The hermit in a tenth-century Irish poem writes of 'excellent fresh springs . . . a cup of water splendid to drink', and a century later a recluse declares, 'though you like your ale with ceremony in the drinking halls, I like better to snatch a drink of water in my palm from a spring'.[5] Sts. Cuthbert and Guthlac carefully avoided all intoxicating liquor, but we are not told they drank only water, although this was probably the case.[6] At the monastery of Lindisfarne Aidan drank only milk and water, and this became the rule for the monks. There is no record that they objected when King Ceolwulf later granted them the licence to drink beer and wine.[7] Monastic rules refer to rations of wine, ale and mead, although perhaps not all monasteries could always provide such drinks for their inmates. The novice of Ælfric's *Colloquy* drinks 'Ale if I have any, or water, if I have no ale' (*Eala gif ic haebbe, oþþe waeter gif ic naebbe ealu*).[8] That the rules do not mention water probably meant it could be drunk freely.

Water certainly was drunk on its own, but it seems that more commonly it was the base for other, more popular, drinks: herb and meat teas, gruels, and various alcoholic beverages. It may have been that pathogenic organisms present in water were destroyed by boiling, or in alcoholic solutions, and that Anglo-Saxon populations appreciated this effect.

Much later, but at a time when the same sources of water existed, the general preference was for fresh water, then well-water, and lastly rainwater kept in cisterns.[9] It appears that spring water was preferred in Anglo-Saxon times, but the present evidence does not allow us to establish a further order of preferences. Wells may primarily have provided water for domestic processes, or on occasion, watering cattle. No doubt the Anglo-Saxons would

---

[1] Mead 1931, 218.
[2] Whitelock 1955, 410.
[3] op. cit., 385.
[4] Napier 1916, 61, 72.
[5] Jackson 1971, 69, 255.
[6] Colgrave 1940, 174; Whitelock 1955, 710.
[7] Colgrave 1940, 345.
[8] Garmonsway 1978, 47.
[9] Moryson 1617, 88, 108, 159.

have used the cleanest drinking water available to them, and this may have meant changing their source of supply from time to time. For example, if animals had paddled the earth round a spring from which household water had been fetched, then the effort of digging a well for water may have been considered worthwhile.

15. Fermented Drinks

Introduction

A wide range of drinks, some of which approximated to those we know today, was available to the Anglo-Saxons. The most important, judging by the number of references, were the fermented drinks: *win*, *meodu*, *beor* and *ealu*. These also give the impression of having been the most prestigious beverages: milk-based drinks seem to have had a rustic flavour, and, to judge by the literature, herbal infusions were probably primarily medicinal. However, in country districts a tradition of making infusions and fermented drinks from the flowers, fruits, leaves and roots of certain plants still exists, and may go back to the Bronze Age.[1] Fruit juices would have been available, but only for a limited period of the year, and a large amount of fruit would have been needed to produce any quantity of liquid. Only one leechdom to be taken internally specifically refers to fruit juice, when an invalid is counselled to drink 'the juice pressed out of blackberries' (*of bramelberian gewrungen*).[2] Water seems to have been a last resort, the preferred drink only of ascetics.

A hierarchy is observable within the group of fermented drinks: *win* was arguably the most desirable, followed by *beor* and *meodu*, then *ealu*. This is not to say that *win* was the most frequently drunk, probably the reverse was true: the more difficult to obtain and the more expensive it is, the more prestige accrues to a drink. Near the bottom of the social scale the novice of Ælfric's *Colloquy* drinks, 'Ale if I have it, water if I have no ale' (*Ealu gif ic hæbbe, oþþe wæter gif ic næbbe ealu*).[3] Soon after the Conquest, labourers on the lands of St. Paul's were supplied with ale to accompany their evening meal.[4] This class distinction was still observable when Moryson wrote severely, 'Clownes and vulgar men only use large drinking of Beere and Ale'.[5]

On a large estate a range of alcoholic drinks seems to have been available, as a blood-thirsty event recounted by Henry of Huntingdon incidentally demonstrates. At a feast in the king's hall at Windsor, Harold son of Godwin, was serving the Confessor with wine, when Tosti, his brother, envious of the fact that Harold possessed a larger portion of the royal favour, seized him by the hair in the king's presence. In a rage Tosti left the company and went to Hereford, where his brother had ordered a great royal feast to be prepared. There he seized his brother's attendants, and cutting off their heads and limbs, placed them in vessels of wine, mead, ale, pigment, morat, and cider. He then sent the king a somewhat ambiguous message that he was going to this farm, where he should find plenty of salt meat, but he had taken care to carry some with him.[6]

---

[1] Sayce 1946.
[2] Cockayne 1851, III *Lac.* 8.
[3] Garmonsway 1978, 47.
[4] Seebohm 1952, 157.
[5] Moryson, 1617, IV 176.
[6] Turner 1828, III 32.

Beor

Beor, translated as beer by Bosworth and Toller,[1] and in the Supplement[2] and Addenda,[3] continued to be so interpreted for some time. Bonser[4] considered it a cereal-derived drink, as he saw *beor* as etymologically derived from *bere* (barley). But although there are references to 'malt for ale' (*alo mealt/mealt aloþ*) in the glosses and leechdoms, there is not a single reference to *beor mealt*.[5] *Beor* glosses *ydromellum* or *mulsum*, sweet honey-based drinks.[6] *Idromellum* is also glossed by *growtt*, (the residue of malt after brewing) or *wurte* (the wort of beer); *mulsum* by *medo* (mead) and *the wyrt of botyr* (probably buttermilk).[7] All are relatively sweet substances. *Leoht beor* is likewise used to gloss *melle dulci*, another sweet drink.[8] Other evidence as to the sweetness of *beor* can be adduced from leechdoms. It was also a strong drink.

Yeast in cider will continue working to concentrations of about eighteen percent by volume of alcohol, making it stronger than ale at about four to six percent, mead at ten percent, and grape wine at eight to twelve percent. This is presumably why a pregnant woman, counselled in general terms not to get drunk, is specifically told to avoid *beor*.[9] The term *gewring* suggests 'juices or liquids that were pressed out', and it would be tempting to relate it to cider-making, but Ælfric uses it to gloss *sicera* (strong drink) and expands: 'all kinds of liquid except wine and water' (*ælces cynnes gewring butan wine and wætere*). An interesting passage in *Leechdoms* states that 'a pint of ale weighs six pence more than a pint of water, and a pint of wine weighs 15 pence more . . . and a pint of *beor* weighs 22 pence less . . . ' (*pund ealoð gewihð vi penegum þonne pund wætres & 1 pund wines gewihð xv penegum mare þonne 1 pund watres . . . ond pund beores gewihð xxii penegum læsse þonne pund wateres*).[10] Alcohol weighs only four-fifths of the same volume of water, and a port at twenty percent alcohol, even if sweet, will weigh noticeably less than the same volume of water. There is therefore no need to assume a copyist's error: in fact, if we could be sure of the volume of an Anglo-Saxon pint, and weighed it against some Anglo-Saxon pennies, it would be possible to discover the alcohol content of *beor*. What this passage makes quite clear is that *ealoð* and *beor* were not synonyms as ale and beer are today, but were very different drinks.[11] Apart from the strength of *beor*, it was probably sweeter than wine, ale or skim-milk, since if the same herbs are to be taken in drink, the last three liquids are to be sweetened.[12] There is only one occasion when *beor* has to be sweetened.[13] If *beor* was sweet, phrases like *biter beorþegn* (a bitter service of *beor*) would gain additional irony.[14]

---

[1] Bosworth & Toller 1898, 85.
[2] op. cit., 1921, 79.
[3] op. cit., 1972, 9.
[4] Bonser, 1963, 358.
[5] e.g. Bonser 1963, 31, 412; Cockayne 1851 III, *Lac.* 37, 89.
[6] Wright & Wulcker 1884, 128, 11, 15; 329, 10, 430, 9; 548, 3.
[7] op. cit., 725, 26; 772, 2; 808, 12; 281, 25; 793, 11.
[8] op. cit., 445, 12; 282, 6; 445, 12.
[9] Cockayne 1851, III xxxvii.
[10] op. cit., II lxvii.
[11] Fell 1975, 85.
[12] Cockayne 1851, II lii 1.
[13] op. cit., III, *Lac.* 59.
[14] Kemble 1848, 89.

15 Fermented Drinks

Returning to the glosses we find that *ofetes wos* (fruit juice) is also used to gloss *ydromellum*, and so is *aæppel win*.[1] This establishes a connection between *beor* and cider. Traditionally other fruit was added to cider: blackberries in the west, cherries in Kent.[2] This may go some way towards explaining the *beor aut ofetes wos* gloss. Historians have presumed that cider was made in Anglo-Saxon England, but not produced an O.E. word for it; *beor* certainly was.[3] William of Malmesbury recorded of Thorney, Isle of Ely, in about 1120, that it was so fully cultivated with apples and vines that it was like the earthly paradise.[4] There is documentary evidence for the consumption of perry in early sixth-century France, as well as in the eighth century, and, according to Charlemagne, in the ninth century, and it may also have been made in England.[5]

Beor occurs as part of one rent: a lease by King Edward and the community at Winchester is made to Bishop Denewulf in return for *twelf seoxtres beoras*, the same amount of sweet Welsh ale and twenty ambers of clear ale.[6] Its comparative scarcity is suggested in leechdoms. Alternatives, water, ale, wine or milk, are usually given on the assumption that *beor* may not be available.[7] There are references to strong *beor*, *leohtes* and *liþon beor*, but it is not qualified with as many terms as ale.[8]

Characters in the literature do go to a *beor sele* (hall), make use of a *beor se[t]le* and become *beore druncen*, but *beor* is clearly less an accurate description than a synonym for strong drink. Beowulf accuses Unferð of being *beore druncen*, but later Unferð cannot remember what he said *wine druncen*. Conceivably he could not remember what he had been drinking, but in *Judith*, Holofernes, *medugal* (drunk on mead), plied his followers with wine. However, he collapsed drunk with wine, while his followers were *medowerige*.[9] There are several instances of this sort of interchange, probably to suit the demands of the alliteration. In *The Fates of Men*, there are compounds of mead, ale and wine in the same sentence:

> . . . *sumum meces ecg*
> *on meodu-bence, yrrum ealo-wosan*
> *ealdor oþþringeð, were win-sadum*

> . . . from one on the mead bench, angry with ale, the sword's edge shall expel life, a wine-sated man.

A *beor byden* was part of the equipment that the reeve was responsible for on a country estate. This suggests the production, rather than just the importation, of *beor*. Cider was certainly made in medieval England. Ten quarters of apples and pears made seven tuns of cider.[10]

---

[1] Wright & Wulcker 1884, 128, 15; 430, 9.
[2] Hartley 1954, 564.
[3] Seebohm 1952, 112, 114.
[4] Ordish 1953, 118.
[5] Roach 1985, 137.
[6] Robertson 1939, 39.
[7] Cockayne 1851, I lxvii 3, xxxix 3, xlvii 2, II lii 1.
[8] op. cit., III xii 1, I lxxi 1,2, *Lac.* 18, *Herb.* CLVIII, CXL 2.
[9] *Beowulf*, l.531, 467; Fell 1975, 83, 82.
[10] Seebohm 1952, 168.

Beor would seem to have continental parallels, though having had evidence of false etymology in the *beor*/beer derivation, we have to be cautious about assuming that words have similar meanings because they sound similar. *Bjorr*, recorded in Denmark during the Viking period as a sweet, strong drink, drunk in the halls of the great, and Valhalla, Roesdahl considers was probably a strongly-fermented cider.[1] Unfortunately the possible etymology of *bjorr*, deriving from the Latin *biber*, a drink, does not give any information as to what it was made from.[2] However, in Normandy, *bère* (usually qualified as *bon bère* or *gros bère*) is still widely used as the dialect term for cider. This is made from pure apple juice, extracted from pulp pressed between layers of straw in a *pressoir*, and then fermented. *Bère* is still made on a number of farms, either for sale, or for the farmer's own use. Until recently, on formal occasions, *bère* was decanted into an earthenware flask which was taken to table, and poured into small, handled cups. These have their parallel in the small drinking cups found in pagan Anglo-Saxon graves dating from the sixth and seventh centuries, and in Danish graves of the eighth- to tenth-centuries and which may have been used for *beor*/*bjorr*.[3] Etymologically *bère* has suffered the same fate as *beor*, which is to say that it is translated, in Norman-to-French dictionaries, as *bière* (beer).

Cider is the one drink in Henry of Huntingdon's list which cannot be accounted for in Anglo-Saxon terms, unless we concede that *beor* is cider. There is no other term for a drink which is used with any frequency, and which would be likely to feature in the preparations for a royal feast. Ælfric wrote that St. Agatha went to a dungeon as gladly as if she was invited to *lustfullum beorscype*, and observed that 'no revelry is seemly at a wake' (*nan gebeorscype ne gebyrað æt lice*).[4] A *beorscype* may reflect Ælfric's idea of a good time, or, more probably, what he believed his readers would think of as one. It may even reflect regional preferences.

Ale

Tacitus writes that the Germans drank a liquor drawn from barley or wheat, and, like the juice of the grape, fermented to a spirit.[5] The Anglo-Saxons had a term (*malt*/*mealt*) for malt, and the technology to malt barley, or other grains, similarly to the way that Markham describes. Presumably barley was usually used: leechdoms usually say simply *wyll on wyrte*, but occasionally they qualify the term, adding *hwætene* (wheaten) to malt or wort.[6] The grain is steeped in water for three nights, left to drain for a day, then piled into a heap for three days. During this time it will begin to sprout. After that, the grain is spread thinly over the malting floor, and turned twice or thrice a day (to prevent the asphyxiation of the grain) for a further two weeks. From this point the grain is referred to as malt. The malt is gently dried over a fire of straw in a kiln before being rubbed clean and winnowed. The dried grains are ground, and are then ready for brewing.[7] This work

---

[1] Roesdahl 1982, 120.
[2] Fell 1975, 77.
[3] op. cit., 90.
[4] Skeat 1881, *Saint Agatha* l. 98; *Saint Swithun* l. 316.
[5] Corran 1975, 23.
[6] Cockayne 1851, II li 1, 2, 3.
[7] Hartley 1954, 540–1.

was presumably carried out in the *mealt-hus*, which glosses *brationarium*.[1] A description of modern procedures gives the additional information that the malt is laid out on a hair cloth over the hearth in the kiln.[2] This gives one very specific use for the 'hair cloth' (*temse*) listed in *Gerefa*, although a hair cloth may also have been used to contain crushed apples in the press during the making of *beor*. Malting the barley makes the grain more assimilable and also gives rise to more nutritionally desirable substances than in the raw state. Malt-fed human beings must have felt better than their contemporaries who did not consume malt, because they were better fed.[3] If ale is hopped, then this involves boiling to incorporate the aromatic principles of hops, and as alcohol is produced during fermentation, the resultant liquor is sterile, and cannot be infected with hostile bacteria.[4] Those Anglo-Saxons who drank ale/beer rather than water or dairy products, which could be infected by various organisms, were clearly less at risk from disease.

The ground malt is placed in a mash tun, then water which has boiled and cooled slightly, or three parts of boiling to one part of cold water are poured over the malt, and the mix is stirred. It is left to stand for three days or so before the wort, i.e. the resultant liquid, in O.E. *mæsc-wyrt*, is drained from the spent grains. If hops are used, then they are boiled in the wort for an hour before being strained off.[5] During mashing, diastase converts the starch in the malt to sugar, on which the yeast, which is now introduced, can feed.[6] Traditionally a bush was used to stir in the yeast, and this was hung up to dry, when the yeast would adhere to the twigs. The bush became the sign of an alehouse. The yeast would have been a top-fermenting variety, which would work well between 58 and 68 degrees Fahrenheit. After some three days, the yeast stops working, and the beer can be cleared and put into barrels. Of the three kinds of fining agents used today, clay was certainly available to the Anglo-Saxons, isinglass and vegetable gums may have been available too.[7]

The water used for brewing makes a great deal of difference to the final product. Soft water from swiftly-flowing springs and rivers, 'white', or moving, water, is preferred, although some living wells are also satisfactory. The bounds of the Charter of Burton Abbey begin 'First from the Trent where thieves hang in the middle of *bere fordes holme*'. *Bere ford* was a common term for a ford carrying a trackway along which barley was transported. The *holme* (water meadow) lay north of the present Trent Bridge, giving rise to speculation that the brewing industry, based on the superior qualities of the water of the Trent, may have been established in Anglo-Saxon times.[8]

The St. Gall abbey plan shows malthouse, kiln, millroom, three breweries and storage cellars. It would seem that each brewery brewed a different brew: *prima melior* for V.I.P.'s and monks, *secunda* for the lay brothers and *tertia* for pilgrims, beggars, and the like.[9] No doubt the brews were progressively weaker, but perhaps there were differences of flavouring as well. Four brewhouses were recorded on the royal

---

[1] Bosworth & Toller 1898, 673.
[2] Corran 1975, 28.
[3] op. cit., 16.
[4] op. cit., 35.
[5] Hartley 1954, 541.
[6] Corran 1975, 12.
[7] McGee 1986, 480.
[8] Hart 1975, 239.
[9] Corran 1975, 27.

domain of Annapes, on the borders of Artois and Flanders before circa 820.[1]
However, there is no evidence to show if they were used for making different brews,
and there seems to be no English evidence as to either the number of brewhouses on
an estate, or the kind of brews made. Present-day brews range from brown and light
ale at 3 and 3½ percent to strong ale at seven percent of alcohol by volume.[2] Strong
brews result from using a large quantity of malt to water.

Unfortunately we do not have any record of how much ale was brewed from a given
quantity of grain for the Anglo-Saxon period, but the Domesday of St. Paul's gives
the information that 67,814 gallons of ale were brewed from 175 quarters each of
barley and wheat and 708 of oats. This must have been a very strong ale: 1,058
quarters were used to produce 1,884 barrels of ale.[3] Adding honey after the initial
brewing would perhaps have further increased the alcohol content, though it seems
unlikely that this would ever have reached twelve percent as D.G. Wilson suggests,[4]
since beer yeasts cannot act if there is more than six percent by weight of alcohol.[5]
The technique of double brewing was evidently known, since a leechdom refers to
twy brownum ealað.[6] The wort would be used instead of water in a second mixture
with more malt, and this second wort would be left to ferment, making a strong brew.
Cockayne thinks that twice-brewed ale would keep until it became 'old' ale, but old
in this context must be a relative term: strong, or hopped brews might also be kept
until they were 'old'.[7] Some leechdoms do call for *eald ealoð* (old ale).[8]

Use of Hops

Eala/ealo/ealu is used to translate the Latin *celia/coelia/celeum/cervise/ceruisia* and
so refers to a cereal-derived drink.[9] *Eala* can be translated as ale or beer, since both
these terms can be used for the same product now, although originally ale had no
admixture of hops. The term 'ale' does seem to have retained a connotation of
strength and goodness, as Professor Fell has observed.[10] This is presumably because
ale had to be strong to have keeping properties. Secondary fermentation, which is
what sours the liquid, can take place if the alcohol content is not great enough to kill
off the yeasts. The inflorescences and nuts of the hop contain the bitter acids
humulone and lupulone which have antibiotic, and hence preservative qualities.[11]
This preservative quality was recorded by Abbess Hildegard of Bingen in the twelfth
century.[12] If hops are used in brewing, then the resulting beer needs to have only half
the alcohol content of ale.[13] Anglo-Saxon *ealu* may have sometimes referred to what
is technically beer, since there is evidence that hops were used in brewing at least in
the late Anglo-Saxon period, and perhaps from before the eighth century.

[1] Rahtz 1979, 8.
[2] McGee 1986, 480.
[3] Corran 1975, 30.
[4] D.G. Wilson 1975, 640.
[5] Corran 1975, 13.
[6] Cockayne 1851, I xlvii, 3.
[7] op. cit., Gloss.
[8] op. cit., I 374.
[9] Wright & Wulcker 1884, 281, 26; 369, 34; 203, 14; 128, 3.
[10] Fell 1975, 76.
[11] D.G. Wilson 1975, 638.
[12] op. cit.
[13] Corran 1975, 45.

The Epinal and Erfurt glosses date from circa 725 and the late eighth/early ninth-century respectively, but have a common ancestor written towards the end of the seventh century. They give *bratium-malt* (malt), *bradigabo-feluuop*; *bratium-malt*, *badrigabo-felduus*.[1] The term *bradigabo/badrigabo* can be explained by reference to later glossaries which give *bradigabo-feldhoppo*, and, (after the terms for malt and ale), *bratigapo-herba quæ admiscetur* (herbs which are mixed with it).[2] Pheifer considers that 'wild hops' is the best translation for *felduuop/felduus*.[3] It could however, perhaps be translated as 'field' or 'cultivated' hops, since hop gardens are recorded on the continent, at Hallertau in 736.[4] A deed of gift to St. Denis from King Pepin in 768 includes *humlonarias* (a hop garden).[5] Charlemagne's *Cartulare*, circa 800, does not list hops as one of the plants to be grown on the royal estates, so perhaps hops were not routinely used in brewing at that time. Strabo, d.849, did not mention hops in *Hortulus*, but this may mean no more than that hops were not seen as a garden plant. In some districts it may have been easier to gather hops from hedges or woods. According to a document of uncertain date, but between 800–1199, certain tenants of the Abbey of La Chapelle aux Planches, Haut Marne, 'must gather hops in the wood' (*debent colligere umblonem in silvam*).[6] Orchards with hop gardens are mentioned in the annals of the Abbey of Freisingen in 859. At about the same time in France monasteries expected dues of hops in such quantities that they imply cultivation. A statute of Abbot Adalhard of Corvey in 882 excludes millers from the task of gathering hops, and a later passage shows that hops were used for brewing. The porter of the monastery was to have a tithing of each malting. 'Of hops also, after they have arrived at the monastery, a tithe for him – the porter – . . . If this is not enough for him he shall obtain for himself some elsewhere to make his ale, so he may have enough' (*De humlone quoque, postquam ad monasterium venerit, decima ei (sc. portario) . . . Si hoc ei non sufficit, ipse . . . sibi adquirat unde ad cervisas suas faciendas sufficienter habeat*).[7] The use of hops presumably continued on the continent, since in 1000 hops are recorded as a rent payment, in 1070 they were apparently grown in Magdeburg, and property rights relating to hops growing wild in hedges are recorded.[8]

Hops were certainly used for brewing in Viking-age Denmark.[9] It may well be that the literal translation for *aste* in *Gerefa* is 'oast house', which would of course be additional evidence for the use of hops.[10] However, as *ast* glosses *siccatorium*, as *cyln* does, this is debatable, and a malting kiln may be implied.[11]

Probably similar conditions prevailed in at least parts of England. The Epinal and Erfurt glossaries suggest that hops were the most favoured, or even the standard addition to beer. The *Herbarium* refers to '*herba brionia* which some call *hymele*'

---

[1] Pheifer 1974, 68.
[2] op. cit., xl.
[3] op. cit., 68.
[4] Corran 1975, 42.
[5] Harvey 1981, 27.
[6] D.G. Wilson 1975, 644.
[7] op. cit.
[8] Corran 1975, 42.
[9] Roesdahl 1982, 119.
[10] Monk 1977, 279.
[11] Bosworth & Toller 1898, I, 55.

(hop) and the Anglo-Saxon translator adds the information, 'that plant is to that degree laudable that men mix it with their usual drinks' (*ðeos wyrt is to þam herigindlic þ hy man wið gewune drenceas gemencgeað*).[1] The complexities of the nomenclature of climbing plants is dealt with by Wilson,[2] but it seems evident that the description of *hymele* is accurate for the hop plant (*Herbarium* LII). *Lacnunga* refers to *hege-hymele* (hedge hop), which implies another sort, possibly the cultivated hop (the *feldhop* of the glosses?). The reference to the *eowu-humelan* (female hop),[3] – recommended as useful against elves, spirits walking at night, and women with whom the devil has sexual intercourse – indicates that there can be no confusion with non-dioecious twining plants, although the bryony with which it is equated in the *Herbarium* shares this characteristic. The names of the two plants continued to be confused for some centuries, but it is not likely that bryony with its poisonous berries was used for brewing.[4] Dues were paid in hops, at least in Kent, where *hopgavel* was apparently a money rent replacing a rent paid in hops.[5] *Hopu* is used to gloss *lygustra* (privet) in Cleop. fol. 57a, and Cockayne thinks that hops are meant; perhaps all we can deduce is that a plant called hop was known to the Anglo-Saxon translator. By the time of Domesday Canterbury was famous for its breweries, and fines were levied on anyone brewing beer 'in any other way than in ancient times' which Wilson thinks may imply the use of hops.[6] Canterbury kept its reputation for centuries, and beer was exported to the continent in the time of Moryson.[7] Perhaps the soils of Herefordshire and Worcestershire, as well as Kent, were already being used for hop growing in Saxon times. The name Himbleton (*hymel tun* – hop enclosure) is recorded in Worcestershire.[8]

Archaeological evidence for hops is now relatively plentiful. Judging from the evidence of pollen grains, hops were possibly cultivated in Norfolk in Saxon times.[9] The boat abandoned at Graveney in the tenth century had contained hops in its cargo, though it has not been established whether they were English hops being traded along the coast, or English hops for export, or even an importation of continental hops.[10] Fragments of Neidermendig lava suggest the boat had crossed the channel, and Flemish hops were later imported into England to supplement native supplies,[11] but the real significance lies not in the provenance, but in the fact that hops were important enough to be traded. The late Saxon site of Hungate, York, produced evidence of hops, and they were relatively abundant on the tenth-century Coppergate site, to where they may have been deliberately brought for brewing, or for the fibre in their stems.[12] It is thought that hops were brought into the town of Hedeby for brewing.[13]

---

[1] Cockayne 1851, *Herb.* LXVIII.
[2] D.G. Wilson 1975, 642.
[3] Cockayne 1851, III lxi.
[4] op. cit., Intro. ix.
[5] D.G. Wilson 1975, 645.
[6] op. cit.
[7] Moryson 1619, IV.
[8] Bonser 1963, 359.
[9] D.G. Wilson 1975, 637.
[10] op. cit., 627; Fenwick 1978, 123.
[11] Moryson 1617, IV 166.
[12] Monk 1977, 297; Hall et al. 1983, 205.
[13] Foote & Wilson 1970, 212.

Hopping beer gave it better keeping qualities, and made it more bitter and thirst-quenching. It may have been, of course, that in winter when the mixture would be less likely to become soured through a secondary fermentation, and when the thirst-quenching properties were less important, hops were not added. When brewing was carried out on a domestic scale hopping might have been less necessary: either going short or making another brew would have been of less moment than in a very large establishment catering for tens or even hundreds of people. Commercial breweries in towns may have found it useful to hop their beer. In one sense hops can be seen as an additive to prolong the life of a food product, and also to increase the manufacturer's profit, since less malt was needed for a brew. The ratio of half- to 3 lb of hops per 34 gallons of beer used nowadays would not be sufficient to preserve beer, so presumably Anglo-Saxon beer would have tasted more strongly of hops.[1]

Other Additions

Before hopping was established in Germany, a mixture of herbs called *gruit*, which included bog myrtle (also known as sweet gale), yarrow and rosemary was employed.[2] Danish beer was perhaps spiced with bog myrtle as well as hops.[3] Boiled with the wort, these herbs would flavour and perhaps help to preserve the beer. It is likely that these herbs were also used in Anglo-Saxon England. Bog myrtle is referred to in a leechdom for a light drink for lung disease where *gagellan* is to be boiled *on wyrte* (presumably the wort of beer) and then fermented with new yeast. Other herbs: helenium, wormwood, betony, march and *ontre* (?radish) were then to be added.[4] Recipes for gale beer are still extant.[5] Another leechdom calls for carline thistle, meadow sweet and agrimony to be boiled in ale and then fermented with yeast.[6] Wilson finds evidence for the use in early brewing of yarrow and rosemary, and, in addition, heather, alecost, and wormwood.[7] Alehoof (*Glechoma hederacea*), also known as ground ivy, was used in brewing. A reference in leechdoms to *tunhoof* suggests a garden variety, perhaps cultivated for brewing.[8] Ash keys were also used as a preservative: it was claimed that by their use small beer could be preserved for two months.[9] Sap from sycamore trees was used to make beer stronger.[10] The traditional use of sappy boughs, particularly those of spruce, in beer-making is widespread in Europe.[11] It may well have been practised in Anglo-Saxon England; some leechdoms call for the bark of trees to be brewed up into a drink.[12] What is certain, is that ale/beer was not a standard product. The flavourings and strength would have varied according to ingredients available, the skill of the brewer, and the preferences of the consumers.

---

[1] McGee 1986, 47 5.
[2] Corran 1975, 42.
[3] Roesdahl 1982, 120.
[4] Cockayne 1851, II li.
[5] Hartley 1954, 544.
[6] Bonser 1963, 358.
[7] D.G. Wilson 1975, 644.
[8] Cockayne 1851, III lx.
[9] Sayce 1946.
[10] op. cit.
[11] Hartley 1954, 546.
[12] Cockayne 1851, *Lac.* LXXI.

Hops may also have been used in non-malted drinks, fermented with water, yeast and honey. Dandelion, sage, nettle, and other plants may have been used to make beers as they have been up to the present.[1] It was perhaps a drink of this kind, described as 'beer with herbs' that a tenth-century Irish hermit enjoyed.[2]

Malt and Ale in Food Rents

Malt and ale often feature in late Saxon rents, gifts to monasteries and leechdoms. Æthelgifu left land to Ælfwold on condition that he gives every Lent 'six *mittan* of malt to Braughing and to Welwyn' (*he selle ælce lengtene to brahingum vi mittan mealtes . . . 7 swa micel into welingum*). Leofsige was to pay either three days' food rent to St. Alban's, or a list of items including sixteen *mittan* of malt.[3] The largest amount of malt referred to seems to have been forty ambers as a yearly donation from the estate of another noblewoman.[4] A fragment from a will from Bury St. Edmunds provided 'five ores for malt and for fuel for the first funeral feast' (*fyf oræ at te fyrræ ærflæ at malt 7 at hældyggæ*). The feasters were presumably to brew their own ale. The will provides 7 pence for ale for the funeral feast when the mourners would have to rely on what was presumably seen as the inferior commercially-produced substance.[5] 'Three bushels of malt' (*iii sceppe mealtes*) were left to Bury St. Edmunds and Abbot Leofstan adds '. . . one bushel of malt' (*Leofstan abb doð to þis fermfultum an sceppe malt*). From Barton the food rent was 'four measures of malt including both mash and grist' (*iiii met maltes under masc 7 grut*).[6] Presumably *grut* was the malted grain still to be milled, and *masc* was the ground malted grain. Æthelwyrd left one day's food rent to the community every year, to consist, *inter alia*, of forty *sesters* of ale.[7] This is comparable to a day's food rent at Peterborough: fifteen *mittan* of clear ale, five of Welsh ale and fifteen *sesters* of *lið*.[8] In about 975 Wulfgeat of Donnington left a brewing of malt to the Church of Worcester. Half was to come from Donnington, half from Kilsall, so perhaps a sizeable amount of malt was involved.[9] The survey of the Manor of Tidenham, Gloucestershire, shows that the *gebur* was to provide six *sesters* of malt at Lammas.[10] Bishop Cuthwulf and the congregation at Hereford leased land in return for rent which included fifteen measures of pure ale, that is, a full cask.[11] According to the services and dues rendered at Hurstbourne Priors, Hampshire, the peasants were to render 'first from each hide . . . six church measures of ale' (*Ærest æt hilcan hiwisce . . . vi ciricmittan ealað*).[12] A lease of land by King Edward and the community at Winchester to Denewulf, Bishop of Winchester, was made in return for an annual rent which included twelve *sesters* of sweet Welsh ale and twenty ambers of clear ale.[13] In

---

[1] Hartley 1954, 545.
[2] Jackson 1971, 69.
[3] Whitelock 1968, 9, 11.
[4] Turner 1828, II 547.
[5] Robertson 1939, 253.
[6] op. cit., 193.
[7] op. cit., 59.
[8] op. cit., 13.
[9] Finberg 1972, 118, 149.
[10] Robertson 1939, 205.
[11] op. cit., 141.
[12] op. cit., 207.
[13] op. cit., 39.

leechdoms ale was regularly used as a basis for herbal drinks, often as an alternative for wine.[1] According to the Bedwyn Guild Statutes, five ambers of ale were part of the compensation to by paid for lying to or cheating a guild-brother.[2] When the members of the Exeter Guild met, which they did three times a year, each guild brother was to have two *sesters* of malt, and each retainer one.[3] This suggests that they were to provide for a brewing.

There is another term, *swatum*, which glosses *cervisia*, and which occurs once in leechdoms, but *swatum* was probably new ale or wort, rather than a distinct sort of ale.[4] It may possibly be swats, the liquor which comes off oatmeal after soaking for 24 hours. Other products of brewing are sometimes called for e.g. *gryt* (the wet dregs of malt liquor), and *alo-malt*.[5]

The payment of ale as rent was common enough for the term *gauel sester*, meaning a measure of rent ale, to be used to gloss *sextarius vectigalis cerevisiæ*.[6] In some areas the *gebur* was expected to pay *ealugafol*.[7]

Ale is seldom referred to in the heroic poetry, and although men in *Beowulf* 'at their ale-drinking told another tale' (*ealo drincende oðer sædan*), they used *ealo-wæge* (ale-cups) on only three occasions, and *ealo-benc* (an ale-bench) twice.[8] There is a solitary *ealowosan* (ale-drinker) in *The Fates of Men*, but the term *ealu* carries very little emotive weight as it is used in the literature.[9] This is hardly surprising if it was the everyday drink of most people.

Brewing

Brewing was attended with difficulties. One problem may have been that the yeast might not work well, another that unwanted bacteria might spoil the brew, which is particularly the case if utensils are not thoroughly cleaned. To ensure that a brewing went well, recourse might be made to superstitious practices. 'It shames us to recount all the shameful sorceries which you foolish men practise . . . in brewing' (*Us sceamað to secgenne ealle ða sceandlican wiglunga þe ge dwæs-menn drifað . . . on brywlace*), wrote Ælfric reproachfully.[10] The objection was probably to 'pagan' (or superstitious) practices, perhaps the use of ale-runes.[11] Leechdoms also dealt with the problem, but the advice 'if ale is spoilt, take lupins and lay them in the four corners of the building and over the door and beneath the threshold and under the ale vat, put holy water into the wort of that ale [?]' (*gif ealo awerð sie genim þa elehtran lege on þa feower sceattas þæs ærnes 7 ofer þa duru 7 under þone werxwold 7 under*

---

[1] Cockayne 1851, II xxviii, liii, lv, lvi 2, *Lac.* LIV, LVIII.
[2] Whitelock 1955, 559.
[3] op. cit., 558.
[4] Cockayne 1851, I ii 19; Bosworth and Toller 1898, 944.
[5] Cockayne 1851, *Lac.* LXXI.
[6] Bosworth & Toller 1898, 363.
[7] Liebermann 1898, 448.
[8] *Beowulf*, l. 11, 481, 495, 1029, 1945, 2021, 2867.
[9] Fell 1975, 80.
[10] Skeat 1881, 100.
[11] Elliott 1963, 67.

þ ealofæt do mid halig wætre þa wyrt on þ eala) is hardly likely to have been effective, even assuming the brewer had supplies of lupins on hand.[1]

The Abbotsbury Guild Statutes also indicate that a brewing might not go well, but here the individual is held responsible for the quality of the brew. The fine of three *sesters* of wheat was probably to deter those who might be tempted to skimp on the amount of malt, or the attention a brewing demands.[2] Brewers in Chester at the time of Domesday were deterred from giving false measure or selling bad ale by a fine of four shillings or being put on the dunghill.[3]

Brewings seem to have been undertaken every month, if not more frequently. According to a law of Æthelstan, the hundred men were to meet 'once a month . . . whether at the filling of the butts or else when it suits them'.[4]

The ale produced was not a standard product, and would have varied from brewer to brewer. Because production was on a domestic basis it was evidently possible to obtain *mealtes smedan* (finely ground malt), new ale before it is strained, *breowende wyrt* (which we know was the liquid wort, since other ingredients are to be boiled in it), mash wort made from wheaten malt, *grut mealtes* (coarsely-ground malt) or dregs.[5] Ale is sometimes qualified as good and/or clear, as sour or new, as well as *wiliscum* (see below), and, as the basis for about a hundred leechdoms, is the liquid most frequently mentioned. Occasionally it is to be avoided: in one instance milk is to be taken instead.[6]

Sites of breweries are recorded in place-names. Hills Bruern, Gloucestershire, derives from *breow ærn*, a place or building used for brewing.[7] *Bruurne*, also in Gloucestershire, and with the same root, was recorded in Domesday and is now Brawn Farm.[8]

It is generally assumed that the products of distillation were not available to the Anglo-Saxons, although there is an opinion that distilling was practised in Ireland in the sixth century, and that the Vikings appreciated distilled liquors imported from the Arab world where the alambic had already been developed (Musée du Cidre, Valognes). Even if there was no distillation, there may have been occasions when the Anglo-Saxons could have drunk alcohol in very high concentrations. If comparatively small barrels of liquor were kept in unheated stores during winter, a hard frost would lock up the water in the form of ice, leaving a quantity of sweet, highly-alcoholic liquid, which could be drawn off.

Although we have no records of the results of drinking bad ale in Anglo-Saxon contexts, the experience of Sedulius in Liège about 840 could probably be duplicated. He was taken in by one Hartgar, whose house he criticises, but, 'Worst of all is the

---

[1] Cockayne 1851, I lxvii 1.
[2] Whitelock 1955, 560.
[3] Turner 1828, III 116.
[4] Whitelock 1955, 389.
[5] Cockayne 1851, I xxxix, III *Lac.* 20, 112, 89; II lii 3, li (1), (2), (3), III xxxix (2), I xxxi 7, III xxviii.
[6] op. cit., II lxv 2.
[7] Smith 1964, III 14.
[8] op. cit. II 152.

really horrible ale. No child of Ceres this, though it has the yellow of her hair . . . a beast of prey in a man's inwards'.[1]

Women presumably did the brewing in domestic situations in Anglo-Saxon times as they did in succeeding centuries, although this may not have been the case in Wales, since if a couple separated, the husband was to have all the liquor vessels and all the tubs, but as he was also to have the iron hob and the baking griddle, the value of the equipment, rather than its association with particular tasks may have been the primary consideration.[2] Surnames connected with brewing which have the feminine occupational suffix survive in Brewster and Malster.[3] On large estates the brewing was probably done by men, as it would have been a full-time occupation, and the various pieces of equipment could have been scaled-up in size. The original measure of water under the *Rule of St. Benedict*, had become a draught of the standard beverage of the country. Although detailed regulations governed the occasions when the monks were allowed to drink, they were allowed alcoholic drinks in some quantity.[4] The daily allowance for a monk was a gallon of good ale, often supplemented by a second gallon of weak ale, and a modest sixteenth-century household brewed two hundred gallons every month, so the quantities involved were considerable.[5] In Domesday *cerevisarii* (brewers) are referred to at Bury St. Edmunds. We do not know whether they were men or women, but presumably they catered for the pilgrims visiting the abbey. At Helston the term probably referred to tenants who paid their dues in ale. Fixed dues would be paid for the right of brewing in a town.[6]

'Welsh' Ale

Ale has a sweetish flavour, as long as the malt sugar in it is not completely fermented.[7] If the ratio of cereal to water is high, sugars will remain after the yeast stops working at about four to six percent alcohol. *Wylisc* (Welsh/foreign) ale may have been of this type, since Denewulf's lease says 'sweet Welsh ale' and was perhaps more like modern barley wine, except that the way the barley was kilned caused it to have a smoky taste too. It was traditionally regarded as being 'glutinous, heady and soporific'.[8] From the evidence of the lease to Denewulf it was more highly-regarded than clear ale, since twelve *sesters* was a much smaller measure than twenty ambers, and the same quantity as the *beor* that was to be provided.[9] Much earlier, Ine's Laws stated that ten hides were to furnish 30 ambers of clear and twelve ambers of Welsh ale. Offa had retained as part of his *feorme* from his estate at Westbury, two tuns of pure ale, a coomb of mild ale and a coomb of Welsh ale.[10] 'Pure' ale may have been clear ale, whereas the sweet ale is likely to have been thick.[11] Clear ale and Welsh ale are two different sorts as an agreement

---

[1] Waddell 1932, 85.
[2] Owen 1841, 523.
[3] Fell 1984, 49.
[4] Knowles 1940, 457.
[5] Corran 1975, 36; Drummond 1958.
[6] Loyn 1970, 383.
[7] Mintz 1985, 136.
[8] C.A. Wilson 1973, 370.
[9] Robertson 1939, 39.
[10] Loyn 1970, 304.
[11] Cockayne 1851, Gloss.

between Ceolred, Abbot of Peterborough, and Wulfred, involved 'two tuns full of clear ale ... ten *mittan* of Welsh ale' (*tua tunnan fulle luhtres aloh ... ten mittan welsces aloð*).[1] Clear ale was not sweet: an invalid was to avoid sweetened ale, and to drink clear ale.[2]

Wylisc/welscum ale is called for in several leechdoms, but much less frequently than ordinary ale.[3] Surprisingly perhaps, lxv 2 calls for the *wylisc ealo* to be 'sweetened with honey' (*swete mid hunige*).

One charter refers to a *coomb of liþes*, translated as 'mild ale'.[4] One day's food rent at Peterborough was to include fifteen *mittan* of clear, five *mittan* of Welsh ale, and fifteen *sesters* of *liðes* (again translated as 'mild ale').[5] Perhaps translators have been influenced by the adjective *liðe*, which means 'pleasant', 'mild'. As *liþ* glosses only the generic Latin terms for strong drink, it is perhaps a reasonable translation.[6] In a recipe from the *Herbarium*, *gladen* is to be taken 'in soft/smooth wine' (*on liþum wine*).[7] A *lið-wæge* was apparently a vessel for *liþ*, and when Cwænburh is cured by John, she invites him to stay for a drink: *þa bær unc mon lið forð 7 wit butu druncon.* This is usually translated as 'then a cup was brought to us and we both drank',[8] but there seems to be no reason why this should not be *lið*, the drink.[9] *Blacan briwe*, named as an alternative solution (to *beor*) in which medicine could be administered, seems to be another case where a drink is distinguished by its qualifying adjective: *blacan* means 'shining', and therefore probably a clear drink.[10]

A land rent paid to the church of Worcester in the time of Offa included three hogsheads of Welsh ale, sweetened with honey. This may have been bragot, honeyed and spiced ale which stood second in esteem only to mead at the Welsh Court, and a parallel to pigment.[11]

Since *wylisc* can mean 'foreign', we need to consider the possible importation of *wylisc* ale from the continent. Certainly ale was traded overseas in later periods, but references are to English ale being exported to the continent.[12] It would be difficult to prove that ale was not imported into Britain from abroad, but, while there are references to the importation of wine, I have come across none to the importation of ale. Moreover, ale was the most important, although not the most prestigious, drink of western Britain, known in Wales as *cwrw* and in Ireland as *courmi*.[13] It retained its individuality even at the end of the eighteenth century.[14] Irish scholars in Cologne and Liège in the ninth century found the continental beer 'abominable', perhaps additional

[1] Robertson 1939, 13.
[2] Cockayne 1851, II lxv 2.
[3] op. cit., I xlvii 3, lxii 2, lxiii, xxxii 4, xlvii 2, lxx, lxv 2, *Lac.* xiva.
[4] Turner 1828, III 31.
[5] Robertson 1939, 13.
[6] Bosworth & Toller 1898, 643, 644.
[7] Cockayne 1851 Herb. LXXX.
[8] Miller 1891, 1 2 392ff.
[9] *Beowulf*, 1 1982.
[10] Bosworth & Toller 1898, 106.
[11] Owen 1841, 391, 675.
[12] Moryson 1617, I 99.
[13] C.A. Wilson 1973, 370; P. Walsh, pers. comm.
[14] C.A. Wilson 1973, 370.

evidence for the superiority of the Celtic product, although their comments may reflect no more than personal preference and nationalistic bias.[1]

Ale seems to have been the commonest drink in Wales according to the evidence of the Laws. The apparitor and the smith were to have the fill of ale of the vessels used in serving, but only the half of bragot and the third of mead.[2] The steward was to have the length of his middle finger of the ale above the lees, of bragot the length of the middle joint of the same finger, and of the mead, the length of the extreme joint.[3] Similar relative values are observable in the rents: one vat of mead is equated with two of bragot and four of ale.[4] Vats full of ale and bragot were included in the winter food rents.[5] The vat had to measure nine spans diagonally, and so was a substantial size.[6] The hierarchy of settlements was reflected in the status of the drink they had to supply: a free *trev* paid mead to the king; a free *trev* where there was no office (? king's building), bragot; and a *tæog* (slave) *trev*, ale.[7]

Wine

Production

Wine is the fermented, cleared and matured drink made from grapes. Wines can be made from other fruits, but to describe these a prefix is used. Grapes have the highest sugar content of any fruit, and so are the most suitable for making wine.[8] A summary of wine-making will demonstrate that there is nothing inherently improbable about the Anglo-Saxons using the same processes. Crushing the gathered grapes by treading them is an ideal method, since the must becomes warm and aerated. The subsequent formation of alcohol precipitates all foreign matter and sterilises pathogenic bacteria.[9] The bloom on grapes is yeast. The most important of these are Saccharomyces apiculatus, which starts fermentation, *S. ellipsoideus*, which carries out the main fermentation, and *S. Pastorianus* which continues working when alcohol inhibits the action of the other two. The alcohol tolerance of wine yeasts is generally around 14%, but some strains are stopped only at concentrations of 20%. It is not necessary to assume because the majority of wild yeasts in this country rarely produce more than 4% alcohol, that Anglo-Saxon wines were weak, and had to be drunk very soon after fermentation.[10] Even if desirable yeasts were not present on the grapes in some vicinities, the Anglo-Saxons could have used baker's yeast, which produces 12–14% alcohol. Certainly if the alcohol level is low – say 7% – wine will not keep well and will not travel, and there is evidence that some wine in Anglo-Saxon England was transported considerable distances. At 10% it is not likely to undergo undesirable secondary fermentation, most commonly by *mycoderma aceti* bacteria which will turn it to vinegar.[11]

---

[1] Waddell 1932, 85.
[2] Owen 1841, 391, 675.
[3] op. cit., 363.
[4] op. cit., 197, 553.
[5] op. cit., 199, 771.
[6] op. cit., 553.
[7] op. cit., 533, 779.
[8] Ordish 1953, 47.
[9] op. cit., 77, 58.
[10] op. cit., 20; Duncan & Acton 1967, 129–30.
[11] Ordish 1953, 53.

Initially the crushed grapes are left uncovered to increase the amount of yeast, then, when air is excluded, the yeast draws oxygen from sugar, breaking up sugar molecules to produce – *inter alia* – alcohols, principally ethyl alcohol. A cool fermentation, (at 70 degrees Fahrenheit or below) is likely in most English autumns, even during warmer climatic periods, and allows yeasts to tolerate higher levels of alcohol, and produce a wine with a more pronounced aroma. Unwelcome microbes are less likely to flourish so there is less likelihood of off-flavours, and the volatile alcohols and esters are less likely to evaporate. Fermentation itself would probably generate enough warmth for the yeasts, which can in any case, work at temperatures down to 43 degrees Fahrenheit.[1]

Wine to be kept a long time must start with grapes with a good acid content, probably the case in England even in the warmer climatic phase known from the ninth to thirteenth centuries. Today English wines are more likely to suffer from excess acid.[2] A pH of approximately 3 is needed to discourage the growth of other microbes. Honey could be added to provide sugars necessary to allow an alcohol content of 10% or so to be reached in a controlled fermentation. In 1669 Sir Kenelm Digby judged that a solution contained enough sugar if a fresh egg floated to a depth of two pence.[3] There is no reason why the Anglo-Saxons could not have used a similar primitive hydrometer. A pint of Anglo-Saxon wine apparently weighed fifteen pence more that the same volume of water.[4] In this case the alcohol content was more than balanced by the presence of substances (presumably mainly sugars) weighing more than water.

If only the free run of grape juice is used, a clear pure wine will result. Usually after crushing and fermenting for one to three weeks the must is pressed. Mechanical pressure will incorporate juice from skin and seeds which contains phenolic, acid and flavour compounds. The eleventh-century Book of Genesis[5] shows a press in use. Wines made from pressed must will tend to be cloudy, but can be fined with gelatin, isinglass, clay or egg-white: all substances available to the Anglo-Saxons.[6]

All vessels used for must or wine have to be sterilised, usually by burning sulphur. *Swefel* (sulphur) was known to the Anglo-Saxons: the merchant of the *Colloquy* imported it. It may have had veterinary and medical uses then as now, but Roman writers known to the Anglo-Saxons, Columella among them, refer to its use in wine-making. Provided this precaution was taken, and the fermenting wine was not in contact with an excessive amount of air, there is no reason to assume that wine more than a year old need have been of very poor quality.[7] In fact 'clear old wine' (*eald win hlutto*) was equated with very good mead or *cæren* (see below).[8] Old wine is called for in several leechdoms, and while wine may have been kept specifically for medical purposes, there is nothing to suggest this. Clear wine is called for in a few leechdoms. This would suggest that the wine had stopped working, and been racked off the lees. *Þicce win* (thick wine) is mentioned once: it is to be avoided.[1]

[1] McGee 1986, 448.
[2] Ordish 1953, 54.
[3] op. cit.
[4] Cockayne 1851, II lxvii.
[5] B.M. MS. Claud. B. IV. fol.17.
[6] McGee 1986, 445, 452; Ordish 1953, 56.
[7] op. cit., 20.
[8] Cockayne 1851, II liii, lv.
[1] op. cit., xliii.

Large wooden casks make possible a controlled, limited contact with the air, thereby allowing the process known as ageing, developing or maturing. Casks of wine illustrated on the Bayeux Tapestry have a bung in the centre of one of their ends. Presumably this does not indicate the position for a spigot: the small barrel could be tipped up, but the large barrel would have to be placed upright on a staging if a spigot was to be used in this position; alternatively the liquid would have to be syphoned out. The bungs may in fact be in holes through which the ullage was filled, and in which spiles would be placed when the supplies in the barrel were being drawn off. If the barrels were kept vertical during this procedure, the area exposed to the air would be much smaller than if the barrel was horizontal. An even temperature, achievable in cellars or storehouses of cob, is ideal for this. Presumably wine was served in flagons, perhaps of pottery (Stamford ware includes some 'flagon' shapes), perhaps of leather. The term *butruce* ('bottle') is sometimes used.[1]

Wines produced in England are usually dry. Relatively few grapes in Europe ripen to the degree required for sweet wine. Very occasionally a period of high humidity may result in infestation by *botrytis cinerea* (*pourriture noble*). This mould injures the skin of the grape through which water then evaporates, producing very high – 30% or more – sugar concentrations in the grape.[2] Sweetness is not one of the qualities of a good wine listed in the Salernian Regimen of Health. 'If you desire good wines, these five things are praised in them: strength, beauty and fragrance, coolness, freshness' (*Si bona vina cupis, quinque hæc laudantur in illis. Fortia, formosa, et fragrantia, frigida, frisca*).[3] This may not have reflected Anglo-Saxon taste, since wines are very often flavoured, and/or used as a base for other drinks.

Imported Wines

Imported and home-produced wines were both potentially available in Anglo-Saxon England. The merchant of the *Colloquy* imported wine, selling it at a profit. At this period wine was certainly imported from France: merchants from Rouen who came to London Bridge with wine had to pay a duty of six shillings on a large ship. This ordinance is reputed to date from the reign of Æthelred, but may in fact date from the last years of Cnut's reign.[4] Wine seems to have been available also from the Rhineland, a wine-exporting area over some centuries which exported to urban centres like Hedeby on the continent too.[5] Sherds of pottery from amphorae customarily used for transporting Rhenish wine have been discovered at *Hamwih* in the same layer as a hoard of eighth-century coins. The wine may have come by way of Dorestad, on the Rhine in the Carolingian period, since remains of relief-band amphorae have been discovered there.[6] Such pottery is found in ninth-century contexts in London, Winchester and Canterbury, as well as in *Hamwih*.[1] Tenth-century layers at Coppergate, York, and Ipswich also yielded fragments of relief-band amphorae from Badorf.[2] In eleventh- and twelfth-century contexts there red-painted

---

[1] Skeat 1881, *St. Maur* 1.273.
[2] McGee 1986, 458.
[3] op. cit., 1986, 463.
[4] Loyn 1970, 93.
[5] Roesdahl 1982, 120.
[6] Van Es & Verwers 1980, 60ff.
[1] Loyn 1970, 88.
[2] Brooks 1980, 41–2.

Pingsdorf ware has been recovered.[1] Typically the amphorae, or flagons, ranged in height from fourteen to twenty-four inches, and from twelve-and-a-half to twenty inches in diameter.[2] Pitchers and beakers were probably a by-product of the wine trade – the Rhenish wine could be served from the spouted pitchers and drunk from matching beakers. Wine was also exported in barrels, recoverable from archaeological contexts when they have been used for lining wells. Silver fir (*abies*) did not grow in Denmark, but well-linings of this wood were found in Hedeby and in Dorestad. The reasonable assumption is that they arrived full of wine from the Rhineland where the silver fir is common.[3] Barrels are illustrated on the Bayeux Tapestry. One large barrel is drawn on a wheeled cart by two men, a smaller barrel is being carried on a man's shoulder.[4] The elongated form of the barrels is paralleled at Hedeby, where a barrel was used as a well-lining.[5] The size and proportions of the smaller barrel are very closely paralleled by barrels used for Calvados in Normandy today. In the early medieval period casks gradually took over from amphorae for the transportation of wine as they take up only 10% (as against 40%) of available cargo space.[6]

Literary evidence for wine includes a letter to Eanbald of York accompanying a gift of wine from Alcuin.[7] When Alcuin returned to England he wrote to his friend Joseph the Irishman who was still at Charlemagne's court, 'But woe is me! There is death in the pot, O man of God! The wine is gone from our wineskins and the bitter beer rageth in our bellies. And because we have it not, do thou drink in our name and lead a joyful day . . . Uinter the physician promised me two crates of wine, excellent and clear . . . ' and he proceeds to the arrangements for its transport.[8] A letter of Daniel, bishop of Winchester, to Boniface talks of the continental Christians as 'possessing fertile lands and provinces fruitful in wine and oil and abounding in other riches', although this does not necessarily imply import of the wine into England.[9] In 1012 however, the Scandinavian army in London were 'very drunk, because wine from the south had been brought there' (*swyðe druncene for ðam ðær wæs gebrohte win suðan*).

In 280 Probus had repealed the edict of Domitian, and restored the privilege of growing vines to most of the provinces to the north and west, specifically including Britain. Presumably Romans then established or re-established vineyards here. In his description of Britain in the middle of the eighth century, Bede stated 'in some places vines grow' (*on sumum stowum wingeardas growaþ*).[10] Vineyards are mentioned in the Laws of Alfred: 'whoever damages the vineyard of another, or his fields or his property, shall thus compensate . . . ' (*si quis damnum intulerit alterius vineæ vel agro vel alcui euis terræ, compenset sicut eius illud altinet*).[1] In tenth-century charters the term *wintreow* (wine-tree) is used as a landmark, indicating the presence of individual

---

[1] op. cit., 40–42.
[2] West 1963, 283.
[3] Roesdahl 1982, 122; Van Es and Verwers 1980, 268.
[4] Wilson 1985, plate 38.
[5] Roesdahl 1982, 185.
[6] Alcock 1987, 90.
[7] Hodges 1982, 128.
[8] Waddell 1932, 68.
[9] Whitelock 1955, 733.
[10] Miller 1898, I 1 26.
[1] Commissioners 1819, 411.

grapevines of some size.[1] In the Domesday survey vineyards are mentioned some 38 times. For example, there are several vineyards listed in Somerset.[2] At *Bistesham*, Berks., on the land of Henry de Ferrières were '12 *arpents* of vines' (*xii arpend uineœ*). (An *arpent* corresponded to an acre.) At Wilcote, Wilts., were *uinea bona* (good vines), and vines were also recorded, for example, at *Holeburne*, Westminster, *Chenetone* in Middlesex, Ware in Hertfordshire, and as far north as Norfolk.[3] References occur to *vinea nouella* (recently-planted vines), as at *Hantun* in Worcestershire. At Stebbing in Essex were two and a half *arpents* of vines, of which only the half was bearing fruit, and at Debden were two *arpents* bearing fruit and another two not bearing. It is possible that the vines not bearing fruit were new, or that they were established vines which had not been properly tended. Svein of Essex had '6 *arpents* of vines, and returns 20 measures of wine if it goes well' (*vi apenni uineœ 7 reddit xx modios uini si bene procedit*). According to Cotton Galba E IV: 'Note that one *arpent* of vines when they produce well for the community (of Christchurch) provides 8 measures of wine, and sometimes 6 and sometimes 10.' (*Memorandum quod una arpenta vini quand vinum communiter bene se habet, respondebit de viii mod vini. Et aliquando de vi et aliquando de x.*) Modern estimates are that 365 bottles on average can be produced every year from one-sixth of an acre.[4] Other vineyards in Essex range from one to ten *arpents* in extent.[5] Almost all are on the manors of landholders, which suggests wine for personal consumption by the lord and his retinue. This may contrast with the situation in France where Neckham declared every peasant should have a wine strainer basket.[6]

It has been argued that as *arpent* was a French term, vineyards were a post-Conquest introduction, but *arpent* is also used as a measure of meadowland, and once of woodland. In four instances vineyards are measured by acre.[7] An estate at Standon, Herts., according to Domesday, has two *arpents* of vines. In 990, Æthelgifu, stipulated in her will that an annual measure of wine should be given from her Standon estate to St. Alban's.[8] This argues for pre-Conquest and continuing wine production.

Few of the great monasteries were without their vineyards, though these were not necessarily near the parent house. Westminster Abbey owned two *arpents* of vines at Staines.[9] Sometimes the vineyards were rented out in return for measures of wine: 'Roald holds Lomer from the abbey. Alfward held it from the abbot and paid him ten *sesters* of wine a year.' (*Ruald ten de abbatia Lamere Aluuard tenuit de abbe . . . 7 reddeto abbi p annu x sextaria uini.*)[10]

William of Malmesbury, recorded of Gloucestershire about 1120: 'This vale is planted thicker with vineyards than any other province in England, and they produce grapes in the greatest abundance and of the sweetest taste. For the wine made in them

---

[1] Harvey 1981, 35.
[2] Thorn 1980, 86d, 90a.
[3] Seebohm 1952, 150.
[4] Ordish 1953, 42.
[5] Commissioners 1819, 411.
[6] Holmes 1952, 201.
[7] Commissioners 1819, 410–11.
[8] Whitelock 1968, 11.
[9] Harmer 1952, 518.
[10] Munby 1982, 43b.

does not twist the mouth by its tartness, and is little inferior to the sweetness of French wines.' (*Regio plusquam aliæ Angliæ provincæ vinearum frequentior densior, proventu uberior, sapore jucundior. Vina enim ipsa bibentium ora tristi non torquent acredine, qippe parum debeat Gallicis dulcedine.*)[1] His own monastery had a vineyard first planted at the beginning of the eleventh century by a Greek monk who settled there and spent all his time cultivating it.[2] He also recorded that Thorney, Isle of Ely, was so fully cultivated with apples and vines that it was like an earthly paradise.[3] These descriptions may also have been true for the Anglo-Saxon period. Certainly at the time of Domesday there was wine production in some quantity at Ely. Verjuice (made from the grapes that were unripe at the end of the season fermented to form a kind of sharp vinegar) was sold off outside the abbey.[4]

There was probably a warmer climatic phase from the ninth- to the thirteenth-century, when the vine would have been easier to grow in England.[5] Earlier, in the Merovingian period, wine was cultivated much further north in France than is the case today.[6] The grape pips discovered at Southampton in late eighth- early ninth-century contexts may have been grown locally, although they may have arrived in imported wine.[7] Wine was one of the blessings asked for at the coronation service of Æthelred II, which would perhaps suggest home production. The translator of *Prognostications* included the section on vineyards, with information that would make it possible to tell each year whether there would be *goda wingeardas*, or whether 'vines will be troublesome' (*wingeardas beoð geswencfulle*).[8] It was also thought relevant to record that it was unlucky to plant vines on one of the *Dies Ægyptiæi*.[9] The terms 'wild vine, wild white vine' (wilde wingeard, hwit wilde wingeard) suggest the Anglo-Saxons were familiar with the idea of a cultivated form.[10] More convincing evidence for the cultivation of vines is provided by Gerefa, which advises the reeve 'to lay out a vineyard/plant vines' (wingeard settan) in spring.[11] On the evidence of William of Malmesbury who wrote of Thorney: 'here land in cultivation is covered with vines which either grow along the ground or, supported by stakes, rise up into the air' (*hic praetexitur ager vineis quæ vel per terram repunt, vel per baeulos palos in celsum surgunt*), there was both low- and high-level cultivation of vines.[12] Because it allows air to circulate freely round the vines, assisting evaporation, high-level cultivation is perhaps more suited to the English climate.[13] High-level cultivation seems to be depicted in the Anglo-Saxon calendar for February, which shows men with hooks pruning very curly trees not unlike vines.[1] The scene may be copied from a continental source, and doubts have been expressed about doing this work so early in the year, (and, by extension, about the Anglo-Saxons' knowledge of viticulture), but a wine grower confirms that to prune vines later would

---

[1] Commissioners 1819, 411.
[2] Wright 1871, 44.
[3] Ordish 1953, 118.
[4] CA Wilson 1973, 328.
[5] Monk 1977, 389.
[6] Talbot Rice 1965, 293.
[7] Monk 1977, 388.
[8] Cockayne 1851, III *Prognostications*.
[9] Bonser 1963, 298.
[10] Cockayne 1851, III Glossary.
[11] Liebermann 1903–6, 454.
[12] Commissioners 1819, 411.
[13] McGee 1986, 483.
[1] Temple 1976.

result in severe bleeding.[1] According to Strutt, Anglo-Saxons called October *wyn monað* (wine month). This is the month in which grapes are still gathered here, although they can be left into November, or, exceptionally, December.[2]

There is a reference to a *vinitor* (vine-dresser) in the Domesday survey.[3] This craft might be assumed to be a Norman innovation, were it not for the fact that in 962 Edgar had given Abingdon abbey a vineyard at Watchet *cum vinitoribus* (with its vinegrowers).[4] A few years before Edwig had donated a vineyard to Glastonbury abbey.[5] Earlier still, Alfred refers to viticulture in terms which suggests he expects his audience to have first-hand knowledge of what is referred to, and this is also true of the writings of Aldhelm and Ælfric. The first writes: 'We well know that the rows of vines and the shoots of the vineyards become leafy and blossom in spring, but in the autumn they soften and grow ripe, with swelling clusters and yellowing grapes'. As Fell points out, the verb *noverimus* could hardly be used if his audience had not seen vineyards.[6] Interestingly, the grapes Aldhelm refers to are white, the general choice for vines grown in England now. Of the four main drinks: *win, beor, eala, medo* (wine, cider, ale, mead), wine has by far the greatest number of compounds; almost three times as many as mead. Of these fifty or so compounds, thirty-five are functional and descriptive, relating to wine production; for example: *winseax, winbeam, wincole* (vine-knife, vine-pole, tub into which the juice pressed from grapes runs).[7]

As one might expect, after William of Malmesbury's description, there are a number of place- and street-names in Gloucestershire which refer to vineyards. Although these are not recorded until after the Anglo-Saxon period: *Le Wyngarde* (1315) and *Le Wingard stret* (1320), for example, are based on O.E. elements and may have existed before the Conquest.[8] There are similar field-names in Devon, Dorset, Oxfordshire, Essex, Worcestershire and Cheshire.[9] Apart from this reference to Cheshire, references to vineyards in Lincolnshire indicate a more northerly cultivation of the vine than recorded in Domesday. *Vineam* was recorded in Lincoln 1103-6, and 'a virgate where the king's vineyard was' (*virgultum ubi fuit uinea regis*) (1156–62).[10] If nothing else, and Fell cautions that a Norman vineyard would have been called *wingeard* by the locals, place and minor names provide evidence for widespread vine-growing in England.[11]

---

[1] Seebohm 1952, 109; Ordish 1953, 36.
[2] op. cit., 41.
[3] Commissioners 1819, 411.
[4] Fell 1981, 8.
[5] op. cit.
[6] op. cit.
[7] Fell 1975, 78–9.
[8] Smith 1964, II 31, 36, 68, 95, 98.
[9] Field 1972, 245, 257, 263.
[10] Cameron 1985, 76, 106.
[11] Fell 1981, 8.

Monastic Vineyards

Vineyards were associated with monasteries, not just because wine was needed for Eucharist, but because the Rules usually laid down a generous allowance of wine. For example, from the *Rule of Chrodegang* in a translation from the second quarter of the eleventh century comes the following extract:

> *... 7 gif se earð sy wynes wæstmbære, sylle man dæghwamlice ælcum breðer fif punda gewihte wines, gif þa unweðru his ne forwyrnað. Gif þonne se eard full win næbbe, sylle ma ælcum þreo pund wines 7 þreo pund ealað, 7 warnien hi wið druncen. Þær þonne win ne byð, wyte se bisceop, oðð se þe under him ealdor byð, þæt hi hæbbon ealswa micel ealoð, swa hi wines sceoldon, þæt hi on þam frofor habban. 7 gif hwa on þam (win)landum for Godes lufon wylle forgan, wite se ealdor þæt he hæbbe ealoð his rihtgemet.*[1]

... and if the land is productive of wine, let each brother receive five pounds by weight of wine a day if bad weather does not prevent it. If the ground does not yield this amount of wine, then let each receive three pounds of wine and three of ale and caution them against drunkenness. There where there is no wine, let the bishop, or those who are in authority under him, see to it that they have as much ale as they should wine, that they may derive comfort from it. And if anyone will abstain from wine out of love of God, let the bishop see that he has the right amount of ale

According to the Regularis Concordia, ministers could partake of mixtum after Communion. However, those who wished to forgo this pleasure in Lent might do so.[2] Wine was saved for certain of the great high feasts at Abingdon in the time of Æthelwold. It seems to have been the case generally that by the time of Dunstan, the evening (in winter) and mid-afternoon (in summer) drinks were sometimes replaced by wine and mead.[3] Before the Conquest wine seems to have been more uncommon than mead, but in the twelfth century it appears as a simple alternative and was consumed on about eighty days in the year. Something of the importance of alcoholic drinks in later monastic contexts is suggested by the fact that post-Conquest Bury St. Edmunds had a cellarer, though he seems to have combined this office with that of bursar (*hordere. i. cellario ut thesaurio*).[4] Even so, it appears that wine was for the senior members of the hierarchy – not for the likes of the novice. That wine was 'for the old and wise' perhaps owes something to Plato: 'But when a man is verging on the forties we shall tell him ... to ask the presence of Dionysus ... the wine cup, which he bestowed on us as a comfortable medicine against the dryness of old age'.[5]

However, there were always those who disapproved of alcoholic beverages. Pliny regretted the misplaced effort that went into the production of wine as well as the effects of drunkenness, a view that was shared by King Alfred – to judge from his additions to his translation of Boethius' *Golden Age*: 'they drank no pure wine' and 'from the various drinks of their cup the raging course of (tyrants') luxury is

---

[1] Napier 1916, 15.
[2] Symons 1953, Sect. 24, 35.
[3] Knowles 1940, 457.
[4] Robertson 1939, 220.
[5] McGee 1986, 427–8.

excited'.[1] Early monastic regimes seem to have been particularly ascetic, perhaps of necessity. The *Rule of Chrodegang* deals with this eventuality.

> *Gif þonne for folces synnum gesceote, swa hit oft gescyt, þæt unwæstmbernys on earð becymð, þæt ma ne mæge þæt drincgemett bringan forð, ne on wine, ne on beore, ne on mede, ne on ealoð, þonne smæge se ealdor hit georne on manifealde þing þæt hi drinc hæbbon; 7 nane ne murcnion, ac mid þancgunge 7 mid glædnysse underfon þæt man him þonne don mage, 7 geþenceon þæt Sanctus Iohannes Baptista ne dranc win, ne medu, ne nan wiht þe him druncennys of come. Þær þær druncen byð, þær byð leahter 7 syn[2]*

If, because of the people's sin it happens, as often befalls, that the earth is infertile, so that it does not produce anything from which drink can be made, either wine, *beor*, mead, or ale, then the senior member of the community is to seriously consider the number of things they have to drink, and no-one is to complain but to receive whatever they may be given with thanks and gladness, and think of St. John the Baptist who never drank wine and was never drunk. Where there is drunkenness, there is vice and sin

After the arrival of King Ceolwulf, for example, the monks at Lindisfarne were given licence to drink wine and beer, instead of milk and water, the tradition established by St. Aidan.[3] On occasion early saints might turn water into wine as Cuthbert did once when those who drank it 'each confessed to the other that they had never before drunk better wine' (*ondette heora ægðer oðrum þæt hi næfre ær selre win ne druncen*).[4] Guthlac, were are told, 'did not taste one draught of intoxicating liquor of any kind of pleasing drink except at the time of communion'.[5] However, he seems to have been quite tolerant of the weakness of others. When two monks came to visit him they hid their flagons of ale under a turf, intending to pick them up on their return journey. This was presumably seen by Guthlac, who, after speaking of many things, and to their great surprise, 'with cheerful voice and laughing face' asked why they had not brought the flagons with them.[6]

Medicinal

There was widespread use of wine as a restorative in Anglo-Saxon times. Herefrith's account of his attendance on Cuthbert in his final illness includes the following passage, 'I also warmed some wine . . . and asked him to taste it, for I saw . . . he was greatly wearied both by lack of food and by disease'.[7] Ælfric, in his *Lives of the Saints*, referred to some particularly praiseworthy individuals who 'had no thought of wine save for the sick' (*wines ne gymdon buton wan-halum*).[8] Averroes had praised the digestive qualities of wine, which may have been one reason it was used as a medium for administering medicines.[9] In one instance it seems to have been equated

[1] op. cit.; Turner 1828, II 36, 53.
[2] Napier 1916, 15.
[3] Colgrave 1940, Ch. 4.
[4] Herzfeld 1900, Mar. 2.
[5] Whitelock 1955, 710.
[6] Swanton 1975, 54–5.
[7] Colgrave 1940, 275.
[8] Skeat 1881, *St. Martin* l.332.
[9] Bonser 1963, 294.

Food Production

for this purpose with good 'Welsh' ale: *do in win oððe in god wealealo*.[1] There are well over a hundred references to wine in leechdoms, more than to ale, the next most frequently-occurring liquor. However, this probably reflects the Mediterranean origin of the texts, rather than the relative frequency with which these drinks were found in Anglo-Saxon England, although only once is the qualification *gif þu hæbbe* added, and that refers to *ealdum* (old) *wine*.[2] Once 'very good mead' is given as an alternative to clear, old wine, and once *cæren* (see below) is an alternative to old wine.[3] The alternatives to wine of vinegar, 'clear ale' (*hluttran ealað*), and *beor* or ale are given.[4] Generally the writer seems to think that his readers will have access to various wines: old and clear, *scearp* (dry), *scearpestan* (driest), clear, *leoht* (light), *liþum* (mild or smooth), best, thin and clear, good and clear, and to as much as a *sester* of 'wine that has been blessed' (*gehalgodes wine*). Moreover he does not give any suggestion that his reader may find it difficult to obtain 'a twig from the top of the vine' (*wingeardes twigu ufeweard*), or 'a vine shoot' (*wingeardes set*).[5]

Sometimes the wine is to be heated: 'good wine heated and clear' (*god win gehæt 7 hluttor*); 'clean and clear red wine very hot and not too dry' (*clæne 7 hluttor win 7 read swiðe gehæt ne si to scearp*).[6] Sometimes the wine is to be heated 'with a glowing/very hot iron' (*mid glowende irene* or *welhat isen*).[7] Occasionally it is used for cooking: one leechdom gives the instruction to take 'chicken meat and stew in wine' (*cicene mete 7 seow on wine*). Other recipes call for apples, fruit and peas, bread, or, more bizarrely, swallow nestlings, to be stewed or taken in wine.[8]

A number of leechdoms are for herbs – fennel, rue, mint and sorrel – for instance, or spices, particularly pepper, in wine.[9] Recipes for 'clear drink' (*hluttor drenc*) with wine, honey, aromatic herbs and spices can be compared with the *luter dranck* for which the twelfth-century abbess, Hildegard of Bingen gave recipes.[10] The gloss *gwyrtod win* for *vinum conditum* suggests the addition of herbs as flavouring was a known practice.[11]

Occasionally wine is to be avoided; if a patient has a fever, for instance, another liquid is to be used as the medium for the dose.[12] One leechdom tells the patient to 'drink nothing new' (*ne drince . . . niwes naht*).[13] This would include new ale as well as new wine. Readers of *Leechdoms* are cautioned against 'drinking a lot of wine' (*micel win gedrinc*) because it 'harms the vision'.[14] But so do 'other sweetened drinks and foods' (*oþre geswette drincan 7 mettas*).

---

[1] Schaumann & Cameron 1977, 292.
[2] Cockayne 1851, II ii 3.
[3] op. cit., II liii, lv.
[4] op. cit., I xviii, *Lac.* 89, *Lac.* II viii, liii, I xlvi 2, *Lac.* LIV, LVIII.
[5] op. cit., II xi, III *Peri Did.* 3.
[6] op. cit., II vi, xvi 2.
[7] op. cit., II xxiv, xlv.
[8] op. cit., III *Peri Did.* 53, II iv, ii 2, xvi 2, I lxxxv.
[9] op. cit., II xxiv, I xviii, II vi, III *Peri Did.* 66, 50, I xli.
[10] op. cit., II 393–4.
[11] Wright 1857, 360.
[12] Cockayne 1851, II xii, xxii, xxiii, xxiv.
[13] op. cit., II xxii.
[14] op. cit., I ii l.

Sweetened Wine

There are several other references to sweetened wine,[1] which tend to contribute to the impression that the wine was naturally dry. Perhaps the belief, or indeed the fact, that 'sweet wine digests better than the rough' (*swete win sel mylt þonne þe afre*) meant that the Anglo-Saxons tried to remedy the deficiencies in their wine by sweetening it.[2] When it was available, the Anglo-Saxons evidently enjoyed drinking the sweet must before fermentation began, or was completed. Alfred, in his translation of Boethius, observes that you cannot press wine in mid-winter, 'though you may greatly desire the warm must' (*þeah ðe wel lyste wearmes must*).[3] (This of course, together with the addition of the technical term 'must' to a metrical translation of Psalm 103, and its use in a homily by Ælfric, is additional evidence for wine production in England). 'Unfermented wine' was noticed at Christchurch by Giraldus.[4] Must was boiled down to produce a very sweet liquid, and there is some evidence that this was done in lead-lined vessels, when lead salts would add to the sweetness of the concentrated grape sugars.

Cæren

According to Palladius, when must had been reduced by one-third it was called *carenum*, by two-thirds, *dulcis sapa*, and if it was boiled until it was thick it was called *defrutum*. However, the Erfurt gloss translates all three terms by *coerim/coerin* and 'must reduced by boiling' is probably the closest translation we can arrive at for *coerin*.[5] The term *cærenes* occurs in leechdoms and Fell deals with other variants.[6] It is clear that *cæren* referred to a prestige drink, suitable for royal feasts, which was so sweet that it could gloss nectar.[7] It could be equated with 'old wine, noble ale, or mulberry wine' (*eald win, æþele alu* or *morað*).[8] This taste for very sweet drinks makes one think that Moryson's comment, 'Gentlemen garrawse only in wine, with which many mix sugar, which I never observed in any other place or any other kingdome . . . the taste of the English is so delighted with sweetenesse' could have applied to Anglo-Saxon nobles too.[9]

Pigment

Spices and honey were added to wine to make pigment, a name derived from the fact it was prepared by *pigmentarii* (apothecaries).[10] It is not referred to in the Anglo-Saxon sources, although it was later described as having been one of the drinks prepared for the royal banquet Harold was going to give at Hereford.[11] It was a popular drink in later medieval times when it was served at the end of a meal with wafers and other delicacies, in the manner of a liqueur.[12]

---

[1] op. cit., I ii 16, 21, xxii, II lix 14.
[2] op. cit., II xvi 2.
[3] Fell 1981, 2.
[4] Knowles 1940, 464.
[5] Pheiffer 1974, 18.
[6] Cockayne 1851, I i 17; Fell 1981, 5.
[7] op. cit., 6,7.
[8] op. cit., 5.
[9] Moryson 1617, IV.
[10] Furnivall 1868, 88.
[11] Turner 1828, III 32.
[12] Furnivall 1868, 157, 356.

Variation in Wine

There would have been little standardisation when it came to wine. Then as now there would have been good and bad years, both in terms of the quantity and quality of the wine produced. Pliny observed that the same vine had different qualities in different places because of soil variation. There are some ten thousand estimated strains of *vitis vinifera*, and while this number includes New World and specially-bred varieties, it indicates that there were almost certainly different strains of vine in Anglo-Saxon England.[1] There are some hundred different strains of several yeast species on the skin or in the released juice of European grapes, which would also lead to variations in finished wine.[2] The wood of the casks in which wine was aged also contributed its own flavour. Greek and Roman wines may have been flavoured with tree resins, as is the case with present-day retsina; or pitch.[3] The silver fir barrels in which Rhine wines were exported may have flavoured the wine to some extent, but Anglo-Saxon barrels were often of oak, which is still used for ageing wine today, for the flavour that it imparts. Occasionally there may have been fine vintages, but if native wine was usually very dry, this may explain why wine was often used as a basis for drinks, which were sweetened and flavoured in a variety of different ways.

Wines other than from Grapes

Most berries will ferment to give wine: the skins of plums and damsons, for example, are covered with natural yeasts and could be fermented in the same way as grapes, if extra sugar in the form of honey was provided, in which case the wine could reach 18% alcohol.[4] In the second millennium B.C. settlers in the foothills of the Alps were making fruit wines from wild grapes, blackberries, raspberries, elderberries, berries of the bittersweet nightshade and cornelian cherries.[5] There seems no reason why the Anglo-Saxons could not have been using the same range of fruits for wine-making, with or without the addition of extra yeasts, although the mulberry is the only fruit we hear of as being regularly used in drinks, apart from grapes and apples. *Moraþ* was apparently made by boiling down and sweetening wine with mulberries, although the term may also have been used for mead with added elderberry juice.[6] The word is cognate with Middle High German *moraz*.[7] It is one of the drinks in which Tosti is reputed to have placed his brother's dead attendants. Less sensationally, it is called for in a leechdom for *circul adl*: a 'dock that will swim' is to be boiled in old *moraþ*.[8] *Eald moroð* is also to be used for external application.[9] Cockayne also thinks that *berigdrenc* (berry-drink) referred to a mulberry-based drink, probably alcoholic.[10] Mulberry wine continued to be popular: Giraldus specifically noted it when visiting Christchurch.[11]

---

[1] McGee 1986, 443.
[2] op. cit., 438.
[3] op. cit.
[4] Ordish 1953, 95.
[5] Helbaek in Brothwell & Higgs 1963, 178.
[6] Bonser 1963, 360; Tickner Edwardes 1917, 17–18.
[7] Bonser 1963, 360.
[8] Cockayne 1851, I xxxvi.
[9] op. cit., III *Lac.* XXXI.
[10] op. cit., II Gloss.
[11] Knowles 1940, 464.

When treated with boiling water, flowers – cowslips, heather, elderflowers, etc., and foliage – from nettles, and burnet, for example, could have been used to make wines, and root wines were also a possibility.[1] The recipes for these wines may never have been written down, and it is unlikely that the refuse from making such wines will be found, or recognised if found, in the archaeological record. Saps were apparently fermented: Bartholomew Anglicus observes that birch and honey would make a strong drink, and sycamore saps could be fermented with ale or yeast.[2]

Conclusion

A comparative rarity as a beverage, wine was served by and to the rich, and there is no evidence wine was taken with water as was customary in Roman times.[3] It seems to have been a prestige product, whether imported or home-produced. This was perhaps because land and labour would be allocated to viticulture only after demands for necessities had been met. It was dear: the novice of the *Colloquy* said, 'I am not so rich that I can buy wine for myself, and wine is not the drink of children and fools, but of those who are old and wise' (*'Ic ne eom swa spedig þæt ic mæge bicgean me win; 7 win nys drenc cilda ne dysgra, ac ealdra 7 wisra'*).[4] It was evidently available to the monks at well-endowed monasteries on feast-days: Æthelwold allowed it to his monks at Abingdon on the great feast days of the church; lesser festivals rated mead.[5] It was presumably drunk at the *caritas*, a light repast of bread and cakes, on about eighty days of the year. Perhaps wine was more readily available after the Conquest as it appears simply as an alternative to mead by the twelfth-century, and the days on which it could be drunk increased greatly.[6] (This may have been the result of Norman influence: the importance of wine is indicated by the invasion scenes on the Bayeux Tapestry in which barrels are featured.)

However, even the poorest Christian Anglo-Saxons would have tasted wine, which it was the responsibility of the priest to provide, at Mass. According to the *Laws of the Northumbrian Priests*, a fine of 12 ores was to be paid by a priest celebrating the Eucharist without wine.[7] The Exhortation of Ælfric and the Laws of Edgar were similarly severe.[8] But this widespread ritual tasting of wine does not detract from the impression that wine was a valuable commodity, an essential part of Anglo-Saxon gracious living. William of Malmesbury, quoting from what he calls an old poem on Æthelstan's coronation, wrote, 'Wine foams everywhere, the great hall resounds with tumult, pages scurry to and fro, servers speed on their tasks'.[9] Wine seems to have been associated with glass vessels, which were probably costly, from early times: there are references to wine being drunk from glass vessels in the *Gododdin*, which dates from the end of the sixth-century, and Bede writes of a sick man who sent to his lord for a *glæsfulne wines* after being cured by Bishop John.[10] If not served in glass vessels, then

---

[1] Ordish 1953, 91–2.
[2] Seebohm 1952, 168; Edlin 1949, 44.
[3] Clair 1964, 48.
[4] Garmonsway 1978, 47.
[5] Turner 1828, III 33.
[6] Knowles 1940, 464, 457.
[7] Whitelock 1955, 436.
[8] Turner 1828, III 502.
[9] Whitelock 1955, 279.
[10] Jackson 1969, 35; Miller 1898, V 398.

wine might be served in goblets of some other valuable material, like gold.[1] Wine was a princely drink, what one might expect from a generous lord, according to the heroic literature. Wine is used in a number of emotive compounds: for example, *winærn*, *winburh*, *winsæd* (wine-hall, a settlement where a prince feasts his followers, sated with wine).[2] Coupled with wine, and mentioned more often in the heroic literature of the Anglo-Saxons and the Welsh, was mead. The men of the *Gododdin* 'set their hands to wine and mead . . . wine and mead was their drink for a year according to the honourable custom . . . choice drink'. One hero 'drank off mead at one draught . . . wine-fed before Catræth'.[3]

Mead

The word 'mead' is cognate with the Sanskrit for honey, and it is therefore probably an ancient drink. Honey-derived drinks seem to have been made throughout Europe in the first millennium A.D. According to Apicius, honey was used as a flavouring in spiced wines, but also as the base for oxymel and hydromel.[4] It is hydromel which seems to equate with mead, since according to classical writers, hydromel was made from one-third honey to two-thirds of rainwater, kept in the sun 40 days at the rising of the dog star. Strabo recorded that in Ireland and other northern lands a drink was made from honey. In Thule men made a drink from honey when they could obtain it.[5]

According to Tickner Edwardes, the method of making mead, 'the common drink of the masses', was to steep in water the crushed refuse of the combs after the honey had been pressed from them. This liquid would subsequently be strained and set aside to ferment – the longer it was kept, the stronger it became. Superior mead, he considered, would be made from pure honey.[6] However, there was still so much wax in the honey from which the mead for the Welsh court was made that it was thought worthwhile to allocate it three ways. Yeast could be added to the liquid to aid fermentation as it was in Sir Kenelm Digby's seventeenth-century version of hydromel. This is similar to the classical recipes except in this particular and in his recommendation of spring – rather than rain – water.[7] Herbs such as sweet gale could be added, in which case the result would be more properly called metheglyn.[8]

Mead was used to translate *defructum* and *mulsum*, concentrated, sweet forms of wine, and so was presumably both sweet and alcoholic.[9] As with *beor*, its sweetness is contrasted metaphorically with the bitterness which might result from the loyalties contracted while drinking it: 'its taste was good, its bitterness was long-lasting'.[10] It is described as bright, sweet, yellow, pale, clarified and fine.[11] Very good mead is equated with clear, old wine in leechdoms.[12] Very few leechdoms call for mead:

---

[1] Jackson 1969, 125.
[2] Fell 1975, 78–80.
[3] Jackson 1969, 110, 125, 106.
[4] McGee 1986, 370.
[5] Frazer 1931, 120.
[6] quoted in Grattan & Singer 1952, 361.
[7] McGee 1986, 371.
[8] Hartley 1954, 569; Furnivall 1868, 107.
[9] Wright & Wulcker 1884, 217,44; 281, 25.
[10] Jackson 1969, 122.
[11] op. cit., 122, 120, 118, 129, 150.
[12] Cockayne 1851, I lvi 1, II lii 1, lii.

meddrosna (dregs of mead) are to be used externally, but with the exception of one reference to pyrethrum to be taken in mead for loss of appetite, alternatives are always given: wine, as above, or clear ale.[1] This suggests that mead was not easily come by, as does the addition to Alfred's *Orosius*, where the situation that there is *swyðe mycel hunig* (a great deal of honey) among the Estonians and that the poor there drink *medo* (mead) is thought worthy of record.[2]

There are references to *sesters* of honey (see Chapter 10) in the Anglo-Saxon food rents, and this may have been important primarily as the raw material for mead. It was obviously more sensible to transport honey than the much greater volume of mead that it would produce, especially as, unlike ale, cider or wine, very little equipment was needed to make it. Guild fines of *sesters* of honey may have been used to make mead for the guild feasts. There is a reference to 'a vessel full of honey or its equivalent in mead' which suggests this correspondence.[3] The notes on the food rents at Bury St. Edmunds include the information that at Abbot Ufi's anniversary we shall have 'forty pence for mead' (*feowerti p to mede*), additional evidence that mead was a drink for special occasions.[4] Mead was allowed on feast days in a monastery when a *sester* was shared between six for dinner, and between twelve for supper.[5] There is evidence that at Abingdon mead was allotted to 'secondary feasts in albs and copes' whereas wine was kept for great feasts, since mead was a more common delicacy than wine before the Conquest, but by the time of Dunstan it was customary on certain days to supply fine wine or mead as an evening drink in winter, a mid-afternoon drink in summer.[6]

Almost all the compounds of mead are emotive, evoking a mood of nostalgia for the revelry associated with drinking. Drink was provided unstintingly by the lord for his retainers as a reward for their past services and to ensure future loyalty.[7] Typical are the words attributed to Ælfwine in *The Battle of Maldon*:

> *gemunað þara mæla þe we oft æt meodo spræcan*
> *þonne we on benc beot ahofon, hælað on healle*

Remember the words we uttered many a time over the mead, when on the bench, made our boasts, heroes in hall.[8]

Once the protagonist of *The Lover's Message* had overcome his troubles he does not lack any lordly possessions or entertainment: 'neither horses, treasure, nor the joys of mead-drinking' (*ne meara ne maðma ne meodreama*). The desertion and dereliction of the ruin in the fragment of the same name, is made more poignant because it was a *meodoheall*, a splendid setting for revelry; a scene for crowds, activity, noise. As a symbol of joyful pastime *medodrince* (mead-drinking) is recalled with nostalgia in changed circumstances: the poet of *The Seafarer* emphasises his isolation when he records:

---

[1] op. cit., XXX, *Lac*. XXXVI, I lvi, 1, II lii 1, liii.
[2] Sweet 1954, 21.
[3] Finberg 1972, 141.
[4] Robertson 1939, 197, 199.
[5] Turner 1828, III 33.
[6] Knowles 1940, 457.
[7] Fell 1975, 80.
[8] Sweet 1954, 117.

> ... *and huilpan sweg fore hleator wera*
> *mæw singende fore mododrince...*[1]

... and the cry of the curlew instead of men's laughter; the scream of the gull in place of the mead-drinking...

Followers who fought in their prince's battles were 'paying for mead'. When three hundred warriors met the English at Catraeth in the late sixth-century 'the pale mead was their feast and their poison' since almost all lost their lives.[2] Warriors were defending the 'woods and mead of Eidlyn'.[3] While it was the warriors' duty to repay their lord for the drink he had provided, the lord had to be liberal with his drink: 'the court of Senyllt did not suffer reproach with its vessels full of mead'.[4] He could offer wine as well as mead, but ale was rarely offered to heroic retainers.[5] Moreover he had to provide a total ambience: a mead-hall; suitable tableware – horns, gold, silver and glass vessels; and candlelight so the drinking could continue at midnight.[6] In this situation drunkenness was the norm.[7] The sixth-century *Elegy of Reged* refers to a deserted hall with the comment, 'More usual on its floor was the mead; and the inebriated warriors'.[8] The strength of mead in particular is conveyed in the Exeter Book Riddle:

> Ic eom weorð werum wide funden
> brungen of bearwum ond of burghleoþum
> of denum ond of dunum dæges mec wægum
> feþre on lifte feredon mid liste under
> hrofes hleo hælað mec siþþan
> baþedan in bydene. Nu ic eom bindere ond
> wingere sona weorpere
> efne to eorþan hwilum ealne ceorl
> sona þæt onfindeð se þe mec fehð ongean
> ond wið mægenþisan minre genæsteð
> þæt he hrycge sceal hrusan secan
> gif he unrædes ær ne geswiceð
> strengo bistolen strong on spræce
> mægene binumen nah his modes geweald
> fota ne folma frige hwæt ic hatte
> Ðe on eorþan swa esnas binde
> dole æfter dyntum be dæges leohte

I am of value to men, found far and wide; brought from the woods and fortress-like hills, from the valleys and downs. In the daytime wings carried me in the air and bore me skilfully under the shelter of a roof. Afterwards men washed me in a tub. Now I am a binder and a scourger and soon become a thrower. Sometimes I cast an old

[1] Fell 1975, 78.
[2] Jackson 1969, 118.
[3] op. cit., 106.
[4] op. cit., 135.
[5] op. cit., 140, 154; Fell 1975, 80.
[6] Jackson 1969, 152, 154, 142, 149, 125, 122,120.
[7] op. cit., 142, 149.
[8] Turner 1828, I 307.

fellow right to the ground. Soon he who grapples with me, fights against my mighty assault, discovers that he must hit the ground with his back if he has not already desisted for his folly. Robbed of his strength, loud in speech, deprived of his might, he has no control, over his mind, his feet nor hands. Discover what I am called who thus bind men upon earth till they are dazed by my blows in the light of day.[1]

Mead was popular at royal feasts referred to in the chronicles, not just in the heroic world of the poetry. On one occasion Æthelstan was due to dine with his relation, Æthelflæd. The royal providers came the day before to see if everything was ready and suitable. Having inspected all, they told her, 'You have plenty of everything, provided your mead holds out'. The king arrived with a great number of attendants at the appointed time, and, after hearing mass, entered joyfully the dining apartment, but unfortunately in the first salutation, their copious draughts exhausted the mead vessel. Æthelflæd prayed to the Virgin Mary, and though 'the cupbearers as is the custom at royal feasts were all the day serving it up in cut horns, and other vessels of various sizes' the liquor was not found to be deficient. According to another source it was Dunstan who answered Æthelflæd's prayers: his sagacity had foreseen the event and provided against it, like the royal fixer he was.[2] The situation does suggest a connection with heroic verse, in that it appears it would have been just as shameful for there to have been a shortage of drink at a real feast, as at one in the heroic literature.

King Edward addresses as one of his free sokemen, 'Payn my mead-brewer' (*Payn min medwrihte*).[3] The Anglo-Saxon kings then may all have had their mead-brewer, but we know far more about the status of the mead-brewer at the Welsh court, where he was the eleventh officer, at the same level in the hierarchy as the footholder, chambermaid, doorward and groom of the rein. He was to have one-third of the wax taken out of the mead vat.[4] The mead vat was one of three things in the palace to have a cover.[5] This covering was apparently tied over the vat in the final stages of brewing, at which point the mead-brewer was entitled to four pence.[6] He presumably made mead from the honey sent from the *mænols* – their lord was not to have the honey because it furnished mead, but he may also have gone round the royal estates making mead, since a free *trev* where there was a royal office was to provide mead for the king; a free *trev* where there was no royal office was to provide bragot (see below).[7] The size of the vats was carefully specified: seven hand-breadths in length diagonally, and nine in breadth.[8] The vat of mead for the king's *gwesta* was to be worth 120 pence, and in case of argument, was to be sufficiently capacious for the king and his elder to bath therein.[9] Mead might have been scarce: if one vat of mead was not available as part of the food rent, then two vats of bragot had to be provided; failing that, four vats of ale were called for.[10] Moreover it seems not to have been drunk as a matter of course. It is recorded that the

---

[1] Mackie 1934, 118.
[2] Whitelock 1952, 58–9; Turner 1828, III 29.
[3] Harmer 1952, 309, 51.
[4] Owen 1841, I 389.
[5] op. cit, 455.
[6] op. cit., 41.
[7] op. cit., 191, 533.
[8] op. cit., 197, 199.
[9] op. cit., 533.
[10] op. cit.

Queen's doorward was 'to take liquor when there shall be mead'.[1] And 'at every feast in which mead is drunk supper silver is apportioned' – the same sort of display is implied as is described in the heroic literature centuries earlier.[2] It was a prestigious enough drink for the allowances for court officials to be laid down in some detail. The Apparitor was to have the third of the vessels used in serving mead; the priest of the household was to receive a hornful of mead from the palace; the chief of the household was to get a hornful of mead from the queen at every banquet; the chief groom was to have the fill of the vessel out of which the king shall drink, the second from the chief of the household and the third from the queen.[3] It is difficult to judge whether the steward did best of all with the length of the extreme joint of his middle finger of mead above the lees, in the vat.[4]

Mead could perhaps have been bought by the end of the period. Richard the mead seller lived outside the west gate of Winchester circa 1120, and paid 12 shillings.[5]

Bragot

Bragot was evidently less valued than mead, more valued than ale, according to the ratios of these drinks in the Welsh food rents and in the steward's allowance, which gave him the depth of the middle joint of his middle finger above the lees of bragot, the depth of the whole finger above the lees of ale.[6] There are no details of how it was to be made in the *Ancient Laws and Institutes of Wales*, but in the later Middle Ages *bragget* was ale with added honey, and spices.[7] Assuming the spices to have been a later addition, honey is the extra ingredient. If supplies of honey-based mead failed, then supplies of bragot might also fail, a situation anticipated in the details of the food rents. The sort of ratios of bragot to ordinary ale, where the later is clearly more readily available, are reminiscent of those of *welisc* ale to ordinary ale in the Anglo-Saxon food rents. It does not seem intrinsically unlikely that *welisc* ale was, in fact, the same as bragot: an ale either brewed with honey, or to which honey was subsequently added.

Sweetened Drinks

Leechdoms counselled that sweetened drinks were bad for the eyes, but good for a 'hardened liver'.[8] At their simplest, sweetened drinks might be 'sweetened water' (*geswettum wætere*), to which the juice of plants might be added.[9] Leechdoms explain the term *mulsa* as 'sweetened drink' (*gemilscede drincan*), and give the recipe for 'sweet/sweetened' (*mylsce/gemilscade*) drink: 'a lot of water boiled with a good deal of honey' (*þis micel dæl bewylledes wateres on huniges godum dæl*).[10] *Mulsum* according to the Roman writers was properly a drink of honey and wine; *aqua mulsum/hydromel* was water and honey, probably fermented to mead.[11] Palladius, and

[1] op. cit., 57.
[2] op. cit., 23.
[3] op. cit., 65, 639, 637, 651.
[4] op. cit., 363.
[5] Barlow et al. 1976, 84.
[6] Owen 1841, 363.
[7] Furnivall 1868, 55.
[8] Cockayne 1851, I ii 1; II xix.
[9] op. cit., I iv 2; xxx ii 2; lxii.
[10] op. cit., II xix; I xlii; II xx.
[11] Frazer 1931, 16, 124, 142.

the writer of *Geoponica*, devote a considerable amount of space to various liquids derived from honey, but although it would have been possible for Anglo-Saxons to drink *oenomel* (must and honey) for example, there is no evidence that they did so.[1] Occasionally leechdoms instruct a wine mixture to be sweetened thoroughly with honey; when the other ingredient is sorrel, which has an acidic taste, this is quite understandable.[2] *Oxymel*, which is referred to as a 'southern' drink, and *þ eced* ('acid', i.e. vinegar) drink, seems to have been made by boiling vinegar and honey together, with or without a proportion of water.[3] One leechdom gives a recipe for making *oxymel* and recommends it 'for almost anything' (*wið ælcere ful neah*),[4] an endorsement which recalls the claims made for cider vinegar and honey in the 1960's. The fact that a recipe is given for oxymel suggests that it was not a regular drink like ale, *beor*, wine and mead, for which no recipes are given.

'Wort' Drinks

'Wort' drinks, mentioned so often in leechdoms were presumably a standard form of drink: herb teas or tisanes made by infusing dried or fresh leaves or flowers in boiling water. The compiler did not consider it necessary to give instructions on making them: one leechdom states simply 'give a wort drink' (*sele wyrtdrenc*).[5] Others just use an adjective: *smeðe* (smooth), *leohte* (light), *scearp* (sharp), *strangne* (strong) to indicate the kind of wort drink to be given, or specify a 'suitable' wort drink.[6] Otherwise they may add that the wort drink is to be *gepiporodne* (peppered).[7] They often give lists of what must have been special ingredients: wormwood, herdwort (and seed?) or rue for a purgative draught, for instance, or fennel, vinegar, aloes and honey.[8] The injunction 'Let him drink good worts' suggest that wort drinks were recognised as beneficial and explain the very large number of wort drinks in this medicinal tract.[9] At the monastery of Llantwit 'It was the custom to bruise herbs from the garden, such as were beneficial for health, in a vessel and serve it out in small porringers by means of a small siphon for their health's sake'.[10] The *The Life of Saint Sampson of Dol* gives the information that the saint was cautious enough to avoid taking the poison someone had slipped into his herb tea.[11] This life was written in the seventh century, and perhaps a knowledge of the properties of herbs and their use in drinks was current throughout the period. Such drinks would have been useful in pre-ascorbutic conditions as a source of vitamins and minerals, and when fermented with yeast, as one of the leechdoms instructs, then they would additionally have contained B-complex vitamins. Sage, horehound, mint, raspberry and blackberry leaves, woodruff, lime, elder, chamomile and rose flowers have traditionally been used to make teas and flower waters.[12]

---

[1] op. cit.
[2] Cockayne 1851, I xli.
[3] op. cit., I lxxix; II xxiii, xxx, xxxix, xl, xliii, lix 12.
[4] op. cit., II lix 13.
[5] op. cit., I xxxv 2.
[6] op. cit., II xlviii, xxix; I iv 5; II xlix, lix.
[7] op. cit., II iii.
[8] op. cit., II xviii, II i 1.
[9] op. cit., I xxxiii 2.
[10] *The Life of Saint Sampson of Dol*, quoted in Bonser 1963, 252.
[11] Davies 1982, 157.
[12] Renfrew 1985, 20; Hartley 1954, 571; Cockayne 1851, II lvi 4.

Miscellaneous

Milk is another important drink. Mother's milk was probably vital to the survival of babies, who may not have been weaned until the age of two or so, and an important food for young children, but this topic is dealt with in *A Handbook of Anglo-Saxon Food: Processing and Consumption*. Women's milk is called for in leechdoms, but for external use.[1] Otherwise the leechdoms contain ten references to goats' milk, perhaps reflecting the Mediterranean origin of the texts, although goats' milk is easy to digest and good for those who suffer from certain allergies; three references to cows' milk; two where cows' or goats' milk will do, and two references to ewes' milk.[2] There is no reference to mares' milk, used fresh or fermented, which is perhaps why Alfred records with evident interest that the nobles in Estonia drunk mares' milk, although this was no doubt fermented to give *koumiss*, which is still made by Kazak peoples in Russian Turkestan.[3] There is one reference to 'skimmed milk' (*þeorfe meoluc*).[4] Sometimes the milk is to be warm from the cow, ewe or goat, to be drawn at one milking, or to be *unsure* (not sour),[5] etc.

The most general use for milk in the leechdoms is as a liquid for boiling herbs in, rather than water. One recipe calls for a broth to be made with milk.[6] In one leechdom it is to be used rather than ale.[7] Sometimes it is to be boiled, or *gewyrð* ('turned') by heating with hot stones and iron, or with rennet.[8]

Bede observed that May was called *tri milchi* (three milkings) because 'they milked their cattle three times a day that month' (*hi on þæm monðe þriwa on dæge mylcedon heora neat*). The same point is noted in the Old English Martyrology, with the observation 'because there was formerly such abundance in Britain' (*fordon swylce genytsumnes wæs geo on Brytone*).[9] The importance of milk, although this may have been as the raw material for butter or cheese rather than as a beverage, is indicated by the fact that it is one of the four main ingredients to be put into the barren field in the *Erce* (or *Æcerbot*) "ceremonial".[10] That a dry cow would have a considerable effect on the domestic economy of a household is suggested by the Welsh Laws: a dry cow is to be compensated for by oatmeal till the feast of St. Curig, thence until the feast of St. Michael by barley meal, and from thence until the calends of winter by rye meal.[11]

The cowherd was entitled to 'the milk of an old cow seven nights after she has newly calved, and the beestings of a young cow for fourteen nights' (*ealdre cu meolc vii niht syððan heo nige cealfod hæfþ, and frymetlinge bystinge xiv niht*).[12] A female slave was allowed 'whey in summer or one penny' (*hwæig on sumera oððe 1 p*). The

---

[1] Cockayne 1851, I ii 1, 5, ii 9, *Lac.* 104.
[2] op. cit., I ii 5; II xxv; III lxv 2; II xxv; Bonser 1963, 111; Cockayne 1851, I lxx.
[3] Tannahill 1973, 134.
[4] Cockayne 1851, II lii.
[5] op. cit., III lxv 2; II ix, xx; I lxvii; II lxv 2.
[6] op. cit. *Peri Did.* 37.
[7] op. cit., II lxv 2.
[8] op. cit., II xix, li 3, II xxv, *Lac.* XLI.
[9] Herzfeld 1900, May.
[10] Cockayne 1851, I 398.
[11] Owen 1841, 273.
[12] Liebermann 1898, 450.

shepherd had the right to a bowlful of whey or buttermilk all summer, and the milk of his herd seven nights after the equinox. The cheesemaker was entitled to all the buttermilk except the shepherd's share.[1] The whey was probably drunk, since, although it could be made into cheese, the female slave probably had neither the time nor equipment to make cheese, and the shepherd's daily bowlful would have hardly warranted turning into cheese. The cheesemaker presumably used his large share of buttermilk for cheese, although he may have drunk – or sold , if he was near a market – some of it. Whey, as a by-product of cheesemaking, was probably readily available in rural contexts, and continued to be part of payments-in-kind after the Conquest, as at Battle and St. Paul's Abbeys where it was received by those performing weeding service and other agricultural labouring work.[2] While the availability of such drinks may have benefited the health of such agricultural workers, bovine tuberculosis could have been transmitted through milk. This could have led to bone deformities, or mental retardation as a result of tubercular meningitis.[3]

Ascetics were another group who drank milk. Boniface criticised over-ascetic priests who chose milk and honey as a diet. Cedd took 'a little milk and water mixed' (*litle meolc wætre gemenede*) in Lent; Ecgberht took a little bread in *þinre* (skimmed?) milk in a fast of three times forty days.[4] St. Aidan allowed milk and water to the monks at Lindisfarne although King Ceolwulf later gave them licence to drink wine and ale.[5] Adamnan's seventh-century *Life of Columba* mentions the white horse that carried the milk from the byre, and St. Eosterwine 'milked the ewes and led the calves to the cows' (*ewa mealc 7 þa cealfas to cuum lædde*), so that certainly there was monastic dairying.[6] In one monastery *lac acidulum* was used from Hokeday to Michaelmas, *lac dulce* from Michaelmas to Martinmas.[7] This may not have been a policy decision, so much as accepting a situation where milk turned sour quickly in warm weather in the absence of sterile utensils. St. Columba reproved Columban for not casting out a demon that was lurking in the bottom of the empty milk pail by making on it the sign of the cross before pouring in the milk. The milk would presumably have been affected but for the saint's action.[8] Leechdoms give a recipe for dealing with a pail that sours milk: 'if milk is spoilt, tie together weybread and githrife and cress; lay them on the milk pail and do not put it down on the ground for seven nights' (*gif meoluc sie awyrð bind tosomne wegbrædan 7 githrifan 7 cersan lege on þone fildcumb 7 ne sete þ fæt niþer on eorþan seofon nihtum*).[9]

A fragment of a will from Bury St. Edmunds provides *fæouer pæniges at milch*.[10] This may have been for drinking with fish or for junkets, which were associated with festive occasions ('junketings'), or some other form of dessert, if it was not just to be used in cooking processes.

---

[1] op. cit., 450–1.
[2] Seebohm 1952, 157.
[3] Burnet & White 1972, 214.
[4] Miller 1890, 232, 244.
[5] Colgrave 1940, 345.
[6] Herzfeld 1900, March 7th; Knowles 1940, 463.
[7] Turner 1828, III 27.
[8] Bonser 1963, 259.
[9] Cockayne 1851, I liii.
[10] Robertson 1939, 253.

Other liquids may have been drunk: ' milk and water in which good worts have been boiled' is called for in one leechdom.[1] This would have been an easily-digested form of broth. Meat teas, made by pouring hot water on to meat, would also have been nourishing and have made less demand on the digestion than broths, but although later medieval recipes for beef tea exist, none is recorded in Anglo-Saxon sources.[2] Bread in water is called for as an invalid drink, and, as pananda, continued in this role into the present century.[3] Oat- and other meals may have been used to make gruels, although these do not seem to be recorded until after the Anglo-Saxon period.[4] *Blenshaw* and *stoorum*, for example were made with meal mixed with a little milk, onto which boiling water was poured.[5]

There is evidence that other liquids were drunk, but these were not standard drinks, and some were officially forbidden. In the late seventh-century *Penitential of Theodore* a woman is forbidden to taste her husband's blood as a remedy.[6] Those who made love philtres for their *wogerum* (wooers) or drinks to harm their wives were warned that they would go to hell.[7] On the other hand, it was perfectly acceptable to make drinks from substances with holy associations: the moss which grew on the cross St. Oswald had erected, or earth from the spot where he had died, or where the water in which his bones were washed was poured out, or some of the wood from the stake on which his head was put.[8]

On Drinking and Drunkenness

Like most societies, the Anglo-Saxons considered drinking very enjoyable. The number of emotive compounds formed with *win*, *beor*, *meodu* and *ealu* give some idea of how intoxicating drinks were regarded.[9] In *Beowulf* at 'the choicest of feasts' 'men were drunk with wine' (*druncon win weras*) (l.1233). Other poems of the heroic courtly life also give many individual instances of men who became 'sated with wine' (*winsæd*). The poem *Be Domesdæge* warns that the joys of this world will depart altogether: 'then drunkenness will cease with feasts' (*þonne drucennes gedwineð mid wistum*) (l.233). This parallels the Celtic view which gave one of the pleasures of the Earthly Paradise as drinking choicest wine while listening to sweet music.[10] Both groups valued the gatherings at which drinking took place. The sixth-century elegy on Urien of Reged speaks of social harmony:

> Where once was the gladness of heroes
> And the horn of the banquet went round:
> It was the solace of the army and the path of melody .[11]

---

[1] Cockayne 1851, II xix.
[2] Hartley 1954, 88.
[3] Cockayne 1851, II i 1; Hartley 1954, 515.
[4] op. cit., 526.
[5] Wright 1898, II 297, 794–5.
[6] Bonser 1963, 221.
[7] Skeat 1881, *On Auguries* l.157.
[8] op. cit., *St. Oswald*, ll. 37, 196, 200, 260.
[9] Fell 1975, 79.
[10] Jackson 1971, 174.
[11] Turner 1828, I 307.

The Seafarer and *The Wanderer* contrast the joys of drinking as one of a lord's retinue with the mutual bonds and obligations of loyalty that this involved, with the isolation of exile, contrasting the noise of revelry with the cry of seabirds. Authors who took a moralistic stance and were not afflicted with regretful nostalgia, found the same sound was unpleasant: 'when wine excites a man's heart, tumult and outcry arise in the company who clamour in speech in various ways' (*þonne win hweteð/ beornes breostsefan breahtem stigeð/ cirm on corpre cwide scralletaþ missenlice*) (Exeter Book, *Warning against Pride*).

Alcuin writes to Charlemagne that he tried to inebriate others with the wine of the ancient classics.[1] But although he was concerned to secure his own supplies of wine, he expresses a general ambivalence about drink: ' to write sacred books is better than to till the soil for the vine, for the one nourishes the soul, the other the stomach'.[2]

Drinking was an element of important social events. It seems to have continued well after a meal: writing of an Anglo-Saxon dinner party, a chronicler stated 'after the meal they went to their drinking, to which the English were too much accustomed' (*Post prandium ad pocula, quibus Angli nimis sunt assueti*).[3] We know that excessive drinking at funerals was a cause of some dismay to church leaders; marriages too seem to have been celebrated with feasting and drinking. When Osgod Clapa, an important individual, gave his daughter in marriage to Tofi, King Hardacnut was enjoying a drink with the bride and some of the guests when he fell senseless to the ground, and subsequently expired: an event that must have cast some gloom over the proceedings.[4]

Drinking parties were not purely pleasurable affairs: accepting drink involved the acceptance of obligations, as the warriors who received wine and mead from golden vessels for a year at Catraeth discovered: 'Of those that hastened forth after the choice drink none escaped but three'.[5] The occasion of offering a drink might well provide an opportunity for treachery. Edward was stabbed at Corfe in 978 when he accepted a cup of drink.

Drinking might lead to various anti-social acts. The Laws of Hlothhere and Eadric, Kings of Kent from 673 to 685, specify the fines to be paid by someone who takes away 'the stoup of another where men are drinking' (*oþrum steop ðær mæn drincen*).[6] More seriously, fighting might break out when men were in their cups. The same law code establishes a fine of twelve shillings payable to the king and one shilling to the owner of the house if a weapon was drawn where men were drinking. If bloodshed resulted, then fifty shillings were payable to the king, and appropriate compensation to the owner of the house.[7] The Laws of Ine (688–94) fined a man who resorted to violence in a quarrel *on gebeorscipe* when his victim did not fight back, the sum of thirty shillings.[8] Not only the king's peace, but the king himself

---

[1] op. cit., III 20.
[2] Talbot Rice 1965, 295.
[3] Wright 1871, 41.
[4] Whitelock 1955, 292.
[5] Jackson 1969, 135.
[6] Attenborough 1922, 20.
[7] Whitelock 1955, 361.
[8] Attenborough 1922, 38.

might be in danger. At the beginning of the seventh century, The Laws of Æthelbert of Kent laid down a double penalty for injuries inflicted where the king was drinking.[1] Drunkenness was a problem throughout the period: in 1008 Æthelred's code stated that overdrinking was to be shunned.[2]

Warriors were expected to be able to take their drink. At one point Beowulf accuses Unferð of being drunk (l.531). It was not considered acceptable to make boasts when drunk that the speaker would not keep to when he was sober.[3] Neither was it a good idea to enter into a contract when drunk: a drunken Dane sold land to a bishop (who had seen to it that his cupbearer deliberately plied him with drink) and subsequently wanted to renege on the deal, but on appeal to the king the bishop was awarded the land.[4] The Welsh Laws, however, did not consider a drunk man bound in this way.[5]

The Fates of Men includes one individual who was slain when drunk, and one who killed himself when he was drunk: both were too hasty in speech. According to *A Warning against Pride*, there are many proud warriors, lovers of company, who, when drunk, are designedly provocative. A homily criticises 'the rich in their feasting [who] practise pernicious scoffing' (*Ða welegan on heora gebeorscipe begaþ derigendlice gafetunge*).[6] Writing to Plegwine, Bede tells of how, at a feast, he was accused of heresy by some who were the worse for drink.[7] In the poem *Juliana* in the Exeter Book, the devil confesses to Juliana that he has led men on to renew old grudges (*beore dru[n]cne*) (when they were drunk); has poured out discord from the cup in the wine-hall, 'that, through the clutch of sword they let forth the soul from the body; dying, they hastened out beset by wounds' (*þæt . . . þurh sweord-gripe sawle forletan/ of flæsc-homan fæge scyndan/ sarum gesohte*). In *Beowulf*, the statement that the son of Ecgðeow was honourable, is amplified by 'he didn't slay his friends when drunk' (*nælles druncne slog heorð-geneatas*), a state of affairs that nowadays one hopes would go without saying.[8] A king might be in the best position to indulge a predilection for drink, but it was considered that he should not give way to this. According to William of Malmesbury, Æthelred the Unready was criticised to Svein by Turketul as being solicitous only about women and wine. Probably the situation was generally like that described some centuries later by Moryson, i.e. in some gentlemen's houses, among the soldiery, and 'the vulgar sort of Citizens and Artisans large and intemperate drinking is used, but in general the greater and better part of the English, hold all excesse blameworthy, and drunkenness a reprochful vice'.[9] The main difference would seem to be in the amount of ecclesiastical drinking. Moryson also observed that in parts of Germany where there was very heavy drinking, quantities of salt meat were consumed.[10] If the Anglo-Saxon diet included a quantity of salt meat, as would seem to be the case, particularly in winter and spring, then liquid intake would have had to have been higher to compensate for this.

---

[1] Turner 1828, III 168.
[2] Whitelock 1955, 408.
[3] *Battle of Maldon* l. 112.
[4] Wright 1871, 41.
[5] Owen 1841, II 425–7.
[6] Bosworth & Toller 1898, 358.
[7] Hunter Blair 1970, 267.
[8] *Beowulf*, l. 2179.
[9] Moryson 1617, IV 176.
[10] op. cit., 29.

On Ceremony

Ceremony, particularly the observation of an order of precedence, was important at formal banquets. The offering of drink followed a strict order, so that any deviation was noteworthy. When St. Martin was feasting with the Emperor Maximus: 'A man carried wine to the emperor in a goblet as was customary. Then he ordered the cupbearer to offer it to Martin first, and he would drink after the bishop had given his blessing. And his mass priest gave him half the liquor that was in the goblet because he knew that it was fitting for the emperor to drink after him' (*man bær þam casere swa swa hit gewunlice wæs win on anre blede. Þa het he þon byrle beodon martine ærest wold æfter ðam bisceope his bletsunge drincan Martinus þa dranc. And his mæsse-preoste sealde hælfne dæl þæs wætan þe wæs on þære blede for-þan-þe he wiste þæt he wurþost wæs æfter him to drincenne*).[1]

On formal occasions the drink was handed to guests by cupbearers. These were women in the early period when courts were still on a domestic scale: according to the Laws of Æthelbert, king of Kent, at the very beginning of the seventh century, if anyone raped 'a nobleman's female cupbearer' he was to pay the relatively large amount of twenty shillings as compensation, considerably more than the twelve shillings compensation to be paid for a man killed on a nobleman's estate. Even though the same offence committed with a ceorl's cupbearer rated a fine of only six shillings, this is the amount for the breach of the ceorl's protection and on a par with compensation paid for men, which indicates the position of cupbearer was an honoured one.[2]

According to the *Gnomic Poem* of the Exeter Book, the wife of a lord should greet her husband first at the mead-drinking, and give the cup promptly into her lord's hand. The mistress of the establishment and her daughters might present the wine cup to those guests they wished to honour.

> *eode wealhþeow forð cwen Hrodgares,*
> *cynna gemyndig grette gold-hro*
> *den guman on healle ond þa freolic*
> *wif ful gesealde ærest east-dena*
> *eþel-wearde bæd hine blidne æt þære*
> *beor-þege leodum leofne he on lust*
> *geþeah symbel ond seleful . . .*
> *. . . ymb-eode þa ides helminga*
> *duguþe ond geogoþe dæl æghwylcne*
> *sinc-fato sealde oþþæt sæl alamp þæt*
> *hio beowulfe beaghroden cwen mode*
> *geþungen medo-ful ætbær*

Wealtheow, Hrothgar's queen went forth, mindful of courtesy, gold-adorned, greeted the man in the hall, and the noble woman offered the goblet first to the king of the East-Danes, bade him be cheerful at the serving of *beor*, beloved of his people, he happily partook of the feast and of the hall-goblet . . . The lady of the Helmings went about to the nobles and the young men, offered the precious goblet to each in turn, until it happened that in hall the queen adorned with bracelets carried the mead-goblet to Beowulf.[3]

---

[1] Skeat 1881, *St. Martin*, l. 630.
[2] Whitelock 1955, 358.
[3] *Beowulf*, l. 612.

Wealtheow's gold ornaments may have included an elaborate and costly wine strainer or sieve spoon, which she used in serving wine.[1] On another occasion she offered wine, saying 'Take this cup, my noble lord' (*Onfoh þissum fulle, freo-drihten min*).[2] Some thirty lines further on is the summary:

Him wæs ful boren ond freond-laþa wor
dum bewægned . . .

To him was the goblet carried, and words of friendship offered).[3]

'*Onfoh dissum fulle, freodrihten min*' seems to have been the formula to accompany offering the cup as it occurs elsewhere in the poem, for example, at line 2343. On another occasion Hrothgar's daughter carried the mead-cup (or ale-cup) to the retainers.[4] There were, however, male cupbearers too at Hrothgar's court:

. . . þegn
nytte beheold se þe on handa bær
hroden ealo-wæge scente scir wered

. . . the thane performed his office, he who carried in his hands the decorated ale-cup, poured the clear measure.[5]

Traditionally Hengist's fair-haired, blue-eyed daughter officiated as cupbearer at the feast to which Gwrtheyrn was invited, and where he became intoxicated with wine and love, until he at last obtained her as his wife.[6] Other evidence of women in this role comes from Bede who writes that after a *gesið's* wife was healed by St. Cuthbert, 'It was a fair sight to see how she who had escaped the cup of death by the bishop's blessing, was the first of all the household of so great a man to offer him the cup of refreshment. She thus followed the example of the mother-in-law of the Apostle Peter . . . '.[7] The suggestion is perhaps that in a large household one might expect a servant to act as cupbearer, so when the lady of the house took it upon herself to perform this function then it showed great respect for a guest.

It seems that to be offered alcohol in a horn was a mark of status, although – the many references to drinking horns in the heroic literature apart – clearer evidence comes from later sources including the Middle English romance of *King Horn*. At her bridal feast a king's daughter is carrying a ceremonial drinking horn round to the guests, but when she is accosted by a man she thinks is a beggar, she offers him instead drink in a large bowl as being more fitting to his condition.[8] In a celebrated eulogy of his warriors by Ywain Cyfeilog, a Welsh prince who died in 1197, he calls for his cupbearer to pour drink from a great horn for each of his warriors. This is reminiscent of *The Gododdin*, and suggests that horns were the ceremonial drinking vessel for those of high status all through the period.[9]

---

[1] Meaney 1980, 88.
[2] *Beowulf*, l. 1162.
[3] op. cit., l.1192.
[4] op. cit., l.1980; 2020.
[5] op. cit., l.494.
[6] Turner 1828, I 261.
[7] Colgrave 1940, 253, 255.
[8] Clark in Fell 1984, 172.
[9] Jackson 1969, 53.

At the courts of the later Anglo-Saxon and Welsh kings the post of cupbearer was held by men. At the Welsh court the page of the chamber was always to act as cupbearer to the king except at the three principal festivals.[1] The Welsh Laws give further details about his post. For example, he was to give everyone the same measure of liquor. He was in charge of the supply of mead, the mead cellar and associated vessels and was to keep the keys. He was to have light without measure for his service, which may be an indication of evening drinking, as well as a dark cellar, and, according to the Dimetian Code, protection from the time when the first tub is begun to be drawn off until the last is drawn.[2] In Scandinavia cupbearers seem always to have been women; in the only case we know of a man serving alcohol, he is offering it to a woman as a prelude to rape.[3] In the will of King Eadred (951–7), 80 mancuses of gold was left to each appointed seneschal, keeper of the wardrobe and butler. Ælfwig, the king's butler, appears in the witness lists of charters from 956. In 959 he witnessed as *regis pincerna*.[4] Asser's *Life of Alfred* contains the information that his mother, Osburh, was noble by birth, being the daughter of Oslac, the renowned cupbearer of King Æthelwulf, and himself of royal stock.[5] Harold Godwinson was cupbearer to Edward the Confessor at a feast and this was seen as a sign of royal favour.[6] He would have had to serve only the king; he would not have been like one of the servers described in the poem about Æthelstan's coronation feast quoted by William of Malmesbury: 'Wine foams everywhere, the great hall resounds with tumult, pages scurry to and fro, servers speed on their tasks'.[7] Princes continued to have their cupbearers for centuries after the Anglo-Saxon period. At the court of the Emperor of Austria, each of his brothers had his own cupbearer.[8]

At the Welsh court, according to the Gwentian Code, the huntsman received a hornful of liquor from the king, or the chief of the household, another from the queen, and the third from the steward at every banquet.[9] The smith was entitled to the first liquor to come into hall, presumably this was an indication of his importance, although there may have been a more practical reason for this privilege.[10] The door-ward was unfortunate enough not to be able to leave his post, so the various drinks were brought to him.[11] It was the steward's job to test the liquors in the palace, and his allowance was the length of his middle finger of ale above the lees, of the bragot, the length of the middle joint of the same finger, and of the mead, the length of the extreme joint. This ensured that everyone else's drink was clear: only by stopping drawing others' drinks well above the lees would the steward ensure that his own drink was palatable.[12] The allowances of ale, bragot and mead were almost always in the ratio of one: half: third respectively, the ratio in which these drinks were supplied in the food rents. Information from the same source shows that the value of drink to be rendered

---

[1] Owen 1841, 33.
[2] op. cit., 45, 355.
[3] Fell 1984, 145.
[4] Hart 1975, 275.
[5] Whitelock 1955, 264.
[6] Turner 1828, III 32.
[7] Whitelock 1955, 279.
[8] Moryson 1617, 254.
[9] Owen 1841, 657.
[10] op. cit., 73.
[11] op. cit., 665, 663.
[12] op. cit., 641, 363.

to the king's court was about one quarter of the value of the total food rent. The usual formula if the food and drink is not 'timely supplied', is that the worth of the king's *gwesta* is a pound, of which 120 pence are for bread, 60 pence for *enllyn* (the 'accompaniment' – meat, cheese and the like) and 60 pence for liquor.[1]

Drinking healths – greeting people and wishing them '*wæs hal*' was practised in religious communities as well as secular contexts. According to the *Regularis Concordia*, on Maundy Thursday the abbot was to go round among the brethren when all were seated in the refectory drinking the health of each. Then the prior was to drink to the abbot and the ministers who assisted him.[2] Responding to such healths could be hazardous. Six hundred and fifty years later when Fynes Moryson was at the Scottish court he had to get the man who had invited him to 'be my protection from large drinking' since the Scottish 'entertaining any stranger, used to drinks healths not without excesse'.[3]

Hospitality

Praiseworthy hospitality involving the supply of unlimited drink – and in this context we remember the court of Senyllt 'which did not suffer reproach, with its vessels full of mead' – could shade into the reprehensible plying of guests with drink..[4] Ælfric wrote reproaching Sigeferd, an Oxfordshire thane, who had urged him to drink 'very much as it were for bliss', since harm could result, and Christ and the Fathers of the Church had forbidden *oferdrenc*.[5] According to the *Rule of Chrodegang*, worse than getting drunk oneself was persuading another to drink more than was good for them. 'Alas, wretched creature who practises this, it is not enough that you are condemned to perdition: you cause the total destruction of others too' (*Eala þu ungesælig þe þis dest, nis þe genoh þæt pu sylf losast, þeah þu uppan þæt oþre ne forspylle*).[6]

After King Eadred had measured out the foundations for the new monastery at Abingdon, abbot Æthelwold invited him to dine in the refectory with his men. The king and his retinue, which included a number of Northumbrians, came to the feast, at which the king was merry, and ordered mead in abundance for his guests. When the doors had been closed so that no-one might hurry away, the servers were all day drawing drink for the feasters, but the drink in the vessel remained at a span's depth, until the Northumbrians were intoxicated (either 'swinishly' or 'after their fashion').[7] This is recounted as evidence for a miracle, but perhaps the monastery's supply of drink was sufficient, or the king had decided to augment it from the royal estate. In any case the event shows that drinking continued all day. It probably continued well into the evening after dinner in court circles. There is a story that when Harold was in Normandy at the court of William, he, William and the duchess used to drink together. Duke William was usually the first to go to bed, but Harold used to stay up late into the night, talking with the duchess.[1] According to William of Malmesbury's

---

[1] op. cit., 533, 769.
[2] Symons 1940, Sect. 42.
[3] Moryson 1617, IV 185.
[4] Jackson 1969, 135.
[5] Bosworth & Toller 1898, 214.
[6] Napier 1916, 74.
[7] Whitelock 1955, 834.
[1] Jones 1980, 132.

Life, Wulfstan had only water to drink after dinner, when the rest had ale or mead before them to drink 'as is the English custom'. Only his servant knew this: the others assumed it was 'some more costly brewage'.

The Laws of Cnut and the Laws of the Northumbrian Priests refer to *drincelean*: '*drincelean* and the lord's legal gift are to remain forever unperverted'. This seems most likely to be a term for a gift of land from the king, a 'reward for drink' made in return for hospitality.[1] It would probably pay not to stint on drink if the king was a guest.

Some men were clearly the life and soul of the party, either as hosts or guests. In *The Endowments of Men*: 'One is witty at wine-bibbing, a good beer-keeper' (*Sum bið gewittig æt wine-þege, beor-hyrde god*), and *The Fates of Men* describes a similar character: 'One shall give pleasure to men in company, delight those who sit on the benches at their *beor* where is the greatest revelry of drinkers' (*Sum scealon heaþe hæleþum cweman/blissan æt beore bencsittendum þær biþ drincendra dream se micla*). Perhaps they were able to tell good riddles, one of the pastimes of men at their drink. Some of those recorded are masterpieces of sexual innuendo, others, ironically, have to do with the effects of drink.[2]

Alehouses

So far drinking parties referred to have been private (if sometimes very well-attended) functions. However, there are several references to alehouses (*ceapealeðelum*) in laws and ecclesiastical canons. These do not seem to have been officially licensed, but some individuals evidently specialised in brewing drink for sale. Guthlac was shrewd enough to guess that the abbot's two servants who had asked for permission to journey by another route had done so in order to call in at the home of a 'certain widow' where they would end up drunk.[3] Perhaps she, and individuals like her, provided the kind of *opene gebeorscipas* (open drinking bouts) that the *Rule of Chrodegang* said were to be avoided.[4]

In Winchester c.1100, lands paid *langabulum* and *brug*, ground rent and payment for a licence to brew – brewgable was paid TRE (in the time of King Edward the Confessor).[5] There are not many references and the business does not seem to have been very lucrative, although Thurstin conveyed to Osbert Cod ten shillings rent, three breweries and *ustilia sua*, for which Osbert paid him 36 shillings.[6] This indicates brewing of ale for sale, perhaps to the travellers and pilgrims to the city, not just domestic consumption.

Wulfstan's *Canons of Edgar* forbade any priest to be an 'ale poet/minstrel' (*ealascop*) or 'to make merry in any other way with others' (*on ænige wisan gliwige, mid him silfum oðrum mannum*). Instead he was to 'be mindful of his holy orders, wise and honourable' (*beo swa his had[e] gebirað, wis and weorðful*).[1] A

[1] Whitelock 1955, 430.
[2] Exeter Book, Riddles 42, 11, 27, 28.
[3] Swanton 1975, 54.
[4] Napier 1916, 76.
[5] Barlow et al. 1976, 14–5, 33.
[6] op. cit., 119.
[1] Fowler 1972, 15.

priest was forbidden by law to eat or drink at a *ceapealethelum*.[1] As alehouses seem to have been places of riotous assembly, this was probably a sensible precaution, although the *Exhortations* of Ælfric merely say no priest should be drunk often in wine-houses, perhaps meaning feast halls.[2]

Edgar attempted to decrease drunkenness by limiting the quantity to be drunk at one time. He ordained certain cups for use in alehouses, which had pins or nails set into them, 'pin tankards', and decreed that anyone who drank past the mark at one draught should forfeit a penny, of which half should fall to the accuser and the other half to the ruler of the town where the offence was committed.[3] This measure would seem to be open to abuse: drinking companions might well connive at drinking past the specified pin, and Archbishop Anselm found it necessary to order 'that priests do not go to taverns nor drink to the pins' (*ut presbyteri non eant ad potationes nec ad pinneas bibant*).[4] Some similar practice seems to be referred to in the Welsh Laws. One of the Privileges of Arven was 'that they drink not stinted measure', though here the measure was 'the depth of the nail joint of the middle finger in the drinking vessel', and not as conveniently indicated by pins.[5]

The Laws of Æthelred 978–1008 deal with the breach of the peace in an alehouse: 'it is to be atoned for, if a man is killed, with 6 half-marks, and if no one is killed, with 12 ores' (*bete man þæt æt deadum menn mid vi healfmarce 7 æt cwicon mid xii oran*).[6] The clientele of an alehouse probably paid no attention to 'Egyptian' days: two days in every month which were very dangerous for drinking any drink as well as for blood-letting. Even the translator attributes this belief to 'old leeches', and seems ambivalent in his attitude.[7]

Ecclesiastical Drinking

Drinking seems to have been rife: Boniface, writing to Cuthbert, Archbishop of Canterbury in 747, had heard that the evil of drunkenness had greatly increased, but bishops, far from checking it, became drunk themselves, and, by offering cups unduly large, forced others to become drunk. The warnings of Luke, Paul and Isaiah against strong drink, are all cited. Boniface saw drunkenness as being peculiar to the heathen and the English: 'For neither the Franks, nor the Gauls, not the Lombards, nor the Romans, nor the Greeks have it'. He enjoined the crushing of this sin, but if this was not to prove possible, then it was at least to be shunned by the priesthood.[8] Alcuin sent one of his pupils to Offa between 787 and 796, asking that Offa should not let him take to drink, but provide him with pupils.[9] Writing to Higbald, bishop of Lindisfarne, and his monks, condoling with them for the sack of Lindisfarne in 793, Alcuin tells them not to blot out the words of their prayers in drunkenness, and to

---

[1] Turner 1828, III 33.
[2] op. cit., 503.
[3] Monson-Fitzjohn 1927, 12–13.
[4] op. cit., 13.
[5] Owen 1841, I 107.
[6] Robertson 1925, 65.
[7] Cockayne 1851, I lxxii.
[8] Kylie 1911, 190.
[9] Whitelock 1955, 779.

hold their banquets in soberness.[1] In a later letter to the monks of Monkwearmouth and Jarrow he instructs the avoidance of secret drunken orgies 'for at such feasts devils are present', which suggests news of unsavoury goings-on had come to his ears.[2] The Penitential of Egbert which also dates from the second half of the eighth century, establishes a fast of 30 days as a penalty for a monk vomiting because of being drunk, 40 days for a presbyter or deacon. If a monk or deacon 'owing to drunkenness or greediness' should vomit the Eucharist, then he should do penance for 60 days, a period extended to 70 days for a presbyter and 80 days for a bishop.[3] The implication is that in terms of sobriety religious establishments left a lot to be desired.

The problem of ecclesiastical drunkenness must have continued since Wulfstan in his *Canons of Edgar* had to lay down that there should be no drinking in church, and that bishops, priests, or any man in orders should either give up drinking to excess or forfeit his status. Priests had not only to avoid getting drunk themselves but 'earnestly dissuade other men from this' (*hit georne belean oðrum mannum*).[4] When Æthelwold was appointed to Winchester he found 'evil-living clerics . . . continually given over to gluttony and drunkenness'.[5] Later still the Laws of the Northumbrian Priests which probably date from 1020–3, stated that a priest should not practise drunkenness, nor become a gleeman, or ale-minstrel, entertaining where men were drinking, under pain of compensation.[6]

Cuthbert sedulously abstained from all intoxicants,[7] but Palladius had declared that to drink wine with reason was better than to drink water with pride, and a number of clerics, including Alcuin, enjoyed wine, and took a moderate amount, like St. Sampson of Dol whom no-one had ever seen drunk although he 'never put away from himself altogether any drink', but John of Salisbury wrote, 'I myself am a drinker [of wine and ale], nor do I abhor anything that can make me drunk.[8] Bede mentions a sinful brother who, although placed in a noble monastery, was very given to drunkenness, but was tolerated because he was a good smith.[9]

The major festivals of the church were to be celebrated on pain of excommunication. The *Rule of Chrodegang* stated that two or three drinks could be taken in the room with a fire but cautioned: 'however great the gladness, see that drunkenness does not prevail' (*locahu þonne seo glædnys beo, huru þær druncen ne rixie*).[10] But *The Penitential of Theodore* excused penance for a priest who drank too much 'for joy of Christmas or Easter or any of the feasts of the saints', especially if he had not taken more than was decreed by his superior.[11] It was no doubt difficult to keep a balance in such matters. Drinking became linked with church festivals to such an extent that several ecclesiastical canons had to be issued inveighing against drunkenness at

---

[1] op. cit., 778, 779.
[2] Bonser 1963, 364.
[3] op. cit.
[4] Fowler 1972, 26, 28, 66, 58.
[5] Whitelock 1955, 835.
[6] op. cit., 437.
[7] Colgrave 1940, 175.
[8] Waddell 1932, 85.
[9] Miller 1898, I 2 442.
[10] Napier 1916, 45.
[11] Bonser 1963, 124.

church wakes, that is, the vigils on the eves of saints' days.[1] It appears that secular festivals also provided occasions for excessive drinking. 'Let none on the Calends of January . . . make feasts lasting all night, nor keep up the custom of . . . intemperate drinking'.[2] Perhaps it was the laity, rather than monks, whom Ælfric was criticising for drinking all night *swiðe unrihtlice* (very unrighteously) at the lying-in of a dead man.[3] The *Rule of Chrodegang* observes somewhat regretfully, it seems: 'we cannot in these days induce them not to drink wine and *beor*' (*we ne magon on þisum dagum gelæran þæt hi win 7 beor ne drincon*), but goes on to say that monks should avoid drunkenness since it divided them from God's kingdom, and to recommend instead a pleasant garden for the monks' recreation.[4]

It was generally forbidden to drink intoxicating liquor in Lent, or on fast days, but retribution can seldom have followed as rapidly as it did in the case of one of Bishop Ælfege's household. This individual 'would drink whenever he wanted in Lent. One day he asked Bishop Ælfege to bless his drink, but the bishop would not, and the fool drank it and went out' (*wolde drincan on lenctene þonne hine lyste. Þa sume dæg bæd he þonne bisceop ælfeh blætsian his ful. He nolde and se dysiga dranc and eode him ut*). The outcome was that a boar ran up against him and fatally injured him.[5] A story like this would presumably have more impact than the statement used to conclude it – that if a man drinks in Lent or on appointed fast-days, his soul shall sorely pay for it. During a period of severe penance too, the penitent was to eschew anything which would make him intoxicated, as well as flesh.[6]

According to The Laws of Wihtred in 695, if a priest was so drunk that he could not carry out his duties, then he was to abstain from his ministry until his bishop sentenced him.[7] It seems that a legal definition of drunkenness was needed; at least, the Spelhelm Council drew one up in the following century. 'This is drunkenness when, the state of the mind is changed, the tongue stammers, the eyes are disturbed, the head is giddy, the belly is swelled and pain follows'.[8] Fasts, proportioned in duration to the status of the offender, were enjoined.[9]

Conclusion

Drunkenness was apparently so prevalent that in large, well-regulated households precautions were taken against it. The falconer at the Welsh Court was to drink only three times in the hall lest the birds were affected by his ebriety. He was, however, to have a vessel in which liquor was to be put and sent to his lodgings.[10] The Apparitor was not to drink at banquets, since it was his job to remain sober and watch out for fire. The risk of this may have been quite high. Bede recounts a case

---

[1] C.A. Wilson 1973, 371.
[2] Bonser 1963, 141.
[3] Skeat 1881, *St. Swithun* 1.313.
[4] Napier 1916, 15.
[5] Skeat 1881, *Ash Wednesday* 1.65.
[6] Turner 1828, III 507.
[7] Whitelock 1955, 362.
[8] Turner 1828, III 32.
[9] op. cit.
[10] Owen 1841, 367.

where a house burns down, except for one post, and the cloak hanging on it, which were protected by some holy mud, because everyone *druncne wæron*.[1]

Homilies, riddles and proverbs all inveigh against drunkenness. St. Paul's letter to the Corinthians was often quoted, for example, by Boniface to Æthelbald, King of Mercia.[2] Gluttony was warned against because it caused sickness and 'death results from immoderate drinking. He destroys his soul too, because often he does not know what he is doing because of the devilish drink' (*to deaðe gebrincgð for ðam ormæten drænce. heo forðeð eac ða sawle forðan he sceal oft done he sylf nat hu he færð for his feond-licum drencum*).[3] The *Rule of Chrodegang* concludes a long section entitled 'Why priests should shun and detest drunkenness' (*Be þam þæt preostas sceolan forbugan 7 asceonian druncen*): 'When a man is drunk he cannot govern the workings of his mind or body' (*Þonne se man druncen byð, ne mæg he gerisenlice begyman naðer ne his geþances ne his lyma færeldes*).[4] The drinking horn criticises those whom it makes drunk: mead can defeat men, and barley can make men talk confusedly, and the general view is, 'If you should do something when drunk, don't blame it on the ale, because you yourself had control of it'.[5] *A Father's Instructions* from the Exeter Book give as the fifth lesson the injunction 'keep yourself from drunkenness and foolish words' (*druncen beorg þe and dollic word*). 'If you want to be healthy, drink in moderation' (*Gif ðu wile hal beon, drince ðe gedeftlice*) was standard advice.[6]

Leechdoms give similar advice: a pregnant woman is not to drink until she is drunk, advice which is now repeated in the light of modern research.[7] The results of eating and drinking to excess are also sensibly dealt with.[8] Roasted swine's lung (five slices to be taken every night) or betony in water (to be taken before any alcoholic drink) were supposedly preventives against drunkenness.[9]

Monastic communities were perhaps more concerned about drunkenness, as well as much more likely to record this, but it does seem to have been a common, rather than a rare, occurrence among those who had the means to indulge a propensity for drinking to excess. If life was nasty, brutish and short, or merely very uncomfortable, a temporary escape from it would have had its attractions.

---

[1] Miller 1898, I 1 180–2.
[2] Whitelock 1955, 752.
[3] Skeat 1881, *Memorial of the Saints*, I.268.
[4] Napier 1916, 75.
[5] Mackie 1972, *Riddles* 11, 27, 28; Swanton 1975, 176.
[6] Kemble 1894, *Dialogue. Sol. & Sat.*
[7] Cockayne 1851, III xxxvii.
[8] op. cit., II xxviii.
[9] op. cit., I lxxx.

II Processing

16. Drying, Milling, Bread Making

Drying & Threshing

Drying kilns were used through the Anglo-Saxon period to harden the grain and facilitate threshing.[1] Kilns which could be substantial structures[2] are often clay ovens of elongated form with domed clay roofs, but these have also been interpreted as malting floors.[3] There seems no reason why such kilns should not have had both functions, although, as they were not particularly efficient at drying grain, they may have indirectly speeded up the adoption of naked wheat varieties.

According to *Gerefa*, threshing was a winter occupation, and the Anglo-Saxon calendar illustrates threshing with flails and winnowing for December.[4] The work was done *on odene* which was thought to be the 'floor of a barn' since it translated Latin *areæ*.[5] But the implication in *Gerefa* is that the two were different: the reeve had to take care of things appropriate to the *scipen oððe to odene* or the effects would be seen *on berne*.[6] Page deals with the problems that the advice 'to build a kiln on the barn floor' (*on odene cylne macian*) would give rise to, and comes to the conclusion that *odene* may represent something more complex than a threshing floor. The suggestion, given by Alfred's version of Augustine's *Soliloquies*, is that it was a place of work, as opposed to a storehouse.[7]

Some structures with opposing doors, as at Chalton, have been interpreted as threshing barns – the draught on a windy day helping with the winnowing.[8] Otherwise a *geflit*, translating the Latin *vannus* (fan), was used. Threshing was probably a humble occupation, which is why it is recorded of St. Eostorwine that 'he threshed corn and winnowed it' (*he corn þærsc and þæt windwode*).[9] Sieving was probably carried out after threshing.[10]

Milling

The process of milling underwent considerable refinement in the Anglo-Saxon period. The simplest method was to pound the grain in a hollow stone with a pestle: 'as a pestle pounds upon barley hulls' (*swylce berenhula punigendum bufan punere*).[11] Saddle querns were also used – the upper stone being rubbed back and forth over the

---

[1] Tannahill 1973, 36; Monk 1977, 26, 260, 338.
[2] Owen 1841, 79, 195, 261, 415, 721; Seebohm 1952, 66.
[3] Jones & Dimbleby 1981, 43, 115.
[4] Traill & Mann 1909, 181.
[5] Grube 1934, 145.
[6] Page 1985, 223.
[7] Whitelock 1955, 845; Seebohm 1952, 105.
[8] Monk 1977, 257.
[9] Herzefield 1900, *March 7*.
[10] Monk 1977, 257.
[11] Grube 1934, 146.

hollow lower stone. Perhaps Alcuin was thinking of a saddle quern when he described teeth as 'the millstones of our food'.[1] Saddle querns and upper rubber stones have been found in several Anglo-Saxon contexts including Southampton.[2] But they were never as popular as the more advanced handmills consisting of two circular stones – the upper moveable with a hole near its circumference for the handle by which it was rotated: 'as one does to the corn – grinds it up – with a pilstaff' (*swa mon corn deð* [*portige*] *mid pilstafe*).[3] Such a mill needed less force to operate than a saddle quern. The moveable stone was a 'quern stone' (*cwyrnstan*): 'the quern stone that turns continually but does not accomplish any journey' (*se cwyrnstan þe tyrnð singallice and nænne færeld ne ðurhtihdð*).[4]

A further development was a mechanically more efficient drive. A long staff replaced the handle of the upper quern stone, with its other end socketed above the stone, perhaps in a hollow in a roof beam. This staff could be turned to whirl the upper stone round. Further improvements included the use of several sockets on the quern in rotation to avoid uneven wear, and even the mounting of a quern on a table, to regulate the fineness of the flour.[5]

Quern stones were made of carefully chosen material. Neidermendig lava seems to have been particularly favoured. Vesicular and hard, it was also light in weight.[6] On the early site of West Stow thirteen Sunken Feature Buildings contained fragments of Neidermendig lava querns.[7] Fragments of rotary querns, often made from Neidermendig/Mayen lavas, have come from most middle and late Saxon sites, including Portchester.[8] Hamwih, Ramsbury,[9] Thetford, Chalton, Canterbury and Ipswich,[10] York from the eighth century on[11] and Cheddar.[12] Native rock traded within the country was also used for querns throughout the period.[13] The late Saxon site of St. Neots produced a number of fragments of Neidermendig lava querns, most from upper stones, and with a diameter of about 18 inches, which seems to have been the standard size.[14] The tenth-century Graveney boat was carrying at least one quern blank of this material and size; it was usual to transport querns as blanks: cutting the central hole weakened the stone.[15]

Grinding corn in a handmill, even for a small family, might take a considerable time.[16] It seems generally to have been women's work.[17] The laws of Æthelbert of Kent which date from the first decade of the seventh century punish the rape of a king's maiden by a fine of fifty shillings. 'If she be a grinding slave, 25 shillings

---

[1] Turner 1828, III 439.
[2] Hope-Taylor 1977, 196; Monk 1977, 266.
[3] Grube 1934, 146.
[4] op. cit., 146.
[5] Thomas 1971, 120; Seebohm 1952, 85.
[6] Crossley 1981, 1.
[7] West 1982, 395.
[8] Cunliffe 1976, 227.
[9] Haslam 1980, 6.
[10] Monk 1977, 226; West 1963, 241.
[11] Kemp 1986, 10.
[12] Rahtz 1979, 234.
[13] West 1982, 64; Crossley 1981, 1; Monk 1977, 266; Cunliffe 1976, 227.
[14] Addyman 1973, 89.
[15] Fenwick 1978, 131.
[16] Kuper 1977, 90; Trow Smith 1951, 66.
[17] Kylie 1911, 86.

compensation, the third class, 12 shillings' (*Gif hio grindende þeowa sio, xxv scillinga gebete. Sio þridde xii scillingas*).[1] This suggests that the grinding servants formed an important group and, while they did not have the status of a hand-maiden, they were above the 'third sort'.

Those who did not possess querns or with limited time might have opted for cracked grain. This, after soaking, might be more quickly reduced to fragments of kernel which could be boiled and served up with butter, milk or vegetables, but it seems likely that those who could, would eat at least some of their cereal food in the form of bread.

Oxen were evidently also used to provide the motive power for mills by the end of the period, since a pound was paid by Bury St. Edmunds for mill oxen.[2]

The water mill may have come to England in the seventh century: dendrochronology indicates a late seventh-century date for the mill at Old Windsor.[3] At Tamworth, a mill which may have been part of Offa's palace complex was radiocarbon-dated to the eighth century.[4]

There is some eighth-century charter and place-name evidence for mills, and this becomes plentiful in the ninth century.[5] If the impetus for mill building came from Kent, then the knowledge spread very rapidly north and west to Mercia; an indication perhaps of the value of water mills to those who had large retinues to feed.[6] Tenth-century leases often refer to mills.[7]

By then most large communities had their own mills.[8] The author of *Gerefa* gives instructions that the reeve was to supervise the construction of the mill in association with the fish weir. By Edward the Confessor's reign, mills had become such a hindrance to road and river traffic that he issued a decree limiting the sites at which they could be constructed.[9] A tide mill, either afloat or worked by a reservoir filled at high water, inconvenienced ships 'in the entrance to the port at Dover' (*in introitu portus de Douere*) according to the Domesday Survey.[10] By Domesday some 6,000 water mills were established in England. Often there was more than one mill in a village. Hatfield, Herts., had four by the time of Domesday, but two-thirds of individual manors were without one.[11] Partnerships in mills were frequent.[12] Ordinarily manorial mills were retained exclusively for the use of the lord and yielded no rental. Entries like that for Borhunte, Hants., where there was a mill paying 42 pence 'and another for the hall' (*7 alt. ad aula*) are quite common.[13] There were relatively small numbers of mills in Devon and Cornwall.[14] Some could only be used

[1] Attenborough 1922, 5.
[2] Robertson 1939, 255.
[3] Wikander 1986, 6; Rahtz in Crossley 1981, 14; Thomas 1971, 124; Baillie 1981, 61-3; Wilson 1976, 276.
[4] op. cit.
[5] Smith 1964, I, 251; Turner 1828, II 571; Seebohm 1952, 105; Whitelock 1955, 474, 487.
[6] Monk 1977, 269; Hodges 1982, 132.
[7] Robertson 1939, 27, 88; Hart 1975, 83; Whitelock 1955, 533-4, 552.
[8] Grube 1934, 147.
[9] Monk 1977, 269.
[10] Commissioners 1819, 412.
[11] C. A. Wilson 1973, 236.
[12] Bennett & Elton 1899, II 114.
[13] op. cit., 115.
[14] Loyn 1970, 357.

in winter, and Marcle Hill in Herefordshire rendered only the sustenance of him who kept it, but two in Cambridgeshire, presumably at Grantchester, produced eight pounds in 1066.[1] Seven mills in Battersea that yielded forty-two pounds, nine shillings, and eight pence or corn to that value, must have produced flour for a substantial number of London bakeries.[2]

The place of female slaves was taken by the male miller, such a one as Wine who was bequeathed in Æthelgifu's will of 980-90.[3] The *molendinarius* seems to be a bondsman of the lord's, permanently attached to the estates. By 1086 Bury St. Edmunds had '75 p' (*pistores*) which perhaps means millers, but could be translated 'bakers'.[4] Provided that a household had the means to pay for milled flour, and easy access to a mill, women would have been freed from an onerous aspect of food preparation.

The expansion of milling may have been associated with demographic decline – resulting in a shortage of slaves – or an increase in population – more mouths to be fed.[5] Or it might reflect investment to provide income: a church should not be like 'a mill for vile toll' (*an mylne for lyðrum tolle*).[6]

Meal

'Meal' (*meolu/melu*) was the term given to corn, or other material, after grinding. Grube considers that the term was applied to ground grain from which 'siftings/bran' (*sifeða*) had been sieved. He bases this interpretation on a passage from Alfred's translation of Boethius: 'so men sift meal – the meal goes through the holes and the siftings are thrown away' (*swa swa mon meolo seft: ðæt meolo ðurgcrypð ælc ðyrel 7 þa syfeða weorðað asyndred*).[7] However, a reference to *þrittig mittan clænes melowes and sixtig mittan oðres melowes* suggests ground corn in general,[8] and substances other than corn were ground into *meolu*. *Mealan stane* seems to have been an alternative term for *cwern*.[9] Unspecified meal was sometimes mentioned in rents.[10]

Meal could be ground more or less fine, and could be sieved then bolted through various grades of cloth to retain or exclude more or less of the bran, and also spiders and the flour moth.[11] *Leechdoms* refer to 'finely sieved meal' (*getemsud melu*), and Cockayne explains *temse* as a fine hair sieve, a term still in use when he wrote.[12] *Hersyfe* and *tæmesplian* (hair sieves) are referred to in *Gerefa*. Appropriately the *getemsud melu* was to be made into a cake as food for a patient with a delicate stomach. Refined meal – the fine flour – was referred to as *smedma* or *smedema*. One

[1] Commissioners 1819, 412; Bennett & Elton 1899, 113.
[2] Loyn 1970, 358.
[3] Whitelock 1968, 6.
[4] Turner 1828, II 369; Bennett & Elton 1899.
[5] Jones and Dimbleby 1981, 115.
[6] Skeat 1881, 253; Robertson 1939, 197, 255.
[7] Grube 1934, 147.
[8] op. cit., 149.
[9] Cockayne 1851, III 215.
[10] Loyn 1970, 304; Whitelock 1968, 8.
[11] Lovell 1988, 1; Holmes 1952, 201; Bosworth & Toller, 1898, I 53.
[12] Cockayne 1851, III 134.

recipe calls for 'fine flour of wheat meal' (*hwætenes meluwes smedman*).[1] *Hlaf smedman* translates 'bread of very fine flour' (*pania smili agineus*), and *smedma* glosses *similia* (the finest wheaten flour). *Pollis* (fine flour) is glossed by *grytt*.[2] Finely divided flour was available in Anglo-Saxon contexts, but it seems probable that only the richer members of society would be able to use it as a matter of course.

Leechdoms are not necessarily representative of substances generally ground into meal, but they are the most prolific source of references. There are ten references to barley meal, plus one to 'fine barley meal' (*smæl beren meal*); six to wheat, plus one to 'fine wheat meal' (*smæl hwætan meolwe*), and one to 'fine wheat flour' (*hwætenes meluwes smedman*); three to rye (as bran, meal, and dust); and one reference each to oat meal and bean meal. All five – barley, wheat, rye, oats and beans – were field crops, and their use for flour is not surprising. 'Worm meal' (*wyrm melo*) was hopefully purely medicinal, but with the mention of 'acorn flour/powder' (*acmeluwes dust*) and 'sieved hazel or alder flour' (*hæsles oþþe alnes asift*) we move into the realm of what might have been used to bulk out flour when more desirable materials were in short supply.[3] The very poorest would have ground up more or less anything edible, including 'weed' seeds and bark, and eaten all of the resultant meal.

Ground grain is rarely recoverable from archaeological contexts. Evidence for flour comes from York where quantities of bran were recovered together with parasite ova, indicating that elements of that population probably ate 100% flour: that is, flour from which nothing had been removed by sieving.[4]

Unleavened Bread

By the addition of salt, water and possibly shortening, Anglo-Saxon populations could have made unleavened bread, which may have taken the form of hard, flat cakes, although it could have resembled flat breads – pitta, nan or chapati.[5] Even when yeast is used but the flour is from grain which has started to sprout, then the resulting loaf will be flat and heavy. Unleavened oaten bread hardened on stands in front of the fire may have been made in some areas.[6] The large round was divided into *feorth-dæls*, or farls.

Baking an unleavened loaf under a pot, rather than on a bakestone or griddle, would draw the dough upwards so that it would rise slightly, resulting in lighter bread.[7] Generally, though, leavened bread is much lighter and easier to digest, particularly when cold, and is likely to have been generally preferred. Moreover, yeast is a good source of B vitamins and lysine, the limiting amino-acid in cereal proteins.[8]

---

[1] op. cit., II 226.
[2] Grube 1934, 149.
[3] Wilson & Foote 1970, 149; Ashley 1928, 58; Moberg 1973, 45ff.
[4] Hall 1981, 5ff..
[5] Tannur in Fenton & Owen 1931, 179.
[6] O'Danachair in Fenton & Owen 1981, 63-5.
[7] David 1977, 155.
[8] McGee 1986, 290.

Leavened Bread

Yeast was potentially available to the Anglo-Saxons from three sources. Wild yeasts are present in the air, and a mixture of meal and water left to stand will begin to ferment, and can be used as yeast.[1] Once a household had fermented dough, a lump (sourdough) could be kept from one day's baking and used to ferment a fresh batch of meal some days later.[2]

However, the discovery that fermenting liquor from brewing produced lighter bread had evidently been made on the continent before the beginning of the Anglo-Saxon period.[3] Perhaps *beorma* (yeast), which is etymologically connected with *breowan* (to brew), referred to this kind of liquid yeast source.[4] The Anglo-Saxons may also have used the sediment from bottom-fermenting yeasts – produced by the fermentation at a low temperature of light beers. This is born out by the fact that one Old English term for yeast, *dærst*, is derived from *dros* (dregs).[5] This yeasty sediment was slow-acting, and resulted in heavy, damp, sour bread.[6] Yeast could also have been dried. Coats of well-washed yeast, whisked up in fresh water, used to be spread on a large wooden platter or in a tub. While the yeast was drying, the platter or tub was inverted to protect the yeast from dust, but in such a way as to allow air to circulate. When each coat was dry, another was added until a layer 2–3 inches thick was achieved. This yeast would keep for several months. Or, as with yeast for brewing, a handful of birch twigs could be dipped in liquid yeast and hung up to dry until the next brewing/baking session when it could be put into wort/water to dissolve off the yeast.[7]

It is possible that *beorma, dærst,* and *hæf* (cf. the modern German brewing term *hefe*) derived originally from brewing; *ðæsma*, which is found translating only *fermentum*, originally meant sour dough, and *gist*, the only term not used in religious literature to translate the idea of leavening, was the dried, relatively pure, form. If liquid, it seems unlikely that *gist* could have been stored in a 'chest, box' (*cist*) (*Gerefa*), and it might make sense of the instruction to take new *gist*, i.e. newly dried and not two or three months old, for a brew.[8] The more general term *teage* (container) was used of holding *beorma*, and the term 'barm' was used until recently to indicate a solution of yeast. Although the terms may reflect different origins, they seem to have been more or less interchangeable in Anglo-Saxon times. In one case *gist* translates 'the froth on the ale' (*spuma cerevisiae*).[9] But the common Germanic character of terms for yeast also points to the early production of leavened bread among Germanic peoples, particularly when there were also common terms for unleavened 'low' bread: Old English *þeorfe* and 'raised' bread, Old English *hlaf*.[10]

---

[1] David 1977, 89; Renfrew 1985, 40.
[2] McGee 1986, 313; David 1977, 293, 156.
[3] Stewart 1975, 45.
[4] Grube 1934, 152.
[5] op. cit., 152.
[6] David 1977, 98.
[7] op. cit., 95.
[8] Cockayne 1851, II li 1.
[9] op. cit., Herbarium 21, 6.
[10] Grube 1934, 151; Tooke 1798-1815, II 155.

The procedures of bread making were presumably commonplace; the instructions given for a salve were 'work it as though it were dough' (*gemang þ hit sie swilc swa dah*).[1] The action of yeast must have been very well-known since it is used as the source of a number of metaphors.[2] 'Dough' is the polite answer to Riddle 45 in the Exeter Book.

On contact with water, i.e. when dough is made, wheat gluten forms a tough rubbery material which traps the bubbles of carbon dioxide gas produced by the yeast. After ageing for one or two months, the light yellow colour of freshly milled corn is bleached, and the bonding characters of the gluten proteins are affected so that they form a stronger, more elastic dough.[3] The oils in wheat germ and bran are susceptible to oxidation and develop rancid odours in a matter of weeks, so if flour is to be kept, thus improving its bead-making qualities, then it is better to sieve it until 'white'.[4] Moreover, germ and bran dilute the bread-making qualities of flour, so for superior bread white flour is best.

Barley gluten tends simply to dissolve into a watery suspension.[5] Rye has its own gluten, but this does little to aid the expansion of the dough. There is no appreciable gluten in oatmeal.[6] These factors explain why wheat was sought after for bread making.

Loaves

The common term for bread was *hlaf* (loaf). The word *bread/bræad* (bread) rarely occurs.[7] The dough could be formed into rolls and loaves of various shapes and sizes.[8] The Anglo-Saxons seem to have had two basic sizes of loaf: small and large. For example, Edward the Elder's will (901-8) refers to 'two hundred large and one hundred small loaves' (*tu hund greates hlafes 7 þridde smales*).[9] The Abbotsbury Guild Statutes refer to broad loaves: one is to be provided by every two guild brothers for common almsgiving.[10] Perhaps these were the same as the *greate* loaves. Judging by illustrations, loaves were round,[11] and on the tables of the gentry, as far as can be gauged, were about the size of a present-day medium-sized loaf. The rule of St. Benedict allowed a pound of bread per day, and this would be represented by a present-day medium/large loaf, but may have been allocated as a portion from a 'broad' or 'great' loaf.[12] Large loaves of leavened dough would be difficult to cook properly, other than in an oven, which would suggest the method of baking.

---

[1] Cockayne 1851, I xlvii 2, II li I.
[2] Swanton 1975, 95.
[3] McGee 1986, 290.
[4] op. cit., 233.
[5] Dr. J. Graham, pers. comm.
[6] David 1977, 67.
[7] Cockayne 1851, II xlix; Robertson 1939, 253.
[8] Wright 1871, 104; Foote & Wilson 1970, 166; Wright 1871, 104.
[9] Grube 1934, 155.
[10] Whitelock 1955, 560.
[11] Temple 1976, figs. 158, 166; Stenton 1957, fig. 49.
[12] Knowles 1940, 462; Ashley 1928, 12.

Baking: Hearths & Ovens

In Asser's version of the story of Alfred and the 'cakes', the loaves are burning at the fire; in the Claud MS. the loaves are on a pan with the fire underneath, while Matthew of Westminster's version has the bread under the ashes of the fire to bake.[1] *Axbakenne hlaf* and *heorðbacen hlaf* are two variants in translations of Gregory's Dialogues.[2] One of the leechdoms instructs 'bake him a warm loaf on the hearth' (*bacan him man þanne wearmen hlaf be heorðe*), but another prescribes 'an oven-baked loaf' (*ofen baocan hlaf*).[3] Ovens were enclosed – in their simplest form an inverted pot covered with embers.[4] A clay-lined oven had been built into the chalk rubble walls of a what was evidently a cooking hut on the sixth/seventh-century site at Puddlehill, Beds.[5] In *The Life of Ceolfrith*, written soon after 716, but probably referring to a time before 674, an oven is lit and then cleansed before loaves are placed in it, suggesting a bread oven on conventional lines in which faggots are lit and the ashes raked out before baking.[6] An *ofenraca* is one of the utensils listed in *Gerefa* and while none has been recovered from an Anglo-Saxon context, beech oven rakes were found in eleventh-century levels in Lund.[7] The sides and lower crust of the bread may have been cut off to get rid of ashes: some manuscript illustrations seem to show four slices cut from the sides of loaves.[8]

Bakehouses

Monastic and other large establishments of the middle period had bakehouses.[9] A bakehouse in which a sequence of ovens had been built at North Elmham has been dated prior to 800.[10] At Fladbury, Worcs., a sunken bread oven with similar dimensions to that at North Elmham – about 2 metres across – was found, and associated timbers were radiocarbon-dated to A.D.851 plus or minus 51 years.[11] By the time of the Conquest there were evidently large communal ovens, like that of the Earl at Norwich,[12] and probably commercial bakeries too.[13]

However, in a peasant's household bread would presumably still have been baked at the hearth fire. An eleventh-century scribe glosses *formacula* (a little oven) with *cylen* (kiln/oven) and *heorþ* (hearth), indicating a continuation of the two methods.[14] A griddle, or a small, circular, long-handled pan, such as are found in Scandinavian contexts, may have been used, particularly in areas where oat bread was common.[15]

---

[1] Turner 1828, I 560ff.
[2] Grube 1934, 153.
[3] Cockayne 1851, III 122, II xxvii.
[4] Bosworth & Toller 1898, 729.
[5] Matthews 1985, 60, 69.
[6] Whitelock 1955, 698.
[7] Foote & Wilson 1970, 166.
[8] Furnivall 1868, 23.
[9] Rahtz 1979, 8.
[10] Wade-Martins 1980, 69ff.
[11] Monk 1977, 27.
[12] Munby 1982, 52d.
[13] Smith 1964, II 135.
[14] Grube 1934, 153.
[15] Foote & Wilson 1970, 166.

Bakers

Women were probably responsible for the bread supply of individual households. The term *hlæfdige* (lady) is etymologically derived from **hlaibadigon* (bread kneader).[1] Old English has both masculine and feminine forms for bakers: *bæcere* and *bæcestre*, and the male baker of the *Colloquy* operates in a domestic, or commercial situation, not a monastic one.[2] By the end of the period, the baker was one of the inhabitants of a large estate.[3]

Apart from the monastic and manorial bakers, it seems that there were bakers who were independent tradesmen.[4] By c.1100 Baldwin, the baker of the High Street in Winchester rented a number of properties; and there were at least five other bakers in the town.[5]

Bread

Asked about the importance of his craft, the baker of Ælfric's *Colloquy* says,

'without my skill every table seems empty and without bread all food is turned to loathing, I gladden the heart of men, I strengthen folk, and because of this, the little children will not shun me'

(buton cræfte minon ælc beod æmtig byþ gesewen 7 buton hlafe ælc mete to wlættan byþ gehwyrfed. Ic heortan mannes gestrangie, ic mægen wera 7 furþon litlincgas nellaþ forbigean me).[6]

This suggests that bread was considered an essential part of a meal and was important for young children, particularly perhaps those who were being weaned. The author of *Leechdoms* also considered bread a strengthening food.[7] Each of the craftsmen of the *Colloquy* tends to exaggerate the importance of his own craft, but there is other evidence pointing to bread as the main constituent of a meal.[8] The standard meal was a loaf and something to eat with it. Possibly bread was already being eaten with butter as one of the 'accompaniments': 'Then give barley bread and pure new butter to the invalid to eat' *(þam mannum sceal sellan ægra to suppane, beren bread, clæne niwe buteran).*[9]

Loaves were often mentioned as part of payments in food, either to be made by tenants to the landlord, inheritors to religious foundations, or masters to their servants. In the time of Ine, ten hides were to provide 300 loaves.[10] The numbers of loaves to be paid to religious foundations are particularly high, and perhaps reflect their large establishments. Osuulf's will leaves yearly '120 wheaten loaves and 30

[1] Grube 1934, 153.
[2] Fell 1984, 49.
[3] Munby 1982, 52b.
[4] Loyn 1970, 324.
[5] Barlow et al. 1976, 16, 45, 77, 94, 126, 133, 135-8.
[6] Garmonsway 1978, 36-7.
[7] Cockayne 1851, II xv 1, xvi 2, xxx, xlix, il.
[8] Whitelock 1955, 385, 390, 410, 559, 560, 760; Miller 1890, I, 1 166; Owen 1841, I 69, 395, 677; Miller 1890, I, 2 244.
[9] Cockayne 1851, II 220.
[10] Whitelock 1955, 371.

without the bran and 120 well-seasoned loaves for almsgiving' (*cxx hwætenra hlafa 7 xxx clenra, cxx gesuflra hlafa to ælmsmessan*), and these categories recur in other ninth-century wills.[1] Such bequests indicate that the estates were expected to produce a surplus, that they had the facilities for baking large numbers of loaves and that wholemeal flour was more frequently used than 'white', and that 'well-seasoned' loaves were in some way special.

Towards the end of the period, the number of loaves specified tends to increase. For example, Bury St. Edmunds was to receive 1,000 loaves annually on September 4th, and Leofstan added another 300 to this number, 'and Thurstan relish for 300 loaves' (*7 Ðurstan syflincge to iii hund hlafe*).[2] Again, this suggests bread as the staple and the 'relish' or accompaniment as secondary, if highly desirable. Sometimes, as with a lease of land to Denewulf, bishop of Winchester, the size of the loaves is specified: 'two hundred large loaves and another hundred small loaves' (*tu hund greates hlafes 7 þridde smales*).[3]

It is possible that loaves paid as rent were a special form of bread or rusk that would still be palatable after a number of days in transit.[4] However, the large numbers of bakers recorded for monastic centres may have been fulfilling contracts for food rents, as well as providing bread for pilgrims.

The title 'Lord' is generally thought to have been derived from *hlaford/*hlaidward* (loaf-keeper).[5] This would accord with the fact that the owners of estates owned substantial food resources, and also with the view of the loaf as the staple food. In the early code of Ethelbert (602–3), the first rank subordinate to the *ceorl* was his *hlafæta* (loaf-eater).[6] *The Dialogue of Salomon and Saturnus* states, 'in twelve months you shall give your servants 720 loaves, besides morning and midday food' (*on xii monðum ðu scealt sillan ðinum þeowan man vii hund hlafa and xx hlafa buton morgemetum and nonmetum*).[7]

Wheaten loaves were regarded as superior,[8] white bread being preferred for the Eucharist.[9] Those who chose to eat barley bread did so from ascetic motives.[10] When Bishop Basil offered Julian barley bread such as he ate himself, the emperor was insulted, 'barley is only fit for horses' (*hors mete is bere*), and offered Basil some grass.[11]

On feast days, at least in religious contexts, the ordinary bread was replaced by a finer kind, or by spiced cakes.[12] Feast-day bread may have been made from enriched dough mixtures. *Gesufel* loaves were bequeathed as an offering on Sundays by Ealhburg and Eadwulf (see above), and the Abbotsbury guild loaves were to be *well gesyfled*.

---

[1] Grube 1934, 154.
[2] Robertson 1929, 13, 193.
[3] op. cit., 39.
[4] Jaine 1987, 78; Imellos in Fenton & Kisban 1986, 74-5; Weaver in op. cit., 354-5.
[5] O.E.D.; Tooke 1805, II 155.
[6] Whitelock 1955, 358.
[7] Kemble 1848, 192.
[8] Owen 1841, 533; Ashley 1928, 129-31; Skeat 1881, *St Eugenia* 1.404-5.
[9] Miller 1898, I, 1 112.
[10] Mellows 1980, 37; Swanton 1975, 45.
[11] Skeat 1881, *St Basilus* 1.212.
[12] Knowles 1940, 464; Connor 1987, 196.

Gesufel seems to mean 'spiced' or 'flavoured'.[1] Guild loaves were also to be *wel besewen*, which perhaps means 'sprinkled with seeds'.[2] Dill, caraway, poppy, fennel and sweet cecily seeds could all have been used. *Leechdoms* give instructions for making 'a cake' (*anne cicel*) of 'finely sifted flour' (*getemsud melu*) into which cumin and march seed was to be kneaded, so perhaps seeds were incorporated in the dough.[3] Such enriched loaves could have been kneaded with milk instead of water (cf. the *Erce* charm), or cream, and had eggs, butter or other fats incorporated in the dough. They may have been sweetened with honey, or contained fruits, preserved in honey or dried.[4] Local variations of enriched loaves and buns may derive from the special breads of Anglo-Saxon feast days.

The crumpet may also have been available to the Anglo-Saxons. *Crompeht* is used to gloss *folialis*, and Schlutter thought this was a form of thin bread. Grube thought that *folialis=foliatus*, and the *crompeht* was a little flat cake with flowers marked on it, as shown in manuscript illustrations.[5] However, it is more likely that *crompeht* is derived from the Celtic *crempog*, meaning a pancake.[6] A leavened batter will produce a crumpet, in effect a small pancake with holes most of the way down from its top surface cooked in a pan or on a griddle.

---

[1] Grube 1934, 156; Knowles 1940, 464.
[2] Grube 1934, 156.
[3] Cockayne 1851, III 63.
[4] Walker & Bennett 1980, 2.
[5] Grube 1934, 156.
[6] David 1977, 341.

17. Dairying

The Milch Animals

The leechdoms contain ten references to goats' milk, three to cows' milk, two where cows' or goats' milk will do, and two to ewes' milk.[1] The more frequent references to goats' milk may reflect the Mediterranean origin of the text, or the fact that goats' milk is comparatively easy to digest, and good for those who suffer from certain allergies. *Rectitudines Singularum Personarum* refers to the duties of the cowherd, shepherd and goatherd:

> 'Concerning the cowherd. His right is to receive the milk of an old cow for seven days after she has calved, and the beestings of a young cow for fourteen days...
>
> Concerning the shepherd. The shepherd's entitlement is to have ...the milk of his herd for seven days after the equinox and a bowlful of whey or buttermilk all the summer.
>
> Concerning the goatherd. The goatherd is entitled to the milk of his herd after Martinmas, and before that a share of the whey...'.
>
> *(Be kuhyrde. Cyhyrde gebyreð, þæt he hæbbe ealdre cu meolc VII niht, syððan heo nige cealfod hæfd, 7 frymetlinge bystinge XIIII niht...*
>
> *Be sceaphyrdan. Sceaphyrdes riht is, þæt he hæbbe ...his heorde meolc VII niht æfter emnihtes dæge 7 blede fulle hweges oððe syringe ealne sumor.*
>
> *Be gathyrde. Gathyrde ge byreð his heorde meolc ofer Martinus mæssedæg, 7 ær þam his dæl hwæges...)*[2]

It is clear that the cow, sheep and goat all provided milk, and other dairy products. Archaeological sites provide evidence for the presence of all three animals, and deductions can be made from the age range of the animals concerned. For example, the age range of the goats at Beckery Chapel, Somerset, suggests a dairy function.[3]

Domesday evidence shows that some manors, for example those of the abbot of Bury St. Edmunds in East Anglia and some royal manors in Devon, had cattle far in excess of the apparent draught needs. This suggests a cattle husbandry in which milk production was important.[4] This may have reflected a preference in which only those with the necessary resources could indulge, and may have been coupled with another preference – the raising of fat cattle for food.

Households in towns and villages may have kept a cow for milk, the food being hay, or grass gathered from hedgerows.[5] Unimproved breeds, such as the small Kerry cow, comparable to Anglo-Saxon cattle, are able to subsist on very scanty fare and to milk on it.[6]

---

[1] Cockayne 1851, I ii 5, II xxv, II lxv (2), II xxv; Bonser 1963, 111; Cockayne op. cit., I lxxv.
[2] Leibermann 1898, 450-1.
[3] Rahtz & Hirst 1974, 81 ff.
[4] Trow Smith 1957.
[5] Mitford 1986, 73-4.
[6] Fream 1952, 520.

Their Young

Presumably not all young were reared: if a dairy animal was kept until it was five or six years old only one of its offspring would need to be reared to replace it during this period, so some lactations may have been available just for dairying, provided that, in the case of cattle, the demand for plough oxen had also been met. Calves, lambs and kids would all presumably have been eaten.

Monasteries may have had more cows' milk (and veal) available than lay establishments in that young calves were killed to provide vellum. The three Pandects or Bibles made for Ceolfrith at Monkwearmouth/Jarrow between 680 and 716 needed the skins of some 1,550 calves, though such a large production was the exception, rather than the rule.[1] The extra milk would have played a useful part in a monastic diet.

Dairy Farms

There are records of dairy farms established by mid-Anglo-Saxon times, though these were for milch animals generally, and were not, as today, concerned exclusively with cattle.[2]

Yield

The closest one can come to estimating the yield of Anglo-Saxon milch animals is by extrapolation from present-day breeds. Kerry or Shetland cattle correspond fairly closely and can convert poor-quality fodder into five to seven gallons of milk a day with 4% butterfat up to 3 months after calving.[3]

Evidence for the yield of an early medieval Welsh cow comes from the *Ancient Laws and Institutes of Wales* indicating a minimum of about two gallons a day.[4] A sheep would give about one-tenth of this.[5]

Beestings, the particularly rich colostrum produced by a cow immediately after calving, was sufficiently valued to be the subject of an allocation: the perquisite of the cowherd, according to *Rectitudines Singularum Personarum*.[6]

Problems of Hygiene

The leechdoms include charms (which are not included in the section from *Apuleius* on which they are based), for milk that has been spoiled,[7] involving plants, often lupins.[8] Plantain, cockle and cress were to be bound together, then laid on the milk pail, which was not to be put down on the ground for a week.[9] It is difficult to know if these herbs would have a disinfectant effect; perhaps allowing the bucket to dry out

---

[1] Dodswell 1982, 94.
[2] Finberg 1972, 105; Loyn 1970, 367; Robertson 1939, 171; Whitelock 1955, 489.
[3] Bowie 1988, 442.
[4] Owen 1841, 271; Herzfeld 1900, *May*.
[5] Seebohm 1952, 126-8.
[6] Leibermann 1898, 450.
[7] Meaney 1981, 56.
[8] Cockayne 1851, I lxvii 1.
[9] op. cit., III liii.

thoroughly would have been helpful.[1] The incident where St. Columba reproves Colomban for not casting out the demon that was lurking in the bottom of the milking pail, by making on it the sign of the cross, is additional indication that the souring of milk was a problem.[2]

A number of outbreaks of disease affecting domestic animals are recorded in the chronicles, and some may have been transmitted to humans, but it is not possible to identify the type of infection with any certainty.[3]

Dairy Workers

On large estates it appears that the men were responsible for milking the animals in their care. The shepherd of the *Colloquy* milked his sheep twice a day and made cheese and butter.[4] According to *Rectitudines Singularum Personarum* the cheese-maker was the only woman specified among the estate workers:

> 'The cheese-maker is entitled to a hundred cheeses, and is to make butter for the lord's table from the whey; and she is to have all the buttermilk except the herdsman's share,
>
> *(Cys-wyrhtan gebyreð hundred cyse, and þæt heo of wringhwæge buteran macige to hlafordes beode; and hæbbe hire þe syringe ealle butan þæs hyrdes dæle.)*[5]

Usually dairy workers are female.[6] This would seem a reasonable division of labour: the various herdsmen would be too occupied with their animals to spend time making dairy produce. The term *dæge/dey* is cognate with *dige* 'kneader' (cf. *hlafdige* 'loaf-kneader, lady'). The working of butter from cream by hand, of butter to expel brine, the pressing of butter into storage tubs and curds into cheese are forms of kneading.

From the law code IV Æthelred, which could be as late as the last years of Cnut, and deals with London, comes the information:

> 'Women who deal in dairy produce – who sell cheese and butter – pay one penny a fortnight before Christmas and another penny a week before Christmas'.
>
> *(Smeremangestrae [quae mangonant in caseo et butiro] XIIII diebus ante natale Domini unum den., et septem diebus ante natale Domini unum allium.)*[7]

This confirms dairying as women's work, and that dairy products were sold in towns, although, as the reference is to the weeks immediately before Christmas, dairy products may have been a delicacy. Perhaps women also brought dairy products into towns in the summer, when milk would have been more plentiful, but they did not then make the kind of price that attracted tolls.

---

[1] Hartley 1954, 467.
[2] Bonser 1963, 259.
[3] Min. of Ag. 1972, 1,2,6; Burnet & White 1972, 214.
[4] Garmonsway 1978, 22.
[5] Leibermann 1898, 451.
[6] Roberston 1939, 257; Whitelock 1952, 113; Owen 1841, 80.
[7] Robertson 1955, 72.

Fresh Dairy Products

A will leaves 4 pence for milk for the anniversary of a funeral feast.[1] It may have been used for frumenty, syllabubs, sweet curds or junkets, which were associated with festivities, or for making butter or cheese, since the anniversary feast, unlike the funeral feast, could be prepared well in advance.[2] But it may have been to drink with the fish or to cook the fish on the menu. Drinking full-cream milk was a luxury, since there were still drinkable liquids (skimmed milk, buttermilk and whey) after milk had been used to produce the valuable commodities of cream, butter and cheese. References to drinking skimmed milk, buttermilk and whey are much more common than to drinking milk.[3] Ascetics tended to drink milk rather than intoxicating beverages, but even then it might be 'skimmed milk' (*þinre meolc*), or 'milk mixed with water' (*meolc wætre gemenede*) which Cedd took in Lent.[4]

The terminology of other fresh dairy products is problematic. *Flete* derives from *fleotan* (to float), and therefore can refer to cream (cf. modern Danish *fløde*), and, in the plural, to curds or skimmings. A fleeter, in Suffolk dialect, is a skimmer for cream.[5] *Ream* also apparently referred to cream, though perhaps to ripened cream, or cream which had been heated in order to preserve and thicken it.[6] Clotted cream, deriving from the Old English *clut*, may have been made in Anglo-Saxon times.[7]

Obviously milk and fresh milk products had a limited life, turning sour quickly in warm weather. Butter and cheese, however, were forms in which milk products could be preserved for weeks and months, for consumption in the winter when there would be a shortage of fresh milk.

Butter

The Anglo-Saxon invaders were already practised in butter making.[8] In order to make butter, milk is skimmed to collect the cream over two or three days prior to making butter.[9] The cream is then churned until granules of butter form. After the buttermilk has been drained off, the butter granules are given several rinses of water, all cold in summer, but the last warm in winter.[10] Then the butter is worked to expel all the buttermilk which would otherwise quickly turn the butter rancid. Unsalted butter may have been made for immediate use, but most butter was salted, since the salter of the *Colloquy* maintains, 'butter and cheese would be lost to you if I was not there to preserve them' (*butergeweor ælc cysgerunn losaþ eow buton ic hyrde ætwese eow*).[11] The salt would be worked into the butter, and if it was to be stored, it would probably have been pressed down into barrels, with layers of salt, to exclude air pockets.[1] It is possible that butterwort (*pinguicula vulgaris*) was also used to preserve butter.

[1] Robertson 1939, 253.
[2] Kuper 1977, 28, 34; Ayrton 1975, 461, 479.
[3] Turner 1828, III 27.
[4] Miller 1890, I, 2 244; Colgrave 1940, 345.
[5] Evans 1969, 104.
[6] Cockayne 1851, III Gloss.
[7] Hartley 1954, 474.
[8] Brothwell 1969, 51.
[9] Wilkins 1982, 1.
[10] Cockayne 1851, I xliv 2.
[11] Garmonsway 1978, 35-6.
[1] Hartley 1954, 481.

17 Dairying

Around 20 to 30 pints of milk (depending on butterfat content), are needed to make one pound of butter, but skimmed and buttermilk are also produced, and the rinsings of buttercurd were traditionally used for fattening pigs.[1] However, cheese could be the primary product, and butter made from the whey, which is the situation described in *Rectitudines Singularum Personarum*: the cheese maker is to make butter from the *wringhwæge*. A good deal of cream may be raised from whey by gentle heating, and this form of butter is little inferior to ordinary butter.[2] The practice seems to have been to make the maximum use of a quantity of milk by using it to make butter then cheese, or cheese then butter. The liquid residue in both cases could be used as a drink.

Buttermilk is slightly thickened and soured by the activity of airborne bacteria during churning, and bacterial cultures may have been perpetuated in the wood of the dairy utensils. Since it has only a short life, it was probably consumed on the farms where the butter was made, although some may have found its way into markets near at hand.

The vigorous activity of churning butter is made the subject of Riddle 54 from the Exeter Book. Like Riddle 45, the respectable answer to which is 'dough', the language is packed with sexual innuendo:

(Hyse se cwom gangan þær he hie wisse
stondan in wincle stop feorran to
hror hægstealdmon hof his agen
hyre stondendre stiþes nathwæt
worhte his willan wagendan buta
þegn unnette wæs þragum nyt
tillic esne teorode hwæþre
æt stunda gehwam strong ær þon[ne] hio
werig þæs weorces hyre weaxan ongon
under gyrdelse þæt oft gode men
ferðþum freogað ond mid feo bicgað.)[3]

'There came a young man to where he knew her to be, standing in a corner. The lusty bachelor approached her, lifted up his clothes and thrust something stiff under her girdle where she stood, had his way, so both of them were shaking. The thane worked hard; his good servant was sometimes useful, but, though strong, he always became tired and weary of tat work before she did. Beneath her girdle there began to grow what good men love in their hearts and buy with money.'

The churn being described here is the knocker churn.[4]

However, *uuellyrgæ* is given as the translation for *smus* (i.e. sinus), 'a vessel in which butter is made' (*uas quo buterum conficitur*). *Uuellyrgæ* is a derivative of *wealwian/wiellan* (roll), and so may refer to a rocker churn.[1]

[1] Wilkins 1982, 4.
[2] Seebohm 1952, 107; Trow Smith 1957, 119.
[3] Mackie 1934.
[4] Wright 1871, 105.
[1] Pheifer 1974, 124; Hartley 1954, 479; Cheape in Fenton & Kisban 1986, 118.

Cheese making

In cheese making, rennet, a natural curdling agent, and sometimes lactic acid bacteria, which cause fermentation, are added to warm milk. When the milk has coagulated to form a 'junket', this is broken up, and the curds separate from the whey. The finer the curd is cut up, the more liquid drains out, and the harder and drier the final cheese will be. If the curds are heated up to between 70 and 130 degrees Fahrenheit they will become progressively more rubbery, and the resulting cheese will be correspondingly denser, and have better keeping qualities. This is likely to have been done in Anglo-Saxon England.[1]

Some soft cheeses, like Roquefort, are not cooked at all. The whey which is drained off can itself be curdled over heat with acid (vinegar, for example), and made into more cheese.[2] Buttermilk, from which most of the fat has been removed, was also used for cheese. Some cheeses have salt, which will slow down the rate of spoilage, added to the curd before pressing in moulds. Other cheeses are put into a bath of brine for a period after pressing. Salt can be rubbed into the surface of a cheese in order to protect it from spoilage. Cheese which is salted very heavily will not ripen, since all micro bacterial activity is brought to a halt.[3]

Anglo-Saxons had rennet available, and lactic acid bacteria were probably present in their wooden utensils.[4] Rennet contains the single enzyme, rennin, of which one part will coagulate five million parts of milk (commercial rennet works only in the ratio of 1:4,500).[5] Flowers of the wild thistle, seeds of safflower and 'lady's bedstraw' (*galium verum*) could also have been used to curdle milk for the preparation of cheese.[6] Boiled nettle and the flower of the teasel can also be used, but, unlike rennet, plant proteases digest more casein than they coagulate, and the result is a soft, weak curd.[7] Vinegar can be used to curdle milk for cottage cheese, although milk will separate naturally as it sours, and the curd so formed can be drained and then salted to make cheese.[8] *Leechdoms* state that milk could be 'turned' (*gewyrd*) by heating with hot stones or a hot iron as well as rennet: 'turn the milk with rennet' (*þa meolc geren mid cys[l]ybbe*).[9] The Anglo-Saxons had access to all the curdling agents that have been mentioned. The evidence from one of the leechdoms is that even new cheese had a relatively firm consistency: 'take new cheese and shred it into boiling water ...and make as it were small cakes and bind to the eyes' (*nim niwne cysan 7 screda hyne on weallendan wætere ...7 maca ealswa litles cicles 7 byd to þan eagan*); this might signify that the cheese was curdled with rennet and the curd heated.[1]

While some cheese was eaten fresh (see below), the addition of salt would seem to have been standard practice. The salter of the *Colloquy* maintained that 'cheese

[1] Oschinsky 1971, 289.
[2] McGee 1986, 44.
[3] op. cit., 47.
[4] Cockayne 1851, 2 376.
[5] McGee 1986, 37, 44.
[6] op. cit., 37; Harris 1961, 82.
[7] Monk 1977, 124; Lodge & Herrtage 1973, Bk VI stanzas 21ff; McGee 1986, 37, 44; Renfrew 1985, 15.
[8] McGee 1986, 35; Renfrew 1985, 15.
[9] Cockayne 1851, II li 3, II xxv, *Lacnunga* 18.
[1] op. cit., III *Peri Didacheon*, 21.

curd' (*cysegerunn*) needed to be preserved with salt.[1] Large dairy farms would have produced more cheese than could have been consumed fresh. The large number of cheeses listed in inventories suggests that they must have been preserved in some way.[2] The Welsh seem to have used the brine bath method for preserving cheese.[3] The cheese was sometimes hung up to keep it out of the way of vermin and domestic animals, but it is possible that it was hung up in order to be smoked, although if it was hung up in the dwelling house it may have been smoked incidentally rather than intentionally.

It is difficult to find any evidence for the size of Anglo-Saxon cheeses. A fragment of a will from Bury St. Edmunds leaves 'eight pence for a cheese' (*viii pe. an. cese*) for the first funeral feast, which suggests a large cheese weighing several pounds.[4]

It is not known if there were any Anglo-Saxon blue cheeses. Certainly in France such cheese was a delicacy, and also a rarity, since when Charlemagne encountered it for the first time he had to be instructed not to throw away the *ærugo* (literally 'the rust of copper', i.e. mould), since this was the best part of the cheese.[5] Presumably this was a Roquefort-type cheese, to which the mould *Penicillium Roqueforti* had imparted its special flavour. This is the same mould that flavours Stilton cheese; it may have occurred in some localities where it could have been incorporated into cheese.[6] Dorset Blue is also known as Blue Vinney, *vinney* being a corruption of *vinew/finew*, from the Old English *fynig* (mouldy).[7] It would seem on linguistic grounds to derive from Anglo-Saxon times, although it could be argued that the Anglo-Saxon population would refer to a blue cheese introduced from France at the time of the Conquest as *fynig*. It is a buttermilk cheese, which suggests the Anglo-Saxon dairying economy.

Cheese making was probably practised on a domestic scale by all households which possessed milch animals. Cheese was certainly made on large estates: the reeve was in charge of the cheese vat, and some cheese was made for sale in local markets or abroad.[8] The more prosperous an establishment, the longer its members could wait for cheese to age. Mature cheese was consumed as a novelty by the rich, whereas the poor ate fresh cheese.[9] Perhaps cheese that was to be kept was more time-consuming to make, and expensive, since more salt would be necessary and probably a press of some kind was needed too.

Dairy Products in Food Rents

Butter is not often referred to in Anglo-Saxon food rents, though Ine's Laws call for the provision of an *amber* of butter from ten hides. Cheeses figure in some of the earliest records of rents. According to Ine's Laws, ten hides were to furnish ten

---

[1] Garmonsway 1978, 35-6.
[2] Robertson 1939, 197, 249.
[3] Owen 1841, 525.
[4] Robertson 1939, 253; D. G. Wilson 1977, 35; Hartley 1954, 486.
[5] McGee 1986, 37-8.
[6] Hartley 1954, 483-7.
[7] O.E.D. IV, 231, X Part II 216.
[8] Leibermann 1898, 455; Poole 1958, 227, 231; Loyn 1970, 96.
[9] McGee 1986, 38; Skeat 1869, 77; Seebohm 1952, 157.

cheeses as well as other food. Forty cheeses were part of an annual food *feorme* retained by Offa from a royal estate at Westbury, Gloucestershire.[1] Cheeses or weys of cheese are often referred to in rents.[2] Religious communities often received cheeses under the terms of wills.[3] As a protein, cheese was of particular importance to monastic communities.

Dairy Products in Remedies

Milk in leechdoms is sometimes to be taken warm from the cow, ewe or goat, to be drawn at one milking, or to be 'not sour' (*unsure*).[4] The most general use for milk is as a liquid for boiling herbs in, or for making broth.[5] It is sometimes to be boiled, or 'turned' (*gewyrð/geren*) by heating with hot stones or iron, or with rennet.[6] The woman who could not feed her child was to take a mouthful of milk from a cow of one colour.[7]

Ripened or newly-skimmed cream is called for in one recipe; in two others hens' eggs are to be mixed with 'cream' (*fletan*), and three pieces of old lard or butter are to be taken with *fletum*.[8]

'Pure, new butter' (*clæne niwe buteran*) is part of an invalid diet, and the instruction 'drink a bowlful of melted butter' (*drican amylte buteran bollan fulne*) is also given.[9] Butter is recommended too as an antidote to wolf's bane.[10] It is to be added to chicken broth.[11] Very common is the instruction to cook items – usually herbs or vegetables – in butter, sometimes with the addition of honey.[12] One leechdom states that butter is better than milk for boiling herbs in.[13]

'Salt butter' (*sealte buteran*) is also specified.[14] In one leechdom butter is an alternative to oil.[15] *Cu buteran* is specified five times, suggesting perhaps that butter made from sheep's or goats' milk was more likely to be met with, but this may reflect the Mediterranean origin of the text.[16]

Cheese was often to be taken internally. For example, cheese with dry bread was part of an invalid diet for an asthmatic and included in the diet of a 'wit-sick' man.[1] Old cheese taken in goats' milk or sometimes roasted was recommended for dysentery.[2]

---

[1] Loyn 1970, 304.
[2] Whitelock 1955, 489; Robertson 1939, 39, 171, 241 ; Whitelock 1968, 10.
[3] Robertson 1939, 59, 193.
[4] Cockayne 1851, III lxv 2, II ix, xx, I lxvii, II lxv 2.
[5] op. cit., *Peri Didacheon* 37; I ix, II lxv 2.
[6] op. cit., II xix, li 3, xxv, *Lacnunga* 17.
[7] op. cit., *Lacnunga* 104.
[8] op. cit., III x, II li, III xiv 1.
[9] op. cit., I i 3, 15, iii 8, viii 2 etc; I xxxi 7, *Lacnunga* XVIIIa, II xxvi, I xl.
[10] op. cit., lxxxiv.
[11] op. cit., III xliii.
[12] op. cit., II li 2,3,4, liii, lvi 1, III xxiii 1, lxv, *Lacnunga* LI, LII, LII, LVI, LX, etc.
[13] op. cit., I ii 22.
[14] op. cit., II lxv 1.
[15] op. cit., *Lacnunga* 3.
[16] op. cit., I I 2, II li 4, lxv 2, *Lacnunga* XXXVII, Lac 29.
[1] op. cit., III *Peri Didacheon* 52, III xli.
[2] op. cit., II lvi 4.

Artefacts

A number of factors militate against the survival and/or identification of dairy equipment but butter and cheese churns were identified at Lund.[1]

Conclusion

Cows perhaps became more common as the dairy animal on estates though peasants may have continued to rely on sheep for their own dairy products and in some areas – the marshes of Essex and Kent, for example – dairying continued to be based on sheep.[2]

The impression is that cheese was the most important dairy product; butter was made from the whey, and the buttermilk drunk. Alternatively butter could be made first, and then cheese could be made from the buttermilk, again this would leave whey to be drunk. Consuming dairy products in this way makes an economical use of the resource. There would have been no standardisation and very great regional diversity, particularly where cheeses were concerned.[3]

If the leechdoms reflect general practice, butter was used primarily for cooking vegetables and herbs. Alternatives for this purpose existed – water, milk, oil and lard – and butter may have been something of a luxury. However, butter was to be produced for the lord's table by the cheese maker of *Rectitudines Singularum Personarum*, which may hint at the same use as today, butter for putting on cooked vegetables or as a relish for bread.

---

[1] Roesdahl 1982, 124; Edlin 1949, 55, 78, 104; Hartley 1954, 481, 486; Liebermann 1898, 455.
[2] Seebohm 1952, 157.
[3] Furnivall 1868, 85.

pulfer camb.

18. Butchery

Nature of the Evidence

The bulk of the information comes from animal bone reports, but these do not follow a standard format, nor do they always explore the same questions or give comparable information. The picture then is necessarily a sketchy one.

Place of Slaughter

All skeletal parts of meat animals were found in domestic waste pits in late Anglo-Saxon Exeter,[1] as at Hamwih, Bedford, and other mid/late urban centres.[2] In these cases complete carcasses could have been brought in from the agricultural hinterland, but it seems more likely that slaughter was carried out in the towns. Slaughter on the consumers' premises would have given them the benefit of all the perishable products.

Butchery: the Butcher

Consumers may have slaughtered their own animals, perhaps with the help of kinsmen and friends, or a professional butcher who would have come to their premises. The slaughterman would kill the animal and hang it up, and may have returned to joint and salt the carcass.[3] It would have made sense to pay a skilled butcher: contaminated or damaged meat will deteriorate quickly.[4]

Payments for this service may have been made in kind. Butchers may then have had meat to sell to people who could not afford a whole animal. Rather than depending on a casual supply of meat, butchers may then have bought animals for slaughter if there was a steady demand. In time the households who had had their own beasts slaughtered, might find advantages in buying from a butcher. There are urban sites where the high percentages of waste bones argue for the presence of specialised butcheries. By the end of the tenth century oxen had to be slaughtered in the presence of two witnesses and it might have been easier to arrange for witnesses in a centre of population.[5] The terms 'slaughterer, flayer' (*hyldere*), 'butcher' (*flæsc tawere*), 'meat market' (*flæsc stræt*) and '[retail] butcher' (*flæscmangere*) were in use by end of the period.[6] In the country farmers no doubt continued to slaughter, process and store their own meat.

---

[1] Maltby 1979.
[2] Bourdillon 1980, 185; Grant 1979, 70ff, 141.
[3] Groves in Kuper 1987, 97.
[4] Walker in Fenton & Kisban 1986, 129, 130.
[5] Whitelock 1955, 404.
[6] Bosworth & Toller 1898, I 581, 291, 290, 291; Barlow et al. 1976, 27.

Evidence for the Sale of Joints

Slaughter was carried on at the late ninth-century Whitehall farm site.[1] There is no evidence that prime – or any – bones had been gnawed or destroyed by dogs, and there is therefore a good case for the dispersal of selected joints: leg and shoulder of mutton, quarters of beef, probably to what was already a substantial market in the city of London.[2] In the case of pigs, the foot bones are in short supply, so trotters may have been disposed of while the main joints of pork were salted.[3] As waste, they could have been fed back to pigs, but they may have been sold as delicacies.

Method of Slaughter

There was a biblical taboo against eating animals that had been strangled, and animals often had their necks severed with an axe.[4] Later, animals were forced to the ground [5]so the sitting cow in the Bayeux Tapestry may represent an animal pulled to its knees prior to slaughter.[6] At Hamwih there was no evidence for pole-axing, so the animals were possibly killed by having their throats cut.[7] One fragment of pig's skull from tenth-century Skeldergate had a round hole 30mm in diameter immediately anterior to the bregma, which may indicate the way it was killed.[8] The pole-axe, with a spike on the back of the blade, was used until very recently in conjunction with a cane, which was inserted through the hole in the skull to destroy the animal's nervous system.[9] At Exeter the fragmentary condition of the skulls of cattle may indicate stunning with a hammer as well as removal of the brain.[10] Presumably cattle were then bled.[11]

Nowadays animals are hung up after slaughter, so that muscles do not set in a contracted position which toughens the meat.[12] There is archaeological evidence that some sheep and cattle were strung up from the middle Saxon period on. Meat is left to age so that the accumulating lactic acid can break down the walls of the cell bodies which store protein-attacking enzymes. These enzymes attack the cell proteins causing them to degenerate into individual amino acids which generally have a strong flavour, and the tissue becomes softer, producing tender meat. This process is best carried out in cool conditions (1–3 degrees Centigrade), and takes from ten days to three weeks for beef, and from one week for lamb.[13] Animals killed in summer would need careful attention or the meat would become high, and this must have given rise to winter as the season for killing. Pork, which goes off more rapidly than other flesh, was traditionally never eaten in summer. A large animal presents the problem of getting the carcass cool quickly from its own body heat. The fact that Anglo-Saxon domestic food animals were smaller than most modern breeds was an advantage when it came to preservation.

---

[1] Chaplin 1971, 127.
[2] op. cit., 126, 135-6.
[3] op. cit., 127, 136.
[4] Owen 1841, 71; Turner 1828, III 36.
[5] Walker in Fenton & Kisban 1986, 129.
[6] D. M. Wilson 1985, Pl. 45.
[7] Holdsworth 1980, 9.
[8] O'Connor 1984, 29.
[9] Walker in Fenton and Kisban 1986, 131.
[10] Maltby 1979.
[11] Walker in Fenton & Kisban 1986, 129; McGee 1986, 96.
[12] op. cit., 98.
[13] op. cit.

Butchery Techniques

There is evidence that the Anglo-Saxons had sharp knives for jointing, and saws may also have been used.[1] The most commonly used instrument for cattle on some sites was a heavy chopper.[2] This technique would be considered heavy-handed in terms of modern butchery practice, where the careful separation of good and poor meat is important, but if the Saxon owner ate all his animal, this was not important.[3]

The Anglo-Saxon period seems to have witnessed a development in the techniques of butchery. On the Flaxengate site, before 900, cattle carcasses were rarely split lengthways to give two sides of beef, but in the tenth-century levels 15–30% of vertebrae had been cloven in the sagittal plane, and this percentage rises to 50% in late eleventh/twelfth-century levels. Sagittally-cloven vertebrae of sheep were also more common after the mid-eleventh century.[4] By the second half of the eleventh century, some cattle vertebrae at Skeldergate were cloven lengthways, indicating some carcasses were butchered as sides by this time.[5] On the eleventh- to thirteenth-century site of St. John's, Bedford, cattle and sheep vertebrae were generally split in this plane.[6] At Portchester the vertebrae were not generally found split, and splitting down the dorso-ventral axis was uncommon at Exeter before the post-medieval period.[7] This major development in technique seems to have been introduced first in the east of the country, so perhaps Scandinavian invaders played a part. Traditional methods seem to have continued beyond the area of this influence.

The Bayeux Tapestry shows a carcass from which the lower limbs have been removed, although the head is still on.[8] This may indicate the pig was to be spit-roasted. The picture reinforces the evidence that the hooves and lowest bones of the legs were regarded as waste, not worth transporting.[9]

On both Flaxengate and Bedford sites the evidence of butchery on pig bones was less extensive than on sheep and cattle, indicating that different joints were required.[10] It may be that the pig meat was to be processed differently, probably by salting.

Bones that were split for marrow extraction, but had not been cooked, indicate that some meat was de-boned before cooking.[11] At Exeter knife cuts on the distal epiphysis and lower end of the humerus were the results of cutting meat off the bone, not severance of the limbs, and there were corresponding cuts on the proximal portions of the radius and ulna.[12] Since this is the case, de-boned meat from substantial joints may have been eaten on sites where there is no trace of it in the archaeological record.

---

[1] Holdsworth 1980, 97; Cunliffe 1976, 272.
[2] op. cit., 273; Grant 1979, 59, 103.
[3] Cunliffe 1976, 273.
[4] O'Connor 1982, 16.
[5] O'Connor 1984, 20.
[6] Grant 1979, 106.
[7] Cunliffe 1976, 272; Maltby 1979, 39.
[8] D. M. Wilson 1985, Pl. 38.
[9] Rahtz 1979, 349; Hope-Taylor 1977, 328; Maltby 1979, 39.
[10] Grant 1979, 106.
[11] Holdsworth 1980, 97.
[12] Maltby 1979, 39.

Tongue & Brain

There is plentiful archaeological evidence for the extraction of the tongue and brain from all the meat animals throughout the period.[1]

Marrow

A practice for which there is both documentary and archaeological evidence is the removal of bone marrow. 'Gather together all the bones you can, and crush the bones with the back of an axe.' (*Ealle þa ban tosomne ðe man ge gaderian mæge, 7 cnocie man þa ban mid æxse yr.*)[2] The 'marrow' (*mearh*) here was to be used externally in salves and ointments, but there can be little doubt that it was generally used to enrich soups and stews.[3]

At Portchester so few whole bones were found, that the tentative suggestion was made that stews were a popular form of meat consumption.[4] At Yeavering in the early part of the period in a kitchen-like dwelling there was an abnormally high number of bone fragments, never more than two inches across, resulting from the chopping of bones laterally and longitudinally.[5] At tenth-century Skeldergate limb bones were reduced to small pieces, the majority having been chopped through lengthways, either specifically to extract the marrow, or to reduce the size of the pieces of bone for boiling in the stock-pot.[6] Chopping and splitting bones was practised on other sites too, and evidently continued all through the period on sites of different status. The chopping up of bones into small lengths presumably indicates stewing rather than roasting, a cooking method which would release the liquid marrow. The need to make full use of the food resource would have made the effort of chopping up meat and bones worthwhile.

Offal

Offal was probably a low-status food in Anglo-Saxon times.[7] None of the food rents makes specific reference to offal, although that could be because it is more perishable than muscle tissue.

Fats

The various forms of fat: 'grease' (*smeru*), 'bacon fat' (*swic*), 'lard' (*rysele*) and 'suet' (*gelyndo*) are mentioned in leechdoms, often for external use, but sometimes such items as 'half a cup of pure bacon fat melted' (*healfne cuppan clænes gemyltes swices*), or 'suet' (*rysle*) or 'unsalted grease' (*unsylt smeoru*) are to be taken.[8]

---

[1] op. cit.; O'Connor 1984, 17; Grant 1979, 106; Hope-Taylor 1977, 328; O'Connor 1982; Holdsworth 1980, 97.
[2] Cockayne 1851, III *Lacnunga* XXXI.
[3] O'Connor 1984, 17; Maltby 1979, 39; Buckland, Holdsworth & Monk 1976, 61ff.; Holdsworth 1980, 97; Cunliffe 1976, 272-3.
[4] op. cit.
[5] Hope Taylor 1977, 105.
[6] O'Connor 1984, 17.
[7] P. E. Jones 1976, 342; Owen 1841, 25, 71, 667.
[8] Cockayne 1851, III *Lacnunga* 116, I Herb. LXXV 5, III *Lacnunga* XXXIX.

Evidence of Site Status

Where there are bones, then they may provide evidence about the status of a site. At one extreme, on the royal site of Yeavering the typical fossil of the early halls is the expensive butcher's joint.[1] In contrast, the heads and feet of older cattle and pigs, and most parts of the low-status sheep seem to 'tell a story of scrupulous making-do' in Viking Age York.[2] However, this interpretation assumes that the inhabitants did not eat boned joints or salt pork, neither of which leaves any trace in the archaeological record.

[1] Hope-Taylor 1977, 327.
[2] O'Connor 1984, 26; Whitelock 1955, 222; Maltby 1979, 39.

19. Preservation & Storage

Some foods keep without any processing, and just have to be positioned away from creatures that would eat them. For short-term storage it was enough to hang some items from the wall or rafters.[1] After processing, meats and cheeses could be hung up in the same way for long-term storage.[2] This chapter is divided into three parts: (i) processing; (ii) storage; and (iii) manufacture and supply of salt.

(i) Processing

Drying

Drying – in the sun, in the open air, by a fire, in an oven or kiln – was perhaps the most important method, since it was used for staple foods: cereal crops and beans. *Leechdoms* give instructions on gathering, drying and powdering herbs.[3] It was assumed that if you could not use fresh herbs, then you would have some dried.[4] Mushrooms and other fungi can be dried threaded on a string.[5] Seaweed can be dried, as can peas and beans.[6]

Meat, birds and fish could also be dried.[7] Into recent times in Scotland fish were dried in different ways.[8] There is no reason why Anglo-Saxons should not have experimented and come up with different methods of preserving fish, each imparting its own taste. Less oily fish like flounder and large cod was probably dried, and made a very good reserve food in that it kept indefinitely.[9]

Smoking

Smoke is a complex substance containing alcohols, acids, phenolic compounds and some toxic substances which inhibit bacterial activity and retard fat oxidization, and impart the characteristic flavour of burning wood to the meat, poultry, fish and cheese it is used to treat.[10] A combination of salt curing and smoking was often used to minimise fat oxidization.[11] There is some evidence for ceramic fish smokers being used to flavour, rather than cure, the fish.[12]

The wood used for smoking would depend to some extent on the supply available. Traditionally birch wood is used for smoking hams and herrings, oak and beech for kippers, York hams and bacon. Hams are sometimes smoked with juniper wood to

---

[1] Colgrave 1940, 268-9.
[2] Owen 1841, 753.
[3] Cockayne 1851, I xxii, lxxii, *Lacnunga* XIVa, III xxii 2.
[4] op. cit., *Peri Didacheon*, II xxxix.
[5] Renfrew 1985, 17.
[6] Cockayne 1851, *Lacnunga* 116.
[7] C. A. Wilson 1973, 113; Severin 1978.
[8] McNeill 1963.
[9] Roesdahl 1982, 120; Tannahill 1973, 216; Horander in Fenton & Kisban 1986, 54; Furnivall 1868, 98; Tannahill 1973, 216.
[10] Lauwerier 1986, 210; Cockayne 1851, II xxiv; Ayrton 1975, 11; Moryson 1617, IV 167; Roesdahl 1982, 120.
[11] McGee 1986, 104.
[12] Moorhouse in Aston 1988.

impart a gin-like flavour.[1] Dried seaweed was also used to smoke bacon in sea-coast counties. Smoking may also have occurred incidentally as foodstuffs were hung from rafters in smoky rooms.

Pickling

Pickling involves impregnating the foodstuff with acid, either directly with vinegar, though whey and various alcoholic liquids may also have been used, or indirectly by brining, which produces a medium in which acid-producing bacteria grow.[2] Salting was such an important means of preservation in Anglo-Saxon times that it is dealt with separately.

Pickling in honey has a similar effect, since a very sugary solution will also draw water across the cell walls and dehydrate bacteria which might otherwise cause food to decay, and was likely to have been used in Anglo-Saxon times.[3]

Boiling

Fruit will keep much longer when boiled down, so the natural sugars are concentrated.[4] The addition of honey before boiling would enhance this effect. The custom of boiling down rose hips and storing the resulting mush in jars, is continent-wide, suggesting its antiquity; the same method was probably applied to other fruit.[5] Such preserves may have been used as a relish.[6]

Salting

Salt draws water across the cell membranes of some bacteria, dehydrating them when they would otherwise cause decay. Salting also causes the foodstuff to be impregnated with acid.[7]

Salting was essential to food preservation in Anglo-Saxon England. The salter is one of the tradesmen of the *Colloquy*, and ranks in importance with the ploughman, fisherman and smith.[8] When asked 'How does your craft benefit us?' (*Hwæt us fremaþ cræft þin?*), the salter replies,

> 'My trade greatly benefits you all. None of you would take any pleasure in your meals or food without my hospitable art. How can anyone appreciate very sweet foods to the full without the savour of salt? Who could fill his cellar or storeroom without my skill? Look, you would even lose your butter and cheese, and you can't even enjoy your vegetables without making use of me.'

> (*Þearle fremaþ cræft min eow eallum. Nan eower blisse brycð on gererduncge oþþe mete, buton cræft min gistliþe him beo ...Hwylc manna þurhwerodum þurhbrycþ mettum buton swæcce sealtes? Hwa gefylþ cleafan his oþþe hedderna buton cræfte*

---

[1] Edlin 1949, 41, 77.
[2] Foote & Wilson 1970, 163; Holmes 1952, 92; Sass 1975, 109, 118-9.
[3] McGee 1986, 370.
[4] op. cit., 171.
[5] Sayce 1946.
[6] Clifton 1983, 19, 32.
[7] McGee 1986, 173.
[8] Garmonsway 1978.

minon? Efne, butergeþweor ælc cygerunn losaþ eow buton ic hyrde ætwese eow, þe ne furþon þæt an wyrtum eowrum buton me brucaþ.)[1]

Leechdoms indicate meat and dairy produce were often salted.[2] As well as preserving fats, fruit and vegetables, salt was important for treating the muscly parts of carcasses.[3]

Bay salt, coarse and heavily polluted with impurities, particularly calcium and magnesium salts, was apparently 'inferior' and did not penetrate meat or fish quickly enough to preserve the flesh.[4] On the other hand it was also said to be 'preferred to finer salts for preserving processes', since fine salt tended to seal the surface tissues, but not to enter further.[5] Traditional recipes reconcile this contraction, since they tend to contain both refined and bay salt.[6] Just how pure Anglo-Saxon salt would have been is a matter of conjecture, although white, i.e. relatively refined, salt seems to have been preferred.[7] Although it was probably not realised in Anglo-Saxon times that saltpetre (potassium nitrate) was useful in the curing process, nitrites would have built up in the wooden utensils and the salting larders.[8]

Dry salting, or curing, would have been more expensive than brining, as more salt is required, and time and energy would be expended in pounding salt to a powder.[9] With this method it is useful to have pepper to coat the knuckle area of hams, to prevent maggots)[10].

Whatever the method used, bacon was produced in quantity. An inventory of Thorney Abbey listed 43 flitches of bacon and to Peterborough were to go 'a hundred flitches and all the delicacies that go with them' (*hundteongig fliccena 7 eal þa smean ðe þerto gebyriað*).[11] The highest quality bacon comes from lean-fleshed primitive breeds like the Tamworth, which has not been crossed with Chinese pigs.[12]

A traditional curing mixture in Yorkshire and Westmoreland was common salt, bay salt, saltpetre, black pepper and honey. All these ingredients were available to the Anglo-Saxons at least towards the end of the period. The hams were turned and rubbed with the mixture twice a week for a month, then soaked for twenty-four hours and hung up to dry.[13] Even with this cure, York hams were considered inferior to those of Gloucestershire and Buckinghamshire, since pigs in these two counties were fed on beech-mast which gave the hams a special nutty flavour.[14]

---

[1] op. cit., 35-6.
[2] Cockayne 1851, II iv, vi, xxxii, *Lacnunga* 39, 112.
[3] Holmes 1952, 92; Sass 1975, 109, 118-9; Kundergraber in Fenton & Owen 1981, 172-3.
[4] Tannahill 1973, 212.
[5] C. A. Wilson 1973, 39.
[6] Hartley 1954, 329ff.
[7] Cockayne 1851, I v, vi, xxxviii 5, II x.
[8] McGee 1986, 509; Hartley 1954, 326.
[9] Horander in Fenton & Kisban 1986, 55.
[10] Kuper 1977, 4.
[11] Robertson 1939, 74-5.
[12] Wiseman 1986, 6, 63, 65.
[13] Ayrton 1975, 79.
[14] op. cit.

If after dry salting the meat was just dried, it was 'green' bacon, but it could then be smoked. Meat pickled in brine could also be smoked subsequently.[1]

A number of animals were probably slaughtered throughout the autumn because they had been fattened up on pasture, or, in the case of pigs, acorns and beech-mast; also flies are absent on cool nights.[2]

Most of the large numbers of fish referred to in food rents must have been preserved, very often by salting.

Other Uses of Salt

Perhaps because of what was seen as its purifying quality, salt was part of a specially consecrated diet for anyone pledged to undergo the ordeal.[3] It was also needed for ecclesiastical ritual, and for the ancient charm addressed to *Erce* for the fertility of land.[4]

Salt was also used much as it is today: as a flavouring with radish, for cooking with beans, with meal and butter to give a savoury pottage, in a marinade for beef, or even for an emetic drink.[5]

Salt intake would need to increase slightly with a predominantly cereal diet, but the Anglo-Saxon population were unlikely to have been short of salt when quantities of salt meat were consumed. The prevalence of salting as a means of preservation perhaps explains the comparatively large drink allowances.

(ii) Storage

Cereals

After harvesting and carting, when they were reasonably dry, sheaves were stacked outside, with heads to the centre of the rick, which was then thatched to keep the rain off, or in granaries (the term *bere ærn* [barn] does not seem to have been used before c.950).[6] Perhaps the owners of large estates had the resources to build barns large enough to accommodate sheaves, and perhaps they needed to do this if they had no one to keep a permanent eye on ricks standing in the open, but a barn came to mean a covered building where a cleaned crop was stored.[7] Peas and beans were also threshed and, presumably, stored in the barn.[8] The official appointed to have charge of the grain was the 'barn-keeper/granger' (*berebrytt*).[9] Those without the resources to build barns, or large supplies of grain or legumes, used pits (not a particularly successful method), or stored the food in their houses.[10]

---

[1] op. cit., 78.
[2] Wiseman 1986, 178.
[3] Whitelock 1955, 385.
[4] Cockayne 1851, I 402.
[5] op. cit., I xvii 2, xxxi 1, lxxxiii, II vii, I lix.
[6] Liebermann 1898, 454; Monk 1977, 278; Owen 1841, 327; Cockayne 1851, III MS. Cott. Vitell. E. xviii. fol. 61; Cunliffe 1976, 126; Bosworth & Toller 1898.
[7] Grube 1934, 145.
[8] op. cit.
[9] Trow Smith 1957, 138.
[10] Monk 1977, 341; Hickin 1964, 89; Turner 1828, II 513.

Like grain, flour and meal had to be kept dry in order to deter insect infestation and the growth of moulds. Flour or meal could be stored in chests or bins, the *cyste* and *mydercan* of *Gerefa*.[1] An ark was generally used for meal, and a bin for flour. It seems likely that the meal ark was a convenient place to store other foods that needed to be kept dry. Moreover, such containers could be padlocked, so that provisions were under lock and key.

Bread could also have been stored in the meal chest, but it was probably not kept for more than a few days, being baked as necessary, although a kind of unleavened bread that would keep for weeks, months, or even years, was traditional in Europe.[2] Such bread may have been baked when there was a surplus of grain, for it was probably a safer way of preserving cereals than leaving them in store in their raw state.

Containers

Storage Jars

'Crock' (*croc*) was probably the Anglo-Saxon term for a storage jar, some of which had a relatively narrow neck and an everted rim, suitable for tying on a cover which may have been greased.[3] Oil or clarified butter may have been used as an airtight seal in the conservation of meat.[4]

Barrels and Boxes

Barrels and tubs were used for the storage of wet and dry goods.[5] Examples of barrels have been found in archaeological contexts, since they were re-used as well linings. It is generally assumed that barrels were used for wine, but the Norman period oval cask found in the bottom of a food storage pit at Pevensey Castle may have been used for pickling.[6] Time-consuming to make, and needing skilled craftsmanship, a new barrel may have been used first for wine, then, if it became tainted, for pickling, before being relegated for use as a well-lining.

The small boxes for which fittings, including locks, were found might have included in their contents particularly valuable spices.[7]

Storage Conditions

Alfred records in his addition to Orosius that Wulfstan told him that 'there is among the Estonians a tribe that can create coldness' (*þær is mid Estum an mægð þæt hi magon cycle gewyrcan*).[8] They used it for preserving dead bodies during a lying-in period, but if 'anyone sets down two vessels full of ale or water, then they cause one or the other to become frozen over, whether it be summer or winter' (*man asette twegen fætels full ealað oððe wæteres, hy gedoð þæt oþer bið oferfroren, sam hit sy sumor sam winter*).[1]

[1] Liebermann 1898, 455.
[2] Weaver in Fenton & Owen 1981, 355; Moberg 1973, II 38-9.
[3] Fenton & Kisban 1986, 114-5; West 1963, 246-72; 1982, 405.
[4] McGee 1986, 104; Bonser 1963, 191; Ayrton 1975, 147-9; CA Wilson 1973, 64-5; Kuper 1977, 38, 41.
[5] Edlin 1949, 72, 99.
[6] Spriggs 1977, 12.
[7] Evison 1987, 103; Ottaway 1985, 7-12.
[8] Sweet 1954, 22.
[1] op. cit.

This can be effected with saltpetre (potassium nitrate), but is recorded because it was evidently not practised in Anglo-Saxon England. In any case, unheated storerooms were likely to have temperatures not much above freezing for some of the winter months. Stores had probably diminished by the time hot weather came, and restocking of dairy goods and meat would not start until the advent of cooler weather.

Butter needs to be stored somewhere cool, since it will become rancid even when salted.[1] Unsalted cheesewould have to be treated as butter, although it would not go rancid as quickly as unsalted butter. In many parts of Britain it was the custom to bury butter in suitable containers, in peat bogs and a similar method may have been adopted for mutton fat in areas of Scandinavian influence.[2] The partial exclusion of air helped keep the fat fresh. Perhaps most households had to make do with cool storerooms. Pots made of porous clay could have been dipped in water which took up heat to evaporate, lowering the temperature of the contents. Salted cheeses could be stored somewhere dry, in the meal chest, for example, or 'hung up'.

Eggs may have been preserved in ash pits, old malt, straw or bran, but results were often less than satisfactory.[3]

Root vegetables could have been stored in cellars or dark storerooms. By spring, when the roots were less palatable, their shoots could be used as early salad.[4]

Storehouses were separate outbuildings, but storerooms could probably be found within large dwellings.[5] The place where salt meat was kept was called, on account of the preponderance of bacon, a 'bacon house' (spic-hus).

Cellars

There is archaeological and documentary evidence for cellars, which are ideal for storage, remaining cool in summer and winter.[6] Ad hoc cellars were probably holes in the ground, like the food storage pit from the Norman period at Pevensey Castle.[7]

Responsibility for Domestic Stores

Girdle hangers found in pagan Anglian graves may represent the bunch of keys worn by Roman women as a symbol of their authority and probably indicated the status of their owner.[8] A chatelaine has generally been seen as evidence of matronly authority, and this would seem to be confirmed by Æthelbert's law code: *Gif friwif locbore leswæs hwæt gedeð ...xxx scll. gebete*. This is translated by Fell as, 'If a freewoman in charge of the keys is found cheating ...then 30 shillings compensation is to be paid'.[9] This law would seem to parallel the Welsh code where

---

[1] Hartley 1954, 481.
[2] Renfrew 1985, 14; Brothwell 1969, 44; Furnivall 1868, 98.
[3] Todd 1987, 175.
[4] Kundegraber in Fenton & Owen 1981, 173.
[5] Colgrave 1940, 346; Olsen & Schmidt 1977, 235; Seebohm 1952, 95.
[6] Hodges 1982, 131; Wiseman 1986, 178; Williams 1984, 133; Biddle 1976, 14, 40, 44, 339-40.
[7] Spriggs 1977, 12.
[8] Meaney 1981, 178-9; Evison 1987, 116-7.
[9] Fell 1984, 60-1.

the freewoman had responsibility for her stores.[1] *II Canute* confirms this since it states when legislating about stolen goods:

> 'But it is her duty to guard the keys of the following – that is her storeroom key and her chest key and her (?)cupboard. If the goods have been put in any of these, she shall be held guilty.'
>
> *(Ac ðara cægan heo sceal weardian, þæt is hire heddernes cæge 7 hyre cyste cæge 7 hire tægan; gyf hit under ðyssa ænigum gebroht byð, ðone bið heo scyldig.)*[2]

Pests

Probably both the house mouse and black rat were present in Anglo-Saxon England.[3] Corn had to be kept from these pests which could make inroads on the stores, contaminate the grain they did not eat and transmit pestilence.[4] The reeve was cautioned not to neglect even a 'a mousetrap' (*musfellan*).[5] The remains of cats are found with remarkable frequency on Anglo-Saxon sites, including the earliest, and an accredited mouser was given a value of four pence in the Welsh Laws.[6] Bones of weasels and polecats found on early medieval sites may indicate their importance in the domestic economy, since they were tamed and trained to catch rats and mice.[7]

Flour, cereals and cereal products, cheese and dried fruits can become infested by the flour mite which causes digestive disorders in those who consume infected foodstuffs.[8] Insects can also transmit moulds from one commodity to another as well as disease.[9] Stores would have to be periodically checked, so that if there was infestation of any sort it could be dealt with before it contaminated quantities of food. On a large estate the reeve was responsible for the stores – their security and condition, cautioned to neglect 'neither grain nor sheaf, meat nor fat, cheese nor rennet.' (*ne corn ne sceaf, ne flæsc ne flotsmeru, ne cyse ne cyslyb*)[10] In monasteries this duty rested with the cellarer.[11]

(iii) Salt Production & Supply

Vessels for Salt

A container made of lead and called a *lead* was probably used for salt production and during the salting process as it would not be corroded by the salt.[12] At Bremesgrave, Worcester, which was in the king's demesne, Domesday records six *plumbi* ('leads') for boiling salt, and at *Terdeberie* were two plumbi.[13] Provided lead was not in direct contact with flames, there was no reason not to use it, as it has a melting point of

---

[1] Owen 1841, 95, 517.
[2] Robertson 1925, 214-5.
[3] Prummel 1983, 245; O'Connor 1988, 39.
[4] Bonser 1963, 76.
[5] Liebermann 1898, 455.
[6] Clutton Brock in Wilson 1976, 384; Bell 1977.
[7] Seebohm 1952, 133.
[8] Hickin 1964, 143.
[9] op. cit., 93, 98, 103.
[10] Knowles 1940, 462.
[11] Liebermann 1898, 453.
[12] Loyn 1970, 108.
[13] Commissioners 1819, 413-14.

327.5 degrees Centigrade. *Gerefa* and inventories list the *lead* with other catering equipment.[1] Archaeological evidence for such containers is likely to be scarce, as lead is a valuable metal, easy to melt down and re-use, but some fairly large lead vessels are known from the middle Saxon period. One from Riby Crossroads (dated by reference to eighth- to ninth-century pottery) is 285mm deep with a diameter of 515mm.[2] Similar are two lead vessels from a large middle Saxon site at Flixborough.[3] The later period also provides evidence for such vessels, that from Westley Waterless, Cambs. for example.[4]

Salt Production

Salt can be made from the ashes of certain plants, and from seaweed.[5] However, there is no evidence that this method was resorted to in Anglo-Saxon England, perhaps because no district was very far from either the sea, or salt-producing areas. Bede mentioned that England possessed salt pits (*Hit hafað eac þis land sealtseaþas*) which may refer to salt springs and/or pits into which the sea flowed at high tide.[6] Water trapped in the pit evaporated in the sun's heat and the wind to leave a deposit of salt. However, in Domesday salt pans were usually conveyed with 'vessels for the boiling of salt'.[7]

Domesday mentions 285 salt pans in Sussex alone, one hundred at *Rameslie*, a lost place-name, and most other seacoast counties have large numbers.[8] In the main the pans ran from Barnstaple in north Devon, round the south coast, and up round East Anglia. The waters of the Bristol channel may have been too turgid for successful salt extraction, or perhaps the superior salt of Worcestershire with its 50 *salinæ* was near enough at hand. There were also *salinæ* in Cheshire (10), Herefordshire (8), Gloucestershire (7), Shropshire (6), Warwickshire (3) and Oxfordshire (1).[9]

The salt from geological deposits in Worcestershire was being extracted from salt springs at least as early as the late seventh century,[10] according to documentary evidence, but excavation has yielded evidence of narrow stone furnaces in a fifth to sixth-century context.[11] Middle Saxon activity involved channelling the River Salwarpe, and the construction of a brushwood trackway carbon-dated between 686 and 788.[12] Charters of the eighth and ninth centuries include salt pits or salt production plant.[13]

Sometimes the Domesday survey indicates that the salt-works were not objects of great importance: some yield scarcely any revenue. The 285 *salinæ* in Sussex averaged two shillings and five-pence halfpenny, but one salt-works in Devon paid

---

[1] Liebermann 1898, 455; Robertson 1939, 75.
[2] Ken Steedman, pers. comm.
[3] Ben Whitewell, pers. comm.
[4] Wilson 1976, 267; Fox 1948.
[5] Kuper 1977, 102; Roesdahl 1982, 120.
[6] Miller 1890, I, 1 26.
[7] Turner 1828, II 547; C. A. Wilson 1973, 29; Darby 1940, 39.
[8] Turner 1828, III 247.
[9] op. cit.
[10] Finberg 1972, 12, 86.
[11] Gaimster et al. 1990, 189.
[12] op. cit.
[13] op. cit., 98, 101.

£13.10s.[1] By way of comparison, a salt pan in Droitwich was worth four shillings when a house in Worcester was valued at one; five salt pans in Halesowen were worth sixty shillings, the mill ten shillings.[2]

At the time of the Domesday survey there seems to have been no standard measure for salt, which is recorded in ambrae, bulliones, mensurae, mittae, *sextaria and summae*.[3] An amber was four bushels, so that we know the production of v salinae de cx ambris salis at Wassington in Sussex to have been 11 tons.

Salt Workers

Salt workers seem to have been men working in a small way, renting their own salt pans. It is likely that many were fishermen or closely associated with fishermen.[4] Some may have been full-time salt-boilers, like Picot Sannarius of Winchester.[5] Block salt required considerable effort to reduce to powder, and the individual, Hack-Salt, who is recorded in the Winton Domesday, may have had an occupational name (though equally, this may be a nickname).[6]

Provision of a Salt Supply

Large establishments were anxious to secure the salt supplies necessary for catering on a large scale. The earliest reference to the important Worcestershire salt trade occurs in a charter of King Wulfhere, who reigned from 657-74. He made over 50 *manentes* at Hanbury with all the meadows, woods and brine pits belonging thereto to Abbot Colman.[7] By effecting an exchange of properties, including salt-works, the king and the community at Worcester seem to have finalised the convenient provision of their salt supply in 716/17.[8] There are other eighth-century references to a salt supply, like the exemption from toll of a ship bearing salt in favour of a Kentish nunnery, and in 732 Ethelbert gave land at Sampton, Kent, suitable for the boiling of salt, to Abbot Dunn, plus 120 laden wagons of firewood annually for cooking the salt.[9] It was common to provide 'wood for boiling salt' (*ligna ad coquendum sal*) with grants of salterns.[10]

Similar grants continued to be made in the ninth and tenth centuries, sometimes in connection with weirs, so provision was made for the fish caught there to be preserved.[11] By the end of the period both Glastonbury and Sherborne Abbeys had procured coastal estates in Lyme, whose importance seems to have rested entirely on the salterns.[12]

---

[1] Commissioners 1819, 413.
[2] op. cit.; Bland, Brown & Tawney 1914.
[3] Commissioners 1819, 415.
[4] Loyn 1970, 106.
[5] Barlow et al. 1976, 85, 115.
[6] op. cit., 96.
[7] Finberg 1972, 12, 86.
[8] Loyn 1970, 106; Whitelock 1955, 450.
[9] Whitelock 1955, 450-1.
[10] Page 1985, 221.
[11] Robertson 1939, 46.
[12] Keen in Haslam 1984, 229.

By the end of the tenth century some ecclesiastical establishments had more than provided for their own needs for salt, and were renting out salt-works as going concerns.[1]

Droitwich, Worcs., the chief salt town of England, was a very specialised community in which, while the majority of the pans belonged to king or earl, many other people had interests.[2] Individuals also negotiated a salt supply. According to the Winton Domesday, Siward the Moneyer owed William of Chesney lodgings, salt and water.[3] Probably most smaller households were dependent on the salt pedlars who transported salt from the salt pans on the coast, or from the wiches of Cheshire and Worcestershire, by way of the extensive system of salt-ways.[4]

Tolls

A cartload of Cheshire salt drawn by two or more oxen and travelling to another county paid fourpence at the time of Domesday.[5] Salt pedlars from Cheshire were given a preferential rate of one penny per cart.[6] The temptation with tolls based on the pack-load, was to load a horse with as much as it could possibly carry.[7] The rate was twopence for a horse-load or eight men's loads.[8] The fact that salt from Droitwich commanded a higher toll than salt from elsewhere perhaps suggests that it was thought superior. The cost of transport and the taxes probably exceeded the price of the salt itself.

[1] Finberg 1972, 110, 126, 133.
[2] Whitelock 1952, 115-6.
[3] Barlow et al. 1976, 106.
[4] Finberg 1972, 73; Hill 1981, map 189; Smith 1964, I 19, 218, 220, 222, III 62.
[5] Langdon 1986, 49.
[6] Whitelock 1952, 116.
[7] Langdon 1986, 49.
[8] Whitelock 1952, 116.

20. Methods of Cooking

Fire

Wood

Securing a Supply

It is sometimes difficult to ascertain for what purpose wood mentioned in grants is intended.[1] 'Wooding' (*uuidigunge*) is the only unambiguous term for fuel.[2]

Cutting and gathering wood is one of the summer tasks listed in *Gerefa*. Wood was taken back to the homestead, sometimes in carts drawn by oxen as illustrated in two early eleventh-century calendars.[3] Splitting the wood was a job for winter,[4] after which it was stacked into a *scidhræc*[5] and kept dry.[6]

A peasant household presumably found its own firewood. *Rectitudines Singularum Personarum* refers to 'the right of cutting wood according to the custom of the estate' (*wuduræden be landside*).[7] A larger household called for more fuel, and the owners of large establishments used their power to ensure that they were supplied with wood. At Hurstbourne Priors, Hampshire, in about 1050, the *ceorlas* had to supply '4 fothers of wood, split and made into a stack in their own time' (*IIII foðera aclofenas gauolwyda to scidhræc on hiora agenre hwile*).[8] Royal charters sometimes granted the right to gather firewood.[9] Tithes and guild dues included firewood.[10]

Different Types Of Wood

Anglo-Saxons who had to make fires for cooking no doubt knew what is now only accessible to most of us in mnemonic poems like 'Logs to Burn'.[11] An analysis of the charcoal in a seventh-century hearth provides evidence of hazel, hawthorn, oak and poplar or willow.[12] Assuming that it is willow rather than poplar charcoal, all the woods are good fuel. Unfortunately there are too many imponderables to make it possible to work out by careful excavation and analysis of hearth material what kind of fire had been made, and therefore what sort of cooking process may have been undertaken.

To spit-roast a pig of 120lb dead weight, the ideal fuel is 15 cwt of large oak logs, a foot long and thoroughly seasoned, cloven into halves or thirds and placed on end to form a bed which will burn steadily. On this 15 cwt of ash with a diameter

---

[1] Robertson 1939, 13; Page 1985, 221.
[2] op. cit.
[3] Temple 1976, no. 199.
[4] Liebermann 1898, 454.
[5] Robertson 1939, 241.
[6] Bosworth & Toller 1898, 213.
[7] Liebermann 1898, 449.
[8] Robertson 1939, 241.
[9] Whitelock 1955, 484; Finberg 1972, 105.
[10] Whitelock 1955, 560; Field 1972, 209.
[11] Edlin 1949, 62-3, 156-7, 170.
[12] Matthews in Hawkes 1985.

of 4-5 inches and in foot lengths (cut at least a month previously) is used to provide local areas of fiercer heat in line with the quarters of the animal.

Other Fuel

Glosses give Old English *col* for *carbo* (coal), and *sinder* for *scorium* (cinder, clinker), and since *col* and *sinder* are Old English words, this suggests they represent things known to the Anglo-Saxons from an early period.[1] Charcoal may also have been used as a domestic fuel, particularly in braziers. Although reeds and straw produce a hot fire, and were used for baking, they burn very quickly, and processes like roasting would have been difficult.[2] It may be that woodland was decreasing during the Anglo-Saxon period, and that some areas of the Midlands, Yorkshire and the Fens had no woodland at all.[3] If this was the case, then other, less ideal, fuels would have had to have been exploited, with a consequent modification of cooking processes.

It seems that even fires which could call on the best fuel were what we would regard as excessively smoky.[4] Soot (*hrum*) was evidently deposited on utensils in some quantity.[5] Food cooked by direct exposure to the heat of the fire, or in open pans may have had a smoky flavour.

Fire Making

Fire-steels are often found in pagan Anglo-Saxon graves, together with flints or pyrites against which the iron could be struck to obtain a spark.[6] These fire-steels very often doubled as pursemounts, the purse almost certainly containing tinder for starting a fire, and sometimes a flint too.[7] These could be prestige items. The grave of a young man, a member of the ruling elite, buried in Sutton Hoo Mound 17 contained a strike-a-light still associated with a leather pouch.[8] They were evidently in use throughout the period, occurring in such late Saxon contexts as the town of Thetford and the palace site at Cheddar.[9] Tinder was often made from touchwood or *punk*, rotten wood decayed by fungal attack, birch bark, dried brushwood, gorse or straw.[10]

'Bellows' (*blestbælg*) were known.[11] Fire tongs are shown also in the Anglo-Saxon calendar, BL Cott. Julius A IV.[12] Pokers and a *fyr-scofl* are recorded.[13] Firecovers were used to keep the fire alive at a time when fires were not particularly easy to light, and to prevent sparks escaping.[14]

[1] Wright 1871, 32.
[2] Corran 1975, 37; Mellows 1980, 2.
[3] Rackham in Biddick 1984, 75.
[4] Owen 1841, 25.
[5] Cockayne 1851, I xi 2, lxxii, for example.
[6] Meaney 1981, 104; Cunliffe 1976, 195; West 1982, 73; Welch 1983, passim.
[7] Brown 1977, 451-77.
[8] Nenk et al. 1992, 266.
[9] Rahtz 1979, 267.
[10] Edlin 1949, 159; Mellows 1980, 2.
[11] Pheifer 1974, 25; Bosworth & Toller 1898, I 82; Riddles 37, 86; Dodwell 1982, 73.
[12] Wright 1871, 32.
[13] Bosworth & Toller 1898, I 354.
[14] Hurst in Cunliffe 1964, 126.

Cooking: Direct Application of Heat

Food could be cooked by direct exposure to the fire, or by heating in a utensil placed in, on, above, under or beside the fire. Such fires were often the domestic hearth for warming a room and its occupants, as well as for cooking. The fires may have been lit directly on an unprepared floor or more commonly on a hearth made of clay, tiles and stones.[1] Bede's account, 'A great fire was kindled in the middle of the house' (*Wæs micel fyr onæled on middum þam huse*) accords with archaeological evidence from West Stow – and elsewhere.[2] Later hearths may have been built against a wall, if this was backed with stone.[3]

There is evidence that hearths were also made in the open.[4] No doubt cooking was carried on outside on suitable days, when the houses could be kept cool and free of smoke.

It is possible that the Anglo-Saxons used chafing dishes and stoves, in effect portable hearths.[5]

Cooking: Indirect Application of Heat

If utensils were available, but were not fireproof, their contents, liquid or semi-liquid, could be heated by 'pot-boilers', stones heated on the hearth and then dropped into the vessels, using tongs or dampened wooden shovels, as was the case at Sutton Courtney.[6] There is evidence that heated stones were used for boiling and roasting material in troughs and hide vessels too.[7] On occasion a heated iron or poker might be used to heat a liquid. Both methods are referred to in leechdoms.[8]

If no utensils were available, then a cooking pit, probably lined with stones, could have been used. Turner deduced that Anglo-Saxons may have cooked their victuals in pits since *seathan*[sic] (to seethe, simmer, boil) was derived from *seath*[sic] (a pit).[9] An experiment in pot-boiler cookery showed that a ten-pound leg of mutton wrapped in clean straw tied with a twisted straw rope, as indicated in early Irish literature, was cooked after 3 hours 40 minutes uncontaminated by ash or mud.[10]

Ovens

Earth Ovens

Earth ovens used the heat from glowing stones heated on a nearby fire. A pit was dug into the ground, was perhaps lined with stones, and either pre-heated with brushwood, or half-filled with red hot stones on which the meat, packed in clay or leaves, was placed. It was then covered with more stones which, as they cooled, may have been replaced, or they may have been covered with earth or turf to retain the heat. In either case the meat would cook in a time comparable to that taken by a modern oven.[11]

[1] West 1982, 37, 38, 41, 62, 71, 141, 194.
[2] Miller 1890, I, 1 180-1; West 1982, 37, 38.
[3] Owen 1841, 523.
[4] Copley 1958, 172-3; Bell 1977, 276-86.
[5] Pheifer 1974, 3; Cockayne 1851, III lxii; Wright 1871, 99.
[6] Copley 1958, 172-3.
[7] Renfrew 1985, 23.
[8] Cockayne 1851, II xxv, xxxiii, No. 59.
[9] Turner 1828, III 34.
[10] C. A. Wilson 1973, 64-5.
[11] op. cit., 64-5; Roesdahl 1982, 124.

Hot-air Ovens

Ovens in which the contents were cooked in hot air were known to the Anglo-Saxons. The *ofn* which was one of the 'many things a farmstead must have' (*fela ðinga sceal to tune*) was probably of this type.[1] There were three main methods of heating an oven. One, still in use today, is to burn faggots of brushwood in the oven, raking out the ashes before putting in the food to be cooked.[2] Another method was to light a fire beneath, or around or on top of an oven – a small 'oven' could be made by inverting a pot and putting embers around and on it. The third method was to heat the oven by building it into a construction where hot air would be conducted round it in flues. The second and third methods are still in use, as is a combination of them.

According to the literature, ovens could be quite large: big enough for a man,[3] as are some ovens in the archaeological record. At the fifth- to seventh-century site of West Stow half a sunken-floored building was occupied by the remains of a large clay oven, 3 feet 6 inches along the surviving axis; its floor consisted of a flat plate of clay 2 ½ inches thick, incorporating a layer of flints, with walls up to 6 inches thick.[4] The mid-period site of North Elmham yielded an oven of comparable size. A mid eighth- to mid tenth-century oven at Portchester in building S11, probably a bakehouse serving the hall, had been built largely of re-used Roman tiles and some lumps of limestone set in clay, with walls approximately 15 inches thick; the floors of the stoking chambers had been worn considerably in use. It had been built over the remains of an earlier oven 3 feet x 5 feet in area and 9 inches deep, the floor of which showed signs of intensive burning.[5]

Ovens were probably a fire risk.[6] It was probably this element, as much as the convenience of having all the baking processes together in a single-purpose building, that caused them to be housed separately.

Use

Perhaps their most important function was to cook bread but they could also have been used for roasting joints, perhaps coated in a flour and water paste which sealed in the juices. After the bread was baked, ovens could have been utilised for a range of dishes that needed long, slow cooking.

Kitchens

Provision of food on a large scale resulted in the use of a detached building as a kitchen, as distinct from a bakehouse.[7] According to Athelstan's Laws, a *ceorl* who had a kitchen could be accounted a thane.[8] From the tenth century the kitchen seems to have been integrated in the manor complex itself.[9]

---

[1] Liebermann 1898, 454.
[2] Jaine 1987, 44.
[3] Herzfeld 1900, *May 3*; Skeat 1881, *St Sebastian* l.291; Bonser 1963, 248; Cockayne 1851, II li.
[4] West 1982, 85.
[5] Cunliffe 1976, 30-1, 58.
[6] Mellows 1980, 52.
[7] Rahtz 1979, 8; Skeat 1881, *St Thomas* l.97; Hope-Taylor 1977, 63.
[8] Turner 1828, III 83.
[9] Cunliffe 1976, 126; Davison 1977, 109, 113; Barlow et al. 1976, 293.

By the tenth-century monasteries had a *coquina* (kitchen).[1] Everyone had to take their turn 'to work in the kitchen' (*of kycenan to þenienne*).[2] At Abingdon Ælfstan prepared food in the kitchen for the builders of the monastery.[3]

In smaller households it is likely that part of the main room was used for cooking.

Cooks

The Old English word *coc* (cook) is a masculine noun and those cooks who are mentioned have male names: 'Ælfsige the cook' (*Ælfsige þene coc*), 'Albold the cook' (*Albold cocus*).[4] The cook of Ælfric's *Colloquy* is also a man and he does not seem to be operating in a monastic context: with his *ge* (you) he seems to be addressing people in general.[5]

A specialist cook is likely to have been male and full-time. Considerable strength was needed to lift large cauldrons and their contents,[6] whilst the quantity of cooking in a large household would have been too great for a part-time worker.[7]

In a peasant household the cooking methods were no doubt adjusted to the amount of time that could be given to this task, which was probably worked in with other jobs. Stews of salt meat and bacon, for example, would have needed little attention, beyond making sure that the fire was kept alight.

The interlocutor in the *Colloquy* suggests most people could cook for themselves: 'we can boil the things that need to be boiled and roast the things that need roasting ourselves' (*we sylfe magon seoþan þa þingc þe to seoþenne synd, 7 brædan þa þingc þe to brædene synd*).[8] Ælfric's cook does not develop the difficulties of his profession, but it is not without significance that one of the dishes he cites – 'rich broth' (*fætt broþ*) may have been a speciality. For providing William I with a dish of farinaceous pottage, his cook, Robert Argyllon, received a carucate of land.[9] *Leechdoms* tell of barley meal or groats 'cooked together as cooks know how' (*togædre gebriwed swa cocas cunnon*) which suggests that some skills were restricted to cooks.[10]

It seems likely that large monastic establishments would have specialist cooks although, according to *The Rule of Chrodegang*, each monk had to take a turn working in the kitchen and to return the *batterie de cuisine* intact and in good condition at the end of his week's work.[11] The *Rule* does however consider the case where 'it is necessary to get in lay cooks' (*neod beo þæt læwede cocas þæder in gan*). They were to leave quickly 'as soon as they had served/done their work' (*swa raðe swa hi geþenod hæbbon*).[12]

---

[1] Symons 1953, xxxi.
[2] Napier 1916, 16.
[3] Whitelock 1955, 834.
[4] Fell 1984, 49; Munby 1982.
[5] Garmonsway 1978, 37.
[6] Whitelock 1955, 235.
[7] Davies 1982, 50; Owen 1841, 47, 49, 355.
[8] Garmonsway 1978,37.
[9] McKendry 1973, 12.
[10] Cockayne 1851, II xxvi.
[11] Napier 1916, 16.
[12] op.cit., 21.

As well as specialist cooks in large establishments, the fact that cooks are recorded in Domesday at Bury St. Edmunds, may indicate that there were also cooks catering for pilgrims, setting up their cookshops in towns which attracted travellers.[1] In Winchester in 1100 Hugh paid the king four pence for his kitchen, and received from it five shillings, which perhaps suggests a cookshop.[2] As well as Theodoric the king's cook, and Herbert the chamberlain's cook, there were seven others simply described as 'the cook' who rented or owned property in Winchester at this time, as well as a confectioner.[3]

Preparation

Some preparation was doubtless done at table: getting oysters or periwinkles 'out of their shells' (*of scellum*), or peeling apples.[4]

A large variety of leaves was eaten as green salad, but was usually picked over to remove poisonous plants: St. Martin 'ate in his food the bitter herb called hellebore' (*on his mete þigde þa ættrian wyrt elleborum hatte*).[5] Most vegetables were probably washed, even when eaten raw.[6]

Some leechdoms call for a 'clean pan, clean container' (*clænne panne, clæne fæt*), but it may have been difficult to clean the various containers used in the preparation of food effectively.[7] This may be why a number of recipes call for new utensils.[8] The success with which metal and soapstone vessels can be cleaned (in comparison with wooden and earthenware containers) added to their value.

After a preliminary scraping and wiping, perhaps with bunches of twigs, leaves or heather, pans could be cleaned with an abrasive sand mixture, or with wood ash.[9] Soap was known at least to later Anglo-Saxons.[10] Presumably the outside of pans was not usually bothered with.[11]

Meat, from large oysters to carcasses, would have needed cutting up with knives or axes.[12] The Anglo-Saxons were able, not only to produce portions manageable enough to be eaten with the fingers, or small enough to be spooned up, but to mince foodstuffs.[13] Minced meat eked out with offal, including such organs as the lights which are not now normally sold for human consumption, cereals, herbs and suet, and sometimes incorporating the blood of a slaughtered – or living – animal, is an ancient dish found in many parts of the British Isles.[14] Mixtures of this type are often put into animal membranes to make sausages or puddings.[15] *Mearh* is used to translate 'a pork

---

[1] Loyn 1970, 370.
[2] Barlow et al. 1976, 98.
[3] op. cit., 13, 18, 47, 91.
[4] Banham 1991, 36; Cockayne 1851, Vol. 1 358, II i 1, xlix.
[5] Skeat 1881, *St. Martin* l.196.
[6] Cockayne 1851, I ii 23.
[7] Cockayne 1851, *Peri Didachaeon 36*.
[8] op. cit., I iii 12, xix, xxi, xliii, xlv 1, xv 5, vi 3, II xli.
[9] Edlin 1949, 117.
[10] op. cit., 159; Cockayne 1851, I xxxii 2.
[11] Herzfeld 1900, *April 3*.
[12] Holdsworth 1980, 131; Roesdahl 1982, 125; Hodges 1982, 132; Owen 1851, 581.
[13] McGee 1986, 108; Hieatt 1980, 298.
[14] Ayrton 1975, 179, 296; C. A. Wilson 1973, 63; Kuper 1977, 51.
[15] op. cit., 51, 171; Hartley 1954, 111, 148.

sausage' (*lucanica*) in the Epinal and Erfurt glosses.[1] *Mearh-gehæcc, mearh-hæccel* are terms for meat puddings; *haccian* means 'to chop up'.[2] Such puddings or sausages could be made from the meat of virtually any edible animal or bird and could be boiled or grilled: in the latter case no further container was necessary.

For invalids and children who were being weaned, it was necessary to reduce food to a pulp. It could be 'ground in a mortar' (*gegnið on mortere*).[3] Bolting cloths, hair and metal sieves and strainers were known.[4]

Salt meat and fish and dried foods were soaked before cooking.[5]

The principle of marinading was known: beef is marinaded in vinegar and herbs.[6] Vegetables and apples were also marinaded – the latter overnight in wine and honey.[7]

Clay was sometimes used for encasing joints, much as a pastry case would do, and for wrapping seabirds, when the feathers would peel off with the clay.[8]

Other miscellaneous instructions in leechdoms read very like modern recipes. Quantities are not given with the same degree of accuracy, but 'a shilling's weight' (*anes scyllinges gewyht*) or 'a handful' (*hand fulla*) give some idea of quantities.[9] 'Work it into a paste' (*clam of þam ilcan wyrc*), 'sweeten with honey' (*geswet mid hunige*), 'beat two eggs in hot water' (*gehrer twa ægru on hatum wæter*), 'shred up new cheese' (*screda niwne cysan*), 'shred the vegetables' (*gescearfa þas wyrto*), 'bind into mouthfuls with honey' (*mid hunige gewealcen to snædum*) are all perfectly comprehensible.[10] Temperature is indicated: 'on warm embers' (*on wærmum gledum*), 'in front of? a gentle fire' (*æt leohtum fyre*), 'smoke on embers' (*berec on gledum*), 'remove from the heat' (*do of heorðe*).[11] While such instructions sound archaic, because an open fire is generally no longer used for cooking, 'boil strongly until reduced by a third' (*welle swiþe oþ þriddan dæl*), 'until it has the consistency of honey' (*oþ huniges þicnesse*) sound perfectly modern.[12]

Cooking Methods

From a survey of Anglo-Saxon utensils, raw materials and methods of heating, it becomes possible to deduce cooking processes and the kind of meals eaten. However, rather than draw up an exhaustive paradigm of possible combinations and processes, I have drawn only a few inferences directly from the source material.

---

[1] Pheifer 1974, 32.
[2] Bosworth & Toller 1898, I 674, 497.
[3] Cockayne 1851, I iv 2, 1 2, 1 3, vi 5, 1 2.
[4] Owen 1841, 723, 725, 95; Cockayne 1851, I i 12, ii 21, xxxi 5, lxiii 1, 3; Bruce-Mitford 1975, 159; Davies 1980, 171-2, 176.
[5] Kuper 1977, 19; Herzfeld 1900, *St. Mary of Egypt* l.663.
[6] Cockayne 1851, II vii; McGee 1986, 108.
[7] Cockayne 1851, III lxvi, II iv.
[8] Alcock 1987, 47; C. A. Wilson 1973, 113.
[9] Cockayne 1851, *Peri Didacheon* no. 49, I ii 23.
[10] op. cit., I i 3, I i 7, I xxxii 2, I iv 3, *Peri Didacheon* 21, III xlviii, II xxxiii.
[11] op. cit., I ii 1, 9, I vi 4, iii 12.
[12] op. cit., I ii 22.

Cauldrons

Cauldrons are in effect metal cooking pots. They could be larger than their earthenware counterparts and had significance as symbols of the kingly provision of food.[1] The Sutton Hoo ship burial contained three cauldrons. The largest, raised from a single sheet of bronze, but with iron fittings, had a rim diameter of 70 cm, comparable in size to cauldrons from London and Taplow, according also with documentary evidence.[2]

Cauldrons were made of various metals or alloys: 'a copper vessel, or a brass or bronze one' (*cyperen fæt oþþe mæstling oþþe bræsen*), and a 'tin vessel' (*tinum fæte*) is also specified.[3] The well-to-do young man at Sutton Hoo was buried with a copper alloy bowl. Copper utensils used over a charcoal brazier do not become oxidised, and need only to be rinsed and wiped.[4] Cauldrons were also made of iron and although these may not have had the prestige value of bronze, copper or brass items, nutritionally they probably contributed significantly to the diet of their owners by preventing anaemia, since cooking acidic food in iron pots increases the iron content of the food by a factor of thirty to a hundred.[5]

Cauldrons (*hweras*) seem to be the cooking vessel most in evidence in the Anglo-Saxon period, and were associated with mass catering.[6] A late Anglo-Saxon monastic inventory included 'a kettle' (*an cetel*) – a metal container for cooking but differentiated from a 'cauldron' (*hwer*).[7] In one leechdom a *cetele* is the vessel to be used for stewing beet to a pulp.[8] The reeve was to have charge of a range of cooking equipment: 'cauldron, container made of lead, kettle, ladle, pans, crocks, firedogs, dishes, vessels with handles' (*hwer, lead, cytel, hlædel, pannan, crocca, brandiren, dixas, stelmelas*).[9]

Cauldrons had to be suspended over, or supported above, a fire. Pot hangers and suspension chains are recorded in documentary sources and from archaeological evidence.[10] When it was part of the hall furniture, the chain might be very elaborate.[11] A different form of suspension is shown in the Bayeux Tapestry where a pole has been passed through the two rings on either side of the cauldron, and then supported on two forked uprights.[12] The eighth-century Epinal gloss gives 'gridiron/tripod' (*brandrad* for *andeda*), and the slightly later Erfurt gloss gives *brondrað*.[13] 'Trivet' (*trefet*) is recorded in an inventory for Yaxley, and trivets are illustrated supporting round-bottomed cauldrons, although these also have suspension loops.[14] Sometimes feet were an intrinsic part of the vessel.[1]

[1] Turner 1828, I 33; Owen 1841, 391.
[2] Bruce-Mitford 1983, 488-90; Wright 1871, 38; Skeat 1881, *St George* l.105; *Maccabees* l.117.
[3] Cockayne 1851, II Faustina AX fol. 115b; II xxxii, *Lacnunga* 112; Owen 1841, 699.
[4] Nenk et al. 1992, 266.
[5] McGee 1986, 623, 548.
[6] Wright 1871, 39; Herzfeld 1900, *April 3*; Hodges 1982, 132; Whitelock 1955, 834; Wright 1871, 100; Owen 1841, 77, 437.
[7] Robertson 1939, 250.
[8] Cockayne 1851, II xxx 2.
[9] Liebermann 1898, 455.
[10] Hodges 1982, 8; Evison in Haslam 1980, 37.
[11] Bruce Mitford 1983, 535-6; Van Es & Verwers 1980, 186; Roesdahl 1982, 122.
[12] Wright 1871, 100.
[13] Pheifer 1974, 3.
[14] Robertson 1939, 75; Wright 1871, 38.
[1] Owen 1841, 697; Pheifer 1974, 11.

Cauldrons, used in conjunction with meat forks and ladles, were presumably used for the production of soups and stews for the household.[1] Fires on a hearth suited a hanging cauldron, or a cauldron supported on its own legs or a trivet, which made 'cauldron food' more or less obligatory.[2]

Soapstone Bowls

Soapstone bowls were desirable as being unbreakable on clay floors, easy to clean with good heat distribution and they did not taint the food. Probably imported from Shetland or Norway they have been found in Anglo-Danish York and elsewhere.[3]

Earthenware Pots

Probably earthenware pots were in general use for cooking throughout the period.[4] Upright pierced lugs on the rims of bowls and horizontal pierced lugs on the shoulders of some of the smaller pots indicate these were for suspension over a fire, and therefore for cooking. Earthenware pots are thought of as being suited to cooking at low temperatures but they were apparently used for boiling too.[5] Good quality pots which were more heat-resistant were imported from widely-spaced centres across northern Belgium and France and Germany into such ports as Hamwih.[6]

Leather Vessels

Leather containers were probably important as cooking vessels.[7] The Anglo-Saxon *sceowyrhta* (shoemaker) made *higdifatu* (leather vessels), and it is likely these were used for cooking.[8]

Boiling & Stewing

The Anglo-Saxons seem to have boiled food which we would expect to be roasted, for example, the goose offered by Cuthbert to the visiting brothers.[9] Boiled meat preserves all its juices, making economical and nutritionally effective use of the foodstuff.[10] It has a less luxurious connotation than roast meat which still keeps its special status. Stewing is the ideal way of cooking any part of a carcass that, because of old age, or hard work – in the case of plough oxen – would be very tough if roasted.[11] In tenth-century Skeldergate, the limb bones of cattle were reduced to small pieces, suitable for boiling in the stock-pot.[12]

Boiling, or stewing, that is, cooking with the addition of water, milk, butter or some other liquid, is likely to be the prevailing mode of cooking when salt meat forms a

---

[1] Seebohm 1952, 157; Dunning, Hurst, Myers & Tischler 1959, 56, 59; Pheifer 1974, 3; Wright 1871, 38; Roesdahl 1977, 194; 1982, 125.
[2] Gamerith in Fenton & Owen 1981, 92.
[3] Roesdahl 1982, 123; MacGregor 1982, 73; Foote & Wilson 1970, 186, 201.
[4] West 1982, 11, 404; Cunliffe 1964, 107, 109.
[5] Cockayne 1851, *Peri Didacheon* 17; Attenborough 1922, Appendix II.
[6] Hurst in Fenwick 1978, 250.
[7] Fenton & Kisban 1986, 117; Moryson 1617, IV 199.
[8] Garmonsway 1978, 35, 57.
[9] Colgrave 1940, 268-9.
[10] Kuper 1977, 225, 6, 8.
[11] Ayrton 1975, 53.
[12] O'Connor 1984, 177.

substantial part of the diet, since if cooked in other ways the meat becomes hard. Traditionally, after soaking for 12–48 hours the meat was wrapped in a floured cloth hung from the handle of a cauldron, and dried peas, or – in the case of bacon – beans and/or barley were also cooked in floured bags in the same cauldron.[1] The vegetables, dried or fresh, would absorb the salt. Probably long, slow cooking was the order of the day: 'stew for a very long time over embers' (*seowe swiþe lange ofer gledum*) is the instruction in a leechdom.[2] Salt fish would also be boiled, traditionally in milk or butter.[3] Boiling was evidently such a common way of cooking meat that a leechdom could give the instruction 'boil three times as strongly as water for boiling meat' (*seow swa swyþe þ hit þriwa wylle swa swyðe swa wæter flæsc*) or simply ask for 'fat meat well-boiled' (*fæt flæsc þ beo wel gesoden*).[4]

Not just meat and fish, but a variety of foods were cooked in various liquids.[5] Where no instructions were given as to the liquid, the presumption is that water was used. The instruction for hard boiling eggs, for example, is simply 'take nine eggs and boil them hard' (*genim nigon ægra 7 seoð hig fæste*).[6] Vegetables were probably usually cooked in salted water, since in one case the salt is to be omitted: 'dry beans and boil them without salt' (*drige beana 7 geseoþ butan sealte*).[7] In one case the instruction was 'boil in milk, butter is better' (*wyl on meolce on buteran is betere*), and in two cases butter was to be used.[8] Honey and butter seem to have been used together in three leechdoms, and honey on its own once.[9] Vegetables were also to be seethed in oil, and seeds in a mixture of oil and ale.[10] 'Many kinds of apples, pears and medlars' (*manigfeald appelcyn peran æpeningas*) were to be stewed in vinegar, wine and water or just wine, on occasion sweetened with honey.[11]

Broth

Broð was the Old English term for broth or soup, which might be enriched with milk or butter.[12] The cook of the *Colloquy* mentions 'fat/rich broth' (*fæt broþ*) as one of the dishes he makes,[13] possibly enriched with bone marrow, as well as dairy products. 'Bean soup' (*beonbroð*) was recommended in *Leechdoms*, as was 'pea soup' (*pysena broþ*).[14] Broths may customarily have included dried pulse,[15] although the recommended *geseaw broðu* were perhaps made from fresh vegetables.[16] Carrot broth and mint broth are also mentioned.[1] *Henne broþe* is referred to, and one recipe for hen and mallow leaf broth confirms the supposition that, like modern soup, Anglo-Saxon

---

[1] Ayrton 1975, 50-1.
[2] Cockayne 1851, I lxxxvi.
[3] C. A. Wilson 1973, 40.
[4] Cockayne 1851, *Peri Didacheon* 33, 37.
[5] op. cit., I ii 2, 11, xxxix 3, lix 14, lxxxv, II xix, xxx 2.
[6] op. cit., Vol. 1 380.
[7] op. cit., I xxxi 1.
[8] op. cit., I ii 22, I ii 15, 20.
[9] op. cit., II li 4, III xiii, xiv, *Lacnunga* LIV.
[10] op. cit., II xxv, xxviii, xxviii.
[11] op. cit., II ii 2, II iv, I i 7.
[12] op. cit., *Peri Didacheon* 37; Jackson 1971, 297.
[13] Garmonsway 1978, 37.
[14] Cockayne 1851, II xxiv, xxxix, lvi 4.
[15] op. cit., II xxiii.
[16] op. cit., II xlix.
[1] op. cit., I xviii.

broth was a relatively thin liquid).[1] Similarly remedies could be taken 'in hot ale or broth or water' (*on hat ala oððe broð oððe wæter*).[2]

Like stews, broth was a convenient food for mass catering. The *Rule of St. Benedict* allowed two dishes of soup every day in monasteries, although peppered broths were classed with dishes of delicacies.[3]

Cereal Pottages

If *broþ* was retained to indicate a thin liquid, the term which supplanted it in the meaning 'pottage', is *briw*. *Briw* originally meant a simple cereal pottage, and even in late Anglo-Saxon times the references of 'make a brewit from rye meal' (*rigenum melwe wyrceað briwas*) and 'new barley meal or groats made into a brewit as cooks know how' (*niwe beren mela oððe grytta togædre gebriweð swa cocas cunnon*) suggest this, even if their preparation seems by this time to have become the province of the professional.[4]

'Groats' (*grytta*) could have been threshed and pounded in a mortar. If the grain had been parched, it needed little further cooking to make it digestible. Unroasted grain soaked in water gelatinises into digestible frumenty.[5] Whole grain preparations are a good source of vitamins A and B, and with milk are a highly nutritious food.[6] Linseed, or other oil-containing seeds, may have been used to enrich cereal-based pottage.[7]

Lacnunga instructs ...'boil [cropleek] in butter, and shred up ...add ...barley meal and plenty of white salt, boil for a long time and eat hot' (*wyll in buteran þas wyrte 7 scearfa smale ado ...beren mela 7 hwites sealtes fela wyl loncge 7 hatne ete*).[8] A similar method is used in other recipes, though with other leaf vegetables and wheat meal.[9] A mixture of 'cream or good skimmings' (*ream oþþe gode flete*) 'good barley meal and white salt' (*god beren mela 7 hwit sealt*) as to be beaten up 'until it is as thick as thin brewit' (*oþ þ hit sie þicce swa þynne briw*) which suggests *briw* was a thick, porridgey mixture.[10]

The serving of cereal or leguminous preparations with meat continues in modern English cooking. Sometimes a direct comparison can be made with an Anglo-Saxon recipe: chicken with a parsley and bread stuffing, for example.[11] Oatmeal (groats) is still used as a thickening agent in stews, as are other flours.

---

[1] op. cit., II lvi 1, III xliii.
[2] op. cit., Vol. 1, 378.
[3] Turner 1828, III 34.
[4] op. cit., 150-1.
[5] Tannahill 1973, 36-8.
[6] Hartley 1954, 520-1.
[7] Renfrew 1985, 16.
[8] Cockayne 1851, *Lacnunga* LI.
[9] op. cit., LX, III xii.
[10] op. cit., III x, I xxxii 2, xxxviii, *Lacnunga* 116.
[11] op. cit., III xii; Ayrton 1975, 50-1, 299-300.

It is possible that such food had a rustic connotation, but while townsfolk may have eaten more cereal as bread, cereals eaten as gruel or porridge probably formed a significant part of the diet in Anglo-Saxon England.[1]

Cereal brewits may also have been fermented.[2] Organic residues from the fermentation process in porridges have been recovered from the Anglo-Saxon period.[3] That such residues have not arisen merely because cereal mixtures were left in pots, is suggested by a traditional Swedish recipe: *blodpalt*, a mixture of salted blood and rye flour fermented for three weeks.[4]

Stews

Stews were the mainstay of the Anglo-Saxon cuisine.[5] In poorer households a stew may have been prepared and reheated with additions over a long period.[6] Such a cooking method would have had much to recommend it to Anglo-Saxons without much in the way of domestic facilities.

Roasting, Grilling & Toasting

These terms are dealt with together, since they cover Old English *gebrædan*: to cook by the direct application of heat from a fire, though an item could also be *gebræde* 'on hot ashes' (*on hatan axan*).[7] Fish could be grilled, so could cheese and apples.[8] Butchery techniques suggest that some cuts of meat may also have been grilled or 'toasted' at a fire. In tenth-century Skeldergate, York, numerous cattle vertebrae were chopped across transversely in a manner consistent with the production of modern fore-rib or T-bone cuts.[9] From the earliest, i.e. ninth-century, levels at Flaxengate, there is archaeological evidence to suggest meat was cooked on the bone and was probably roasted.[10] It has been assumed from the butchery remains at Yeavering that spit-roasted beef was a major item of diet.[11] As well as the cost of the metalwork and a large enough piece of meat for spit roasting, this method is expensive in terms of fuel and time. (A 120lb pig takes about eight hours to cook, it must be turned constantly and the fire also has to be regulated.)

Roasting spits have been found in Viking-age Scandinavia,[12] but the only complete cooking spit known in Britain is from the 'pagan lady' burial at Peel Castle, Isle of Man. It was accompanied by a goose-wing (with feathers) and some seed-bearing plants. Perhaps spit, wing and herbs belong together as a roasting kit, indicative of the prestige of their owner (Graham-Campbell forthcoming). Poultry and other foods are illustrated being delivered to the table on spits in the Bayeux Tapestry.[13] In another

[1] Seebohm 1952, 157; Bonser 1963, 357.
[2] Vaduva in Fenton & Owen 1981, 338; Gamerith in op. cit., 87ff.
[3] Arrhenius 1984, 343.
[4] op. cit., 344.
[5] Hieatt 1980, 295-6; Holdsworth 1980, 97; Cunliffe 1976, 286.
[6] Moryson 1617, IV 27, 59; Kuper 1977, 224.
[7] Bosworth & Toller 1898, I 375.
[8] Herzfeld 1900, *March 27*; Evans 1969, 45, 66; Cockayne 1851, II lvi 4, I lxi 1; Bonser 1963, 222.
[9] O'Connor 1984, 17.
[10] O'Connor 1982.
[11] Hope-Taylor 1977, 327.
[12] Roesdahl 1977, 190; 1982, 124; Foote and Wilson 1970, 164.
[13] Wilson 1985, pl. 46.

scene food on spits is being passed from a stove to what may be a sideboard.[1] A tenth-century manuscript shows three diners, two of whom are being offered food on spits by kneeling attendants. The food here is cylindrical in form, and not immediately recognisable, though it may consist of lengths of sausage, or, more probably, eel.[2]

Griddles/Frying

Food was cooked at or over the fire on a solid support: a griddle or a toasting/baking stone, for example.[3] Griddles/pans occur in the archaeological record in Scandinavia (e.g. Graham-Campbell 1980, no. 48), but were presumably well-known utensils in England since Bede refers to the different cooking methods their use entails in his commentary to the *First Book of Samuel*: 'We are being nourished on food cooked on a griddle when we understand literally, openly and without covering ...upon food cooked in the frying pan when, by frequent turning over the superficial meaning and looking at it afresh we comprehend what it contains...' (quoted in Hunter Blair 1970, 300).

In some places in Ireland a shallow pan was used to cook bread.[4] So a frying pan could be used without fat, but a flat griddle could take only a smear of fat to prevent sticking. A frying pan was a necessity if food was to be cooked in any quantity of fat. The Epinal and Erfurt glosses give *bredipannæ* and *breitibannæ* respectively for *sartago* (frying pan).[5] This was presumably the same utensil as the *brade pannan* which was to be 'greased inside with pork fat' (*gesmyre innewearde mid þan rysele*).[6]

Frying pans are found in archaeological contexts from the early ninth century.[7] A much patched iron pan was finally relegated to a rubbish pit in tenth-century York. It has a diameter of 30–35cm and there were clear signs where the handle had been attached. It may have been used for cooking buckwheat cakes.[8] Sheet metal from the iron dish of a smaller pan was also recovered from Anglo-Scandinavian York.[9] A complete iron frying pan of late ninth- early tenth-century date was recovered at Winchester.[10]

Rysele (lard/pork fat/dripping) used for greasing a frying pan, was probably a common medium for frying.[11] Oil and butter were also used.[12]

The term *afigæn/afigan* was used to translate 'fried' (*frixum*) in the Epinal and Erfurt glosses of the late eighth-early ninth centuries.[13] Elsewhere the term for frying seems to have been *gehyrstan*, as in the instruction *gehyrste on hatte pannan*.[14] From written

---

[1] op. cit., pl. 47.
[2] Wright 1871, 35; Banham 1991, 36.
[3] Roesdahl 1977, 194; Bruce-Mitford 1975, 161.
[4] O'Danachair in Owen & Fenton 1981, 63.
[5] Pheifer 1974, 46.
[6] Cockayne 1851, I iv 5.
[7] Evison in Haslam 1980, 37, 39.
[8] Hall 1982, 21; Ottaway 1983, 22.
[9] McGregor 1982, 84.
[10] Roesdahl et al. 1987, 169, J12, with illus.
[11] Cockayne 1851, *Peri Didacheon* 58.
[12] op. cit., II li, li 3, lix 9, xxxviii, *Lacnunga* 3; Holmes 1952, 135.
[13] Pheifer 1974, 23.
[14] Cockayne 1851, I lxviii.

sources it seems that fried dishes often consisted of eggs. *Leechdoms* contain detailed instructions for a sage omelette. 'Take a handful of sage and grind it very small, and twelve peppercorns and grind them up fine; then take eggs and beat them up with the sage and the pepper. Take a clean pan and fry the mixture in oil.' (*Nim salvian ane hand fulle 7 cnuca hy swiþe smale 7 nim twelf piper corn 7 gnind [read grind/gnid] hy smæle 7 nim þanne ægru 7 swing ho togædere mid þam wyrtum 7 mid þan pipor. Nim þanne æne clæne panne 7 hyrste hy mid ele*).[1] Another recipe in *Leechdoms* is also a form of vegetable omelette.[2]

Baking

Abacen is applied to meat as well as bread.[3] Oven-roasted meat may have been encased in a flour-and-water paste before baking so that, technically, it was steam-baked.[4] Baking would also have been the method of cooking complicated composite dishes like 'oyster loaves' (*osterhlafas*), probably made by filling a hollowed out loaf with oysters, suet, minced meat, egg and seasoning.[5]

Anglo-Norman recipes are more complex than those in the French sources and may derive from the Anglo-Saxon cuisine.[6] They include a '*soutil brouet d'Angleterre*': chestnuts, hard-boiled egg yolks, and pork liver ground up and made into a paste cooked with spices and saffron. Another unusual combination is cherries, ground chicken and hard-boiled egg yolks.[7] These mixtures were presumably baked.

Desserts

Sweet omelettes containing flowers or fruit were also a possibility, as were egg custard mixtures.[8] Certainly the Anglo-Saxons enjoyed dishes of milk/cream/curds, sometimes with wine, or with the addition of meal.[9] Summer puddings which use bread to contain fruit, often blackberries, raspberries or whortleberries, are also archaic. Cereal-derived flummery produced a slightly acid, solid jelly, and cows' heels and calves' feet may have been used to make jellies.[10]

Sweet dishes – *eft-mettas* (literally 'after-meats', so, desserts) – were regarded as morally dubious.[11] They were seen as a temptation to gluttony, and could result in the stimulation of other appetites. In the Epinal and Erfurt glosses, *sperwyrt* (elecampane) glosses *gallengar*, i.e. galingale, the preserved root of the cypress used in cookery and as a sweetmeat.[12] Elsewhere *sperwyrt* glosses *veneria*, roots used as a confection.[13] Perhaps it was the apparent implications of this semantic association that called down condemnations.

[1] op. cit., *Peri Didacheon* 63.
[2] op. cit., 58.
[3] Turner 1828, III 34.
[4] Weaver in Fenton & Kisban 1986, 44.
[5] Cockayne 1851, II xxiii; Ayrton 1975, 245-6.
[6] Hieatt 1980, 295-6.
[7] op. cit.
[8] Ayrton 1975, 418; McGee 1986, 56.
[9] Cockayne 1851, III x.
[10] Furnivall 1868, 34.
[11] Turner 1828, II 36, 102.
[12] Pheifer 1974, 134.
[13] op. cit., 56.

Cakes & Biscuits

Fats and oils were almost certainly used as shortening in biscuits and cakes.[1] The glossing of *crustulla* (a flat cake) by *halstan/heallstan* (hall-stone, possibly hearth- or baking stone) might suggest a mistranslation.[2] However, *halstan* could have been something like a round of shortbread, and the name a humorous one like 'rock' cakes. The French *gastel*, a type of biscuit or cake recorded in the twelfth century was compared to a flat, round stone.[3] This was made from flour, shortening and honey, and would have been similar to shortbread. The low temperature needed for cooking would have been available in an oven after the bread had been baked, or at the hearth-side. Enriched breads (see Chapter 16) provided another sort of cake.

Other Anglo-Saxon cakes were small: at least *cicel* (cake) is glossed by *pastillus* (a little cake) in one of the later word-lists.[4] *Peri Didacheon* prescribes new cheese pared into boiling water and made into little *cicles* to be bound to the eyes overnight. Here a 'little cake' would only be an inch or so across: perhaps the standard cake size was 2–5 inches in diameter, our bun or scone size. Grube considers that cake was known to the Germanic peoples long before the Migration period.[5] He thinks that on occasion the term *æppel* (apple) was used to signify a dumpling, as in 'knead it together so that you make it into an apple/a dumpling' (*cnuce tosomne þan gelice þe þu æppel wyrce*).[6] On occasion these may have been sweetened to produce some sort of cake since *hunig æppel* (honey dumpling) glossed Latin *pastellus*.[7] In the post-Conquest period types of cake were made by assembling and binding together ready-cooked ingredients,[8] suggesting the *hunig æppel* of Anglo-Saxon times.

Sauces

A comparison of two later medieval recipes for green sauce, one French, the other English, suggests that the English either had more native herbs or at least appreciated them more.[9] There are several mentions of sorrel in leechdoms, and this was possibly used as a sauce then as it is today.[10]

Some fruit sauces are traditionally served with meat and fish dishes.[11] Fruit sauces are useful in that they 'cut the fat', aiding digestion. Strawberry sauce for boiled meat, recorded in an Anglo-Norman recipe is reputedly subtle and very good.[12]

Vinegar, honey and herbs (cf. modern mint sauce) are mentioned in *Leechdoms* as an appetising sauce, there is no reason to suppose that such sauces were not used as part of the normal diet in Anglo-Saxon times.[13]

[1] Holmes 1952, 135.
[2] Pheifer 1974, 16.
[3] Holmes 1952, 91.
[4] C. A. Wilson 1973, 250.
[5] Grube 1934, 156.
[6] Cockayne 1851, I 250.
[7] Wright & Wulcker 36, 7, 468,18.
[8] Peacocke in Jaine 1986, 58.
[9] C. A. Wilson 1973, 40; McGee 1986, 130.
[10] Cockayne 1851, I xii, xxxix 3, xli, xlvii 1, II li 3, liii.
[11] Ayrton 1975, 182, 206-7, 284.
[12] Hieatt 1980, 298.
[13] Cockayne 1851, II vi.

'Prepared mustard' (*gerenodne senep*) was apparently used as a flavouring with bread or other food (op. cit.). A mixture is to have 'the form in which mustard is tempered for flavouring' (*þa onlicnesse geworht þe senop bið getemprod to inwisan*), and we learn that this could be spooned up, and so had the pasty consistency that made mustard has today. Cumin is also mentioned as an ingredient in a sauce, and both mustard and cumin were found in the Oseberg ship burial in Norway.[1]

Conclusion

Anglo-Saxon cookery seems to have been based on boiling, a method practised particularly in subsistence economies, where all parts of the animal have to be utilised.[2] The nobility may have been able to indulge a preference which is now widespread for tender joints which do not need stewing. Barley and other cereals, dried beans and legumes were commonly used in stews, brewits and soups.

Some basic procedures were already established in Anglo-Saxon times: clarifying butter, whipping cream, salting vegetables and serving them with butter, or with oil and vinegar, for example, but one important difference is a quantitative one: numerous herbs were used to flavour Anglo-Saxon dishes. That the cuisine used the resources to hand imaginatively, is emphasised by a comparison between Anglo-Norman and early medieval French recipes. The Anglo-Norman recipes make a considerable use of fruit and flowers not found in any French recipes. They are also far more specific and discriminating in the spicing of different dishes.[3] Features of the Anglo-Norman recipes which arguably represent the native English tradition are custard tarts with dried fruit, strawberries, blackberries and pears, hawthorn and rose flowers; white meat stews with elderflowers, mulberries or pears; red meat stews with rose petals, hawthorn blossoms, cherries and strawberries.[4] There seems to have been a predilection for sweet dishes, as a number of the recipes include fruit or honey.[5] There are dessert dishes: hazel nuts used in flour, and flour, milk and elderflowers used to made a pottage, for example.[6]

As well as fruit sauces and seasonings, colourings and garnishes were seen as important as part of the overall visual effect.[7]

This evidence for skilled cookery would seem initially to contradict the *Colloquy*, where the cook is summarily dismissed: 'We don't consider we need him, because we can stew ourselves anything that needs stewing, and roast those things that have to be roasted' (*We ne reccaþ ne he us neodþearf ys, forþan we sylfe magan seowan þa þingc þe to seoþenne synd, 7 brædan þa þingc þe to brædene synd*).[8] The response might be the same today: even if we don't feel we can turn our hand to ploughing or smithing, we feel we can manage to cook for ourselves. However, professional cooks then as now will have produced delicacies – indeed, kings and nobles were certainly able to command a variety of dishes.

---

[1] Foote & Wilson 1970, 163.
[2] Kuper 1977, 51.
[3] Hieatt 1986, 860.
[4] op. cit.; Ayrton 1975, 251.
[5] op. cit.
[6] Hieatt 1986, 875ff.
[7] Hieatt 1980, 296.
[8] Garmonsway 1978, 37.

III Distribution

21. Food and Administration

Landowners

In the early stages of settlement, family groups probably laid claim to land to support themselves. The more powerful a group, the larger the area they could retain. Chieftains with a force of armed men could control a large area which then gave them the means to provide for their retainers. Large land units were proportionately more valuable, since control of the surplus cereals produced from large fields formed the basis of all wealth and power.[1] The king could reward followers with gifts of land which would usually, after one or more lifetimes, revert to the crown.

The invading Vikings in turn did as the Angles, Saxons and Jutes had done. In 876 Healdene shared out the lands of the Northumbrians and the invaders proceeded to plough and support themselves.[2] Therefore they were not prepared to take part in Guthrum's invasion of Wessex. He later conquered and divided East Anglia among his soldiers and they cultivated it.[3]

It is clear from Bede's letter to Archbishop Egbert in 734, that he considered a young thane had a right to expect an endowment of land from his prince so that he might marry and set up an establishment of his own.[4] If a gift of land was not forthcoming, it seems that some individuals did not scruple to appropriate monasteries, to judge from a letter from Boniface to Cuthbert, archbishop of Canterbury, in 747 deploring the fact that 'a layman . . . should seize for himself a monastery . . . and begin to rule in the abbot's stead, and . . . take into his possession the money that was gathered by the blood of Christ . . . such a man [is] a plunderer . . . a murderer of the poor'.[5] Although King Alfred's preface to his version of St. Augustine's soliloquies observes: 'Every man, when he has built a settlement on land leased to him by his lord . . . likes to stay in it sometimes, and to go hunting and fowling and fishing and to support himself in every way on that leased land . . . until the time he may acquire bookland', which suggests more peaceful times, the lord of the manor may not have hesitated to draw upon the poor man's stocks in Anglo-Saxon times as he did later, according to Piers Plowman:

> Bothe my gees and my grys his gadelynges fecceth
> I dar nougte for fere of hym fygte ne chyde . . .
> and bereth awey my whete
> And taketh me but a taille for ten quarters of otes.[6]

---

[1] Tebrake in Biddick 1984, 172.
[2] Whitelock 1955, 179, 181.
[3] op. cit., 181.
[4] Whitelock 1952, 36.
[5] Kylie 1911, 189.
[6] Whitelock 1955, 844; Skeat 1869, 37–8.

A landowner might build a church with a graveyard and then legitimately give the third part of his tithe to his own church.[1] In effect, since his priest was a dependant, and could be a slave, the lord gained a rebate. Being a landholder conferred independence, whereas at court, paid in kind, one was seen to be a dependant. Bookland was free from royal dues (see below), and this advantage was readily paid for.[2]

The landscape was structured in basic resource units consisting of arable, river-grazing areas, an intercommoning area, a large tract of rough pasture and woodland, some of which could be used for emergency cultivation or transhumance.[3] Cheddar, Wedmore and Axbridge were the principal components of a royal estate jointly providing a share in the firma unius noctis in the eleventh century.[4] Together they contained the types of area that could produce sheep, pigs and cattle as well as cereal crops and honey. It was customary for Merovingian great estates to be complementary, and clearly it was advantageous for the same principle to be followed in England, as seems to have been the case.[5]

Landowners were protected by the laws, which deal with, for example, the penalties for those who withheld from another his rights in bookland or folkland.[6] While landholders were responsible for enclosing their property, they were protected against those who allowed their cattle to break through hedges and wander on cornland, in that they were entitled to kill the animal, though its flesh and hide had to be returned to the owner.[7] Those leaving their portion of common unfenced, with the result that animals ate up the crops belonging to others, had to pay compensation.[8]

Land measurement was in terms of the amount of land that would support a ceorl's household. This was the origin of the hide, though from the beginning of the Anglo-Saxon period Kent was assessed in *sulungs*, the area which could be worked by an eight-ox plough. There were 120 acres to the hide in the East Midlands in the tenth century, although in the west country hides were barely half this size.[9] Bede said that Sussex, which extended from Kent to the borders of Wessex contained the land for seven thousand.[10] Hild was given 'land for a household to the north of the River Wear' (*anes heowscipes stowe to norðdæle Wiire þære ea*).[11] Obviously the number of dependants made a considerable difference to how well as family lived on their holding, but no doubt even small children were engaged in agricultural work that was more or less productive.[12]

Those who took a homestead as well as land at a rent from their lord owed him agricultural services in addition. A *gebur's* holding was a quarter of a hide together with two oxen, one cow and six sheep, seven acres already sown, tools for his work and utensils for his house supplied by the lord. In return, after the lapse of a year, he was to

---

[1] Robertson 1925, 164–5.
[2] Whitelock 1952, 154.
[3] Biddick 1984, 107ff.
[4] Rahtz 1979, 8.
[5] Talbot Rice 1965, 293.
[6] Attenborough 1922, I Edward No. 2.
[7] Whitelock 1955, 368–9.
[8] op. cit., 368.
[9] Whitelock 1952, 68, 97.
[10] Miller 1890, I 2 300.
[11] op. cit., 332.
[12] Loyn 1970, 347.

give two days' work every week, and three days at harvest time, and from Candlemas to Easter, unless he was using his horses on the lord's service. He was also to take his turn keeping watch at the lord's sheepfold between Martinmas and Easter. In addition he had to plough one acre a week in the autumn ploughing, fetch seed from the lord's barn, and plough three acres extra as boon work, and two acres in return for his pasture rights. He was to plough a further three acres and sow them with his own seed. Together with another gebur he was to keep a staghound for his lord, and to give six loaves to the lord's swineherd when he drove the herd of swine to the mast pasture. As well as producing enough food for his own consumption, he had to contribute indirectly to his lord's food supply and also had to pay a rent of various food items. *Cotsetlan* might hold as few as five acres, for which they paid no rent, but did services, some of which would have contributed to their lord's food supply. The highest ranking tenants rendered services of a non-agricultural kind.[1] It is as though status is indicated by the distance of an individual from involvement in the production of food, or payment in food; feasting with the king being the exception to this.

Food Rents

Landlords were paid in kind for the use of their land. For example, according to the Laws of Ine, if one takes pannage in pigs, then one is to take a third with bacon (fat) three fingers thick, a fourth with it two fingers thick, the fifth with it a thumb thick.[2] The same laws give the food rent from ten hides (*Æt x hidum to fostre*) as 'ten vats of honey, three hundred loaves, twelve ambers of Welsh ale, thirty of clear ale, two full-grown bullocks, or ten wethers, ten geese, twenty hens, ten cheeses, an amber full of butter, five salmon, twenty pounds of fodder and a hundred eels' (x fata hunies, ccc hlafa, xii ambra wilisc ealað, xxx hluttres, tu eald hriðeru oððe x weðeras, x gees, xx henna, x cesas, amber fulne buteran, v leaxas, xx pundwæga fodres 7 hundteonig æla).[3] As barley-rent, six weys had to be given for each labourer.[4] Details of the remission of the royal food rent at Berkeley in 883 confirm the food items collected: clear ale, beor, honey, bullocks, swine and sheep.[5] In circa 1050, workers on an estate at Hurstbourne Priors rendered 40 pence, six church *mittan* of ale, three *sesters* of wheat for bread, three pounds of barley, and two ewes and two lambs at Easter, as well as ploughing, sowing and harvesting three acres and bringing the corn to the barn, mowing half an acre of meadow, making a hayrick, and stacking four fothers of split wood as well as other work.[6]

These lists are very similar to the food items paid to Welsh chiefs: a horseload of wheat flour, an ox, seven threaves of oats, a vat of honey; from the tæogs, a sow, a salted flitch, sixty wheaten loaves, a tub of ale, twenty sheaves of oats in winter; in summer, a tub of butter, twelve cheeses and bread.[7] At the time of Domesday, manors in Gwent rendered a food rent of forty-seven sesters of honey, forty pigs,

---

[1] Whitelock 1952, 100–1.
[2] op. cit., 369.
[3] Robertson 1939, 58.
[4] op. cit.
[5] Finberg 1972, 49–50.
[6] Douglas and Greenaway 1953, 816–7.
[7] Seebohm 1952, 57.

forty-one cows and twenty-eight shillings for hawks.[1] In general, English renders are substantially greater, but this perhaps indicates the fertility of the soil was better, rather than that English food rents were particularly severe (but see below).[2]

According to *Rectitudines Singularum Personarum*, the *gebur* had to pay twenty-three, or more probably, twenty-four, *sesters* of barley and two hens at Martinmas, a young sheep or two pence at Easter. On one estate the *geburs* would pay *gafol* in honey, and on another in food (*metegafol*), on another in ale (*ealugafol*).[3] Contributions from the *geburs* on an estate at Tidenham, Glos., directly or indirectly connected with the provision of food, included half a *sester* of honey after Easter, six *sesters* of malt at Lammas and a ball of good net yarn at Martinmas.[4] Payment was also to be made at every weir on the Severn or Wye of every alternate fish to the lord of the manor. There was also the obligation to inform the lord, when he was on the estate, whenever a fish was to be sold for money, presumably so the lord could exercise an option on this delicacy.[5]

The holder of large estates could expect to receive a quantity of food, including prestigious items, without working on its production himself. The only food-getting activities the lord was likely to engage in were recreational pursuits, where the game caught, though desirable, was not the necessary end of such activity. Additionally his tenants might also, as in the case of the *gebur* providing loaves for the lord's swineherd, contribute to the food for his servants, and his hounds, which enabled the lord to hunt for prestigious food items. Moreover, his tenant had to leave more than half the land sown (twelve hides on twenty hides, six on ten hides) when he left.[6] Some land had to be surrendered with all its men, livestock and produce.[7] Land was normally bequeathed with all the provisions and standing crops, and very often with its labour force too.[8]

Food was an important component, if not the most important, of the king's revenue. All lands in the realm unless specifically exempted had to contribute food to the king. The unit was the farm of one night, that is the food and drink necessary to support the king and his court for one day. An estate of sixty hides at Westbury in Gloucestershire, was inherited by Offa, who retained the royal *feorm*, although he granted the estate to the church of Worcester. This food rent was two tuns of pure ale, a coomb of mild ale, a coomb of Welsh ale, seven oxen, six wethers, forty cheeses, six long *þeru*, thirty ambers of unground corn, and four ambers of meal.[9] In 866 Burgred leased land at Seckley to Wulferd and his heir for, *inter alia*, eight oxen, fifty swine, the corn from two hundred acres and thirty bushels of barley, threshed and winnowed, annually.[10]

---

[1] Seebohm 1883, 207.
[2] Davies 1982, 46.
[3] Harmer 1952, 491.
[4] op. cit., 460.
[5] op. cit.
[6] op. cit.
[7] Turner 1828, III 89.
[8] Whitelock 1955, 496.
[9] op. cit., 467.
[10] Finberg 1972, 105.

Others leased land while reserving the payment of food, for example, the four oxen or cows and the four vessels of honey due from Aldington to Winchcombe.[1] Ealhmund, bishop of Winchester at the beginning of the ninth century, leased land in Farnham reserving two nights' entertainment in Farnham and ten measures of honey annually.[2]

The king's food rent could be transferred to other, almost always religious, institutions. Offa willingly bestowed his food rents for three years, that is six 'entertainments' (i.e. two 'farms of one night' a year) to the Church of Worcester.[3] According to the Laws of Alfred, if any guilty party fled to one of the monastic houses to which the king's food rent belonged, or some other privileged community which was worthy of this honour, he was entitled to three days' respite.[4]

The king was more ready to grant exemption from his other rights than from the royal food rent. Other rights due to the king included the provision of hospitality for his messengers, huntsmen and falconers, feeding his dogs or hawks, or the 'Welsh expedition'. However, obtaining exemption from the latter right was costly. Ealhhun, bishop of Worcester, paid three hundred silver shillings for this exemption in 855, but was still liable to feed huntsmen of the king and ealdormen 'who are in the province of the *Hwicce*'.[5] There are a number of such immunity charters. One for Archbishop Wulfred in 822 frees *Mylentun* from the entertainment of the king, bishop, ealdormen, reeves, tax-gatherers, keepers of dogs, or horses, or hawks, and the feeding or support of all those who are called *fæstingmen*.[6] Lands of the monastery of Hanbury were freed from the entertainment of the king and ealdormen and *fæstingmen* in 836; land at Pangbourne was to be free from the entertainment of ealdormen, *fæstingmen*, men who bear hawks or falcons, or lead dogs or horses.[7] *Fæstingmen* seems to refer to those who had a right to claim lodging as they went about the king's business. They may have been travellers on their way to the king's court who were entitled to claim hospitality on route, or royal messengers. While we have no details of what the *fæstingmen* were entitled to, the envoys of Charlemagne could exact on their own and their servants' behalf forty loaves, a pig or sheep, two sucking pigs, four hens, twenty eggs, eight pints of wine, two measures of ale, and two measures of oats for their horses.[8] If similar amounts of food were provided for *fæstingmen*, the term may have been jocular, since these individuals had to be very well fed, or possibly it was because, by their consumption of substantial food resources, they reduced their host to fasting.

That the king had not entirely sold off his rights to the indirect provision of food for himself, as well as the feorm, is indicated by Domesday records. Six counties, Leicestershire, Oxfordshire, Northamptonshire, Warwickshire, Wiltshire and Worcestershire each paid the king ten pounds for a hawk, and twenty shillings for a sumpter horse, while Oxfordshire and Warwickshire paid twenty-three pounds for

---

[1] op. cit., 98.
[2] Gelling 1979, 153.
[3] Whitelock 1955, 466.
[4] op. cit., 374.
[5] op. cit., 486–7.
[6] op. cit., 474.
[7] op. cit., 478, 481.
[8] Whitelock 1952, 56; Talbot Rice 1965, 291.

dogs, and three royal manors in Bedfordshire paid from one hundred and thirty to sixty-five shillings for dogs.[1]

Domesday also records that the king could still ask for services which included the provision of food for his servants from the towns and counties of his realm. At Torksey, if the king's messengers arrived, men of the town were to conduct them to York with their ships and the sheriff was to find the messengers' and the sailors' pay out of his farm.[2] An annual charge of sixpence per house at Colchester could be devoted to provisioning the king's mercenaries or an expedition by land or sea. In Berkshire a man from every five hides could be sent with provisions for two months, or four shillings, from each hide.[3]

The Welsh Laws give details of those officials who were entitled to progresses of their own during the year. For example, the falconer, grooms and huntsmen were allowed an annual progress, but not together.[4] Perhaps the huntsmen and falconers of the Anglo-Saxon kings were also entitled to a specific progress, and it is hospitality for this that the laws refer to, rather than hospitality on an *ad hoc* basis if they happened to be hunting in the vicinity. The ealdormen also seem to have had the right to demand hospitality for their retainers, increasing the burden on food producers.

It seems that payment of the royal food rent was a great burden, at least in the time of Cnut, since his second law code states:

Ðis is ðonne se lihtingc ðe ic wylle eallon folce
gebeorgan, ðe hig, ær ðyson mid gedrehte wæron ealles to swyðe.

1. Ðæt is ðonne ærost, þæt ic bebeode eallum minan gerefan þæt hig on
minon agenan rihtlice tilian 7 me mid ðam feormian, 7 þæt him nan man
ne ðearf to feormfultume nan ðingc syllan, butan he sylf wille.

2. And gyf hwa æfter ðam wite crauian [wille], beo he his weres scyldig wið
ðone cyningc.

Now this is the mitigation by means of which I desire to protect the general public in cases where, until now, they have been far too greatly oppressed.

1. The first provision is that I command all my reeves to provide for me in accordance with the law from my own property and support me thereby, and that no man need give them anything as purveyance unless he wants to.

2. And if any of my reeves shall demand a fine in such a case he shall forfeit his wergild to the king.[5]

The king's food rent had presumably grown out of the spontaneous feasting offered the king as he toured his domain, but had been incorporated in the law codes and strictly exacted, to the distress of those who had insufficient means to pay it and maintain their own food supply.

[1] Whitelock 1952, 65–6.
[2] op. cit., 65.
[3] op. cit., 73.
[4] Owen 1841, 771–3, 673.
[5] Robertson 1925, 208.

The *firma unius noctis* for manors and outlying lands in Somerset was worth about one hundred pounds when commuted to a money payment at the time of Domesday;[1] North Petherton, South Petherton and Curry Rivel made up a farm of one night, paying the equivalent of £42.8s.4d., £42 and 100d, and £21 and 50d. respectively. Part of their payment was made up from other tributary estates, for example, Cricket St. Thomas paid six sheep, six lambs and a bloom of iron from each man to South Petherton; Brickenhall paid five sheep and five lambs to Curry Rivel, while one hide at Hatch owed one sheep and one lamb.[2] In Hampshire the *firma unius noctis* recorded was £76.16s.8d. before the Conquest, and about one hundred pounds at the time of Domesday.[3] Other manors seem to have paid less: Writtle in Essex which paid ten nights' provisions and ten pounds before the Conquest had its contribution commuted to one hundred pounds by weight and one hundred shillings in gifts.[4] Brightlingsea and Harstead between them paid two nights' provisions set at £25 before the Conquest and £22 at the time of Domesday.[5] However, when even this lower figure is compared to the four shillings for two months' provisions for a soldier, it is apparent both that the king had a large retinue and that they ate well.[6]

The king, or landowner, went round to his estates in turn with his retinue, eating up the provisions gathered for him. He would stay in the main dwelling, to which corn, provisions, cattle and dairy produce were sent from the collecting centres, often called bartons, berewicks and herdwicks.[7] By studying the distribution of *sulungs* round royal tuns at the time of Domesday, it is possible to reconstruct the system by which the Kentish kings were maintained at the time of their independence.[8] While he was present on an estate the lord had first call on all perishable prestigious food items. For example, we have seen that no-one had the right to sell any fish for money on the estate at Tidenham when the lord was there without first telling him about it.[9] Bede describes the progress made between his cities, villages and provinces by Edwin of Northumbria.[10] Bede mentions three *villæ regiæ* or *regales* 'royal townships', one by the River Derwent, one at Yeavering and at Compodunum near Dewsbury, centres for this peripatetic court to which tribute in kind would be brought.[11] Eddius reports of King Ecgfrith that the king with his queen was making a progress through the chief towns, forts and townships, with worldly display and daily rejoicing and feasting.[12] After Egbert's accession the *gemot* was convened at London, Kingston, Wilton, Winton, *Clofesho*, Dorchester, Cirencester, Calne, *Ambresbury*, Oxford, Gloucester, *Æthelwaraburgh*, *Kyrtlesham* and other places.[13] Presumably these meeting places were chosen for their convenience to the king, and therefore depended on his residence at the time. A

---

[1] Rahtz 1979, 18.
[2] Thorn 1980.
[3] Poole 1912, 29.
[4] Thorn 1980.
[5] op. cit.
[6] op. cit.
[7] Seebohm 1952, 103.
[8] Joliffe in Loyn 1970, 311.
[9] Loyn 1970, 361.
[10] Whitelock 1952, 49.
[11] Alcott 1987, 291.
[12] op. cit., 162.
[13] Turner 1828, III 212.

witness list of thirty-seven to a charter at Cheddar in 968 suggests a gathering of several hundred people, some of whom had travelled long distances to get there.[1] In 1006 we are told that the king had gone across the Thames into Shropshire and received there his food rents in the Christmas season.[2]

There is nothing inherently improbable in this state of affairs since there is evidence that roadways were well-defined, and in good repair.[3] There were some eight to ten thousand miles of Roman road, and Icknield Way, Ermine Street, and Fosse Way were regarded as being under the king's special protection.[4] King John travelled an average of twelve times each month throughout his reign, but was a noted traveller in his own time.[5] Edward I's nine moves a month may have been closer to the general average for the royal court in medieval times.[6] It is difficult to tell whether the statement in *Prognostications* that when the moon is fourteen days old 'it is good to travel to a new homestead' (*god . . . on niwne hired to færenne*) means that it is a good time to move to a new home or a different one.[7]

Records show that the estates of King Edward and Queen Edith in 1066 and those of Earl Harold were widely scattered.[8] This may have been conscious strategy, in that any local crop failures might be offset by good harvests elsewhere. Sometimes estates were granted as resting-places on frequently made journeys. Edgar gave estates to Kenneth of Scotland so he could stay on them on his way to the English court, and Ecgfrith of Northumbria is said to have granted Crayke, Yorkshire, to Cuthbert as a stop-over point on his way to court.[9] Many estates from the tenth century onwards had properties in neighbouring, or even quite distant, boroughs. Many Surrey properties had connections with Southwark.[10]

A substantial landowner at the end of the tenth century, Æthelgifu had ten estates in three different counties, each with at least two men and in some cases more than twenty workers. Between them, these estates had several herds of swine, about a hundred cattle and over six hundred sheep, and produced cereal crops, honey and wine.[11] Stockholdings of this size were presumably not uncommon, since the case of Ohthere is worthy of remark. 'He was among the first men in that land, though he had no more than twenty cattle, twenty sheep and twenty pigs' (*He wæs mid fyrstum mannum on þæm lande: næfde he þeah ma ðonne twentig hryðera, and twentig sceapa, and twentig swyna*).[12]

Domesday gives details of Queen Edith's estate at Leominster, Herefordshire. It had thirty ploughs on the demesne, and two hundred and thirty others, and there were eight reeves, eight beadles, eight *radcnihts* (*geneatas*), two hundred and thirty villeins (*geburas*), seventy-five bordars (*cotsetlan*) and eighty-two persons of unfree birth.

---

[1] Rahtz 1979, 16.
[2] Whitelock 1955, 218.
[3] Hindle 1982, 6.
[4] op, cit., 6–7.
[5] op. cit., 10.
[6] op. cit.
[7] Cockayne 1851, III.
[8] Hill 1981.
[9] Whitelock 1952, 56.
[10] op. cit., 128.
[11] Whitelock 1968.
[12] Sweet 1954, 19.

The villeins ploughed 140 acres of the lord's land and sowed it with their own wheat seed; they paid eleven pounds and fifty-two pence. The *radcnihtas* gave fourteen shillings and fourpence and three *sesters* of honey. There were eight mills worth seventy-three shillings and thirty sticks of eels. The woodland rendered twenty-four shillings in addition to pannage. In general make-up this estate agrees closely with *Rectitudines Singularum Personarum*.[1] Both Æthelgifu's and Queen Edith's estates would have produced surpluses over and above what was necessary to feed their owners well and the workers adequately.

Royal income and the income of major landowners in the form of food could come additionally from the non-payment of tithes. According to *1 Cnut*, two-fifths of the total produce (i.e. four times the amount of the tithe) of the defaulter was to go to the lord of the manor.[2]

The inheritor of land might find that by accepting the bequest he was liable for providing a food rent, usually payable to a religious foundation. Prince Æthelstan left estates to his brother from which one day's food rent and a hundred pence was to go annually to Ely. In default the estates were forfeit to Ely.[3] According to the will of Æthelgifu, Ælfnoth was to receive land, livestock and slaves on condition that he sent annually 'three days' food rent to Hitchin' (*hyccan þreo dægfeorma*). Ælfwold was to receive land at Munden provided he 'gives each Lent to Braughing six measures of malt and meal in addition and fish, and as much to Welwyn, and to each minster four pigs at Martinmas. Leofsige is to provide from the two estates for the community at St. Alban's three days' food rent annually or sixteen measures of malt and two of meal and a *sester* of honey and eight wethers, and six lambs and bullock for slaughter and thirty cheeses and an oman of wine and twenty cheeses and six pigs and a bullock for slaughter and a barrel of ale' (*selle ælce leng tene to brahingum vi mittan mealtes 7 þær meolo to 7 fisc 7 swa micel into welingum 7 to ægðeran mynstere iiii swin to mærtines mæssan . . . Leofsige . . . gefeormige of þam twam tunum þone hired æt sce albane iii dægas ælce gere oððe xvi mittan mealtes 7 ii melwes 7 anne sester huniges . . . 7 viii weþeras 7 vi lomb 7 an slegeryþer 7 xxx cysa 7 . . . anne oman wines . . . 7 xx cysa 7 vi swin 7 an hyrðer . . . 7 ælce geare . . . ane tunnan fulle ealoð*).[4]

The Marketable Surplus

It is evident that estates produced a surplus, and first call on this was made by the landowner for his own and his household's consumption. However, it is likely that food rents were set at a level that could be realistically met in all except the worst years. In this case, it is likely there was a surplus over and above the food rent, which could be sold or traded most years. The Axbridge Chronicle, a fourteenth/fifteenth century compilation writing of the times of 'Æthelstan, Edmund, Eadred, Edgar and St. Edward' stated that there were at that time 'Governors in each Borough, who at that time were called Wardemen, that is, Port Reeves, constables, and other officials

[1] Whitelock 1952, 101–2.
[2] Robertson 1925, 165.
[3] Loyn 1970, 222.
[4] Whitelock 1968, 9, 11.

who in the name of the king were to supply victuals, to wit, wheat, wine and barley, sheep and oxen and other cattle of the field and fowls of the air and fishes of the waters, for the time that the king with all his following ordered a stay in the appointed Borough. But if it happened that the king did not come there, then all the supplies were sold in the market of the aforesaid Borough, and the money received therefrom shall be carried to the king's treasury'.[1] This is not necessarily at odds with another post-Conquest account which confirms that food, not money, was transported to the royal courts: 'kings received not sums of gold or silver from their manors, but only *victualia* for the daily necessaries of the king's household. And the officials appointed for the business knew how much was appointed from each manor . . . I have myself seen people who have seen provisions brought up to the court at appointed times from the king's manors . . . the king's officials accounted for them to the sheriff reducing them to a sum of money, as for a measure of wheat for bread for a hundred men one shilling, for the carcass of a grass-fed ox one shilling, a ram or ewe four pence'.[2] Some food from estates near at hand may indeed have been supplied to the court. The *gebur* was obliged to keep a horse for carrying service on his lord's behalf, and may have transported food. But 'counted money' also came in from payments by agreement.[3] It may well have been more convenient for large estates to sell surpluses for cash, and transport the money, rather than the much more bulky goods.

Trading and marketing was established by the time of Ine, since his laws have a section dealing with the necessity of witnesses for transactions made by 'a trader dealing inland' (*ciepemon uppe on folce ceapie*), and such conditions were also encoded later to make it difficult to dispose of stolen goods.[4] A comprehensive system of marketing was evidently in operation by the time of *VIII Æthelred* which declares 'Sunday marketing shall be strictly forbidden, under pain of the full civil penalty' (*Sunnondage cypinga forbeode man georne be fullan worldwite*)[5] (See also Chapters 20 and 21).

Payment in Food for Services Rendered

Whereas status is generally indicated by the distance of an individual from the production of food, or payment in food, the notable exception to this rule is the provision of food for his retainers by the king. The 'war-band', a bodyguard of picked and trained professional warriors, had the special task of defending the king in battle with their lives; their memory would be disgraced if their leader was killed and they had not died fighting to save him. In return they were supplied with board and lodging, as well as weapons and other gifts. Feasting in hall was the supreme form of this, summed up metaphorically as their 'mead'. In *The Fight at Finnsburgh* (ll. 41–2), the poet says, 'Nor did ever retainers pay better for their sweet mead than did his liegemen repay Hnæf', and in *Beowulf* (l. 2633 on), a warrior declares, 'I remember the time when we used to accept mead in the banqueting hall, when we promised our lord who gave us these arm-rings that we should repay him for our war

[1] Rahtz 1979, 10.
[2] Poole 1912, 27.
[3] op. cit., 62.
[4] Attenborough 1922, 45.
[5] Robertson 1925, 122.

equipment if ever straights like this befell him'. It is still a potent metaphor in the poem written to celebrate the battle of Maldon in 991:

> Gemunað þara mæla þe we oft æt meodo spræcon
> þonne we on bence beot ahofon,
> hælað on healle, ymbe heard gewinn:
> nu mæg cunnian hwa cene sy.
> Ic wylle mine æpelo eallum gecyþan
> þæt ic wæs on Myrcon miccles cynnes,

Remember the times when we often spoke at the mead drinking, when we spoke boastingly, heroes in hall, about hard strife. Now he who is brave may prove it. I will make known to all my nobility, that I was of a mighty race of the Mercians.[1]

The idea of deserving one's mead is common to the heroic poetry of the Welsh and English in the Dark Ages.[2] In return the chief was to be generous with food and drink, an idea found also in Scandinavian sources. To be described as mean with food was a great insult to a king, and a leader's hold over his followers was proportionate to his success in obtaining not only plunder but food.[3] The head of the household had a particular responsibility as the maintainer of life – the loaf-keeper or 'hlaford'. The control of food supplies conferred special prestige and authority, but also a responsibility for hospitality. Her husband's status also affected a wife's right to control food supplies. In the Welsh laws the wife of a freeman was permitted by law to give away her meal, cheese, butter and milk without asking her husband's advice, while the tæog's wife could give away nothing without her husband's permission.[4] The English laws were less specific, but suggest similar privileges.

Tacitus wrote of the Germanic chief's followers that feasting in the lord's household was a return for their service.[5] Anglo-Saxon 'hearth-companions' (heorð-geneatas), the band of retainers who shared the 'joys of the hall' in times of peace, were bound closely to their lord.[6] The closeness of this bond is indicated by the laws of Æthelbert, king of Kent (c.602–3). The king's fedesl is to be paid for with twenty shillings. If anyone kills a ceorl's hlafæta he is to pay six shillings compensation.[7] It seems likely that while the picked band of retainers ate with the king, other officials or workers were entitled to food from the hall, but did not necessarily join in the feasting. This was the case at the Welsh court where, for example, the smith had victuals for himself and his servant, and the chief huntsman had a meal and a hornful of liquor in his lodging.[8] However, on great feasts more dependants were allowed to eat in the hall.

---

[1] Sweet 1954, 117–8.
[2] Jackson 1969, 36–7.
[3] Foote & Wilson 1970, 143, 338; Talbot-Rice 1965, 268.
[4] Owen 1841, 517, 747–9, 95.
[5] Whitelock 1952, 29.
[6] op. cit., 31.
[7] Whitelock 1955, 357, 358.
[8] Owen 1841, 681, 657.

Free labourers had no homes of their own, and while they contributed their labour to increase their lord's food supply, the lord supplied them with 'food, shoes and gloves' (*mete 7 scoung 7 glofung*).[1] However, a slave might better his lot: since 'if he can earn more, then he may enjoy the fruits of his labours' (*gyf he mare geearnian mæig, him bið sylfum fremu*).[2] There was a fixed standard of what was due to a bondsman for his labour, and local variations increased his allowance. Rectitudines Singularum Personarum counsels that, since 'land-rights vary' (landlagu syn mistlice), one should find out the local entitlements. 'Workers' entitlements are many and various: in some places Christmas and Easter feasts, feasts at harvest, ploughing, haymaking and rickmaking, a log of wood from each load of wood, a 'rick cup' at corn carting, and so many things that I cannot tell you them all' (*Feola syndon folcgerihtu: on sumre ðeode gebyreð winterfeorm, Easterfeorm, bendform for ripe, gytfeorm for yrðe, mæðmed, hreacmete, æt wudulade wæntreow, æt cornlade hreaccopp 7 fela ðinga, ðe ic getellan ne mæig*).[3]

A specialist workman often received perquisites related to his post. An unfree swineherd was entitled to 'a young sty-fed pig and his chitterlings after he has seen to the bacon, and otherwise the rights that the bondsmen are entitled to' (*stifearh 7 his gewirce ðonne he spic behworfen hæfð 7 elles ða gerihtu ðe þeowan men to gebyriað*).[4] These seem to have consisted of a 'food allowance' (*metsunge*) of 'twelve pounds [see below] of good corn, and two sheep for food and one good cow for food and the right to cut wood' (*XII pund godes cornes 7 II scipætenras 7 I god metecu, wuduræden be landside*). A female slave received 'eight pounds of corn for food, one sheep or three pence for winter food, a *sester* of beans to eat in Lent, whey on summer or one penny' (*VIII pund cornes to mete, I sceap oðða III p. to wintersufle I syster beana to lægtensufle, hwæig on sumera oðða I p.*).[5] In addition, 'All bondsmen are entitled to extra food at midwinter and Easter, to an acre for ploughing and a 'harvest handful' as their due.' (*Eallum æhtemannum gebyreð Midwintres feorm 7 Easterfeorm, sulhæcer 7 hærfesthandful toeacen heora nydrihte.*).[6] The sower was entitled to 'a seed-lip full of each kind of seed that he sowed well over the year' (*ælces sædcynnes ænne leap fulne, ðonne he ælc sæd wel gesawen hæbbe ofer geares fyrste*). The oxherd was allowed to pasture two or more oxen with his lord's herd, and with his oxen was to earn enough to provide his own shoes and gloves. The cowherd was entitled to 'the milk of an older cow for seven nights after she has calved, and the beestings of a young cow for fourteen nights after calving' (*ealdre cu meolc VII niht, syððan heo nige cealfod hæfð. 7 frymetlinge bystinge XIIII niht*).[7] His cow was allowed pasture with the lord's cows. The shepherd received twelve nights' dung at midwinter (presumably by folding the flock on his land), 'and one lamb born during the year and a bell-wether's fleece and the milk of his herd for seven days after the equinox and a bowl of whey or buttermilk all through the summer' (*7 I lamb of geares geogeðe 7 I belflys 7 his*

[1] Liebermann 1898, 450.
[2] op. cit.
[3] op. cit., 452.
[4] op. cit., 449.
[5] op. cit., 450.
[6] op. cit.
[7] op. cit., 450–1

hearde meolc VII niht æfter emnihtes dæge 7 blede fulle hweges oððe syringe ealne sumor). The goat herd was similarly entitled to milk from his herd but not until 'after Martinmas and before that he gets his share of the whey and one kid from those born that year, provided he tends his herd well' (*ofer Martinmas mæssedæig ær ðam his dæl hwæges 7 I ticcen of geares gegoðe, gif he his heorde wel begymeð*). The cheesemaker was entitled to 'a hundred cheeses: she is to make butter for the lord's table from the whey pressed from the cheese, and she is to have all the buttermilk except for the herdsman's share' (*hundred cyse, 7 þæt heo of wringwæge buteran macige to hlafordes beode, 7 hæbbe hire ða syringe ealle butan ðæs hyrdes dæl*). The overseer of the grain was entitled to all the corn which fell at the door of the barn in harvest, but, presumably because this perk was particularly liable to abuse, it had to be confirmed by the *ealdorman*, although he was also entitled to a portion of land too. The woodward was entitled to all trees that were blown down.

However, there is evidence that bondsmen did not always receive their food rights, since Archbishop Wulfstan considered the disregard of these rights as one of the abuses that had brought down God's wrath in the form of Viking invasions.[1] Perhaps labourers did not always receive the perquisites they were entitled to, especially as there was a pool of poor available as cheap labour, since famines resulted in free men selling themselves as slaves to a landowner in return for food. A will sets free 'those who had sold their heads in return for food in hard times'.[2]

However, it is apparent that the workers of a farm would be likely to trade some of their perks among themselves, or even to sell the excess food.

At Watton, Yorks., each shepherd on the estate received a bell-wether's fleece in 1641, as in Saxon times, indicating the long continuance of such customs.[3] It is possible that where payment in food is recorded in post-Conquest documents, this would relate also to the Anglo-Saxon period. For example, at Glastonbury in 1250 the swineherd received the interior parts of the best pigs slaughtered and the tails of all the others killed.[4] At Sturminster Newton, the cowherd received all the milk the calves did not take from the older cows, and the same from the heifers for four weeks.[5] These examples suggest the form that the additional local privileges mentioned by *Rectitudines Singularum Personarum* might take. At Glastonbury the food for mowing service for the men of the village was a she-lamb, four cheeses and two loaves.[6] For shearing service each received a cheese made in the lord's hall the same day. At Battle Abbey the carrier of a thousand dried herrings or two loads of hay or ten rods for fence making, or he who ploughed an acre, were all entitled to two loaves and six herrings; while at Bright Walton, which belonged to Battle Abbey, weeding service was payable with barley bread, broth and whey at noon and bread and whey in the evening.[7] At Boile on the Canterbury lands, the provision was three quarters of wheat, a ram, a pat of butter, a piece of cheese of second quality from the

---

[1] Whitelock 1952, 109.
[2] Loyn 1970, 350.
[3] Seebohm 1952, 235.
[4] op. cit., 138.
[5] op. cit., 142.
[6] op. cit., 157.
[7] op. cit., 167, 157.

lord's dairy, salt, oatmeal for cooking a stew, and all the morning milk from all the cows in the dairy.[1] On the lands of St. Paul's, the allowance for two men was two loaves at noon, one white, one maslin, and a piece of meat; in the evening a small maslin loaf and two pieces of cheese and ale, though at a 'dry request' when no drink was supplied, workers received two large loaves, pottage, six herrings, a piece of some other fish, and water.[2] These examples perhaps suggest how the various *feorms* referred to in *Rectitudines* might be made up. At Bright Walton, the swineherd received *inter alia* the intestines of one pig at killing time – the fat was needed for the larder, as in *Rectitudines*.[3]

Probably it was not only agricultural workers who received payment in food. In south-east Wales by the eleventh century grave diggers received food and income from sanctuary, and relic keepers received four pence or an ewe and a lamb.[4] As monasteries received food rents as income, it is obvious this food could be directly passed to employees as payment.

Conclusion

The early Anglo-Saxon social systems were chiefly hegemonies, but these gave way to simple state systems with grants of land to nobles and churches. The seventh century saw the multiplication of positions of power at intermediate levels.[5] The control of food supplies thus came into the hands of more individuals, though not necessarily on an equitable basis. In 746 when Eadwulf allotted swine pasture to St. Andrews at Rochester he took it from the ancient commons, thus depriving the commoners of food for their pigs, and indirectly, themselves.[6] Food rents, which had their origin in the custom of feasting the chief or king on circuit became incorporated in legal codes, and payment was no longer voluntary.

The food allocated to a wife separating from her husband after less than seven years is codified in the Welsh Laws.[7] This suggests the importance of food as a primary resource, although a wife's entitlement is not codified in the English laws.

That livestock were central to the early economy is indicated by the belief that the difference between the Kentish and West Saxon shilling indicated a difference in reckoning between an economy where the ox was the unit and one in which sheep were the unit in which important transactions were reckoned.[8] Livestock could not be maintained without a landholding, and the landowner was a powerful figure:

> staþolæhtum steald stepgongum weold
> swylce eorþe ol

I possessed estates; where I stepped I controlled whatever the earth produced.

---

[1] op. cit., 157.
[2] op. cit.
[3] op. cit., 142.
[4] Davies 1982, 166.
[5] Biddick 1984, 107ff.
[6] op. cit.
[7] Owen 1841, 753.
[8] Loyn 1970, 206.

but the self-satisfied, even arrogant, lord of the *Rhymed Poem* fell on hard times.[1] When harvests failed, peasants would have to live off the countryside, apparently a possibility in the time of Chaucer, since we learn that Grisildis, daughter of a poor peasant, collected

> Wortes and other herbes times oft
> The which she shred and sethe for hire living.[2]

The position of the *gebur* with his holding of some thirty acres was not secure. A run of bad harvests, murrain or an enemy raid might deprive him of his plough oxen and he would sink to the level of a cottar.[3] If flourishing, he could hire the services of a poorer neighbour. By dint of his plough oxen he could benefit from a cereal surplus. Cottars, with five acres or less, eked out a living by gardening and keeping poultry. They were employed as tradesmen on the lord's estate. Some may have had a very small holding indeed. When slaves were freed, they were usually given a homestead and some land, with a cow and corn for food. Without a landholding they would be unable to maintain themselves. A failure in food supply could lead to a dramatic change in status: free men entered slavery in order to survive; but those who had food resources improved their position in a time of dearth.

Withholding food was an important means of reinforcing the law. According to *II Cnut* 'If anyone unlawfully maintains an excommunicated person, he shall deliver him up in accordance with the law, and pay compensation to whom it belongs, and to the king a sum equivalent to his wergild. If anyone keeps and maintains an excommunicated person or an outlaw, it shall be at the risk of losing his life and all his property.' (*Gyf hwa Godes flyman hæbbe on unrihte, agyfe hine mid rihte 7 forgylde ðam ðe hit gebyrige, 7 gylde ðam kynincge þe wergilde. Gyf hwa amansodene man oððon utlagene hæbbe 7 healde, plihte him sylfum 7 ealre his are.*)[4] Hospitality could be demanded by the ties of kinship, but *II Edmund* sets this aside in order that the kin of a murderer might escape involvement in a vendetta: 'If his kindred abandon him and will not pay compensation on his behalf, it is my will that, if afterwards they do not give him food or shelter, all the kindred, except the delinquent, shall be free from vendetta.' (*Gyf hine ðonne seo mægð forlæte 7 him forgyldan nellan, ðonne wille ic þæt eal seo mægð sy unfah, buton ðam handdædan, gif hy him syððan ne doð mete ne munde.*)[5]

Food was an important means of payment: for some, the only payment they received. Professionals could also be paid in food. Ælfric Bata's *Colloquy* suggested payment for a well-written book could be made in gold or silver, or horses or mares or oxen or sheep or swine or provender or clothes or wine or honey or grain or vegetables. The passage is a vocabulary exercise, and so the list may be extra long on this account, and the wise seller chooses pennies or silver because with silver you can buy what you please.[6] This suggests that food too could be bought. Alfred added to his translation of Boethius' *Consolations of Philosophy* that

---

[1] Gollancz & Mackie 1934.
[2] Robinson 1957, 103.
[3] Seebohm 1952, 122.
[4] Robertson 1925, 206.
[5] op. cit., 9.
[6] Loyn 1970, 116.

a king must have sustenance for his tools, i.e. the three orders: men who pray, soldiers and workmen, and that sustenance consists in land to live on, and gifts and weapons and food and ale and clothes and whatever else these three orders require.[1] 'And without those things he cannot hold those tools, nor without those tools do any of the things that he is charged to do.'

Mercenaries were paid in part with food from the beginning of the period. Hengist and Horsa and about one hundred *cniten* were promised food and clothing, (*hi him andlyfne 7 are forgeafen for heora gewinne*), but demanded larger supplies: 'they made it known to him [Vortigern] openly, saying that unless they received more food, they would themselves take it by plundering'.[2] According to Æthelred's treaty with the Viking army in 991, they were to be supplied with food 'as long as they are with us', helping defend the country against any other fleet which harried it.[3] In 1012, the forty-five ships from the Viking army promised the king to defend England in return for food and clothing.[4] And the following year Svein demanded provisions as well as tribute for his army that winter, and Thorkel demanded the same for his army which lay at Greenwich.[5] The problem of an adequate food supply for the English army occurs when the serving force under Alfred came to the end of its term but disbanded before the relief division arrived because it had used up its provisions (see Chapter 26). Shortage of rations could evidently modify the conduct of a campaign.

Temporary servants, like the local bodyguard called up for six days if the king stayed in Canterbury or Sandwich, would be paid in food and drink.[6]

Royal servants continued to be paid in food as late as the thirteenth century, when the master of the writing office received ten pence a day, one salt simnel and half a sextary of ordinary wine. The servants of the Chapel received 'each a double portion of food' as did the ewerer, so they could in turn have a servant or dependant to whom they gave food.[7] Some, like the king's tailor and the chamberlains were entitled to a meal in the house.[8] This may reflect an earlier custom. The Welsh Laws indicate a strict hierarchy: some were allowed dishes of meat, others simply a loaf with its 'accompaniment' (*enllyn*); some individuals were allowed to eat with the king, some allowed food from the palace, while some received their food 'in ordinary'. Some received three hornsful of the best liquor, others received only one, while lesser employees received no drink.[9] A monetary value seems to have been placed only on the mediciner's food, which was to be worth a penny half-penny.[10] According to the Welsh Laws, only the *edling* was allowed food and drink without measure, and there may have been some sort of hierarchy of provision in the English court; while some royal retainers would be extravagantly provided for, slaves would receive only the basic necessities.

---

[1] Whitelock 1955, 846.
[2] Miller 1898, I 1 52.
[3] Whitelock 1955, 401.
[4] op. cit., 202.
[5] op. cit., 223.
[6] Whitelock 1952, 85.
[7] Poole 1912, 96–7.
[8] op. cit.
[9] Owen 1841, 9, 13, 19, 31, 37, 47, 65, 67, 69, 71, 73, 367.
[10] op. cit., 43.

Food almost always had to be earned. Free support was given by the English Laws only to children and foreigners (see Chapter 26). The Welsh Laws define a foreigner as one ignorant of the language and also give free support to the aged, and details of where the allowance was to come from.[1]

Strong emotional ties grew up between those who habitually ate together. Food could be tainted by the evil eye, so sharing a meal implied faith in those you ate with.[2] Sixth- and eighth-century Celtic sources, like the twelfth-century Book of Carmarthen, indicate that through the justice of the ruler of the land it was made fruitful, thus chiefs had a special responsibility for their land and followers.[3] In late Anglo-Saxon England too there is a concept that people could expect plenty only if they lived their lives in accordance with moral and spiritual laws, though the onus seems to be on monastics rather than kings.

---

[1] op. cit., 549, 553.
[2] Sayce 1946.
[3] op. cit.

22. Measures

Reckoning And Measuring Amounts

Measures for the remedies or invalid diets in leechdoms are very often imprecise: 'a good handful' (*gode hand fulle*), 'as much as you can pick up with the tips of three fingers' (*swa micel swa þu mæge mid þrim fingrum foreweardum geniman*), 'as much as an olive' (*swa micel swa ele berge*), 'as much as three beans' (*swa bið þreo beana*), or even 'as much as you think' (*swa micel swa þe þince*).[1] But this way of indicating quantity is understandable, and still used today in recipes: a pinch of salt, a nut of butter, etc. Occasionally measures are proportional: three times as much of one substance than another.[2] Sometimes they are more precise: 'an eggshell full' (*ane ægscylle fulle*), 'four spoonsful' (*feower cucleras full*) and sometimes exact: 'two pennyweights' (*tu pening wæge*), 'three shillings' weight' (*þreora scyllinga gewyht*).[3] Once the instruction to 'weigh in a balance' (*weh on wæge*) ochre, salt and pepper to make up an eye salve, is given.[4]

The Erfurt and Epinal glosses give the Anglo-Saxon terms for *exagium* (a small scale or balance – *handmitta*), *lanx* (scale of a balance – *helor*), *momentum* (bar of a balance – *scytil*) and *patena* (scale of a balance – *holopannæ*).[5] Roman objects possibly associated with the Anglo-Saxon occupation at the fifth to seventh-century site of West Stow include a bronze steelyard bar with suspension loop.[6] Small weighing balances have been found in Anglo-Saxon graves, together with sets of weights.[7] While their primary use was probably checking coin, those households owning such balances could weigh to the precision demanded by some leechdoms. The *Leechbook* also gives a list of comparative weights for a given volume, that of the pund, where the differences are in pennyweights. 'A pint of oil weighs twelve pence less than a pint of water, and a pint of ale weighs six pence more than a pint of water, and a pint of wine weighs fifteen pence more than a pint of water and a pint of honey weights thirty-four pence more . . . a pint of butter eighty pence less . . . a pint of *beor* twelve pence less . . . a pint of meal one hundred and fifteen pence less . . . a pint of beans fifty-five pence less and fifteen pints of water go to the *sester*' (*Pund eles gewihð xii penegum læsse þonne pund wætres 7 pund ealoð gewihð vi penegum mare þonne pund wætres 7 i pund wines gewihð xv penegum mare þonne i pund wætres 7 pund huniges gewihð xxxiiii penegum mare þonne pund wætres 7 i pund buteran gewihð lxxx penegum læsse þonne pund wæteres 7 pund beores gewihð xxii penegum læsse þonne pund wætres 7 i pund melowes gewihð cxv penegum læsse þonne pund wætres 7 i pund beana gewihð lv penegum læsse þonne pund wætres 7 xv pund wætres gaþ to sestre*).[8]

---

[1] Cockayne 1851, II lxi 1, II ii 2, II xxx, I xxxi 5.
[2] op. cit., II lxv 2.
[3] op. cit., *Lac.* XVIIIa, I xliii, I lii, *Peri Did.* 36.
[4] op. cit., Vol. 1 374.
[5] Pheifer 1974, 21, 33, 34, 42.
[6] West 1982.
[7] Bonser 1963, 304.
[8] Cockayne 1851, II lxvii.

The *Pund* and the *Sester*

Using Anglo-Saxon pennyweights and substances approximating to what might have been found in Anglo-Saxon England, it might be possible by means of this table to arrive at the approximate volume of the *pund*. Cockayne suggests the final clause should read 'there are fifteen ounces to the *sester*' (*xv yntsan gaþ to sestre*), but this seems untenable since in one leechdom one and a half pounds of fennel was to be put into a *sester* and a half of vinegar, hardly possible if a *sester* was only fifteen ounces.[1] Connor also supposes that the *sester* was close to the Roman *sextarius* of about one pint, but a *sester* was the amount of mead allowed by Æthelwold between six monks at dinner, and between twelve at supper on feast days.[2] Although Æthelwold was given to austerity, two-and-a-half pints/ one-and-a-quarter pints per drinker would seem a reasonable allowance (although it may have been only three-quarters of this amount in imperial measure – see below), rather than two-and-a-half and one-and-a-quarter ounces, and 'pint' would seem a reasonable translation for *pund* in this case. In fact the *sester* of wine mentioned by *Fleta* in the thirteenth century was four gallons, i.e. 24 imperial pints, an amount neatly divisible between twelve and six.[3] The peg tankard known as the Glastonbury tankard, and reputedly Anglo-Saxon, contains when full exactly two quarts, Winchester measure, divided by pegs into equal portions of half a pint each suggesting the pint was a recognised measure.[4] The reference to *huniges þus lytle pund* in *Leechdoms* Cockayne explains as the pound by weight, not the measured pint.[5] The Apothecaries' pound contained twelve ounces and was Troy measure based on the Roman denarius, and was already an established system by the beginning of the Anglo-Saxon period in Britain, and used in Anglo-Saxon England.[6] The early medieval pound seems to have been made up of twelve ounces, according to the addition made to Walter of Henley's *Husbandry* in the translation attributed to Robert Grosseteste, but perhaps there was already a larger pound of fifteen ounces, the heavier 'commercial pound' mentioned in the mid-thirteenth century White Book of Peterborough and other documents of the period; there is considerable evidence that the pound was not increased to sixteen ounces until the fifteenth century.[7] The text goes on to say: '*viii pound makith a galon and viii galones makithe a bushell*'.[8] In fact eight avoirdupois pounds of wine generate a volume very nearly equal to that of the old Guildhall gallon of 224 cubic inches.[9] This again argues an equivalence of *pund* and pint. The larger gallons of later medieval times were generated by producing containers for stricken measures which would provide a volume equivalent to heaped measures, reaching a size of 268 cubic inches by the time of Henry VII.[10]

In the mid-ninth century, a charter of Bishop Cuthwulf of Hereford granted land in return for an annual rent which included '15 measures of pure *beor*, that is, a full

---

[1] op. cit., II xii.
[2] Connor 1987, 149; Turner 1828, III 34.
[3] Connor 1987, 149.
[4] Morison-Fitzjohn 1927, 65.
[5] Cockayne 1851, II lix 8.
[6] Connor 1987, 119.
[7] op. cit., 126, 27.
[8] Lamond 1890.
[9] Connor 1987, 158.
[10] op. cit., 288, 159.

cask'.[1] Assuming the measures were *sesters* of 15 pints, then the cask would have contained just over 28 modern gallons, but if the *sesters* were made up of *punds* of twelve ounces, then the cask would have contained about 22 gallons, the amount of the Winchester bushel or 'tub' of oysters. However, there must have been a much larger pound, which was used for the annual amount of corn as food for slaves (*XII pund godes corn* for a male, *VIII pund* for a female), and for the twenty pounds of fodder which were part of Ine's food rent from ten hides.[2] Liebermann translated *pund* by *wispel*, a German measure of about 24 bushels.[3]

According to *Husbandry*, a bushel was made up of 64 pounds of 12 ounces, i.e. 48 modern pounds, whereas the modern bushel is of 56 pounds. According to the fifteenth-century *Boke of Curtayse*, twenty loaves could be made from a London bushel, so these were presumably made from 2.4 modern pounds of flour, unless the larger bushel was used, in which case 2.8 modern pounds of flour would go to each loaf.[4]

The twelfth-century French *sestier* was nearly fourteen pints, or possibly two gallons and therefore would approximate to an Anglo-Saxon *sester* of fifteen pints.[5] A *sester* of this size would seem a reasonable quantity for measuring honey and malt as in various guild statutes. Each guild brother at Exeter was to produce two *sesters* of malt for the tri-annual feasts, and any member of the thegns' guild in Cambridge was to provide a *sester* of honey if he sat within the *stig*.[6] It is also the measure commonly used for honey in the Domesday survey (two or three times only for corn or flour), although there seem to be *sesters* of different capacities, and sometimes the term *sester* seems to mean no more than 'measure'. At the time of the Conquest the city of Gloucester paid (*inter alia*) 'twelve *sesters* of honey according to the measure of that town' (*XII sextaria mellis ad mensura ejusd bergi*), *Chenemartune* paid 'eight *sesters* of honey – royal measure' (*VIII sextaria mellis ad mensuram regis*), while Warwick 'renders twenty-four *sesters* of honey – with the larger measures of the town six *sesters* that is to say, for fifteen denarii' (*redd XXIII sextar mell cu majori mensura be Bergo VI sextar mell sextar scilicet pro XV denar*).[7] The term *sester* is further defined in *Peri Didachaeon*: 'the *sester* shall weigh as much as two pounds of silver' (*se sester sceal wegan twa pund be sylfyr gewyht*).[8] Later, Henry of Huntingdon defines the *sester* as the burthen of one horse, in which case the *sester* used for dry measure was considerably larger than that for liquid measure.[9] This may explain the discrepancy between the two sizes of Domesday *sester* for Warwick: six *sesters* of fifteen pints would come to approximately two London bushels whereas the burden of a horse (the *sester* of Henry of Huntingdon) was eight London bushels.[10] The ratio 4:1 is that of the two sizes of *sester*. The *summa* or *seme*, a horse load, is used in the survey for salt, corn, flour, malt, peas and fish.[11]

---

[1] Finberg 1972, 141.
[2] Liebermann 1898, 449–450; Whitelock 1955, 371.
[3] op. cit.
[4] Furnivall 1868, 198.
[5] Holmes 1952, 196; Bosworth & Toller 1898, 866.
[6] Whitelock 1955, 558.
[7] Commissioners 1819, 415.
[8] Cockayne 1851, *Peri Did.* 16.
[9] Bosworth & Toller 1898, 866.
[10] Commissioners 1819, 415.
[11] op. cit.

The Amber and *Mitta*

Like *sester*, the term *mitta* indicated a measure. When Benedict gives St. Maur his holy rule, he gave 'the weight of their bread and the measure for their wine' (*heora hlafes gewiht and heora wines gemett*).[1] *Handmitta* was used to translate *exagium* (scale, balance that could be held in the hand) in the Erfurt gloss.[2] When Christ turned water into wine, each vat (*fæt*) held two or three *mittan* which suggests the *mitta* was also a measure of a particular size.[3] The *fæt* was an unofficial measure of a quarter (of nine bushels) used in London early in the fifteenth century.[4] This would relate to a *mitta* of four bushels (see below). A passage in one of the charters speaks of 'thirty ambers of good Welsh ale which are equal to fifteen *mittas*'.[5] The *mitta* was often used as the measure for salt: at Hadesore, Worcs., seven *salinæ* yielded one hundred and eleven *mitts*. of salt.[6]

A minimum of three and possibly five *ambru* could be boiled in a *cytele*.[7] The term *ambras* is used to translate *cados* (casks, barrels) in the Epinal gloss.[8] The Bedwyn Guild Statutes specified five ambers of ale as a fine, but this does not help towards defining an amber, and neither does the instruction in *Leechdoms* that the patient is to 'drink enough of an amber full of new ale to make him spew', although in both cases 'barrel' would seem a reasonable translation.[9] In an extent of the manors of Crowhurst & Fylesham, Sussex, *8 Edward I*, we are given the information 'twenty-four ambers which make twelve quarters of the second London measure. An amber therefore is four bushels' (*xxiiii ambrae ... quae faciunt xii quarteria secundum mensuram Londoniae. Ambra igitur quatuor modios*).[10] Four bushels liquid measure were made up of 32 gallons, the capacity of the standard ale barrel of the fifteenth century (the standard barrel is now larger at 36 imperial gallons).[11] A hogshead was twice this amount at 63 gallons, thus a *mitta*, being twice an amber (see below), was a hogshead (which would have contained 52 and a half imperial gallons). Barrels have been used traditionally as containers for butter, meal and ale, substances referred to in food rents. It is unwise to assert in the face of the evidence that the Anglo-Saxon amber could not contain as much as four bushels 'otherwise the donations and land rents in kind of ecclesiastical foundations would have been enormous'.[12] There is evidence that food rents had to be substantial to support the size of establishments (see above). Besides if the amber is represented by four bushels approximately 18" in diameter and 8" deep, then the amounts are not excessive. Moreover a measure of this size relates to the Welsh Laws when amounts for food rents are to be paid in measures three handsbreadths deep (vertically or horizontally) and three handsbreadths wide (in Gwentian Law the thumb is to be standing), and to such *ad hoc* measures as 'a

---

[1] Skeat 1881, *St Maur* 1.68.
[2] Pheifer 1974, 21.
[3] Herzfeld 1900, Jan. 6.
[4] Connor 1987, 363.
[5] Bonser 1963, 305.
[6] Commissioners 1819, 415.
[7] Cockayne 1851, III xxxix 2.
[8] Earle 1884, 91.
[9] Whitelock 1955, 559; Cockayne 1851, II lii 3.
[10] Commissioners 1819, 414.
[11] Connor 1987, 199.
[12] op. cit., 149.

dish of butter, the dish as broad as the largest in the *trev* and two handsbreadths in depth'.[1] The vat of mead supplied to the king 'ought to be sufficiently capacious for the king and his elder to bathe therein'.[2] Since there is no reason why Welsh food rents should have been greater than English ones, this argues that the amber probably is the 'large' measure that Connor discounts.[3]

An amber of four bushels then was two hundredweight, i.e. a modern 'sackful' and equivalent to a *combe/coomb*.[4] Since a *mitta* was twice the size of an amber, it was equal to a quarter of corn (which weighed four hundredweights), although some writers put the *mitta* at ten bushels, i.e. five hundredweights.[5] The term *cumb* originally meant 'a vessel', translating *dolium*,[6] but it came to be a measure of volume, since it seems to have varied with the grain. A coomb of oats weighed 12 stones, of barley 16 stones, and wheat 18 stones, and while only the volume of barley weighs two hundredweight, the other amounts are each likely to have made up a sackful.[7] A bad harvest was when there was not as much as three coombs per acre of barley, a good yield of wheat was ten coombs per acre.[8]

Another measure used in medieval times was the thrave, a quantity of twenty-four sheaves.[9] The gifts of Bishop Æthelwold to Peterborough included tithes in the ratio of a fother of corn containing eight thraves for every plough.[10] The size of sheaves almost certainly varied, though it is likely that a sheaf was of a size manageable by one individual. At Longbridge on the estates of Glastonbury, after the Conquest, the hayward could challenge any sheaf which appeared 'less than is right', by putting it in the mud and then, taking hold of his hair above the ear, having it drawn through his arm. If this could be done without soiling his clothes or hair then the sheaf was adjudged insufficient.[11] This method would presumably discourage the hayward from finding fault lightly.

Weys

The wey seems to have been a very large measure, originally a wagon load, and a quarter was quarter of a wey, which was therefore a ton.[12] A wey of wool, according to Edgar's Code at *Wihtbordesstan*, was to be sold for half a pound.[13] A wey of barley now contains six quarters, a wey of other grains five quarters.[14] However, the wey of tallow was 28 cloves of six pounds each, i.e. 168 pounds.[15] A wey of 168 pounds/pints would correspond roughly to the Anglo-Saxon Winchester bushel of 21 gallons, one quart and half a pint, (i.e. 170½ pints) which corresponds to the 'tub' of

[1] Owen 1841, 199, 771.
[2] op. cit., 533.
[3] Connor 1987, 149.
[4] *Manshead Magazine* No 23; H. Newman pers. comm.
[5] Commissioners 1819, 415.
[6] Cockayne 1851, III liii.
[7] Evans 1960, 143.
[8] Evans 1969, 72.
[9] Seebohm 1952, 142.
[10] Robertson 1939, 75.
[11] Seebohm 1952, 144.
[12] Connor 1987, 170.
[13] Whitelock 1955, 397.
[14] Attenborough 1922, 191.
[15] Jones 1976, 148.

oysters. All other measures for oysters, whelks, shrimps, winkles and cockles are merely sub-divisions of this old standard of capacity.[1] In the thirteenth century a wey of cheese was a hundredweight (of a hundred and twelve pounds).[2]

Other measures, like *bulliones* (fifteen made a horse load of salt) are mentioned very rarely in the Domesday survey and are not dealt with here.[3] The *oman* of wine, part of the food rent given to St. Alban's by the terms of Æthelgifu's will, and the long *þeru* which was part of the food rent retained by Offa are both unknown quantities.[4]

Standardising Weights and Measures

The custom of estimating weight without weighing was common up to the eighteenth century, and local measures were common until the accession of Victoria.[5] Probably 'unofficial' measures were used for a number of transactions which did not involve royal or ecclesiastical food rents or tithes. After the Conquest some measures continued on an *ad hoc* basis. For example, payment for a tenant's service in 1310 included drinking with his fellows 'so long as five candles of tallow each a shaftment in length are burning together'.[6] The shaftment (O.E. *scæftmunde*) was the length of two clenched fists size by side with extended thumbs touching.[7]

Welsh Laws tend not to refer to weights and measures *per se*, but to 'loaves as broad as the elbow to the wrist and so thick as not to bend in holding them by the edges'; 'a dish of butter, the dish to be as broad as any in the *trev* and two handsbreadths in thickness'; 'one milking from all the milch animals in the *trev* is to be made into cheese'.[8] There are references to measures three handsbreadths deep and three handsbreadths broad, sometimes the second length is a diagonal one, and according to the Gwentian Code, the handsbreadths were 'with the thumb standing', obviously a larger measure.[9] English Laws on the other hand refer to particular measures (except when this is impracticable: both codes refer to 'fingers' thickness' for measuring the fat on pigs).

Anglo-Saxon Laws attempted to standardise weights and measures. *IV Edgar* stated: 'and there shall be one system of measurement and one standard of weights such as is in use in London and Winchester' (*7 gange an gemet 7 an gewihte, swilce man on Lundenbirig 7 on Wintaceastre healde*).[10] (His earlier codes had referred only to the system of measurement as observed at Winchester.) Æthelred's Code of 1008 declared deceitful deeds and hateful abuses were to be strictly shunned, and false weights and wrong measures are the first of these to be mentioned.[11] But he did not succeed in wiping out these abuses since, according to *II Cnut*, 'measures and weights shall be carefully corrected, and an end put to unjust practices' (*Gemeta 7 gewihta rihte man*

[1] Lever 1916, 18.
[2] Connor 1987, 139.
[3] Commissioners 1819, 414.
[4] Whitelock 1968.
[5] Connor 1987, 1, 48.
[6] op. cit., 30.
[7] op. cit., 28–9.
[8] Owen 1841, 199.
[9] op. cit., 199, 771.
[10] Robertson 1925, 29.
[11] Whitelock 1955, 408.

georne 7 ælces unrihtes heonan forð geswice).[1] It must have remained a problem, and William decreed that weights and measures should be stamped (*signatas*), a form of certification which has continued to the present.[2] In practice, localities and organisations had their own sets of measures. According to *Episcopus*, a tract thought to be inspired by Wulfstan, the priest had the task of seeing that all weights and measures were properly made, with the bishop called in to settle the matter in the case of dispute.[3] This explains references to *ciricmittan* (church measures).[4] Payments of corn to the Abbotsbury Guild were to be made in guild-*sesters*.[5]

Materials and techniques for making containers and measures remained the same after the Conquest, and these are likely to have been related to what could be easily rolled or carried. Traditionally cylindrical measures for corn have been made from willow cleft into thin bands, a technique that could have been used by the Anglo-Saxons.[6] Very large vessels were available for liquids. A *cyfe* or an *hwer* were both large enough to take a man.[7] The Anglo-Saxon calendar shows corn being carried to the barn in a deep wicker basket, which was perhaps a measure since the load is being checked on a notched stick by the reeve.[8] At a size of approximately four bushel measures 18 inches in diameter and 8 inches deep, an amber may be intended.

According to the *Tractatus de Ponderibus & Mesuris* of 1302–3, a penny was to weigh 32 grains of wheat, from the middle of the ear, twenty pennies were to equal one ounce and there were to be twelve ounces to the pound.[9] Four grains of wheat equalled three grains of barley (nowadays the weights of the two grains are equal), so a penny weighed 24 Troy grains.[10] That this was still so in 1936, demonstrates the strength of tradition in measuring systems. (However, now it has been realised that the moisture content is significant in determining the weight of grain).[11] If there had been very distinct changes in the size of measures after the Conquest some mention of the fact is likely to have been noted. What seems likely is that the names amber and *mittan* were replaced by the French bushel and French/Old English hogshead, the *pund* became pint/pound, while the *sester* would have become two gallons.

---

[1] op. cit., 178.
[2] op. cit., 246.
[3] Loyn 1970, 238.
[4] Robertson 1939, 207.
[5] Whitelock 1955, 560.
[6] Edlin 1949, 104.
[7] Skeat 1881, *Forty Soldiers* l. 150; *St George* l. 105, *Maccabees* l. 117.
[8] Seebohm 1952, 113.
[9] Connor 1987, 360.
[10] op. cit., 358.
[11] op. cit., 4.

23. Theft

Deterrence: Compensation and Punishment

The attempt by landowners to secure a food supply was threatened from time to time by bad weather or diseases of crops or livestock. While the effects of these natural calamities could perhaps be minimised if stores had been built up from previous years, they could not be legislated against. However, the other main threat to food supplies, theft, is frequently the subject of laws, from the earliest recorded code, that of Æthelbert, king of Kent (602–3), onwards. In Æthelbert's laws, and those of Hlothhere and Eadric (673–685) and Wihtred (695), we are not told that the property which might be stolen included provisions, though this is a reasonable assumption. In the Laws of Ine and subsequent codes, livestock are frequently cited as the objects of theft. Apart from their intrinsic value, livestock did not have to be transported, since they could be led or driven away, (although they did leave tracks by which they were sometimes traced), and they could quickly be rendered into meat, which the rightful owner could not positively identify. Coming across stolen meat which had been hidden away was a common enough occurrence to warrant a section in Ine's Laws. The finder 'if he dare . . . may swear that it is his', (*gif he dear . . . mot mid aðe gecyðan þæt he hit age*) but anyone tracing the meat was entitled to 'an informer's reward' (*meldfeoh*).[1] The effect of making payable compensation of several times the value of the goods was no doubt a deterrent one. With compensation for stealing from a bishop set at eleven-fold, and nine-fold for a king, as compared with three-fold for a freeman (which fine in any case went to the king), kings and bishops were perhaps less likely to be stolen from: another instance where those in power used it to safeguard their supplies.

According to the Laws of Ine,

> *Gif ceorl ceap forstilð 7 bireð into his ærne, 7 befehð þærinne mon, þonne bið se his dæl synnig butan þam wife anum, forðon hio sceal ealdore hieran: gif hio dear mid aðe gecyðan þæt hio þæs forstolenan ne onbite, nime hire ðriddan sceat.*

> If a *ceorl* steals a beast and carries it into his house, and it is seized therein, he shall forfeit his share [of the household property] his wife only being exempt, since she must obey her lord. If she can declare, with an oath, that she has not tasted the stolen [meat], she shall retain her third [of the household property].[2]

> *Gif hwa stalie, swa his wif nyte 7 his bearn, geselle LX scill. to wite. Gif he ðonne stalie on gewitnesse ealles his hiredes, gongen he ealle on ðeowot. X wintre cniht mæg bion ðiefðe gewita.*

> If anyone steals without the cognisance of his wife and children, he shall pay a fine of sixty shillings. If, however, he steals with the cognisance of all his household, they shall all go into slavery. A ten-year-old child can be regarded as accessory to a theft.[3]

---

[1] Attenborough 1922, 40–1.
[2] op. cit., 54–5.
[3] op. cit., 56–7.

The forfeiting of household goods, and a heavy fine would undoubtedly be a deterrent, and accomplices might be hard to come by if slavery were the punishment. Slavery evidently remained a punishment for theft, since the law code *II Edward* also refers to it.[1]

Suspected thieves might be put to the ordeal, the choice of ordeal by water or iron being at the discretion of the accuser, according to *III Æthelred*.[2] Slaves, who were unlikely to be able to pay compensation, were more likely to be put to the ordeal, or to be killed. Slaves who formed themselves into robber bands were severely punished: on capture the leader was killed or hanged, while 'each of the others shall be scourged three times and have his scalp removed, and his little finger cut off as a sign of his guilt' (*aliorum singuli verberentur ter et extoppentur et truncetur minimus digitus in signum*).[3]

I Ethelred stated that a slave found guilty at the ordeal should be branded the first time, but should be killed if found guilty on a second occasion.[4] According to *II Cnut*, a proven thief was not entitled to sanctuary, and this code also lay down more extensive mutilations for thieves, (cutting off hands and/or feet at a second offence, for example) without indicating this was restricted to slaves.[5]

It seems likely, however, that some thieves met summary justice. The same code states that:

> *Se ðe ðeof slihð, he mot aðe gecyðan, þæt he hine fleondne for ðeof sloge, 7 þæs deadan mægas him swerian unceases að. Gif he hit þonne dierne, 7 sie eft yppe, þonne forgielde he hine.*

> He who kills a thief shall be allowed to declare with an oath that he whom he killed was a thief trying to escape, and the kinsmen of the dead man shall swear an oath to carry on no vendetta against him. If, however, he keeps it [the murder] secret, and afterwards it comes to light, then he shall pay for him.[6]

VI Æthelstan seems to have encouraged such executions, rewarding 'who is before others in killing a thief, shall be the better off for his action and initiative by twelve pence' (*se ðe þeof fylle beforan oðrum mannum, þæt he wære of ealra feo XII pænig þe betera for dæda 7 þon anginne*).[7] With the possibility that a trial might be thus pre-empted, it was in the interest of the innocent to keep clear of any suspicion.

IV Æthelstan confirmed the death sentence for stealing goods worth more than twelve pence, and *III Æthelred* states 'let him be killed by breaking his neck' (*slea man hine, þæt him forberste se sweora*), which suggests beheading or hanging.[8] Moreover the dead thief could not be buried in consecrated ground.[9]

---

[1] op. cit., 120–1.
[2] op. cit., 66–7.
[3] op. cit., 14–5.
[4] op. cit. 54–5.
[5] Robertson 1925, 190–1.
[6] Attenborough 1922, 46–7.
[7] op. cit., 162–3.
[8] op. cit., 157, 66–7.
[9] op. cit., 54–5.

Most people would want to avoid even the suspicion of theft, since according to the same laws, anyone charged with stealing cattle had to clear himself by an oath of 60 hides if accused by a Welshman, or 120 hides if the charge was brought by an Englishman.[1] The magnitude of this oath, as well as the punishments detailed above, indicate the anxiety with which theft was regarded. This is understandable since it put the attempts to secure a food supply at risk.

Registration of Ownership

As well as the deterrent effect of punishments, and the size of oaths required to clear oneself of a charge, the laws aimed at crime prevention, by requiring that cattle were exchanged only in the presence of trustworthy witnesses. For example, *II Æthelstan* stated:

> *7 nan mon ne hwyrfe nanes yrfes buton ðæs gerefan gewitnesse oððe mæssepreostes oððe londhlafordes oþþe þæs horderes oððe oþres ungelygnes monnes.*

> And no one shall exchange any cattle unless he has as witness the reeve, or mass-priest, or the landowner, or the treasurer, or some other trustworthy man.[2]

If this ruling was disregarded, then a fine of thirty shillings was payable, and the cattle were forfeit to the landowner. Anyone bearing false witness was never to witness again, and in addition was to pay a thirty-shilling fine.[3] Later laws, like those of William I, forbade the buying and selling of livestock outside towns, though this was also an anti-tax evasion measure, as much as to ensure title was properly witnessed.[4]

If anyone set out to buy cattle they were to inform their neighbours of what they planned, and were to bring the livestock to the common pasture within five days 'with his village's cognisance' (*mid his tunscipes gewitnysse*).[5] This way a community would get to know its cattle.

If someone was taking possession of livestock to which he was legally entitled, he had still, as stated in *II Æthelstan*, to get one of five men nominated from among his neighbours to swear that he was acting in accordance with the law. However it seems that anyone could maintain his claim to livestock so attached by calling on two of ten nominated men to swear 'that the livestock was born in his possession' (*þæt hit on his æhte geboren wære*).[6]

As an additional precaution *III Æthelred* laid down that no-one should kill a cow unless he had two trustworthy witnesses, and the hide and head of a cow (or a sheep) should be kept for three days.[7] If the animal had been stolen, this gave the owner three days in which to track down its hide, though it was a little ingenuous to imagine that a thief would keep the hide by which an animal could be recognised. Perhaps it was more a case of being able to refute an accusation that the slaughtered animal had been stolen, by producing its skin which witnesses could swear to.

---

[1] op. cit., 51.
[2] op. cit., 132–133.
[3] op. cit.
[4] Robertson 1925, 238–9.
[5] Attenborough 1922, 34–5.
[6] op. cit., 132–3.
[7] op. cit., 69.

Detection and Law Enforcement

Law codes, like that of *II Edward*, lay down procedure to be followed when cattle were stolen:

> *Eac ic wylle, þæt ælc man hæbbe symle þa men gearowe on his lande, ðe lædan ða men ðe heora agen secan willen, 7 hy for nanum medsceattum ne werian, ne ful nawar friðan ne feormian willes ne gewealdes.*

> It is also my will, that everyone shall have always ready on his estate men who will guide others wishing to follow up their own [cattle]; and they [the trackers] shall not for any bribes whatsoever hinder them; nor shall they anywhere shield crime, nor willingly and deliberately harbour [a criminal].[1]

III Edmund further lay down that anyone who refused to help with the pursuit should pay 120 shillings to the king.[2]

If the trail passed beyond a landowner's boundary, then the owner of the second estate was to take up the trail until it passed beyond his boundary in turn. If, however, he could not do that then, according to *V Æthelstan* 'the trail shall serve as the oath of accusation if he [the plaintiff] charges anyone on the estate' (*stande þæt spor for þone foraþ, gif he ðærinne hwæne teo*).[3] *VI Athelstan* contained further details. If the trail was lost, one man or two men were to be provided from one or two tithings, unless more were needed, to go on foot or on horseback in whatever was considered the most likely direction. Moreover the quest was not to be abandoned until everyone who had a horse had ridden out once.[4] *I Edgar* provided positive encouragement for tracking down a cattle thief. After the value of the stolen livestock had been paid to the owner, half the thief's property, exclusive of his men, was to be paid to the Hundred.[5]

The Laws of Ine dealt with the situation where those who caught the thief allowed him to escape. They were to make compensation 'according to such terms as they can arrange with the king and his reeve' (*swa hie geþingian mægen wið cyning 7 his gerefan*).[6]

Insurance

VI Æthelstan seems to establish compulsory insurance on a Hundred basis for all those with property worth thirty pence, for a premium of four pence. It seems as though a further shilling was payable, perhaps to meet the expenses of a search for stolen goods, though there is an exclusion clause relating to 'poor widows who have no-one to work for them, and no land' (*earmre wudewan, þe nænne forwyrhtan næfde ne nan land*).[7] This would ensure that no-one who had a modest amount of property in the first place would unexpectedly lose his livestock as a result of theft, but the poorest group of people seem to have been without this protection.

---

[1] op. cit., 120–1.
[2] op. cit., 12–3.
[3] op. cit., 154–5.
[4] op. cit., 161.
[5] op. cit., 16–7.
[6] op. cit., 60–1.
[7] op. cit., 158–9.

Conclusion

VI Æthelstan says that all the regulations for crime prevention and detection must be obeyed, and moreover any suggestions for improving the situation will be accepted, otherwise 'the thieves will tyrannize over us even more than they did in the past' (*þas þeofas willað rixian gyta swyðor þonne hig ær dydon*).[1] However, his laws were apparently effective, since Edmund, his successor, was able to say: 'Further, I thank God and all of you, who have supported me, for the immunity from theft which we now enjoy' (*Eac ic ðancie Gode 7 eow eallum ðe me fylston, ðæs friðes we nu habbað æt ðam ðyfðam*).[2] However, Edgar, his successor in his turn was having to issue elaborate measures to make cattle stealing more difficult.[3] No doubt factors like the scarcity of food, and presence of Viking raiders, who provided useful cover, as well as stealing on their own account, caused the incidence of theft to increase, and cattle rustling was a problem for most of the period.

Boniface writing to King Æthelbald of Mercia (745–6), quotes *Proverbs VI* 30–8: 'Men do not despise a thief if he steal to satisfy his soul when he is hungry: but if he is found, he shall restore seven-fold: he shall give all the substance of his house'.[4] But this attitude seems to have hardened. Severe punishments instituted for theft were appropriate when thieves were described by Ælfric as living like savage wolves and since 'they often-times snatched away from the righteous their subsistence' (*þam rihtwisum ætbrudon heora bigleofan foroft*).[5]

---

1 op. cit., 166–7.
2 Robertson 1925, 11.
3 op. cit.
4 Kylie 1911, 164.
5 Skeat 1881, *Achitophel & Absalom*, l.160.

24. Food Supply for Monastic Communities and Religious Households

The Acquisition of Land

The seventh century saw the beginning of the establishment of monasteries and nunneries which were provided with lands for the support of their inhabitants. It was in the interest of monastic communities to preserve documentary evidence of their entitlement to land, and a relatively large number of such wills and charters have been preserved.

This land might be donated by a landowner: Æthelwald, son of King Oswald who ruled Deira, gave lands so that Cedd could found a monastery; King Æthelwalh gave bishop Wilfred eighty-seven hides of land at Selsey for himself and his followers.[1] In 746 Eadwulf allocated swine pasture in the Weald to St. Andrew's, Rochester, but in so doing he took land from the ancient commons, concentrating it in monastic hands.[2] In c.757 Uhtred, under-king of the Hwicce, granted *Uverabyrig* (Overbury) to the cathedral clergy of Worcester to provide for their board, and this was shortly followed by a gift of land at *Sture* made by Offa.[3] Worcester continued to receive gifts of land including one specifically 'for the board of the brethren' from subsequent kings of Mercia, including Beorhtwulf, Burgred and Ceolwulf.[4] Eanswith, consort of Burgred, granted Croombe to the cathedral clergy 'for their dairy farm'.[5]

However, ecclesiastics with the necessary funds also bought lands to establish monasteries as bishop Colman did in Ireland.[6] By the close of the eighth century there is evidence that monastic estates had been in being for some time. An agreement was made in the synod of *Clofesho* in 803, between Deneberht, bishop of Worcester and Wulfheard, bishop of Hereford, concerning their respective rights in the ministers at *Celtanham* (Cheltenham) and *Beccanford* (Beckford) which the church of Hereford had 'long held on lease'.[7] Theodred, bishop of London in the mid-tenth century bequeathed St. Osyth to St. Paul's 'as an estate to provide sustenance for the community', and other estates including one 'with all the fishing that belongs to it'.[8] In the first half of the eleventh century Æthelric, bishop of Dorchester, granted lands in Cambridgeshire and Huntingdonshire to Ramsey abbey, for the support of the monks.[9]

While originally the estate which supported the community surrounded the church, by the end of the period monks in some cases drew on the surpluses of distant estates, although these may have retained some renders as hospitality obligations, so monks travelling in the area would have board and lodging.[1] For example, Edward the

---

[1] Miller 1890, I 2 230, 306.
[2] Biddick 1984, 107ff.
[3] Finberg 1972, 92, 93.
[4] op. cit., 103–5.
[5] op. cit., 105.
[6] Miller 1890, I 2 274.
[7] Finberg 1972, 43.
[8] Whitelock 1955, 510.
[9] Hart 1975, 61.
[1] op. cit., 164–5.

Confessor leaves twenty-two estates in Kent to Christchurch, Canterbury, two in Sussex, four in Surrey, four in Essex, two in East Anglia, one in Buckinghamshire and two in Oxfordshire.[1] Drawing food from such a wide area would have helped mitigate the effects of local crop failure. Not only the members of the community, but households far distant from a minster, might be dependent on its landholding. Ely, with an income of £800 or more, had farming lands in a hundred villages in six counties. In addition some 1,200 landholders, great and small, in more than two hundred villages were dependent upon it.[2]

Monasteries endeavoured to keep their lands free of the usual encumbrances. In the second half of the eighth century Offa freed monastic land at Beckford and Ripple from secular dues.[3] Renewals of this freedom are recorded, as at Chilcomb where Edgar confirmed the freedom for Æthelwold on behalf of the Old Minster.[4] The church at Much Wenlock purchased immunity from secular dues with lands at Stanton Long, although these were subsequently regranted to the monks in 901 to provide 'for their board'.[5]

The eleventh-century leases of land made by Worcester and Evesham indicate that monasteries could be major landholders.[6] Occasionally land was leased to the king, so that 'he might be a better friend' to a community.[7]

The leasing of land in return for money rents, as the abbot and community at Bath let thirty hides of land at Tidenham to Archbishop Stigand for his lifetime in return for ten marks of gold, would seem to indicate that the monastery in question had enough other land to provide food for its own needs.[8] Occasionally land was granted with the proviso that it should be given back to a community for their board if the need arose.[9] In some cases the rent was to be aid in food, like the three *mittan* of wheat bishop Werfrith negotiated to be paid to Cleeve.[10] A mid-ninth-century lease required an annual rent of fifteen measures of pure beer, that is a full cask, a vessel full of honey, or its equivalent in mead . . . one plough beast, one hundred loaves, one sheep and one pig.[11] By the eleventh century one of the estates of Bury St. Edmunds, Tivetshall, was to provide 'one measure of malt including mash and grist, and one *lepene* of wheat and a quarter of beef and half a pig and one goose and five hens' (*i met maltes under mascc 7 grut 7 i lepene hwæte 7 feorðendæl an ryðer 7 an half swin 7 an gos 7 v hennen*).[12] A more comprehensive food rent also payable to Bury St. Edmunds consisted of 'three bushels of malt, half a bushel of wheat, one bullock for slaughtering, five sheep, ten flitches of bacon and a thousand loaves, to be ready on September 4. Abbot Leofstan adds this additional contribution to the old food rent – one bushel of malt and three hundred loaves, and six flitches of bacon and another six

1 Robertson 1939, 182.
2 Poole 1959, 215.
3 Finberg 1972, 93.
4 Robertson 1939, 69.
5 Finberg 1972, 148.
6 op. cit., 126–8, 130–2.
7 op. cit., 103.
8 Robertson 1939, 219.
9 Finberg 1972, 148.
10 Robertson 1939, 31.
11 Finberg 1972, 141.
12 Robertson 1939, 200.

to complete it, and ten cheeses, and Brihtric the prior the same amount, and Leofstan the same amount, except for the ten cheeses, and Thurstan relish for three hundred loaves, and two ores to the kitchen and Brihtric sixteen pence' (*III sceppe mealtes 7 healf sceppe hwæte an slægryþer V scep X fliccen 7 X hund hlafe þ sceal beon gære on þridie NONAS Septembris Leofstan abb doð to þis fermfultum an sceppe malt 7 III hund hlafe 7 VI fliccen 7 oþer VI to fyllincge into þan ealdan fyrme 7 X cesen 7 eallswa mycel Brihtric þe 7 eallswa mycel Leofstan buton X cesen wane 7 Đurstan syflincge to III hund lafe 7 twegen oran into kycene 7 Brihtric XVI pen*).[1] The abbot and community at *Medeshamstede* (Peterborough) leased an estate at Sempringham for an annual rent which included firewood and 'two casks of clear ale and two cattle for slaughter and six hundred loaves and ten measures of Welsh ale . . . and one day's food rent: fifteen measures of clear ale and five measures of Welsh ale and fifteen measures of mild ale' (*tua tunnan fulle luhtres aloh 7 tua slegneat 7 sex hund lafes 7 ten mittan Welsces aloð . . . 7 hine ane niht gefeormige fiftene mitta luhtres aloð v mitta welsces aloð fiftene sestras liðes*).[2] This was possibly a more effective use of the land than for the community to farm it themselves.

Monastic, like lay, estates would endeavour to become possessed of such assets as would make them self-supporting. Glastonbury and Sherborne abbeys both had coastal estates in Lyme, whose importance seems to have rested entirely on the salterns.[3] The monastery at Pershore owned saltworks at Droitwich.[4] At Canterbury a *parvus burgus* of a seasalter 'belonging to the abbot's kitchen' probably provided the brethren of Christchurch with salted fish.[5] Christchurch also owned 8 fisheries and a part of the royal forest of Blean, which would have provided wood for evaporating the seawater.[6]

Bequests of land often include a formula damning anyone who attempted to take even part of the estate from the monastery. When Æthelstan granted an estate at Uffington to St. Mary's at Abingdon he threatened excommunication to any such individual, and that he should be 'cast into the abyss of hell for ever without end' (*gesceorfen into helle grunde aa buton end*).[7] Such strong feeling seems to be evidence less of a disinterested wish to provide for the inhabitants of a monastery, than of an implicit reciprocal arrangement whereby the benefactor's soul would have the advantage of the community's prayers. That such curses were taken literally, at least by the devout, is evidenced by the countess of Earl Godwine, who refused to eat any of the food grown on the estate at Berkeley, Glos., because of the destruction of the minster. Her husband had to buy an estate at Woodchester for her to live off whenever she was at Berkeley.[8]

However, provision might be made for exchanging a bequeathed estate. Ceolwin granted fifteen hides at Alton, to Winchester, 'and she commands, in the name of God and St. Peter, that the community shall never give it away from their refectory

[1] op. cit., 192.
[2] op. cit., 12.
[3] Keen in Haslam 1984, 229.
[4] Finberg 1972, 117.
[5] Tatton Brown in Haslam 1984, 32.
[6] op. cit.
[7] Robertson 1939, 44.
[8] Whitelock 1952, 87–8.

for money, unless they give it in return for another estate which is nearer and more convenient for them' (*hio he bebot on Godæs naman 7 sce þetres ðet ða hiwan hit næfre utt ne syllan of hira bæddern wið nanan feo buton hi wið oðre lande sullan ðæ him gehændre beo 7 behefre*).[1] Brihthelm, bishop of Wells exchanged lands at Kennington for seventeen hides at Creedy Bridge with Æthelwold, abbot of Abingdon.[2] Æthelwold, when bishop of Winchester, exchanged lands at Moredon for two acres within the town wall of Winchester.[3] This argues a sufficiency of food, since agricultural land was exchanged for a much smaller urban site. He also exchanged an estate at Washington with Wulfstan Uccea, receiving in exchange lands at Yaxley and Ailsworth which he then gave to Thorney and Peterborough respectively. The estate at Ailsworth had belonged to a widow and her son, who had driven an iron pin into an image of one Ælfsige. Forfeit to the king on account of this witchcraft, the estate was given to Ælfsige, whose son Wulfstan exchanged it as outlined above. This indicates one – but not, it seems, a common – way, that estates could come into monastic ownership.[4]

Not all lands granted to monasteries were necessarily to provide food directly. Christchurch, Canterbury, was to receive an estate at Halton after the death of Toki, but this is without any particular conditions.[5] Other bequests were quite specific. Evenlode was purchased by abbot Mannig and the monk Athelwig of Evesham 'for the monks' table' (*ad mensam fratribus*).[6] Christchurch received from Archbishop Æthelnoth an estate at Godmersham 'for sustenance of the community in their refectory for my soul's sake' (*þan hirede to bigleofan into heora beodderne for mine sawle*).[7] Christchurch was the recipient of an estate at Chartham granted by Edward the Confessor 'to supply food for the community that serves God therein' (*þan hirede to fosterlande þe þærinne Gode þeowað*).[8] An estate at Chart 'with produce and men exactly as it stands' (*mid mete 7 mid mannum ealswa hit stande*) was likewise to go to Christchurch after the deaths of archbishops Eadsige and Æthelric 'to provide food and clothing for the servants of God' (*þam Godes þeowan to fostre 7 to scrude*).[9] Ælfgifu, mother of King Edward, acquired the estate at Newington from the king, and granted it to Christchurch 'to provide food for the community' (*þan hirede to fosterlande*).[10]

Other monastic establishments received similar endowments. In 770 Uhtred left five hides to Æthelmund and two heirs which were then to be given to the church at Worcester, for their table, without any contraction 'as alms for me and us all'.[11] In the mid-tenth century Theodred, bishop of London, granted estates at St. Osyth, Tilingham, Dunmow and Southery to provide sustenance for the community of St. Paul's. The fishing is specifically mentioned as with some other estates

---

[1] op. cit., 30.
[2] Robertson 1939, 58.
[3] op. cit., 110.
[4] op. cit., 69.
[5] Robertson 1939, 174.
[6] Finberg 1972, 69.
[7] Robertson 1939, 174.
[8] op. cit., 180.
[9] op. cit., 188.
[10] op. cit., 182.
[11] Whitelock 1955, 463.

bequeathed to monastic foundations.[1] Stow St. Mary was endowed with land by Earl Leofric and Godgifu 'to provide food and clothing for the brothers there' (*þam gebroðran þe þær binnon beoð to fotnode 7 to scrud*), but even so the bishop was to have two-thirds of this food that came into the monastery, the priests the remaining third.[2] Æthelstan granted three estates, fifty hides in total, to the Old Minster, Winchester, 'to the community to supply them with food and clothing' (*þam hiwum to hira beodlandæ 7 to hregltalæ*).[3] Abbot Wulfwold also gave land, to St. Peter's minster in Bath for the provision of food and clothing for the monks.[4] King Edward gave an estate at Lessness to Westminster to 'for food for the monks' (*ðæra muneca fodan*).[5] At the end of the tenth century Bishop Ælfwold of Crediton granted land with produce at Sandford to the minster as payment for his soul.[6] According to Ælfric's *Life of Æthelwold*, King Eadred gave him the abandoned monastery of Abingdon, possessing only 40 hides. He collected a flock of monks, over whom he was ordained abbot, and to whom the king gave a royal property of 100 hides he had owned in Abingdon 'to augment the daily provisions, and he assisted them with money, but his mother did so even more generously'.[7]

As well as bequests of land for the production and provision of food, food rents were also left to monastic communities. At the end of the tenth century, Wulfwaru desired the heirs to her property to furnish a food rent for Bath 'every year for ever, as good as they can afford', whenever it was most convenient for them.[8] The will of Æthelwyrd left the estate at Ickham that he was leasing from Christchurch to Eadric on condition that he paid an annual rent of 'five pounds and one day's food rent consisting of forty *sesters* of ale, sixty loaves, a wether sheep, a flitch of bacon and a haunch of beef, two cheeses, four hens and five pence' (*v pund 7 ælce gære æne dæg feorme in hiowum þ is ðonne xl sæstra ealað lx hlafa weðær 7 flicce 7 an hriðres læuw ii cesas iii hæn fugulas 7 v þænningas*).[9]

Grants of land sometimes included the specification that the anniversary of the death of the benefactor should be commemorated. Wulfgar bequeaths an estate to Æffe (presumably his wife), for her lifetime, as long as she provided 'three days' food rent to God's servants where my body rests on the anniversary' (*feormige þrie dagas þa Godes þeowas þær min lic reste on þone gemynddæg*).[10] His estate at Inkpen was also to go to Æffe for her lifetime though a quarter of the crops and a three-day food rent were to go to the community at Kintbury, to commemorate Wulfgar himself, his father and grandfather. A three-day food rent was to go from another estate left to Æffe for her lifetime to the community at Winchester at Easter.[1] These food rents were almost certainly to furnish the raw materials for feasts, although the wording of Bishop Wulfrith's grant of land with all the profits

---

[1] op. cit., 510.
[2] Robertson 1939, 214.
[3] op. cit., 48.
[4] Harmer 1952, 134–5.
[5] op. cit., 343.
[6] Whitelock 1955, 536.
[7] op. cit., 833–4.
[8] op. cit., 524.
[9] Robertson 1939, 58–60.
[10] op. cit., 52.
[1] op. cit.

from fisheries and meadowland to the community at Worcester in 922 was somewhat circumspect: 'and every year also to a certain degree they shall remember the anniversary of my death with the profits which they gain from that land' (*ælce gere of ðæm londe ec be sumum dæle gemyndgien ða tide mine forðsiðes mid þæm nytnessum ðe hio on ðæm londe begeten*).[1]

Specific foods were sometimes mentioned. As well as leaving estates in general terms to Burton, the will of Wulfric Spott, dating from the beginning of the eleventh century, granted the lands between the Ribble and the Mersey in Wirral to two heirs, each of whom was to pay annually three thousand shad to the monastery at Burton. One of these beneficiaries was also to receive an estate at Conisborough, on condition that he arranged for the monks to have one-third of the fish.[2] Fish was particularly important to monastic establishments where fasts were to be strictly observed, and when they leased land with fisheries then a yearly render of fish, fifteen good salmon on the first day of Lent, in one instance, was sometimes specified.[3] The gift to a monastery of half a fishery with its buildings and the fishermen's tofts is also recorded.[4]

The late tenth-century will of Æthelgifu leaves to St. Alban's in return for her burial there thirty oxen and twenty cows as well as gold and other property.[5] She also left three days' food rent to Hitchin, and 'fifty ewes with their lambs to Hitchin from Langford, and fifty sheep to Bedford and thirty to Flitton and twenty to Ashwell and ten to Henlow' (*l ewna mid heora lombum into hiccan of langaforda 7 l sceaþa into bedaforda 7 xxx to flittan 7 xx to æsceswellan 7 x to heanhlæw*). Land was left to Ælfwold on condition that he paid 'each Lent to Braughing six measures of malt and meal and fish in addition, and the same amount to Welwyn and to each minster four pigs at Martinmas' (*ælce lengtene to bratingum vi mittan mealtes 7 þær meolo to 7 fisc 7 swa micel into welingum 7 to ægðeran mynstere iiii swin to mærtines mæssan*).[6] Four oxen were to go both to Hertingfordbury and to Welwyn, with four oxen and two cows to Braughing. These cattle may not necessarily have been intended as food, but both oxen and cows could be used in food production. Estates at Tewin and Offley were to provide St. Alban's with 'three days' food rent each year or sixteen measures of malt and three of meal and a *sester* of honey . . . and eight wethers and six lambs and a bullock for slaughter and thirty cheeses and from Standon one *oman* of wine and twenty cheeses and six pigs and a bullock and this same amount is to be taken from each of her estates for the thirtieth day' (*iii dagas ælce gere oððe xvi mittan mealtes, 7 iii melwes 7 anne sester huniges . . . 7 viii weþeras 7 vi lomb 7 an slegeryþer 7 xxx cysa 7 of standune anne oman wines 7 xx cysa 7 vi swin 7 an hryðer 7 nyme man of æghwilcum tune to þam þryttyguþan*).[1] The thirtieth day was the 'month's mind', a commemoration of the burial. Another estate was to provide 'each year a barrel full of ale' (*ælce geare an tunnan fulle ealoð*) for St. Alban's.

---

[1] op. cit., 42.
[2] Whitelock 1955, 542.
[3] Finberg 1972, 135.
[4] Turner 1828, II 547.
[5] Whitelock 1968, 6.
[6] op. cit., 9.
[1] op. cit., 11.

According to a grant of 847, on the anniversary of bishop Ealhhun's death the community at Worcester were to have three barrels full of ale, three casks of Welsh ale (one of them sweetened with honey), three barrels of mead, three fat cows, six wethers, six hams, sixty cheeses, sixty loaves of white bread, plus four large candles and oil for all the lamps of the minster.[1] Wulfgeat of Donnington c.975 left a brewing of malt to the church of Worcester and a bullock to *Cliftune* (Clifton-on-Teme), another to Bromyard and four full-grown bullocks to Leominster.[2] A ninth-century nobleman left one hundred pigs to a church in Canterbury for the sake of his soul, and the same to Chertsey abbey.[3] The will of king Alfred ends by requesting that 'such payment be made for the good of my soul as is possible and is also fitting' from his livestock.[4] The will of Ætheling Æthelstan, eldest son of king Æthelred, dating from 1015, granted a day's food rent to the community of Ely on the festival of St. Æthelthryth, and that one hundred pence should be given to the monastery and one hundred poor people fed there on that day. He requested that this charitable bequest be performed yearly, whoever should hold the estate.[5] Abbot Ufi of Bury St. Edmunds provided half a pound for fish and forty pence for mead and two measures of wheat for an annual feast on the anniversary of his funeral.[6] Abbot Baldwin granted half a pound to supply fish on the anniversary of the death of King Edward, half a pound for food (unspecified) on the anniversary of his becoming abbot.[7] He also granted half a pound from the rent of two mills for the Nativity of St. Mary, six ores for the festival of St. Dionysius, six ores for the festival of St. Nicholas plus two fat pigs or three ores for lard.[8] The anniversary of the death of bishop Denewulf was to be celebrated by the annual rendering from an estate of twenty hides that he had bequeathed, of 'twelve *sesters* of beer and twelve of sweet Welsh ale and 20 ambers of clear ale and 200 large loaves and another hundred small loaves and two bullocks, one salt the other fresh, and six wethers and 4 pigs and four flitches of bacon and twenty cheeses. If it falls in Lent, then the value of meat shall be taken in fish unless this is impracticable' (*twelf seoxtres beoras 7 twelf geswettes wilisc ealoð 7 twentig ambra hluttor ealoð 7 tu hund greates hlafes 7 þridde smales 7 tu hrieðeru oþer sealt oþer ferse 7 six weðeras 7 feower swin 7 feor fliccu 7 twentig cysa gyf hit on lencten gebyrige þ þæ þonne þære flæscum geweorð on fisce gestriene buton þ þis forgenge sie*).[9] At the beginning of the eleventh century Wulfrun gave to the church of Ramsey on the summer feast of St. Benedict (11 July) annually for her lifetime ten measures of malt, five of groats, five of threshed wheat flour, eight hams, sixteen cheeses and two fat cows from her land at Hickling, and eight salmon for the brothers at Lent.[1] Another noblewoman made a similar annual grant consisting of forty ambers of malt, an old ram, four wethers, two hundred and forty loaves, one weight of bacon and cheese, four cartloads of

---

[1] Finberg 1972, 103.
[2] op. cit., 118, 143.
[3] Turner 1828, III 147.
[4] Whitelock 1955, 495.
[5] op. cit., 549.
[6] Robertson 1939, 197.
[7] op. cit.
[8] op. cit.
[9] op. cit., 38.
[1] Hart 1975, 102.

wood and twenty hen fowls.[1] Four thousand eels were a yearly gift from the monks of Ramsey to those of Peterborough, and according to another charter some twenty fishermen furnished Peterborough with sixty thousand eels annually.[2]

Benefactors were naturally anxious to ensure the livelihood of their dependants, and so Gracechurch with the church and its endowments was to go to Christchurch after the deaths of Brihtmær, his wife and two children.[3] Badanoth Beotting's will of c.845 entrusted his widow and children to the community at Christchurch. His heirs were to enjoy the estate of sixteen yokes of arable and meadow land during their lifetime, and to provide the community with a food rent on the anniversary of his death 'the best they can afford' (*swa hie soelest ðurhtion megen*). After their death, the estate was to be given 'to their refectory as a perpetual gift, to be used as they think fit' (*to heora beode him to brucan on ece ærfe swa him liofast sie*), and any future tenant was to honour the arrangements for the anniversary feasts.[4]

Monastic Income

Monastic income came from the monasteries' own estates, but their main income came from the dues paid to them.[5] Royal dues were granted to monasteries, as Edward granted the third part of the toll on horse-loads and of the toll on market sales to St. Mary's, Worcester.[6] These dues included tithes: although there was some debate as to whether monks could possess tithes, in practice monasteries in England owned tithes by the eleventh century, if not earlier.[7] In 667 the tithe is a voluntary payment but by the end of the seventh century, one-tenth of the corn produced was regarded as a reasonable contribution to the church.[8] Not long afterwards, the Laws of Ine state that if church scot was not given by Martinmas then a fine of sixty shillings was payable and church scot was to be paid twelve-fold. It was to be paid from the 'thatch and hearth' (*healme* and *heorðe*) where one resided at midwinter.[9] Church scot properly signified the first fruits of the grain crop, and was often paid in According to Cnut's ordinance of 1027 it was 'payable at Martinmas' (*primitie seminum*) and therefore distinct from the tithe of the fruits of the earth, including uncultivated produce, payable by the middle of August. Wulfstan's *Canons of Edgar* state that the priests were to remind the people at Easter, Rogation and mid-summer that they should pay God's dues on 'in tithes and other things; first plough alms – one penny for every plough team – fifteen days after Easter, and a tithe of new-born livestock by Pentecost, and a tithe on crops by All Saints . . . and church scot by Martinmas' (*teoðungum and on oðrum þingum: Ærest sulhælmessan xv niht onufan eastron, and geoguðe teoðunge be pentecosten, and eorðwestma be ealra halgena mæssan, . . . and ciricsceat be Martinus mæssan*).[1] According to *I Edmund*, anyone

---

[1] Turner 1828, II 547.
[2] op. cit., III 23.
[3] Robertson 1939, 216.
[4] op. cit., 10.
[5] Whitelock 1952, 167.
[6] Finberg 1972, 128.
[7] Whitelock 1952, 167; Constable 1964, 33.
[8] op. cit., 167; Loyn 1970, 255.
[9] Whitelock 1955, 365, 371.
[10] Loyn 1970, 235.
[1] Fowler 1972, 13.

who did not pay the tithe or church scot was to be *amansumnod* (excommunicated).[1]
Perhaps this was not enough of a deterrent, since Cnut's laws stated that anyone
resisting by force the payment of ecclesiastic dues should pay 'a fine for breach of
the law in the Danish area, or the full fine among the English or acquit himself'
(*lahslit mid Denum 7 fulwite mid Englum oððe geladige him*).[2] VIII Æthelred
declared that one third of the tithe should be used for the relief of 'God's poor and
destitute slaves' (*Godes þearfum 7 earman þeowetlingan*), and part of the income
from fines from unpaid tithes should go to the relief of poor men.[3]

Oswald, bishop of Worcester, leased land to a thegn of his in 963, 'on condition that
each year he plough two acres of that land and sow therein his church scot and
afterwards reap and garner it'.[4] Evidence on Worcestershire in Domesday indicates
that church scot remained payable in grain: 'from every hide of land . . . the bishop
ought to have on St. Martin's day one load of grain, of the best that is grown there.
But if that day should pass without the grain being rendered, he who has kept it back
shall render the grain and shall pay elevenfold; and the bishop moreover shall receive
such penalty as he ought to have from his land'. The same amount, one load of grain,
had to be paid to the church of Aylesbury, Bucks., by every sokeman possessing one
hide of land or more in any of the surrounding hundreds.[5]

The tithe was also paid to priests of churches which were not associated with
monasteries. In order to free a priest for the full-time spiritual care of his
congregation, provision had to be made for his support. A priest might have family
or a household with several dependants to be provided for before he administered to
the needs of the poor of the parish and the upkeep of the church.[6] Churches were
also in receipt of benefactions, and the 'entitlement' (*gerihta*) of the church on the
royal manor at Lambourne, Berks., included a hide of land free and quit . . . and the
tenth acre in the king's land, the produce of two acres at harvest, the tenth lamb and
the tenth young pig; at Michaelmas a wey of cheese, at Martinmas two *sesters* of
corn and one pig, and at Easter fifteen pence. Pasture was to be provided for the
priest's oxen, cows, his sheep, pigs and horses. Every day wood was to be brought
for his fire. Tithes and church tax were to be paid to him.[7]

That tithes were not readily paid, or had been diverted to more recently-established
churches, is indicated by Edgar's decree at Andover: 'And all tithes shall be paid to
the old churches to which obedience is due; and payment shall be made, both from
the thane's demesne land, and the land held by his tenants – all that is under the
plough' (*7 man agife ælce teoðunge to ðam ealdum mynstrum þe seo hyrnes to
hyrð; 7 þæt sy þonne swa gelæst, ægðer ge of ðegnes inlande ge of neatlande, swa
hit seo sulh gegange*).[1] Plough alms were to be rendered fifteen days after Easter;
the tithe of young animals by Pentecost, and that of the fruits of the earth by the
equinox, so that all church dues were rendered by Michaelmas under pain of the full

[1] Robertson 1925.
[2] Robertson 1939, 200.
[3] Robertson 1925, 120; Whitelock 1952, 167.
[4] Whitelock 1955, 518.
[5] Whitelock 1952, 166–7.
[6] op. cit., 168; 1968, 12–15.
[7] Harmer 1952, 241.
[1] Robertson 1939, 20.

penalty prescribed by the law. Anyone refusing to render tithes in accordance with the code, was liable to lose nine-tenths, instead of the one-tenth he should have paid. In this case the church was to have its tithe, and the bishop was to have two-fifths of the property. Two-fifths also went to the lord of the manor, so that major landowners too, benefited from defaulters.[1] Cnut required his bishops and reeves to ensure that full payment of church dues had been made before he came to England in 1027, or they would be exacted by royal officials sternly and without remission.[2]

However, people must still have been unwilling to pay tithes, since Edgar's code at *Wihtbordesstan* declares that laymen have resisted the frequent admonitions which our teachers have given about our Lord's tribute, namely our tithes and church scot. The latter was to be paid in grain, but Loyn suggests that the lesser tithe on the young animals, vegetables, and poultry was more personal in many ways, and became more bitterly resented.[3] Alcuin wrote of the difficulty of exacting tithes from converts, and perhaps not surprisingly this remained a problem.[4] Tithing probably entailed some abstinence on the part of those tithed unless they had large landholdings, as Ælfric likens the fast of Lent to tithing days 'when we tithe our bodies with abstinence'.[5]

The 'plague' (*færcwealme*) which befell the land in 962, was attributed particularly to the withholding of tithes.[6] However, almost any disaster, natural or man-made, could be ascribed to the non-payment of tithes. According to Gregory of Tours, the hermit Hospitius who lived near Nice in the late sixth century attributed the Lombard invasions to the wickedness of the people and their failure to pay tithes, with the result that 'the poor are not nourished . . . the pilgrims not received in the guest house and adequately fed'.[7] There are several early references to the tithe being used to support the poor and pilgrims as well as the clergy, and this situation is confirmed by the laws of Æthelred and the writings of Ælfric.[8] Bede reports that Eadberht who succeeded Cuthbert as bishop of Lindisfarne in 687, in accordance with the law gave a tenth part to the poor every year not only of animals but also of all crops and fruits and also of clothes.[9] Anyone who misused tithes was styled a slayer of the poor, for the very good reason that the poor were likely to starve without the charity provided by the church.[10] Edgar does enjoin that the servants of God who received the dues should *libban clænan life* (live a wholesome life), so they could intercede more effectively for their contemporaries.[1]

Income also came from fines: these normally went to the king, or the lord of the manor, but were sometimes granted to religious institutions. Bishops were to see that the fines they were entitled to from religious offences were to be put to good use. In part they were to pay for the maintenance of the indigent, and to cloth and feed 'those

---

[1] op. cit., 22.
[2] Robertson 1925, 152–3.
[3] Loyn 1970, 256.
[4] Constable 1964, 33.
[5] Loyn 1970, 255.
[6] Robertson 1939, 28.
[7] Constable 1964, 22.
[8] op. cit., 27, 50.
[9] op. cit., 22.
[10] op. cit., 49.
[1] op. cit., 30.

who serve God'.[1] In *VIII Æthelred*, the king's reeves are enjoined: 'in every locality to support the abbots with all their worldly needs as you best can, and if you desire God's favour and mine, help their stewards everywhere to obtain their rights, so that they themselves may constantly remain secure in their monasteries and live according to their Rule' (*on æghwilcere stowe þat ge þam abbodan æt eallum worldneodum beorgan swa ge betst magon 7 be þam þe ge willan Godes oððe minne freondscipe habban, filstan heora wicneran æghwar to rihte, þæt heo sylfe magon þe oftor on mynstrum fæste gewunian 7 regollice libban*).[2] This follows a section dealing with the behaviour of abbots and monks, desiring them to live according to the Rule. As it was felt their intercessions on behalf of ruler and people would be less effective if they were living a worldly existence, it was at least in the spiritual interest of the king and his servants to keep them supplied within their communities.

The Size of Monastic Establishments

It is difficult to be certain of the size of early monastic establishments, but by the mid-seventh century, thirty brethren from the monastery in the province of the East Saxons went to settle at the monastery of Lastingham, and were welcomed by the monks there.[3] Since we are not told that all left, the original strength was presumably well over thirty. Bishop Colman established a monastery at Inishboffin for thirty English and an unspecified number of Scots 'all the Scots that he gathered on Lindisfarne as well' (*ealle þa Scottas þa he on Lindesfarena ea gesomnade*).[4] According to one account, the communities of Monkwearmouth and Jarrow, to which Ecgfrith granted seventy hides in 672, and a further forty in 681 for the second monastery, had more than six hundred brethren with estates of one hundred and fifty hides when abbot Ceolfrith departed in June 716.[5] However, there were much smaller establishments: around 678 'Dicul had a small monastery in which there were five or six brothers serving the Lord in a life of poverty and privation' (*Dicul hæfde ... medmicel mynster ... 7 in þæm wæron fif gebroðor oððe syxe in þearfendum life 7 earmlecum Drihtne þeowiende*).[6]

There are few details of the size of religious communities in the middle and late periods, but, in contrast to the seventh century when the numbers of monks were relatively large and monastic estates small, tenth and eleventh-century monastic establishments had small numbers of monks, but large estates (with the exception of Christchurch, Canterbury).[1] Between 965 and 1066, the monks at the Old and New Minsters, Winchester, averaged about forty or fifty, and there were only twenty-six monks at St. Benet's of Holme in 1020.[2] But by this time many of the monasteries were great landholders with the need for numerous dependants to maintain their buildings and work their estates.

---

[1] Loyn 1970, 260.
[2] Robertson 1925, 126.
[3] Miller 1890, I 2 232–4.
[4] op. cit., 272.
[5] Whitelock 1955, 706.
[6] Miller 1898, I 2 303.
[1] Dodwell 1982, 67.
[2] op. cit.

Evidently a careful control had to be kept on numbers. At St. Maur the monks agreed to keep their numbers at one hundred and forty, 'no more, no less ... in case there should not be enough food for the brothers' (*ne læs ne ma ... þe læs þe ðam gebroðrum bigleofan ateorode*).[1] Bucge, one of the corespondents of Boniface, writes that her religious community is troubled, not only by discord, but by poverty, in that it did not have enough land to support it, and she and her mother have no kin living to help them.[2] The various administrative problems, and the community's precarious existence induce in Bucge a wish to embark on a pilgrimage to Rome as a means of achieving peace of mind. Evidently the resources of a monastery might not be sufficient to feed all those who wished to enter. The Old English version of *The Rule of Chrodegang* had a section devoted to this very problem.

> *Miclum is to warnienne þam preuoste 7 þæs mynstres ealdre þæt hi na ma broðra into heora geferrædene underfon þonne þæs mynstres ar acuman mæge, þe læs hi mid ungesceade gesamnion swa fela swa hig begiman ne magon ne mid gerysnon forð bryngan. Witodlice manege syndon þe for manna ydelon gylpe micele geferrædene gesamniað, 7 þonne naðer ne (þære) sawele þearfe ne gymað, ne þæs lichaman frofres. Þonne witodlice þa þe þus beoð gegaderode, þonne hi nabbað æt heora ealdrum þa lichamlican þearfe þe him gebyreð to hæbbene, þonne forlætað hi heora rihtgesetednysse 7 þone godcundan þeowdom 7 þæs mynstres inwununge 7 gefeðrrædene, 7 farað ut 7 wyrðað wydscridole 7 hygelease, 7 gimað untidæta 7 druncennysse 7 oðra geflearda, 7 eal þæt him list, þæt hig lætað alyfedlic þing. For þi þonne is þam ealdrum miclum to warnienne on swilcum þingon, þæt hi mid miclum gesceade na ma (ne) underfon on heora geferrædene þonne þæs mynstres ar aberan mage; ne eft þæt hig for heora agenre gytsunge nanne þæra forlætan þe hi to mynstres þearfe behofiað 7 þe hi forð magon bringan mid gesceade.*

The priests and elders of the minster are to be very careful that they do not receive into their fellowship more than the benefice can provide for, in case they unwisely assemble so many that they are not able to continue to support them fittingly. Certainly there are many who – in vain – gather a great congregation out of vainglory and neither heed their souls' need nor the comfort of the body. Then indeed those who have been assembled in this way, when they do not have enough to supply their bodily needs, then they forgo right-living and the divine service, living properly in the fellowship of the minster, and leave and wander abroad, careless, indulge in excessive eating and drinking and other ridiculous things, and do just as they wish and give up lawful practices. Therefore the elders are greatly to be warned against such things, that they with great discernment may not receive into their fellowship more than the minster's resources can support, nor again, that they for their own desire will not forsake those who have need of the minster's support and that they may treat them still with discretion.[1]

[1] Skeat 1881, *St Maur* 1.265.
[2] Fell 1984, 111.
[1] Napier 1916, 10–11.

A particular aspect of the problem is aired in Alcuin's letter of 801 to Calvinus and Cuculus, where he displays his concern over the excessive number of thegns in the retinue of Eanbald, archbishop of York, 'He seems to maintain them out of pity. He is harming the monastic folk who receive him with his following . . . [the thegns] have more of the common sort, that is lowborn soldiers, than is fitting . . . [Æthelbert of York] allowed no-one of his followers to have more than one such, apart from the heads of his household who had two only. That pity is imprudent that benefits a few – and those perhaps criminals – and harms many – and those good men'.[1]

St. Eufrasia asked how many there were in a particular minster, and receiving the answer, 'Three hundred and fifty-two', asked if the abbot would receive anyone who wanted to enter. On receiving an affirmative reply, she promises many possessions to the minster if the abbot will admit her.[2] It seems likely that a novice who was also a landowner would be particularly welcomed, especially when their resources would effectively subsidise others. In 656 Oswin, king of Northumbria, on the occasion of his daughter's dedication to the religious life, grants six estates, each of 10 *familiae* in Deira, and six similar estates in Bernicia for the needs of the monks.[3] At the beginning of the eighth century, Puch, a *gesith*, granted the manor of Walkington to the church of Beverley when his daughter Yolfride became a nun there.[4] King Alfred bequeathed to Shaftesbury a hundred hides 'with produce and men, as they stand (*mid mete 7 mid manne al so it stant*) and his daughter Æthelgifu along with the inheritance, since she took the veil on account of ill-health. And the profits of jurisdiction to the convent – namely the fines for obstruction and attacks on a man's house and breach of protection'.[5] The income from the estates that made up the hundred hides would obviously be able to support a number of other inmates besides Æthelgifu herself. A charter of about 1060 of an estate to Peterborough abbey by Burred and his parents sounds like a gift accompanying the presentation of Burred as a novice at the monastery.[6] The eleventh-century *Life of St. David* suggests that fees normally had to be paid on admission to a community.[7]

An idea of the comparative size and wealth of the monasteries is given by their gross income recorded in Domesday. This varies from the £840 for Glastonbury, and £790 for Ely, to £278 for St. Alban's, to a calculated £54.16s.0d for Muchelney, £17.8s.4d for Buckfast and £2 for Swavesey. Of the post-Conquest foundations, Battle with an income of £212.3s.2d was the most important.[8]

According to Domesday, in 1066 Bury St. Edmunds held three hundred manors and had an annual income of over six hundred pounds. The basic food supply by this time was made in terms of a month's food rent, which might be supplied by one estate, e.g. Rougham, or might be produced by two or three estates together, e.g. 'from Rickinghall a month's food rent together with Stoke and Brockford' (*On*

[1] Whitelock 1955, 797.
[2] Skeat 1881, *St Eufrasia* 1.63, 145.
[3] Hart 1972, 131.
[4] op. cit., 134–5.
[5] Robertson 1939, 24.
[6] Hart 1975, 65.
[7] Davies 1982, 154.
[8] Knowles 1940, 702–3.

Ricyncgahale anes monðes ferma mid Stoca 7 Brocaforde).[1] Perhaps lunar months were referred to, since the total comes to thirteen months.[2] Moreover seventy-five workpeople: bakers, brewers, tailors, washerwomen and cooks waited daily on the saint, the abbot and the brethren.[3] While some specialists may have been monks, clearly a number who worked for the community were lay people, and there may have been other permanent dependants, like the boys mentioned in Ælfric's *Colloquy*.[4] For some or all of these, the community may have provided food.[5]

Eleventh-century figures show an increase after the Conquest. There were twelve monks at Westminster under Dunstan, but eighty by 1085.[6] Christchurch had over sixty at the time of Domesday, but ninety by 1090, Evesham: twelve (1059), thirty-six (1077), sixty-seven (1095); Worcester: twelve (1060), fifty (1088).[7] The newly established community of Battle was about sixty strong by 1080.[8] Other figures, with the year they were recorded are Durham: twenty-three (1083); Ely: fifty (1110); Glastonbury: seventy-two (1160); Gloucester: eleven (1072); Norwich: sixty (1100); Peterborough: sixty (1125); Rochester: sixty (1110); Tewkesbury: fifty-seven (1105); Winchester (New Minster): about forty (1040).[9]

The Monastery as a Self-Contained Unit

The monastery described by the Benedictine Rule is a completely self-contained and self-sufficient unit, both economically and constitutionally, supported by the produce of its fields and garden, and having within its enclosure all that is necessary to convert the produce into food.[10] Presumably early Saxon monastic communities were, or aimed to be, self-supporting, with the monks taking it in turns to carry out the various tasks. There was conflict at Inishboffin as the Scottish monks left for the summer, leaving the English the task of harvesting, but expected to return to enjoy the stores.[11] At Monkwearmouth/Jarrow in the abbey of Eosterwine the monks produced and processed all the grain needed for food as well as cultivating crops of vegetables, including leeks, and raising sheep and cattle for milk, butter and cheese.[12] Eosterwine himself was reputed to enjoy the tasks of threshing and winnowing.[13] However, the fact that Bede specifically records of the monastery of Maigeo in Ireland which held a number of monks *of Ongolcynne*, that they lived 'by the labour of their own hands' (*heora agnum hondgewinne*) suggests that not all monks did so.[1] Although the Rule suggested that monks shared the duties of the kitchen and bakehouse, in later years it was accounted praiseworthy that Æthelwold took his turn as one of the *hebdomadarii coquinæ*, to labour in the kitchen, or for his week obeyed the orders of the *hordere* (steward), and

---

[1] Robertson 1939, 194–6.
[2] op. cit.
[3] Dodwell 1982, 68; Poole 1958, 215.
[4] Davies 1982, 156.
[5] op. cit., 165.
[6] Whitelock 1955, 700; Knowles 1940, 714.
[7] op. cit..
[8] op. cit., 713.
[9] op. cit., 714.
[10] op. cit., 4.
[11] Miller 1890, I 2 274.
[12] Hunter Blair 1970, 208.
[13] op. cit., 177.
[1] Miller 1890, I 2 274.

sweated in the hayfield, the fallow or the garden.[1] This suggests that in general monks occupying higher positions in the monastic hierarchy, may have left the work of producing and processing food to others. In fact, the community which was too small to specialize, and to benefit from intensively labouring at busy times, can have had little time for activities other than those of self-support.[2]

By the end of the twelfth century the great monasteries of Glastonbury, Bury, Evesham and Abingdon had between thirteen and twenty officials in charge of various functions, some at least of which had existed in pre-Conquest times.[3] For example, all four had a cellarer and a refectorer, three had a kitchener, and the same three a pittancer, whose responsibility was the provision of extra dishes – the number varied with the grade of feast – on feast days.[4] In post-Conquest times the cellarer was the provider of all foodstuffs for monks, guests, poor and servants, save in so far as special contributions of food and drink came in directly to departmental officials from certain manors or tenants. His business was to maintain stocks of the great staples: flour, fish, beans and beer, from which other departments drew.[5] The kitchener was the immediate caterer for the monks. He received directly a number of perishable foodstuffs: honey, eggs, milk from the farmer, and the rest, such as flour and dry vegetables he drew from the cellarer. He was responsible for the food while it remained in the kitchen.[6] Abingdon had also a chamberlain, and a pittancer of the farmer, but no master of the guests, a post in the other three, although it had a hosteler. Three had established the post of gardener, and one a keeper of the granary, while all four had an almoner, responsible for the poor.[7]

A section of the Old English *Rule of Chrodegang* is devoted to the post of *hordere* (translating the latin *cellarius*), which indicates the importance of this official in pre-Conquest times:

> Se hordere sceal him God andrædan, 7 beon syfre 7 na druncengeorn, ne ceaslunger, ne wearmod, ac gemetfæst, on þeawum wær, 7 getrywe, ne modig, ne sleac, ne myrrend, ne idelgeorn, ac healde georne swa hwæt swa under his gymene to preosta neode betæht beo, þe læs þa þenas þe under him beoð to broðra neode gesette, þara broðra god þurh stæling ætferion, oððe on ænige wisan amyrron. Þa wicneras sceolon beon gecorene of þam getrywestan mynstres þeowum, 7 hi man þonne geornlice ty þæt hi gode bæcystran beon 7 to ælcum meteþingum clængeorne þe to broðra behofe belimpe. 7 ealswa we wyllað þæt þa cocas clængeorne beon 7 wel getyde.[8]

The cellarer shall be god-fearing, sober and not given to drunkenness, nor quarrelsome or choleric, but modest, aware of the general practice of the community, and trustworthy, not proud or slack, obstructive or lazy, but shall diligently look after everything committed to his charge that is to supply the brothers' needs, in case the servants that are under him to supply

[1] Symons 1953, Sect 64; Cockayne 1851, III 408.
[2] Davies 1982, 152.
[3] Knowles 1940, 713.
[4] op. cit., 430.
[5] op. cit.
[6] op. cit.
[7] op. cit.
[8] Napier 1916, 19.

the brothers' needs should steal the brothers' supplies or dissipate them in any way. The stewards shall be chosen from the most trustworthy of the minster's servants, and they shall be carefully instructed in how to be good bakers, and to be cleanly when it comes to dealing with any of the brothers' food. And we also require that the cooks shall be concerned with cleanliness and well skilled.

The resources were not necessarily shared. It is recorded of the monastery at Whitby under the rule of Hild 'that after the example of the primitive church no-one there was rich or poor, but all were equal and no-one regarded anything as his own' (*þæt in bisene þære frymþelecan ciricean nænig þær welig wæs ne nænig wædla; ac eallum wæron eal gemæno, 7 noht agnes ængum gesegen wæs*).[1] Had this been standard procedure it is unlikely that Bede would have commented on it. The Old English *Rule of Chrodegang* has a section 'That those in a religious establishment should all have the same to eat and drink' (*Be þam þæt on preosta geferrædene ealle gelice onfon ætes 7 wætes*) which goes on to suggest that those members of communities who would have enjoyed superior food and drink in secular circumstances attempted to preserve that privilege when they joined a monastery.

> *Hit is gewuna on manegum preosthiredum þæt mid miclum ungesceade 7 ungefade sume þa preostas þe woroldwelan habbað, 7 lytle oððe nane nytwyrðnysse doð on mynstre, scolon maran 7 creaslicran fodan habban on mynstre þonne þa þe ealne þone godcundan þeowdom for(d)dod, 7 we þæs nane bysne nabbað ne on boca gesceadnyssum, ne on haligra fædera hæsum. Witodlice hit is gesceadwislic 7 rihtlic for Gode 7 for worolde þæt on ælcum preosthirede fram þam gingstan oð þæne yld(e)stan ealle (gelice) æt 7 drinc underfon þe þære geferrædene beon 7 ænigre note nytte magon on mynstre beon. Þeah on manegum oðrum þincgum þa ealdras sceolon wyrðuncge ætforan heora underþeoddum habbað, on þisum þincgum we nellað nane twislunge habban nanes hades, ac sy gelic eallum seald æt 7 drinc efne ætsamne.*[2]

It is customary in many religious communities that – with great unreason and indecorum – those priests who have worldly wealth and do little or nothing that is useful in the minster, have more and better food than those who perform godly tasks, and there is no authority for this either in the teachings of books or the commands of the holy fathers. Indeed it is reasonable and right in the sight of God and the world that each member of the religious community, from the youngest to the oldest, shall share the same food and drink out of fellowship and any benefit that there may be in the minster. Though in many other matters the elders shall closely pay heed to their subordinates, in this matter we shall not permit any deviation according to rank, but each shall be given exactly the same food and drink.

Monastic property was an easy prey for the rapacious, and Bede complains that kings and bishops were taking away monastery lands which would provide not only for the monks and their servitors, but for travellers and the poor.[1] Writing to Cuthbert,

---

1 Miller 1890, I 2 334.
2 Napier 1916, 13.
1 Turner 1828, III 493.

archbishop of Canterbury in 747, Boniface deplores the – apparently current – abuse whereby a layman seized a monastery and its money. Such a man was a 'murderer of the poor'.[1] This suggests that the charitable relief of the poor from excess produce was a major function of the monastery, but also that the monks received sufficient sustenance themselves. The attaching of monastic lands by powerful individuals seems to have continued. We learn that Eadwig, who died in 959, 'through his childish ignorance', 'distributed the land belonging to holy churches to strangers and robbers' (*halegra cyricena land incuþum reaferum todælde*).[2] Such actions perhaps prompted the law of Edgar that all tithes and church scot were to be paid to the old minster to which obedience was due. Landowners tended to build churches on their own estates and to use the income which they generated. Rather than the excommunication invoked by Edmund, Edgar introduced penal legislation for this offence, and it was reaffirmed by Æthelred and Cnut.[3] However, this did not put an end to the abuses. 'King Harold had Sandwich taken from Christchurch for his own use, and held it himself for about a year – and at any rate for two whole herring seasons' (*Harold king let beridan Sandwic of Christes cyrcean him sylfan to handa and hæfde hit him wel neh twelf monað 7 twegen hæringc timan swa þæh fullice*).[4]

Conclusion

The provisioning of monasteries was not only to provide food for the monks, but was also to supply food for others who might be present. The Benedictine Rule stressed the importance of providing service to those in the guesthouse – travellers or the poor (*peregrinis, pauperibus*).[5] This redistribution of resources was an extremely important function of the monastery, making food available to numbers of people who would otherwise have starved. By providing provisions for guests, monasteries supported travel by various sections of the community, rather than just landowners who could call on food resources at their various estates.

Establishment of tithing incorporated into legislation what was otherwise an *ad hoc* arrangement. According to Æthelred's laws, one-third of the tithe was to be spent on the repair of churches, one-third was to go to the servants of God, and the remaining third was to go to the poor and poverty-stricken slaves.[6]

The gifting of food, either *per se* or as potential produce from gifts of land, for the monks or their benefactions had a spiritual dimension. Either explicitly or implicitly, this was one side of a reciprocal arrangement, which ensured prayers for the soul of the donors. Unneeded material resources were traded for spiritual reserves.

This is one area where there is still very little in the way of archaeological evidence. Only a small proportion of the seventh- to ninth-century monastic sites have been excavated, and until recently only four of the later tenth- and eleventh-century monasteries had been investigated.[1] It is difficult to relate archaeological evidence to

---

[1] Kylie 1911, 189.
[2] Cockayne 1851, III.
[3] Loyn 1970, 255; Whitelock 1955, 165–6.
[4] Robertson 1939, 174.
[5] Symons 1953, Sect. 63, 64.
[6] Loyn 1970, 255.
[1] Cramp in Wilson 1976, 203.

the provision of food in any quantifiable way, but skeletal evidence seems to indicate a likelihood that high status clerics at Wells were obese.[1] The well-fed monk caricatured in the later Middle Ages perhaps had his antecedents in the Anglo-Saxon period. A plentiful supply of desirable food may have made the church a relatively attractive career prospect.

The food provided for funeral and anniversary feasts confirms fish, fatty meat, hams, poultry, cheeses, white bread, ale (particularly sweet Welsh, clear or mild), and honey as delicacies.

---

[1] Rogers & Young 1994, S114.

25. The Food Supply in Towns

This chapter is concerned with the food supply of those who could not draw directly upon the land for their sustenance, either because they were not involved in subsistence agriculture on their own account, or because they were not members of landowning establishments, secular or religious. Some such individuals – craftsmen and traders – may have lived in rural locations, but most would have lived in towns.

The criteria of a medieval town have been listed as follows: defences; a planned street system; (a) market(s); a mint; legal autonomy; a role as a 'central place'; a relatively large and dense population; a diversified economic base; plots and houses of urban types; social differentiation; complex religious organisation; a judicial centre.[1] Biddle considered that a place possessing three or four of these features merits serious consideration as a town.[2] However, a definition of a town as permanent human settlement in which a significant proportion of the population is involved in non-agricultural occupations, and which forms a social unit more or less distinct from the surrounding countryside is helpful in being more comprehensive. In the context of the provision of a food supply, I am concerned with settlements where even a small proportion of the population was involved in non-agricultural occupations, and so the term 'town' here includes what would now be thought of as villages.

In contrast to the Roman economy, which was based on central places, Germanic institutions tended to be focused on central persons.[3] The manors of nobles, like royal estates, became centres of population, as did religious foundations.[4] A topographical pattern centred on royal residences and religious foundations can be traced back to the eighth century in some areas.[5] Proto-urban settlements were developing round royal centres, and no doubt monastic ones too, in the ninth century.[6] Royal residences provided the basis for settlement and expansion.[7] One such basis for settlement was the surplus of food that such establishments provided.[8] However, documentary evidence for this is extremely rare. One contemporary example is continental: at Annapes the palace gardens produced something to the value of 11 sous before c.820.[9] The fourteenth- fifteenth-century Axbridge Chronicle refers to the duties of the royal officials in the time of Æthelstan, Edmund, Eadred, Edgar and St. Edward as being to gather victuals for the king's stay. If the king did not arrive, these were to be sold in the market, and the money sent to the treasury.[10] Obviously such surpluses could have fed 'artisan and bureaucratic' classes.[11]

---

1 Hodges 1982, 21.
2 quoted in Haslam 1984, 203.
3 Hodges 1982, 29.
4 op. cit., 171.
5 Astill in Haslam 1984, 89.
6 Haslam 1984, 276.
7 Keen in Haslam 1984, 230.
8 Haslam 1984, 138.
9 Hodges 1982, 132.
10 op. cit., 168.
11 op. cit., 130.

The Burghal Hidage indicates towns, even if these were 'new towns', such as Barnstaple and Totnes in Devon, in the time of Edward the Elder, 891–911.[1] On the evidence of mints and the Domesday Book, the chief boroughs towards the end of the Anglo-Saxon period were London, York, Winchester, Lincoln, Chester, Worcester, Norwich and Ipswich.[2] Other centres of importance were Gloucester, Tamworth, Stafford and Warwick.[3] By the end of the period there were more than a hundred places with some claim to be regarded as towns, and which contained an estimated ten percent of the population. Of these, seventy-one were not on royal estates or on the estates of ecclesiastical or secular lords.[4] From the late seventh century, the Anglo-Saxon economy was money-based, and from 973, as a result of deliberate policy, no inhabitant of England south of the Humber would find himself more than a reasonable journey from a mint.[5] Recovery of coins is influenced by many factors – coins found do not necessarily reflect the numbers of transactions taking place; *sceattas* were a large-scale currency.[6] Domesday references to markets which provided income, to burgesses, or, as in the case of Glastonbury, to eight smiths, may all indicate towns.[7]

Since it is impossible to attempt a comprehensive review, most of the evidence concerns London, *Hamwih* and York, with occasional reference to other towns. This serves to identify the main features and problems of the topic. London was in origin a Roman town, and British squatters were likely to have used its declining facilities until the mid-sixth century, although its original economic function may not have continued beyond the end of the fifth century.[8] London became the capital of Essex at the beginning of the seventh century, and this may indicate the revival of trade along the Thames. By the 640's London had once again become a commercial centre, with issues of gold *thrymsas* and silver *sceattas* in the second half of the century, and was trading with Quentovic, Dorestad and Domburg.[9] In the law codes of Hlothhere and Eadric (673–85), the city is called *Lundenwic*, (the market town of London) and the kings of Kent have a hall there.[10] Bede wrote that 'London is a market for many people coming by land and sea' (*Lundenceaster . . . is monigra folca ceapstow of londe 7 of sæ cumendra*).[11] Fitzstephen's description of London in about 1183 refers to goods brought by 'merchants from every nation under heaven'.[12] There was then continuity of trading, even if this was temporarily disrupted by such upheavals as Viking raids and the Conquest. Traders could buy provisions for their ships in London, and when, in Ælfric's *Lives of the Saints*, Malchus buys all their food for the Seven Sleepers in Rome, this passes without comment.[13] Presumably it was assumed that one could buy food readily in a major city.

---

[1] Aston in Haslam 1984, 178; Haslam 1984, 279.
[2] Whitelock 1952, 130.
[3] Biddle in D.M. Wilson 1976, 133–4.
[4] op. cit., 141.
[5] Loyn in Blackburn 1986, 2, 6.
[6] Hinton in op. cit., 20, 26.
[7] Aston in Haslam 1984, 178.
[8] Whittock 1986, 172.
[9] op. cit., 173.
[10] Robertson 1925.
[11] Miller 1890, I 1 104.
[12] Poole 1958, 226.
[13] Skeat 1881.

A writer of about 1000 said that York (*Eoforwic*) had a population of 30,000 adults, a figure which may be greatly exaggerated.[1] A number of eighth-century coins known as 'porcupine stycas', a medium of international trade, have been discovered there, indicating the site was visited by, or was the home of traders.[2] The impression given by the recent excavations of Anglo-Scandinavian York, is of a large number of small tenements, indicating that there was considerable pressure on land within the town in the tenth century. By 975–8 land in Winchester had become expensive, since the community of the Old Minster was ready to relinquish 12 hides which they were holding at an annual food rent, in order to obtain a plot of only 2 acres in the city.[3] On a conservative estimate of five persons to a tenement Norwich had a population of 6,600 in 1066.[4]

Like London, Lincoln seems to have been almost continuously occupied, and to have had a commercial function. When Paulinus preached in Lindsey in the 620's he met a *præfectus*, a reeve, which implies some degree of civic life, and he went on to build a 'stone church of fine workmanship' there.[5] Excavations at Flaxengate revealed buildings used in the Anglo-Saxon period, and perhaps a remnant of the population continued to live in the town up to the time Paulinus met the reeve. By the end of the period Lincoln was an important urban centre.[6]

Hamwih flourished from the late seventh century to some point in the ninth. Its wooden houses were built quite close together, closer than at the contemporary continental port of Dorestad.[7] Trade may have been disrupted by Viking incursions, but whatever the reason, the settlement moved a short distance across the peninsula to what became Southampton.[8]

There was some food production within the towns: townsfolk could pasture their cattle on the town common.[9] Most people could perhaps keep pigs in sties near their houses, and poultry too could be kept on a domestic scale. There were crofts and gardens within and around the walls.[10] In Northampton a timber hall dated by a St. Edmund memorial penny unlikely to have been deposited after 917, was associated with a small cultivated plot.[11] Vegetables and fruit could be grown, and this was presumably the case even in the most populous centres like London, since as late as 1345 the gardeners of various nobles and citizens were creating a nuisance selling off their masters' pulse, cherries, vegetables and other wares around the gate of St. Paul's churchyard.[12] Some magnates could afford to keep land for gardens into a later period still: the bishop of Ely's garden in Holborn was famous for its strawberries.[13]

---

[1] Whitelock 1952, 130.
[2] Kemp 1986, 11.
[3] Whitelock 1952, 129.
[4] op. cit., 130.
[5] Whittock 1986, 178.
[6] O'Connor 1982.
[7] Bourdillon 1980, 181.
[8] Haslam 1984, 163.
[9] Whitelock 1952, 131.
[10] op. cit.
[11] Williams 1984, 113.
[12] Drummond & Wilbraham 1958.
[13] *Richard III*, III iv 32ff.; *Henry V*, I i 60.

No doubt there were farms at hand which produced protein surplus to the requirements of their occupants, and which could be disposed of to the non-agrarian section of the community and to visitors.[1] Periodic markets, weekly or annual, were probably the precursors of permanent shops. Held where numbers of people lived/assembled, they were therefore likely to have been found in royal or religious centres. Canterbury was both, and a 'market place' (*venalis locus*) was established there by the eighth century.[2] Charters of 923 and 1002 refer to a 'cattle-market' (*hrypera ceap* or *ryperceap*), and the cattle market operated until 1955 on the same site just outside the eastern walls.[3] Oat and salt markets in Canterbury were recorded in the twelfth century and may have existed earlier.[4]

There was probably a system of markets, the days on which local markets were held being arranged so as not to conflict with each other. This pattern is still observable in some areas. At Hoxne, Suffolk, in the days of King Edward there was a market which continued to be held on a Saturday in the time of King William. When William Malet made his castle at Eye, he held a market there on Saturdays, whereby the bishop's market declined so that it was worth little.[5] Markets tend to be mentioned only when they were the subject of a dispute, as in this case, or for the amount of income they brought in. Annual markets, 'fairs', tended to attract a large number of people. The annual fair at *beorna-wyl* (Barnwell), Cambridgeshire, was held on the eve of the Nativity of St. John the Baptist, and 'on account of the number of girls and boys who gathered there it grew a custom for a crowd of sellers and buyers to assemble on the same day for the purpose of commerce'.[6] This fair probably attracted traders from abroad; the fair of St. Denys near Paris was visited by Anglo-Saxons from the middle of the seventh century.[7] The Welsh Laws declared that proclamations were to be made in every fair and market, which indicates the large numbers of people present.[8]

Cheapside, London, was associated in the twelfth century with the food markets of Honey Lane, Bread, Milk and Friday (i.e. Fish) Streets, and the Poultry. These had originated in the sale of surplus food rents rendered to the Chapter of St. Paul's at the western end of the street.[9] Estates established town houses as convenient centres for marketing or as storehouses for buying as well as residences.[10] There were almost certainly permanent shops in the major towns by the end of the Anglo-Saxon period. Winchester had its Fleshmongers' Street before about 1000, and there was also Ceap Street.[11] Street names in York suggest organised marketing on a comparatively large scale in Anglo-Scandinavian times. *Bootham* meant at the booths/stalls, and Cook Row was established by 1377.[12] One butchers' lane survives as The Shambles, deriving from *flæsc-scamol* (a stall on which meat is sold), and is mentioned in Domesday as a food market. There was also *Haimanghergate* (the street of the hay-

---

[1] Prummel 1983, 254–5.
[2] Poole 1958, 240.
[3] Tatton-Brown in Haslam 1984, 8.
[4] op. cit.
[5] Loyn 1970, 370.
[6] Wright 1871, 80.
[7] Hodges 1982, 90.
[8] Owen 1841, II 541.
[9] Dyson and Schofield in Haslam 1984, 304.
[10] Loyn 1970, 109.
[11] Biddle in D.M. Wilson 1976, 125–7.
[12] Palliser 1978.

sellers), and *Kethmangergata*, from *kiotmangari* (meat sellers).[1] However, *ket* means horseflesh, and it is possible that Scandinavian tastes were being catered for.[2] By 1100 the king was drawing the sum of £3.1s.4d. from stalls in Winchester High Street, and Queen Edith had owned shops in front of a tenement there.[3] A kitchen gave the tenant an income of five shillings – much more than he paid in rent.[4]

By 1183 there was a cookshop in London which sold a great variety of hot meals for rich and poor. Fitzstephen lists some of the delicacies available and calls it appropriate to a city.[5] It is hard to tell whether he means that the extensive menu was appropriate to a city, or whether he is referring to the cookshop itself. It seems likely that cookshops would have opened, at least on market days, in centres where there was a demand for ready-cooked food.

Flour was probably produced within towns. Fourteen mills were mentioned in the Domesday record for Derby, and the tenth-century boundaries of a small site in Winchester include the west, east and old mills.[6] At Lewisham, Kent, the eleven town mills had the custom of the rural population as well as the townsfolk.[7]

Town-dwellers could probably have bought flour relatively easily, provided they could afford it, and no doubt many made their own bread. However, bread was probably one of the first ready-cooked foods available for sale. Time-consuming to make, and much improved by cooking in a purpose-built oven, it would have been likely to find a ready market. Free burgesses were recorded as working as bakers in the *pistrinum* (bakery) of the earl.[8] They may have cooked bread for sale, as well as for the lord's household. By 1100 Winchester had Robert, Roger, Seaman, Hugh and Baldwin as bakers, and a William Sourloaf is recorded.[9]

Other food may have been baked in bread ovens. The residual heat after baking was probably used for cooking dishes which needed a gentler heat for a longer period of time. In Victorian England, poorer members of the community who did not have an oven and were rarely able to afford the kind of food that demanded cooking in an oven, would take any special joints to be cooked at the bakers (cf. the Crachits' Christmas goose). This amenity of town life would probably have been available in Anglo-Saxon times. Charcoal was on sale in Paris in the thirteenth century, and was to be bought up for re-sale between Easter and All Saints.[10] It would have been a convenient fuel in Anglo-Saxon towns too since it was less bulky and would burn at a higher temperature than wood.

The meat supply in middle-Saxon towns seems to have been similar to that in contemporary settlements on the continent. As at Dorestad, almost all the meat at *Hamwih* came from domesticated mammals, and beef provided more than half the

---

[1] cf. Mod. Danish kød – meat.
[2] *Interim* Vol 2, No. 1 48–9.
[3] Barlow 1976, 27, 38.
[4] op. cit.
[5] Drummond and Wilbraham 1958.
[6] Whitelock 1952, 131.
[7] Bennett & Elton 1899, 115–6.
[8] op. cit., 116.
[9] Barlow 1976, 16, 45, 94, 126, 135–8.
[10] Holmes 1952, 135.

meat consumed.[1] At Hamwih the fragment count gave 53% cattle, 32% sheep and 15% pig. A good sufficiency of sizeable cattle indicates sound provisioning, for a solid surplus of cattle places more demands on pasture and organisation than sheep or pigs.[2] A high ratio of cattle to pigs is the strongest indication of the substantial provisioning of the town, and the ratio of 2·5:1 is greater than the 1·25 growing to 1·5:1 at Haithabu.[3] The percentage of cattle was still growing at the end of *Hamwih*'s existence.[4] This indicates the rural base was well able to supply the demand for cattle; cattle do not dominate pigs again until the sixteenth century.[5] The animals were quite large, which is another indication the town was drawing on a well-stocked and well-run countryside.[6] There was a dearth of younger animals and old animals which were common on rural sites in the region, like Ramsbury, Wilts..[7] The animals coming into *Hamwih* were of an age and size produced by a good period of successful rearing before their selection for provisioning the town.[8] The same sort of age range is found later at Exeter, where 46–78% of the sheep were younger than 25 months old, but lambs dying in their first year were under-represented.[9] In tenth-century Skeldergate, cattle, sheep and pigs were slaughtered at an age when they had attained something close to their adult body size. They would have yielded carcasses of prime meat.[10] In Anglo-Scandinavian York cattle bones are again much more numerous than those of sheep/goat or pig.[11] The evidence suggests that towns could command high-quality meat, and that beef was preferred. The term *mete*, still meant food generally in Anglo-Saxon times, gaining its modern meaning about 1300, but perhaps a taste for fresh meat was already growing in Anglo-Saxon towns where consumers could exercise choice over their diet.

Animals were almost certainly brought in to towns on the hoof, a practice continued into this century. At Skeldergate, and Anglo-Scandinavian York there is evidence that the animals were slaughtered within the town, since there are large numbers of horn cores and cattle skulls.[12] Presumably Archbishop Ælfheah was near a slaughteryard in London when pelted with bones and ox-heads.[13] At *Hamwih* the meat presumably came in on the hoof, but the flesh was then trimmed from the bone, the bones chopped to release their fat and marrow before being quickly cast into pits. The bones were probably never cooked.[14]

Hamwih judged by its animal bone was homogeneous, with no clear differences in social usage or in custom between one area and the next.[15] One cannot generalise from one town, but perhaps one might expect town-dwellers to share a similar

---

[1] Prummel 1983, 248.
[2] Bourdillon 1980, 182.
[3] op. cit., 183–4.
[4] op. cit., 185.
[5] op. cit., 186.
[6] op. cit.
[7] Haslam 1980, 47–9.
[8] Bourdillon 1980, 185.
[9] Maltby 1979.
[10] O'Connor 1984, 19.
[11] Hall et al. 1983, 186.
[12] O'Connor 1984, 19; Kemp 1986, 11.
[13] Whitelock 1955, 222.
[14] Bourdillon 1980, 185.
[15] op. cit., 182.

standard of living, as their status was similar. Perhaps this would be more true of a recently-established settlement than one where differentials had operated over a period of time: with successful artisans and traders raising their standard of living relative to that of others.

The fisherman of Ælfric's *Colloquy* sold his catch *on ceastre* (which translates *civitate* – city), to the *ceasterwara* (city folk). The demand outstripped the supply: 'I cannot catch as many as I could sell' (*Ic ne mæg swa fela swa ic mæg gesyllan*).[1] Unfortunately he does not give us the additional information we would like to have. Did the townsfolk want to add variety to their diet? Was fish wanted as alternative protein for fast days? Was fish a convenience food – quick to prepare and with a short cooking time demanding less fuel? The high price put on whale was perhaps related to its high fat content, important nutritionally for those who ate very lean meat. The archaeological record shows that at *Hamwih* fish were important to the diet: eels, plaice and flounder proving the commonest species, with few fish brought from deeper water. Ælfric's fishermen seldom went to sea 'because it means too much rowing' (*forþam micel rewyt*), and clearly as he had a very good market for the estuarine fish he caught, there was little point in putting in the extra effort.[2] Fish were caught in sea ponds in the Solent when the tide fell, and these were associated with saltworks in Domesday.[3] Oysters, also gathered by the fishman, were eaten at *Hamwih*.[4] At York cod, herring and eel were the common species.[5] According to Domesday evidence, eels caught from the Thames in Buckinghamshire were transported live to London.[6] By 1100 Winchester had at least three herring-mongers.[7] *Craspois*, whale blubber, which was imported into London, and perhaps other ports, would leave no trace in the archaeological record. The same is true of stockfish, an important part of the diet in the latter middle ages. One town may have grown up around its oyster market: Whitstable possibly derives from the Norman French *huitre* (oyster) and the Old English *staple* (market).[8] More surprisingly, inland towns too included fish in their diet. In 1202 the Lord of the Manor of Winwick, Northants., had been taking toll in kind from carts of eels, green fish, salmon and herrings.[9] Since neither fishing techniques nor transport had changed much since Anglo-Saxon times (although more packhorses may have been used at the end of the period, and this would have speeded up deliveries), there is no reason why the same sort of fish could not have been available earlier in such inland areas.[10]

It is difficult to assess the rate of travel. Treasure carts in winter averaged 12 miles a day (which Stenton thinks was comparatively fast) and while travel was probably faster in summer, so was the rate of decomposition of fish and some at least of the Northamptonshire fish was described as *green* (fresh). Perhaps fish were

[1] Garmonsway 1978, 27.
[2] op. cit., 28.
[3] Currie in Ashton 1988, 283.
[4] Bourdillon 1980, 182.
[5] Hall et al. 1983, 186.
[6] Croft & Pike in Ashton 1988, 235.
[7] Barlow 1976, 39.
[8] Tatton-Brown in Haslam 1984, 34.
[9] Stenton 1936, 19.
[10] Langdon 1986, 27.

transported to inland towns primarily in winter. Certainly Lent when fish would certainly be consumed, is often a cold period. Packhorses could average around thirty miles a day, but carts were used to transport the fish in the instance cited.[1] The upkeep of roads and bridges was a charge on estates in Anglo-Saxon times, and a *port stræt*, leading to a town or market was one of the classified roads, obviously regarded as more important than local tracks like 'the foul way', or 'the clay way'.[2] The Old English Law was primarily concerned with the roads that lead 'from cities to cities, from boroughs to boroughs, by which men go to markets, or about their other affairs'. In other words, public opinion concentrated on the road which served the local market.[3] This suggests that the market, and the sale of at least some foodstuffs there, was important to the local community.

It seems that women sold dairy products in London since Æthelred established the rate of toll on cheese and butter in the two weeks leading up to Christmas. Eggs and hens were also sold. The toll exacted was one hen or five eggs per hamper (see Chapter 8). Small numbers of hen and goose bones have been recovered from town sites, but sometimes, as in York, the bones of domestic fowl and geese are moderately common.[4]

There are very few wild bird remains from urban sites like *Hamwih*, a situation which is general in continental urban centres too.[5] The hawker of the *Colloquy* says that his hawks feed themselves and him in the winter, but he does not say that he sells any of the wild birds or animals they caught.[6] It seems to have been a hobby: from the beginning of Lent until the autumn when he had tamed that year's young birds, the hawker too was dependent on other sources of food. Only a king or noble could afford the expense of keeping hawks all year (see Chapter 9).

The remains of game in *Hamwih*, or in contemporary Dorestad, for that matter, are very sparse.[7] There were no food remains of wild animals recovered from tenth-century Skeldergate (antler was present), although some bones of hare were recorded from Anglo-Scandinavian York.[8] The testimony of Ælfric's hunter perhaps explains why this is so. He is the king's servant, and so the deer, boars and hares he caught were given to the king.[9] These were prestige foods, and therefore were likely to be consumed by the court. The York hares may have been taken by the owners of greyhound-like dogs, who were not necessarily professional hunters.

By the end of the seventh century, London was trading with Quentovic, Dorestad and Domburg.[10] There were contacts with other foreign centres too (see Chapter 12). The inhabitants of towns which were also ports were most likely to have contacts with foreign merchants and the chance to acquire imported food, but traders also travelled inland. Their presence tended to be recorded only when something untoward

[1] op. cit., 17.
[2] op. cit., 2–3.
[3] op. cit., 3–4.
[4] Hall et al. 1983, 186.
[5] Bourdillon 1980, 189; Prummel 1983, 256.
[6] Garmonsway 1978, 32.
[7] Bourdillon 1980, 182; Prummel 1983, 256.
[8] O'Connor 1984, 19; Hall et al. 1983, 186.
[9] Garmonsway 1978, 24–5.
[10] Whittock 1986, 172.

happened. Irish merchants came to Cambridge (perhaps to the annual Beorna-wyl fair), with their wares in the time of King Edgar and a priest of the place stole some of their merchandise.[1] We do not know that these particular merchants were selling food, but there is no reason why merchants should not have imported food items valuable in relation to their size. The merchant of the *Colloquy* imported 'spices, wine and oil' (*wytgemangc, win 7 ele*).[2]

The moves to confine all buying and selling of livestock to market towns were based in a desire to stamp out theft (and perhaps to raise revenue from taxes and fines), rather than to enhance the provisioning of towns. Æthelstan's *Laws at Grateley* stated that no-one was 'to exchange any livestock without the witness of the reeve or the priest or lord . . . or the treasurer . . . or other trustworthy man'. This did not necessarily mean the transaction had to be carried out in a town, though there might be more likelihood of finding the necessary witnesses in a centre of population. Thirty shillings was the fine for breaking this decree, and the lord of the estate was to succeed to the exchanged property.[3] *I Edward* [*be ceapunge* (concerning trading)] extended the concept by saying that as well as having his warrantor, or witness, 'No man is to trade except at a market town, and he must have the witness of the reeve of the market or other men of credit who can be trusted, and if anyone buys and sells outside the town, then he is to give the king the fine for insubordination' (*nan man ceapige butan porte, ac hæbbe þæs portgerefan gewitnesse oððe opera ungeligenra manna, ðe man gelyfam mæge 7 gif butan porte ceapige, ðonne sy he cyninges oferhyrnesse scyldig*).[4] However, goods worth less than twenty pence seem to have been exempt from this regulation.[5] William's Laws repeated the requirement for trading to take place in market towns so that the customs could not be defrauded, and all things would be done openly and legally.[6] The Welsh Laws also declared that there should be no privileged markets except in the legitimate corporate cities.[7]

Marketing was not allowed on Sundays. Injunctions against it are repeated in one law code after another. Wulfstan's *Canons of Edgar* state: 'and we instruct that people refrain from Sunday marketing' (*And we læraðþæt man geswice sunnadæges cypinge*).[8] *Æthelstan II*: 'that no marketing is done on Sundays; if anyone does so, he shall lose his goods and pay thirty shillings fine' (*þæt nan cyping ne sy Sunnondagum; gif hit ðonne hwa do, polige ðæs ceapes 7 gesylle xxx scll. to wite*) introduces the idea of punishment.[9] The fine for this offence was 'twelve ores for a Dane' (*twelf orena mid Denum*).[10] *Æthelred VII* seems to recognise a civil penalty is being exacted for what is at bottom a religious offence: 'Sunday marketing is strictly forbidden under pain of incurring the full civil penalty' (*And Sunnondaga cypinga forbeode man georne be fullan world wite*).[1] The fact that this offence is mentioned so

---

[1] Wright 1871, 90.
[2] Garmonsway 1978, 33.
[3] Whitelock 1955, 383.
[4] Attenborough 1922, 114–5.
[5] op. cit., 134.
[6] Robertson 1925, 249.
[7] Owen 1841, II 515.
[8] Fowler 1972, 6.
[9] Attenborough 1922, 140.
[10] op. cit., 106.
[1] Robertson 1925, 123.

often seems to suggest that it was common. In terms of the townsman's food supply, it points to a situation similar to that prevailing generally not long ago this century, and still true for some areas: that is, that food shopping would be done on Saturday for the Sunday.

It is possible that the situation prevailing by the thirteenth century was already growing up, whereby the king's servants had the right to buy until 3 p.m. Moreover, no hucksters of meat or fish were allowed to go out of the city to make a deal with suppliers and increase the price, exploiting their knowledge of food shortages and what the market would bear.[1]

There were tolls to be paid on the sale of food. An Anglo-Saxon manuscript of the Psalms[2] contains a representation of a man taking toll in the market or at the gates of a city. He carries scales to weigh the money, and has a substantial sack for his takings.[3] Men from Flanders and France had to pay *sceawing* (a toll payable for the privilege of displaying goods for sale), before any sales took place.[4] A few examples will indicate the range of tolls and beneficiaries. 'The third part of the toll on horseloads and market sales' (*Þe tridde deles wyrþe of semtolne 7 of chyptolne*) was granted to St. Mary's minster, i.e. Worcester cathedral, by King Edward, probably in 1062. When the market at Hoxne, Suffolk, was referred to as the bishop's market, this was because he had the benefit of the tolls.[5] It was relatively common for the king to grant some proportion of the toll which belonged to him to religious foundations; Æthelred and Æthelflæd granted half their rights in the market and streets of Worcester, the toll of a shilling on cartloads and a penny on packloads of salt at *Saltwic* (Droitwich).[6] The foundation of SS Peter and Paul at Winchester had been granted all the trading dues from the market at Taunton, and this was renewed by King Edgar.[7] Another charter also refers to toll on cartloads of salt, and it seems the toll was exacted on loads just passing through the town: presumably another was payable at the point of sale.[8] At Lewes there was an extra impost of a halfpenny to the reeve on an ox, and the same from the buyer.[9] In the case of an ox valued at thirty pence, this represents a tax of something under four percent, but it is difficult to know what percentage such tolls added to the overall cost of food for those who had to buy it in.

At *Hamwih* the human bone remains seem to indicate the population was extremely well-nourished. This was predicted from the animal bone remains which indicated the town was plentifully supplied with meat.[10] The remains from Anglo-Scandinavian York seem to indicate more straightened circumstances, but since the apparent diet has not been linked to human remains, there is no evidence as to whether the townsfolk were actually short of food.

---

[1] Walford 1976, 130.
[2] MS Harl. 603.
[3] Wright 1871, 91.
[4] Harmer 1952, 83.
[5] Loyn 1970, 370.
[6] Finberg 1972, 106–7.
[7] Robertson 1939, 93.
[8] op. cit., 106.
[9] Loyn 1970, 371.
[10] Bourdillon 1980, 185.

The post-Conquest surveys of Winchester show a town served by four butchers in the High Street (known as *ceapstræt* from the beginning of the tenth century) by the eleventh and twelfth centuries. There were also two fishmongers, bakers, cooks, a confectioner, brewsters and a water-seller. Richard the mead seller lived outside the west gate. There was probably a sheep market, and in 1096 the Fair of St. Giles was granted to Bishop Walkelin.[1]

Once consumers were no longer able to oversee the production of their food, they could be exploited by those who sold them provisions. Unless they bought an entire animal and had it slaughtered by someone who would recognise a diseased carcass, they would not necessarily know the circumstances under which an animal had died. The many references to the sale of bad meats in the post-Conquest period coincide only with the recorded times of murrain.[2] It was not until 1319 that the wardens of the city of London were appointed to oversee the flesh market and destroy putrid carcasses.[3] Murrains were recorded in the Anglo-Saxon Chronicle too, and bad meat may have been on sale at such times.

Sometime between 884–901 Æthelred and Æthelflæd granted to the bishop of Worcester the fines for dishonest trading.[4] This could have ranged from selling underweight and giving short measure to adulterating food and drink. Piers Plowman complained:

> . . . Brewesteres and bakesteres bocheres and cokes;
> For þise aren men on þis molde þat moste harme worcheth
> To þe þore peple þat parcel-mele buggen.
> For they poysoun þe peple priueliche and oft.

> . . . brewers and bakers, butchers and cooks; for these are the people who do most harm on this earth to the poor folk who buy piecemeal, since they often poison them secretly.[5]

Similar exploitation probably went on in Anglo-Saxon times, although it may have been less common in smaller communities where people were known as individuals. No doubt there were always those ready to profit by cheating their fellows.

Townsfolk had to have the money (or objects to barter) to buy their provisions. These provisions were the producers' surpluses. In time of dearth, the townsfolk would be the first group to lose their supplies. The poor tradesmen who could only afford to buy *parcel mele*, and were therefore without substantial stores, must have been one of the most vulnerable groups in Anglo-Saxon society. Their recourse in time of hardship might have been to contract themselves as slaves to landowners, or to ask for relief at religious or royal establishments (see Chapter 19).

---

[1] Barlow 1976, 202, 285, 432, 431, 84, 460, 286.
[2] Sabine 1933, 337–8.
[3] Drummond and Wilbraham 1958.
[4] Finberg 1972, 106.
[5] Skeat 1965, 26.

26. Provision of Food Away from Home

Who the Travellers were

Anglo-Saxon populations were not static, locked into small, totally self-sufficient communities they never left. Even allowing for considerable hagiographical exaggeration, the story of Guthlac's birth (written before 749), indicates the possibility of considerable and rapid contact between communities. On the day he was born 'a hand of the fairest red colour appeared from heaven, holding a golden cross . . . and behold, before the sun set, it was known and famous all over middle-England' (*ane hand on þam fægerestan readan hiwe of heofunum cumende; and seo hæfde ane gyldene rode . . . and efne ær þon þe sunne on setl eode hit wæs ofer eall middel Engla-land cuð and mære*).[1] Navigable rivers and major roads[2] indicate the main lines of communication.

Slaves may not have left the estate on which they worked, although when they were left in wills to new owners on other estates they may have had to make substantial journeys.[3] The freemen living at subsistence level may have had no economic reason for travel, but if their existence became marginal, they may have been forced to leave their holdings and to beg for charity and alms (see following chapter). Even those groups who did not travel might at times, particularly during mowing or harvest, have been working at a distance from home which made return for at least one meal of the day difficult. If they became more prosperous, then they may have travelled to sell their surplus food in local markets, like the women who sold their dairy products and poultry in London. Men of standing in their communities travelled to gatherings of the hundred, to courts, and, in the later period at least, to guild meetings. Most of these return journeys were probably short enough to be accomplished in the space of a day. Perhaps it was quite usual to contemplate a long day's walking without food. As late as 1594 when Moryson was on the road from Genoa to Milan, he set off on a 22-mile leg, and only received food by chance from a begging friar whom he met.[4]

Opportunities for long journeys in relative comfort may have been restricted to the king and other rich landowners. We do not have records of all royal journeys but the known itineraries of kings are extensive.[5] In times of peace landowners were able to follow a planned circuit from manor to manor. Even if only a proportion of estates were visited by their owners, the fact that, for example, Queen Edith or Earl Harold held lands in most counties nevertheless suggests a certain amount of travelling by nobles.[6] Moreover, estates that were not visited would have to send men with tribute in one form or another. When hostilities broke out kings and nobles may have been forced to flee like Oswald or Alfred, or to pursue an enemy force around the country. Viking troop movements covered most of the country.[1] Nobles also had to travel to

---

1   Goodwin 1848, 10.
2   Hill 1981, maps 15, 199.
3   Whitelock 1968, 6–16.
4   Moryson 1617, I 361.
5   Hill 1981, maps 70, 145–7, 154–5, 160–3.
6   op. cit., maps 180, 181.
1   op. cit., maps 58–61, 120–129.

court for royal assemblies, as did bishops who also attended synods. During the period of the conversion some bishops undertook missionary journeys, as Cuthbert did in Scotland and the north of England, but they might also be called to do some *ad hoc* travelling: Eardwulf, who had St. Cuthbert's body with him at the time, was forced to keep on the move ahead of the Danish invaders for nine years, 'in great toil and penury' until his death in Chester-le-Street in 899.[1]

Some royal servants, like the king's huntsmen, hawkers, and *fæstingmen* were on the move most of the year. Messengers carried presents and letters, carriers took provisions as tribute, rents or gifts from one estate to another or to monasteries.

Traders brought salt along the saltways, merchants travelled in England, and abroad, sometimes trying to pass as pilgrims when this enabled them to avoid tolls. Gleemen travelled freely from household to household, a circumstance exploited by Alfred and Æthelstan when they wanted to spy in the camps of their enemies.[2] They also travelled from country to country, according to *Widsith*, a poem in the Exeter Book:

> *swa scriþende gesceapum hweorfað*
> *gleomen gumena geond grunda fela*

Thus roving with their songs the entertainers of men travel over many lands.[3]

Invalids were taken by families and friends to holy men – or their relics – to be cured. Pilgrims of all ranks travelled to shrines and abroad to Rome. Others more religious journeyed to serve God in a foreign land or merely set sail, trusting to God to provide them with a suitable landfall.

Involvement with the law might enforce absence from home, either in support of the right: tracking down cattle thieves, attending courts as an oath-taker, or, on the wrong side of the law, in seeking sanctuary, in prison, or exile.

Men who had to serve in the army or as 'shipmen', sometimes had to travel long distances to meet up with the king's forces, or to the coast where they were to join a ship.[4] These men had to be provided with food for the journey and the campaign. Danish invaders plundered the countryside for food.

The Anglo-Saxon View of Travel

Journeys were generally seen as times of privation, away from the comforts of home and the society of congenial folk. When journeys lasted any length of time it is particularly the loss of the joys of feasting in hall that is regretted. In the elegiac poem *The Wanderer* the speaker asks,

> *Hwær cwom symbla gesetu? Hwær sindon seledreamas? Eala beorht*
> *bune . . .*

Whither has gone the place of feasts? Where are the joys of hall? Alas, the bright cup . . . [1]

---

[1] Whitelock 1955, 251.
[2] Wright 1871, 47.
[3] Mackie 1934.
[4] Hill 1981, Map 165.
[1] Sweet 1954, 151.

By leaving home, the traveller was separating himself from a relatively assured food supply. A sea voyage was especially hazardous. *The Seafarer*, companion piece to *The Wanderer*, treats various hardships, and states,

> .... *hungor innan slat*
> *merewerges mod*

hunger rent within the mind of the sea-weary man.[1]

Ensuring a Food Supply

The usual procedure seems to have been to take provisions for a journey with you. According to *The Fates of Men* in the Exeter Book,

> *Sum sceal on feþe on feorwegas*
> *nyde gongan ond his nest beran*

Another shall of necessity travel on foot on distant paths and carry his food.[2]

The Laws of the Northumbrian Priests forbade all carrying of goods on a Sunday, whether by wagon, or by horse, or on one's back. He who did any of these things was to pay the penalty appropriate to his status, except for travellers, who were permitted to carry 'sustenance for their needs'.[3] When some brothers came to visit Cuthbert for some days, he told them to cook and eat a goose hanging on the wall before they went back, but because they had brought plenty of food with them, they did not trouble to take the goose as he had commanded them.[4] Food would have had to be portable, with keeping qualities depending on the length of the journey, and needing only the minimum of preparation in terms of utensils.

In Europe generally, bread was traditionally taken as food on journeys for times when it was not possible to prepare cooked meals.[5] The bread may have been dried out to produce a form of rusk or hard tack, like ship's biscuit. Hard tack lasts much longer than conventional bread, and is still edible after weeks and months.[6] The sixth-century Byzantine historian, Procopius, whose works were known to the Anglo-Saxons, gave instructions for making hard tack in his book *On Wars*. 'Bread, which the soldiers shall eat in the camp, should be placed twice on the damper and be so carefully baked that it is longer preserved and is not soon decayed.' He also recorded the fact that hard tack lost three-quarters of its weight when it was dried out like this.[7] Hard tack could have been eaten without any further treatment, but as it is very hard it could have been soaked in water before eating. As a lasting, sustaining, easily portable, and not easily damaged food, it would have been very useful to travellers, but, while we might assume that the Anglo-Saxons made use of it, there is no definite evidence. Unfortunately the etymology of 'tack' is doubtful, and so the philological approach yields no information.

---

1 op. cit., 152.
2 Mackie 1934.
3 Whitelock 1955, 438.
4 Colgrave 1940, 269.
5 Kowalska-Lewicka in Fenton & Kisban 1986, 92.
6 Imellos in op. cit., 74.
7 op. cit., 75.

Having to transport the necessary food would restrict journeys, unless the traveller had money to buy food, which would mean he could not travel though areas of very low population, and areas of poor land where there would be no surpluses to sell, or unless he was prepared to trust to hospitality and charity. The obligations of hospitality, enjoined by Christian tenets, were not always fulfilled. The boy accompanying St. Cuthbert on a missionary journey along the river Teviot did not expect to get a midday meal since he knew none of their kindred along the way and did not hope for any sort of kindness from unknown strangers.[1] The Welsh Laws allowed a traveller to steal, if he was refused food at a certain number of dwellings (see next chapter). The hall of a rich man, especially if he was known to be charitably disposed, would be an obvious point of call for a traveller without means. It seems that the provision of hospitality was related to status: the concept of *noblesse oblige* was in operation, so that strangers were admitted to the lord's table without question. That this came into conflict with a need for security is demonstrated by the return of an exiled bandit called Leofa to King Edmund's manor of Pucklechurch, in Gloucester. At dinner Leofa sat beside one of the important nobles of the court, and only the king recognised him, but in attempting to eject Leofa King Edmund was mortally wounded.[2] After the establishment of religious communities, the monastery guesthouse would provide an alternative feeding station, since they had similar food resources to important lay landowners.

Catching or gathering food on the journey was a third possibility, and the Welsh Laws allowed for such a contingency: a traveller on the road might wound an animal in the king's forest, and then continue to pursue it as long as he could see it. If he overtook the animal he was entitled to take it, but if it went out of sight he was not to continue the hunt.[3] To judge from a twelfth-century Welsh account success in the hunt was unusual. Gereint and his travelling companions met a young lad carrying a bundle wrapped in cloth and a small blue pitcher and cup. The boy's observation was, 'I suppose that your state [in the wood] last night was not good, and that you got neither food nor drink'. 'No, before God,' agreed Gereint. Thereupon the boy offered the travellers bread, meat, and wine – the meal he was carrying to some mowers working nearby, 'and if you wish it, sir, they shall get nothing'. 'I do wish it,' replied Gereint, unsurprisingly in the circumstances. The addition, 'and God reward you', suggests an absence of immediate financial return for the food.[4]

This story also indicates that agricultural workers were often brought meals out in the fields by someone, like the boy of this story, who was not strong enough to join in the work. Taking meals 'up the field' is still part of farm life at harvest-time. Sometimes the workers may have taken food with them. They could have used very small oak 'beever' barrels as they did into this century.[5] Food could have been carried in birch boxes, still made in Scandinavia for this purpose, baskets, or a cloth, as in the Welsh tale. I suspect it was a packed lunch of this kind that St. Cuthbert miraculously discovered on one of his journeys. He probably knew where he could normally expect

---

[1] Colgrave 1940, 85–7.
[2] Wright 1871, 34–5.
[3] Owen 1841, 497.
[4] Jackson 1971, 177–8.
[5] Edlin 1949, 99.

hospitality on a journey, but once, when travelling in winter, he found a settlement deserted, because it was used only in spring and summer, and so there was no man to feed him or his horse. Tethering his horse inside the dwelling, he saw it seize part of the thatch of the roof, and there fell out a warm loaf and meat carefully wrapped up in a linen cloth. Fortunately Cuthbert was convinced his good angel had left it there for him, and he was not inhibited by the notion that he might be eating someone-else's meal.[1] Picturesque cloth-wrapped bundles, usually carried on a stick over the shoulder, have been the traditional sign of a traveller: they probably contained his food for the journey.

Travellers who had ready cash could perhaps have bought food, but it was probably only in towns that food was regularly for sale. It is possible that some of the food that was sold was inferior. This was certainly the case after the Conquest when a number of precautions had to be taken; for example, to see that putrid carcasses and the carcasses of animals that had died from disease were not sold and that fair weight was being given. (See Chapter 22).

Provisions for Those Travelling on Business

Those employed on official business were most sure of receiving food. The food that the servants of the Anglo-Saxon kings were provided with, seems not to have been specified, which contrasts with the continental situation. As we have seen, Charlemagne's 'royal envoys' (missi dominici) could exact on their own and their servants' behalf an allowance of 40 loaves, a pig or sheep, 2 sucking pigs, 4 hens, 20 eggs, 8 pints of wine, 2 modii of ale, and 2 modii of oats for their horses.[2] Charles the Bald decreed that a bishop on his pastoral progress could requisition at each halt 50 loaves, 10 chickens, 50 eggs and 5 sucking pigs.[3] The demand on behalf of the Apparitor of the Welsh court was very modest by comparison: he was to have only a loaf and its ellyn (accompaniment) at any house to which he went on an errand.[4] When the porter went to the king he was to have a handful of herrings.[5] Food payments for those who had to undertake journeys continued to be provided after the Conquest. The twelfth-century carrier of a thousand dried herrings to Battle Abbey was to have 2 loaves and 6 herrings.[6]

Probably, the servants of the Anglo-Saxon kings also lived relatively modestly when travelling on their own, rather than in the royal retinue, since only royal food rents compare with the continental examples. Even so, providing food for these servants, and their animals, was evidently an onerous duty, since a number of landowners paid substantial amounts to be freed from it. In 781 Offa freed an estate from all royal tribute and the duty of provisioning with food.[7] In 836 Wiglaf, king of the Mercians, freed Hanbury Minster from the entertainment of the king and ealdormen and the support of fæstingmenn (?emissaries) in return for 40 hides and, according to a contemporary

---

[1] Colgrave 1940, 71.
[2] Talbot Rice 1965, 291.
[3] Tannahill 1973, 112.
[4] Owen 1841, 395, 677.
[5] op. cit., 67.
[6] Seebohm 1952, 167.
[7] Hart 1975, 76.

endorsement, 600 shillings in gold to the ealdorman Sigred.[1] The community at Bredon bought immunity from entertaining *fæstingmen* six years later in return for a large and well-wrought silver dish, 120 mancuses of pure gold, and 100 psalters and 120 masses chanted 12 times over for the king, his friends and all his people.[2] Alhwine paid 300 silver shillings in 855 to exempt Blockley Minster from feeding the king's or ealdorman's huntsmen, the Welsh expedition and all mounted men, English or foreign.[3] In 875 Wærfrith, bishop of the Hwicce, seems to have struck a better bargain in that he freed his diocese from feeding those who led the king's horses in exchange for making intercession and reciting the Lord's prayer daily for the king, then Ceolwulf II.[4] Other exemptions are from the provisioning of hawks, huntsmen, horses and their attendants, but ambassadors or messengers still had to be given a meal.[5] In a comprehensive exemption of 845 Beorhtwulf freed an estate from provisioning the king, his princes and junior retainers, entertainment (i.e. overnight accommodation) and feeding of royal huntsmen, horses, falcons, hawks, and the servants that lead the hunting dogs.[6]

Wulfstan's *Canons of Edgar* instructed clergy who attended an annual synod to take 'books and vestments for divine service and ink and parchment for their instructions and provisions for three days' (*becc and reaf to godcundre þenunge, and blæc and bocfel to heora geræðnessum, and þreora daga biwiste*).[7] The Welsh Laws give food and drink at the beginning of a list of conveniences which the planning of a convention had to take into account.[8] Wulfstan's solution to the problem seems an eminently practical one from the organiser's point of view.

Professional entertainers travelled from court to court, literally singing for their supper. According to Widsith in the Exeter Book,

> simle suð oþþe norð sumne gemetað
> gydda gleawne geofum unhneawne

north or south they always find an appreciative patron, generous with his gifts.[9]

Travelling Abroad

Travelling well-trodden routes, for example to Rome, it might have been comparatively easy for someone with money to obtain food, since the main routes were well provided with hostelries.[10] In Rome itself Ine's *Borgo Saxonum*, founded in 725, was a hostelry for pilgrims who included the young Alfred, and Cnut.[11] Travel further afield presented more of a risk: when Ingulf went to Jerusalem by way of Germany and Greece in the eleventh century he and his companions went out thirty fat horsemen and returned scarcely twenty emaciated pedestrians.[1]

---

[1] Finberg 1972, 101.
[2] op. cit., 102.
[3] op. cit., 48.
[4] op. cit., 49.
[5] Hart 1975, 68.
[6] op. cit., 76.
[7] Fowler 1972, 2.
[8] Owen 1841, 499.
[9] Mackie 1934.
[10] Whitelock 1952, 175.
[11] op. cit.
[1] Turner 1828, II 375.

In the early eighth century Ceolfrith set off for Rome, having procured a sufficiency of things which might be necessary for so great a journey.[1] He had about eighty men in his company, and ordered his attendants that any of his followers without provisions should be given immediately either food or money. After Ceolfrith's death at Langres, Gangulf provided supplies for those who wished to continue the journey to Rome, and means of subsistence for those who stayed on.[2] Bishop Dalfinus of Lyons provided Wilfred with provisions for the journey to Rome, and again, on the way back, for the journey home.[3] Not all pilgrims were as lucky. Bishops could rely on help from fellow ecclesiastics, but Boniface was concerned at the number of female pilgrims who apparently ran out of money and became 'adulteresses or harlots'.[4] Charlemagne wrote to Offa that pilgrims who wished to go to Rome should be free to go in peace, bearing with them the necessities for their journey;[5] tolls had earlier been exacted from them as though they were merchants. Anglo-Saxons at Rome could find food and shelter in their national *scola* – as could Frisians, Franks and Lombards.[6]

If a foreigner arrived in England he might be able to buy food and shelter, though it seems from the *Gnomic Verses* that these comforts might be denied him:

> ceap eadig mon cyning wic þonne
> leodon cypeð þonne liþan cymeð
> wudu ond wætres nyttað þonne him biþ wic alyfæd
> mete bygeþ gif he maran þearf ærþon he to meþe weorþe
> seoc se biþ þe to seldan ieteð þeah hine mon on sunnan læde
> ne mæg he be þy wedre wesan þeah hit sy wearm on sumera
> ofercumen biþ he ær he acwele gif he nat hwa hine cwicne fede
> mægen mon sceal mid mete fedan morþor under eorþan befeolan
> hinder under hrusan þe hit forhelan þenceð

A wealthy man will sell property and the king a dwelling to a man when he comes on his voyage. He has the use of wood and water when a dwelling is granted him. He buys food if he needs more before he becomes too faint. He who eats too seldom will be ill. Even if he is led into the sun, he cannot exist on good weather, even if it is warm in summer. He will become exhausted and then die unless he knows someone who will keep him alive by feeding him. One should nourish strength with food, and he who proposes to conceal it, shall bury murder under the earth, down under the ground.[7]

The Welsh Laws also suggest the difficulty of obtaining food. 'Foreigners' (*alltuds*), were not to be put to death for taking either victuals or any other thing during three nights and three days, but they were to pay for what they had.[8] Elsewhere the laws mention that the *alltud* was granted 'spear allowance; that is, a grant from the country and the lord, lest he die by famine and cold, until he shall be placed in his station in respect to country and kindred'.[1] Peasants in the countryside who had no surplus food

[1] Whitelock 1955, 702.
[2] op. cit., 707.
[3] Miller 1890, I 2 455.
[4] Whitelock 1952, 174.
[5] Whitelock 1955, 781.
[6] Riché 1978, 31
[7] Mackie 1934, II 107.
[8] Owen 1841, 257.
[1] op. cit., 553.

would not welcome a stranger who might put their own provisioning at risk. If food was generally short in the area, then even money payments would have held little attraction. A foreigner's best course would usually have been to seek out the king's court: one more in a large entourage would have more chance of being fed, and a foreigner probably had a novelty value. At the court of Alfred, foreigners, like Othhere and Wulfstan and the three Scots who set out from Ireland, were made welcome.[1]

Food on Board Ship

Boats plying a coastal or cross-channel trade could keep themselves reasonably provisioned, but provisioning a long sea voyage presented problems. His king addresses St. Andrew (in the poem *Andreas*) in some bewilderment:

> Hu gewearð þe þæs wine leofesta
> þæt þu sæbeorgas secan woldes
> merestreama gemet, maðmum bedæleð,
> ofer cald cleofu ceoles neosan.
> Nafast þe to frofre on faroðstræte
> hlafes wiste ne hlutterne
> drync to dugoðe is se drohtað strang
> þam þe lagolade lang cunnað

How does this come about, dearest friend, that you want to seek out the mountainous sea, the limit of the sea-streams, and, devoid of treasure, want to go beyond the cold cliffs to see a ship? You will have no comfort on the sea, no sustenance from bread, nor bright drink to sustain you. It is a harsh existence for one who undertakes a long sea voyage.[2]

The Graveney boat yielded remains of sheep or goat (larger than the Soay type), remains of a young pig and cattle, and what were possibly fragments of horse.[3] A law code of about 1000 which deals with the trade of London, allowed foreign traders to buy London wool and melted fat, plus three live pigs for provisioning their ships.[4] No doubt merchants who regularly put into ports knew where they could get supplies.

On long voyages fish and birds could be caught. According to the account of St. Brendan's voyage mackerel and cod were both caught at sea, and so were fulmars. Dried fish, whale meat, blubber and lamb had been laid in for the voyage, together with supplies of plants and roots. When they made landfalls they were able to catch more birds, and once to salvage a dead whale which provided meat for three months.[5] Successful saints could rely on divine providence. When St. Cuthbert and his companions were delayed from sailing by bad weather, they found on the shore three portions of dolphin's flesh as though they had been cut by a human hand with a knife and washed with water. The 'wonderful sweetness' of the flesh is recorded, and there was enough for three men for three days and nights.[1] The death from starvation of holy men probably went unrecorded.

---

[1] Sweet 1954, 17–22; Whitelock 1955, 184.
[2] Kemble 1843, 19.
[3] Fenwick 1978, 162.
[4] Whitelock 1952, 119.
[5] Severin 1978, 87, 137, 156, 269, 261.
[1] Colgrave 1940, 85.

In 891 three Scots came to Alfred's court in a boat without any oars from Ireland 'because they wished for the love of God to be in foreign lands, they cared not where'. They had taken with them enough food for seven days. Fortunately they landed in Cornwall just as the seven days were up.[1] That this should be regarded as the major happening of that year suggests that it was considered that a miracle had occurred, but also that it was unusual to want to leave your own country. However, it may simply be that Alfred received few (if any) Irish visitors in the normal course of events, let alone any who travelled in such an unorthodox a manner and with limited provisions.

Liquid Refreshment

It seems unlikely that a traveller would have had to go thirsty for very long: watercourses are relatively numerous in England, and even during a period of warmer, drier summers as is thought to have occurred in the later part of the period, the water table must have been higher than it generally is today, when more demands are being made on the aquifers. Anglo-Saxon Laws do not refer to the ownership of water in natural features, and I assume anyone was free to drink it. The Welsh Laws as they have come down to us, are much more comprehensive, and they state that 'Three things are free to every person, whether he be a native or a stranger, and it is not right, according to law, to debar them therefrom: water from a spring, or brook, or river . . . .[2] Another law extended this concept to water from a well, or other artificial feature: ' . . . three things which every person can take without consent of another: water not in a vessel . . . '.[3] The assumption that anyone could drink from springs and streams is confirmed by the action of Eadwine of Northumbria, who had formerly been a fugitive throughout Britain for some years, when he came to the throne. Where there were clear springs by frequented roads he had posts set up from which drinking cups were hung for the use of travellers.[4] This benefit was not abused, but conditions in Eadwine's reign were relatively civilized, and from Bede's comments we gather they did not appertain to his day.

It was possible to carry liquid in flagons as two monks did when they visited St. Guthlac at Crowland. They were surprised when Guthlac

> *mid bliþum andwlitan and hlihhendre gespræc . . . cwæþ to heom For hwon behydde git þa flaxan under an tyrf, and for hwon ne læddon ge hi mid inc*

> with a smiling face and laughing words said to them, 'Why did you hide the flagons under a turf and why didn't you bring them with you?'.[5]

The answer, which Guthlac presumably guessed, was because they were filled with *ælað* (ale), and Guthlac was famed for the austerity of his life.

We know from the legislation concerning them that alehouses existed. Perhaps one reason that quarrels arose so often in alehouses was that they were places where travellers (and therefore strangers) might impinge upon the life of a community. A traveller might be entertained there by singers, musicians or other entertainers as well as getting a drink. Food seems to have been secondary to drink in alehouses, but

---

[1] Whitelock 1955, 184.
[2] Owen 1841, II 523.
[3] op. cit., 329.
[4] Miller 1890, I 1 129, 144.
[5] Goodwin 1848, 65.

perhaps it was available on an informal basis, if a traveller was prepared to wait and eat with the host. It is not until FitzStephen's *Description of London* in 1183 that we hear of a cookshop, but in fact it sounds like a superior restaurant with a very extensive menu where all sorts of delicacies could be bought.[1] Perhaps this is why FitzStephen recorded it: more modest cookshops could have existed previously. It has generally been assumed that the cook in Ælfric's *Colloquy* was a household servant, but there is nothing in his testimony that rules out his being a cookshop cook, combining waiting duties with his cooking, but unfortunately what he does say is of too general a nature to draw definite conclusions. Chaucer's unpleasantly unhygienic cook seems to be a self-employed cookshop owner, and Piers Plowman's

> *Brewsteres and baksters*
> *Bochiers and cokes*

must have been serving the public, rather than in the employ of some individual, or Piers would not have wanted them punished for their cheating.[2]

Guesthouses

It seems more likely that lodging houses where travellers stayed over night would have offered food to guests, and such establishments are referred to in the Welsh Laws, since we learn that three things were not to be paid for though lost in a lodging house – they were a knife, sword and trousers. Perhaps the logic was that the traveller should keep all three about him, since the management appears to have accepted responsibility for other items.[3]

Apart from privately-owned inns, guesthouses where a monk was appointed to minister to guests were attached to monasteries. At Ripon Cuthbert was the guest-master. One winter day he welcomed a man, washed his hands and feet, warmed his feet, and invited him to stay until the third hour to take food. However, this offer was refused because of the urgency of the traveller's journey until Cuthbert abjured him in the name of Christ. Cuthbert set out a table and spread on it such food as he had, and went to the monastery for a loaf. When he returned to the guesthouse, he discovered that the traveller had in fact been an angel, and had left three, superior, warm loaves.[4]

Bede uses the term *cumena-bur* to translate *hospitale*: the place where strangers, including pilgrims, but also the old and infirm, were provided with hospitality.[5] The hospital of St. Peter at York was founded, according to generally accepted tradition, through the munificence of King Æthelstan in about 937 (although it was refounded after the Conquest at St. Leonard's), and endowed by one thrave (i.e. 20 sheaves) of corn from every carucate of land in the bishopric of York. Another hospital was at Flixton in Holderness, founded by a noble called Acehorn in the time of Æthelstan. Two other hospitals dating from Anglo-Saxon times were in Worcester; one was said to be founded by St. Oswald, the bishop of Worcester who died in 992, the other was founded

---

[1] Ayrton 1975, 12.
[2] Robinson 1957, 20–21; Skeat 1965, 26.
[3] Owen 1841, I 451.
[4] Colgrave 1940, 77–9.
[5] Bonser 1963, 95.

just after the Conquest by Wulfstan, the last Anglo-Saxon bishop, and bore his name.[1] Leland says that two other hospitals – St. Giles at Beverley and St. Nicholas at Pontefract – were of pre-Conquest date, and mentions an almshouse dedicated to St. Chad at Shrewsbury, but there appears to be no contemporary evidence for these. There is no evidence to show that these hospitals were connected with monastic establishments.[2] A traveller in the middle or late Saxon period might plan his route so that he could eat and stay at monasteries and at guesthouses, which had the advantage over the king's court of being stationary and, for the most part, permanent.

Food for Military Expeditions

Imma, a young follower of King Ecgfrith who was seized by his enemies:

> ondred he ondetton þæt he cyninges þegn wære, ac sæde, þæt he folclic mon wære 7 þearfende 7 gewiifad hæfðe; 7 þætte he forðon in þa fyrd cwome, þæt he sceolde cyninges þegnum heora ondlifen 7 mete lædan mid heora heafodgemæccum

> feared to acknowledge that he was a thegn of the king, but said that he was an ordinary man and was poor, and married, and that he had joined the expedition in order to fetch supplies and food to the king's followers.[3]

This suggests that people were employed to fetch provisions from estates, the obvious source of bulk supplies, although if there were large enough markets at hand, some supplies could have been bought.

The Bayeux Tapestry shows tuns of wine and a carcass, a man carrying a sack of what were presumably provisions for the campaign on his shoulder, and a pack pony with panniers.[4] There are also illustrations of animals about to be slaughtered, and wineskins. Turner considered that William encouraged the spirits of his army by an abundance of provisions, and this morale-boosting strategy was the reason he did not stay at Pevensey, but went straight on to Hastings for more food.[5] Certainly the supply of food to the numbers involved in the invasion – an estimated 14,000 Normans in the camp at Dives-sur-Mer, and probably a larger number of English, must have presented logistical problems.[6] William used a centralised system of collection, storage and distribution of supplies as used by Roman and Byzantine forces.[7] Probably some 28 tons of unmilled wheat, assuming cold wheat gruel to be the staple diet, and 14,000 gallons of clear water was needed per day.[8] William's strategy to keep Harold's forces mobilised from late spring, and especially throughout July and August, so that, by early September a lack of supplies would require demobilisation was successful.[1] Harold's fleet, which would have provided opposition to William's invasion, had to disperse on 8th September for want of provisions.[2]

[1] op. cit., 96.
[2] op. cit., 96.
[3] Miller 1890, I 2 326.
[4] Wilson 1985, plates 38, 39, 46.
[5] Turner 1828, II 400.
[6] Bachrach in Allen Brown 1985, 4.
[7] op. cit., 10.
[8] op. cit., 11.
[1] op. cit., 9.
[2] Turner 1828, II 397.

Another, this time potentially disastrous, example of provisioning determining strategy had occurred in 893 while the English were besieging the Danes on an islet in the Colne (Æthelweard calls it Thorney, which has been identified as an island near Iver, Bucks.). The English force had completed their term of service and had used up their provisions, and so went home before the king and the divisions which had been newly called-up, arrived. In fact the Danish king had been wounded badly, and could not be moved, otherwise the Danes might have escaped.[1] Alfred's campaigns against the Danes were successful in part because he effectively deprived the Danish force of provisions. He besieged them at Buttington on the Severn over several weeks during which time they were forced to eat their horses to survive, although many died of starvation.[2] Alfred's siege of Chester was also based on depriving the Danes of provisions by driving away all the cattle in the vicinity and consuming or burning all the corn. This aggressive campaign had to be coupled with defending his own subjects so they could gather in their harvest. One autumn saw him at London to make sure the Danes would not prevent the harvest being gathered in.[3] Subsequent events in the Anglo-Saxon Chronicle emphasise the importance of securing a food supply. In 914 the Danes were besieged on the island of Steepholme until they became very short of food and many men died of starvation.[4] In 917 a great Danish army assembled from East Anglia and Mercia and went to the borough at *Wigingamere* and besieged and attacked it . . . and seized the cattle round about.[5] But although the Danes threatened food supplies, as an invading force in a foreign country they had to fight for their own provisions. In 994 they were in the ascendant and were provisioned throughout all the West Saxon kingdom as well as receiving 16,000 pounds in money.[6] In 998 the Danes avoided confrontation, staying for a period in the Isle of Wight and getting their food from Hampshire and Sussex.[7] An agreement in 1002 arranged for provisions and tribute, and in 1006 they were supplied with food throughout England at a time when the English levy too seems to have caused a drain on resources.[8] In 1016 the Scandinavian army successfully procured provision for themselves, and drove both their ships and their herds into the Medway.[9] When Æthelred made a treaty with the Viking army, one condition was that all were to help fight any fleet that might harry England. In return the soldiers were to be provided with food 'as long as they are with us'.[10]

Land was rarely exempted from the obligation to furnish men to fight in the royal army. In Wales the men were to serve for three days and three nights in the royal host, taking their food with them.[1] In the first half of the period particularly the supply of camp rations may have been uncertain, since it is recorded as a miracle that when Cuthbert lived in camp in the army he yet lived abundantly all the time.[2] Domesday Book records

---

[1] Whitelock 1955, 186.
[2] op. cit., 187.
[3] op. cit., 188.
[4] op. cit., 195.
[5] op. cit., 197.
[6] op. cit., 214.
[7] op. cit., 215.
[8] op. cit., 216, 219, 218.
[9] op. cit., 226.
[10] op. cit., 401.
[1] Davies 1982, 131.
[2] Colgrave 1940, 73.

in detail payments that were to be made towards the maintenance of the royal army. In Colchester the burgesses paid six pence from each house for the maintenance of the king's soldiers or for an expedition by sea or land.[1] If the king should send an army anywhere, one soldier should go from every five hides in Berkshire and for his victuals and pay every hide was to give him four shillings for two months. The money was given directly to the soldier.[2] This presupposes that he was going to be able to buy food readily. Twelve burghers were to go with the king when he went with the army by land. If the expedition was a maritime one, they were to send him four horses as far as London to carry their arms and necessaries.[3] In Wiltshire, if the king went on an expedition by land or sea, he had from the borough of Wilton, either twenty shillings to feed his *huscarls* or one man from every five hides.[4]

Claiming Sanctuary

Sanctuary was a special circumstance in which the normal home food supply was foregone. If a man, attacked by his enemies, could reach sanctuary – according to the laws of Alfred this included every church consecrated by a bishop – then

> *þæt hine seofan nihtum nan mon ut ne teo . . .*
> *gif he for hungre libban mæge.*

he shall not be dragged out for seven days . . . if he can live despite hunger.

The elder of the church was to see that no-one gave him any food during this period.[5] However, some churches had special privileges, particularly if they possessed relics of famous saints. As St. Cuthbert foresaw, men of every sort would flee to his body, and when it was brought to Durham the right of sanctuary continued to be exercised there. Fugitives were fed at the expense of the house for thirty-seven days.[6]

Food in Prison

According to Alfred's laws, which were largely a compilation of the laws of previous kings, if a man failed to keep a pledge, then he was to hand over his weapons and possessions to friends,

> *7 beo feowertig nihta on carcerne on cyninges tune ðrowige ðær swa biscep him scrife, 7 his mægas hine feden, gif he self mete næbbe . . . Gif he mægas næbbe oððe þone mete næbbe fede cyninges gerefa hine*

and remain forty days in prison at a royal manor and undergo there whatever the bishop prescribes for him; and his relatives shall feed him if he has no food himself . . . If he has no relatives and has not the necessary food, the king's reeve shall feed him.[1]

Details like this emphasise the difficulty of obtaining a food supply when the domestic routine was broken.

---

[1] Loyn 1970, 380.
[2] Turner 1828, III 174.
[3] op. cit.
[4] op. cit.
[5] Attenborough 1922, 66–7.
[6] Colgrave 1940, 278, 355–6.
[1] Attenborough 1922, 63.

Conclusions

A way of life which included a number of fast days probably made it easier for the Anglo-Saxon traveller to cope with the lack of regular food. In fact Sir John Harrington in the sixteenth century was recommending occasional days of complete fasting for, 'By this meanes . . . your bodies shall be better accustomed to endure and suffer hunger and fasting, eyther in iourneyes or wars'.[1] Unless travelling under the aegis of the king or a noble, in which case arrangements were made, travellers had to be resourceful individuals – there was no systematic provision made for them, though probably, as demand grew, food and even meals could be bought by the end of the period. Transactions would be purely commercial, since the traveller would not be able to reciprocate in kind, and would have no previous or current relationship with those who provided him with food. The guesthouses of monasteries probably provided the best food, most hygienically cooked, and there seems to have been no obligation to pay. Even if the traveller had food, he might regret the absence of the social framework in which meals were normally taken. Any disruption to the normal routine meant that arrangements for a food supply had to be specially made. The hardships suffered by Bishop Eardwulf highlight the additional difficulties of travelling in a war-torn countryside. The success or otherwise in provisioning a large force was perhaps the most important single factor in military campaigning, and the common soldiery may well have been on short commons some of the time.

---

[1] Furnivall 1868, 142.

27. Hospitality and Charity

Judging from *Beowulf* and other heroic age verse, generosity was thought of as having been a virtue in the pagan period before it was seen as part of the Christian ethic. Generosity included hospitality, so that King Æthelbert of Kent could say to Augustine: ' . . . we will receive you heartily as guests, will provide for your maintenance and supply your necessities' ('. . . *we willað eow eac fremsumlice in gestliðnesse onfon, 7 eow ondlifen sellan 7 eowre þearfe forgifan*').[1] Only those with sufficient resources could provide hospitality, so that being a generous host was also, or perhaps mainly, a matter of demonstrating status. The once-prosperous lord of the *Rhymed Poem* in the Exeter Book looks back regretfully to a time when feasts never failed and when he could provide for guests.

In the Christian period the English correspondence of St. Boniface shows how hospitality was recognised as an obligation for which biblical illustrations were cited: . . . 'the Holy Scriptures show how great is the reward of hospitality and how acceptable it is to God to discharge kind offices to strangers'. The stories of Abraham and Lot entertaining strangers who turn out to be angels are related with the comment, 'Receiving the servants of God, you receive Him, for he hath promised, "He that receiveth you, receiveth me"'.[2] Bede writes approvingly of the Scots who gave 'daily maintenance without charge' (*dæghwamlice onlifne buton ceape*) to men of God of English descent in Ireland.[3] An incident in the life of St. Eustace is recounted to show his hospitality. 'Then Eustace led them into his guest-house and brought them wine to drink because of their great fatigue. Then he went to the lord and said, 'I know these men which is why they have come to me. Give me food and wine and I will pay you back from my earnings,' and he gladly granted him this, and then Eustace ministered to them' (*Eustachius þa gelædde hi into his gesthus and utgangende bohte him win and him scencte for heora micclan geswince þa cwæð he to þam hus-hlaforde þas men synd me cuðe and hi for-þi comon to me. Gif me nu mettas and wine and ic hit þe gilde eft of mine hyre and he him þa glædlice tiþode and he þa eustachius him þenode . . .*).[4] Various saints were credited with hospitality. Anastasius fed a leper; Gallicanus, although a great man, washed men's feet and 'carried water for their hands and served them with food' (*wæter bær to handum and mid wistum þenode*); Rufus provided food for a bishop, and Taurus 'provided him with food for four years' (*hine . . . afedde feower gear mid wistum*), others 'with their offerings protected widows and step-children from hunger' (*mid ðam lacum widewan and steop-bearn bewerian mid hunger*).[5]

Aidan would not give money to 'powerful/rich' (*ricum*) men, 'but only food and hospitality to those who visited him; but rather he gave the gifts and money rich men gave him for the use of the poor' (*nemne mete 7 swæsendo þæm þe him sohton ac he*

---

[1] Miller 1890, I 1 60.
[2] Kylie 1911, 47.
[3] Miller 1890, I 2 292.
[4] Skeat 1881, *St Eustace* ll. 257.
[5] op. cit., *St Basil* l. 482, *St Agnes* l.389, *St Apollinarius* l. 126, 188, *Maccabees* l. 754.

ma ða gife 7 þa feoh þe him rice men sealdon, oðþe þearfum to are gedælde).[1] Bede records that Cuthbert was appointed guestmaster at Ripon where he pressed hospitality on strangers.[2] As a bishop Cuthbert observed St. Paul's dictates on how a bishop should behave – he was a lover of hospitality and took in strangers and fed the hungry.[3] His last words were reputedly, 'Do not despise those who come to you for the sake of hospitality, but see you receive them as such, keep them, and send them away with friendly kindness'.[4]

One could expect to receive hospitality at a monastery since, according to the Pope's answer to Augustine, one quarter of a bishop's income was for the bishop and his household to entertain and receive guests and strangers – the same proportion as was to be spent on the repair and improvement of churches.[5] According to the *Regularis Concordia*, the tenth-century monastery had a guesthouse, and hospitality to strangers, the care of guests and the poor is legislated for.[6]

Hospitality began by washing the feet of the traveller in warm water. An early eleventh-century manuscript from Canterbury shows this being done in a very large, handled, bowl, but later illustrations of c. 1120 and c.1150 show what look like elaborate low-level fonts being used for this.[7] Boniface gave an Anglo-Saxon prelate what must have been a forerunner of the towel (a 'shaggy' present) to dry the feet after washing. Warm wine was sometimes administered to the newly-arrived guest.[8]

Monasteries apart, no-one could be sure of receiving hospitality. A traveller with a bag of holy dust was received by the owner of a house where a feast was in progress, and a convivial evening resulted, but he certainly knew the district, and so may have been known to his host.[9] Certainly the boy travelling with St. Cuthbert said he did not know of any of their kindred along that way, and he did not hope for any sort of kindness from strangers.[10] Probably travellers avoided areas known to be poor. When Cuthbert was abbot of Melrose, he went into remote areas which others were afraid to visit and whose poverty and ignorance deterred teachers.[11] Clearly some people could not afford to offer hospitality; to have done so might have imperilled their own existence.

Throughout the period kings were expected to be generous with their hospitality. Alfred devoted one sixth of his income to foreigners 'whether they demanded it, or awaited its voluntary descent'.[12] Florence of Worcester records that in 1037 when Ælfgifu was expelled from England, she was received with honour by Count Baldwin of Flanders. He supplied her needs for as long as necessity demanded 'as

---

[1] Miller 1890, I 1 162.
[2] Colgrave 1940, 176.
[3] op. cit., 243.
[4] op. cit., 283.
[5] Miller 1890, I 1 65.
[6] Symons 1953, xxxiv.
[7] Temple 1976, figs. 207, 37, 28.
[8] Turner 1828, III 118, 57.
[9] Miller 1890, I 1 181.
[10] Colgrave 1940, 87.
[11] Whitelock 1955, 668.
[12] Attenborough 1922.

became such a man'.[1] Over three centuries later Chaucer's Franklin is providing lavish hospitality:

> It snewed in his hous of mete and drynke,
> Of alle deyntees that men koude thynke.[2]

To substantiate his claim to status, his table was always standing ready for food to be served.

It appears that on the continent itinerant monks claiming to be on pilgrimages abused the hospitality enjoined by St. Paul. An eighth-century commentator on St. Benedict gives a long description of these vagabonds for whom 'many chicken give up the ghost under the knife'. On the morning of the third day when the host took himself off to his work instead of to the kitchen, the *gyrovagus* would realise he was no longer welcome and take what he could not get his host to give him.[3] One of the laws of Wihtred, King of Kent c.695, seems to suggest a parallel situation in England. 'If a tonsured man, not under ecclesiastical discipline wanders about looking for hospitality, once only shall it be granted to him, and unless he has permission, he shall not be entertained further' (*Gif bescoren man steorleas gange him an gestliðnesse gefe him man ænes; 7 þæt ne geweorðe, buton he leafnesse habbe, þæt hine man læng feormige*).[4] Three hundred years later Æthelred was still trying to get monks back in their cloisters, which in itself indicates they were accorded hospitality, even if this was perhaps from moneyed relations rather than strangers.[5]

A householder might have been more willing to take in a monk, whose way of life was, at least theoretically, godly, than other strangers, since from the time of the earliest laws he was responsible for the behaviour of his guests. The laws of Hlothhere and Eadric (673–685) stated: 'If a man entertains a stranger – a trader or anyone else who has come over the border – for three days in his own home, then supplies him with food from his own store, and [if] he [the stranger] then does harm to anyone, the man shall bring the other to justice, or make amends on his behalf' (*Gif man cuman feormaþ III niht an his agenum hame, cepeman oþþe oðerne þe sio ofer mearce cuman, 7 hine þonne his mete fede, 7 he þonne ænigum mæn yfel gedo, se man þane oðerne æt rihte gebrenge oþþe riht forewyrce*).[6] While there was a moral obligation to provide hospitality, one had to be careful about harbouring fugitives from justice. If one fed an outlaw the fine was five pounds according to the laws of Cnut, unless one could clear oneself on oath.[7] When the son of Hygelac received a party to a feud, he too became involved and lost his life.[8] Much later Edmund warns that if any of his kinsmen harbour a murderer, they are liable to forfeit all they own to the king.[9] Clearly the intention was to 'starve out' the murderer, but family ties and obligations to provide hospitality would be in conflict with the legal code.

---

[1] Whitelock 1955, 289.
[2] Robinson 1957, 20.
[3] Waddell 1932, 183.
[4] Attenborough 1922, 27.
[5] Whitelock 1955, 406.
[6] Attenborough 1922, 21.
[7] Robertson 1925, 180.
[8] *Beowulf* l. 2385.
[9] Whitelock 1955, 392.

The provision of hospitality was left to the discretion of the householder. The Laws of Ine state 'Every man may deny entertainment.' (*Ælc mon mot onsacan fyrmþe*).[1] This must have been partly because of the element of responsibility for a guest that he incurred, partly perhaps because he had to decide whether or not he had enough food to provide for a guest. However, it was compulsory to provide hospitality for the king and various of his agents. Only someone with considerable power could have imposed what was apparently an onerous burden. There are a number of recorded cases where the owners of estates have bought out these rights at considerable cost. A charter of 836 frees a bishop's estate from – *inter alia* – hospitality to the king or ealdormen. It notes that 'the bishop gave to Ealdorman Sigred 600 shillings in gold and to Ealdorman Mucel 10 hides of land at Crowle'.[2] In 855 Ealhhun, bishop of Worcester, paid 300 shillings in silver to free the monastery at Blockley 'from the feeding and maintenance of those men whom we call *walhfæreld* and from lodging them and from lodging all mounted men of the English race and foreigners, whether of humble or noble birth'.[3] Sometimes the king himself would release land from this burden. Ninth-century Mercian charters grant immunity from feeding *fæstingmen* and the minders of hawks, dogs and horses. An example is the charter of Brihtwulf in 844 where monasteries are to be free from the entertainment of ealdormen and from the burden of *fæstingmen*, and from the entertainment of men who bear hawks or falcons, or lead dogs or horses.[4] In 875 Ceolwulf II freed the diocese of the Hwicce from the charge of feeding the king's horses and those who led them, in return for spiritual benefits and the lease of 6 hides of land of four lives.[5] A grant of land of 848 freed a monastic estate from provisioning huntsmen, but stated that foreign ambassadors or messengers from the West Saxons or Northumbrians were to be given a meal if they arrived at the monastery between tierce (9 a.m. and midday) or after 3 p.m. They were also to be fed before they set out in the morning.[6]

This enforced hospitality was different to that freely offered to a traveller or a stranger (often one and the same). In the latter case the host presumably might feel that some prestige accrued to him, particularly if his guest was a man of rank or wealth, and it may have been that a stranger provided entertainment in the form of news from beyond the immediate district. The host would eat with his guest, and perhaps a special meal – like the chicken provided for the *gyrovagus* – would be cooked.[7] Bishops behaved like other great landlords in providing hospitality. A charter of Æthelwulf to Bishop Swithun of Winchester allows him 30 *cassati* at Brightwell for the expenses of hospitality to distinguished foreign visitors, or, in the intervals of these, for the relief of paupers.[8]

---

[1] Bosworth & Toller 1898, 353.
[2] Whitelock 1952, 79.
[3] Whitelock 1955, 486.
[4] Gelling 1979, 26, 28.
[5] Whitelock 1955, 491.
[6] Hart 1975, 68.
[7] Waddell 1932, 183.
[8] Gelling 1979, 28.

When Bishop Cedd excommunicated an unlawfully wedded *gesíð*, he ordered everyone 'not to go into his house nor to eat meals there' (*þæt heo in his hus ne eodon, ne of his swæsendum mete þege*).[1] The king chose to disregard this sentence, and later met his death in that same house.

Charity was not different in kind to hospitality: one person was still providing food for another, but whereas the king and his servants could rely on hospitality by right, and a prosperous traveller was likely to be accorded hospitality, the poor could only wait until someone else took action. The charter to Bishop Swithun implies there was no shortage of the poor, even if distinguished foreign visitors were at times in short supply. The recipients of charity were unlikely to be invited to eat with their benefactor. Ceolfrith's father, an important noble, prepared a very magnificent banquet for the king, and when he could not come, caused the poor, strangers and sick to be summoned – he served the male guests and his wife the women.[2] The fact that this is recorded of him suggests it was not common practice, even if it was undertaken for the sake of 'eternal reward'. A manuscript illustration[3] shows a lord and his lady distributing food to the impoverished and infirm from the steps of their hall. Drink is also being given out, presumably by servants.

In the early part of the period it seems likely that the food the poor received was the 'left-overs'. The king's court was probably a focus for the destitute of quite a large area. King Oswald appointed one of his attendants to take charge of the poor, of whom there was 'a great crowd' (micel menigeo). Sitting at table with Bishop Aidan at his 'early meal' (undernswæsendum) he is told the street outside is full of the poor sitting and begging for alms. 'Then at once the king bade the meat and the victuals set before him to be taken and carried to the poor, and also ordered the dish to be broken in pieces and distributed to them' (*Þa het se cyning sona neoman þone mete 7 þa swæsendo, þe him to aseted wæs, 7 beran þam þearfum; 7 eac bebead, þæt mon þone disc tobræce to styccum 7 þæm þearfum gedælde*).[4] That such generosity was unusual is implied by Aidan's response: 'he was pleased with the king's pious action, took him by the right hand, kissed it and said, "May this hand never grow old"' (*þa licode him seo arfæste dæd þæs cyninges; genom hine þa big þære swiðran honda 7 cyste, 7 þus cwæd: Ne forealdig þeos hond æfre*).[5]

Left-overs were still important enough to be legislated for towards the end of the period when other forms of relief had been established, which perhaps hints at the lavish nature of some meals. The leavings after the monthly feasts of the hundredsmen were to be distributed to the poor, according to the tenth-century ordinance of the bishops and reeves of the London district: 'And then 12 men shall dine together and shall supply themselves as they think fitting, and distribute all the leavings for God's sake'.[6] However, it may have been that the trencher and uneaten bread made up a substantial part of the leavings, as was the case in the later medieval period. *The Boke of Curtayse* circa 1430–40 contains the following verse:

---

[1] Miller 1890, I 1 22.
[2] Whitelock 1955, 706.
[3] Harleian MS No. 63, fol. 57 verso, reproduced in Wright 1871, 26.
[4] Miller 1890, I 1 166–7.
[5] op. cit.
[6] Whitelock 1955, 389.

Byt not on thy brede and lay it doun,
That is no curteyse to use in town;
But breke as myche as þou wylle ete,
The remelant to pore þou shalle lete.[1]

Almsgiving was enjoined on men as a Christian duty and as a way of lessening sins. The poem *Giving of Alms* in the Exeter Book points out that it is well for the man who has a generous heart 'that by means of his almsgiving he removes the wounds of sins and heals souls' (*swa he mid ælmessan ealle toscufeð synna wunde sawla lacnað*). Particularly charitable saints were cited as examples of Christian living, although St. Eustace 'distributed every necessity to those who had need' (*ealle nyd-behæfnysse he wæs dælende þam þe þæs behofoden*) while he was still pagan.[2] St. Cuthbert cared for the poor, fed the hungry, and took in strangers. One of his successors, Eadberht, was careful to give the tithe 'according to Moses' law, not only of four-footed beasts but also of corn and fruit . . . he gave the tenth portion to God as almsgiving to the poor' (*æfter Moyses æw nales ðæt aan feðerfotra neata ac swylce eac ealra wæstma 7 æppla . . . ðone teoðan dæl for Gode to ælmessum ðearfum sealde*).[3] Bede praises Pope Gregory because 'he assuaged the hunger of the poor with food' (*earmra hungur he oferswiðe mid mettum*).[4] He also praises Aidan as being generous to the poor.[5] Boniface writes to King Æthelbald of Mercia in 745/6 congratulating him on giving to the poor. Alcuin's letters to fellow ecclesiastics stress the giving of alms and care of the poor.[6]

Probably most charity during the early and middle periods was of a random, *ad hoc* nature, exercised by those whose own food resources were considerable, although occasionally alms-giving is incorporated in a legal agreement. For example, the tenant of land that had been given to the church at Worcester was to give alms daily for the souls of King Burgred and Bishop Ealhhun, the donors of the land.[7] As the charter is not specific as to the amount to be given, the recipients of this charity must have been dependent on the generosity of the tenant. As the alms were to be given daily, this suggests left-overs, rather than substantial quantities of food.

Making a will was, then as now, an obvious occasion to think of charitable bequests. The will of Werhard, a *presbyter*, made provision for *pauperes* at several estates, including five at Harrow.[8] According to Asser, King Æthelwulf enjoined his successors – until the day of judgement – to always supply with food, drink and clothing, one poor man, whether native or a foreigner, from every ten hides throughout all his hereditary land, provided that the land was occupied by men and herds and had not become waste land.[9] In 1015 the Old English will of Ætheling Æthelstan, the eldest son of King Æthelred, stated that each year there should be paid one day's food rent (from a particular property) to the community at Ely on the

[1] Furnival 1868, 178.
[2] Skeat 1881, *St Eustace* 1.9.
[3] Miller 1890, I 2 374.
[4] op. cit., I 1 94.
[5] op. cit., 1 60.
[6] Whitelock 1955, 203.
[7] Finberg 1972, 108.
[8] Gelling 1979, 104.
[9] Whitelock 1955, 265.

festival of St. Æthelthryth and that 100 pence was to be given to that monastery and 100 poor people fed there on that day.[1] Whereas this will seems to be referring to the provision of ready-to-eat food, Æthelstan's dictate to his reeves refers to the raw materials for meals: 'for the forgiveness of my sins, [that] it is my wish that you shall always provide a destitute Englishman with food, if you have such a one or if you find one [elsewhere]. From two of my rents he shall be supplied with an amber of meal and a shank of bacon or a ram worth four pence every month' (*for minra sinna forgyfenesse, þæt ic wille, þæt ge fedaþ ealle wæga an earm Engliscmon, gif ge him habbaþ, oþþe oþerne gefindaþ. Fram twam minra feorma agyfe mon hine elce monaþ ane ambra meles 7 an sconc spices oþþe an ram weorþe IIII penigas for twelf monþa ælc gear*).[2] The tenth century shows a further development: from the raw materials to financial relief. Money is provided to buy food and these funds are to be administered by the church. The will of Bishop Theodred (942–951), granted ten pounds to be distributed for his soul in his episcopal demesnes, in London and outside London; ten pounds at Hoxne, and that the stock at Hoxne was to be taken and divided in two, one part for the minster and the other distributed 'for my soul'.[3] The will of King Eadred (951–955) granted 1600 pounds to his people 'that they might redeem themselves from famine and from a heathen army if they need'. The archbishop at Christchurch is to receive 400 pounds for the relief of the people of Kent and Surrey and Sussex and Berkshire . . . Ælfsige, bishop at the see of Winchester, is to receive 400 pounds, 200 for Hampshire, 100 for Wiltshire, and the other for Dorset . . . Abbot Dunstan is to receive 200 pounds for the people of Somerset and Devon . . . And Bishop Ælfsige is to receive the 200 pounds which is left over and keep it at the see of Winchester for whatever shire may need it . . . Bishop Oscetel is to receive 400 pounds . . . for the Mercians . . . And 2000 mancuses of gold are to be minted; and the archbishop is to receive one part, the second, Bishop Ælfsige, the third, Bishop Oscetel, and they are to distribute them throughout the bishoprics for the sake of God and the redemption of my soul . . . Then it is my wish that from each of these estates twelve almsmen shall be chosen, and if anything happens to any one of them, another is to be put in his place. And this is to continue as long as Christianity shall last . . . '.[4]

However, although by the end of the tenth century members of the Thegns' Guild in Cambridge were donating two pence each on the death of a member 'for the almsgiving, and from it the fitting amount is to be brought to St. Æthelthryth's', in the eleventh century members of the Abbotsbury Guild were still donating food: on the eve of the feast of St. Peter 'from every two guild-brothers, one broad loaf of good quality and well supplied with something to eat with it for our common almsgiving'.[5]

Christianity probably did improve the situation considerably for the poor in the middle Saxon period, even if their benefactors were primarily acting out of a form of self-interest, but its greatest impact would have occurred towards the end of the period when its tenets were codified. The Laws of Æthelred, drawn up, it is thought, by Archbishop Wulfstan, are particularly comprehensive: 'and that they should

[1] op. cit., 549.
[2] Attenborough 1922, 126–7.
[3] Whitelock 1955, 511.
[4] op. cit., 512.
[5] op. cit., 557, 560.

comfort and feed the poor of God. And that they should not be constantly oppressing the widow and orphan, but they should diligently cheer them. And that they should not vex and oppress strangers and men come from afar' (*7 þæt hy Godes þearfan frefrian 7 fedan. 7 þæt hy widewan 7 steopcild to oft ne ahwænan ac georne hi gladian. And þæt hi ælþeodige men 7 feorran cumene ne tyrian ne tynan*).[1] Religious fines were to be used for religious purposes including the maintenance of the indigent.[2] Wulfstan's *Canons of Edgar* state: 'It is right that every fast should be accompanied by alms-giving' (*And riht is þæt ælc fæsten beo mid ælmessan gewurðod*).[3] The impression remains that charity continued to be of an *ad hoc* nature, even if it was on a national scale. Æthelred's edict, drawn up when 'the "great army" invaded' (*se micel here com to land*), stated that the food that would have been eaten during the three days of fasting he ordained, was to be given as charity.[4]

Tithes could have proved a substantial source of provisions for the poor in good years after Æthelred's decree: 'the third portion to God's poor and poverty-stricken slaves' (*þridde Godes þearfum 7 earman þeowetlingan*).[5] According to Wulfstan's *Canons of Edgar*, priests were to distribute alms. 'And we teach that priests are to distribute the alms . . . we teach that the priests are to sing psalms as they distribute alms, and exhort poor men to intercede for the people' (*And we lærað þæt preostas . . . dælan folces ælmessan . . . we lærað þæt preostas sealmas singan þonne hi ða ælmessan dælan and þa þearfan georne biddan þæt hig for þæt folc þingian*).[6] However, it would be a mistake to think of this system as a proto-Welfare state with priests acting as Benefits Agency officers, since the variations in harvests, the effects of murrains on domestic stock, and the changing political conditions must have made it virtually impossible to provide regular relief. Moreover, the vision of hell seen by Adamnan and recounted in the eleventh century included 'stewards of monasteries who . . . being in charge of the gifts and tithes of the church embezzle those treasures instead of devoting them to the guests and the needy ones of the Lord'.[7] Fortunes could change dramatically. At one point when he was in hiding with his wife and one thegn, Alfred was reduced to one loaf and a little wine.[8]

This story was in fact recounted to demonstrate Alfred's generosity, since, reserving a part for his friends who were out hunting, he gave the rest to a beggar since he thought his need was greater than his own. That beggars were not generally treated as generously seems to be implied by the eponymous subject of *The Exile's Prayer* in the Exeter Book. Forced to live on charity 'increasing his misery' (*ycaþ his yrmþu*), 'he endured all that bitter reproach' (*he þæt eal þolað sarcwide segca*).[9] The Welsh Laws take into account that a beggar might not receive the aid he asked for: 'One of the three thieves who shall escape for an acknowledged theft' was a beggar 'who shall traverse three *trevs* and nine houses in each *trev*, without obtaining either alms or *gwesta* to relieve him, though he be caught with stolen eatables in his possession, he

---

[1] Robertson 1925, 105.
[2] op. cit.
[3] Fowler 1972, 13.
[4] Robertson 1925, 114–5.
[5] op. cit., 121.
[6] Fowler 1972, 13, 15.
[7] Jackson 1971, 293.
[8] Turner 1828, I 569.
[9] Mackie 1934, I. 93.

is still free by law'.[1] The Anomalous Laws were more lenient still. The 'destitute pauper' who had stolen meat to the value of three score pence had only to prove that he had been refused alms or relief in three houses that day to be allowed to go free.

By the end of the period some individuals may have received regular relief as guild members[2] or almsmen. Such a condition of dependence was probably deeply felt, particularly by those who had fallen on hard times from a position of relative wealth, as being the antithesis of the lordly ideal of the provider. Those in conditions of abject poverty who were unable to obtain charity, had to steal food to live, sell themselves into slavery to obtain rations, or starve to death.

There seems to have been a gradual development in the form charity took, from leavings and meals, to provisions and money with which to buy food, so that by the end of the period all four types of charity co-existed. The tenth-century *Regularis Concordia* not only recommended charity to the poor, but insisted attendance on them was the common duty of all. A special place was to be reserved for the reception of poor strangers. But it was also taken for granted that each monastery would support a number of poor men from whom three would be chosen everyday to receive the Maundy, and partake of food from the monks' table.[3] The function of the monasteries in providing hospitality to travellers and charity for the sick and poor seems to have been well-established by the end of the period. The Peterborough Chronicle refers to a refectory for feeding the poor in the twelfth century.[4] Forethought and organisation went into the provision of large-scale relief. This was obviously more significant than individual, random acts of charity, although these may have been very important for the recipient – even a matter of life and death.

---

[1] Owen 1841, I 463.
[2] Whitelock 1955, 557.
[3] Symons 1953, xxxvii.
[4] Mellows 1980, 52.

IV Consumption

28. Meals

Mealtimes

Taking meals at regular times was seen as a good thing in moral terms: 'every mouth needs food; meals shall take place at their proper time' (*muþa gehwylc mete þearf mæl sceolon tidum gongan*).[1] Gluttony consisted of eating before the time of the meal, as well as taking too much.[2] Regular mealtimes seem to have been seen as evidence of an ordered, civilised life.

Moreover, in large establishments, serving meals at set hours would have saved time. Punctual meals were particularly important in monasteries where the offices had to be observed.[3]

When meals were taken, or even how many meals a day there were, varied according to the calendar, social class, and personal preference. The novice of the *Colloquy* seems to eat first soon after midday.[4] The novice is being interrogated at this point in his day, so we do not hear the time of any later meals, although this evidence may reflect the fact that children had their main meal at midday. The midday meal is referred to in other monastic contexts.[5]

The *Regularis Concordia* mentions the *prandium ad sextam* at noon, and a *cena* between Vespers and Compline allowed daily from Easter until Whitsun. From Whitsun until September 14 (apart from certain fast days which included Wednesdays and Fridays) and on all Sundays and feasts of twelve lessons there were also two meals a day but the *prandium* was not taken until *none* (3 p.m.).[6] A single meal *ad nonam* between Nones and Vespers was the rule for the winter period from September 14 to Lent; in Lent and on Quarter Tense days the one meal was *ad vesperam* (after Vespers).[7] So it appears there was a main, midday meal, though this might be put back to mid-afternoon, or later, for which the term was *gereordung* or *non-mete*.[8]

According to the Old English *Rule of Chrodegang*, if *preostas* ate twice a day then it was at midday and evening, and at Æthelwold's monastery the monks had dinner and supper.[9] There are other references to 'the evening meal' (*æfen-gereord, æfen-gyfl, æfen-mete and æfen-þenung*).[10]

---

[1] Bloch 1961, 74; Mackie 1934, *Gnomic Verses* l.124.
[2] Skeat 1881, Mem. of the Saints l.268; St Mary of Egypt.
[3] op. cit., *St. Martin* l.331.
[4] Garmonsway 1978, 44.
[5] Whitelock 1954, 704.
[6] Logeman 1888, Chapter 41; Miller 1890, I, 1 162.
[7] Symons 1953, xxxv.
[8] Wright 1871, 33.
[9] Napier 1916, 14; Turner 1828, III 33.
[10] Wright 1871, 33, 184.

In monasteries a drink was allowed just before *collatio* (the reading at 6 p.m.). By the time of Dunstan, this drink, probably ale, was replaced on certain days by a superior beverage (called the *caritas*), which was accompanied by finer bread and cakes.[1] Frequency of the *caritas* grew to twice a week, and the provision of wine or mead for this was laid as a charge on all the administrative officials.[2]

An earlier meal than dinner or supper is referred to – the *undernswæsendum*. *Undern* was roughly the period of dawn.[3] Aidan was sitting with King Oswald at an *undernswæsendum*.[4] However, this was on Easter Sunday, and 'we eat on Sundays early in the morning and in the evening because Sunday is such a holy day' (*we etað on þam sunnan dagum on undern and on æfen forðan þe se sunnan dæg is swa halig*), so, if there was not to be a midday meal, breakfast may have been eaten instead.[5]

In contrast to the monastic regimen where the main meal was at or around midday, it is possible that in a secular time-table, main meals were at the third hour and again at supper time, to allow a full day's activity between them.

A number of individuals, usually for religious reasons, chose to have only one meal a day. There may have been others whose meals were similarly limited from lack of resources, but we do not hear of them.[6] King Alfred added to his translation of Boethius on the Golden Age, 'They lived naturally and temperately. They always ate but once a day, and that was in the evening'.[7] Everyone was supposed to observe fast days, particularly the period of Lent, and to cut down to one meal a day, but in monasteries dietary observations were strictly observed, so the Old English *Rule of Chrodegang* refers to both eventualities: 'whether the priests eat once a day or twice' (*swa hwæðer preostas ætan on dæg swa æne swa tuwa*).[8]

The ideal meal was the feast, taken in hall, with tables and seating. No doubt most nobles and senior members of their retinues managed to sit at table for their meals, even if the exigencies of campaigning meant this was, on occasion, improvised.[9] Al fresco meals, eaten at a table with servants in attendance, are depicted in manuscripts, but this may reflect Mediterranean artistic influence. Some workers almost certainly ate their meals in the fields.[10]

An anonymous letter to one Brother Edward asks him to try to stop countrywomen at their feasts from eating and drinking in privies.[11] It was the element of gluttony that concerned the writer: eating should be done at table, and perhaps publicly. However, it seems that some saints did not sit at table for meals in order to avoid gluttony.[12]

[1] Knowles 1940, 456-7.
[2] op. cit., 430.
[3] Bosworth & Toller 1898, I 424.
[4] Miller 1890, I, 1 164.
[5] Skeat 1881, *Ash Wednesday* 1.3.
[6] op. cit., *St Aethelthryth* 1.42; Miller 1890, I, 2 244, 318.
[7] Turner 1828, II 36.
[8] Napier 1916, 14.
[9] Wilson 1985, pl. 47.
[10] Colgrave 1940, 70.
[11] Swanton 1975, 29.
[12] op. cit., 57.

Diet & Composition of Meals

The composition of meals is hard to assess, though they almost certainly included bread when possible. There was a sound nutritional reason for this. If meat is not accompanied by calorie-rich carbohydrate foods, the protein in the meat will be used as a source of energy and will not be available for other physiological functions.[1]

The baker of the *Colloquy* is pleading a special case, but his reply to the question, 'Can we live without you?' must be close to the truth or it would have been commented on: 'You may for a period of time, not for long, or very well. Indeed without my trade every table would seem empty, and without bread all food turns to loathing. I strengthen the heart of man and am the strength of men. Even the little ones will not despise me.' (*Ge magon þurh sum fæc buton na lancge ne to wel: soplice buton cræfte minon ælc beoð æmtig byþ gesewen, 7 buton hlafe ælc mete to wlættan byþ gehwyrfed. Ic heortan mannes gestrangie ic mægan wera 7 furþon litlincgas nellaþ forbigean me.*)[2]

The legal 'accompaniment' to bread, according to VI Athelstan, might be 'meat or cheese or beans, or what ever one eats with bread according to the season'.[3] Ælfric's *Homily on the Life of St. Benedict*, observes of the Italians 'they eat oil …with their food as we do butter', which means that bread was generally eaten with butter.[4] Bread seems to have been eaten with any kind of *smeoru* (literally: smearing), including dripping, new cheese or lard. If there was nothing more substantial, bread might be eaten with a relish of herbs like *gitte* (black cumin), 'the southern wort that is good to eat on bread' (*suþerne wyrt sio is god on hlafe to þicgenne*).[5]

Even royal meals on feast days included bread.[6] We probably would not know the constituents of two particular meals nor their cost if they had not been itemised for legal purposes in a will, of which only a fragment remains. The first funeral feast was detailed as follows: '7 pence for ale and 2 ores, 1 ore for bread and another ore for a flitch of bacon and for a buck' (*seuen peniges at hale 7 twa ore 7 an ære at bræad 7 hoþær hæræ at an flychca 7 at an buch*).[7] At the second funeral feast, when more time could be spent on the preparations, 5 ores were to be provided for malt and fuel and 42 pence for bread, and 17 pence for a pig and 2 ores for a bullock and 1 ore for 3 bucks and 8 pence for a cheese and 3 pence for fish and 4 pence for milk.[8]

At the bottom of the social scale were the destitute. According to Athelstan's ordinance, one destitute Englishman on each of the royal estates was to receive one amber of meal and a shank of bacon or a wether worth fourpence every month.[9] The meal could have been consumed as bread or pottage. According to *Rectitudines Singularum Personarum*, a male slave was to receive, *inter alia*, about 3½ pounds of corn per day, and a female slave

---

[1] Harris 1986, 27.
[2] Garmonsway 1978, 36-7.
[3] Whitelock 1955, 390.
[4] Wright 1871, 37.
[5] Cockayne 1851, II xxxix.
[6] Miller 1890, I, 1 166.
[7] Robertson 1939, 252.
[8] op. cit.
[9] Attenborough 1922, 127.

2½ pounds.[1] This roughly equates to the '4lbs of bread by weight' (*feower punda gewihte hlafes*) provided every day by *The Rule of Chrodegang* for everyone 'from the youngest to the eldest' (*fram þam gingstan oð þone yldstan*).[2]

Bread 'went without saying'. Asked what he eats, the novice replies: 'I still eat flesh-meat because I am still under tutelage …vegetables and eggs, fish and cheese, butter and beans and all things that are not taboo I eat very gratefully.' ('*Gyt flæscmettum ic bruce forðam cild ic eom under gwrda drohniende ...wyrta 7 ægra, fisc 7 cyse, buteran 7 beana 7 ealle clæne þingc ic ete mid micelre þancunge.*')[3] The Bury St. Edmunds will fragment and the novice's testimony suggest the kind of food that might make up a meal: bread, bacon or pork, beef, cheese, fish, vegetables, eggs, butter, beans and, for special occasions, venison; milk dishes or milk to drink, or ale, or failing that water, with wine for the older, wiser and richer.[4] However, one might be expected, at least under normal circumstances, to limit oneself to one or two dishes.[5]

The monks might not have eaten as well as individuals in a noble household, but probably enjoyed a good diet most of the time. The agricultural labourer of *Rectitudines Singularum Personarum* lacked the variety and choice of the monastic table, but as well as the allowance of meal, the male slave received two sheep carcasses and a good cow, the female one sheep or 3 pence for winter food, one sester of beans for Lenten food and whey in summer or one penny.[6] Both received food at Christmas, Easter, and harvest, and had a strip of land in which to grow vegetables. The swineherd had a pig in a sty and the perquisites when he prepared the bacon. The cowherd, shepherd and goatherd all had some milk from their animals, in some cases beestings and whey too. No doubt some bartering went on, so some butter, cheese and other white meats, would be added to the diet.

The Anglo-Saxon peasant's evening meal may very often have taken the form of broth, then chopped meat.[7] Perhaps this was on the lines of the French *pot-au-feu*, which includes a beef marrow bone to provide marrow to spread on the bread served with the broth, and would help to account for the number of split marrow bones found on Anglo-Saxon sites.[8]

About 25kg. of meat per head p.a. may have been consumed, as compared to the present national average of 63.5kg. More than half would have come from beef, pigs provided the second largest amount with sheep providing only a small percentage, although (as has been noted) animal bone evidence takes no account of salt meat. Venison seems to have been a fairly scarce meat. Wildfowling provided a continuous supply of meat, and, if small in amount, more birds were available in winter when food supplies were short. Fish are often shown whole in illustrations of feasting. Perhaps this is because fish are easily recognisable, as well as because they were a desirable food.[9] Poultry – fowl and goose – was also present on sites throughout the period.

---

[1] Douglas & Greenaway 1953, 815; Whitelock 1952, 109.
[2] Napier 1916, 14.
[3] Garmonsway 1978, 46.
[4] Robertson 1939, 252; Garmonsway 1978, 46-7; Napier 1926, 14-15.
[5] Garmonsway 1978, 46-7.
[6] Liebermann 1898, 449-50.
[7] Fell 1984, 144.
[8] David 1960, 184.
[9] Garmonsway 1978, 27.

Regional Variations

Inhabitants of coastal districts would probably have included more salt-water fish and shellfish in their diet.[1] Those living near large rivers, or lakes would probably have consumed a fair proportion of fresh-water fish, including eels.

The wetter western and northern counties were more suited to growing oats or barley, and therefore breads and cereal pottages would be likely to include these grains. In the region round Worcester rye was apparently used more than elsewhere. In the eastern counties bread would be more likely to be based on wheat.

Those in western and south-western counties with a climate suited to cattle-raising and dairying based on the cow, may have consumed more beef and dairy products.[2] However, the consumption of beef probably depended more on who you were than where you were.

Seasonal Variations

These were very significant, especially for those with slender resources. A winter diet of bread, salt meat, legumes, with some cheese, was probably short in antiscorbutic foods, but fresh vegetables, particularly early types of cabbage, onions and leeks, but also including 'wild' plants, like Chenopodium, may have been eaten, although these would not necessarily feature in the written record. Lent would have been a time of short commons for some, though vegetables, together with fish, cereals and some fruit and nuts were available. Easter was technically a feast day, and could have been celebrated with fresh meat, probably lamb, eggs, salads of green shoots. The stock-pot could be used again for stews of salt meat, lamb and veal. By midsummer some 'grass beef' was ready for eating, and mackerel were plentiful. Dairy products were available, and various white meats were eaten fresh. There may have been a dearth just before harvest. From the summer into autumn various fruits, which may have been eaten with cream, and nuts were available.[3] By Michaelmas fat mutton was available, and at Hallowmas pork, sprats and smelts were in season.

Courses

The Old English *Rule of Chrodegang* refers to courses, so that a meal might have consisted of soft (?new) cheese, then 'delicacies' (i.e. meat puddings/sausages), then fish or vegetables as the *priddan sande* (lit: third sending), or the order might be meat puddings/sausages, then cheese then vegetables or stewed meat.[4] The Benedictine Rule decreed the *prandium*(lunch) should consist of two cooked dishes and a third of fresh vegetables and fruit.[5] By the end of the period great feasts in rich monasteries might run to a number of courses. Secular meals in important households would seem to have consisted of four to five courses.[6]

---

[1] Holdsworth 1980, 131; Bell 1977.
[2] Davies 1982, 23.
[3] Furnivall 1868, 85.
[4] Napier 1916, 14-15.
[5] Furnivall 1868, 131, 152ff.
[6] Knowles 1940, 463.

Drinks with Meals

The four pence for milk for the second funeral feast detailed in a will fragment from Bury St. Edmunds may have been to make white meats, or it may have been to drink, particularly with the fish after which it is mentioned, since the Danish custom was to eat fish with milk.[1] Food allowances never give fish with ale.[2] The monastic diet at Llancarfan included plenty of fish and milk.[3] Otherwise wine (for the senior members of society), ale, mead, cider/fruit wines, or water were drunk.

Conclusion

Monotony may have been a characteristic of the Anglo-Saxon diet. Until recently peasants in central Europe ate the same dishes, basically farinaceous, on five days of each week.[4] Penitents were often given a deliberately monotonous diet, perhaps bread, salt and pease pudding.[5] Hunger would have made repetitious meals more acceptable, and we know that famines did occur.[6]

[1] Groundes Pearce 1971, 12.
[2] Ashley 1928, 126-7; Seebohm 1952, 157.
[3] Davies 1982, 35.
[4] Gamerith in Owen & Fenton 1981, 86.
[5] Davies 1982, 35.
[6] Napier 1916, 15.

29. Fasting

In Anglo-Saxon society an annual pattern of fasting and feasting was enjoined on the population as a Christian duty; periods of fasting were followed by periods of feasting, and single feast days were preceded by a day of fasting. Fasts were observed by the laity as well as clerics; those exempt were children and the infirm.

The three main forms of fasting were to limit the diet to certain items, to limit the daily amount of food consumed, usually by delaying eating until a certain time, and consuming only one meal a day, but also by limiting the ration of food, and adulterating food with unpalatable additions.

Reasons for Fasting

It has been suggested that there were practical reasons for instituting fasting and that one effect would be the overall saving of food resources, but this can hardly have been a prime concern in a system which also enjoined feasting. However, if food supplies were comparatively short for most of the population at particular times of the year, then there would at least be a psychological benefit if those forced to limit their food intake felt they were gaining merit by so doing. To some extent the pattern of feasts and fasts follows the pattern of the seasons, but a period of fasting is sometimes followed immediately by a period of feasting.

Theoretically at least, fasting freed food for almsgiving, so that food was redistributed to those who needed it most.[1]

In the background was the vision of the ideal world in which man would be freed from the necessity of consuming earthly food. The patristic tradition saw fasting as union with the angels, and that it made the soul clear for the reception of divine truth.[2] Meat eating was seen to reflect Cain's primal crime, and as proof of human weakness and cruelty.[3] To abstain from meat was to go some way to recovering primal innocence. Old Testament models offered pure hearts to God by fasting, and the forty-day fast of Christ in the desert was the model for the forty-day fast of Lent.[4]

Fasting was in some measure reparation for Adam's sin, which was seen as one of 'gluttony' (oferfylle), as much as disobedience.[5] It is evident that fasting was a means of purification, and it was so used in various ceremonies (see below).

Apart from these theoretical considerations, it was observed that fasting moderated lust.[6] St. Augustine maintained that the body was excited by the full satisfaction of the appetite, but acknowledged the difficulty of keeping the balance between

---

[1] Whitelock 1955, 410.
[2] Bynum 1987, 36.
[3] McGee 1986, 83.
[4] op. cit.; Dembinska in Fenton & Kisban 1986, 153.
[5] Cockayne 1851, III *Lar* 1.40, 1.74-5; Turner 1828, III 505.
[6] Swanton 1975, 177.

suppression of lust and enfeeblement of the body.[1] Other writers point out the difficulty of carrying out one's duties when following a very ascetic regime.[2] Boniface complained of the perversity of priests who did not eat of the foods which God gave, and others, whose interpretation of the bible was perhaps over-literal, fed on milk and honey, rejecting bread and animal foods.[3]

Fasting was employed to get God on one's side and thereby bring about desired results.[4] The tenth-century *Institutes of Polity* suggest that if misfortune befell the people, then they should consult how amends might be sought from Christ with cleansing fasts and with frequenting churches.[5] There was a belief that choosing a lack would induce God to give plenty.[6]

The Regular Fasts

Some fasts were only day-long. The important weekday fast was on Fridays, though Saturday was also a day of fasting in anticipation of the following feast day. Some monastic institutions also observed a fast on Wednesdays. The ancient church followed the Jewish custom of fasting on two days a week, but instead of Monday and Thursday, altered the fast days to Wednesday and Friday.[7] Bede tells us that Aidan and his community observed both these days: 'it became their habit through the year, except for the fifty days after Easter, to fast till the ninth hour on the fourth and sixth days of the week' (*þæt hi him to gewunan genamen þæt heo þurh eall ger buton fiftig neahta ofer Eastron þæt heo þy feorðan wicdæge 7 þy syxtan feaston to nones*).[8] Possibly Cuthbert observed the Wednesday fast too, but in the sense that he did not eat until the ninth hour, since he did not abstain from flesh on Fridays.[9] There was much variation in the matter of abstinence, especially among the laity in the early medieval church.[10] The eves of feast days were observed with a fast. The periods of fasting were Lent, September and Advent. The eves of feast days are specifically mentioned in Ethelred's Code of 1008, which states that all festivals of St. Mary are to be diligently observed, first with a fast and afterwards with a festival, and the same for festivals of every apostle, except there should be no fast for the festival of SS Philip and James because of the Easter festival.[11] The *Regularis Concordia* of a few decades earlier had specifically stated that the fast should not be observed on the Vigil of the Epiphany, so perhaps by imposing a fast then too, the law code was simplifying matters by removing exceptions.[12] Ethelred's Code went on to say that there should be a fast every Friday, except when it was a feast day.[13] The Lent and Ember Day fasts were specifically mentioned in the *Be fæstene* (Concerning Fasting), section of the later Code of Canute: 'That one must observe fasts, whether it be the Ember Day fasts, or the Lenten fast, or if it be any other fast, with all conscientiousness' (*Þæt*

[1] Bynum 1987, 79.
[2] Dembinska in Fenton & Owen 1986, 153; Skeat 1881, *Prayer of Moses* l.104.
[3] Kylie 1911, 116, 122.
[4] Davies 1982, 168.
[5] Bonser 1963, 5.
[6] Bynum 1987, 39.
[7] Colgrave 1940, 344.
[8] Miller 1890, I, 1 162.
[9] Colgrave 1940, 344.
[10] op. cit.
[11] Whitelock 1955, 407.
[12] Cockayne 1851, III.
[13] Whitelock 1955, 407.

man ælc beboden fæsten healde, sy hit ymbrenfæsten, sy hit lenctenfæsten, sy elles oðer fæsten, mid ealre geornfulnysse).[1] The Council of Placentia in 1095 confirmed the Ember day fasts as the Wednesday, Friday and Saturday following the first Sunday in Lent, Whitsun, 14th September and 13th December.

Periods of Fasting

According to VII Æthelred c.1009, the nation was to fast for three days on bread and herbs and water on the Monday, Tuesday and Wednesday before Michaelmas (and other penitential actions were to be performed). Slaves were to be freed from work during these three days so that they might more willingly observe the fast.[2] This was to 'obtain God's mercy and his compassion that we may through his help withstand our enemies', with the food that would otherwise have been consumed being given to the sick and needy.[3] Saints are recorded as practising or prescribing the three-day fast.[4] The three-day fast perhaps paralleled the three-day feast: both were serious matters. The week-long fast was called for on some occasions.[5]

The Lenten Fast

A fast lasting a few days before Easter was practised in the second century, emerging in the fourth century as a fast of 36 days. This was expanded to 40 days in the seventh century in the west.[6] According to the *Old English Martyrology*, Pope Telesphorus was the first to decree 'that one fast for seven weeks before Easter in Rome' (*þæt man fæste on rome syfon wucan ær eastran*).[7] It was not until nearly fifty years after the arrival of Augustine's mission that a Kentish king ordered the final suppression of paganism, and 'that the forty-day fast be held before Easter on pain of punishment' (*þæt feowertiglice fasten healden beon ær Eastrum bi witerædenne*).[8]

It seems that violating the Lenten fast might invite more than legal punishment, and the following cautionary tale was recorded for the beginning of Lent. 'In that same week some buffoon came to the bishop's household and went to the kitchen while the bishop was saying mass and began to eat. He fell down backwards in a faint at the moment when he took his first mouthful, and vomited blood and his life was preserved only with difficulty.' (*On þære ylcan wucan com sum trud to þæs bisceopes hirede se ne gymðe nanes lenctenes fæstenes ac eode him to kicenan pa hwile ðe se bisceop mæssode and began to etenne. he feoll þa æt dærne forman snæde under-becc geswogen and spaw blod ac him gebyrede swa ðeah þæt feorh.*)[9]

The fact that a *presbyter et Scottus* had eaten meat in Lent caused Charlemagne enough concern for him to mention it in a letter to Offa. Charlemagne sent him to be

[1] Robertson 1925, 65, 166.
[2] Whitelock 1955, 409.
[3] op. cit.
[4] Skeat 1881, *St Basilus* l.235; *St Sebastian* l.206.
[5] op. cit., St Eufrasia l.211; St Martin l.1284; The Chair of St Peter, l.262.
[6] Bynum 1987, 37.
[7] Herzfeld 1900, *Jan. 2*.
[8] Miller 1890, I, 1 172.
[9] Skeat 1881, *Ash Wednesday* ll.59.

judged by the bishop, as he could not remain at his post because of the infamy of the sin, and the fact that others might be induced to violate the sacred fast.[1]

On the other hand 'Many deeds foolishly injure mankind …like those do who foolishly fast beyond their strength in Catholic Lent as we ourselves see until they become ill.' (*Fela dyslice dæda deriað mancynne …swa swa men doð þe dyslice fæstað ofer heora mihte on gemænelicum lenctene swa swa we sylfe gesawon oð þæt hi seoce wurdon.*) Ælfric went on to explain that England was on the outer edge of the world and therefore not as strong as lands in the middle and there men might fast more easily. Moreover 'men now are not as strong as they were in the beginning' (*ne nu nis man cynn swa mihtig swa men wæron æt fruman*).[2]

The later medieval period records a period of fasting called the 'Lent of Pentecost' which ended on SS Peter and Paul's Day, June 29, but this is not often referred to in the Anglo-Saxon sources.[3] One occasion where it does occur, is when Ecgberht says that he will keep to a very strict diet 'the forty days after Pentecost' (*for þæt feowertig daga æfter Pentecosten*).[4] The other sustained fast period in Anglo-Saxon England was the forty-day Advent fast, beginning on November 14, which developed originally as an expression of penance at the year's end, but then became seen as the forerunner of the Christmas feast.[5]

Although there were three forty-day fast periods, most references are made to the Lent fast. Bede gives an account of how Bishop John used to retreat to an oratory and church for the Lenten fast, with a few companions whom he asked to find 'a poor and needy man suffering from great infirmity and poverty, so they might have him with them at that time, and give him alms. For it was his custom always to do this' (*sumne earmne ðearfan, se ðe wære micel untrumnisse 7 woedelnisse hefigað, ðæt hie meahton in ðæm dagum mid him habban 7 mid him ælmesse doan. Forðon his gewuna wæs, ðæt he symle swæ dyde*).[6]

However, while Bishop Eadberht also took himself off, this time to an island, for the Lent fast, he did the same for the forty days before Christmas, so he could live in great abstinence, fervent prayers and outpourings of tears.[7]

Instructions as to the observation of a fast are given with reference to the Lenten fast, which may indicate its importance, although, as the first feast of the year, it would be logical to give regulations about fasting at that point. The Old English version of the *Rule of Chrodegang* gives the following details:

'We beg that on the forty days before Easter our community conduct itself with all soberness of mind and body and eats only one meal and takes drink with the abstinence that God decrees, and each day except Sunday from the beginning of Lent until Easter eats after evensong in the refectory and everyone is to keep to the food that the bishop and the prior has appointed and not to eat elsewhere, either in the

[1] Turner 1828, I 416.
[2] Skeat 1881, *Prayer of Moses* ll.91, 106.
[3] Bynum 1987, 37.
[4] Miller 1890, I, 2 242-4.
[5] Bynum 1987, 37.
[6] Miller 1890, I, 2 388.
[7] op. cit., I, 2 376-7.

town, or in the minster or in any place, nor even in their own house during these forty days, except out of necessity, in that they do not have enough time to get back for the brothers' meal.'

(We beodað þæt on þam feowertigum dagum ær Eastron mid alre syfernysse modes 7 lichaman ure preosthyredas hi sylfe gehealdon 7 an metes þigene 7 drinces habbon swa micle forhæfednysse swa him þonne God geunne 7 ælce dæg butan sunnandæge fram Lenctenes aginne oð Eastron æfter æfensange etan on beoderne 7 fram þam metton dricum hi forhæbbon hi [þe] se bisceop 7 se ealdor þonne gesetton 7 elles nahwer ne an þære ceastre ne an þam mynstrum ne on nanum stowum, ne furðon on heora agenum husum þissum feowertigum dagum ne gereordigen hi, butan hwa for hwiclere nytwyrdnysse swa feor beo þæt he þam gefenlicum tidum to broðra gereorde cuman ne mage.)[1]

It is clear that laymen were to observe fast days, but it is also evident that lay fasting, fasting practised by monastics, and the virtuoso performances – admired if not emulated – of saints were different in degree, and so I propose to deal with these three types of fasting separately.

Fasting for Laymen

Evidence for fasting is almost entirely documentary, though there is a possibility that stones sometimes found in the boxes which were excavated from tenth-century Fyrkat (Denmark), and normally belonged to women, were sucking stones to relieve hunger or thirst, and they may have been used during fasts.[2]

The attitude laymen took towards fasting varied considerably. Alfred added to his translation of Boethius on the Golden Age, 'They lived naturally and temperately. They always ate but once a day and that was in the evening'.[3] In this he seems to have been more abstemious than the clerics with whom Cuthbert was dining one Christmas. Exhorted by Cuthbert to 'earnestly engage in prayers and vigils' they understandably replied, 'You give us good, yea excellent, instruction, but nevertheless, because the days of fastings, prayers and vigils abound, today let us rejoice in the Lord'.[4]

The fast-day food of the poor may not have been very different from their normal diet. In the fifteenth century in the west, the poor on fast days ate mainly vegetable foods, since fish was more expensive and even a comparative rarity.[5] This is likely to have been the case in Anglo-Saxon England. The nobility and rich religious establishments took pains to secure a supply of fish, fish featured at feasts, and were in short supply (see previous chapter). Some dried cod or salted herring may have been available; these were eaten by the poor with linseed or rape oil in later medieval Europe as fast-day food.[6]

[1] Napier 1916, 42-3.
[2] Roesdahl 1977, 194.
[3] Turner 1828, II 36.
[4] Colgrave 1940, 247.
[5] Kisban in Fenton & Kisban 1986, 3.
[6] Dembinska in Fenton & Owen 1981, 162.

Originally a religious requirement, fasting became a legal one. According to the *Laws of Wihtred*, 'If a man gives meat to his household during a fast, he shall redeem free a slave by payment of his *healsfang*' (*Gif mon his heowum in fæsten flæsc gefe, frigne ge þeowne halsfange alyse*). 'If a slave eat of his own accord, he shall pay six shillings or be lashed.' (*Gif þeow ete his sylfes ræde, vi scll oþþe his hyd.*)[1] Later Laws repeat and amplify the legal requirement for fasting. It was obviously important that people should be told when the fasts were, and apparently this was the duty of the parish priest. The legislation enacted by Alfred and Guthrum states 'If a mass-priest misinforms the people about feasts and fasts, he shall pay thirty shillings in an English district, three-and-a-half marks in a Danish one.' (*Gif mæssepreost miswyssige æt freolse oððe æt fæstene, gylde xxx scill. mid Englum 7 mid Denum þreo healfmarc.*)[2] It continued: 'If a freeman break an official fast, he is to pay compensation. If a slave does this, he is to suffer a beating, or pay a fine in lieu.' (*Gif frigman rihtfasten abrece gylde wite oððe lahslite. Gif it þeowman gedo, ðolie his hyde oððe hydgylde.*)[3] The same situation is recorded in Canute's Laws, in that if a free man were to break a legally ordained fast, he was to pay a fine. Fasting is here further defined in that it was wrong to eat during a time of fast before the mealtime, and worse still to defile oneself with fleshmeat. If a slave was to do this, he was to suffer a flogging, or redeem himself from one, in proportion to the wrong-doing.[4] Canute's proclamation of 1020 repeated that 'all men, poor and prosperous ...should observe strictly the legal fasts and conscientiously celebrate saints' days, as the mass-priests tell us' (*ealle men, earme 7 eadige ...ælc beboden fæsten geornlice healdan 7 þa halgan georne weordian þe us mæssepreostas beodan sceolan*).[5] This again confirms the responsibility of the masspriests. The purpose of right observance was so that all 'may attain to the joy of the heavenly kingdom' (*to heofena rices myrðe becuman*).[6] About the same time the Laws of the Northumbrian priests also specified a fine for anyone violating a festival or a legal fast, fixing the amount at 12 ores.[7] King Edgar's Code at Andover (959–63) had repeated that ordained fasts were to be observed with all diligence, and added that the fast every Friday was also to be observed, unless it was a festival.[8] Evidently the importance of observing fasts was felt from the mid-seventh century on, since most law codes referred to it. Fasting as an institution presumably met with resistance from some individuals, since penalties for breaking fasts had to be imposed.

Fasting by Monastics

Whereas laymen were to observe only the legal feasts and were otherwise free to eat what and when they wanted, monastics generally were restricted as to diet, as to mealtimes and quantity. Moreover, their regime on fast days was probably more austere than that of laymen. According to the *Rule of Chrodegang* there was some restriction on diet for almost all the year:

---

[1] Attenborough 1922.
[2] op. cit., 102-4.
[3] op. cit.
[4] Whitelock 1955, 425-6.
[5] Attenborough 1925, 144.
[6] op. cit.
[7] Whitelock 1955, 438.
[8] op. cit., 396.

'From Easter to Pentecost the brothers eat twice a day and can eat flesh with permission except for Wednesday and Friday. From Pentecost till the birthday of John the Baptist they also eat twice a day but forgo flesh. From John the Baptist's birthday until the anniversary of St. Martin's death, they also eat twice a day and forgo flesh on Wednesdays and Fridays. Then from Martinmas to midwinter, they forgo all flesh and fast till nones and on all of those days they eat in the refectory, and during that period they forgo flesh on Wednesday and Friday. If one of those days is a festival it lessens the fast, and if the prior gives permission they may eat flesh for the sake of their health.'

(Fram Eastron of Pentecosten tuwa on dæg etan preostas 7 etan flæsc be leafe, butan þa dædbetendan buton Wodnesdæg, 7 Frigedæge. Fram Pentecosten oð Sancte Iohannes gebyrdtide þæs fulwihteres, ealswa eton tuwa on dæg 7 forgan flæsc. Fram Sancte [Iohannes] gebyrdtide of Sancte Martinus forsiðe ealswa eton tuwa on dæg 7 Wodnesdæge 7 Frigedæg forgan flæsc. Þonne fram Sancte Martinus mæssan oð midne winter forgan ealle flæsc 7 fæstone to nones 7 ælce þara dage eton on beoderne 7 on þone timan Wodensdæge 7 Frigedæge forgan flæsc. Gif þonne þam dagum hwilc freolsdæg gescyt, gif se ealdor lifð hi moton flæsc etan for untrumnysse.)[1]

However, a Vegan diet was not encouraged, perhaps because it weakened members of the community who would not then be able to do their share of the work. This effect was recognised as early as the fourth century on the continent, and caused concern, since it ultimately diminished the amount of food available to the whole community.[2]

'Indeed abstinence in these days consists in giving up almost all delicacies and in living soberly and ascetically. He who is genuinely able to abstain from eggs and cheese and butter and fish and wine is of great strength/virtue. He who cannot really abstain from them because of weakness or any other reason may eat them; provided he solemnly fasts until evening before a feast and doesn't get drunk on wine, they may be consumed to preserve his body. He who abstains from cheese and milk and butter and eggs when he is not fasting is very wrong and completely mistaken. Truly wine and every intoxicating drink and gluttony is forbidden, but not milk and eggs. Certainly the apostle did not say "Don't eat milk and eggs"; what he said was, "Don't get drunk on wine, gluttony lies there".'

(Forhæfdnes soðlice on þysum dagum sceal beon forneah ealra esta 7 syferlice and clænice to lybanne. Se ðe soðlice fram ægrum 7 cyse 7 buttan 7 fixum 7 wine forhabban mæg he is mycles mægenes. Se ðe witodlice fram þæm for untrumnesse oððe ahwylcum weorce forhabban ne mæg, he bruce, for an þ he þæt fæsten of æfen symbellice breme, 7 win næs to drucenesse, ac he gereorde his lichaman nyme. Ðæt hwa fram cyse 7 meoluc 7 buteran 7 ægrum forhæbbe 7 ne fæste is gedwolenlicost 7 fram eallum gesceade ascyred. Soþlice wines 7 ælces wætan druncennes 7 galne synt forbodene, næs meoluc 7 ægru. Ne cwæð witodlice se apostol, 'Nellen ge þicgan meoluc 7 ægru,' ac he cwæð, 'Nellen ge beon gynddrencede of wine, on þam is galnes'.)[3]

---

[1] Napier 1916, 43-4.
[2] Dembinska in Fenton & Kisban 1986, 153.
[3] Napier 1916, 114-115.

The very austere regimes of the east where dry eating and raw eating were practised seem to have been admired. At the monastery where Zozimus went to live the brothers kept themselves alive 'on bread and water' (*mid hlafe and mid wætere*) to demonstrate their devotion.[1] But there was the realisation, voiced by Ælfric, that such a diet was not sufficient for monastics in the colder climate of England. Towards the end of the period the larger abbeys secured supplies of eels for Lent. They were Lenten food at Abingdon, and the abbot and brethren of Ramsey, who probably had a plentiful supply of eels for themselves, were to give 4,000 in Lent to Peterborough.[2]

Monastics who ate outside the cloister were presumably able to avoid some of the restrictions imposed on those who ate in the refectory, which is why monks were expected to make the effort to eat together in the refectory during fasts, unless it was too far for them to get back to. Bishops presumably could have eaten out on a number of occasions: when a gesith invited Bishop John to a meal 'the bishop refused, saying his minster was near, and he ought to go there' (*widsoc se biscop 7 cwæth þær his mynster neah wære þæt he scold þyder faran*). However, he did ultimately accept the invitation when the gesith promised to fast and give alms to the poor.[3] A section in the report of the Legates to Pope Hadrian prohibits ecclesiastics taking food in secret.[4] This was presumably to limit the abuse whereby an individual might appear to be observing food restrictions, but was in fact consuming extra rations. On the other hand, an individual could not elect to fast without the permission of the abbot.[5] In both cases the food resources of the monastery were affected, either directly, as in the first case, or indirectly, if the faster could not maintain his contribution to production.

Monastic meals in mid-fifth-century Gaul consisted of two cooked dishes, one a vegetable/cereal soup, the other a puree of pulses with oil, flour or cheese, and a third dish of raw vegetables with salt, oil and vinegar. Bread was also available, but was probably hard dried rusk, which had to be softened in liquid before it could be eaten. Meat was generally prohibited but some wine was permitted.[6] The strict fasting diet consisted of restricting intake to one meal of this sort per day taken in the evening, or to bread and water only. Those who could not comply with this regime were allowed to divide their meal into two, one part to be eaten not before three in the afternoon, and the other in the evening. In the mid-sixth century Benedict laid down the 190–200 fast days in the year. Periods of strict fasting included the forty days of Lent, from Whit Sunday till the autumn equinox, and thirty days before Christmas. There were additionally the two or three fast days each week (Wednesdays, Fridays and in some communities, Mondays) and the eves of twenty-five holidays particular to the monastery, when abstinence from fats, eggs, cheese and fish was called for. When two meals a day were still taken quantitative restrictions were achieved by serving the normal single ration in one bowl which was then shared by two monks.[7] This was probably close to the fasting regime for early Anglo-Saxon monasteries. According to

---

[1] Skeat 1881, *St Mary of Egypt* 1.93.
[2] Cockayne 1851, III; Harmer 1952, 265.
[3] Miller 1890 I, 2 394.
[4] Whitelock 1955, 771.
[5] Dembinska in Fenton & Kisban 1986, 154.
[6] op. cit., 153.
[7] op. cit., 154.

the later *Regularis Concordia*, the Lenten abstinence from milk and eggs was to be observed from Quinquagesima, and on the Ember Days.[1] However, it proved necessary to increase the amounts of food available under the strict fasting diet, since it did not allow for the fulfilment of duties.[2] Fish were originally classed as 'delicacies' (*deliciae*), to be eaten only with the abbot's permission on holidays. Later in the period after monasteries had acquired grants of land and rights to the fish in lakes, rivers and ponds fish became a fasting dish.[3] The growing wealth of monasteries in England and on the continent led to some degree of laxity. The regime laid down by Benedict of Nursia was reformed by Benedict of Aniane, although this rule in turn was relaxed, since Cluny was founded in the tenth century to revive the strictness of the original Benedictine Rule.[4] In England too, reforming ecclesiastics like Æthelwold worked to bring back a more rigorous regime.

The *Regularis Concordia*, produced in the reign of Edgar, confirmed that flesh was prohibited, but the evidence of the novice of Ælfric's *Colloquy* 'I still eat meat because I am a novice' (*Gyt flæscmettum ic bruce, forðam cild ic eom under gyrda drohniende*), indicates that the importance of an unrestricted diet for growing children was recognised.[5] According to *The Rule of Chrodegang*, 'no food or drink is to be taken before or after mealtimes, except by the sick and children if permission has been previously given by the prior' (*ær tide oððe æfter tide naht metes oððe drinces hi na underfo ut asyndrodum untrumum 7 cildrum þæra wacmodes fram þam ealdre is toforan sceigende*).[6]

Fasting by Saints

Saints, and others not officially canonised, either observed fasts more strictly than was ordained, or followed a regime of deprivation, the rationale being that increasing austerities increased merit. No doubt fasting was also used as a demonstration of moral superiority, and to try to influence opinion.

The fact that the early saints of the Christian church tended to fast strictly must have influenced their later followers. For example, Mary of Egypt 'lived on vegetables' (*be þam wyrtum leofode*), and on one occasion was satisfied with a pinch of dried peas.[7] Bread and water was a standard diet.[8] St. Eufrasia occupied herself in fasting and vigils day and night and 'was very thin on account of her strict and austere life' (*wæs swiðe geþynnod for þære micclan and stiðan drohtnung*).[9] Some individuals emulated these practices with similar results: a twelfth-century hermit who ate nothing but roots became so thin from fasting that he could hardly stand.[10]

---

[1] Cockayne 1851, III.
[2] Dembinska in Fenton & Kisban 1986, 157.
[3] op. cit., 155.
[4] op. cit., 163.
[5] Garmonsway 1978, 46.
[6] Napier 1916, 123.
[7] Skeat 1881, *St Mary of Egypt* 1.569.
[8] Herzfeld 1900, July 9, January 17, July 7, June 2.
[9] Skeat 1881, *St Eufrasia* 1.173, 236.
[10] Holmes 1952, 125.

Consumption

On occasion the fasts might not be voluntary, as when St. Ananias was imprisoned for twelve days without food by Diocletian, or when St. Thomas told Migdonia to fast earnestly for seven days.[1] Or they might be incidental: Enbolus was so desirous of Basil's doctrine 'that he had no wish for any food ... for three days ... he took no heed of any meals' (*þæt he hlyste nanes metes ...ðry dagas ...ætes ne gymdon*).[2] But fasting seems to have been an attribute of saintliness, and not the prerogative of one or two individuals.[3]

During the Lenten fast Ecgberht 'only ate once a day, and then only had a small loaf and some thin milk' (*æne siða in dæge gereorde 7 elles ne þeah nemne medmicel hlafes mid þinre meolc*), while Bishop Cedd ate only half a loaf and a hen's egg and milk in the evening.[4]

Cuthbert, who from other evidence was a man of considerable bodily strength and stamina, found it difficult in his early years to fast for long periods, lest he should become unfitted for the labour required of him.[5] He did not abstain from flesh on Fridays, but always fasted until nones.[6]

Once he had settled at Crowland, Guðlac 'tasted nothing except barley bread and water and when the sun was set, then he ate the food on which he lived' (*nahwiht ne onbyrigde buton berenne hlaf and wæter; ond þonne sunne wæs on setle, þonne þigede he þa andlyfene þe he bigleofode*).[7] He rejected the suggestion of two devils that he should fast for seven days 'instead he took a moderate meal, that is the barley loaf, and ate it and preserved his life' (*ac feng to medmycclan bigleofan, þæt wæs to þam berenan hlafe, and þone þigede and his lif bileofode*).[8] A passage in the Exeter Book tells us that 'Guðlac loved fasting and was refreshed by that noble meal', i.e. the Eucharist (*Guðlac fæsten lufiað ead-mod þy æplan gyfle*) and certainly he did not begrudge the visiting brethren their *beor*, since he found amusing the incident where they buried the container so they could recover it after visiting him.[9] The fiends by whom he was persecuted had warned him that 'hunger and thirst will be hard foes' (*beoð hungor and þurst heard gewinnan*), but he said that God sent by the hand of men his necessities each day.[10] Presumably procuring the blessing of so holy a man by taking him what was a relatively cheap food, was motive enough to ensure that individuals took him enough to eat.

Neither Aidan nor Guðlac generally accepted invitations to eat out, though Aidan did on occasion eat with the king, and Guðlac dined with the bishop who ordained him 'though it was not his habit to do so' (*þeah hit his life ungeþeawe wære*).[11]

---

[1] Herzfeld 1900, Jan. 19; Skeat 1881 *St Thomas* 1.296-7.
[2] Skeat 1881 *St Basilus* 1.43-4.
[3] op. cit., 1. 478.
[4] Miller 1890, I, 2 244, 232.
[5] Bonser 1963, 113.
[6] Colgrave 1940, 344.
[7] Goodwin 1848, 27.
[8] op. cit., 35.
[9] Mackie/Gollancz 1972, *Guthlac*; Swanton 1975, 54.
[10] Mackie/Gollancz 1972, *Guthlac*
[11] Miller 1890 I, 1 162; Goodwin 1848, 27.

According to Bede, Aidan influenced all monastics of his time in the matter of fasting.

> 'By the example of this holy man at that time, all religious people, whether men or women, were so confirmed, that it became their habit throughout the year, except during the fifty days after Easter, to fast up to the ninth hour on the fourth and sixth days of the week'.
>
> *(Mid þyses halgan mannes bysenum wæron getrymeðe on þa tid gehwilce æfeste ge wæpnedmen ge wimmen, þæt hi tim to gewuman genaman, þæt heo eall ger buton fiftig neahta ofer Eastron, þæt heo þy feorðan wicdæge 7 þy syxtan feaston to nones.)*[1]

Bede cites a number of saintly individuals who fasted strictly, like Cenred who 'in prayers and fasting and almsgiving lived until his last day' (*on gebedum 7 on fæstenum 7 on ælmesdæum awunade oð ðone ytmestan dæg*).[2] Dryhthelm, having seen a vision of heaven, purgatory and hell, was so shocked, that he embarked on a regime which 'by daily fasts' (*dæghæmlice fæsteno*) left him 'exhausted and subdued' (*swæncte 7 temede*).[3]

Columba once fasted on a diet of nettle soup because a poverty-stricken old lady living nearby was reduced to this extremity. However, his cook added milk to the broth, and when Columba was complimented on how well he was looking, the deception was discovered. Far from being annoyed with the cook, he blessed him.[4]

Monastic situations were generally perceived as too lax by saintly individuals. In the mid-fifth century, Sampson, dissatisfied with the life he had tried at three monasteries for this reason, withdrew to an isolated community, and then used to retreat to a cave for seven-day fasts, when the brethren provided him with food (though of course no meat or alcoholic drink).[5] This withdrawal from even a strict monastic regime was paralleled by Cuthbert's retreats to Farne, after he was made bishop of Lindisfarne.[6] Occasionally an abbot like Æthelwold succeeded in imposing a more austere regime against considerable opposition. Æthelwold only ate the flesh of animals and birds once for three months when forced by infirmity, and this, moreover, at the command of Archbishop Dunstan, and again during the sickness from which he died.[7]

Anglo-Saxon women are also recorded as practising lives of austerity. Leoba, Boniface's chief woman helper in his mission, ate and drank very sparingly, though she practised the greatest kindness to others. The little cup from which she used to drink was called 'the little one of the loved one'. In her case fasting was accompanied by hospitality: she would produce a feast while fasting herself.[8] After Ætheldrida had received the veil, 'seldom, except at greater festivals and seasons or in case of greater need, would she touch food more than once a day' (*seldon, buton maran symbelnysse 7 tidum oðþe maran nydþearfe, ma þonne æne siðe on dæge þæt heo wolde mete þycgan*).[9] Eadgyth, the sister of Athelstan, remained strong to the end of her life, at

---

[1] Miller 1890 I, 1 162.
[2] op. cit., I, 2 448.
[3] op. cit., 436.
[4] Jackson 1971, 279.
[5] Davies 1982, 152.
[6] Miller 1890, I, 2 360.
[7] Whitelock 1955, 837.
[8] op. cit., 722.
[9] Miller 1890, I, 2 318.

Polesworth, in fasts and vigils.[1] Perhaps the lives of those important by virtue of their family connections are more likely to have been recorded, but we do hear occasionally of other individuals, like a certain widow called Oswyn, who lived near the burial place of St. Edmund in prayers and 'fasting for many years afterwards' (*fæstendum manega gear syððan*).[2]

Fasting as Penance

The view that fasting was an efficacious penance presumably received a boost from the account of purgatory given by a Northumbrian, who returned from the dead to say that souls could be aided by – inter alia – the fasting of other men so that they could be rescued before Doomsday.[3] After the death of a much-hated prioress at Wimborne, the younger nuns danced on her grave, and the consequent subsidence was seen as evidence of the dead woman's sinfulness. In order to obtain absolution for her, the mother of the community enjoined a three days' fast for her soul, together with psalm singing and prayers. The depression in the grave duly filled with soil, indicating the success of their penance.[4]

However, fasting is mostly mentioned as penance to be carried out by an individual to atone for his own misdeeds. Fasting was given as penance for such crimes as administering a love potion, passing a child through a hole in the earth for the sake of its health (40 days' bread and water), fasting in honour of the moon on health grounds (1 year's bread and water).[5] These were presumably more likely to be lay misdemeanours, but the lazy monks of Winchester who refused to get up and sing the *Te Deum* every time St. Swithin effected a cure, were threatened by the bishop that they 'should heavily atone for it with seven days' fasting' (*sceolde hit mid fæstene seofon niht on an swarlice gebetan*).[6] According to Wulfstan's *Canons of Edgar*, 'The regulation says if any man in orders goes hunting then if he is a cleric he must abstain from fleshmeat for one year, a deacon for two years, a masspriest three, and a bishop seven.' (*Se canon segð gyf hwylc gehadod man on huntaþ fare, gyf it bid clerec forga xii monað flæsc, diacon twa gear, mæssepreost þreo, bisceop vii.*)[7]

As in Wales, penance might involve a limited diet for days or years.[8] Monastic penances ranged from missing one meal to foregoing flesh and alcohol and most fats for several years.[9] Welsh sources give in detail the fasting diet for the monastic priest or deacon found guilty of a sexual offence: bread without limitation and a titbit fattened slightly with butter on Sunday; on the other days a ration of dry bread and a dish enriched with a little fat, garden vegetables, a few eggs, a British cheese, a Roman half-pint of milk in consideration of the body in this age, also a Roman pint of whey or buttermilk for his thirst, and some water if he is a worker.[10] According to the

[1] Whitelock 1955, 257.
[2] Skeat 1881, *St Edmund* 1.191.
[3] Miller 1890, I, 2 432.
[4] Whitelock 1955, 720-1.
[5] Bonser 1963, 149, 240, 249.
[6] Skeat 1881, *St Swithun* 1.261.
[7] Fowler 1972, 15.
[8] Davies 1982, 192.
[9] op. cit.
[10] op. cit., 151.

Old English *Rule of Chrodegang*, no-one was to sleep in the interval between *utsange* and *dægeredsange* (a period of time in which a man may say forty or fifty psalms), but 'if he does, then he must abstain from that day's drink' (*gif hwa elles do, sy he ascyreð fram þæs dæges drince*).[1] Or for various 'small offences' (*litlum gultum*) 'he must abstain from meals …and eat his food after the brothers' meal, so that …if they eat at midday he must eat at 3pm , and if they eat at 3pm he must wait until the evening' (*ascyreð fram gereorde …7 ete ana his mete æfter broðra gereorde, swilce …gif broðra etan to middæges ete he to nones, gif broðra to nones, he to æfenes*).[2]

'Adamnan only took meat and meals on Sundays and the fifth day of the week …the other days he fasted' (*Adamnan næfre mete onfeng ne swæsendo þeah, buton Drihtenlecan dæge 7 þy fiftan wiicdæge …oðrum dagum he swa fæstende awunade*).[3] This austere existence was imposed on him by a priest who said that a week of fasting was excessive and 'two or three days' fasting is enough to observe' (*twydæglic fæsten oðþe þreodæglic fæsten is genoh to healdenne*), and that he would shortly return and tell Adamnan how long his penance should continue. However, he suddenly returned to Ireland, and as the penance was not rescinded, Adamnan continued with the regime, first 'on account of divine terror' (*for intingan þæs godcundan eges*) and then on account of the eternal reward.[4]

An example of penitential fasting is recorded from 735 when a lady of noble family in Oxford is recorded as mortifying herself by lying on the ground and subsisting on broth made of the poorest herbs and a small quantity of barley bread.[5]

According to Edgar's Laws, part of the penance of a rich man was that he should fast on bread, green herbs and water, and that he should eat no flesh nor drink anything intoxicating.[6]

Special penitential bread was sometimes eaten. In monastic institutions it was made from the lower grades of the unsifted flour of rye, barley, oats and pulses, or a mixture of these flours.[7] Individuals like Gwynllyw and his wife ate barley bread with added ashes.[8] The Cistercian Rule established in the eleventh century envisaged bread made of bran with some bitter herbs added.[9]

Those who chose to fast were probably always outnumbered by those who preferred not to. Even though ascetics were held in very high regard, they were no doubt seen as different by most people who were not prepared to emulate them, even though fasting was a route to eternal feasting. Fast day dishes could be elaborate delicacies, so that even if a noble was observing the fast legalistically, and limiting himself to fish, he might be able to enjoy a luxury meal. This problem was commented on by – inter alia – St. Thomas Aquinas. Moreover with a certain amount of sophistry one could have reclassified the tail of the beaver, frogs, puffins and barnacle geese as fish,

[1] Napier 1916, 24.
[2] op. cit., 35.
[3] Miller 1890, I, 2 352.
[4] op. cit.
[5] Turner 1828, III 27.
[6] op. cit., 30.
[7] Dembinska in Fenton & Kisban 1986, 154.
[8] Davies 1982, 192.
[9] op. cit.

and unborn or newly born mammals as 'not meat' as had happened by the fifteenth century.[1] There is no evidence for these evasions in Anglo-Saxon England, but we do not have a menu for a 'fish feast' (like that held for the Archbishop of Canterbury in 1504-5) where these items are listed.

Bishop Theodred imposed a penance on himself (for having thieves at St. Edmund's shrine hung there and then) and then called on the people 'that they fast completely with him for three days' (*þæt hi him mid fæstan fullice þry dagas*).[2] Alcuin thought that a fast should be declared because Æthelheard had fled his post as Archbishop of Canterbury in 797. The whole people were to join in this, and in addition, prayers were to be said, masses celebrated and alms given.[3]

Fasting as Part of Particular Rituals

Fasting was used to sanctify places and occasions. Cedd fasted to purify the site for his church, and various ceremonies were consecrated by fasting. As Lent was a sanctified period, the fine for breaking and entering according to Alfred's Laws, was to be doubled if these offences were committed 'during the Lenten fast' (*in lencten fæsten*).[4] In a sense, feast days were sanctified by the fast on the preceding day(s). The *Canons of Edgar* stated that 'we instruct that any man who has eaten, unless because of illness, may not take communion' (*we lærað þæt ænig unfæstende man husles ne abirige buton hit for oferseocness sy*).[5] Individuals were expected to refrain from eating and drinking in church, but 'Now men nevertheless will foolishly weaken very often and recklessly drink within God's house ...he who wants to drink and make a foolish noise let him drink at home, not in the Lord's house.' (*Nu doð men swa þeah dyslice foroft þæt hi willað wacian and wodlice drincan binnan Godes huse ...and seðe wile drincan and dwæslice hlydan drinc him at ham na on drihtnes huse.*)[6]

The protagonist of the ordeal was expected to prepare for the ceremony with three days' fasting. 'If anyone is committed to go to the ordeal, he shall come three days before to the mass priest who is to consecrate it, and live off bread and water and salt and herbs until he has to go to it.' (*Gif hwa ordales weddige, ðonne cume he þrim nihtum ær to þam mæssepreost þe hit halgian scyle, ond fede hine sylfne mid hlafe 7 mid wætre 7 sealte 7 wyrtum, ær he togan scyle.*)[7] According to another account, an equal number from each party were allowed to enter the church as witnesses, 'all having fasted' (*beon ealle fæstende*).[8]

There are several instances in *Leechdoms* where the patient is to fast before taking a cure.[9] This may have been to make the remedy more effective – taking the medicine before meals, but equally it may have been to purify the patient and consecrate the treatment. Proverbs declared quite sensibly that 'If you want to be healthy, drink in

---

[1] Furnivall 1868, 37; Tannahill 1973, 112.
[2] Skeat 1881, *St Edmund* 1.229.
[3] Whitelock 1955, 789.
[4] Attenborough 1922, 82.
[5] Fowler 1972, 8.
[6] Skeat 1881, *Prayer of Moses* 1.72.
[7] Attenborough 1922, 138.
[8] op. cit., 172.
[9] Cockayne 1851, II vi, xxv, xxxii, etc.

moderation; all surfeit and all idleness nourishes sickness'.[1] Fasting was supposed to dry up bodily humours, and put demons to flight, so that it was seen as medicine for the body and the soul.[2] Gluttony was the first of the eight sins that troubled man, because it brought about sickness and caused early death through immoderate drinking.[3] One of the chief virtues on the other hand, is 'Temperance, which is moderation in English, that is that a man be moderate and does not eat or drink too much, nor eat before mealtimes ...but a wise man shall observe his mealtimes ...then may he overcome such as gluttony.' (...*temperantia þæt is gemetegung on englisc þæt is þæt man beo gemetegod and to mycel ne ðicge on æte and on wæte ne ær timan ne gereordige ...ac se gesceadwisa man sceal cepan his mæles ...þonne mæg he oferswiðan swa þa gyfernysse.*)[4]

Commuting Fasting

Although fasting could be carried out for the sake of others, fasting as a penance is most often referred to as atonement for one's own sins. Preventing a penitent from feasting cut him off from a normal social life, and reduced his prestige. Donating land, saying psalms, paying for masses to be said, or paying fines were alternatives to fasting. However, it was theologically acceptable to transfer a fast to another individual.[5] This made it possible for a powerful man to avoid fasting for any length of time or making any payment. If fasting was imposed for seven years, he could get twelve men to fast three days on bread, green herbs and water. Then he could get 7 x 120 men to fast for three days, thus making up as many days of penance as there are in seven years.[6]

Conclusion

Fasting and feasting gave an eating rhythm to the week and to the year. However, 'some fasted as though they scorned eating, but on the next day they ate greedily' (*sume fæston eac swa þæt hi forsawon to etanne buton on ðone oðerne dæg and æton þonne grædelice*).[7] Extremes were eschewed: 'eat every day with moderation' (*ælce dæg eton mid gedafenlicnysse*).[8]

One had to be sure of the dates: it was not safe merely to fast, since feast days had to be observed, and 'he who fasts on that day through self-will is to be excommunicated' (*ðe on þam dæge fæsten wile þæt he beo amansumod gif he hi hit for his anwylnysse deð*).[9] It was the mass-priest's duty to tell his communicants the dates of fasts: misinformation was punished by a fine. This is one reason why copies of calendars which gave the dates of fast and feast days were in demand.

---

[1] Swanton 1975, 177.
[2] Bynum 1987, 41.
[3] Skeat 1881, *Memorial of the Saints* l.267.
[4] op. cit., l. 314.
[5] Miller 1890, I, 2 233.
[6] Turner 1828, III 86.
[7] Skeat 1881, *Prayer of Moses* l.96.
[8] op. cit.; Napier 1916, 123.
[9] Skeat 1881, *Ash Wednesday* l.4.

Like the feast, the fast brought Christians together. To violate the Friday fast was the clearest, most visible way of rejecting the faith.[1] In *Sermo Lupi ad Anglos*, the failure to observe fasts and festivals occurs time and time again and is seen as being in some measure responsible for the state of the country.[2]

Fasting was always supposed to be accompanied by almsgiving: 'then is his fasting pleasing to God' (*þonne bið his fæsten God gecweme*).[3] In theory, those who had food voluntarily forwent some in order that those without food could have something to eat, but it seems unlikely that almsgiving was regularly and generously practised. Altruism was not a prime motive: those who submitted themselves to a rigorous regime of deprivation seem to have been looking ahead to heavenly feasting.[4] For the poor who scarcely had enough to keep themselves alive, visions of the heavenly feast, though infinitely desirable, must have seemed cold comfort.

---

[1] Bynum 1987, 41.
[2] Whitelock 1955, 858; Swanton 1975, 120.
[3] Fowler 1972, 13.
[4] Mackie/Gollancz 1972, The Wonders of Creation I.95; The Phoenix; Soul Addressing the Body I.36.

30. Feasting

Feasts in hall offered a variety of sense impressions – taste, smell, warmth, music and entertainment, the play of light on tableware, colours of hangings, the clothes of the guests. Companionship, a confirmation of one's position in the community, reward, the chance to drink and escape day-to-day concerns were all part and parcel of feasting, and the potent appeal of the feast derives in part from them, as well as the rich and plentiful food.

The Function of Feasting

Although the feast was not primarily a gastronomic event, but a ritual – with religious, aesthetic, legal and societal ramifications – the provision and consumption of food and drink was central. The 'chieftain' provided food and drink that was prestigious in kind and plentiful in quantity. The term *gegadorwiste* meant 'assembly for feasting': *wiste* meant 'plenty' as well as 'feast'.[1] That the image of the king, as a provider of feasts was a particularly important and resonant one, is suggested by the fact that in feeding the five thousand Christ is described in these terms.[2]

The function of royal feasts was to emphasise the ruler's power, and through a lavish display of wealth, attract followers and supporters. Those who partook of the feast were declaring or confirming their obligations to the provider. In return for sustenance, they were pledged to fight to the death for him, sustaining him in his position of power, but also obliging him to continue to provide well for them. Feasting was functional: by keeping his retainers well-fed on a variety of foods, the leader ensured that he had, quite literally, strong supporters. A retainer who ate with the king gained a legal status, but the term *fedesl* used for such an individual occurs elsewhere only in the sense of a fatted animal, and implies special feeding.[3]

A noble king not only provided amply for his retainers, but created a splendid occasion; an image of plenty and assured harmony in a world where shortage, uncertainty and conflict were the experience of many.[4] The feast retained its symbolism as a unifying force, even when the guests were not dependent on the king for sustenance and support.[5]

The lord of the *Rhymed Poem* comments that, when prosperous, 'feasts never failed, guests came and went', and certainly people apart from the king had the resources for a social life that included feasting.[6] The visit of guests was celebrated with a feast, though if the king was the visitor, the royal provisioners would arrive the day before to see everything was ready and suitable.[7] The king could not have his status compromised by attending a feast at which the supplies were insufficiently lavish, or the mead might run out.[8]

---

[1] Zupita 1959, 1.1735-6.
[2] Kemble 1848.
[3] Whitelock 1955, 357-8.
[4] Zupita 1948, 1.2431; Huizinga 1977, 24.
[5] Whitelock 1955, 258, 280; Turner 1828, III 29, 234.
[6] Mackie 1973, *Rhymed Poem*; Miller 1890, I, 1 180-2, I, 2 396-8.
[7] Turner 1828, III 29.
[8] op. cit.

Sometimes the guests may have been visiting specifically to consume the food payable as the food rent.[1]

Most people probably only arranged feasts for special occasions, which could be personal, celebrating the arrival of a guest, celebrating or commemorating rites of passage, or seasonal, called forth by the time of year or the date of a religious festival.[2] Victories and coronations were celebrated with feasting.[3]

Funeral feasts and feasts on the anniversaries of deaths are most frequently mentioned. In pagan times the dead person seems to have been propitiated by a grand burial feast.[4] Funeral feasts continued to be held after the introduction of Christianity, and ultimately had to be incorporated into the Christian scheme.[5] Anniversary feasts were often held, particularly in religious establishments.[6]

The Calendar of Feast days

Gregory realised that pagan religious feasts, being an important part of the life of the people, would be difficult to eradicate.[7] A calendar of feasts commemorating Christian festivals took the place of pagan celebrations.[8] Festivals were holidays and feast days, and while the Church could not enjoin feasting, it could at least state (as above) that there should be no fasting during feast days. The council of all the greater men was summoned to the royal court for all the great festivals, with the Easter feast being the most frequently mentioned.[9] It was the Easter feast which provided the illustration for April in the Anglo-Saxon Calendar.[10]

A well-endowed monastery would have been able to feast on a large number of saints' days, as well as anniversaries of its benefactors' deaths. The arrival of bequests of food was timed to coincide with feasts.[11] *The Rule of Chrodegang* states that those in monasteries would be able on feast days to 'eat twice a day with everyone having plenty to eat' (*eton tuwa on dæg 7 hæbbe ma to eallum þysum fulle þenuncge*).[12]

The seasonal feasts associated with the completion of agricultural tasks and given by the landowner to his workforce were perhaps the only feasts likely to be attended by those of lower classes, including slaves. According to *Rectitudines Singularum Personarum,* 'There are many folk-rights: some are entitled to a winter feast, Easter feast, a feast to celebrate the binding of the sheaves at harvest, a feast at which the drink flows for ploughing, a reward for mowing, food for making ricks, the 'wagon-favour' when loading wood, the 'rick-cup' at corn carting, and many things that I am

---

[1] Davies 1982, 165.
[2] Bonser 1963, 109.
[3] Skeat 1881, *St Eustace* l.387.
[4] Meaney and Hawkes 1970, 31-2, 53.
[5] Bonser 1963, 135; Whitelock 1955, 557, 707.
[6] Kylie 1911, 200; Robertson 1939, 199.
[7] Bonser 1963, 123.
[8] op. cit., 125; Miller 1890, I, 2 314; Whitelock 1952, 24; Seebohm 1952, 100-11; Skeat 1881, *The Exaltation of the Cross.*
[9] Turner 1828, III 210.
[10] BL MS., Cott. Tib. B5.
[11] Whitelock 1968, 8.
[12] Napier 1916, 81.

not able to enumerate'. (*Feola syndon folcgerihtu: on sumre deode gebyreð winterfeorme, Easterfeorm, bendform for ripe, gytfeorm for yrðe, mæðmed, hræcmete, at wudulade wæntreow, at cornlade hreaccopp 7 fela ðinga ðe ic getellan ne mæig.*)[1] The very poorest probably did not participate in feasts directly, though they gathered when and where there was feasting in expectation of leftovers, and they might, on occasion, do much better than that.

Guild Feasts

Feasting together confirmed the unity of those present. Guilds were voluntary associations whose members, usually substantial members of the community, provided mutual support. The benefits were similar to those arising from kinship obligations, and guilds provided a valuable social service in the very late Anglo-Saxon period, in settlements where a substantial part of the population were recent immigrants, without families at hand.[2] Officials of the peace guild in London at the time of Athelstan were to meet once a month and 'feed themselves as they themselves think fitting', an early instance of a civic banquet. The meal was evidently a substantial one since they were to 'distribute all the leavings for God's sake'.[3] The regulations for the guilds at Cambridge, Exeter, and Abbotsbury all refer to feasting.[4] Some of the feasts were fixed for church festivals, others were funeral feasts held at the interment of a member.[5]

Holding a Feast

A feast was arranged and guests *gelaðod* (invited/bidden/summoned).[6] They dressed in their best clothes 'guests …beautifully dressed' (*giestas …lustum glendon*), according to the *Rhymed Poem* of the Exeter Book, or perhaps their most splendid armour, like the *byrnwiga* of *The Wanderer*.[7] The writer of *The Ruin* saw in hall:

> ....*beorn monig*
> *glædmod and goldbeorht gleoma gefrætwed*
> *wlonc and wingal wighyrstum scan*

(many men, joyful and bright with gold, splendidly adorned, proud and gladdened by wine; their armour shone).

According to Cynewulf in his image of the Ascension, the radiant garments of the angels were appropriate to the great feast which was held in heaven to greet Christ's arrival.[8]

---

1 Liebermann 1898, 452-3.
2 Barlow et al. 1976, 335; Turner 1828, III 98; Whitelock 1955, 558.
3 op. cit., 389.
4 op. cit., 557-60.
5 op. cit., 558.
6 Bosworth & Toller 1898, 407.
7 Sweet 1952, 1.151.
8 Clemoes & Hughes 1971, 294.

Summoning the Guests

Presumably the guests foregathered, and then a horn was blown to summon them to the feast.[1] Such a use of the horn may have been strictly functional, or it may have played some further part in the ceremonial.[2] Hand-washing was the first and necessary part of the ceremonial of feasting.

The Hall

The scene of feasting was the great hall, furnished with trestle tables and benches, and guarded by door-keepers who turned away gate-crashers and prevented anyone from entering while the meal was in progress.[3] The number of compounds using synonyms for hall, e.g. 'hall-cup' (*sele-ful*), 'wine-hall' (*wine-ærne*), 'mead-hall' (*medo-ærne*), 'wine-hall' (*wine-reced*), indicates the importance of the hall for the feasting that took place there.[4] The archaeological record provides much evidence of halls, e.g. one of these at Yeavering was over 80' long and 40' wide and the walls were white-plastered on the inside,[5] whilst at Cheddar there was a hall about 75' long dating from the mid-ninth century.[6]

Other business was also carried on in the hall at mealtimes, so that Harold might receive news of William's landing when he was dining at York, and when Cnut was at table in hall at the end of a feast a crowd of petitioners was occupying his ear, while a bard wanted to sing him a poem he had just composed.[7] In these circumstances it is not surprising that, although communal feasting in hall continued, in the late period we hear that the lady of the household, and sometimes the lord retired to a private room to eat.[8] Some people were no doubt grateful for their entitlement to sleep in the hall after the feast.[9]

Hangings & Table-linen

Hangings, sometimes interwoven with gold, were used to decorate halls from early in the period.[10] Tablecloths were in use, at least on the continent, by the early ninth century.[11] Table napkins (*cneorift* – knee-covering), known of by the eighth century, were certainly in use by the tenth century.[12]

[1] Bosworth & Toller 1898, I 431.
[2] Wilson 1985, pl. 48; Jones & Jones 1949, 162.
[3] Whitelock 1955, 299; Owen 1841, 79; Zupita 1959, l.67 ff.
[4] Riddles 55, 56; Whitelock 1955, 559; Barlow et al. 1976, 336, 335; Turner 1828, III 32.
[5] Hope-Taylor 1977, 130, 140.
[6] Rahtz 1979, 50.
[7] Turner 1828, II 344.
[8] Owen 1841, 51, 669; Wilson 1985, pl. 3; Turner 1828, III 29.
[9] Jackson 1969, 157; Owen 1841, 47.
[10] Dodwell 1982, 120-9; Turner 1828, III 50; Whitelock 1968, 12; Fell 1984, 46-7.
[11] Hodges 1982, 132; Furnivall 1868, 92-3; Knowles 1940, 452.
[12] Wright & Wulcker 1884, I; Wright 1871, 36, 42; Banham 1991, 32.

Heating & Lighting

The hall was described as being desirably warm: 'while you sit at the meal with your nobles in the winter and the fire is alight and your hall warmed, while it rains and snows and storms outside' (*swylc swa þu æt swæsendum sitte mid þinum ealdormannum 7 þegnum on wintertid 7 sie fire onælad 7 þin heall gewyrmed 7 hit rine 7 sniwe 7 styrme ute*).[1] Some retainers were known as 'hearth-companions' (*heorð-geneatas*), and while this may have been merely a poetic epithet, it may have indicated those whose status entitled them to a seat near the fire, or to sleep in hall. Braziers may have been used in upper rooms; this may possibly have been the case in the first-floor hall at the Cheddar palace site.[2]

The hall was probably lit by lamps and candles, as well as firelight.[3]

Precedence & Seating

A royal feast had some of the elements of a superior dinner party today: fine table-linen, lighted candles, shining tableware. But, aesthetic enjoyment apart, how one fared in hall depended on rank. A visitor to a feast did not necessarily qualify for the rarer dishes unless he was a person of some rank.[4] A thegn was entitled to a seat in the king's hall, but it might be necessary to have had 'high rank' (*heanne had*) before one could say, 'I lacked nothing in hall' (*ne wæs me in healle gad*).[5]

There is evidence that an order of precedence was insisted on in early medieval England as well as Wales.[6] It was possible to buy your way in at a guild feast. If a retainer, as opposed to a guild brother, wanted to sit within the *stig* (possibly a railed-off dais) at a feast of the Cambridge Thegns' Guild, then he could pay a sester of honey to be accorded the privilege.[7]

Hrothgar bids Beowulf, 'sit now to the feast' ('*site nu to symle*'), and we learn that the *medu-benc* is 'decorated with gold' (*gold-geregnað*).[8] Later we are told, 'then the glorious ones sat on the bench, rejoiced in the feast' (*bugon þa to benc blæd-agande/fylle gefægan*).[9] Tenth- and eleventh-century illustrations depicting feasting, show diners sitting on settles or benches which seem to be cushioned.[10] 'Seat coverings' (*setl hrægl*) were bequeathed in wills, so at a feast one might expect to sit on a cushioned or, at least, covered seat.[11] The end of the bench was, for obvious reasons, a desirable position.[12]

[1] Miller 1890, I, 1 134-6.
[2] Rahtz 1979.
[3] Jackson 1969, 120, 122; Owen 1841, 669; Roesdahl 1982, 113; Crane 1983, 241.
[4] Holmes 1952, 114.
[5] Mackie 1973, *Rhymed Poem* l.15.
[6] Furnivall 1868, 365, 70-1, 170-1; Owen 1841, 77, 96-8, 363, 641; Garmonsway 1978, 25; Miller 1890, I, 1 196.
[7] Whitelock 1955, 558.
[8] Zupita 1959, l. 489, 774.
[9] op. cit., l.1010.
[10] Temple 1976, illus. 158, 197.
[11] Turner 1828, III 51; Whitelock 1968, 12.
[12] Jackson 1969, 134, 131.

Retainers

Guests seem to have been allowed to bring companions to a feast.[1] A guest who arrived with a large retinue assumed his host had considerable resources.[2] If anyone brought a *fotsetla* to a feast of the Cambridge Thegns' Guild, then he was to pay a sester of honey.[3] Whatever sort of retainer the *fotsetla* was (and he could have been a minstrel, since these are recorded as sitting at the feet of their lords, or even a foot-warmer such as the Welsh king had), in the context of a guild feast where the members had to provide the food and drink, he was to be paid for.

Servants

The emphasis on those who 'sat to' the feast was perhaps because sitting down was a privilege in itself, for some of those present at a feast, including the servers, were not entitled to sit, such as the unfortunate apparitor of the Welsh laws, who, though a court official, was not allowed to sit while the king was eating and drinking in hall 'lest the house be burnt while the king is at meat'.[4] At a great feast the servants had to 'scurry to and fro ...speed on their tasks'.[5] What they might be doing is illustrated in manuscript illustrations – bringing food on spits from the kitchens and kneeling with it in front of the diners who then helped themselves, serving drink, etc.[6]

Almost all the evidence as to who served food comes from Celtic sources and indicates that men were in charge of the great hall and the serving of food in large establishments.[7] Rank was observed among servants too; high ranking servants served diners of high status. It is possible that men served men with food, women, women.[8]

On occasion it seems to have been the women who served the drink to men at feasts. The *Gnomic Verses* outline the duties of a queen:

> ....*meodorædenne*
> *for gesiðmægan symle æghwær*
> *eodor æþelinga ærest gegretan*
> *forman fulle to frean hond*
> *ricene gereacan ond him ræd witan*

(always everywhere before the band of comrades at the mead-drinking, she shall first of all greet the protector of the nobles, quickly offer the first cup to her lord's hand, and know good counsel).[9]

In Beowulf it is the queen who offers the cup to Hrothgar and his guest. The wife of a noble who was cured of an illness was then well enough to carry out her duties as hostess and brought the cup to the bishop and the rest of the guests, serving them all until dinner was finished.[1]

---

[1] Miller 1890, I, 1 162; Owen 1841, 491, 673.
[2] Jackson 1971, 30.
[3] Whitelock 1955, 558.
[4] Owen 1841, 65, 393.
[5] Whitelock 1955, 279.
[6] Turner 1828, III 36.
[7] Jackson 1969, 34; Owen 1841, 355, 643.
[8] Whitelock 1955, 706.
[9] Mackie 1973, *Gnomic Verses* l.87 ff.
[1] Miller 1890, I, 2 396.

In the early period, high born women perhaps poured imported wine through the delicate and expensive sieve spoons which indicated their status and were buried with them.[1] Women's graves also contained bucket pendants, which perhaps symbolised the female role as servers of drink, though buckets were more likely to have been used as intermediate vessels for the serving of mead, *beor* or ale, than wine, which was imported in flasks or casks.[2] Female servants who held the office of 'cup-bearer' (*byrele*) are referred to in the seventh-century laws of Æthelbert, since an *eorl* was entitled to twelve shillings compensation if anyone slept with his cup-bearer; a *ceorl* was entitled to half this amount.[3] What had traditionally been a female role would of course have to be filled by a man in a monastic household.[4] However, it seems that towards the end of the period high-born women were eating with the men at feasts and were not required as servers.

Blessing Food and Breaking Bread

While Hrothgar simply invites Beowulf to sit down and enjoy the feast, after the conversion food was blessed before the eating started.[5] After grace the most important guest seems to have broken the bread or divided the food.[6]

Manners

By the end of the period table-manners were a matter of concern and interest to some.[7] It was not considered polite to gulp down or gobble your food for which the pejorative word *fretan* is used.[8] This word is used to show that it was not the done thing to pick up and eat any morsel of food that had fallen on the floor:

> ðonne snottrum men snæd oddglideð
> ða he be leohte gesihð, lueð æfter,
> gesegnað and gesyfled and him sylf friteð

(when a chunk of food slips from the hand of one of these clever men, he spots it in the light, bends down to pick it up, blesses it, covers it with seasoning and actually consumes it).[9]

At Coppergate in York the evidence of the faecal layers which contained fruit stones, apple core fragments and fish bones, is that food was bolted, or at least eaten in uninhibited fashion.[10] There is no way of knowing whether hunger was the reason for these foods being bolted, or whether this method of eating was habitual to the inhabitants of Viking York.

---

[1] Meaney 1981, 87-8.
[2] op. cit., 247.
[3] Attenborough 1922, 6-7.
[4] Fell 1984, 50.
[5] Miller 1890, I, 1 166; Wilson 1985, pl. 48.
[6] Turner 1828, III 420.
[7] Holmes 1952, 89; Jackson 1969, 128, 100; Magnusson & Palsson 1960, 117; Garmonsway 1978, 46.
[8] Page 1985, 14-15.
[9] op. cit.
[10] Jones 1987, 29.

The Food

It seems that feast-day food was anticipated with some pleasure, and then enjoyed: Athelstan 'entered joyfully the dinner apartment', and Hrothgar gladly partook of the 'feast and hall-cup' (*symbel* and *sele-ful*).[1] It seems that one might expect better food at a feast – rarer items and choicer cuts – and plenty of it. The better cuts of meat could be roasted, especially as the diners would be on hand to eat the meat as soon as it was done.

Poultry and pork were suitable foods.[2] Beef, particularly from specially fattened bullocks, was feast-day food.[3] The fact that sheep are not mentioned could be an accident of the non-survival of evidence, but is perhaps accounted for by the fact that pigs and cattle will more readily put on weight to give fatty, tender meat.

The game taken by hunting and fowling was considered suitable for feasts since it was expensive to obtain.[4] Fish was also a delicacy, as were broth and cheese.[5]

Bread was the standard constituent of all meals, and specified for funeral feasts, as above; ordinary bread was probably replaced by a finer kind on feast days. A number of festival cakes based on enriched dough mixtures are known from across Europe from Roman times on (Chapter 2).

The most complete picture of food for a feast is that provided by the listing of the major ingredients of the funeral feasts at Bury St. Edmunds (see above). The first feast consisted of ale, bread and meat; the second of ale (this time brewed specially for the feast), bread, meat, cheese, fish and milk.[6]

While one might expect Anglo-Saxon feasts to be hearty Homeric affairs, the impression from the documentary evidence is that considerable skill was exercised by cooks to produce delicacies: 'the strange diversity of sumptuous food'.[7] Eating to show social status was a well-developed phenomenon of the medieval period, but was evidently established early in Anglo-Saxon England.

Duration

Day-long feasts were common.[8] It was not generally acceptable to leave before the end of a feast.[9] Some banquets seem to have continued overnight.[10] St. Eligius exhorted people – ineffectually as it has turned out – not to make feasts lasting all night nor to indulge in intemperate drinking on the Calends of January.[1] The three-day feast seems to have been the standard for any great celebration.[2]

---

[1] Turner 1828, III 29; Zupita 1959, l.619.
[2] Fell 1984, 144; Davies 1982, 35; Liebermann 1898, 454; Hawkes et al. 1985, 103; Robertson 1939, 199, 252.
[3] Davies 1982, 23; Robertson 1939, 252; Whitelock 1968, 10.
[4] Robertson 1939, 252.
[5] op. cit.; Douglas & Greenaway 1953, 817; Garmonsway 1978, 27; Davies 1982, 35.
[6] Robertson 1939, 252.
[7] Whitelock 1955, 279, 777; Kylie 1911, 42-3.
[8] Zupita 1959, l. 2103ff., 2115ff.; Turner 1828 III, 29, 32; Whitelock 1955, 235; Mellows 1982, 42.
[9] Miller 1890, I, 1 162; Whitelock 1955, 234.
[10] Turner 1828, II 154.
[1] Bonser 1963, 141.
[2] op. cit., 140.

The Drink

It is clear from the references to feasting that drink was as important as the food. *Ealu* (ale), *beor* (probably fermented fruit-based drinks, including cider), *meodu* (mead) and *win* (wine) are the four drinks frequently mentioned, and all occur in compounds with, for example, *sele/heall* (hall) and *benc* (seat). *Gebeorscipe* was a common term for feasting. The over-riding concern was that there should be plenty of drink.[1]

Drunkenness

The consumption of unlimited quantities of alcohol tended to militate against the preservation of an image of harmony which the feast was calculated to further. Men 'drunken with *beor* renewed old grudges', and in extreme cases the conflict might threaten the king's peace, so this had to be protected by severe penalties.[2] Fines for murder committed at a feast were much higher than if the act was done at an open grave, when feelings might be expected to have been running high.[3]

Gluttony

Although feasting became incorporated into the Christian scheme, the problem was that feasts could and, according to a number of accounts, did lead to the sin of gluttony. Gluttony in respect of Anglo-Saxon feasting was the concern of ecclesiastical writers from the eighth century.[4] When Æthelwold was appointed to Winchester, clerics given over to gluttony and drunkenness attempted to poison him when he introduced a more austere regime.[5] In 1008 Æthelred's law code specifically outlawed over-eating and drinking.[6] The sermon of Wulfstan declares that it was in part gluttony which was causing the destruction of the country.[7] England as a whole had a reputation for heavy eating and drinking all over the continent by the end of the Anglo-Saxon period.[8]

Some people must have had a somewhat ambivalent attitude to feasts: pleasurable as they undoubtedly were, ecclesiastics denounced them as sinful. One way of partially resolving this conflict was to dispose of the leftovers charitably.[9]

Treachery

Eating with someone implied reciprocal social and even legal bonds. Hospitality carried with it a number of obligations – not just the provision of food but the protection of guests. Feasts were used as a cover for premeditated treachery on a number of occasions throughout the period.[1]

---

[1] Turner 1828, III 29; Owen 1841, 63.
[2] Gollancz/Mackie 1973, *St Juliana*; Attenborough 1922, 4; Whitelock 1955, 361.
[3] Turner 1828, II 507.
[4] Kylie 1911, 42-3, 169; Whitelock 1955, 777, 790.
[5] op. cit., 835.
[6] op. cit., 408.
[7] Swanton 1975, 122.
[8] Knowles 1940, 463; Whitelock 1955, 291.
[9] op. cit., 389.
[1] Turner 1828, I 264, 419; Whitelock 1955, 323, 835.

Entertainment

Despite the possibility of violence, people went to feasts expecting to enjoy themselves. The sound of people having a good time is mentioned a number of times in the literature; perhaps most dramatically, Grendel is overcome with rage and jealousy when he 'heard the sounds of enjoyment' (*dream gehyrde*) in Heorot.[1] The drink obviously helped people enjoy themselves and everyone might be expected to contribute to the entertainment at a feast. In this connection the story of Caedmon is well known.[2]

Harping must have been a common pastime at feasts since it is used as a metaphor for feasting.[3] The poetic epithet for the harp/lyre was 'the wood of joy' (*gleobeam*), suggesting association with the pleasures of feasting in hall.

Minstrels

It seems that the professional minstrel or the amateur singer ideally accompanied himself on a harp or lyre. According to the professional scop Widsith,

> þonne wit scilling sciran reorde
> for uncrum sigedryhtne song ahofan
> hlude bi hearpan hleoþor swinsade
> þonne monige men modum wlonce
> wordum sprecan þa þe wel cuþan
> þæt hi næfre song sellan ne hyrdon

(when Shilling and I, with clear voice raised the song before our victorious lord – loud to the harp our speech made music – then many men bold of heart who well knew, declared in words that they had never heard a better song).[4] Listening to the feast in Heorot, Grendel distinguishes

> Hludne in healle ...hearpan sweg
> swutol sang scopes

(loud in the hall ...the sound of the harp and the sweet song of the minstrel).[5]

The phrase to learn or say *by rote* apparently comes from the practice of reciting to harp accompaniment, since one of the types of harp was called a *rota*.[6]

The harp of a chief was a valuable instrument, probably decorated with gilt mounts, like the lyre found at Sutton Hoo.[7] This instrument had been kept in a beaver-skin bag, which was probably valuable in itself, since the Welsh Laws give the value of a beaver skin at 120 pence, that of a stag, fox or wolf as eight pence.[1] At the Welsh court the harp of the chief of song (provided for him by the king) and the harp of the king were both worth 120 pence according to the Welsh Laws, while the harp of the *gwrda* was worth 60 pence.[2] A

---

[1] Jackson 1969, 149; Zupita 1959, l. 88.
[2] Miller 1890, I, 2 343.
[3] Mackie 1973, *Rhymed Poem*, l.25 ff.
[4] Gollancz/Mackie 1973, *Widsith* l.103 ff.
[5] Zupita 1959, l. 88ff.
[6] Whitelock 1955, 766.
[7] Bruce-Mitford 1983, 724-5.
[1] Owen 1841, 948.
[2] op. cit., 679, 77, 723.

harp was one of the three pledges that never lapsed, and the fee for tuning the keys was 24 pence, so that it was a prestige object.[1] It seems to have been in the keeping of the chief of the household at the Welsh court – at least, he was to place the harp in the hands of the bard on the three principal festivals, and was entitled to a song from the bard whenever he wanted one.[2] (However, if the queen wanted a song, then the bard had to sing it in a low voice, so that the hall should not be disturbed by him.)[3]

The form of harps is indicated in the manuscript illustrations. There seem to have been a large harp of seven or twelve strings which was held on the knee and the *rota*, a zither-like harp of five strings.[4] The two sorts are shown in a manuscript of between 1030–1050.[5] One has a narrow trapezium shape, while the other is rectangular. One illustration from the mid-eighth century shows King David playing the lyre,[6] and harps are also shown in later manuscripts, like one dating between 1030–50.[7] There is considerable archaeological evidence for harps/lyres. As well as the example from Sutton Hoo, there was also a lyre in the burial of Tæppa, a chieftain or minor king buried at Taplow.[8] This confirms the documentary evidence that harping was a fashionable accomplishment. Dunstan, for example, was accustomed to play his *cythera* "which we in the native language call 'harp'" to entertain a noblewoman and her ladies.[9] Only the bone yoke facings from an instrument survive in a mid-fifth century immigrant's grave at Abingdon.[10] The remains a lyre, consisting of two metal plates, plain and undecorated, in a poorly furnished burial at Burgh Apton, and remains at other sites, Morning Thorpe, and Buckland, Dover, may indicate the grave of a professional scop.[11]

According to the Welsh Laws, the professional bard was entitled to protection in his 'circuit of minstrelsy'; bardism and the science of a harpist, together with metallurgy, were the three domestic skills with special rights.[12] The chief harper seems to have trained minstrels who then set out on their own account as professionals.[13] According to *The Fates of Men*:

> Sum sceal mid hearpan æt his hlafordes
> fotum sittan feoh þicgan
> ond a snellice snere wræstan
> lætan scralletan sceacol se þe hleapeð
> nægl neomegende biþ him neod micel

(one shall sit at his lord's feet with his harp, receive wealth, and ever pluck the strings rapidly, let the leaping plectrum, the ringing nail shrill loudly, great is his eagerness).[1]

[1] op. cit., 341.
[2] op. cit., 13.
[3] op. cit., 33, 35.
[4] Holmes 1952, 235.
[5] Camb. Univ. Lib. MS Ff. 1.23 f.4 v. illustrated in Temple 1976, fig. 249.
[6] Durham Cathedral Lib. B11.30 fol. 81 v.
[7] Bruce-Mitford 1983, 687-8; Temple 1976, No. 249.
[8] Bruce-Mitford 1983, 683, 701.
[9] Whitelock 1955, 234.
[10] Bruce-Mitford 1983, 718.
[11] Evison 1987, 121.
[12] Owen 1841, 475, 477.
[13] op. cit., II 19.
[1] Gollancz/Mackie 1973, *The Fates of Men* l.80 ff.

This suggests a permanent post with a lord, and Deor was the minstrel of the Heodnings for many years, until he was replaced by Heorrenda, 'a man skilled in song' (*leodcraftig monn*).[1] However, the minstrel Widsith had been to very many courts:

> ....*folgaðe wide*
> *forþon ic mæg singan ond secgan spell*
> *mænan fore mengo in meoduhealle*
> *hu me cynegode cystum dohten...*

(I served far and wide so I can sing, tell my story, declare before the company in the banqueting hall how men of high rank were noble, generous to me).[2]

He sang the praises of Queen Ealhhild 'throughout many lands' (*geond londa fela*),[3] and concludes:

> *Swa scriþende gesceapum hweorfað*
> *gleomen gumena geonde grunda fela*
> *þærfe secgað þoncword sprecað*
> *simle suð oþþe norð sumne gemetað*
> *gydda gleawne geofum unheawne*
> *se þe fore duguðe wile dom aræran*
> *eorlscipe æfnan oþþæt eal scæceð*
> *leohte ond lif somod lof se gewyrceð*
> *hafað under heofonum heahfæstne dom.*

(Roving thus as is their destiny, the minstrels of men wander over many lands. They tell their need, they speak words of thanks. North or south, they always find someone skilled in lays who wishes to exalt his fame among his retinue and do heroic deeds until all passes away, light and life together. He gains praise and enduring glory under the heavens.)[4]

This passage establishes the fact of the wandering minstrel, readily admitted to the feasts of the great, as were also Alfred, Athelstan, and Olaf, who were able to trade on this, and disguising themselves as minstrels, were received into enemy camps where they managed to do some useful spying.[5] The old poem about Athelstan's coronation feast quoted by William of Malmesbury suggests with its juxtaposition of 'stomachs are filled with delicacies, minds with song' that the music accompanied the meal.[6] The story of Olaf confirms that the singing went on during the meal, and once the nobles had eaten enough, the conversation turned to war, and he was ordered out.[1] It also confirms the connection between feasting, and adding to the prestige of the ruler, since the minstrel was paid in many cases to sing his employer's praises: 'one makes the harp resound, another contends with praises'.[2] There is also a link between the feasting, the minstrel and the pagan concept that a man's immortality would rest in the commemoration of his deeds after his death.

---

[1] op. cit., *Deor* l.36 ff.
[2] op. cit., *Widsith* l.53 ff.
[3] op. cit., l. 99.
[4] op. cit., l. 135 ff.
[5] Turner 1828, III 62; Wright 1871, 47; Whitelock 1955, 278.
[6] op. cit., 279.
[1] op. cit., 278.
[2] op. cit.

Widsith received a jewelled bracelet from Guðhere of the Burgundians, as a reward for his song.[1]

This was a suitably noble reward, within the heroic tradition. A ninth-century Irish poem complains of a boorish patron that he does not give horses for songs of praise 'but what is natural to him – a cow', but we also hear of a chief praised because he did not leave his court deliberately on the calends of January, and so was a profit to the minstrels of Britain, since the New Year's feast was when gifts were traditionally given to minstrels, among others.[2] So while employing a minstrel was prestigious, a suitable return had to be made for their services. The names of famous minstrels were recorded, like that of Gorthyn who provided song at a New Year's feast.[3] Grants of land are recorded to minstrels: 'to Æthelweard, my faithful minstrel' (*meo fideli ministro Æthelweard*), or 'to Ealdbert, my minstrel' (*Ealdberhto ministro meo*).[4] William the Conqueror gave his minstrel 3 vills and 5 carucates of land in Gloucestershire.[5] More immediately, the minstrel seems to have been given a horn of liquor as soon as he finished his song.[6]

The council of 'Clofesho' in 747 decreed that monasteries must not be *ludicrarum artium receptacula*, and these arts are defined as those of versifiers, harpers, minstrels or buffoons. The canon law forbade the clergy from having anything to do with mimes, jesters or play actors. The word 'minstrel' applied to all these variety performers associated with bawdy songs and comic acts, as well as to the respectable gleemen who recited epics.[7]

However, it was not so easy to eradicate minstrelsy from the religious life. Wulfstan's *Canons of Edgar* were still trying to prevent priests from being an *ealu-scop* (ale-minstrel) or acting the *gliwige* (gleeman).[8] *Gliwig-manna* (gleeman) glossed *ganeones*, a term which covered vagabonds, ribalds and jokers.[9] *The Laws of the Northumbrian Priests* in c.1020 repeated that if a priest practised drunkenness or became a gleeman or ale-minstrel he was to compensate for it.[10]

---

[1] Gollancz/Mackie 1973, *Widsith* l.65 ff.
[2] Jackson 1971, 132.
[3] Jackson 1969, 100.
[4] Turner 1828, III 567.
[5] Waddell 1932, 210.
[6] Gordon 1954, 307.
[7] Poole 1958, 605; Colgrave 1940, 246-7, 352.
[8] Fowler 1972, 14-5.
[9] Wright 1871, 47.
[10] Whitelock 1955, 437.

Musicians

While the minstrel had his harp, the Welsh Laws refer to two other Chiefs of Song to be provided with appropriate instruments by the king. These were a *crawd* and pipe.[1] A riddle in the Exeter Book, describes a bagpipe which:

> *siteð æt symble sæles bideþ*
> *hwonne ær heo cræft hyre cyþan mote*
> *werum on wonge ne heo þær wiht þicgeð*
> *þæs þe him æt blisse beornas habbað...*
> *hwæþre hyre is on fote fæger hleoþor*
> *wynlicu wodgiefu*

(sits at the feast and awaits the time when it may first make known its art to men on earth. It receives nothing there of what men have for their enjoyment yet it has in its foot beautiful music, a gift of pleasant sound.)[2]

Manuscript illustrations show other instruments.

It is possible that, while the minstrel sung to his harp during the meal, after the eating louder instruments were played, since the horn, trumpet, drums and the flutes, which could be played two at a time, were hardly likely to have been used as continuo.[3] A short trumpet, curved horn and organs are also shown in illustrations, and Bede mentions a drum and cymbals.[4] A violin-like instrument with four strings played with a bow is also shown.[5] The other instrument illustrated is a bell.[6] *Clochetes*, a series of small bells strung on a rod and played with a hammer from a sitting position were known from twelfth-century France.[7] The musicians *heapere* (harper), *bymere* (trumpeter), *pipere* (piper), *fithelere* (fiddler), and *horn-blawere* (horn blower) are all recorded.[8] The feminine forms *fidelestere, hleapestre* and *sangstere* (fiddler, dancer and singer) all appear in the glosses, and as we find a manuscript illustration of a *hleapestre*, there may have also been female musicians and singers.[9]

Dancing, Juggling & Jesting

Professional entertainers, jesters, actors and dancers as well as singers and other musicians, were employed as part of their establishment by those who could afford them.

The manuscript Cot. Cleo. C. 8 shows two men in martial gear with a horn player and a female dancer.[10] *Tumbian* is the word used for dancing – Herodias' daughter *tumbude* before Herod, hence the term 'tumbler'.[1] Harl. MS 603 also shows dancing.[2] The cup-

---

[1] Owen 1841, II 19.
[2] Gollancz/Mackie 1973, Riddle 31 1.12.
[3] Turner 1828, III 59.
[4] op. cit., 455 ff.
[5] op. cit., 59.
[6] Temple 1976, fig.305-6.
[7] Holmes 1952, 235.
[8] Turner 1828, III 61.
[9] Fell 1984, 54.
[10] Turner 1828, III 59.
[1] op. cit., 61.
[2] op. cit.

bearer is serving out wine, a man and a woman seem to be dancing together, another on her own, to the accompaniment of two horns, one larger than the other, a harp, either played by two men, or played by one and supported by a second, and a violin. The step-mother of the young King Edward had in her service a dwarf, a minstrel skilled in various modes of dancing who was sent to entice the young king to her home.[1] Juggling may have been performed to a musical accompaniment, since an illustration in the manuscript Cot. Tib. C. vi shows a juggler with three balls and three knives, and a musician playing a fiddle with a bow.[2] The same illustration shows King David playing one of the larger eleven-stringed harps, a musician with a curved horn, and another with a straight pipe resting on some sort of support.[3] There are also illustrations of dancing animals and what may be *buffones* (clowns).[4]

Dancing was not just the province of professional entertainers any more than harping or singing was. In the account of the murder of King Ethelbert in 792 we are told that the royal party after dinner spent the whole day with music and dancing in great glee.[5]

At the time of the Winton Domesday John *ioculator* (the jester) paid the king fourpence.[6] A riddle describing a jay or jackdaw has the lines 'who, like an actress, loudly mimic the ways of a clown' (*þe swa scirenige sceawendisan hlude onhyrge*), so there may also have been actresses.[7] Adelina *joculatrix* held lands in Hampshire at the time of Domesday.[8] These two late references would be out of place in the man's world world of heroic feasting where the woman's function was virtually that of barmaid.

Riddles

The asking of riddles seems to have been part of the entertainment at a feast since Riddle 42 of the Exeter Book ends:

>............*nu is undyrne*
>*werum æt wine hu þa wihte mid us*
>*heanmode twa hatne sindon*

(now it is revealed to men at their wine how those two mean-spirited creatures are named among us).

Riddles are easy to devise, but the skill lies in providing more and more clues without making the answer easier, and also in ambiguity. A number of Anglo-Saxon riddles have an obvious ribald answer, and a less obvious polite one. Feasts were also occasions for storytelling.[9]

---

[1] Wright 1871, 47.
[2] Turner 1828, III 59.
[3] illustrated in Wright 1871, 48.
[4] Turner 1828, III 59.
[5] op. cit., 61.
[6] Barlow et al. 1976, 96.
[7] Fell 1984, 54.
[8] op. cit.
[9] Colgrave 1940, 246-7.

Nostalgia

Most people saw feasting as an infinitely desirable pastime. Hagiographers even made use of this fact in their writings. St. Agatha 'went as cheerfully to the dark dungeon as if she were invited to a pleasant banquet' (*eode þa bliðelice to than blindum cweaterne swylce heo wære geladod to lustfullum beor-scype*), though she was perhaps outdone by some brothers who 'went as gladly to their own deaths as to a banquet' (*swa bliþelice eodon to heora agenum slege swylce to gebeorscipe*).[1] It is the dramatic contrast of the feast in the warm hall where the king sits with his retainers around him and the cold darkness outside that is drawn on for an analogy of human life.[2]

The loss of prosperity evokes nostalgia for feasting. The lord of the *Rhymed Poem* says that, when rich,

> secgas me segon symbel ne alegon
> feorgiefe gefegon

(men gazed upon me, feasts never failed and they rejoiced in the gift of life).

> giestas gengdon gerscype mengdon
> lisse lengdon lustum glengdon

(guests came and went, mingled their talk, lingered over delight, adorned themselves richly).[3] The *Seafarer* regrets that he hears now

> huilpan sweg for hleahtor wera
> meaw singende for medodrince

(the cry of the curlew instead of men's laughter, the scream of the seagull in place of the mead-drinking).[4]

The regret for the silent, deserted ruin which was once 'a meadhall full of the sounds of music' (*meadoheall monig mon dreama full*), a place where people had gathered and feasted, where the horn was passed round, is found also in the Celtic literature.[5] The hall was a centre of companionship: the isolated exile has no-one 'who knows my mind in the meadhall' (*þe in meoduhealle min mine wisse*).[6] It is in *The Wanderer* that nostalgia for the joys of feasting finds its most eloquent expression. The lament refers to several essential elements of the noble feast:

> Woriað þa winsalo waldend licgað...
> Hwar cwom symbla gesetu? Hwær sindon seledreamas?
> Eala beorht bune! Eala byrnwiga eala þeodnes þrym...

(The wine-hall crumbles, the walls decay... Where is now the place of feasts? Where are the joys of hall? Alas for the bright cup! Alas for the armed warriors, alas for the might of the nation...)[7]

---

[1] Skeat 1881 *St Agatha* 1.97 ff.; *St Cecilia* 1.228.
[2] Miller 1890, I,1 134-6.
[3] Gollancz/Mackie 1973, *Rhymed Poem* 1.5 ff, 1.11 ff.
[4] Gordon 1960, 35.
[5] Gollancz/Mackie 1973, *The Ruin*; Davies 1982, 30; Turner 1828, I 307 *Elegy on Urien of Reged.*
[6] Sweet 1965, 149-151.
[7] op. cit.

31. Special Regimens

This chapter is divided into three sections: special regimens for infants, invalids, and monastics.

(i) Infants

Children were probably breast-fed until they were about two. A woman who could not lactate, and could not employ a wet nurse, would probably lose her child. A leechdom counsels the woman who cannot feed her child to 'take the milk of a cow of one colour in her hand and then fill her mouth with it and go to running water and spit the milk in and then ladle up with the same hand a mouthful of the water and swallow it' (*nime þonne anes bleos cu meoluc on hyre handæ 7 gesupe þonne mid hyre muþe 7 gange þonne to yrnendum wætere 7 spiwe þær in þa meolc 7 hlade þonne mid þære ylcan hand þæs wæteres muð fulne 7 forswelge*). After that she was to recite some words, but the element of sympathetic magic was no doubt important.[1]

According to Bede, it seems to have been the case that a couple should not resume sexual relations until their child was weaned: 'her man must not go to her bed before the newborn child is weaned from milk' (*to hire gerestscipe þonne hire wer ne sceal gongan, ær þon þæt acennde bearn from meolcum aweneð sy*). However, this tended not to be observed. 'A culpable custom has grown up between the married pair in that the wife neglects to feed her child and gives it to other women to feed.' (*An unriht gewuna wel hwær is arisen betweoh gesinhiwum þæt wiif forhycgað heora bearn fedan þa ðe heo cennað 7 heo oðrum wiifum to fedenne sellað.*)

The late seventh-century Laws of Ine suggest that wet nursing was established. The Laws allow a *gesith*-born man to take with him his reeve, and his smith and his *cildfestre* if he moves elsewhere.[2] *Cildfestre*, translated 'children's nurse' literally means 'child's feeder', and is unlikely to mean simply a nursemaid who would have been easy to replace.

The milk of cattle, goats and sheep, and the whey from cheese making may have been given to babies and young children.[3] The latter is rich in nutrients and easy to digest. Traditionally cows' horns were used as feeding bottles for babies, but there must have been a considerable risk of gastroenteritis as there is no evidence that utensils would have been sterilized, although experience with dairying may have shown the importance of cleanliness. A mammiform vessel with a perforated teat-shaped base was excavated from an infant's grave dated c.550–675 at Barton-on-Humber, suggesting a case when artificial feeding proved unsuccessful.[4] The likelihood would be that a mother breast-fed her baby, supplementing as the child grew older with cereal porridges for which the grain could be finely ground.

---

[1] Cockayne 1851, *Lacnunga*, 104.
[2] Whitelock 1955, 371.
[3] Bonser 1963, 302; Holmes 1952, 200.
[4] Neuk et al. 1991, 168.

Food for Young Children

Babies were probably weaned onto finely ground cereal mixtures. The Welsh Laws provided wheat to be made into pap for a child during the first year of its life, and the 'pan with feet', which was also to be provided, was probably for cooking this gruel.[1] Pap could also be made by soaking bread in milk or water. Probably babies were given bread to suck/chew as soon as they had teeth.[2]

Bread was probably the basic food for children. The baker of the *Colloquy* claims 'I make men strong, and because of this the little ones will not shun me' (*Ic mægen wera 7 furþon litlincgas nellaþ forbigean me*)[3]. Bread was all that the children at the monastery of Abingdon had to eat when Queen Edith came to visit them and decided to make provision for better food.[4] A tradition at St. Albans assigned a gift of land in Æthelred's day to the provision of milk and cheese 'for food for the young monks' (*ad alimenta monachorum juniorum*).[5]

Older children, like the novice of the *Colloquy* drank ale or water, not wine because 'wine is not the drink for children or the foolish, but for the older and wiser' (*win nys drenc cilda ne dysgra ac ealdra 7 wisra*).[6]

Relaxation of Dietary Observance

Children were not made to fast. The *Penitential of Ecgbert* states, for example, 'if he is a grown man, he is to fast one year' (*gyf hit geweaxan man sy fæste 1 gear*). The rigour of the Benedictine Rule was to be relaxed for children and the old on account of their 'feebleness' (*wacmodness*). 'This is to be a kind consideration of them, and permission is to be given them to anticipate the regular hours'.[7] Ingulf says of Editha at the royal court that she used to send him to the larder for refreshment when he was a boy.[8] Lanfranc's *Statutua*, perhaps codifying earlier practice, legislate for a mid-morning breakfast for the children and those monks unable to fast longer, and children could breakfast during the monks' chapter)[9].

The novice of the *Colloquy* says 'I still enjoy meat because I am a child under instruction ...vegetables and eggs, fish and cheese, butter and beans and all permitted things I eat with great thankfulness' (*Gyt flæscmettum ic bruce, forðam cild eom under gyrda drohtniende ...wyrta 7 æigra, fisc 7 cyse, buteran 7 beana 7 ealle clæne þingc ic ete mid micelre þancunge*). He is not 'such a great glutton that [he] eats all kinds of food at one meal' (*swa micel swelgere þæt ...ealle cynn metta on anre gereordinge etan mæge*).[10] It was important that the children were allowed to eat meat, otherwise they could have suffered from zinc deficiency, leading to arrested growth.[11]

[1] Owen 1841, 51.
[2] Kylie 1911, 95.
[3] Garmonsway 1978, 36-7.
[4] Knowles 1940, 457.
[5] op. cit.
[6] Garmonsway 1978, 47.
[7] Bonser 1963, 91.
[8] Turner 1828, II 354.
[9] Knowles 1940, 45.
[10] Garmonsway 1978, 46.
[11] Morgan 1975, 4.

Malnourishment

Infanticide was not accounted a crime in the earlier Anglo-Saxon period because it was considered better in times of stress, that a child should die as soon as it was born, rather than that it should linger a short time to die of starvation. By the time of the Penitential of Theodore infanticide was accounted a serious crime, although more excusable if carried out by an impoverished mother.[1]

Wells suggested that enamel hypoplasia affecting the canines and second molars most often among the Anglo-Saxons indicates that periods of morbidity occurred between the ages of 2 and 4 years, perhaps due to nutritional disturbances associated with weaning.[2] However, Harris's lines in the early Anglo-Saxon communities at Burgh Castle and Caistor, Norfolk, indicate increased frequency around the ages of 4–6 and 8–12.[3] This is probably evidence of the more general 'bread-winner effect'. As in other agricultural communities which depend on the strength of adult males for the heavy agricultural work, children probably ate afterwards with the women.[4] If supplies were scarce, the women and children went short.

(ii) Invalid Diet

A tradition of doctoring, using herbs as the main treatment, was established by the middle of the period, though medical writings date from the late period.[5] The wort drinks so often recommended, are prescriptions rather than food, but so many recipes are given – some hundreds in *Leechdoms* – that they must have been a very common way of treating complaints. They would have been important as a valuable source of vitamins A and C in particular, as well as minerals, apart from containing active principles which may have been effective against the particular complaint for which they were taken. 'Good herb drinks such as doctors make' (*godum wyrtdrencum swa læces wyrcað*) elsewhere called *oxumellis*, contained vinegar and honey, a combination still recommended.[6]

Instructions for invalid or special diets are sometimes given in very general terms: 'eat fresh meat where it is fattest' (*ete fersc flæsc þær þær hit fætost sie*) for example, and there are a number of references to fat meat.[7] 'Light foods' (*leohte mettas*) which included 'juicy broths and fresh peas and beaten eggs and bread broken into hot water and periwinkles removed from their shells with peas' (*geseaw broþu 7 geseawe pysan 7 geslegen ægru 7 bread gebrocen on hat wæter winewinclan adon of scellum mid pysum*) are also called for, and 'delicate food and good drink' (*hnesce mettas 7 godne drincan*).[8]

Sometimes the instructions are specific and worth quoting in full, since they are the nearest we get to Anglo-Saxon recipes, or to an idea of diet: 'he is to eat dry bread and cheese …bake a warm loaf for him' (*sceal he etan drigne hlaf 7 cyse …baca hym*

---

[1] Bonser 1963, 87.
[2] Wells 1964.
[3] op. cit.
[4] Kuper 1977, 103-4, 107, 164, 175.
[5] Turner 1828, III 4.
[6] Cockayne 1851, II i 1; II xxiii; Hills 1988, 70.
[7] Cockayne 1851, III lxv, lxxii; *Peri Didacheon* 37, 38, II vi, vii.
[8] op. cit., I xlix; *Peri Didacheon* 40, 44.

man þanne wearmen hlaf);[1] 'stew chicken in wine and then add walnut oil and drink that' (*cicene mete ...seow on wine do þanne ele to þe beo of frencissen hnutu 7 drince þæt*).[2] Beef broth made from beef marinaded in vinegar and oil, cooked with salt, dill and leek was recommended for stomach trouble.[3] So was a diet which included apples, pears and peaches, bread in water, salmon, goose giblets, and pigs' trotters, and another leechdom recommends the flesh of small birds, stewed and roasted; apples, pears, medlars, and peas cooked in vinegar or sharp wine.[4] Salt meats, hares' and boars' flesh, roots of rue, cresses and easily digested meats were recommended for an invalid with 'a hard swelling of the stomach' (*heardum swile þæs magan*).[5] He was also to be given sweet apples, marinaded in wine, then stewed and sweetened with honey and peppered.[6] An internal stomach injury was treated by giving the patient 'eggs to sup up, barley bread, clean new butter and new barley meal or groats made into a brewit as cooks know how' (*ægru to supanne beren bread clæne niwe buteran 7 niwe beren mela oððe grytta togædre gebriwed swa cocas cunnon*).[7] 'Fresh milk sweetened with honey' (*niwe molcen meoluc mid hunige gesmeþed*), and 'oven baked bread' (*ofen bacen hlaf*) were recommended for other gastric complaints.[8]

Meats 'that make good blood' (*þe god blod wyrceað*) were thought to be 'shellfishes, finned fishes and domestic and wild hens and all the birds that live on the hills, and pigeons, that is, the young chicks of culvers, half-grown pigs' and goats' flesh and the juice of peas with honey somewhat peppered' (*scilfixas finihte 7 ham wilda hænna 7 ealle þa fugelas þe on dunum libbað 7 pipiones þeod culfrena briddas 7 healfeald swin 7 gate flæsc 7 pisena seaw mid hunige hwæt hwega gepiperod*).[9] The recommendation of fish was not in the original Greek, and fish remains an 'invalid' food today, as does chicken, recommended elsewhere.[10] The value of eggs, dairy produce and vegetables seems to have been recognised.[11]

'Bullocks' meat, goats' and harts, bucks' and rams' and bulls' and the meat of all old four-footed animals, and birds that have hard flesh – peacock, swan, and duck' (*hryþeres flæsc gæten 7 hiorota buccena 7 ramma 7 fearra 7 þa þe swiðe ealde beoð on feoporfotum nietenum 7 fuglas þa þe heard flæsc habbað pawa swan æned*) are all recommended in one case.[12]

Avoidance

A pregnant woman was sensibly warned against 'eating salt or sweet things or *beor* or pork or anything fat or drinking to excess' (*sealtes ete oððe swetes oþþe beor drince ne swines flæsc ne naht fætes ne druncen gedrince*).[1]

---

[1] op. cit., 52.
[2] op. cit., 53.
[3] op. cit., II vii.
[4] op. cit., II i; ii 2.
[5] op. cit., II iv.
[6] op. cit.
[7] op. cit., II xxvi.
[8] op. cit., II xxvii.
[9] op. cit., II xxxvii.
[10] op. cit., II xvi, III lxxii, *Peri Didacheon* 51.
[11] op. cit., II xvi 1, xxv, xxvi, xxvii, li, *Peri Didacheon* 37.
[12] op. cit., II xvi.
[1] op. cit., III xxxvii.

Instructions about what food is to be avoided is sometimes given in general terms: 'avoid anything sour or salt' (*forga sur 7 sealtes gehwæt*), for example.[1] Food to be avoided by a man with liver disease is given first in general terms: nothing too sharp, bitter or purgative and then in detail: 'all broth must be avoided ...eggs are forbidden ...crumb of bread can be taken provided it is moistened or sodden ...but not to excess. Other moist ?wheaten ?meat-preparations and cookings-up must be forbidden and all moist and greasy things and oyster pies and all sweet things that create wind ...no apples or wine' (*ælc broþ is to forganne ...ægru sint to forganne ...hlafes cruman gif hie beoþ ofþænde oþþe gesodene ...ac na to swiþe. oþre wætan mete gearwa 7 cocnunga ealle sint to forbeodanne 7 eal þa wætan þing 7 þa smerewigan 7 osterhlafas 7 eall swete þing þe wyrcað aþundenesse ...æppla ne win*).[2]

Other leechdoms warned against vinegar, peas, beans, turnips, apples and nuts because they caused wind.[3] Sometimes 'cold oysters and apples and various vegetables' (*cealde ostran 7 æppla 7 missenlice wyrta þigð*) were to be avoided, elsewhere leek and cabbage are singled out.[4] Cheese, goose, eel, pork, fish and waterfowl could be eaten if salted.[5] Another leechdom forbade 'freshwater fishes and sea fishes that have hard flesh ...bullocks' flesh, or pork or mutton ...or goat or kid meat' (*fen fixas and sæ fixas þa þe habbað heard flæsc ...hriþeres flæsc ne swines ne sceapes ...ne gate ne ticcenes*). It also counselled against drinking *þicce win*.[6] Asthma sufferers were given the comprehensive instruction to avoid 'many kinds of meat and drinks and roasted meat and the meat of every kind of animal that chews the cud' (*feala cunna metas 7 drencas 7 wið gebræd flæsc 7 wið ælces orffes flæsc 7 þe cudu ceowe*).[7]

Relaxation from Religious Rule

The Rule of St. Benet allowed the flesh of quadrupeds only to the very weak and sick.[8] Æthelwold ate meat for three months when he was ill only at the command of Dunstan, and again during his final illness.[9] The *Rule of Chrodegang* allowed an invalid 'to take food and drink whenever he wants to or is able to, when he cannot observe the proper mealtimes' (*on ælcne sæl æt 7 wæt þicge þonne hine lyste oððe he mæge, þonne he gedafenlicum tidum ne mæg*).[10]

(iii) Monastic

Some Christian hermits, like Old Testament prophets, led a life of austerity in which a restricted, even eccentric, diet played a part.[1] The growth of communal monastic living necessitated meals that were acceptable to a group of individuals. The most famous rule was that instituted by Benedict of Nursia in the sixth century. The

---

1 op. cit., I iv 5, 6, xv 2, ii 1, II xliii.
2 op. cit., II xxiii.
3 op. cit., II xxiv, xxxix.
4 op. cit., II xxxvi, I ii 1.
5 op. cit., II xxii; I xxxvi.
6 op. cit., II xliii.
7 op. cit., *Peri Didacheon* 52.
8 Logeman 1888, Ch. 39.
9 Symons 1953, xxxv; Knowles 1940, 458.
10 Napier 1916, 47-8.
1 Turner 1828, III 27; Whitelock 1955, 749.

standard meal was bread and its accompaniment, as in lay households, and a second dish was offered at mealtimes so that 'he who perchance cannot eat of the one, may make his meal of the other'.[1]

A restricted diet was thought unlikely to inflame the passions, and gluttony and drunkenness would also be avoided.[2] *The Rule of Chrodegang* declared: '...feasts ...are to be avoided. But let bread with vegetables and fruit make a pleasant evening meal and if anyone has a fish let it be accounted a great delicacy. He who wishes to reign with Christ, does not care if he consume expensive food and drink which are excreted as dung and urine' (*...gebeorscipas ...synt to fleonne ...Ac sy eadelic æfenmete, hlaf mid ofæte, 7 amang þam gif ma fisc hæbbe healde þæt for healicne est. Se þe mis Criste wilnað to rixigenne, ne recð he na swiðe hwæþer he of deorwyrðum mettum 7 drincum þæt meox his argancges 7 his micgan gesamnige*).[3] However, there was a problem in balancing food intake so that bodily lusts would be subdued, but the monks would have enough energy to carry out their work. According to *The Rule of St. Benet*, 'Everyone hath his proper gift from God, one thus, another thus. For this reason the amount of other people's food cannot be determined without some misgiving'.[4] Fixing reasonable rations was difficult and laxity tended to creep in because no absolute standard could be established.[5]

The capital question concerned the abstinence from flesh meat as Benedict supplied matter for argument. The term 'flesh' was taken not to include fat (*pinguedo*) since an incidental enactment forbids this only during the Advent and Lenten fasts. Because the word 'quadruped' was used, the flesh of birds was considered lawful.[6] The *Regularis Concordia* does not include a chapter expressly devoted to diet, but announces that the Benedictine Rule is to be followed absolutely: that is, the two cooked dishes and one of fruit or vegetables, or, if the field labour was especially severe, other dishes at the abbot's discretion.

A number of religious, or quasi-monastic, communities were established in Anglo-Saxon England as early as the seventh century, among them Canterbury, Ripon, Winchester, Gilling, Whitby and *Icanho*.[7] However, the numbers of men and women living under the monastic rule varied throughout the period, and the dietary regulations were not always observed. At Monkwearmouth and Jarrow, for example, Biscop compiled his guide from the observances of seventeen different monasteries he had visited.[8]

Ascetic individuals, like Cuthbert, and later Æthelwold, who 'thought to subdue himself by abstinence', were revered by their contemporaries.[1] They had their adherents, ready to follow their example, and Æthelwold gave impetus to a movement for monastic reform. However, the respect accorded such individuals on account of their asceticism argues that it was not widespread, even among monastics.

---

[1] Matt & Hilpisch 1961, 114.
[2] Garmonsway 1978, 46; Napier 1916, 40.
[3] op. cit., 69.
[4] Logeman 1888, Chap. 39, 40.
[5] Knowles 1940, 150.
[6] op. cit., 458.
[7] op. cit., Appendix III; Whitelock 1955, 152, 696, 697; Matt & Hilpisch 1961, 149.
[8] Knowles 1940, 23.
[1] Colgrave 1940, 70; Whitelock 1955, 837.

Timetabled Meals

The times of meals, and their number, varied according to the time of year (see Chapter 29), but meals had their place in a regular routine, not to be interrupted by personal circumstances, or the exigencies of work or weather. It is this element of regularity which characterises the monastic regimen. There was a formal, ritual quality to a meal in the refectory.[1] According to *The Rule of Chrodegang*, after washing their hands in silence, a bell would be rung after which the brothers were to kneel and pray, then take their seats one by one. After blessing the food and drink, the prior was the first to eat. The Rule was to be read, and no-one else was to speak.[2] This regimented existence may have been irksome to some of the inmates, but for those who were not guaranteed sufficient food by their personal circumstances, regular meals may have been an attraction.

Food allowed by the Rule

After the *Regularis Concordia*, abstinence from flesh meat was general throughout the monasteries of England until well after the Conquest.[3] Fat, in the form of lard, suet and dripping was eaten, though it was a luxury and therefore to be renounced from Septuagesima till Easter, and in Advent, save on Sundays and feasts.[4] Lent was a time for fourfold abstinence and *pinguedo* (lard) was one of the four items to be abstained from (milk and eggs were two other items specifically mentioned, the fourth was presumably poultry).[5] The flesh of birds and fish could normally be consumed while still keeping to the letter of the law.[6]

The midday meal, the *prandium*, became the chief meal, to consist of two cooked dishes, *twa gesodene sylfian/ twa gesodene sufel*, to be eaten as an accompaniment to bread. These would have been of cereals, beans or other pulse, eggs, cheese and the like. There was to be a third dish of fresh vegetables and fruit if such were available. Bread was the mainstay of the diet with the individual ration set at a pound a day. St. Benedict nowhere gave details of the second meal, but it may be supposed that it was a lighter version of the other, since a third of the daily ration of bread was kept back for it.[7]

This information may be amplified by the details given in the plan for the monastery garden of St. Gall. Apple, pear, plum, service, medlar, bay, chestnut, fig, quince, peach, hazel, almond, mulberry and walnut trees all featured, and the eighteen great beds of the kitchen garden were to contain onions, leeks, celery, radish, carrots, garlic, shallots, lettuce, parsnip, cabbage, parsley, dill, chervil, marigold, coriander, poppy and corn campion.[1] The vegetables would have made suitable flavourings for cereal or bean dishes or could have been served as an accompaniment to bread.[2]

---

[1] Symons 1953, Sect. 26.
[2] Napier 1916, 125-6.
[3] Knowles 1940, 460.
[4] op. cit.
[5] Symons 1953, xxxv.
[6] Knowles 1940, 460.
[7] op. cit., 462.
[1] Stewart 1975, 46.
[2] Cockayne 1851, III 408.

The Rule of Chrodegang is interesting since it gives a more generous allowance of bread, and mentions 'animal flesh' (*flæsc*) foods:

'give each …four pounds by weight of bread, and …for their midday accompaniment for their bread let each two have a dish of fleshfood and offer other delicacies (e.g. meat puddings and sausages). If there are no delicacies, then let them be given two meat dishes. And for their evening meal let every couple have a meat dish or other delicacies. And at that time they must forego meat, and in Lent, then at midday day every couple shall have sufficient soft cheese and some delicacy, and if fish or vegetables are available, let them have them as a third course. And in the evening, each couple is to have soft cheese and some delicacy, and if the food is plentiful, humbly thank eternal God. When they only have one meal a day, then each couple is to have a delicacy and a serving of soft cheese and vegetable or some kind of stewed meat (?food) as a third course.'

(sylle ma ælcum …feower punda gewihte hlafes; 7 …heora middæges sufle, twam 7 twam an[e] flæscsande, 7 syddan oðre smeamettas. Gif man næbbe smeamettas, sylle man twam 7 twam twa flæscsande. 7 [to] heora æfenþenunge sylle man twam 7 twam ane flæscsande oðde oðre smeamettas. On þam tidum þe hi sceolon flæsc forgan, ealswa on Lengtenne, þonne sylle man to middægþenunge twam 7 twam an tyl cyssticce 7 sumne smeamete; 7 gif man fisc hæbbe oðde wyrta, sylle ma him to þriddan sande; 7 on æfen twam 7 twam an cyssticce 7 sume smeamettas; 7 gif it rumre cymð, þancion eadmodlice þæs æcum Drihtene. Þonne hi etaðf to anes mæles on dæg, þonne sylle man twam 7 twam sumne smeamete 7 tyl cyssticce, 7 wyrta oðde sumes cynnes gesodenne mete to þriddan sande.)[1]

There are no precise and authentic data for reconstituting the daily monastic meals in the times of Dunstan and Lanfranc.[2] So far as can be ascertained, the arrangements for the common meals remained unchanged between 960–1216, modified only by the addition of more feast days in winter. How far the observance was relaxed in the decades before the Conquest must remain a matter of doubt.[3] When information becomes plentiful, it is clear that, erected upon the basis of an ordinary day's fare of bread, cheese, vegetables, and two or three dishes of cereals, beans or eggs, a considerable fabric of extra dishes had sprung up. The most general form taken by these additions was the pittance, a small dish, usually of eggs or fish, served to each monk or pair of monks. A separate official, the pittancer, had charge of the material for the pittances.[4] At Glastonbury by the end of the period the monks had two pittances on Sundays, Tuesdays, Thursdays and Saturdays, and one on the remaining days of the week. At the same time the Abingdon dietary also allows two pittances on the same four weekdays, and three or four pittances on feast days, with two dishes of vegetables, one or two of *pulmenta* (cereals/beans) and one *generale* of eggs and fish.[1] In the opening years of Edgar's reign some men had been attracted to Abingdon by its reputation for stricter observance, so other monasteries may have been more lavish in the matter of food, or, perhaps more probably, the laxity had crept in over the ensuing decades.[2]

---

[1] Napier 1916, 14-15.
[2] Knowles 1940, 462.
[3] op. cit., 457.
[4] op. cit., 464.
[1] op. cit., 463.
[2] Symons 1953, xix.

Wealthy individuals made provision for feasts in particular monasteries on the basis that the monks were to intercede for their souls (see above). Æthelgifu left St. Albans '16 measures of malt and 3 of meal and a sester of honey …7 wethers and 6 lambs and a fattened bullock ready for slaughter and 30 cheeses …one *oman* of wine and 20 cheeses and 6 pigs and a bullock …from each estate for the thirtieth day [i.e. after burial – the 'month's mind']' (*xvi mittan mealtes 7 iii melwes 7 an sester huniges …7 viii weþeras 7 vi lomb 7 an slegeryþer 7 xxx cysa …anne oman wines 7 xx cysa 7 vi swin 7 an hryðer 7 nyme man of æghwilcum tune to þam þryttguþan dæge).*[1]

Laxity & Reforms

There were ideals, but normal practice was not attuned to them. Bede complained to Egbert in 734 that 'certain bishops …are given to laughter, jests, tales, feasting and drunkenness' .[2] He maintained the double abbey at Coldingham was destroyed by fire because of 'gluttony and drunkenness and idle gossip and other unlawful transgressions' (*oferæta 7 druncennesse 7 leasspellunge 7 oðerra unalefedlecra scylda).*[3]

Æthelred instructed in 1008 that clerics, where there was property such that they could have a refectory, were to obey the Rule, but he had to follow this up in 1014 by declaring 'henceforth we desire that abbots and monks live more according to the Rule than they have been accustomed to do until now' (*heonan forð we willað þæt abbodas 7 munecas regollicor libban þonne hi nu ær ðisan on gewunan hæfdon).*[4] The tendency towards laxity was a feature of monastic establishments, although this was checked by a number of individuals throughout the period.[5]

There was an infrastructure of lay servants at monasteries.[6] Cynesige, a monk who was archbishop of York, is recorded as living very temperately when his clerks or household officers were daily feasting in great luxury and splendour.[7] Although there is some confusion over whether those who were feasting were in fact clerics or lay officials, the source indicates the potential for good living in an important ecclesiastical household, even when its head was an ascetic.

Since a monastery contained categories of inmates not bound to observe the Rule, it is not surprising, for instance, that the stores of the monastery of Bury St. Edmunds contained flitches of bacon and associated delicacies since the flesh of domestic animals may have been used for guests, servants and the sick, while the lard went to the monks.[8] It is possible to maintain that there is no trustworthy evidence to show meat was ever allowed in the common refectory of a Benedictine monastery between 960 and 1216, even if certain relaxations had begun to come in outside the refectory.[9]

[1] Whitelock 1968, 11.
[2] Whitelock 1955, 737.
[3] Miller 1898, I, 2 354.
[4] Robertson 1925, 126.
[5] Symons 1953, xvi, xxi; Whitelock 1955, 836; Knowles 1940, Appendix III.
[6] Symons 1953, Sect. 24, 55, 60.
[7] Mellows 1980, 37.
[8] Knowles 1940, 460; Robertson 1939, 199.
[9] Knowles 1940, 458-63.

Consumption

The *Regularis Concordia* stated that all should feed together in the refectory (except in case of illness) and neither prelates not their subordinates should ever presume to be present at worldly feastings, unless perhaps in the case of unexpected hospitality when travelling.[1] However, this dispensation was obviously open to abuse.[2] The difficulty was that high status in lay society was indicated by the consumption of prestige foods in quantity and in the presence of numbers of guests or subordinates.

Monasteries were major landowners, and therefore generally had access to a plentiful food supply. Monks very often came from the ranks of a class used to conspicuous consumption: 'nobly-born men who had been used to eating delicacies' (*æþel-boren weras ...þa wæron estlice afedde*).[3] The fact that they subjected themselves to 'the austerity that prevailed in the monastery' (*þære stiðnysse þa þær stod on þam mynstre*) is seen as admirable, and even surprising. In a society where kings, nobles and landowners rewarded their retainers and servants and demonstrated their status by holding feasts, it proved to be difficult to prevent a movement towards feasting in monasteries.

---

[1] Symons 1953, xxxi.
[2] op. cit.
[3] Skeat 1881, *St. Martin* 1.355.

32. Food Shortages & Deficiency Diseases

Hunger

Steorfan did not yet mean 'to starve' but simply to die, though *of hungor/hungre/hungær* was sometimes adjoined, but of the synonyms used for 'to die' only *stearfan/steorfan* and *sweltan* seem to have been commonly employed in the 'of hunger' connection.[1]

Bede mentions hunger and thirst as the first infirmities of nature, following from the sin of the first man.[2] *The Fates of Men* refers to the individual eaten by a wolf, and then states 'another shall be wasted by hunger' (*sumne sceal hungor aliþan*).[3] The eventualities listed by the poem, though perhaps not commonplace, were distinct possibilities. A woman writing to her absent lover feels constrained to point out:

> *Wulf min wulf wena me þine*
> *seoce gedydon þine seldcymas*
> *murnende mod nales meteliste*

(Wulf, my Wulf, it was my longing for you, your long absences and my sad heart that have made me sick, not lack of food).[4]

A golden age of plenty was looked back to, but times had changed.[5] Life on earth was 'hard and spent in sweating toil and wearied by hunger' (*geswinc-ful and on swate wunad ...and on hungre gewæht*).[6] Some of the writings about hunger are particularly vivid:

> *Þa wæs wop hæfen in wera burgum*
> *hlud heriges cyrm hreopon friccan*
> *mændon meteleaste meðe stodon*
> *hungre gehæfte. Hornsalu wunedon*
> *weste winræced welan ne benohton*
> *beornas to brucanne on þa bitran tid*
> *gesæton searuþancle sundor to rune*
> *ermðu eahtigan.*

('Then was weeping uplifted in the towns of men, the loud outcry of the host, heralds shouted, they moaned the famine, weary they stood, bound by hunger. The spired halls remained, the winehouses empty, wealth needed not men to enjoy in that bitter tide. The wise of thought sat apart in council to investigate on their misery'.)[7]

One way of dealing with misfortune 'through enemy invasions or hunger, through plague or mortality, through crop failure or bad weather' (*þurh here oðþon hunger, þurh stric oððe steorfan, þurh unwæstm oððe unweðer*) according to the tenth-century

---

[1] Bosworth and Toller 1898, I 917; Jember 1975, 21.
[2] Miller 1890, I, 1 78.
[3] Gollancz/Mackie 1972, *The Fates of Men* l.15.
[4] op. cit., *Wulf and Eadwacer* l.13.
[5] Skeat 1881, St Maurice & his Companions l.160.
[6] op. cit., *St Cecilia* l.143.
[7] Kemble 1848, l.2311.

Institutes of Polity was to 'earnestly consult how amends could be sought from Christ, with pure fasts and with frequenting churches'.[1] Hunger was seen as a punishment for evil living. If monks and their superiors cared for worldly things then God would manifest his disapproval: 'if men cast away the monkly life and hold God's services in contempt what shall we come to but disease and hunger?' (*ða þa man towearþ munuc-lif and godes biggengas to bysmore hæfde buton þæt us com to cwealm and hunger*).[2]

One specific incidence of famine is recorded by Bede, since for three years before Bishop Wilfred came to Sussex 'there had been no rain and consequently a very severe famine had weakened the people and they died a cruel death. It is said that often forty or fifty people at a time suffering from starvation and in their misery, took each other by the hands, and jumped together from the cliffs, in order to kill themselves by the fall or drown themselves' (*þær nænig regn ...cwom 7 þonon se grimmesta hungor þæt folc wæs wæcende 7 heo mid arlease cwale fylde wæron. Secgað men þatte oft feowertig monna oðþe fiftig somed, þa ðe mid þy hungre gewæcte wæron, þæt heo earmlice bi honum noman 7 ealle ætgædre of sæsofre ut feollan, 7 woldan heo sylfe oðþe offyllan oðþe adrencan*).[3] Wilfred showed the people how to fish, since they knew only how to take eels. What were apparently suicide pacts may have been heathen sacrifices, but the rationale was presumably the same.

Scarcity may also be deduced from the laws relating to stolen food. Thieves were severely punished because 'they have snatched away very often the sustenance of the righteous'. Religious writings too confirm scarcity. Alcuin complains to Æthelred of Northumbria in 793 that 'some are inundated with delicacies and feastings like Dives, clothed in purple, ...and Lazarus dies in hunger at his gate. Where is brotherly love, where the pity which we are admonished to have for the wretched? The satiety of the rich is the hunger of the poor'.[4]

Relief of Hunger

Some charitable individuals of means did make efforts to relieve hunger. A king orders his reeves to supply one poor man on each of his estates with an amber of meal, a flitch of bacon or a wether worth one penny every month.[5] King Alfred left fifty pounds in his will to poor men in need, and another fifty pounds to poor servants of God.[6] Hunger continued a problem in the tenth century, since King Eadred left sixteen hundred pounds in his will to his people that they might be able to buy relief for themselves from famine, and from the heathen army if they had need. Wulfwaru in her will directs her legatees to feed twenty *freolsmen*, presumably freedmen, formerly slaves, on her lands.[7] Another testator left by will that a hundred poor men were to be fed at Ely, annually on St. Audrey's day.[8] There was no comprehensive system of organised relief for the hungry, and it is unlikely that relief reached all those who needed it.

---

[1] Bonser 1963, 4-5.
[2] Skeat 1881, *Prayer of Moses* l.139, l.152.
[3] Miller 1890, 1, 2 302-4.
[4] Whitelock 1955, 77.
[5] Whitelock 1952, 104.
[6] Whitelock 1955, 494.
[7] Kemble 1876, 220.
[8] Whitelock 1952, 104.

Special Circumstances

An individual like Cuthbert, living the life of a recluse and refusing an attendant, was at risk from hunger, if not starvation, if he fell ill. Cuthbert had in fact only consumed half an onion of the five he had with him when he took to his bed.[1] But when the brethren were, after a tempest of five days, able to reach him one of them observed 'I saw by his face that he was greatly wearied by lack of food as well as disease' (*videbam ...in facie eius quia multum inedia sinnul et languore erat defessus*).[2]

Famine Effecting a Change in Economic Circumstances

Theodore's Penitential states 'a father may sell his son aged under seven as a slave if necessity forces him to do so, after that he must have the agreement of the child' (*pater filium suum septem annorum, necessitate compulsus, potestatem habet tradere in servitium; deinde sine voluntate filii licentiam tradendi non habet*).[3] This was not as callous an act as at first appears. Selling oneself into slavery in exchange for food was an established practice throughout the period.[4] Under the terms of her will, written in a hand of the late tenth century, Gætflæd set free 'all the people who sold themselves for food during those evil days' (*ealle ða men ðe heonon heora heafod for hyra mete on ðam yflum dagum*).[5] Slaves who were already part of an estate might be in a reasonably good position in times of dearth. The land would not afford any profit to its owner if it were not worked, and so it was in the landowner's interest to see that workers were fit enough to work.

Monastic

In times of famine gold and silver were stripped from reliquaries, and crucifixes and chalices were melted down – presumably for the poor.[6] St. Æthelwold in the tenth century declared that he could not endure the sight of men, created in the image of God, dying of starvation and want, so broke up the church plate to buy food for those in distress.[7] Leofric at St. Albans did the same, probably in 1005, adding to the church plate gold and silver vessels from his own table.[8]

Causes of Famine

Weather

After a bad season food might be scarce, but a succession of bad years would bring about serious famine and probably pestilence.[9] Walford made a comprehensive analysis of the causes of famines recorded in the annals and found inclement weather the most serious factor.[1]

---

[1] Colgrave 1940, 276-7.
[2] op. cit.
[3] Kemble 1876, 199.
[4] Miller 1890, I, 1 54; Walford 1879, 7.
[5] Kemble 1876, 196; Whitelock 1955, 563-4.
[6] Dodwell 1982, 219.
[7] op. cit., 7.
[8] op. cit., 108; Mellows 1980, 70.
[9] Bonser 1963, 86.
[1] Walford 1879, 20ff; Whitelock 1955, 242, 290.

Entomological & Zootic Factors

There were occasional plagues of insects – 'locusts' according to the sources, which consumed quantities of the harvest. More important perhaps were the murrains which afflicted cattle and other animals periodically. They may have been influenced by poor pasture and reduced supplies of provender, so that a shortage of animal products might coincide with a reduced crop yield and compound the problem of securing sufficient food.

Human Factors

Walford's 'defective agriculture' may have played a part in food shortages, but the consequences of warfare were a decisive factor.[1] The land itself might be ravaged by troops or agricultural workers might be away campaigning.[2] Transport was certainly not organised on a comprehensive enough basis to make feasible the supply of provisions to an area suffering a shortfall.[3] No doubt landholders with large scattered estates either went to their properties where there was sufficient food or organised supplies to be transported to them.

In some cases there may have been a lack of technological knowledge when it came to exploiting food resources. There is nothing intrinsically unlikely in the fact that the starving inhabitants of Sussex, used to taking eels by spearing them or catching them in weirs of brushwood, did not know how to net fish at sea.

Famine Years

Occurrences of famine were recorded in copies of the Anglo-Saxon Chronicle. These were kept at various religious houses, and local outbreaks may have been recorded in only one copy.[4] The most important, together with comments from the sources, are listed below.

439　after a comet
466　caused by 'bad fatal air'
515　'most afflictive'
590　caused by a tempest which raised a great flood
592　caused by a drought from the 10 January to September, and locusts
605　caused by heat and drought
625　'grievous'
680　caused by three years of drought
681　at Selsey, Sussex.[5]
688　Bede says that Cædwalla abdicated and went on a pilgrimage for the good of his soul, but Matthew Paris gives another reason in a marginal gloss. He says it was on account of a widespread famine in England that he fled from the country.[1]
695　famine and pestilence 'so that men ate each other'.[2]

---

[1] Walford 1879, 108.
[2] Whitelock 1955, 255.
[3] Walford 1879, 107.
[4] Bonser 1963, 14.
[5] Walford 1879, 5.
[1] Bonser 1963, 87.
[2] Walford 1979,5.

−700   In the second half of the seventh century the Yellow Plague was raging, and according to Adamnan's *Life of Columba*, about 684 there was 'a mortality upon all animals …for the space of three years so that there escaped not one out of the thousand of any kind of animal'.[1] While there is no record of famine in the chronicles for this year, supplies of animal food must have been scarce, even allowing for sensationalising on the part of the writer. Perhaps this confirms that cereal crops were the principal food resource.

730   great famine.[2]

737   a great drought made the land unfruitful.[3]

793   after many meteors, immense whirlwinds and flashes of lightning.[4] The fact that the pagan invaders slaughtered sheep and oxen no doubt contributed to the natural effects.[5]

800   Contemporary evidence no longer exists for an extensive murrain of cattle in 800, but such is recorded by Roger of Hovenden, who was perhaps using a local copy of the chronicle no longer extant.[6] *Brut y Twysogion* recorded a great mortality of the cattle of the island of Britain for 810.[7]

820   The harvest was spoilt by continuous heavy rains and many men and cattle died. Floods prevented the autumn sowing.[8]

821   harvest devastated by hail, pestilence among men and cattle. The story was told of a town that was afflicted 'each year very frequently by hail so that their crops were destroyed before any reaper could gather the harvest' (*ælce geare oftost þurh hagol swa heora æceras ær wæron aþroxene ær ænig ryftere þæt gerip gaderode*).[9] While this presumably happened in France since St. Martin prayed for the afflicted and there was no more hail there during his lifetime, it indicates how devastating hailstorms were for the harvest.

867   a great dearth.[10]

868   a great famine with mortality of men and cattle.[11] There were almost certainly local shortages that went unrecorded, but the great plunder of cattle the invading Danes made in 870 on their way to Peterborough would have taken some seasons to replace, to take only one example.[12] Danish campaigns would certainly have disrupted supply in the areas they were conducted, even if famine is not necessarily recorded as a result.

872   'from ugly locusts'.[1]

879   universal famine.[2]

887   grievous two years.[3]

---

[1] Whitelock 1955, 690.
[2] Walford 1879, 5.
[3] Whitelock 1955, 259.
[4] Walford 1879, 5; Whitelock 1955, 167, 247.
[5] op. cit., 242.
[6] Bonser 1963, 87.
[7] op. cit.
[8] Turner 1828, II 55.
[9] Skeat 1881, *St Martin* l.1215.
[10] Walford 1879, 6.
[11] Turner 1828, II 550.
[12] op. cit., I 524.
[1] Walford 1879, 6.
[2] op. cit.

893   The invading Danes were surrounded at Buttington on the Severn and were reduced to eating their horses, but even so a number died of starvation.[2] (Many Danes also died of hunger in 914, when similar tactics were employed).[3]

896   The English people were much more seriously afflicted by the mortality of cattle and men than by the Danes in these three years.[4] In 894 they had been 'oppressed with lack of food' (*mid metelieste gewægde*).[5]

900   famine.[6]

        In the reign of Athelstan Olaf and his Northmen set fire to crops, 'the green crops withered in the fields, the blighted cornfield mocked the husbandman's prayers'.[7]

954   great famine which lasts four years.[8]

962   famine caused by frost.[9]

969   all grain burnt by the winds.[10]

975   a very great famine recorded in the major versions of the chronicle, interpreted as the vengeance of God.[11]

976   great famine in England, the *micla hungor*.[12] This followed a period of frost, from the 1st November to the end of March.[13]

986   great mortality of cattle (*yrfcwealm*) in England.[14]

988   famine from rain and barren land.[15]

989   great drought and famine followed a period of much snow and rain when there could be no sowing.[16]

1004   such a famine as no man could remember.[17] (This is presumably the famine referred to for 1005).

1005   great famine throughout England – such that no man ever remembered one so cruel.[18] Perhaps this is what motivated the departure of the Danish fleet.

1012   endless multitudes died of famine in England and on the continent.[1]

1016   famine throughout Europe because of hail, thunder and lightning.[2]

1025   famine because of rains.[3]

1031   famine because of great rains and locusts.[4]

---

[1] op. cit.
[2] Whitelock 1955, 187.
[3] op. cit., 195.
[4] op. cit., 188.
[5] Bosworth & Toller 1898, I 463.
[6] Walford 1879, 6.
[7] Whitelock 1955, 209.
[8] Walford 1879, 6.
[9] op. cit.
[10] op. cit.
[11] Whitelock 1955, 209.
[12] op. cit., 210; Walford 1879, 6.
[13] Turner 1828, II 551.
[14] op. cit.
[15] Walford 1879, 6.
[16] Turner 1828, II 551.
[17] Walford 1879, 6.
[18] Whitelock 1955, 218.
[1] Walford 1879, 6.
[2] op. cit.
[3] op. cit.
[4] op. cit.

1041 weather inclement all the year, great mortality among cattle.[1]

1044 a dreadful famine in England and on the continent so that a sester of wheat cost above 60 pence.[2] Henry of Huntingdon says that a sester of wheat was the burthen of one horse. The famine lasted seven years.[3]

1047 great famine from snow and frost.[4]

1051 an extreme dearth in which many thousands perished.[5]

1054 terrible famine after a comet, wheat at fifteen shillings a quarter.[6] This compared with an average price for the previous fifty or so years of three shillings and sixpence.[7]

1065 'Morkere and his horde from the north harried Northamptonshire, burnt corn, took all the cattle so that the shire and other shires near were for many winters the worse'.[8]

In the south-eastern counties which suffered most from the campaigns which followed Hastings, there is frequent reference to the reduction in hidage on account of the waste and devastation.[9] This was the background to the famines recorded after the Conquest, and presumably led to local shortages.

1068 famine (and plague) after a severe winter.[10]

1069 after harrying by William I the northern countries and other parts of the realm suffered a great dearth.[11]

1073 famine followed by mortality so fierce the living could neither take care of the sick nor bury the dead.[12]

1086 murrain of animals and intemperate weather.[13]

1087 pestilence followed by famine.[14]

1093 great famine and mortality.[15]

1096 famine from summer rain, tempests and bad air.[16]

1099 famine from rains and floods.[17]

Famine Foods

The likelihood is that if supplies were short, important foods like flour would be bulked out with less desirable additions: beans and peas, acorns and ground bark, for example (see Chapter 16). Diseased meat that might normally have been rejected may have been consumed, in some cases infecting the eater. Fruit that was unripe or bad would normally have been rejected, but in times of famine it was probably eaten.

---

[1] Turner 1828, II 551.
[2] op. cit.
[3] Walford 1879, 6.
[4] op. cit.
[5] Turner 1828, II 325.
[6] Walford 1879, 6, 257.
[7] op. cit.
[8] Douglas and Greenaway 1953, 140.
[9] Loyn 1970, 312.
[10] Walford 1879, 7.
[11] op. cit.
[12] op. cit.
[13] op. cit.
[14] op. cit.
[15] op. cit.
[16] op. cit.
[17] op. cit.

Herbs and roots (nettles and wild skirret, for example) would be gathered from the hedgerows to eke out a scanty existence.[1]

In extreme conditions, as were recorded for 695–700, 'men ate each other'.[2] Cannibalism is also recorded in the post-Conquest period. The *Liber Eliensis* records 'consequent famine prevailed with the result that men ate horses, dogs, cats and human flesh' (*fames secuta praevaluit ut homines equinam, caninam, catinam et carnem commederent humanam*).[3] This pattern seems to be generally followed during times of severe famine; taboos play little part when existence is at stake.[4]

Some famine foods, in particular dark green (i.e. high carotene) leaves, including Chenopodium, were nutritionally valuable, high in iron (4mg per 100gm), Vitamin A (3,000IU per 100gm), ascorbic acid (100mg per 100gm), and contained valuable amounts of the B vitamins, thiamine, riboflavin, and nicotinamide. Other leaves with medium or low carotene would also contribute to a healthy intake.[5] Wild rose hips would be a particularly valuable source of ascorbic acid, with an average of 700mg per 100gm.[6] Blood, and human flesh in particular, would have also been valuable nutritionally. However, it seems likely that without the bulk of cereals or dried legumes for bread or stews, the population would gradually have weakened.

Malnutrition

Lack of Vitamin A

The probability is that Anglo-Saxon populations suffered from vitamin A deficiency with consequent skin, eye and urinary tract diseases.[7] The vitamin is present in butter, fish liver, offal and eggs.[8] The vitamin A value of dairy produce and eggs is highest when cows are out at pasture and hens are running loose on grass. Cows fed on dried hay yield milk which becomes progressively poorer in vitamin A. In winter the supply was greatly reduced and consequently reserves in the body would be depleted, so that many may have been in a condition of mild or sub-acute deficiency in the spring.[9] This might explain the high demand for fish experienced by the fisherman of the *Colloquy*, and also the demand for eggs, and fatty foods generally .[1]

Lack of Vitamin C

In the winter and spring a shortage of fresh meat and vegetables may have meant some of the population were in a pre-scorbutic state, suffering from symptoms which included bleeding gums, ulcers and bloody dysentery.[2] A leechdom states: 'there is no time for bloodletting as good as the beginning of Lent when the evil liquid which has

---

[1] Drummond 1958; Fenton & Kisban 1986, 123-4. [2] Walford 1879, 5. [3] op. cit., 229. [4] Victor 1955, 146. [5] Platt 1968, 14-15. [6] op. cit., 36.
[2] Walford 1879, 5. [3] op. cit., 229. [4] Victor 1955, 146. [5] Platt 1968, 14-15. [6] op. cit., 36.
[3] op. cit., 229. [4] Victor 1955, 146. [5] Platt 1968, 14-15. [6] op. cit., 36.
[4] Victor 1955, 146. [5] Platt 1968, 14-15. [6] op. cit., 36.
[5] Platt 1968, 14-15. [6] op. cit., 36.
[6] op. cit., 36.
[7] Bonser 1963, 375, 382, 400.
[8] Platt 1968, 20-1, 24-5.
[9] Drummond and Wilbraham 1958.
[1] Garmonsway 1978, 27.
[2] Holmes 1952, 226.

been absorbed during the winter has accumulated' (*nis nan blodlæstid swa god swa on foreweardne lencten þonne þa yfelan wæten beoð gegaderode on wintra gedruncene beoð*).[1] This is not an isolated reference: a second leechdom refers to various complaints, including skin complaints and leprosy, the bacillus of which can feed on human tissue in the absence of vitamin C, and continues 'therefore men should cleanse away the evil humours before the evils come and grow in the winter and run through the limbs' (*Forþon sceal mon ær clænsian þa yflan wætan aweg ær þon þa yfelan cuman 7 geweaxan on wintra 7 þa limo geond yrnen*).[2]

The beet, mallow, brassica, nettle and elder leaves recommended, contained vitamin C which would remedy the deficiency.[3] It may have been that in the warmer phase towards the end of the Anglo-Saxon period, green plants had a longer growing season than at present, and were readily available in early spring. The numerous green herbs and sometimes bark used in leechdoms may well have been beneficial by reason of their ascorbic properties.[4]

However, the likelihood is that scurvy was prevalent; Bonser considered that during the Danish invasions the populace was always afflicted by a mixture of diarrhoea, dysentery and scurvy.[5] They may also have been affected by relapsing fever which was a famine fever, as is dysentery.[6] In general there is little evidence of scurvy in archaeological material, since it affects soft tissue, rather than bone, but it has been tentatively diagnosed in seven out of 350 Anglo-Saxons from East Anglia, in skeletons at Portchester and a skull from West Stow.[7]

The symptoms of scurvy include anaemia, lassitude, loss of muscle tone and tendency to sudden death on slight exertion. Trouble with sore gums, loosening and loss of teeth was also likely to occur and the Anglo-Saxons had recipes for 'sore of teeth' and 'looseness of teeth', and 'bone-wort' (*banwyrt*) was recommended for 'canker of the teeth from which the teeth fall out'.[8]

Lack of Minerals

Fluorine in the water or from fish would prevent tooth decay. The number of teeth lost *ante mortem* indicates that the teeth of the population at Monkwearmouth were healthier than those of the inhabitants of Jarrow, who would presumably have had a similar diet, but whose water supply would not have contained fluorine.[1] Both groups lost fewer teeth than Anglo-Saxon populations in general, perhaps because of the importance of fish in the monastic diet.[2] It may also have been because the eating habits of monastic groups were more refined, or because they were less likely to use their teeth as tools.

---

[1] Cockayne 1851, I lxxii.
[2] op. cit., II xxx; McNeill 1977, 175.
[3] Cockayne 1851, II xxx.
[4] Bonser 1963, 9; Bosworth & Toller 1898, I 344.
[5] Bonser 1963, 86.
[6] McArthur 1949, 169.
[7] Wells 1975, 756; Cunliffe 1976, 240, 255; West 1982, 197.
[8] Bonser 1963, 390.
[1] Wells 1964.
[2] op. cit.

Zinc is particularly necessary for growing children, pregnant and lactating women, and is easily absorbed from animal foodstuffs.[1]

Ignorance was still an element in malnutrition.[2] The bread which young children were given probably did not provide all the nutrients necessary.

Indications of Famine

Evidence of malnutrition came from a number of skeletons from early, mid- and late-period communities in East Anglia of which more than two-thirds were affected in the early and mid periods, about half in the late period.[3]

Fe/male Differences Including Life Expectancy

What evidence we have indicates that girls suffered more than boys from illness, despite their more favourable chromosome pattern, and more from carious teeth; they were probably less valued and had to content themselves with leftovers.[4]

Amenorrhoea is one obvious response to malnutrition, and leechdoms dealing with this condition prescribe, among other things, hot herb drinks fairly rich in iron.[5]

On a number of sites the average age of women at death seems to have been several years less than that of the men. That malnutrition was the main cause of earlier deaths is supported by the frequency of enamel hypoplasia and Harris's lines. Women no doubt died from complications of childbirth. At Buckland Anglo-Saxon cemetery most women died in the 20–30 age range, then the 30–45 range, with few surviving to old age.[6] The likelihood is that most of these deaths would not have occurred if the women had been well-nourished from birth: obstetric failures are more likely in malnourished women. The greater increase in male stature over female, from the Roman sample to the sixth-century Saxon sample found in Hampshire cemeteries indicates that the roles, and importance, of each sex in society varied considerably.[7]

Life expectancy derived from the skeletal series indicates an almost complete absence of elderly people (i.e. over the age of 50 or so). The picture is complicated since there is some evidence that conventional methods for dating skeletal material give the age at death as being younger than was the case.[1] Even so, a larger percentage of Anglo-Saxon adults reached old age than in English parishes in 1800, and the child mortality rate was lower.[2] In fact the Anglo-Saxon statistics for mortality are closer to those of modern Europe, though this may reflect the fact that the Anglo-Saxons were not exposed to as many diseases as later populations so may not simply indicate superior nutrition.

Results of Famine

[1] Morgan 1975, 4.
[2] Eydoux 1966, 81.
[3] Wells 1964, 277.
[4] op. cit., fig. 31; Kuper 1977, 107; Harris 1986, 241; Bosworth & Toller 1898, I 348.
[5] Fell 1984, 51.
[6] Evison 1987, 128.
[7] Arnold 1984, 137.
[1] Ascadi & Nemeskeri 1970.
[2] Brothwell in Brothwell & Higgs 1963, 328.

A longer-lived population indicates higher living standards and a more productive workforce. One serious shortage could start a vicious circle of early death, inability of the community to produce enough food, and further early deaths.[1] The usual reaction to shortage is irritability, complaint and unrest, then lack of initiative, and apathy.[2] So those suffering from a shortage of food would not be in a condition to organise themselves effectively to deal with the situation.

Leechdoms suggest that 'if a woman who is four or five months pregnant often eats nuts or acorns or any fresh fruits then it sometimes happens that her child is stupid because of this' (*gif wif biþ bearn eacen feower monoð oþþe fif 7 heo þonne gelome eteð hnyte oþþe æceran oþþe ænige niwe bleda þonne gelimpeð hit hwilum þurh þ þæt þ cild biþ disig*).[3] It may be that a woman eating nuts, acorns, etc., was scavenging because supplies of the staple foods were not available, and the baby's subsequent defects may have been caused by malnutrition, rather than these particular items.

New-born children may have been killed, since infanticide in times of dearth was not accounted a crime.[4] Those who survived famine during their growing years were likely to be smaller and weaker than those who had not experienced this trauma.[5] However, the stature of Anglo-Saxons was greater than that of either Iron Age or later medieval populations.[6]

The occurrence of famine and pestilence might be stressed as a cause of England's weakness in the time of Æthelred the Unready. The country may have succumbed to Swein and Cnut in part because of the demoralised condition of the people. No outbreaks occurred in the reign of Cnut when the devastation wrought by the Danes ceased with the accession of their own king.[7]

Resistance to disease is lowered by inadequate nutrition and there is a correlation between famines and plagues in Anglo-Saxon times: most pestilences did follow famine.[8] The situation may have been exacerbated by the fact that some people are likely to have moved around in search of food in time of famine.[9] While immune to every common pathogen in their own environment, leaving it to seek food could lead to an outbreak of disease since individuals would then be exposed to different pathogens. Other people might be on the move too, increasing the range of infections.[1]

As well as the plagues which were dramatic in their effects, poor food, combined with poor housing, probably gave rise to chronic 'lowering' diseases, where the sufferer lost strength over a period of months or even years before finally succumbing.

Conclusion

---

[1] Davies 1982, 42.
[2] Drummond 1958.
[3] Cockayne 1851, III.
[4] Bonser 1963, 87; Whitelock 1955, 754.
[5] Brothwell in Ucko & Dimbleby 1971, 534; Jackson 1969, 117.
[6] Wells in Brothwell & Higgs 1963, 363.
[7] Bonser 1963, 52.
[8] op. cit., 85, 63-4.
[9] Sayce 1946.
[1] Burnet & White 1972, 82, 146, 153.

Consumption

The number of references to hunger in the literature, chronicles and legal documents implies that it was probably a normal experience of life in Anglo-Saxon England, even if it was only the hunger of waiting for mealtimes. In the dialogue of Alcuin and Pepin, the answer to the question, 'What makes bitter things sweet?' is 'hunger'.[1] This probably explains how it was the Anglo-Saxons found palatable food that we would reject today. The higher incidence of caries may indicate not a greater reliance on cereals but the reverse: a dependence on rougher food: siliceous vegetables and stringy meat.[2]

A proportion of the population, in particular women, probably had to make do with a less than adequate diet throughout the period. Some upsets of the metabolism connected with bad diet were probably effectively treated with medicinal herbs.[3]

On a domestic level, the better a woman was as a manager, the more likelihood of her family surviving.[4] Keeping the stores in good condition would be a vital task. The Lenten fast was probably a case of making a virtue of necessity. Easter, when the consumption of eggs and poultry would bring relief, probably brought to an end a season of hunger. Providing the rations laid down in *Rectitudines Singularum Personarum* were met in full and were complemented by vegetables, estate workers may have lived reasonably well most of the time.[5] There is archaeological (as well as documentary) evidence that monastic communities were comparatively well-nourished.[6]

The devastation and disruption caused by Viking raids took its toll on the general health of the people, creating conditions favourable to outbreaks of hunger and pestilence.[7] Bad weather had the same result.[8] Shortages of cereals and hay might mean that their owners could live on the carcasses of their animals for a season, but the following year they would be short of stock.[9] A dearth might take a year or two to make its effects felt, after which it might take several years to re-establish an adequate food supply.

If exacted harshly, the food rents paid by the poor to the rich could lead to very short commons for the poor. Even wealthy men wanted to buy out the right of food farms for considerable sums. Cnut relieves his subjects from what he calls this 'burden'. The powerful were able to strengthen their position during a time of famine by providing food, not as a charitable gift, but as a way of buying slaves.

---

[1] Turner 1828, III 439.
[2] Brothwell in Ucko & Dimbleby 1971, 537-8.
[3] Sergo in Fenton & Owen 1981, 264-5.
[4] Sayce 1946.
[5] Fenton & Owen 1981, 161.
[6] Wells 1964.
[7] Bonser 1963, 4.
[8] op. cit., 57-8.
[9] Fenton & Owen 1981, 161.

33. Adulteration: Damage Caused by Dietary Elements

Poisons

Of adulterants poison was perhaps the most dramatic in its effects. It might be taken accidentally: 'at that time Martin ate with his food the poisonous plant called hellebore' (*Martinus on þære tide on his mete þigde þa ættrian wyrt þe elleborum hatte*).[1] As green-leaf salads were served, some knowledge of plants was advisable. If food was short, plants not usually eaten might be tried, which would have increased the likelihood of poisoning. There are also a number of leechdoms in case a man eats or drinks something poisonous. In these cases the poisoning was presumably accidental since there are separate remedies in case you suspect someone may try to poison you, as happened to Æthelwold.[2]

Coccel (cockle) translating 'tares', was presumably corncockle, (*agrostemma githago*). It contains githagenin, which predisposes those who consume it to leprosy, and can be fatal. Corncockle was recognised as a 'baneful weed' of corn at least by the eighth century.[3] Corncockle would need to be rooted up before harvest since the seeds are produced at about the same height and time as ears of corn, and are difficult to separate from cereal grains by sieving as they are not much smaller.[4] As Anglo-Saxon grain size was smaller than that of modern cereal varieties, this difficulty would have been exacerbated. Corncockle seeds turn up in quantity on middle and late urban sites.[5] Perhaps farmers were less concerned with the purity of their corn if they were going to sell it, or the anti-helminthic qualities of corncockle may have been known, and the Anglo-Saxons who consumed it may have been trying to rid themselves of the heavy worm burdens most of them carried (see below).[6] Moreover, the githagenin is probably reduced or destroyed by prolonged heating, so contaminated samples could have been used in stews and porridges.[7]

Ergot (*claviceps purpurea*) was established as a fungus disease of cereals in Europe before the beginning of the Anglo-Saxon period.[8] Ergotism, also known as *ignis sacer*, St. Anthony's fire, or erysipelas, was one of the common complaints dealt with in *Leechdoms*, and could produce convulsions, gangrene and abortions in humans and stock.[9] There are several possible instances recorded by chroniclers of the sixth and eighth centuries.[10] Anglo-Saxon populations may have suffered in areas where rye was the main crop: parts of the West Midlands, for example, since ergot is much more common on rye than other cereals.[11] Ergot flourishes in damp weather which is likely

[1] Skeat 1881, *St Martin* l.196.
[2] Cockayne 1851, II lxv 2, III xliii, I p.84, *Lacnunga* XXVIII, X; Whitelock 1955, 835.
[3] Kylie 1911, 116, 123.
[4] Hall 1981, 5ff.
[5] Monk 1977, 293 ff.
[6] Hall 1981, 5 ff.
[7] op. cit.
[8] Brothwell & Higgs 1963, 178.
[9] Deegan 1986, 20.
[10] Brothwell 1969, 190.
[11] Dickens 1974, 1, 3.

to cause low yields, and so populations may not have been able to afford simply to dispose of contaminated samples. Rye was probably more susceptible to ergot in damper British conditions than on the continent, which may be why wheat became the preferred species.

Moulds which secrete dangerous aflatoxins grow on damp grain, meal and flour.[1] Mouldy samples might not be discarded if food was short.

Parasites

The smoking of cured pork would not have killed trichinae (*Trichuris trichiura*), also known as whipworms, with which it was often infected, because the temperature reached was not high enough.[2] Large numbers of whipworm can lead to moderate to severe diarrhoea.[3] In children the irritation leads to sleeplessness and loss of condition. Whipworm eggs were discovered at West Stow and Anglo-Scandinavian York.[4] Ascarids (*Ascaris lumbricoides*) also known as large roundworms, or maw worms, generally cause little damage to the host, though migrating larva can produce hepatitis and damage the lung tissues, and cause serious trouble if they enter other organs.[5] If these worms are numerous, the symptoms may be severe, simulating those of gastric and duodenal ulcer.[6] A coprolite from Anglo-Scandinavian York was parasitized by a heavy infestation of maw worm and whipworm by today's standards, though it was well within the limits of human tolerance.[7] From the large numbers of parasite ova discovered in York, it seems likely that most people carried worm burdens for most of their lives.[8] It is possible that worm infestation was heavier in urban populations where there was more pressure on space.[9] King Alfred indicates that he also was familiar with internal parasites, since to Boethius he adds, 'the small worms that crawl within and without [man] even sometimes nearly kill him'.[10]

Bacterial Infections

There was, as one might expect, bacterial contamination of dairy products or brewings.[11] Eating food that had 'turned' was recognised as leading to problems.[12] St. Gregory told the story of the nun who swallowed a devil through eating a lettuce without making the sign of the cross over it first.[13] Presumably the 'devil' produced unpleasant symptoms, probably the result of eating the unwashed leaves. A general lack of hygiene may have made itself felt in terms of infections.

---

[1] Renfrew 1985, 27; Erlichman 1986, 143.
[2] Kuper 1977, 39.
[3] West 1982, 310.
[4] op. cit.; Jones 1980, 9; Jones in Hall et al. 1983, 228-9.
[5] West 1982, 310; Jones 1980, 11.
[6] op. cit., 11.
[7] Jones in Hall et al. 1983, 228-9.
[8] Jones, undated paper.
[9] West 1982, 309.
[10] Turner 1828, II 34.
[11] Cockayne 1851, I lxvii 1, 2.
[12] op. cit., *Lacnunga* 90.
[13] Bonser 1963, 259.

The common and lesser houseflies are likely to have been significant as carriers of disease. Disease organisms are transferred from faecal matter (which was almost certainly more in evidence in Anglo-Saxon times) to uncovered food.[1] Insects and mice which infested stores could act as vectors of disease [2] (see Chapter 19).

Cured pork was a common source of botulism in Europe in later medieval times.[3] There is a strong likelihood that the same situation prevailed in Anglo-Saxon England.

Physical Damage

The teeth of Anglo-Saxons from a number of sites showed marked wear, an indication of a coarse, fibrous diet, probably containing abrasive materials.[4] They suffered from two kinds of tooth decay which arose as a complication of tooth wear, and both gave rise to abscesses.[5] These types of caries differ substantially from caries in modern man and have a different aetiology.[6] In 260 individuals from two cemeteries dating from about 600 and 800, practically all the caries was of the wear-fracture type.[7]

The evidence of arthritis on mandibles also points to a diet which contained tough and chewy materials, perhaps a combination of smoked or salted meat, siliceous vegetable fibres and hard breads or bannocks containing quern dust.[8] Female jaws were more commonly affected which partly reflects the problem the relatively lighter female jaw would have coping with tough food, but may also imply that women took second-best as far as food was concerned.[9]

Cooking & Preserving Methods

There was a high incidence of chronic sinusitis among the Anglo-Saxons.[10] This may reflect the inclement weather, and the winter-long nasal irritation from peat or log fires burning in badly-ventilated rooms.[11] Since cooking was done over such domestic fires, the household cooks, probably women in most cases, may have suffered more from sinusitis and, as a result, from general ill-health.

As well as poisons of vegetable or fungal origin, there is a possibility that Anglo-Saxon populations may have absorbed lead from processing equipment. Salt was evaporated in *leads*, and was probably contaminated with lead in consequence. This contaminated salt might then be used for salting meat in lead containers. Brining creates an acidic medium which can dissolve metal. Lead-lined cider presses and vats may have caused outbreaks of colic and lead poisoning.[1] Brazen cooking equipment may have led to poisoning by copper salts.

---

[1] Hickin 1963, 118.
[2] op. cit., 103; Bonser 1963, 76.
[3] McGee 1986, 512.
[4] Bonser 1963, 338-9, 390; Holdsworth 1980, 79; Wells 1964, 60, 125; Rahtz and Hirst 1974, 85, 87.
[5] Miles 1972, 309.
[6] Miles 1969, 1313.
[7] op. cit., 1314.
[8] Wells 1964, 60; Miles 1969, 1315.
[9] Wells 1964, 60.
[10] op. cit., 81.
[11] op. cit.
[1] Redfern 1987, 16.

Smoke contains a number of carcinogens which are imparted to food preserved by smoking, a traditional method of preservation. The assumption might therefore be that an individual who ate a large amount of smoked food might be at risk from various cancers of the alimentary canal and intestines. On the other hand, if that individual also ate food rich in fibre, any carcinogens would probably not remain in contact with the walls of the digestive tract for long enough to have any serious effect. Since there are so many imponderables, it does not seem to be particularly helpful to deal with the number of scenarios which might conceivably have arisen.

Conclusion

In this area perhaps more than any other, the evidence is incomplete. However, the significant points are that food was contaminated by various substances. In some cases this had a minimal effect on the consumers; in other cases it could have caused ill-health or proved fatal. While ignorance of the effects of, for example, lead poisoning would have been general, possibly most kinds of contamination were less likely in affluent establishments, where sub-standard food samples could be discarded, more tender vegetables and animals were eaten, and where hygiene was practised to some degree.

V Conclusion

The intention of this synthesizing study has been to gather information about the production, processing, distribution and consumption of Anglo-Saxon food and drink from Old English sources, archaeological, place- and field-name evidence, to see what could be established about the Anglo-Saxon food supply and the ways this might affect the population. It has also been to try to discover what part the production and distribution of food played in social organisation and to discover changes over the period.

From the vast number of references – many more than were expected – it is clear that food production for home consumption was the basis of economic activity throughout the Anglo-Saxon period. The unit of land division was that needed for subsistence by a family group. The demands of food production influenced the work of most countrymen, the division of tasks, and even the organisation of Alfred's army. Although the royal food rents seem large, plentiful for a king and his retinue, they seem to have been relatively modest in terms of the area which had to supply them, so that peasants were not exploited and over-worked.[1] It has been estimated that the population rose steadily from fewer than 300,000 in c.600 to a million by the time of the Conquest.[2]

Moreover, the provision of food and eating together was central to social, and sometimes legal, obligations.

Changes over the Period

There were, however, other changes over the period. The skeletons of the early Anglo-Saxons of East Anglia show the results of very hard work, hoeing and mattocking. As settlement progressed, an agricultural system that was community-based could develop, bringing with it the establishment of plough teams and an increase in cereal production for bread and ale, and perhaps the fattening of beef cattle. Towards the end of the period landowners with capital were effecting improvements, as with the reclamation around Glastonbury. The references to *tunnaep* and *tuncaers* indicates the bringing into cultivation, into 'enclosures' (*tuns*), of previously wild plants with a good food potential. The interest in agriculture extended to the writing of treatises.

As the acreage of cultivated land increased, the habitat of wild animals and birds decreased. For example, at *Hamwih*, the proportion of wild animals in the diet dropped by half over a period of a few decades, probably because woodland in the immediate vicinity had been lost.[3] Developing preferences were indulged in by those who could afford them, e.g. for lighter wheaten bread, for tender, specially-bred beef, and for certain cuts of meat. The rich were unlikely to have been hungry, and therefore preferred lighter foods that were easier to eat. This factor may account for

---

[1] Hodges 1982, 138.
[2] op. cit., 164.
[3] Holdsworth 1980, 99.

the relative scarcity of rye in the later period, although the prevalence of ergot in a damp climate, as compared to drier conditions in the continental homeland where it was an important crop, is perhaps more significant.

While there is insufficient evidence to trace the development of particular breeds of farm animals, it is worth recording that rare or 'primitive' breeds, though smaller than modern animals, are in general hardy and thrifty, suited to outdoor systems. Whereas modern breeds of dairy cattle, for example, need good food, Shetland cattle are able to convert poor quality fodder into excellent beef and milk with a 4% butterfat content up to three months after calving.[1] The Norfolk Horn sheep which shares some of the characteristics of Anglo-Saxon sheep was able to flourish on the heather and poor quality pasture of the Breckland.[2] In general primitive breeds have superior maternal qualities and the meat is considered to be better than that from the popular modern breeds.[3]

Archaeological evidence suggests the development of the deep-water drift net increased the catch in the ninth and tenth centuries.[4] Fish, for which we know the demand exceeded the supply, probably formed an important part of the diet in coastal and riverside towns. Most rivers had brushwood weirs, so many that by the end of the period they constituted a problem. For reasons to do with survival and recovery, fishbones are unlikely to reflect the importance of this item of diet.

However, the period does not show a consistent increase in the amount of food available to the population. Food production was precarious, and was disrupted by bad weather and political disturbance, in which case famine and death resulted. The yield from land in cultivation for long periods may have diminished, and the protein content of the grain that was produced would have gradually lessened without adequate fertilizer. Domestic animals suffered from various infections, resulting in high mortality in certain years. Malnutrition does not only result in a high death rate, but also in lowered fertility and a low birthrate as well as a general lowering of resistance to disease. In times of famine, when people left their homes in relatively small communities to look for food, they would have come across pathogens to which they had not developed immunity.

The Role of Women

Eating and drinking seems to have been stereotyped as a male activity, whereas in domestic situations women seem to have prepared and cooked the food, and to have offered drink to guests.[5] There is evidence that women and girls suffered the brunt of shortages, and in this were no different to females in a number of societies.[6] Death in childbirth may have been higher for women who had been undernourished, and there may have been high peri-natal and infant mortality rates for babies of such women.

---

[1] Bowie 1988, 442.
[2] Cassidy 1989, 43.
[3] Cloke 1989, 39.
[4] Hodges 1982, 143.
[5] Bynum 1987, 190–1.
[6] Cole-Hamilton & Lang 1986, 2, 65.

The Importance of Bread

Bread was the staple food without which 'any table seems empty' (*aelc beod aemtig byþ gesewen*), and 'without bread all food is unpalatable' (*buton hlafe aelc mete to wlaettan byþ gewyrfeð*).[1] This seems to have been the case in England into the last century. Tastes and textures of the 'accompaniments' usually contrast noticeably with the taste, texture and dryness of bread.[2] These are often oily, have ingredients that are dried, fermented, cured, smoked, salted, or are fresh. Fat and salt (sometimes together as butter) were used to flavour the bread, or the relish might very often be fatty meat, butter, or cheese. The preference for fatty foods can be explained by the fact that the assimilation of fats slows the digestive process, and thus delays the recurrence of hunger.[3] Poorer classes probably had access to bread and some accompaniment, or cereal stews if they were unable to make bread, or vegetable stews with some cereal. The rich were likely to have been the only group with the choice to alter the general pattern of 'bread and its accompaniment', elevating the 'accompaniments' to the most important element of a meal.

Securing a Food Supply

Securing a food supply was a constant preoccupation in Anglo-Saxon times. Æthelred's coronation ceremony included a prayer for 'the fatness of the earth, abundance of corn, wine and oil . . . the blessing of the suckling and the womb; with the blessings of grapes and apples . . . By Thy blessing may his land be filled with apples and with fruits . . . from the apples of the eternal hills and from the fruits of the earth and its fullness . . . '.[4] The charm beginning *Erce, Erce,* (Mother Earth, Mother Earth) reflects the closeness of the Anglo-Saxon to his environment – his need to eat what it produced. By sympathetic magic the earth is fed with oil, honey, yeast, milk, holy water and 'part of every plant known by name except ?buckbean' (*ælcre namcyþe wyrte dæl butan glappan*) in order that it will be fertile.[5]

Whereas early sources suggest it was the responsibility of the chief to rule well and justly to ensure the land was fruitful, in the later period the onus was upon the people, and particularly monastics, to live their lives in accordance with moral and spiritual laws to ensure plenty.[6]

Any interruption to routine meant special provision had to be made. While travellers at the beginning of the period would have had to take food with them, they were later provided with food at monasteries and, especially at centres of pilgrimage, trade or administration, were catered for by cookshops as supply developed in answer to demand. In Winchester, a religious and administrative centre, seven cooks were mentioned by name in the survey of c.1100 in addition to Theoderic, the king's cook, and Herbert, the chamberlain's cook.[7]

---

[1] Garmonsway 1978, 36.
[2] Mintz 1985, 11.
[3] McGee 1986, 530.
[4] Turner 1828, III 156.
[5] Cockayne 1851, III.
[6] Sayce 1946.
[7] Barlow et al., 1976, 47, 76, 88, 112, 113, 226, 133.

Conclusion

Those in positions of power were able to do most to ensure an adequate and varied diet: drawing on food rents from different parts of the country, kings and nobles were not at the mercy of local crop failures. The itineraries of the kings of Wessex and Mercia, although not exhaustive, give the impression that the king operated from a number of bases. Later, the estates of King Edward, Queen Edith and Earl Harold were still scattered widely. Certain foods, fish and honey, for example are established as luxuries since the king or chief had first claim on them. By exacting rights in connection with hunting, the king or lord must on occasion have made those whose food supply was not assured, contribute high status food to his own plentiful larder. Cnut recognised the hardship contributing to the royal food supply could occasion, and made contributions voluntary.

The diet of the rich was not limited to what could be produced here. Wine, oil, some species of fish and spices were all imported.[1] The importance of traders in maintaining the status of the rich is indicated by the traders' *wergild*, a large part of which was payable to the king.[2]

Spices would have made dubious meat acceptable, or perhaps they were more commonly used for adding variety to bland and repetitious food. It is possible that the tradition of Mediterranean cookery with its large number of highly-seasoned sauces as evinced by Apicius, was not evident in England until after the crusades, although spices were highly valued in Anglo-Saxon England. That they were used sparingly was to do with the cost of a limited commodity. Those without the money to buy spices seem to have made use of native herbs, fruits, and to a lesser extent, flowers as an accompaniment to meat.

At the lower end of the social scale, inability to command a food supply led to diminished status or death. The poorest would have been dependent on charity, which, although enjoined as a Christian duty, could be arbitrary. Some were ready to accept slavery for themselves and their family as an alternative to starvation. It is perhaps not too cynical to suggest that some of the appeal of a religious way of life might have been the likelihood of a regular food supply, although asceticism was recognised as a sign of sanctity. There is evidence that monastic establishments were concerned that their numbers should not outstrip their food resources.

A number of saints have a connection with food provision. Cuthbert provides food for himself and his companions, Wilfred teaches the starving folk of Sussex sea-fishing. The Welsh saints David and Cadog were both sources of plenty.[3] Food is a powerful source of imagery for religious writers. Ædiwald writing to Aldhelm at the beginning of the eighth century begins an extended metaphor by saying that Aldhelm 'has nourished him . . . strengthened him with the more delicate food of his industry . . . '.[4]

---

[1] Hodges 1982, 54.
[2] op. cit.
[3] Davies 1982, 178.
[4] Kylie 1911, 39–40.

Conclusion

Feasting

The ritual of feasting was well established and reflected social status very closely. Only the *hlaford* had access to plentiful food and with this he could repay his retainers. If a *ceorl* had social aspirations, he had to own, *inter alia*, a kitchen, and be able to make provision for his own, and others', retinue. This suggests Chaucer's Franklin: '*It snewed in his hous of mete and drynke*', who was also aspiring to join the ranks of the nobility.[1]

The lord's diet might include beef, mutton, veal, lamb, kid, pork, wild boar, venison, hare, pigeons, fowls, ducks and geese both tame and wild, and other wild birds, and fish (freshwater and sea). These foods might be available in fresh and preserved states. Fruit, nuts, honey, dairy products, cereal food, including wheat bread, and eggs were also likely to be available. If he could, the lord would provide such wildfowl as crane and curlew for a feast, since they indicated his ability to pay for and keep expensive hawks, and the presence of venison and wild boar flesh would indicate that his resources enabled him to maintain a pack of hounds. Since the food value of these prestige foods was outweighed by the food resources that went to keeping hawks and hounds, they were symbolic of the conspicuous consumption that would confirm his power. The admission of strangers to royal feasts without question indicates generosity with food was a virtue as well as a measure of status.

Preferred foods that are 'good to think' in Lévi Strauss's dictum are foods that have a more favourable balance of practical benefits over costs (in the widest sense) than foods that are avoided because they are 'bad to think'. Apparently baffling preferences and avoidances are in fact, quite rational.[2] Privileged groups maintain high standards of nutrition and the possession of food is a source of power. Access to animal foods bestows health and well-being above and beyond mere survival, as meat is a concentrated source of vitamins and minerals – the only source of B12.[3] A higher percentage by weight of cooked meat, poultry, fish or dairy foods consists of protein than plant foods. This protein is also of a higher quality than any vegetable protein the Anglo-Saxons would have had access to, since the ten essential amino acids occur in ratios which make more of them available for use in the human body.[4] Roast meats were highly desirable in cultural terms as well as nutritionally. 'Good' cuts of meat that can be roasted were top of the food hierarchy. Food provided for feasts confirms the popularity of fish, fatty meat, hams, poultry, cheeses, white bread, ale (particularly sweet Welsh, clear or mild), honey (for mead), milk which could be fermented, perhaps for drinking with salt fish as fjøll milk is consumed in Norway and Sweden today or used to make a buttermilk soup with raw eggs and other additions as in Denmark.[5]

References to feasting in the literature are so emotionally loaded as to make one realise that such indulgence in food and drink probably took place against a background of deprivation. Feasting was also a way of reinforcing social bonds,

---

[1] Robinson 1957, 20.
[2] Harris 1986, 15.
[3] op. cit., 22, 35.
[4] op. cit., 31–3.
[5] S. Hawkes & J. M. Hagen, pers. comms.

particularly the loyalty to the death owed by a retainer to his lord. Virtually every band or village society studied by anthropologists expresses a special esteem for animal flesh by using meat to reinforce the social ties that bind campmates and kinsfolk together.[1] Sharing food is known to reduce individual and intragroup tensions and it was the fellowship experienced during such feasting that would unify retainers into a fighting band if need be.[2]

In a situation where long-term planning was difficult, and storage uncertain, there must have been pressure to celebrate times when food was plentiful, and to indulge the gratification of the moment. Such a feeling would be in conflict with the need to eke food out during the winter months and possibly through the following year if the harvest failed. Feasting for poorer groups was more modest and seems to have been regulated by being connected to the completion of agricultural tasks and holy days. The fact that the church enjoined feasting on occasions made it possible to indulge without guilt, and to endure periods of fasting.

Fasting

Fasting was one way in which God could be propitiated.[3] In *Sermo Lupi ad Anglos* reference to the failure to observe fasts and festivals occurs time and again. This failure was seen as in some measure responsible for the state of the country.[4]

Fasting was connected explicitly with charity: the food one saved through restricting intake should be given to the destitute. However, for the poor fasting might have been unescapable, even on Sundays: only he who fasted 'through self-will' (*for his anwylnysse*) was to be excommunicated.[5] It seems likely that the Lenten fast to some extent reflected the non-availability of food, a clear case of making a virtue of necessity. Once again the rich were able to escape the effects of fasting in that they could obtain allowed and acceptable food. Also, if a fast was inflicted as penance, they could pass the fast on to others.

Religious communities found it difficult to make the compromise between allowing food that would provide the necessary calories for labouring work and the necessity of subjugating the body, and particularly sexual appetites, by means of fasting. Adjustments, usually additions, or increased measures, were made to the diet, and this may have reflected the increasing prosperity of religious foundations.[6]

Charity and Hospitality

Montesquieu wrote, 'Luxury is a necessity: if the rich do not waste much of it, the poor will starve'. Much of the food collected for the chief and his retinue may have been given in alms, perhaps as raw ingredients from the heap near the kitchen, or as cooked food.[7] Virtues praised on the rune stones set up to celebrate lords in Viking

[1] Harris 1986, 27.
[2] Marshall 1961, 236.
[3] Bynum 1987, 34–5; Whitelock 1955, 858.
[4] op. cit.
[5] Skeat 1881, *Ash Wednesday* l.4.
[6] Dembinska & van Winter in Fenton & Kisban 1986, 152ff., 612–3.
[7] Fenton 1986, 122.

Conclusion

Age Denmark include generosity with food, and in post-Conquest times the baron's *fole largesce* or excessive generosity was also seen as a virtue, and the post-Conquest English kings had to have a force of bailiffs to keep at bay the crowd who would have seized food between kitchen and hall and pestered guests.[1] Clearly the crowds who gathered outside King Oswald's hall were not without expectations, and Alfred made provision for the entertainment of foreigners. Strangers seem to have been admitted without question to some royal feasts.

Greater Dietary Range and Flexibility

The greater dietary range and flexibility in Anglo-Saxon times when compared with the situation today is striking, and there were a number of reasons for this. Firstly, perishable products were near at hand for most of the population. Offal was widely eaten and would have included a wider range of items than is now considered acceptable. A similar situation pertained to dairy products, with beestings, whey and buttermilk all being consumed. The availability of all these products was seasonal. It is likely that a family with an excess of perishable products, for example blood and offal when a pig was killed, would give some of them away; the recipients were then bound by an obligation to reciprocate when they killed a pig. Thus a number of families received manageable amounts of fresh meat. This is a sensible way to husband resources, and underlines social ties.[2]

Towards the end of the period this situation was beginning to change. Tenemental divisions in Canterbury by 839, renewed activity in ninth-century Winchester and the construction of a wharf in ninth-/early tenth-century London are amongst pointers to the development of an urban society.[3] With the growth of urban development, some consumers were distanced from the sources of production, and only the less perishable supplies would be brought in from outside towns. The situation is indicated by references to tolls, and presumably food bought in towns cost more.

Secondly, there was little standardisation. For example, there would have been a great range of grades of flour, which could contain all the grain, or be sieved and sifted until it was almost white. One cereal was frequently mixed with another, and flour could be more or less contaminated with the dust of querns or millstones, and chemically with the alkaloids of ergot, and the seeds of corncockle or other weed seeds that could not be easily sieved or picked out. Both grain and flour could have been contaminated during storage by rodents or insects. Baking was attended by some risks, and some batches of bread would fail to rise.

Processing was necessary to preserve surpluses. Milk, from sheep as well as cows, was converted into butter and cheese, both of which will keep longer than milk. While the poor probably ate green cheese, the rich could afford to wait and enjoy matured cheese, even blue cheese. Preservation of meat and fish was also necessary, and salting, smoking and wind-drying were effective methods, but different local circumstances and varying conditions from year to year would have resulted in different flavours. Food was not uniformly fresh or well-preserved, and there is evidence that it was eaten in what would now be an unacceptably 'high' state.

[1] Roesdahl 1982, 27; Holmes 1952, 257, 37.
[2] Yoder in Fenton & Owen 1981, 413.
[3] Hodges 1986, 152.

Thirdly, a much wider range of plants, birds and animals was eaten than now. This was in part because they were at hand, whereas now some of the animals and birds (the wild boar, bear, crane, etc.), are extinct in this country, and may have been getting scarcer and therefore have become prestige items for feasts during the Anglo-Saxon period. A number of plants which we think of as inedible are not only eatable, but rich in vitamins and minerals.[1] Gerard mentions more than thirty salad herbs as being in use in the sixteenth century, and some of these, salad burnet and borage, for example, are coming back into fashion.[2] Moreover, plant lore which gave substitutes: nettles for rennet, for example, or ground ivy in the place of hops, has never entirely died out.[3] Some idea of the importance of gathering wild produce and the weight of tradition attached to this, is suggested by modern law. This allows the gathering of wild fruit and vegetables under the 1968 Theft Act.[4] However, one item of diet – horse – had to be relinquished during the period because of religious pressure.

Seasonal variation would have been apparent, particularly in relation to plants, which would not have been available during the winter, apart from one or two exceptions like colewort and leeks. The tender shoots of spring would give way to the much more siliceous, and in the case of bracken, poisonous, mature leaves. A summer diet: bread, milk, curds, butter, vegetables, for example, might give way to a winter diet of bread, butter, cheese, salt meat, dried peas and beans.[5] If fish was part of the diet, then the varieties available changed with the seasons. Wildfowl were more likely to be trapped in winter. The dates for which game is in season may reflect Anglo-Saxon customs. The rhythm of the agricultural year governed not only what food was eaten, but the times of day at which meals were taken.[6]

Regional variation was probably an important factor. Nearness to the sea would mean fresh fish and shellfish could be added to the diet. Closeness to a river could mean the addition of fish, fresh-water mussels and eels. Dairying based on cattle became established in the south-west.

Natural circumstances imposed variation on meals, but so did the church. It decreed periods and days of fasting and feasting which were closely regulated and therefore probably observed by most people. Feast-day and fast-day meals were different in kind as well as quantity.

There was no such thing as a standard water supply: water varied with its source. In turn this would affect the drinks brewed. Moreover, each region had its characteristic yeasts which infected ale or wine spontaneously, and were then passed on from batch to batch.[7] Drinks were probably made not only from malted barley, but from other cereals. Oats were used until recently in Scotland.[8] Whey from butter- or cheese-making would also have been drunk, and that too could be left to ferment. Fruit-based drinks would vary from year to year, as they do now, but probably differences were even more marked in Anglo-Saxon England.

---

[1] Harris 1961, passim; Ayrton 1975, 304; Monk 1977, 124, 131.
[2] Ayrton 1975, 304.
[3] Monk 1977, 124, 131.
[4] Section 4.2.
[5] Fenton & Owen 1981, 161.
[6] op. cit., 162.
[7] McGee 1986, 434.
[8] McNeill 1963.

Finally, necessity resulted in people eating what was not normally considered food. Cereal flour was bulked out with ground peas, beans or acorns. Grass and the bark of trees may in fact have had some nutritive value, but these foods were not resorted to if there were more palatable alternatives available.

Nutrition

It is difficult to arrive at any definite conclusions as to how nutritious was the Anglo-Saxon diet. Certainly crops were organically grown, and free from pesticide residues. It was thought that the protein content of wheat may have been higher than in modern varieties, but in fact this would have depended on the ground being sufficiently manured, since this is the factor which largely determines protein content.[1] What we know of the composition of meals: meat with vegetables or cereal products, suggests the Anglo-Saxons were aware empirically that such combinations were more satisfying without realising the scientific explanation – that these made available a greater proportion of the protein in the foods. The preference for white, leavened bread also made nutritional sense in that the effect of phytic acid, present in the outer layer of the grain, which prevented the absorption of essential minerals (iron, zinc and calcium) was lessened.[2] Certainly wheat bread was preferred, since it will rise more than other breads, and in consequence, be lighter.

Fermented drinks were especially valuable. Yeast cells synthesize proteins and vitamins as they grow, and make a fruit juice or cereal mash much more nutritious. Today yeast cells tend to be skimmed or filtered out, but these beverages when consumed 'whole' or 'live' are a valuable part of the diet.[3] Liquid intake was probably higher because of the consumption of items preserved by salting.

Relatively small amounts of milk, butter or cheese (3–4 oz. daily) will supply the recommended daily allowance of calcium, which is also present in significant qualities in oysters and some greens.[4]

A lack of fresh vegetables may have meant that some of the population were in a pre-ascorbutic condition by the spring of some years; others may actually have suffered from scurvy. The Lent *ratten* described in leechdoms suggests scorbutic sores. Lack of vitamin C may also have disposed individuals specifically to leprosy. Because of a general lack of hygiene, it seems likely that many people ingested the ova of parasitic worms, which made their own demands on the food consumed by their host. Teeth seem to have been at risk from stone dust in flour, tougher meat and vegetables as well as less inhibited table manners. There is direct archaeological evidence of this kind of damage, and the presence of beaver teeth in late pagan Anglo-Saxon graves may be related to encouraging the growth of strong teeth.[5]

In bad years a lack of adequate food caused a number of deaths, but it seems likely that a proportion of the population was perpetually undernourished and therefore able to work at less than optimum efficiency, as well as being more susceptible to disease. In some

[1] Ucko & Dimbleby 1971, 80; Dr. J. Graham, pers. comm.
[2] McGee 1986, 284; Weicholt 1987, 53–7.
[3] McGee 1986, 437.
[4] op. cit., 546.
[5] Meaney 1981, 136–7.

monasteries, *The Rule of Chrodegang* seems to imply, food might be short, and rations vary according to the harvest. Probably those well-endowed monasteries, where hygiene was better, would offer the members of their communities a healthier than average life.

In general the rich had a good diet of some variety. Æthelgifu's will from the end of the tenth century allows us to reconstruct her establishments, and we see that she would have had access to quantities of meat from domestic animals, including cattle reared specifically for beef. She had a dairy which provided her with cheese, from her sheep or cattle. She was provided with wine and ale, honey and fish, as well as cereal products.[1]

The poor probably had a monotonous and inadequate diet. Unfortunately records of the diet of the poor are lacking, but although *Piers Plowman* was not written until the fourteenth century, Piers' lament probably echoes his Anglo-Saxon forebears:

> *I haue no peny . . . poletes forto bigge,*
> *Ne neyther gees ne grys but teo grene cheses,*
> *A fewe cruddes and creem and an hauer cake,*
> *And two loues of benes and bran ybake for my fauntis.*
> *And yet I sey, by my soule I haue no salt bacoun,*
> *Ne no kokeney, by cryst, coloppes forto maken.*
> *Ac I haue percil and porettes and many kole-plantes,*
> *And eke a cow and a calf . . .*
>
> *And bi þis lyflode we mot lyue til lammasse tyme;*
> *And bi þat, i hope to haue heurest in my croft;*
> *And þanne may I digte þi dyner as me dere liketh.*

I have no money to buy pullets, no geese or pigs, only two fresh cheeses, a few curds and cream and an oatcake and two loaves of beans and bran baked for my children. I have no bacon or eggs by Christ, but I have parsley and leeks and many cabbages and also a cow and a calf . . . and I must sustain myself on this fare till Lammas when I hope to have harvest in my barn, and then I can have the kind of meal I like.[2]

It was the cereal addition that was desired, and that the church celebrated Lammas (*hlaf-maesse*) as a festival underlines the importance of bread. Piers was probably better provided than some, whose diet may have resembled that within the living memory of an old Cornish woman: 'When the meat's short we puts plenty of pot herbs (carrots, onions, turnips) . . . and when the pot herbs is short we puts plenty of salt. Salt and water's never short round these parts'.[3] Over the centuries the stand-by of the poor seems likely to have been the open fire and one pot.

Incidentals may have contributed to the nutrition of the rich. Most people can actually benefit from additional dietary iron; iron deficiency is the commonest form of malnutrition in the USA today.[4] Cooking acidic foods in cast iron pots, which were more likely to be possessions of the wealthy, multiplies the iron content of food by a

---

[1] Whitelock 1968.
[2] Skeat 1879, 77.
[3] Ayrton 1975, 311.
[4] McGee 1986, 623.

factor of thirty to a hundred.[1] On the other hand, if the brazen pots they possessed were for cooking, the ingestion of copper may have been damaging to health.

Food as a Medium of Exchange

Towards the end of the period food seems to have decreased in importance as a medium of exchange. A currency had been established and was more or less strictly controlled. *IV 6 Æthelred*, repeating earlier codes, stated that 'no-one shall refuse pure money of the proper weight, in whatever town in my kingdom it be coined, under pain of incurring the fine for insubordination'. Ælfric Bata wrote, 'A wise man chooses gold or silver as he can buy anything with it'. Landowners bought out the king's right to food rents for considerable sums. Food rents were sometimes commuted to payments in honey and money, honey having in common with money the quality of being valuable in proportion to its bulk, and that it does not deteriorate with keeping over a number of years. However, the payment of agricultural specialists was in kind, in such quantities that some foodstuffs must have been bartered. Harvest rations continued to be supplied into the nineteenth century, and at court payment in food – two meals a day at the king's table, bread and wine – for some officials continued at least until the end of Henry I's reign.[2]

Table-Manners

It is apparent that the knife was used almost exclusively at table, and that eating from communal plates and using a communal wine jug was standard practice.[3] It seems to have been considered politic to bless food, by making the sign of the cross over it, in the Christian era. Grace was said before meals in monasteries and visiting ecclesiastics to a secular meal seem to have said grace and blessed the food.

Comparisons and Contrasts

There are some elements of Anglo-Saxon food and drink that are familiar to us: meat and two vegetables, meat with fruit sauces, green salads with onions, garlic, oil, vinegar and salt dressing. Candle-lit dinners, with imported glassware, wines, exotic foods, fine table-linen and silver tableware are still occasions for impressing guests. Feasts were occasions for escaping the concerns of everyday life:

> lyt him geþenceð
> seþe him wines glaed wilna bruceð
> siteð him symbelgal siþ ne bemurneð
> hu him aefter þisse worulde weordan mote

he little thinks, gladdened with wine, enjoying pleasures, flushed at the feast, what must become of him after this life.[4]

References to the fertility of the earth, particularly after the winter, a time of scarcity, are heartfelt and lyrical: 'The noble field flourishes under the heavens, blooming with

---

[1] op. cit., 548.
[2] Douglas & Greenaway 1953, 422.
[3] Freeman 1970, 192.
[4] Mackie 1934, *The Day of Judgement*.

delights' (*Se aeðela feld wripað under wolcum, wynnum geblowen*); 'he saw blossoming groves adorned with flowers' (*geseh he geblowene bearwas blaedum gehrodene*).[1]

There were those who mourned the passing of feasts, and good fellowship in the meadhall, but there were those for whom heaven would be the only 'dwelling place of plenty'.[2] Anglo-Saxons were only too aware on a personal level of the importance of food as 'a primary and recurrent want', recognising more acutely than their descendants that 'our transitory life is sustained by food' (*Ure hwilendlice lif biþ mid mettum gefercod*).[3]

---

[1] Jackson 1971, 129; Bosworth & Toller 1898, 402.
[2] Jackson 1971, 251.
[3] Richards 1932, 1; Bosworth & Toller 1898, 391.

Bibliography

Addyman, P. 1973 Late Saxon Settlements in the St Neots Area *Proc. Camb. Antiquarian Soc.* LXIV 45–99.

Agricultural Research Council: *Institutes and Units of the Agricultural Research Service* n.d.

Alcock, L. 1987 *Economy, Society & Warfare among the Britons & Saxons* Cardiff.

Allen Brown, R. 1985 ed. *Anglo-Norman Studies VIII: Proceedings of the Battle Conference* The Boydell Press.

Arnold, C. J. 1984 *Roman Britain to Saxon England* Croom Helm.

Arrhenius, B. 1985 Chemical analyses of Organic Remains in Archaeological Contexts *ISKOS* 5 339–343.

Ascardi, G. & Nemeskeri, J. 1970 *History of Human Lifespan & Mortality* Budapest.

Ashley, Sir W. 1928 *The Bread of our Forefathers* Oxford.

Aston, M. 1988 *Medieval Fish, Fisheries & Fishponds in England Part ii* BAR British Series 182 (ii).

Attenborough, F. L. 1922 *Laws of the Earliest English Kings* Cambridge.

Austin, Thomas 1888 *Two Fifteenth-Century Cookery Books* EETS reprinted 1964.

Ayrton, E. 1975 *The Cookery of England* Book Club Associates/Andre Deutsch.

Bachrach, B. S. in Allen Brown 1985 Some observations on the military administration of the Norman Conquest 1–25.

Bailey, R. N. 1980 *Viking Age Sculpture in England* Collins 1980.

Baillie, M. 1981 Dendro-chronology: the Irish view & Horizontal Mills *Current Archaeology* Vol. 7 No. 2 August 1980, Mag. No. 73 61–3.

Bammesberger, A. 1985 ed. *Problems of OE Lexicography: Studies in Memory of Angus Cameron* Regensburg.

Banham, D. 1990 *Anglo-Saxon Food Plants* University of Cambridge Ph.D. thesis.

Banham, D. 1991 *Monasteriales Indicia* Anglo-Saxon Books.

Barlow, F., Bidden, M., von Feilitzen, O., Keen, D. J. 1976 *Winchester in the Early Middle Ages: an edition & discussion of the Winton Domesday* Winchester Studies 1 ed. M. Biddle Oxford.

Barton, F. T. 1912 *Cattle, Sheep and Pigs: their practical breeding and keeping* London.

Barton Lodge, Rev. 1872, 1879 *Palladius, On Husbondrie* EETS

Battiscombe G 1949 *English Picnics* Harvill Press London.

Beasley, Brown & Legge 1987 Ageing cattle by their teeth *Ark* January 22–25.

Bell, M. 1977 Excavations at Bishopstone, Sussex. *Sussex Archaeol. Collections* Vol. 115.

Bencard, M. 1984 ed. *Ribe Excavations 1970–6* Vol. 2 Esbjerg.

Bennett, R. & Elton, J. 1899 *History of Corn Milling* Vol II London.

Biddick, K. 1984 ed. *Archaeological Approaches to Medieval Europe* Kalamazoo.

Bingham, S. 1977 *Dictionary of Nutrition* Barrie & Jenkins.

Bishop, S. n.d. Bishophill *Interim* Vol. 2 No. 2 14–16.

Blackburn, M. A. S. 1986 ed. *Anglo-Saxon Monetary History: Essays in memory of Michael Dolley* Leicester Univ. Press.

Bland, A. E., Brown, P. A., Tawney, R. H. 1914 *English Economic History – Select Documents* G. Bell & Sons London.

Bloch, M. 1961 *Feudal Society* Routledge & Kegan Paul.

Bonser, W. 1963 *The Medical Background of Anglo-Saxon England* Wellcome Historical Medical Library.

Boorde, A. 1542 *A Compendyous Regyment or a Dyetary of Helth* R. Wyre for John Goughe London.

Bosworth, J. and Toller, T. Northcote 1898 An *Anglo-Saxon Dictionary* (I) and *Supplements* (II) OUP.

Bourdillon, J. 1980 Town Life & Animal Husbandry in the Southampton Area *Proc. Hants. Field Club & Archaeol. Soc.* 36 181–191.

Bibliography

Bourdillon, J. & Coy, J. 1980 (in Holdsworth 1980) *Statistical Appendix to Accompany the Animal Bone Report on Material from Melbourne Street*

Bowie, S. H. U. 1988 December Cattle for Calf raising *Ark* 442.

Brett, G. 1968 *Dinner is Served* Rupert Hart-Davis.

Brillat-Savarin, J.-A. 1970 *The Philosopher in the Kitchen* Penguin.

Brinklow, D. 1979 Sites Review: Walmgate *Interim* Vol. 6 No. 2 YAT 27–32.

British Ornithologists' Union 1971 *The Status of Birds in Britain & Ireland* Blackwell Scientific Pubs.

Brøndsted, J. 1940 *Danmarks Oldtid* Copenhagen.

Brooks, C. 1980 Pot Spot: Torksey Ware *Interim* Vol. 6 No. 4 YAT 39–42.

Brothwell, D. & P. 1969 *Food in Antiquity* Thames & Hudson.

Brothwell, D. & Higgs, E. eds. 1963 *Science in Archaeology* Thames & Hudson.

Brown, L. 1987 *Three Course Newsletter* No. 4 March.

Bruce-Mitford, R. 1975 ed. *Recent Archaeological Excavations in Europe* Routledge & Kegan Paul.

Bruce-Mitford, R. 1983 *The Sutton Hoo Ship Burial* British Museum Publications Vol. 3 i & ii ed. A. Care Evans.

Buckland, P. C., Holdsworth, P. and Monk, M. 1976 The Interpretation of a Group of Saxon Pits in Southampton *Jour. Archaeol. Science* 3 61–9.

Bullough, D. 1984 in L. Fenske et al. *Institutionem, Kultur & Gesellshaft in Mittelalter* Sigmaringen Albuinus deliciosus Karoli regis 73–92.

Burnet, Sir Macfarlane & White, D. O. 1972 *Natural History of Infectious Disease* CUP.

Bynum, C. W. 1987 *Holy Feast & Holy Fast: the religious significance of food to medieval women* Univ. California.

Cameron, K. ed. 1975 *Place-name evidence for the Anglo-Saxon Invasions & Scandinavian Settlements* English Place Name Soc.

Cameron, K. 1985 *Place-Names of Lincolnshire* Part 1 English Place-Name Soc.

Campbell, J. 1962 ed. *Chronicle of Æthelweard* Nelson.

Carter & West see East Anglian Archaeology Report 1980.

Cassidy, P. 1989 Food for thought *Ark* April 115; What, How Many, Where & Why June 195.

Casteel, R. W. *Estimation of size . . . by means of fish scales* in Clason, A. T. 70–86.

Chaplin, R. E. 1971 *The Study of Animal Bones from Archaeological Sites* Seminar Press London & New York

Chapman, N. & D. 1970 *Fallow Deer* British Deer Soc.

Clair, C. 1964 *Kitchen and Table* Abelard-Schuman.

Clarke, H. & Carter, A. 1977 *Excavations in Kings Lynn 1963–1970* Society for Medieval Archaeology Series Monograph 7.

Clarke, H. (1986–7) in A. Williams, ed. Agriculture in Late Anglo-Saxon England.

Clarke Hall, J. R. 1950 *Beowulf & the Finnsburgh Fragment* 3rd ed. Allen & Unwin.

Clason, A. T. 1975 ed. *Archaeozoological Studies* North Holland Publishing Co. Amsterdam.

Clemoes, P. & Hughes, K. 1971 *England before the Conquest* CUP.

Clemoes, P. 1972 *Anglo-Saxon England* I CUP.

Clifton, C. 1983 *Edible Flowers* Bodley Head London.

Cockayne, O. 1851 *Leechdoms, Starcraft & Wortcunning* I–III Rolls Series reprint 1961 Holland Press.
Re: *Lacnunga*. Roman numerals refer to Bonser's numbering.

Cole-Hamilton, I. & Lang, T. 1986 *Tightening Belts: A Report on the Impact of Poverty on Food* London Food Commission.

Coles, J. M. & Simpson, D. 1968 *Studies in Ancient Europe presented to Stuart Piggott* Leicester University Press.

Colgrave, B. 1940 *Life of St Cuthbert, Anon. Life of St Cuthbert* CUP.

Commissioners 1819 *Reports from the Commissioners...respecting the Public Records of the Kingdom 1800–19.*

Connor, R. D. 1987 *The Weights & Measures of England* HMSO.

Constable, G. 1964 *Monastic Tithes from their Origins to the Twelfth Century* CUP.

Copley, G. J. 1958 *An Archaeology of SE England* Phoenix House London.

Bibliography

Corran, H. S. 1975 *A History of Brewing* David & Charles.

Cox, Charles J. 1905 *The Royal Forests of England* Methuen & Co.

Crane, Eva 1983 *The Archaeology of Bee-Keeping* Duckworth.

Crabtree, P. 1984 *Studies in Medieval Culture* XIII The Archaeozoology of the Anglo-Saxon Site at West Stow, Suffolk 223–235.

Cramp, R. 1984 *Corpus of Anglo-Saxon Stone Sculpture* Vol.1 OUP.

Creighton, C. A. 1891 *History of Epidemics in England* Two vols. CUP reprinted 1965.

Crossley, D. W. 1981 *Medieval Industry* CBA Report No. 40.

Cunliffe, B. 1964 *Winchester Excavations* 1949–60 Vol. 1 City of Winchester Museums & Libraries Committee.

Cunliffe, B. 1976 *Excavations at Porchester Castle* Vol. II Saxon Soc. of Antiquaries of London Reports of Research Committee 33.

Darby, H. C. 1940 *The Medieval Fenland* David & Charles.

Darby, H. C. & Terrett, I. B. 1954 *The Domesday Geography of Midland England* CUP.

David, E. 1960 *French Provincial Cooking* Penguin.

David, E. 1977 *English Bread & Yeast Cookery* Penguin.

Davies, S. M. 1980 Old Down Farm, Andover Part I *Proceedings of the Hants. Field Club and Archaeol. Soc.* 36 161–180.

Davies, W. 1982 *Wales in the Early Middle Ages* Leicester Univ. Press.

Davison, B. K. 1977 Excavations at Sulgrave, Northants. 1960–76 *Archaeol. Journal* CXXXIV 105–114.

Deegan, Marilyn 1986 '...sing a chant against a curly worm' *Popular Archaeology* Feb. 1986 16–21.

De Vriend, H. J. 1984 The *OE Herbarium & Medicina de Quadrupedibus* EETS.

Dickens, J. S. W. & Mantle, P. G. 1974 *Ergot of Cereals & Grasses* MAFF Advisory Leaflet.

Dimbleby, G. W. 1967 *Plants & Archaeology* John Baker.

Dix, J. draft (in Bedford Museum) *Wells at Harrold and Odell, Beds.*

Dix, J. 1981 *Saxon wells near Harrold* Beds. Mag Vol. 18 No. 138 69–71.

Dodwell, C. R. 1982 *Anglo-Saxon Art: a new perspective* Manchester Univ. Press.

Dony, J. G. 1974 *English Names of Wild Flowers* Butterworth.

Douglas, D. C. & Greenaway, G. W. 1953 *English Historical Documents 1042–1189* Eyre & Spottiswoode.

Drummond, J. & Wilbraham, A. 1958 rev. edn. of:

Drummond, Sir J. & Wilbraham, A. 1939 *The Englishman's Food* Jonathan Cape.

Duncan, P. & Acton, B. 1967 *Progressive Winemaking* The Amateur Winemaker.

Dunning, G. C., Hurst, J. G., Myres, J. N. L. & Tischler, F. 1959 *Anglo-Saxon Pottery: A Symposium* CBA Research Report 4 (reprinted from *Medieval Archaeology* III).

Dyer, A. 1984 What to Read on Medical History *The Local Historian* Vol. 16 No. 1 Feb. 1984.

Earle, J. 1884 *Anglo-Saxon Literature* Soc. for Promoting Christian Knowledge.

East Anglian Archaeology Report 1980 No. 9. ed. Carter & West Norfolk Museums Service, Gressenhall.

Eckwall, E. 1960 *The Concise Oxford Dictionary of English Place-Names* Oxford.

Edlin, H. L. 1949 *Woodland Crafts in Britain* Batsford.

Elliott, R. M. W. 1963 rep. *Runes* Manchester Univ. Press.

Ellis Davidson, H. R. 1964 *Gods & Myths of Northern Europe* Penguin.

Ellis Davidson, H. R. & Webster, L. 1967 The Anglo-Saxon Burial at Coombe (*Woodnesborough*) Kent *Medieval Archaeology* 1967 II 1–41.

Erlichman, J. 1986 *Gluttons for Punishment* Penguin.

Evans, G. Ewart 1960 *The Horse in the Furrow* Faber.

Evans, G. Ewart 1969 *The Farm & the Village* Faber.

Evershed, R. P. et al 1991 Epicuticular wax components preserved in potsherds as chemical indicators of leafy vegetables in ancient diets *Antiquity 65* 540–44.

Evison, V. I. 1981 *Angles, Saxons & Jutes* Oxford.

Evison, V. 1987 *Dover: the Buckland Anglo-Saxon Cemetery* Hist. Buildings & Monuments Comm. for England Archaeol. Report No. 3.

Eydoux, H.-P. 1966 *The Buried Past* Weidenfeld & Nicolson.

Bibliography

Fell, Christine 1974 *OE Beor Leeds Studies in English New Series* Vol. VIII 76–95.

Fell, Christine 1981 A note on OE Wine Terminology: the Problem of *Cæren Nottingham Medieval Studies* 1–12.

Fell et al. 1983 (C. Fell, P. Foote, J. Graham-Campbell, R. Thomson, eds.) *The Viking Age in the Isle of Man* UCL London.

Fell, Christine 1984 *Women in Anglo-Saxon England and the impact of 1066* with contributions by Cecily Clark & Elizabeth Williams Colonnade Books.

Fenton, A. & Kisban 1986 *Food in Change: Eating Habits from the Middle Ages to the Present Day* John Donald with National Museums of Scotland.

Fenton, A. & Owen, T. M. 1981 eds. *Food in Perspective* Edinburgh.

Fenwick, V. 1978 *The Graveney Boat: a tenth-century find from Kent* BAR British Series 53.

Field, J. 1972 *English Field Names: A Dictionary* David & Charles.

Finberg, H. P. R. 1972 *The Early Charters of the West Midlands* Leicester Univ. Press.

Flower, B. & Rosenbaum, E. 1958 *Apicius, A Roman Cookery Book* Harrap.

Foley, W. 1974 *A Child in the Forest* BBC Publications

Foote, P. G. & Wilson, D. M. 1970 *The Viking Achievement* Sidgwick & Jackson.

Fowler, P. J. 1981 Farming in the Anglo-Saxon landscape: an archaeologist's review *Anglo-Saxon England* No. 9 263–80 CUP.

Fowler, R. W. 1972 *Wulfstan's Canons of Edgar* EETS.

Fox, C. 1948 *The Archaeology of the Cambridge Region* (with supplement) Cambridge.

Fraser, H. M. 1931 *Bee-Keeping in Antiquity* London.

Fraser 1955 rev. edn of above.

Fream, W. 1932 *Elements of Agriculture* John Murray.

Freeman, S. T. 1970 *Neighbors: The Social Contract in a Castilian Hamlet* Univ. Chicago Press.

Furnivall, F. J. *Early English Meals & Manners* 1868 London.

Gaimster, D.R.M., Margeson, S. & Hurley M., Medieval Britain & Ireland in 1989 in *Medieval Archaeology* XXXIV 1990.

Gair, R. & Lee, J. E. 1978 *Cereal Pests & Diseases* Farming Press Ltd.

Garmonsway, G. N. 1978 *Aelfric's Colloquy* Univ. of Exeter.

Garmonsway, G. N. 1953 *Anglo-Saxon Chronicle* J. M. Dent & Sons.

Gelling, M. 1979 *The Early Charters of the Thames Valley* Leicester Univ. Press.

Gerard, J. 1597 *The Herball or Generall Historie of Plants* London.

Godwin, H. The Ancient Cultivation of Hemp *Antiquity* XLI Part 161 42–49.

Gollancz, I. see Mackie.

Good, G. L., Jones, R. H. & Ponsford, M. W. eds. 1991 Waterfront Archaeology. Proceedings of the third international conference on waterfront archaeology held at Bristol, 23–26 September 1988.

Goodwin, C. W. 1848 *The Anglo-Saxon Version of the Life of St Guthlac, Hermit of Crowland* John Russell Smith.

Gordon, I. L. 1960 ed. *The Seafarer* Methuen OE Texts.

Graham-Campbell, J. & Kidd, D. 1980 *The Vikings* BM Publications.

Graham-Campbell, J. 1980 *Viking Artefacts: a select catalogue* BM Publications.

Grant, Annie 1974 (unpub.) *Excavations at St John's, Bedford* (Bedford Museum).

Grant, M. 1996 *Anthimus, On the Observation of Foods*, Prospect Books, Blacktawton.

Grattan, J. H. G. & Singer, C. 1952 *Anglo-Saxon Magic & Medicine* London.

Green, F. J. 1975 Plant Remains in Excavations at Westgate St., Gloucester *Medieval Archaeology* Vol. 23 186–90.

Green, F. J. 1979 Ed. Collection & Interpretation of Botanical Information from medieval urban excavations in Southern England in *Festschrift Maria Hopf Archaeophysika* Vol. 8 35–55.

Gregory, V. L. 1974 Excavations at Becket's Barn, Pagham, W. Sussex *Sussex Archaeological Collection* 114 207–17.

Grigson 1984 ed. *Five Hundred Points of Good Husbandry: Thomas Tusser* OUP.

Groundes-Peace, Z. 1971 *Mrs Groundes-Peace's Old Cookery Notebook* David & Charles.

Grübe, F. W. 1934 Cereal Foods of the Anglo-Saxons *Philological Quarterly* XIII 1934 140–158.

Hall, A. 1981, The cockle of rebellion... *Interim* Vol. 8 No. 1 5–8 YAT.

Bibliography

Hall, A. R. & Kenward, H. K. 1982 *Environmental Archaeology in the Urban Context* CBA Research Report 43.

Hall, A. R., Kenward, H. K., WIlliams, D., Greig 1983 JAR *The Archaeol. of York Vol. 14* Fasc. 4 *The Past Environment of York* CBA for YAT.

Hall, R. 1979, Sites Review: Coppergate *Interim* Vol. 6 No. 2 9–17 YAT.

Hall, R. 1982, Sites Review: Coppergate *Interim* Vol. 8 No. 2 16–24 YAT.

Hall, S. 1989 Running Wild *Ark* January 12–15.

Hamilton, N. E. S. A. 1870 ed. William of Malmesbury *De Gestis Pontificum Anglorum* iv Rolls Series.

Harcourt, R. A. 1974 The Dog in Prehistoric & Early Historic Britain *Journal of Archaeological Science* Vol.1. Part 1 151–175 .

Harmer, F. E. 1952 *Anglo-Saxon Writs* Manchester Univ. Press.

Harris, B. 1961, *Eat the Weeds* Keats Publishing Corp. New Caanan Conn.

Harris, B. E. 1987 *The Great Roll of the Pipe for the fourth year of the reign of Henry III* Pipe Roll Soc.

Harris, M. 1986 *Good to eat: riddles of food and culture* Allen & Unwin.

Hart, C. R. 1975 *The Early Charters of Northern England and the N. Midlands* Leicester Univ. Press.

Hartley, Dorothy 1954, *Food in England* Macdonald.

Hartley, Dorothy 1978 *Water in England* Macdonald & Jane's.

Harvey, J. 1981 *Medieval Gardens* Batsford.

Haslam, J. 1980 with L. Biek & R. F. Tylecote et al. A Middle Saxon Iron Smelting site at Ramsbury, Wilts . *Medieval Archaeology* XXIV 1–68.

Haslam, J. 1984 ed. *Anglo-Saxon Towns in Southern England* Phillimore.

Hawkes, S. C., Campbell, J., Brown, D. eds. 1985 *Anglo-Saxon Studies in Archaeology & History* No. 4 Oxford see Matthews & Hawkes.

Heighway, C. M., Garrod, A. P., & Vince, A. G. 1975 The Plant Remains in Excavations at Westgate, Gloucester *Medieval Archaeology* XXIII 186–90.

Helbaek, H. 1959 Comment on *Chenopodium Album* as a Food Plant in Prehistory *Berichte Geobotanischen Institues Der Eidgenossischen Technischen Hochschule Stiftung Rubel* Vol. 31 16–19.

Henderson, P. 1959 ed. *The Poems of John Skelton* Dent London.

Henel, H. ed. 1970 reprint Aelfric's *De Temporibus Anni* EETS.

Henson, Elizabeth 1982 *Rare Breeds in History* RBST.

Herzfeld, G. 1900 *An Old English Martyrology* EETS.

Hickin, N. E. 1964 *Household Pests* Hutchinson.

Hieatt, C. B. 1980 The Roast, or Boiled, Beef of Old England *Book Forum* 5 294–99

Hieatt, C. B. & Butler, S. 1985 *Curye on Inglisch* EETS.

Hieatt, C. B. & Jones R. F. 1986 Two Anglo-Norman Culinary Collections ed. from BL MSS Addit. 32085 & Royal 12.C.xii *Speculum* 61/4 859–882.

Higgs, E. S. & White, Peter J. 1963 Autumn Killing *Antiquity* Vol. 37 282–9.

Hill, David 1981 *An Atlas of Anglo-Saxon England* Blackwell.

Hill, J. 1939 *Wild Foods of Britain* Adam & Charles Black London.

Hills, M. 1988 *Curing Illness the Drug-Free Way* Sheldon Press.

Hinde, T. 1985 *The Domesday Book, England's Heritage Then & Now* Hutchinson.

Hindle, B. P. 1982 *Medieval Roads* Shire Archaeology.

Hobhouse, H. 1985 *Seeds of Change* Sidgwick & Jackson.

Hodges, R. 1982 *Dark Age Economics: the Origins of Towns & Trade* Duckworth.

Hodges, R. & Hobley, B. eds. *The Rebirth of Towns in the West AD700-1050*, CBA Research Report 68 CBA 1988.

Hodgson, P. 1960 *The Franklin's Tale* CUP.

Holdsworth, Jane n.d. Pot Spot: Tating Ware *Interim* Vol. 2 No. 3 36–7.

Holdsworth, P. 1980 *Excavations at Melbourne St., Southampton 1971–76* Published for Southampton Archaeol. Research Comm. by the Council for British Archaeology.

Bibliography

Holdsworth, P. 1981 Hamwih *Current Archaeology* No. 79 Vol.7 No. 8 October 243–249.

Holmes, U. T. Jr. 1952 *Daily Living in the Twelfth Century* Univ. Wisconsin Press.

Hooke, Della 1988 ed. *Anglo-Saxon Settlements*, Blackwell.

Hope-Taylor, B. 1950 Excavations on Farthing Down, Coulsdon, Surry *Archaeological Newsletter* Vol. 2 Part 10 170.

Hope-Taylor, B. 1977 *Yeavering: An Anglo-British centre of early Northumbria* Dept. of the Environment Archaeological Reports No. 7 HMSO.

Howes, F. N. 1948 *Nuts* Faber & Faber.

Huizinga, J. 1970 *Homo Ludens: A Study of the Play Element in Culture* Temple Smith London.

Jackson, K. H. 1969 *The Gododdin* Edinburgh Univ. Press.

Jackson, K. H. 1971 *A Celtic Miscellany* Penguin.

Jaine, T. 1987 ed. *The Barefoot Baker* T. Jaine, Blackawton, Devon.

Jember, G. K. et al. l975 *English-Old English, Old English-English Dictionary* Boulder, Colorado.

Jessen, K. & Helbaek, K. 1944 *Cereals in Great Britain & Ireland in Prehistoric & Early Historic Times* Copenhagen.

Jones, A. 1980 in *East Anglian Archaeology Report No. 9* (North Elmham) ed. Carter & West Norfolk Museums Service, Gressenhall.

Jones, Andrew K. G. undated paper ?1985 *The End Product* York Environmental Archaeology Unit.

Jones, G. 1980 *Eirik the Red and other Icelandic Sagas* OUP.

Jones, G. & Jones, T. 1949 *The Mabinogion* Dent.

Jones, J. 1988 Pridings Farm *Ark* December 430–432.

Jones, M. & Dimbleby, G. W. eds.1981 *The Environment of Man: the Iron Age to the Anglo-Saxon period* British Archaeology Reports British series 87.

Jones, P. E. 1976 *The Butchers of London* Secker & Warburg.

Kemble, J. M. 1843 *Poetry of the Verceeli Codex comprising the Legend of St. Andrew London.*

Kemble, J. M. 1848 *The Dialogue of Salomon & Saturnus* Aelfric Soc.

Kemble, J. M. 1879 *The Saxons in England* London.

Kemp, R. 1986 Pit your 'wics' *Interim* Vol. 11 No. 3 8–16 YAT.

Kenward, H. K. & Hall, A. R. (& Williams, D.) 1982 *The Archaeology of York* Environmental Evidence from Roman deposits at Skeldergate Vol. 14 Fasc. 3 CBA for YAT.

Kenward, H. K. 1990 A skeptical view of the Coppergate 'beehive' *Interim* Vol. 14 No 4 20–24 YAT.

Ker, N. R. 1957 *A Catalogue of Manuscripts containing Anglo-Saxon* OUP.

Knowles, Dom. David 1940 *The Monastic Order in England* 943–1216 OUP.

Kuper, J. 1977 ed. *The Anthropologist's Cookbook* Routledge & Kegan Paul.

Kylie, E. 1911 *The English Correspondence of St Boniface* Chatto & Windus.

Lamb 1981 Climate from 1000BC to AD1000 in Jones & Dimbleby 1981 53–66.

Lamond, E. 1890 *Walter of Henley's Husbandry together with an Anonymous Husbandry, Seneschaucie & Robert Grosseteste's Rules* Longmans, Green & Co.

Langdon, J. 1986 *Horses, Oxen & Technological Innovation* CUP.

Lappe, F. Moore 1971 *Diet for a Small Planet* Ballantine Books.

Lauwerier, R. C. G. M. 1986 The Role of meat in the Roman diet *Endeavour* New Series Vol. 10 No.1 208–212.

Laver, H. 1916 *The Colchester Oyster Fishery* Colne Fishery Board.

Le Roy Ladurie, E. 1978 *Montaillou* Penguin.

Leslie, R. F. 1966 *The Wanderer* Manchester Univ. Press.

Lester, R. *The Fruitful Interaction: the Food Producer & the Engineer* 62nd Thomas Hawksley Lecture for the Institution of Mechanical Engineers.

Lethbridge, T. C. 1936 A Cemetery at Shudy Camps, Cambs. *Proc. Camb. Antiquarian Soc. xxxvi.*

Lethbridge, T. C. & Tebbutt, C. F. 1933 Huts of the Anglo-Saxon period *Proc. Camb. Antiquarian Soc. xxxiii* 133–51.

Lever, C. 1977 *The Naturalised Animals of the British Isles* Hutchinson.

Levison, W. 1946 *England and the Continent in the Eighth Century* Oxford.

Lévi-Strauss, C. 1972 *From Honey to Ashes* Jonathan Cape.

Lévi-Strauss, C. 1973 *Introduction to a Science of Mythology* Vol.3 Jonathan Cape.

Bibliography

Liebermann, F. 1898 *Die Gesetze der Angelsachsen* Vol. 1 Halle.

Lodge, B. & Herrtage, S. J. 1872, 1879, reprint.1973 *Palladius on Husbandrie* EETS.

Logeman, H. 1888 *The Rule of S. Benet* EETS.

Lovell 1988 Barefoot Baker 1 T Jaine Blackawton, Devon.

Lowe, P. R. 1933 The Differential Characters...of *Gallus* & *Phasianus...Ibis* 332–43.

Loyn, H. R. 1970 *Anglo-Saxon England & the Norman Conquest* Longman.

Mabey, R. 1972 *Food for Free* Collins.

Mackie, W. S. 1934 *The Exeter Book* EETS.

Mackie, W. S. & Gollancz I. 1972–3 reprint The Exeter Book EETS.

Mackreth, D. F. n.d. *Saxons in the Nene Valley* Nene Valley Research Committee.

MacNeill, J. T. & Gamer, H. M. 1938 *Medieval Handbooks of Penance* Columbia Univ. Press.

MAFF 1972 rev. *Brucellosis* Advisory Leaflet No. 93.

Magnusson, M. & Palsson, H. 1960 *Njal's Saga* Penguin.

Magnusson, M. & Palsson, H. 1965 *The Vinland Sagas:Graenlendinga Saga and Eirik's Saga* Penguin.

Maltby, J. M. 1979 *Faunal Studies on Urban Sites: The Animal Bones from Exeter 1972–5* Exeter Archaeology Reports No. 2 Univ. of Sheffield.

Marchenay, P. 1979 *L'homme et L'abeille* Berger Levrault Paris.

Margeson, S. 1983 (in Fell et al.) On the iconography of the Manx crosses 95–106.

Marshall, L. 1961 Sharing, Taking and Giving: relief of social tensions among Kung Bushmen *Africa* 31 231–49.

Masefield, G. B., Wallis, M., Harrison, S. G., Nicholson, B. E. 1986 *The Oxford Book of Food Plants* OUP.

Mason, E. 1980 *The Beauchamp Cartulary Charters 1100–1268* Pipe Roll Soc.

Matthews, C. L. R. & Hawkes, S. C. 1985 Early Saxon Settlements & Burials on Puddlehill, Nr. Dunstable, Beds. *Anglo-Saxon Studies in Archaeol. & Hist.* No. 4 59–115.

Mawer, A. and Stenton, F. M. 1969 in collaboration with F. T. S. Houghton *The Place-Names of Worcestershire* CUP.

McArthur, W. P. 1949 The Identification of some pestilences recorded in the Irish Annals *Irish Historical Studies* 6 169–188.

McGee, H. 1986 *On Food and Cooking: The Science and Lore of the Kitchen* Allen & Unwin.

McGraill, S. & Switsur, R. 1979 Log Boats *Medieval Archaeology* XXIII 229–31.

McGregor, A. 1982 Anglo-Scandinavian Finds from Lloyds Bank, Pavement & other sites *The Archaeology of York* Vol. 17 Fasc. 3 CBA for YAT.

McKendry, M. 1973 *Seven Centuries of English Cooking* Weidenfeld & Nicolson.

McNeill, F. Marion 1963 *The Scots Kitchen: its lore and recipes* Blackie.

McNeill, W. H. 1977 *Plagues and Peoples* Basil Blackwell.

Mead, W. 1931 *The English Medieval Feast* Allen & Unwin.

Meaney, A. L. & Chadwick Hawkes, S. 1970 *Two Anglo-Saxon Cemeteries at Winnall, Winchester* Soc. *Medieval Archaeology* Monograph series No.4.

Meaney, A. L. 1981 *Anglo-Saxon Amulets and Curing Stones* BAR 96.

Mellows, W. T. 1980 *The Peterborough Chronicle of Hugh Candidus* Peterborough Museum Soc.

Miles, A. E. N. 1969 The Dentition of the Anglo-Saxons *Proc. Royal Soc. of Medicine* 62 1311–1315.

Miles, A. E. N. 1972 Some morbid skeletal changes in the Anglo-Saxons *British Dental Assoc. J.* 133 309–311.

Miller, T. 1890–1 *OE version Bede's Ecclesiastical History* Vols. I & II EETS.

Miller, W. 1965 *Russia* Newnes.

Min. of Ag. see MAFF.

Mintz, S. 1985 *Sweetness and Power* Elisabeth Sefton Books/Viking.

Mitford, M. 1986 *Our Village* Sidgwick & Jackson London.

Moberg, V. 1973 *A History of the Swedish People* Vol. II Heinemann.

Monk, M. 1977 *The Plant Economy & Agriculture of The Anglo-Saxons in southern Britain with particular reference to the 'mart' settlements of Southampton & Winchester* Univ. of Southampton thesis.

Bibliography

Monson-Fitzjohn, G. 1927 *Drinking Vessels of Bygone Days* Herbert Jenkins.

Morgan, J. 1975 Nutrition: trace element deficiencies *Medical News* June 26 4.

Morris, C. 1983 A late-Anglo-Saxon hoard of iron & copper artefacts from Nazeing, Essex. *Medieval Archaelogy* XXVII 27–39.

Morris, C. 1985 Pole-lathe Turning *Woodworking Crafts Magazine* Issue 16 Aug/Sept/Oct 1985 20–4.

Morris, I. 1990 Surviving with Soays *Ark* XVII, No. 11 Nov. 401–3.

Moryson, F. 1617 *An Intinerary* Vols. I–IV Glasgow 1907.

Moss, P. 1958 *Meals through the Ages* Harrap.

Moulden, J. & Tweddle, D. 1986 Catalogue of the Anglo-Scandinavian sites s.w. of the Ouse *The Archaeology of York* Vol. 8 Fasc. 1 CBA for YAT.

Munby, J. ed.1982 *Domesday Book Vol. 4: Hampshire* Phillimore.

Musty, J. 1969 The Excavation of two barrows, one of Saxon date, at Ford...Wilts. *Antiquaries J.* 49 98–117.

Napier, A. 1916 *The OE Version of the Rule of Chrodegang* EETS.

Nenk, B., Margeson S., Hurley M. Medieval Britain & Ireland in 1990 in *Medieval Archaeology* XXXV 1991.

Nenk, B., Margeson S., Hurley M. Medieval Britain & Ireland in 1990 in *Medieval Archaeology* XXXVI 1992.

Nix, J. 1985 *Farm Management Pocket Book* Wye College, Kent.

Noddle, B. A. 1975 *A Comparison of the Animal Bones from Eight Medieval sites in Southern Britain* in Clason AT 248–260.

Noddle, B A 1977 Animal Bone in *Excavations in Kings Lynn 1963–1970* Clarke, H. and Carter, A. eds. 378–403.

O'Connor, T. P. with Wilkinson, M. 1982 *The Animal Bones from Flaxengate, Lincoln c.870–1500* The Archaeology of Lincoln CBA Vol. XVIII–1.

O'Connor, T. P. 1984 *Selected Groups of Bones from Skeldergate & Walmgate* The Archaeology of York Vol. 15 Fasc. 1 CBA for YAT.

O'Connor, T. P. 1984 Archaeogastronomy *Interim* Vol. 10 No.1 26–7.

O'Connor, T. P. 1985 Shellshock *Interim* Vol. 10 No. 2 29–32.

O'Connor, T. P. 1988 The Case of the Absent Rat *Interim* Vol. 13 No. 4 39–41.

Olsen, O. & Schmidt, H. 1977 *Fyrkat: en jysk vikingeborg* Vol.1 Copenhagen.

Ordish, G. 1953 *Wine Growing in England* Rupert Hart-Davis.

Ordish, G. 1977 *Vineyards in England and Wales* Faber.

Oschinsky, D. 1971 *Walter of Henley and other treatises on estate management & accounting* Oxford.

Ottaway, P. 1983 Any old iron *Interim* Vol. 9 No. 1 20–4 YAT.

Ottaway, P. 1985 We're getting it off our chests *Interim* Vol. 10 No. 4 7–12 YAT.

Owen 1841 A *The Ancient Laws & Institutes of Wales* Record Commission.

Page, R. I. 1985 *Anglo-Saxon Aptitudes* Cambridge.

Page, R. I. 1985 Some Problems of Meaning in Bammesberger, A, 221–7.

Palliser, D. M. 1978 The Medieval Street Names of York *York Historian* No.2 2–16.

Palsson, H. 1971 *Hrafnel's Saga & other stories* Penguin.

Pennant, W. 1772 *Tours in Wales.*

Petch, A. 1987 *Newsletter* p.1 Kings Nympton, Devon.

Pheifer, J. D. 1974 *Old English Glosses in the Epinal-Erfurt Glossary* Clarendon Press Oxford.

Platt, B. S. 1968 *Tables of representative values of foods commonly used in tropical countries* HMSO.

Platt, C. 1969 *Medieval Archaeology in England: A Guide to the Historical Sources* Pinhorns.

Platt, C., Coleman-Smith, R. et al. 1975 *Excavations in Medieval Southampton 1953–1969* Leicester Univ. Press.

Poole, A. L. 1958 *Medieval England* Oxford.

Poole, R. L. 1912 *The Exchequer in the Twelfth Century* Frank Cass (Blackwell, Oxford).

Pope, J. C. 1967 *Homilies of Aelfric* EETS.

Prummel, W. 1983 *Excavations at Dorestad* 2 Amersfoort.

Bibliography

Pullar, Philippa 1970 *Consuming Passions* Hamish Hamilton.

Rackham, O. 1984 in Biddick 1984 The Forest: Woodland and Wood Pasture in Medieval England 70–101.

Radley, J. 1971 Economic Aspects of Anglo-Danish York *Medieval Archaeology* XV 37–57.

Raffald, E. 1784 *The Experienced English Housekeeper* printed for R. Baldwin London.

Rahtz, P. & Hirst, S. 1974 *Beckery Chapel, Glastonbury 1967–8* Glastonbury Antiquarian Soc.

Rahtz, P. 1979 *The Saxon & Medieval Palaces at Cheddar Excavation* 1960–2 BAR Series 65.

Rahtz, P. 1990 *Review: The Mills of Medieval England by Richard Holt* in *Medieval Archaeology* XXXIV

Rare Breeds Survival Trust *Soay Sheep* undated.

Redfern, M. 1987 Killer of Kings & Emperors *The Listener* 5 March 16.

Renfrew, Jane 1985 *Food and Cooking in Prehistoric Britain* English Heritage.

Riche, P. 1978 *Daily Life in the World of Charlemagne* Univ. of Pennsylvania.

Richards, A. 1932 *Hunger and Work in a Savage Tribe* Routledge.

Roach, F. A. 1985 *Cultivated Fruits of Britain: their origin & history* Blackwell.

Robertson, A. J. 1925 *The Laws of the Kings of England from Edmund to Henry I* CUP.

Robertson, A. J. 1939 *Anglo-Saxon Charters* CUP.

Robertson-Smith 1889 *Lectures on the Religion of the Semites* D. Appleton New York.

Robins, D. 1988 A spin through the past *New Scientist* 25 Feb. 1988 49–52 London.

Robinson, F. N. 1957 *The works of Geoffrey Chaucer* Cambridge.

Roesdahl, E. 1977 *Fyrkat: en jysk vikingeborg Vol. II* Copenhagen.

Roesdahl, E. 1982 *Viking Age Denmark* B.M. Publications.

Roesdahl, E. et al. 1987 *The Vikings in England.*

Rogers, J. & Young, P. 1994 'Bone formers' – Positive correlations between osteophyte and enthesophyte formation. *Homo* 45/Suppl. Gustav Fischer Stuttgart.

Rogerson, A. ed. 1976 *East Anglian Archaeol. 2* Norfolk Museums Service.

Rothamsted Experimental Station Library Catalogue of Printed Books & Pamphlets on Agriculture 1471–1840.

Rowley, T. 1981 *The Origins of Open Field Agriculture* Croom Helm.

Rumble, A. 1983 *Essex Domesday* Phillimore.

Ryder, M. L. 1961 Livestock Remains from Four Medieval Sites in Yorkshire *Agric. Hist. Review* 9 105–110.

Ryder 1987 Feral Goats – their origin & uses *Ark* September 305–11.

Sabine, E. L. 1933 Butchering in Medieval London *Speculum* 8 335–353.

Salisbury, C. 1980 The Trent, the story of a river *Current Archaeology* No. 74 Vol. VII Pt. 3 88–91.

Sass, Lorna 1975 *To the King's Taste* John Murray.

Sayce, R. U. 1946 Food through the Ages *Montgomeryshire Collections* XLIX Part II.

Schaumann, B. & Cameron, A. 1977 A Newly found leaf of Old English from Louvain *Anglia* XCV 289–312.

Seebohm, F. 1883 *The English Village Community* Longmans, Green & Co.

Seebohm, M. 1952 rev. ed. *The Evolution of the British Farm* Allen & Unwin.

Severin, T. 1978 *The Brendan Voyage* Book Club Associates.

Simpson, A. W. B. 1984 *Cannibalism and the Common Law* Univ. Chicago Press.

Skeat, W. W. 1869 *Piers the Plowman* OUP.

Skeat, W. W. 1881 *Ælfric's Lives of the Saints* EETS.

Small, A., Thomas, C., Wilson, D. M. 1973 *St Ninian's Isle & its Treasures* OUP.

Schmidt, M. 1980 *Eleven British Poets* Methuen London.

Smith, A. H. 1964 *The Place-Names of Goucestershire* Parts 1–3 CUP.

Smith, A. H. 1970 *The Place-Name Elements 1 & 2* CUP.

Southampton Archaeological Research Committee 1980 *Saxon Southampton: the Archaeology & History of the port called Hamwih* S A R C.

Spencer, P. J. 1979 Fish that men gnawed upon *Interim* Vol. 6 No. 1 9–11.

Spriggs, J. 1977 Roll out the barrel *Interim* Vol. 4 No. 4 11–15.

St Clare Bryne, M. 1925 *Elizabethan Life in Town & Country* Methuen.

Bibliography

Steane, J. M. & Bryant, G. F. 1975 Excavations at the DMS at Lyvenden, Northants. *Northants. Museum Journal* 12 3–160.

Stenton, F. M. 1936 The Road System of Medieval England *Econ. Hist. Review* Nov. 1936 1–21.

Stenton, D. M. 1965 *English Society in the Early Middle Ages* 4th ed. Penguin.

Stevenson, W. H. 1929 *Early Scholastic Colloquies* Oxford.

Stewart, K. 1975 *Cooking and Eating* Hart-Davis Macgibbon.

Stone, L. 1977 *The Family, Sex and Marriage in England 1500–1800* Weidenfeld & Nicolson.

Storms, G. 1948 *Anglo-Saxon Magic* Martinus Nijhoff The Hague.

Stratton, J. M. 1969 *Agricultural Records AD 220–1968* John Baker.

Svensson, O. 1987 *Saxon Place-Names in East Cornwall* Lund.

Swanton, M. 1975 ed. *Anglo-Saxon Prose* Dent.

Symons, T. 1953 *The Monastic Agreement of the Monks and Nuns of the English Nation* Nelson.

Talbot-Rice, D. 1965 ed. *The Dark Ages* Thames & Hudson.

Tannahill, Reay 1973 *Food in History* Methuen.

Tannahill, Reay 1975 *Flesh and Blood: A History of the Cannibal Complex* Hamish Hamilton.

Taylor, T. 1925 *The Life of St Sampson of Dol* London.

TeBrake, W. H. 1984 Early Medieval Agriculture in Coastal Holland: The Evidence from Archaeology & Ecology in Biddick 171–189.

Temple, E. 1976 *A Survey of Manuscripts illuminated in the British Isles 900–1066* Harvey Miller.

Thomas, C. 1971 *Britain & Ireland in Early Christian Times AD 400–800* Thames & Hudson.

Thompson, M. 1989, Poultry Evolution & Development *Ark* Jan. 25 24–5.

Thorn, C. & F. 1980 *Somerset Doomsday* Phillimore.

Thorpe, B. 1843 ed. *The Homilies of Aelfric* Aelfric Soc.

Thorpe, L. 1978 *Gerald of Wales* Penguin.

Ticehurst, N. F. 1923 Some birds of the fourteenth century *British Birds* 17 29–35.

Tickner, Edwards 1917 *The Lore of the Honey Bee* 8th edn.

Todd, M. 1975 *The Northern Barbarians 100BC–AD300* Hutchinson Educational.

Todd, M. 1987 *The South-West to AD 1000* Longmans.

Tooke, J. Horne 1805 *The Diversions of Purley* London.

Trow-Smith, R. 1951 *English Husbandry from the Earliest Times to the Present Day* Faber & Faber.

Trow-Smith, R. 1957 *British Livestock Husbandry to 1700* London.

Turner, Sharon 1828 *The Anglo-Saxons* London.

Tusser, Thomas 1984 reprint *Five Hundred Points of Good Husbandry* OUP.

Tylecote, R. F. 1962 *Metallurgy in Archaeology* Edward Arnold.

Tylecote, R. F. 1967 The Bloomery Site at W. Runton *Norfolk Archaeology* 34 187–214.

Ucko & Dimbleby 1971 *Domestication and Exploitation of Plants & Animals* Duckworth.

van Es, W. A. with Verwers, W. J. H. 1980 *Excavations at Dorestad Vol. 1. The Harbour: Hoogstraat 1* Nederlandse Oudheden 9 R.O.B. Amersfoort.

Victor, Paul-Emile 1955 *The Great Hunger* Hutchinson.

von Matt, L. & Hilpisch, S. 1961 *St Benedict* Burns & Oates London.

Waddell, Helen 1932 *The Wandering Scholars* Penguin.

Wade-Martins, P. 1984 Excavations in Thetford 1948–59 & 1973–80 *East Anglian Archaeology 22* Norfolk Museums Service.

Wade-Martins, P. 1986 Breeding Manx Loghtans: is it worth it? *Ark* May 168–171.

Walford, C. 1879 *The Famines of the World Past & Present* Statistical Soc of London.

Walker, C. & Cannon, G. 1986 *The Food Scandal* Century Arrow.

Walker, M. & Bennett, H. 1980 *Somerset Folklore* Somerset Rural Life Museum.

Wartburg, W. von 1928 reprint 1948 + suppl. 1969 *Franzosisches Etymologisches Worterbuch* Bonn & Leipzig.

Waterman, D. M. 1954 Excavations at Clough Castle, Co. Down *Ulster J. of Archaeol.* XVIII Third Series 103–168.

Webster, L. 1975 Medieval Britain *Medieval Archaeology* XIV 220–60.

Weicholt, R. P. 1987 Barefoot in the Netherlands *Three Course Newsletter* No. 4 March 1987 52–47.

Welch, M. G. 1983 *Early Anglo-Saxon Sussex* BAR 112 (i).

Welch, M. G. 1992 *Anglo-Saxon England* English Heritage.

Bibliography

Wells, Calvin 1960 Animals bones assoc. with cremations at Illingworth, Norfolk *Antiquity* XXXIV
No. 133 March 1960

Wells, Calvin 1964 *Bones, Bodies & Disease* Thames & Hudson

Wells, Calvin 1975 Prehistoric & historical changes in nutritional diseases and associated conditions
Progress in Food and Nutrition Science No. 1 756.

Wells, Calvin 1977 Disease of the Maxillary Sinus in Antiquity *Medical Biology Illustrated* Vol. 27
173–8.

West, S. E. 1963 Excavations at Cox Lane (1958) and at the Town Defences, Shire Hall Yard,
Ipswich (1959) *Proc. Suffolk Institute Archaeology* 29 233–303.

West, Stanley 1982 *The Early Saxon Site at West Stow (5th–7th centuries)* Doctoral Thesis Birkbeck
Coll. London.

Wheeler, Alwyn 1969 *The Fishes of the British Isles and N.W. Europe* Macmillan.

Wheeler, Alwyn 1979 *The Tidal Thames: the History of a River and its Fishes* Routledge & Kegan Paul.

Wheeler, A. & Jones, A. K. G. 1976 Fish remains Excavations on Fuller's Hill, Great Yarmouth,
East Anglian Archaeology 2 131–245.

Whitelock, D. 1952 *The Beginnings of English Society* Penguin.

Whitelock, D. 1955 *English Historical Documents Vol. 1* c.500–1042 Eyre & Spottiswoode.

Whitelock, D. 1968 *The Will of Æthelgyfu* New Collection Roxburghe Club.

Whittock, M. J. 1986 *The Origins of England* Croom Helm.

Wikander, Orjan 1986 *Archaeological Evidence for Early Water Mills – an Interim Report* History
of Technology Lund.

Wilkins 1982 *Butter-making* Acton Scott Farm Museum

Wilkinson, M 1979 *The Fish Remains* in Maltby 1979

Wilkinson, M 1986 *Withowinde* LXXVII 16.

Williams, A. 1986–7 ed. The Great Domesday Allecto Historical Editions London

Williams, J. 1984 From Palace to Town: Northampton & Urban Origins *Anglo-Saxon England* XIII
113–136.

Wilson, C. Anne 1973 *Food & Drink in Britain* Constable.

Wilson, D. G. 1975 Plant Remains from the Graveney Boat & the Early History of *Humulus
Lupulus L.* in W. Europe *New Phytologist* LXXV 627–648.

Wilson, D. G. 1977 *The Making of the Middle Thames* Spur Books.

Wilson, D. M. 1960 *The Anglo-Saxons* Thames & Hudson.

Wilson, D. M. 1964 *Anglo-Saxon Ornamental Metalwork, 700–1100, in the British Museum* BM
Publications.

Wilson, D. M. ed. 1976 *The Archaeology of Anglo-Saxon England* CUP.

Wilson, D. M. 1984 *Anglo-Saxon Art: from the Seventh Century to the Norman Conquest* Thames &
Hudson.

Wilson, D. M. 1985 *The Bayeux Tapestry* Thames & Hudson.

Wilson, D. M. 1986 Trade *Proceedings of Spoleto Conference.*

Wilson, J. 1909 *The Evolution of British Cattle* Vinton & Co.

Wiseman, J. 1986 *A History of the British Pig* Duckworth.

Wiseman, J. 1988 Comments on Corsican Pigs *Ark* May 176–9.

Wolters, J. B. 1967 *Wijster* Palaeohistoria XI Groningen.

Wright, T. 1871, *The Homes of Other Days* London.

Wright & Wulcker 1884 see

Wright, T. & Wulcker, R. P. 1968 reprint *Anglo-Saxon & OE Vocabularies* Vols. I & II Second
Edition Darmstadt.

Wycliffe-Goodwin, Charles 1851 *Saxon Legends of St Andrew & St Veronica* Camb. Antiquarian
Soc. Series 1.

Yonge, C, M. 1966 *Oysters* New Naturalist Series Collins.

Zeuner, F. E. 1963 *A History of Domesticated Animals* Hutchinson.

Zinsser, Hans 1934 *Rats, Lice and History* Little, Brown & Co. Boston Mass.

Zupita, J. 1959 *Beowulf: facsimile and notes...*EETS.

Personal Communications

B. Adams, Verulam Museum
A. Cook, A. Cook & Son, Heddon, Filleigh, Devon
Dr. D. J. Drewry, Scott Polar Research Institute, Cambridge
The late Professor J. McN. Dodgson, UCL
J. Fensom, Northend Farm, Stagsden, Beds.
Dr. J. Graham, Shuttleworth Agricultural Institute, Old Warden, Beds.
R. K. Hagen, Manshead Archaeol. Soc., Dunstable, Beds.
J. M. Hagen, Porthcawl, Glam.
Mrs S. C. Hawkes, St. Cross College, Oxford.
P. Holdsworth, Formerly Director, Southampton Excavats.
Sir Bernard Ingham, Purley, Surrey.
D. Maule, R & D, Whitbreads Brewery, Luton, Beds.
A. Milton, Chapelton Barton, Umberleigh, Devon.
The late H. Newman, Village Farm, Stagsden, Beds.
I. Newman, Village Farm, Stagsden, Beds.
D. Smallridge, Chasestead Engineering, Letchworth, Herts.
W. Smallridge, Instow, Devon.
Ken Steedman, Humberside Archaeological Unit.
P. Walsh, Guinness Museum, Dublin.
R. Ward, University of Exeter.
Ben Whitwell, Humberside Archaeological Unit.

Index

Index

Albold the cook, 289
alcohol, 147, 200, 203, 204, 210–14, 224, 238, 239, 275, 276, 403, 404, 417
alcoholic drinks, 197, 199, 210, 211, 220, 224, 226, 245
Alcuin, 43, 55, 177, 216, 235, 242, 243, 248, 342, 345, 382, 406, 436, 445
alder flour, 251
Aldhelm, 179, 219, 454
Aldington, 305
Aldwinkle, 194
ale, 41, 81, 90, 91, 125, 129, 151, 154, 197, 199–246, 219–33, 238–45, 252, 279, 294, 295, 199–246, 309, 314, 316, 319, 322, 335, 199–246, 350, 367, 371, 388, 389, 390, 392, 415, 416, 417, 426, 451, 455, 458, 460; minstrel, 421
alecost, 207
alehoof, 207
alehouses, 203, 241–42, 371
ale-minstrel, 243
ale-runes, 209
Alexandria, 178
Alfred, 24, 62, 77, 111, 116, 135, 138–40, 144, 152, 166, 175, 180, 181, 185, 186, 192, 216, 219, 220, 223, 227, 232, 239, 301, 305, 315, 316, 339, 345, 363, 364, 138–40, 375, 378, 384, 451, 457
Alfred, Ealdorman, 30
Alfred, King, 247, 250, 254, 279, 388, 397, 398, 420, 436, 448; laws, 406
Alfward, 217
Alhuun, 111
Alhwine, 137, 368
All Saints, 340, 355
allium, 44, 45
almond: tree, 431
almonds, 62
alms, 336, 340, 347, 363, 373, 381–85, 456
almsgiving, 253, 256, 393, 396, 400, 403, 406, 408
aloes, 178, 180, 181, 231
Alternan, 166
Altfrid, 150, 174
Alton, 335
Alveston, 160
amber, 265, 283, 389, 436
amber (measure), 30, 37, 108, 201, 208, 209, 211, 303, 304, 322, 323, 325, 339, 383
Ambresbury, 307
amenorrhea, 444
amino acid, 270
anaemia, 292, 443
Ancient Laws and Institutes of Wales, 260
Andover, 66, 73, 94, 185, 341, 398
Andreas, 183, 370
Andred, 99, 108

Andrew, St., 370
Angerton, 71
Angles, 301
Anglo-Danish, 71, 100
Anglo-Norman recipes, 298–300
Anglo-Saxon Chronicle, 19, 90, 154, 361, 374, 438
Angmering, 82
animal, 104–6, 265, 267, 268–72, 278, 285, 290, 291, 300, 390, 403, 409, 428, 429, 432, 433, 438, 439, 441, 446, 450; bone, 269, 390; dancing, 423; food, 394, 439, 443; membranes, 290; milch, 259, 260, 265; product, 438
animal bone, 85, 94, 105, 116, 119, 126, 127, 356, 360
animals, 16, 17, 20, 23, 26, 27, 30, 35, 36, 37, 39, 48, 57, 59, 65–84, 65–84, 65–84, 104–6, 110, 113, 116–19, 65–84, 143, 164, 167, 168, 65–84, 187, 189, 192, 198, 302, 324, 329, 341, 342, 65–84, 361, 65–84, 373, 451, 452, 455, 456, 458, 460
aniseed, 54, 180
Annals of Ulster, 154
Annapes, 46, 55, 128, 148, 204, 351
Anselm, St., 181, 242
anthrax, 68
Apicius, 178, 226, 454
Apothecaries' pound, 320
apparitor, 414
apple, 290, 291, 294, 296, 299, 428, 429, 431; core, 415; dumpling, 299
apples, 45, 55–58, 59, 60, 179, 188, 201, 202, 203, 218, 222, 224, 453
Apuleius, 260
Arabia, 175, 178, 180, 210
arable, 24, 109, 302, 340
ard, 25
Ardenfield, 152
ark, 279
arpent, 217
arthritis. *see osteo-arthritis*
artichoke, 51
Artois, 204
Arvon, 114
ascarids (roundworms), 448
ascorbic acid, 442–43
ash, 70, 147
ash keys, 207
ash, ashes, 254, 282, 285, 287, 288, 290, 296, 405; pit, 280
Ashburton, 185
Ashridge, 116
Ashwell, 338
Asia, 178
assarting, 99

Index

Index

Index

Index

Index

The English Warrior from earliest times till 1066
Stephen Pollington

This is not intended to be a bald listing of the battles and campaigns from the Anglo-Saxon Chronicle and other sources, but rather it is an attempt to get below the surface of Anglo-Saxon warriorhood and to investigate the rites, social attitudes, mentality and mythology of the warfare of those times.

> "An under-the-skin study of the role, rights, duties, psyche and rituals of the Anglo-Saxon warrior. The author combines original translations from Norse and Old English primary sources with archaeological and linguistic evidence for an in-depth look at the warrior, his weapons, tactics and logistics.
>
> A very refreshing, innovative and well-written piece of scholarship that illuminates a neglected period of English history"
>
> *Time Team Booklists* - Channel 4 Television

Revised Edition
An already highly acclaimed book has been made even better by the inclusion of additional information and illustrations.

£16.95   Hardback   304 pages

The Mead Hall The feasting tradition in Anglo-Saxon England
Stephen Pollington

This new study takes a broad look at the subject of halls and feasting in Anglo-Saxon England. The idea of the communal meal was very important among nobles and yeomen, warriors, farmers churchmen and laity. One of the aims of the book is to show that there was not just one 'feast' but two main types: the informal social occasion *gebeorscipe* and the formal, ritual gathering *symbel*.

Using the evidence of Old English texts - mainly the epic *Beowulf* and the *Anglo-Saxon Chronicles*, Stephen Pollington shows that the idea of feasting remained central to early English social traditions long after the physical reality had declined in importance.

The words of the poets and saga-writers are supported by a wealth of archaeological data dealing with halls, settlement layouts and magnificent feasting gear found in many early Anglo-Saxon graves.

Three appendices cover:
- Hall-themes in Old English verse;
- Old English and translated texts;
- The structure and origins of the warband.

£19.95   296 pages

First Steps in Old English
An easy to follow language course for the beginner
Stephen Pollington

A complete and easy to use Old English language course that contains all the exercises and texts needed to learn Old English. This course has been designed to be of help to a wide range of students, from those who are teaching themselves at home, to undergraduates who are learning Old English as part of their English degree course. The author has adopted a step-by-step approach that enables students of differing abilities to advance at their own pace. The course includes practice and translation exercises, a glossary of the words used in the course, and many Old English texts, including the *Battle of Brunanburh* and *Battle of Maldon*.

£16-95   272 pages

Old English Poems, Prose & Lessons   2 CDs
read by Stephen Pollington

These CDs contain lessons and texts from *First Steps in Old English*.

Tracks include: 1. Deor. 2. Beowulf – The Funeral of Scyld Scefing. 3. Engla Tocyme (The Arrival of the English). 4. Ines Domas. Two Extracts from the Laws of King Ine. 5. Deniga Hergung (The Danes' Harrying) Anglo-Saxon Chronicle Entry AD997. 6. Durham 7. The Ordeal (Be ðon ðe ordales weddigaþ) 8. Wið Dweorh (Against a Dwarf) 9. Wið Wennum (Against Wens) 10. Wið Wæterælfadle (Against Waterelf Sickness) 11. The Nine Herbs Charm 12. Læcedomas (Leechdoms) 13. Beowulf's Greeting 14. The Battle of Brunanburh 15. A Guide to Pronunciation.
And more than 30 other lessons and extracts of Old English verse and prose.

£15   2 CDs - Free Old English transcript from www.asbooks.co.uk.

Wordcraft: Concise English/Old English Dictionary and Thesaurus
Stephen Pollington

This book provides Old English equivalents to the commoner modern words in both dictionary and thesaurus formats. The Thesaurus presents vocabulary relevant to a wide range of individual topics in alphabetical lists, thus making it easily accessible to those with specific areas of interest. Each thematic listing is encoded for cross-reference from the Dictionary. The two sections will be of invaluable assistance to students of the language, as well as to those with either a general or a specific interest in the Anglo-Saxon period.

£9.95   A5   256 pages

An Introduction to the Old English Language and its Literature
Stephen Pollington

The purpose of this general introduction to Old English is not to deal with the teaching of Old English but to dispel some misconceptions about the language and to give an outline of its structure and its literature. Some basic knowledge of these is essential to an understanding of the early period of English history and the present form of the language.

£5.95   A5   48 pages

Anglo-Saxon Runes

John. M. Kemble

Kemble's essay *On Anglo-Saxon Runes* first appeared in the journal *Archaeologia* for 1840; it draws on the work of Wilhelm Grimm, but breaks new ground for Anglo-Saxon studies in his survey of the Ruthwell Cross and the Cynewulf poems. It is an expression both of his own indomitable spirit and of the fascination and mystery of the Runes themselves, making one of the most attractive introductions to the topic. For this edition new notes have been supplied, which include translations of Latin and Old English material quoted in the text, to make this key work in the study of runes more accessible to the general reader.

£5.95 A5 80 pages

Looking for the Lost Gods of England

Kathleen Herbert

Kathleen Herbert sifts through the royal genealogies, charms, verse and other sources to find clues to the names and attributes of the Gods and Goddesses of the early English. The earliest account of English heathen practices reveals that they worshipped the Earth Mother and called her Nerthus. The tales, beliefs and traditions of that time are still with us in, for example, Sand able to stir our minds and imaginations.

£5.95 A5 64 pages

Rudiments of Runelore

Stephen Pollington

This book provides both a comprehensive introduction for those coming to the subject for the first time, and a handy and inexpensive reference work for those with some knowledge of the subject. The *Abecedarium Nordmannicum* and the English, Norwegian and Icelandic rune poems are included in their original and translated form. Also included is work on the three Brandon runic inscriptions and the Norfolk 'Tiw' runes.

£5.95 A5 Illustrations 88 pages

Anglo-Saxon FAQs

Stephen Pollington

125 questions and answers on a wide range of topics.

Are there any Anglo-Saxon jokes? Who was the Venerable Bede? Did the women wear make-up? What musical instruments did they have? How was food preserved? Did they have shops? Did their ships have sails? Why was Ethelred called 'Unready'? Did they have clocks? Did they celebrate Christmas? What are runes? What weapons and tactics did they use? Were there female warriors? What was the Synod of Whitby?

£9.95 128pages

Organisations

Þa Engliscan Gesiðas

Þa Engliscan Gesiðas (The English Companions) is a historical and cultural society exclusively devoted to Anglo-Saxon history. Its aims are to bridge the gap between scholars and non-experts, and to bring together all those with an interest in the Anglo-Saxon period, its language, culture and traditions, so as to promote a wider interest in, and knowledge of all things Anglo-Saxon. The Fellowship publishes a journal, *Wiðowinde,* which helps members to keep in touch with current thinking on topics from art and archaeology to heathenism and Early English Christianity. The Fellowship enables like-minded people to keep in contact by publicising conferences, courses and meetings which might be of interest to its members.

For further details see www.tha-engliscan-gesithas.org.uk or write to: Membership Secretary, Þa Engliscan Gesiðas, BM Box 4336, London, WC1N 3XX England.

Regia Anglorum

Regia Anglorum is an active group of enthusiasts who attempt to portray as accurately as possible the life and times of the people who lived in the British Isles around a thousand years ago. We investigate a wide range of crafts and have a Living History Exhibit that frequently erects some thirty tented period structures.

Our site at Wychurst has a large Anglo-Saxon hall – defended manor house - which has been reconstructed using the best available evidence. Members can learn weapon skills with accurate copies of weapons of the period. We own and operate six full scale vessels ranging from a 6 metre Faering to a 15 metre ocean-going trader!

We have a thriving membership and 40 branches in the British Isles and United States - so there might be one near you. We especially welcome families with children.

www.regia.org   *General information* eolder@regia.org   *Membership* join@regia.org

The Sutton Hoo Society

Our aims and objectives focus on promoting research and education relating to the Anglo Saxon Royal cemetery at Sutton Hoo, Suffolk in the UK. The Society publishes a newsletter SAXON twice a year, which keeps members up to date with society activities, carries resumes of lectures and visits, and reports progress on research and publication associated with the site. If you would like to join the Society please see website: www.suttonhoo.org

Wuffing Education

Wuffing Education provides those interested in the history, archaeology, literature and culture of the Anglo-Saxons with the chance to meet experts and fellow enthusiasts for a whole day of in-depth seminars and discussions. Day Schools take place at the historic Tranmer House overlooking the burial mounds of Sutton Hoo in Suffolk.

For details of programme of events contact:-
Wuffing Education, 4 Hilly Fields, Woodbridge, Suffolk IP12 4DX
email education@wuffings.co.uk   website www.wuffings.co.uk
Tel. 01394 383908 or 01728 688749

Places to visit

Bede's World at Jarrow

Bede's world tells the remarkable story of the life and times of the Venerable Bede, 673–735 AD. Visitors can explore the origins of early medieval Northumbria and Bede's life and achievements through his own writings and the excavations of the monasteries at Jarrow and other sites.

Location – 10 miles from Newcastle upon Tyne, off the A19 near the southern entrance to the River Tyne tunnel. Bus services 526 & 527

Bede's World, Church Bank, Jarrow, Tyne and Wear, NE32 3DY

Tel. 0191 489 2106; Fax: 0191 428 2361; website: www.bedesworld.co.uk

Sutton Hoo near Woodbridge, Suffolk

Sutton Hoo is a group of low burial mounds overlooking the River Deben in south-east Suffolk. Excavations in 1939 brought to light the richest burial ever discovered in Britain – an Anglo-Saxon ship containing a magnificent treasure which has become one of the principal attractions of the British Museum. The mound from which the treasure was dug is thought to be the grave of Rædwald, an early English king who died in 624/5 AD.

This National Trust site has an excellent visitor centre, which includes a reconstruction of the burial chamber and its grave goods. Some original objects as well as replicas of the treasure are on display.

2 miles east of Woodbridge on B1083   Tel. 01394 389700

West Stow Anglo-Saxon Village

An early Anglo-Saxon Settlement reconstructed on the site where it was excavated consisting of timber and thatch hall, houses and workshop. There is also a museum containing objects found during the excavation of the site. Open all year 10am (except Christmas) Last entrance summer 4pm; winter 3-30pm. Special provision for school parties. A teachers' resource pack is available. Costumed events are held on some weekends, especially Easter Sunday and August Bank Holiday Monday. Craft courses are organised.

For further details see www.weststow.org or contact:

The Visitor Centre, West Stow Country Park, Icklingham Road, West Stow, Bury St Edmunds, Suffolk IP28 6HG   Tel. 01284 728718

Lightning Source UK Ltd.
Milton Keynes UK
UKOW02f0603030913

216430UK00002B/44/P